# Svay

May Mayko Ebihara

# Svay

## A Khmer Village
## in Cambodia

Edited by Andrew Mertha

With an introduction by Judy Ledgerwood

SOUTHEAST ASIA PROGRAM PUBLICATIONS
an imprint of
Cornell University Press
Ithaca and London

First published 2018 by Cornell University Press

Printed in the United States of America

Library of Congress Cataloging-in-Publication Data

Names: Ebihara, May, author. | Mertha, Andrew, 1965– editor.
Title: Svay : a Khmer village in Cambodia / May Mayko Ebihara ; edited by
    Andrew Mertha ; with an introduction by Judy Ledgerwood.
Description: Ithaca, New York : Southeast Asia Program Publications, 2018. |
    Originally presented as author's thesis (Ph.D)—Columbia University, 1971. |
    Includes bibliographical references and index.
Identifiers: LCCN 2017020651 (print) | LCCN 2017044735 (ebook) |
    ISBN 9781501714801 (pdf) | ISBN 9781501714719 (epub/mobi) |
    ISBN 9781501715112 (hardback) | ISBN 9781501715129 (paper)
Subjects: LCSH: Khmers—Cambodia—Svay Riĕng. | Village communities—
    Cambodia—Svay Riĕng. | Svay Riĕng (Cambodia)—Social life and customs. |
    Svay Riĕng (Cambodia)—History—20th century.
Classification: LCC GN635.C3 (ebook) | LCC GN635.C3 E25 2018 (print) |
    DDC 959.604—dc23
LC record available at  https://lccn.loc.gov/2017020651

Cornell University Press strives to use environmentally responsible suppliers and materials to the fullest extent possible in the publishing of its books. Such materials include vegetable-based, low-VOC inks and acid-free papers that are recycled, totally chlorine-free, or partly composed of nonwood fibers. For further information, visit our website at cornellpress.cornell.edu.

# CONTENTS

# ILLUSTRATIONS

## Maps

## Tables

## Charts

# PREFACE

I was formally trained as a China scholar. Becoming a student of Cambodia occurred midcareer, coinciding with my arrival at Cornell in 2008. Once I realized that extending my scholarship beyond China to Cambodia was not an indulgence but a serious research strategy, I set about reading every book, article, and unpublished paper I could find on this intoxicating country.

As I read, one citation kept popping up, over and over again, that of May Ebihara's (1934–2005) doctoral dissertation, "Svay: A Khmer Village in Cambodia," defended in 1968. Although widely cited in the literature, locating a physical copy was somewhat of a chore. It was never published as a book. Rather, it remained in the format of a doctoral dissertation. It was written long before the digital age (in a time when graduate students would routinely keep their unfinished dissertations in the freezer at home, the one place they could survive a house fire!) and was only available on microfilm or as a dissertation reprint. I painstakingly photocopied the dissertation, in all of its blurry Courier typeface glory, directly from the film, capturing two generations' worth of dust, smudges, and scratches in the process.

It was unbelievable to me that a work of such importance had never been published. Yet it was immediately clear that it needed to be. *Svay* is an indispensable window into a particular time and place in Cambodia, one that has long passed into the ether of history. It provides a rich, granular description of a single village just before the country slid into civil war (1970–75) and experienced the horrors of the Khmer Rouge (1975–79). Since it was one of only two ethnographies of pre–Khmer Rouge Cambodia ever committed to paper, *Svay* provides a unique time capsule as well as a precious baseline for comparison for all that has happened since.

In her introduction to this volume, Judy Ledgerwood makes a strong case for why *Svay* should be considered an ur-text in the study of rural Cambodia. Ebihara's scholarship represents an intersection of several key approaches of her day, notably models from British social anthropology, functionalism, and structural-functionalism. "Materialist" rather than "ideational," it enriches our knowledge of key facets of everyday Cambodian life: kinship, social organization, gender, and religion, among many others. And it holds up remarkably well today.

Indeed, one of the most striking things about *Svay* is its accessibility. Each academic discipline develops its own tribalisms, with obscure, arcane jargon providing the secret handshake that keeps outsiders at arm's length. My own discipline of political science is no exception; neither is anthropology. Ebihara's presentation is devoid of the verbal calisthenics that make up so much of scholarship today. Her fluid prose has been described by Ledgerwood as "fine description" (akin to the "fine" in "fine art"). In reading *Svay*, one is drawn directly into the village, becoming a part in the lives of the individuals she lived among and documented so meticulously. It is almost possible to hear the cicadas, to smell the faint scent of burning wood, or to feel the freshness in the air following a monsoon downpour.

This volume opens with Ledgerwood's introduction, then presents the complete text of *Svay*, and closes with a reprint of Ebihara's 2002 essay, "Memories of the Pol Pot Era in a Cambodian Village," which is based on research conducted on her return visits to Svay between 1989 and 1996, a generation after her initial fieldwork.

A number of people worked very hard on the volume. Ledgerwood wrote the introductory essay and provided important materials and editorial assistance, as well as arranged permissions to reprint here Ebihara's essay from *Cambodia Emerges from the Past: Eight Essays* (Dekalb: Northern Illinois University, Center for Southeast Asian Studies, 2002). She also graciously gave permission to use photos that Ebihara took of Svay during her time there. Alexandra Dalferro retyped the entire manuscript. Hannah Phan graciously provided the Khmer words for the updated glossary. Sarah Grossman of SEAP Publications at Cornell University Press shepherded this project from start to finish. The Center for Khmer Studies (CKS) provided the initial platform from which to embark on this project and will soon be translating it into Khmer.

Many of the names of individuals and places in the text have been changed in order to maintain their anonymity. Adding an extra layer of anonymity to protect the residents of Svay, the pseudonyms used in the main text are different than the ones used by Ebihara in "Memories of the Pol Pot Era in a Cambodian Village." Apart from a few minor editorial touches, the format and the organization of the text remain unchanged.

Andrew Mertha

# INTRODUCTION

May Ebihara's dissertation, *Svay: A Khmer Village in Cambodia,* now being published in book form for the first time, is foundational for much of the anthropological work done by scholars of my generation who wish to address key questions in the study of Cambodian history, society, and politics. Ebihara writes in her introduction that the dissertation's primary purpose is description and analysis of the "round of life" (p. 6) in Village Svay. What follows is a remarkably detailed description of what life was like in one village in Kandal province in 1959–60—including social structure, economic organization, rice cultivation, animal husbandry, credit, property holdings, religious institutions, political organization, and the village—in relation to the surrounding area and the city of Phnom Penh. For me, rereading the dissertation is personal, like embracing an old friend. My dog-eared copy is filled with sticky notes and underlining. I remember specific lines I have cited in my own publications, and descriptions that introduced me to people whom I would later come to personally know. Ebihara was my mentor and my adopted aunt ("ming" in Khmer); she and I conducted research together in Svay in 1990, 1991, 1994, and 1996. I have continued to do research there in the 2000s, including most recently in 2012. When Ebihara died in 2005, I inherited her field notes and papers. Currently, I am at work on the project that she could never bring herself to do, writing the story of the village across the years before, during, and after the maelstrom of the revolution. The publication of this dissertation as a book more than fifty-five years after the research was conducted, and its planned translation into Khmer, will make this important touchstone work available to a new generation of foreign and Khmer scholars.

## EBIHARA, ANTHROPOLOGY, AND HISTORY

In the early 1960s, when Ebihara finished writing *Svay,* she could not have fore-seen the devastation that was soon to befall Cambodia. It would not be possible for her to conduct any follow-up research for thirty years. She also could not have antici-pated that when she did go back in 1989, half of the people she had known would have died in the violence of war and revolution. The importance of this book is that it is one of the only detailed glimpses we have of prewar life at the village level; Ebihara was one of only three professional anthropologists to conduct research in Cambodia before the war and one of only two to write a detailed ethnography.[1] Svay thus became

---

[1] See Ebihara 1968, 1973, 1974, 1977, 1987, 1993a, 1993b, 2002, and Ebihara and Ledgerwood 2002. The other village ethnography is Martel 1975. In appendix A Ebihara summarizes the French literature to the date of her research, emphasizing that much of this work was focused on the archaeology of the Angkor region. Of course much of the literature on Cambodia in the last four decades has focused on the Democratic Kampuchea era.

something she never intended, a prototypical village used as a foundation for academic understandings of prewar Cambodian society—in contrast to the reign of terror of Pol Pot's Khmer Rouge and what has occurred since. Ebihara dealt with the reasons why Svay was not "typical" in her introduction: it was a village of unique individuals, near a normal school with foreign teachers, close enough to Phnom Penh for people to easily seek seasonal wage labor, and in a region very densely populated relative to the rest of the country; yet it was a rice-growing village, entirely ethnic Khmer, Theravada Buddhist, and Khmer-speaking, so it shared many characteristics with other rural villages. She wrote, "it cannot, of course, be claimed that the entire, rich range of Cambodian society and culture is mirrored in Village Svay" (p. 9). Because Ebihara included in her work the connections with surrounding communities and the city (chapter 7 and 1973), we are presented with Svay not in complete isolation, as was common in many ethnographies from this era, but as part of a larger social milieu.

The importance of Ebihara's work does not lay in her theoretical contributions but in her descriptions of daily life. In a 2005 interview Ebihara said that she was influenced by Harold (Hal) Conklin, who was still at Columbia when she was a student. It was because of him that she included so much detail on agriculture and developed an interest in irrigation, landholdings, and rice varieties. In a 2007 volume dedicated to Conklin, the authors praise his work as "fine" description, both in the sense of detailed and in the sense of "fine" art (Kuipers and McDermott 2007, x), noting that even though he often did not address broader theoretical issues, the hot theoretical issues of his day (like those in vogue on peasant studies when Ebihara did her work) are long forgotten anyway. Instead, the force of Conklin's work "comes from the attention to fine detail, to accuracy in the research underlying the prose. It comes from its evidence for having come as close as possible to the impossible objective of 'truth' in culture" (Kuipers and McDermott 2007, xv). Today, in an era where all social research is understood to be subjective and positional, Ebihara's work is similarly "fine," cautiously and conscientiously written, in what anthropologist John Marston has lauded as the "precision of her tone" (2011c, 8).

In part this focus on ethnographic description, of what Ebihara called the "round of life," arises from her position within the field of anthropology, as a person of her time, and from her training at Columbia University. Anthropology as a discipline was born of late nineteenth-century cultural evolutionary models; all societies were imagined as passing through stages of savagery and barbarism to reach (Western) civilization. In reaction to these evolutionary models, Franz Boas, the Columbia University–based "father" of American anthropology, proposed a new theoretical paradigm that took anthropology down into the detailed context of daily life. While he called his model "historical particularism," the focus was largely synchronic: recording the details of dance, song, story, and ritual, primarily of Native American societies, before they could be lost. Boas's call to understand local history and a diversity of cultures (in the plural, not a singular ideal "civilization"), emphasizing cultural relativism, remains at the core of American anthropology.

In the first half of the twentieth century, anthropology also came to be dominated by models from British social anthropology, functionalism and structural-functionalism. With an emphasis on detailed fieldwork, Malinowskian functionalism located the purpose of specific beliefs, objects, and practices in the part they played in fulfilling the basic needs of the individual. A. R. Radcliffe-Brown, Edward Evans-Pritchard, and others diverged from this form of functionalism into explicating the social structures of a particular society and analyzing how the components of the structure maintained and reinforced the structure itself. Fieldwork in both approaches was similar, involving intensive participant observation immersion in village life to the extent that this was possible. Indeed, George Stocking, the preeminent historian of anthropological theory, writes that in the "classical" period (1925–65) the most distinctive feature of Anglo-American anthropology was the central role of ethnographic fieldwork: "participant observation in small-scale communities, conceived holistically and relativistically" (1992, 357). The roots of Ebihara's work lay in these three schools of anthropological thought. While she saw herself as more "Boasian," following the Columbia approach more so than that of the University of Chicago where there was a Radcliffe-Brown legacy (Marston 2011b, 195), all three schools emphasized parallel ethnographic methods.

At midcentury, when she was conducting her fieldwork, important shifts were taking place in anthropological theory. Structural-functionalism was being critiqued for being too static, focusing on structures rather than processes, incapable of explaining social conflict or historical change. Evans-Pritchard (1950) issued a call for a reintegration of history into anthropology, writing that any good anthropologist is also a historian. In the same piece, Evans-Pritchard makes the case for anthropology as a humanity rather than a social science; the anthropologist as a writer is creating a set of abstractions when she describes another culture, and these abstractions are imaginative constructs of the anthropologist herself. This important transition midcentury, from studying objects and structures to studying ideas and patterns that take place in the mind, led to the symbolic and interpretive anthropology paradigms of the second half of the twentieth century. Ebihara's thesis research stands on the earlier side of this divide; her study is materialist rather than ideational, focused on structures and patterns of behavior, not ideologies. In Ebihara's dissertation, as in most anthropological work of this time, anthropology was framed as a science, the goal being to gather the rich details of daily life for the ultimate purpose of doing comparisons, seeking generalizable patterns of the human condition, and then developing new theories.

Finally, to place Ebihara in the context of the anthropology of her time, one should note the place of the individual within her analysis. In much of the structural-functionalist writing of this era individuals are subsumed. People are talked about in relation to their position within a social structure, as a mother's brother or a father or a member of an age set. They are the indistinguishable, generic "natives" who remain nameless. Ebihara analyzes villagers' lives in general terms, but she also gives specific examples of actions and characteristics of named individuals. Active agents populate the dissertation; her generalizations about social relations are based on aggregate data and the stories of individuals woven together through descriptions of daily interactions.[2] Individual personalities can be seen to influence events and decisions. This of course becomes even more the pattern in the follow-on research that she did in Svay in the 1990s when she collected the stories of individual lives through the Democratic Kampuchea (DK) period.

It is interesting, and perhaps ironic, that Ebihara's dissertation, a synchronic vision of lives in 1959–60, now becomes a tool for the study of localized Cambodian history. The aggregation of detail, from records of the agricultural cycle to the

---

[2] Victor Turner's work on the Ndembu was one of the first to use actor-focused research to show process as well as social structure; see Turner 1967.

donations people gave at Buddhist festivals, provides a foundation for our understanding of Khmer society as it was before the cataclysm.

## Why Is the Book Important?

In order to demonstrate the influence of Ebihara's *Svay*, let me highlight aspects
of Ebihara's thesis that became the basis for subsequent research topics, debates,
and discussions in Cambodian studies. Researchers build out from Ebihara's work
on such topics as analysis of the roots of the DK regime, Khmer kinship, social organization and local-level leadership, gender, and Buddhism. Particular passages and
descriptions of individual people have prompted entire lines of inquiry and academic
conversations. This discussion is not meant to be comprehensive, but to provide some
key references to the wider literature on these topics.

### Understanding Democratic Kampuchea

Scholars across a wide range of disciplines have turned to Ebihara's portrait of life
in Svay before the revolution to help explain what came next. Perhaps no questions
are more contentious than those of how the process of revolution and the violence of
war brought Pol Pot's Khmer Rouge to power, and why the resulting regime caused
the deaths of so many Cambodians. Was DK a Marxist regime, and the horrific death
toll the result of class-based violence, as David Chandler (1993), Steve Heder (2004),
and others have argued? Or was the revolution not primarily Marxist/communist, but
primarily "racist" or a "peasant revolution" as Ben Kiernan (2008) and Michael Vickery (1984) have argued respectively.[3] While Ebihara's work does not answer these
larger questions, she provides a rich trove of data for a single location that serves as a
unique lens through which to view the upheaval of this period.

Although Khieu Samphan and Hou Youn, prominent Cambodian scholars who
joined the Khmer Rouge movement, characterized Khmer rice farmers as exploited
and ripe for revolution prior to 1975, most Cambodian peasants were small landholders, not landless sharecroppers or indentured labor. Khieu Samphan's thesis (1979)
in fact notes that most Cambodians were what he termed "middle peasants" who
owned between two and seven hectares of land. Alexander Hinton writes that Khieu's
research overemphasized areas of the country where there were larger concentrated
landholdings. Khieu further argued that even the majority who were landowners were
kept indebted and exploited by moneylenders (2004, 54). But indebtedness too varied
widely across the country. Jean Delvert found that the severity of indebtedness ranged
from 10 percent to 78 percent in various parts of Cambodia but was lowest near Phnom
Penh where people could earn some extra cash from wage labor, and was particularly
low south of the city (1961, 522). This coincides with Ebihara's data. While the area
she worked in was more densely populated and landholdings were smaller (only one
household owned four hectares, and four households had two hectares), indebtedness
tended to be infrequent and relatively minor. Most people borrowed small amounts,
often in the form of rice rather than cash, from their relatives and neighbors (p. 118;
Hinton 2004, 55). In 1960 in Kandal, Ebihara did not find large numbers of landless

---

[3] See Heder 1997 for a summary of these disagreements.

peasants ripe to rise up against the exploiting classes; most peasants were subsistence farmers who were poor but grew enough rice to live.

Svay falls within an area that Vickery calls the "central rice-growing and gardening zones," which he links closely with urban areas, in sharp contrast to the rest of the more distant dark and unstudied countryside (1984, 5). According to him, those who see the violence of the DK period as an anomaly do not understand the poverty, arbitrary violence, and deep urban/rural animosity that characterized earlier historical periods. Despite Svay being in this more urban zone, Vickery makes use of Ebihara's data to argue several points. First, he cites her to document a decline or disregard for religion, including her comments that Buddhism for villagers integrated ideas about ghost and spirits, and popular Buddhism focused primarily on merit making to obtain a better life. Further, Ebihara documented a dramatic decline in the number of men becoming ordained as monks during the time of her research.[4] Vickery builds on this observation to say that among his colleagues when he taught in 1960–61, religion was openly ridiculed and monks seen as social parasites, an attitude previously attributed only to the Khmer Rouge. This decline in Buddhism, he argues, continued when it was manipulated by the Lon Nol Regime (1970–75) to foster violence against ethnic Vietnamese. Finally, he says, Buddhism did not serve as a deterrent to violence either before or during DK (Vickery 1984, 9–12).

Vickery also uses Ebihara's description of labor-exchange networks, the difficulties of water allocation across adjacent fields, and the fact that in one tough year farmers only provided rice porridge (*baba*) for labor-exchange workers in their fields to argue that elements of the DK regime were not such a dramatic departure from prewar rural life:

> Thus for the Cambodian peasants in that area the conditions of existence imposed cooperative labor, but made outbursts of inter-family violence inevitable, and at certain times of the year forced them to accept a diet which since 1975 has become a symbol of communist oppression in Democratic Kampuchea. (Vickery 1984, 16)

While Ebihara does say that cooperative labor-exchange practices were necessary (hence "imposed" in a sense), she does not report any forms of "inevitable" family violence. In fact it is notable that living in the village for a year, she never witnessed any domestic or other forms of violence. And in the footnote where she references workers being fed rice porridge in 1959 because the harvest had been poor, she also notes that it came with dried fish, and in fact in many instances, "especially if the coworkers were relatives or good friends," rice continued to be part of the meal (p. 105). Furthermore, this was a lunch taken in the fields for those doing collaborative labor. The farmers would have then gone home in the evening and eaten a regular meal of rice. The comparison to the DK pattern of feeding rice gruel at every meal for weeks or months with all other food sources collectivized and therefore restricted, resulting in mass malnutrition and starvation, is a perverse comparison.

---

[4] According to Malada Kalab's (1976) research, this decline was reversed in the 1960s, before the disruption of the war, once the Ministry of Cults included the study of secular lessons as part of the monk education system. Thereafter boys could get credit in the national school system for classes in temple schools; thus poor boys could get a free education and rise through the monk education system. While it was technically free to attend state schools, in fact there were local fees and book and uniform costs.

Much has been made of Ebihara's comments, by Vickery and others, that Svay residents were highly distrustful of strangers, that there was a "basic insularity and parochialism" in their attitudes toward others (p. 228). Hinton links this to peasant distrust of city people and discusses how DK propaganda exploited this distrust with a discourse that labeled urbanites as corrupt and sinful, as immoral foreign lackeys as opposed to the "clean" peasantry (2004, 78).[5] The rice farmers of Svay, because they fled to Phnom Penh in the early 1970s to escape fighting in their region, were labeled as "new people" or "April 17th people" when the city was evacuated by the Khmer Rouge in 1975. Ebihara writes:

> The villagers found themselves under suspicion because they had fled to Phnom Penh instead of joining the revolutionary forces . . . although the villagers answered truthfully that they were peasants, they were suspected or accused of having been Lon Nol soldiers, urbanites from higher social classes or even CIA. (1993a, 153)

Even though they knew how to do heavy agricultural labor like plowing and transplanting, and had the dark skin and calloused hands of peasants, they were viewed as city people. And like the other city evacuees, they died in large numbers. In 1960 Svay had 159 inhabitants, sixteen of whom died of old age or illness before 1970 and four of whom died in the civil war, leaving 139 people. Of these, seventy (50 percent) died during the DK regime (Ebihara 1993a, 158).

Vickery has called the city evacuees "spoiled, pretentious, contentious, status-conscious at worst, or at best simply soft, intriguing, addicted to city comforts and despising peasant life" (1984, 26); since these were the stories more likely to be told, we "inevitably" have a distorted view of what life was like in the revolutionary regime. Indeed almost all of the first-person narratives that have been published on the DK era have been written by wealthy, urban elites.[6] Ebihara's work after she was able to return in the late 1980s and 1990s, allowed for another range of voices to be heard. She found that Svay villagers, like the urbanites from higher socioeconomic classes, also suffered in the DK period, telling Ebihara "it was all suffering" and "it was beyond suffering" (1993a, 152). They recounted the relentless pace of the work regimes, the separation from family members, the collective dining that resulted in constant hunger, relocation (in some cases) to the northwest where there was even less food, and the persistent purges intended to locate and eliminate the perceived enemies of the regime (Ebihara 1993a, 1993b, and 2002). Ebihara's work on prewar society and on the same village during and after DK gives us a unique perspective on this era, allowing us to see change across time in the lives of individuals, and helps to document what was taking place at the local level in the notorious southwest zone. This helps to answer Vickery's (1984) and Chandler's (1993) calls for us to better understand variations across time and geographical regions during the period of DK rule.

---

[5] Zucker uses Ebihara's comments as a starting point from which to build an analysis of trust and distrust in the wake of the violence of the 1970s, 1980s, and 1990s (2013, chap. 3). See discussion below. See also Erik Davis's 2011 article on the resentment of rural villagers when city relatives come bearing gifts at the Pchum Ben holiday.

[6] See, for example, U and McCullough 2005, Panh and Bataille 2013, Ung 2012, Yathay 2013, Szymusiak 1986, Ngor and Warner 1987, Criddle and Mam 1987, Him 2001.

## CAMBODIAN KINSHIP

Ebihara describes in detail the kinship system of the Khmer, listing all the terminology, when and how it is used to reference and address individuals (see appendix E), and patterns of behavior regarding how people act toward kinsmen (*bong p'aun*). This is one of the hallmarks of the dissertation, because her analysis of Khmer kinship terms, and her understanding that kinship was revealed through patterns of behavior, upended the prevailing understanding of kinship in the academic literature on Cambodia.

The earliest ethnographic writings on Cambodia were written by colonial officials. From these French works at the end of the nineteenth century and beginning of the twentieth comes the notion that Cambodian culture was matrilineal (that kinship was traced through women), often conflated with the idea that it had also been matriarchal (that women possessed political power).[7] Following the classic Orientalist pattern, this notion was repeated down through the decades, each "expert" on Cambodian culture citing the one before them that the Khmer were matrilineal. It is only when one looks back up the chain of citations to contemporaries of nineteenth-century evolutionists Lewis Henry Morgan and Edward Tyler do we find that Cambodia was placed in the categories "matrilineal" and "matriarchal" primarily because these patterns were thought to be clustered in one "stage" of unilineal evolution. Such models were abandoned in Anthropology more than a century ago.[8]

Ebihara's detailed work, however, clarified that Khmer kinship is bilateral, and nearly every scholar who has conducted research in Cambodia since Ebihara's groundbreaking work has confirmed this finding. Kinship connections are traced through both men as fathers and women as mothers. Relatives on both sides can be considered *bong p'aun* or "relatives," an emic category for the circle of people to whom one is related, and therefore on whom one may rely in times of distress, and with whom one may have reciprocal exchange responsibilities (see Martel 1975; Kalab 1968; Kobayashi 2005, 2008; Derks 2008; Zucker 2013; Ledgerwood 1990).[9] While Ebihara's approach to kinship is structural—in the sense that she saw bilateral as a categorical type (like matrilineal or patrilineal)—her thinking was not restricted to static social structures. She was able to appreciate the limits of Western models as definitive categories for what she was seeing. Her discussion of residence patterns, for example, contrasts ideal versus actual patterns. While Khmer will say the ideal is uxorilocal (also called matrilocal) residence with the family of the bride after marriage, the reality is far more complex. In the thesis and in her 1977 piece, "Residence Patterns in a Khmer Peasant Village," Ebihara finds that the answer to the question varies across time; the young

---

[7] See, for example, Finot 1916, Przyluski 1925, Barth 1885, Aymonier 1904.

[8] A detailed discussion of the arguments on this issue (including the term "of one grandmother" to mean cousin, and the use of the prefix *me* in terms connoting leadership) is too extensive for this introduction; for a review of the "matriliny" question, see Ledgerwood 1995 and Parkin 1990.

[9] One of the exceptions is Jacques Népote (1992) who continued to argue for matrilineality in Cambodian society. He is dismissive of Ebihara's work, claiming that she was "brainwashed" by the American anthropologist George Murdock about the prevalence of bilateral systems, that she was just a young graduate student when she did her research, and that she herself honestly discusses how difficult it was to conduct village-level research (Népote 1992, 48–57). Ethnography is not a tool suited for the study of Cambodian society, he argues; observing daily life at the village level would just be incomprehensible (5).

couple may reside with the wife's or the husband's relatives initially, but then set up their own separate household later.

Cambodians she interviewed were very practical, she argued, settling where they were most likely to inherit land, which may explain why there were inmarrying men at the time of her research and why there are so many outmarrying people in recent years when landholdings are now so small due to population growth after the land distribution of 1989. While Ebihara found a preference for village exogamy, she noted that three-quarters of those who married beyond the village married someone from within a fifteen-kilometer radius. She links this to villagers' suspicion of strangers and unknown regions and their desire to know the families to which they will be bound by kinship obligations. Ebihara's detailed work on kinship groups, household composition, and marriage arrangements has been used to understand changes to marriage under the Khmer Rouge (see LeVine 2010, especially chap. 3), post-war social organization after DK in Cambodia (Ovesen, Trankell, and Öjendal 1996; Frings 1997; Marston 2011c; and below), and also changing Khmer familial relationships in the United States (Ledgerwood 1990; Smith-Hefner 1999; Ong 2003).

## Social Organization, Community, and Leadership

One of the most often cited quotations in the Ebihara dissertation is "a striking feature of Khmer village life is the lack of indigenous, traditional, organized associations, clubs, factions, or other groups that are formed on non-kin principles" (p. 80). She writes that aside from cooperative work teams that were formed for agricultural labor, other carefully calculated labor exchange, and temporary groups formed to organize religious rituals, there were no formal groups or factions in the village: "in sum, then, the family and household are the only enduring and clearly defined units in West Svay" (p. 82).[10]

Further, she argued that it was a homogeneous community with a basic sense of "egalitarianism." Villagers say, "We are all people of the rice fields," "We are all poor" (p. 83). Yet even given the relative egalitarianism of the villagers, there were some differences in status within the community. Ebihara outlines the "mosaic of elements" (p. 84) that differentiates status, including sex, age, occupation or specialization, official position, wealth, and individual character and personality. In another crucial paragraph she describes Kompha:

The "most important person" in West Svay, according to general consensus, is Grandfather Kompha. Although he holds no official position, he is the true leader of the hamlet and possesses considerable informal authority. Age sixty-six, he had once been a monk for seven years and is a devoted supporter of religious activities, as well as being a lay priest (*achaa*) much in demand for healing and for conducting life-cycle and other private ceremonies. He is also fairly well-off (a *neak kuĕsóm*), and his gentle yet vigorous and commanding personality enables him to organize and direct activities in a competent manner. And, perhaps most important of all, Kompha possesses exceptional "good character" that is widely admired. (p. 88)

---

[10] For an extended discussion of the concept of community in relation to Ebihara's work, see Marston 2011a.

Ebihara's discussion of community groups and village solidarity, or lack thereof, and her emphasis on leadership roles as linked to moral standing and systems of reciprocity have spawned a variety of discussions in the academic literature. In the 1990s, it was used by development non-governmental organizations (NGOs) who were trying to find local community leaders with whom to connect to organize grass-roots development programming. The idea of *me kyal* (literally "a leader of the wind"), someone who took on a temporary leadership role, such as for organizing a particular ritual, became a target for neoliberal community development workers looking for local partners (see, for example, Collins 1998, Vijghen and Ly 1996).

Others questioned whether there had ever been any sense of village community. Ovesen, Trankell, and Öjendal postulated in *When Every Household Is an Island* that on the one hand social relations had been so badly damaged by the violence of the DK years that even kinsmen no longer helped one another, and on the other that perhaps there had never really been much sense of community in the prewar years (1996, 7). Ebihara and I coauthored a response to this and other similar arguments, for while post-war poverty may have restricted the help that people could provide to one another, we did see the reestablishment of systems of exchange (including labor exchange) and mutual aid in Svay in the 1990s (Ebihara and Ledgerwood 2002; see also Kim 2011). Kobayashi Sotoru (2005, 2008) has argued that Ebihara, like other scholars of Southeast Asia of this era, was biased toward finding harmonious communities rather than seeing conflict, so she was predisposed to find cooperation. This may well be true. Yet it is also true that because she had known people well across a long period of time, she may have been told about or seen forms of collaboration that would not necessarily have been visible to someone conducting research in a village for a week or a month—as when one is researching and writing NGO reports.

Furthermore, as more research has come in from other areas of Cambodia in the 1990s and 2000s, including, for example, Eve Zucker, Soizick Crochet and Kim Sedara's work in a volume dedicated to Ebihara's memory (Marston 2011a; see also Zucker 2008, 2013; Kobayashi 2008; Biddulph 1996, 1999), part of the answer is that these issues of social solidarity vary widely around the country. In Svay and other villages on the central plains near Phnom Penh, people who knew each other from before the revolution returned to their villages and took up their lives among those with whom they had dense kinship ties (as well documented by Ebihara's subsequent work). In other areas, villages were often new amalgamations of those who had fled or been relocated who returned, but who now lived among new outsiders, often including those who had fought on the Khmer Rouge side. Zucker's (2013) ethnography is a particularly powerful look inside the dynamics of a village up on the edge of the forest where those living together today had fought on opposite sides in the 1970s, 1980s, and 1990s, and where specific individuals are blamed for the deaths of current residents' loved ones. Here trust is thin and the wounds much more raw and open than in Svay.

John Vijghen and I (2002) used the status of a village "helpful grandfather" as a starting point in our discussion of how local-level leadership and patron–client relationships changed over time through the opening of the country to development aid, the arrival of international NGOs, and other external factors in the 1990s. While we found dramatic changes in the underpinnings of legitimacy of local rulers and how they exercised power, we argued that there was still a sense in which local leadership was still linked to the moral responsibilities of leaders and followers grounded in religion (Ledgerwood and Vijghen 2002, 110). Patrons, in their elevated positions due to meritorious behavior in this or previous lives, are obliged to provide gifts to their clients to demonstrate their generosity and enhance their karmic status. Ebihara never used the word "patron"; she did not see the level of social differentiation in the village in 1959–60 that would justify the use of that term. But she did see the development of patronage systems that reached from the city back into the village when she did follow-up work in the 1990s (Marston 2011b, 207; see also Ledgerwood 2012).

Dramatic changes in local-level leadership accelerated in Cambodian rural communities across the 2000s. Decentralization brought the election since 2002 of commune (*khum*, what Ebihara called sub-district) level councils; while at the same time new actors, including thousands of international and local NGOs and more recently local community-based organizations (CBOs) arose, and large-scale business operations penetrated into rural areas. Decentralization has been analyzed closely by a number of researchers affiliated with the Cambodia Development Resource Institute (CDRI);[11] and a book edited by Caroline Hughes and Kheang Un (2011) offers a range of perspectives on how local government works and how accountable local leaders are to their communities.

Hughes and Un find many of the personnel in the new electoral system are the same as, or relatives of, the Cambodian People's Party leaders who have governed local communities since the 1980s. Interestingly, they also found that when the kinship terms *mae* and *ov*, mother and father, were used to refer to local leaders, it referenced a kind of ideal relationship parallel to that of a parent and child. The ideal village chief or *ov* took care of the villagers, "advising and guiding them on matters of personal conduct and morality, guarding their interests in the sphere of development and offering an example to the young" (Hughes and Un 2011, 251). But among the forty-six local leaders identified across three communes they surveyed, only one leader was said to fulfill this ideal; in every other case the parental ideal was used to critique individuals whose behavior was found to fall short. While Hughes and Un think that the term *ov* may refer to the "father of the nation" model, fostered by Norodom Sihanouk in the 1950s and 1960s, I would argue that the roots were also there at the local level in the model of generous moral exemplars like Grandfather Kompha. The authors conclude that this may be an unrealizable goal based on nostalgia for another era, but that it highlights how difficult it is for leaders to be seen as responsive and caring in this period of extremely rapid transformation (Hughes and Un 2011, 251).

Kim Sedara and Joakim Öjendal have written about the growth and changing nature of CBOs. There are now not only temporary groupings that arise and fade away, such as temple committees and funeral fundraising committees, but local CBO groups focused on natural resources, such as groups designed to protect local forestry and fishery resources. Membership in such groups tends to begin with enthusiasm, but participation wanes over time. This is in part because personal benefits may not accrue, particularly in the short term, and indeed, there can be dangers (2011, 275–76). CBO leadership is sometimes associated with outside groups, be they international NGOs or a technical department of the government, instead of only members of local communities. The article concludes that CBOs can in fact succeed in demanding services and accountability from local commune councils. While the council may not have the resources to exercise their authority, "there is no doubt that the idea of downward accountability is emerging in rural Cambodia, driven by decentralization

---

[11] See the extensive bibliography in Hughes and Un 2011.

trends and the process of allowing community-based schemes to emerge. This amounts to a political transformation—downward accountability has never been a dominant feature in (rural) Cambodia—with far-reaching democratic and development consequences" (287).

Far less optimistic, Roger Henke's piece in the same volume (2011), finds that the NGOs, "established specifically to contest neo-patrimonialism in the name of good governance," are undermined by their own insistence on certain forms and priorities. He writes that the "NGO-ization" of civil society ends up supporting state dominance, and that donors are complicit in the creation of the neopatrimonial state and the "further marginalization of the poor" (308). The only ideological influence of Buddhism that Henke sees is not the moral obligation to help one's fellow villagers or "clients," but an emphasis on a magical (*boran*) form of Buddhism that provides access to power. Politicians seek to accumulate *bareamey*, a kind of spiritual energy, by making donations to temples and undertaking religious construction projects, which then makes them invincible. Henke reports, as in earlier articles by Öjendal and Kim (2006) and Hughes (2006), that the gift giving that happens around election time in Cambodia is a combination of "generosity and menace" (Henke 2011, 290). He writes that in a distortion of the idealized patron–client relationship, the voter must accept the gift and then also accept the obligation that they must vote for the giver and must respect the giver's authority when they win. Yet, as Erik Davis writes, because political gifts "can never be adequately repaid with a single vote," one then comes to resent the "continuous subservience" that having accepted the gift brings (2011, 327). The ideal of the helpful grandfather whom everyone respects has been distorted beyond recognition by a wide range of influences, from Khmer Rouge violence, communist state models, the penetration of transnational capitalism, imposed foreign models of civil society, and the contemporary neopatrimonial state.[12]

## GENDER

Ebihara's thesis work on kinship and the life cycle, and an important appendix on the sexual division of labor in common activities (appendix H), as well as her article "Khmer Village Women in Cambodia" (1974) continue to provide a backdrop to discussions of gender, and especially women's roles in prewar society. In late 1994, I was asked to present at a workshop on women's roles in Cambodian society at the CDRI. The participants included many women from the new State Secretariat for Women's Affairs, both women from the old Revolutionary Women's Association of the People's Republic of Kampuchea and women who had returned from the border camps and from overseas who were associated with the opposition FUNCINPEC and Buddhist Liberal Democratic parties. As a reading for this workshop, CDRI staff translated Ebihara's 1974 piece on Khmer village women into Khmer. Like the dissertation, it describes people's lives across the life cycle, as children, young adults, full adults, and elders. The workshop participants, who perhaps could agree on little else (having essentially been at war with each other for a decade), embraced the piece as accurate, saying it had "really" been like that in the time of their mothers, or in the time of their youth. Ebihara's use of stories from individual women at different stages of life,

---

[12] There is also an extensive literature on a national level version of adapted patron-clientism or neopatrimonialism that in many ways is systematic and monetized; see for example Un 2005, Un 2006.

perhaps drawing on Margaret Mead's work on enculturation, provides memorable models for thinking about women's lives.

Ebihara describes how infants are indulged, the process of weaning, the games and responsibilities of children as they age, beliefs around a woman's first menses, ideas about physical maturation, the expected shyness of young women, and the prohibitions on premarital sex. In the image of the parents calling out to the young child Mias to "dance" and her waving her hands with her fingers bent back, I recall two generations of children I have known, jumping and turning to the amusement of the elders in exactly the same way. I also envision the grown woman Mias I knew in the 1990s, who moved to the city and married a cyclo driver, and the elder Mias, now a grandmother—but forever frozen in that moment of dancing as a small child by Ebihara's description. Clifford Geertz (1973) writes that what anthropologists do is "fix" people in time by describing their actions and words. Like Mias dancing, here is the adolescent San in 1960 shy on the day of her wedding, and young wife Nara sitting at her loom—some of the frozen moments still clearly resonating in contemporary society while other behaviors and beliefs have long faded to memories of a past age.

Cambodian conceptions of gender parallel those across the other dominant lowland groups across Southeast Asia. Annuska Derks writes that Cambodian society has been characterized as having "male dominance, relative equality, complementarity between men and women, and 'high status' and 'considerable authority' of women" (2008, 37); and while these statements may appear incompatible, they reflect the complex and fluid nature of notions of gender. In addition, as Trudy Jacobsen argues, there have apparently always been greater differences between social classes than there have been between men and women in Cambodia (2008, 4), and in the region, there are some shared social patterns that are seen as giving prestige to women.

First, the bilateral kinship system, which traces kin linkages through both men and women, affords women greater standing than patrilineal patterns common in much of Asia. Uxorilocal residence as an ideal form highlights the importance of the women's relatives in the social milieu. In previous generations Cambodians practiced bride service, where the inmarrying man had to live with and work for the girl's family before the marriage. This has been replaced by "bridewealth," payments from the groom's family to the bride's (or to the new couple), but in either case the status of the women is relatively better off than in dowry systems where money moves from the woman's side of the family to the man's. In dowry systems, girl babies are often seen as a burden on the family, and thus boy children are preferred. Because of the close relationship between mothers and their children, especially their daughters, it has been argued that there is a matrifocal bias in Cambodia (and other Southeast Asian societies), in which women, especially women as mothers, are seen as more important than fathers.[13]

Second, women are seen as relatively equal because of their complementary work roles in Cambodian society; they work alongside men in agriculture, still roughly in line with the duties outlined in Ebihara's appendix though some activities have now been mechanized (see also Martel 1975, 101–2). Women raise small animals while men and boys tend oxen. Women also own property, including their own agricultural

---

[13] It is this "matrifocality" that Népote (1992) focuses on, leading him to assert matrilineality. For a discussion of "matrifocality" across the region, see Tanner 1974. A Cambodian proverb says, a father is worth a thousand friends, a mother is worth a thousand fathers (Leclère 1899, 352).

fields; they take property into a marriage, and if the marriage ends in divorce they have the right to take property out of the marriage. Further, women keep and handle the money in the family; when men earn a wage, the common pattern is for them to give it to their wives for safekeeping and for use in managing the household budget. Women make daily decisions about purchasing food and other supplies, and men and women jointly decide many major decisions. Women also dominate as sellers in local-level markets, with Southeast Asia being one of three areas in the world where women control local-level business (the others being West Africa and the Caribbean). Ebihara's descriptions of men's and women's labor influenced work on post-war rural work patterns and how the division of labor had changed after the war when the sex ratio meant more women than men in the adult labor pool (Chanthou Boua 1982; Ledgerwood 1996).

The relative independence of women in economic activities, as traders and as those who handle money, also presages contemporary women as wage laborers. While women also worked for wages when Ebihara did her initial research, it was far more common for men to go to the city to pedal cyclos or work in construction. Since the early 1990s, the garment industry has expanded rapidly, so that today more than seven hundred thousand people, mostly women, are employed in the industry, which generates $5.7 billion dollars a year (Human Rights Watch 2015). Most of the women have migrated from around the country to work in Phnom Penh, but young women in Svay mostly commute, leaving early in the morning when it is still dark and arriving home after it has become dark again in the evening. In Svay this extra family income has had dramatic effects, allowing families to purchase pumps and additional agricultural inputs, which beginning in the 1990s has led to increasing yields and income. Women from further away in the countryside who migrate to work must spend most of their salary on living expenses and are able to send only small amounts home to their families (see Derks 2008). At the same time the phenomenon of labor-exchange groups, which Ebihara and I used to document social solidarity in the post-war era, have largely disappeared. There are no young women to join such teams, and villagers have taken to paying field labor or planting using broadcasting rather than transplanting methods, which in turn brings down yields. The age-range ratio in the village is now skewed with many young people, men and women, permanently moving to the city, leaving the elders to farm in Svay. In a country where 46 percent of the population is under eighteen, nearly 70 percent of the villagers in Svay are over eighteen (Ledgerwood 2012, 199).

Third, a woman's status is tied to her sexuality; the unmarried woman should be a virgin, innocent, and therefore vulnerable. Ebihara's description of young women being afraid of "bad-smelling talk" and "great shame" (1974, 314–15; p. 190) was taken in 1959–60 as a strong motivation to refrain from premarital sex. My thesis (1990) discussed how ideal images of women, including these ideas about kinship, work relations, and the control of women's sexuality, continued to provide ideal models for behavior among Cambodian Americans in the United States. Derks (2008) builds on Ebihara's work and mine to analyze the lives of young Cambodian women factory workers, food sellers, and prostitutes who have migrated to the city. As in the work of Mary Beth Mills (1999) on Thailand, Derks finds young women torn between their obligations to their families and desire to appear as good, traditional women, and the longing to be "modern," to shed a backward provincial image, and to enjoy the commodities and comforts that come with being "up to date" (2008, chap. 7).

Ebihara's work gives us not only a prewar model from which we might measure change, but also introduced us to women across different stages of their lives and across different personalities, so that we see them as active participants in negotiating gender roles.

## RELIGION

Much of the exciting new work on Cambodian religion in the last two decades (for example, Marston and Guthrie 2004; Hansen 2007; Kent and Chandler 2008; Harris 2005) makes little mention of rural practice. It has focused on the broad historical sweep, the development of philosophical ideas, cosmological categories, and the history of religious institutions, rather than the small scale of daily practice. When Ebihara's work is cited, it is often either to note her famous observation that Buddhism and spirit beliefs are not different religions, but "a single religious system" (p. 153), or to note her stress on the importance of the five precepts, and in particular the importance of the injunction against killing (p. 163; see Harris 2005, 79; Davis 2016, 223).

Even among anthropologists, Marston and Guthrie have written that new research on religion has specifically tried to move away from accounts of religion in agricultural communities: "A new generation of anthropologists has questioned the implicit timelessness and autonomy of traditional models and sought new ways of framing ethnographic descriptions" (2004, 127). They tend to focus instead on social change in the wake of the Pol Pot period and the "wholesale destruction and reinvention of religious practice" (127).

Kobayashi Satoru is one of the only anthropologists who builds on Ebihara's work on "village" Buddhism, even as he critiques her work as too structural (2005, 2008). Kobayashi wants to combine research based on long-term fieldwork that gives "full consideration to local community conditions" with consideration of historical perspective—avoiding the notion that Cambodia is a "changeless entity" (2005, 493). He argues that Ebihara's work was overly influenced by the American models of her time, including the "loosely structured social system" analysis of Thai society (Embree 1950), which provided an inherent bias toward the notion of stable communities (as indeed her wider theoretical training would have made her less likely to focus on change or conflict, as noted above).[14] Kobayashi notes that Ebihara did revisit the village in the 1990s and wrote about some aspects of social change in the post-DK era, but he writes that these articles provide little empirical data (2005, 493).

In his 2008 piece, Kobayashi questions Ebihara's comment that the temple is the center of the community; he problematizes the notion of *chamnoh*, or supporters of a particular temple. Rather than a single or stable community, he finds these to be a "multi-layered spectrum" of participants that vary over time across geographical space. A temple "community" may appear to be outwardly calm and peaceful, but in fact he finds most rural Buddhist temples to be "characterized by tension and negotiation among the participants of various backgrounds, young monks and old monks, the rich and the poor, the so-called modernists and the so-called traditionalists" (515). Marston, in the same edited volume (2008b), also addressed the complexities of temple loyalties and histories in a piece that explores the story of one historical figure and how local and outside support for this temple had changed over time (see also Marston 2008a).

---

[14] See Ebihara's comments on the difficulty of getting a handle on the "social organization" in the data she was analyzing, and how she found the notion of "loose" structure helpful (Marston 2011b, 206).

In that same volume, Kent and Chandler's *People of Virtue,* I contributed a piece comparing village-level practice in 1960 and 2003, using data from a field school conducted in the latter year and framed using Ebihara's original discussion of the importance of the precepts and the making of merit. The piece documents how in many ways villagers do discuss Buddhism as unchanging, including the importance of the relationship between monks and the laity, elders and the primary actors, and the role of monks in performing ritual. The physical movements involved in practice— the walking of alms rounds, the visit to the *wat* to take the precepts on holy days, the lighting of incense, and the ritual bowing before the monks and images of the Buddha—serve as physical acts of remembrance of how things were before the war. The celebration of ritual serves to "rebuild a sense of community lost in the upheavals of the 1970s and 80s" (Ledgerwood 2008a, 159). At the same time people do discuss Buddhism as having changed; most importantly there is a perceived general decline in the morality among the laity as well as the notion that the monks are now lax in their discipline.

Framed partly in response to Kobayashi's 2008 piece, I published a chapter in 2011 on the two temples where Svay residents are *chamnoh.* The piece compares the two temples, one Mohanikay and one Thommayut, using data from Ebihara's original research and from 2003 and 2007 field schools. The reasons people attend one temple over another include family history of association with a particular temple, including where they or their father had ordained, where their ancestors' ashes were interred, the personalities of the current abbots, and other kinds of personal preferences. In the conclusion I agreed with Kobayashi that "villagers may choose to participate in the activities of a number of temples, depending on their own personal preferences and beliefs, creating a 'fluid, flexible situation'" and second, that "'sharing merit-making ideology facilitates cooperative activity' even as 'questions of identity frequently lead to competition and conflict'" (Kobayashi 2008, 177, 189, cited in Ledgerwood 2011, 126).

Zucker's work (2013) on a village in upland Cambodia further interrogates the degree to which ritual can "rebuild a sense of community" and the role of religion in post-war Cambodian society. Initially when she saw villagers preparing for the local Bon Dalien festival, she found that the camaraderie and enthusiasm called into question her assumptions about the effects of the war on social cohesion. But after the ritual activities were concluded, "the aftermath did not yield that heightened sense of solidarity that Turner claims is the product in such rituals. Instead, a certain emptiness permeated the atmosphere, lighted perhaps by the warm memories of the festival and the glimpse of what might be possible for the future" (Zucker 2013, 167). She concludes that through the effective reproduction of the Bon Dalien, the destruction of the last decades is "at least partially negated" (170) but suggests in her epilogue that perhaps only the death of the members of the generation who survived the violence will heal the rifts within the disrupted communities.

## EBIHARA AND THE IMPORTANCE OF SVAY

A political scientist colleague of mine once told me that as an anthropologist I have to read his work—to understand the wider political context—but that he didn't have to read mine: after all, what broad lessons can one draw from a single village? The comment was only partly in jest. What can we learn from trying to understand one single community over time? Ebihara went back to Svay and conducted research in the 1990s to give us local stories from one rural place before, during, and after the war and revolution (Ebihara 1990, 1993a, 1993b, 2002; Ebihara and Ledgerwood 2002). Many volumes have now been published by urban Khmer evacuated to the countryside in 1975, but there are almost no accounts from rural survivors who were not considered "base people." Ebihara's work in the 1990s took us inside one community where people were rice farmers but had close ties to the city and had fled to the city during the civil war. This combination of factors led to the particularly high death rate for West Svay. Ebihara used her genealogy data to ask about each person from her earlier research to find out their fate. This research was often emotionally exhausting, for the researchers and the person telling their stories, but they very much wanted to tell Ebihara so that she would understand clearly what had happened to those she had known. It is the only complete story from a single community across a fifty-year time span that included DK.

As I wrote in Ebihara's obituary, Svay residents saw Ebihara as a witness, a person who could understand the depth of their loss because she knew what their lives had been like before; she had known their mothers, husbands, and other relatives who had been lost. They wanted her to write their stories. Ebihara told me once that she was teaching a class at the CUNY Graduate Center and she used the phrase "giving voice to" rural peasants who had not told their stories to the rest of the world or even the rest of Cambodia. But her students, good post-modernists, objected to the phrase, asking what right had she to "appropriate" peasants' voices? She said she was stunned. She had not "taken" their stories; they had wanted her to tell their stories. This incident of course reflects a much wider tension in contemporary anthropology; Stocking describes how the map at the University of Chicago with pins in all the countries where students were conducting their field research came to be seen as a kind of schematic for imperialism—another country being exploited by forms of neocolonialism (1992, 363). What the anthropologist should feel toward those they study is arguably guilt.

Ebihara said that she felt a tremendous sense of guilt and of debts still owed:

> I think for many, many years, all those years I did not go back, I felt this sense of guilt in a way, that they gave me so much, and what did I give them in return? I think precious little, you know, aside from little gifts every time now and then which are insubstantial compared to what they gave me. And when I went back the first few interviews I did about the Pol Pot years, I was extremely depressed, because I realized that I was able to get up and walk out of there and lead a very comfortable life. They had to stay there and suffered tremendously. So that made me feel really quite terrible. (Marston 2011b, 211)

She goes on to say that the one thing that she was able to do that people in Svay appreciated very much was to give back copies of photos that she had taken in 1959–60. Since most people had lost all their prewar photos, these were the only copies they had of lost loved ones. The village headman told her, "Our grandchildren would not know what their grandparents looked like without these photos" (Marston 2011b, 211). So this gave her some sense of having given something in return. I think the donations that she made to the local temple over the years and the money she gave to individuals in time of need also served to help repay her obligations to those who shared the stories of their lives.

Perhaps with the publication of this dissertation turned book, the debt is further repaid; though I think this is not at all certain. With the translation of the book into Khmer, there is the possibility that individuals could be identified and be unsettled by their portrayal. There are moments in the dissertation where people appear in a less than favorable light, hence the decision was made to use pseudonyms rather than real names. Perhaps when this book appears in Khmer, descendants of those described will have comments on how their relatives are portrayed. The book that follows, however, is as it was written by Ebihara: voices from another time.

Judy Ledgerwood

## REFERENCES

Aymonier, E. 1904. *Le Cambodge*. Vol. 3: *Le groups d'Angkor et l'histoire*. Paris: E. Leroux.

Barth, A. 1885. *Inscriptions sanscrites du Cambodge*. Paris: Imprimerie Nationale.

Biddulph, Robbin. 1996. "Participatory Development in Authoritarian Societies: The Case of Village Development Committees in Two Villages in Banteay Meanchey Province, Cambodia." Master's thesis, Development Administration, Australian National University.

———. 1999. "Ref. Panel Members for the Concept of Community Conference." In *Conference on the Meaning of Community in Cambodia*, 1:137–38. Phnom Penh: Working Group on Social Organization in Cambodia.

Boua, Chanthou. 1982. "Women in Today's Cambodia." *New Left Review* 131:45–61.

Chandler, David P. 1993. *The Tragedy of Cambodian History: Politics, War, and Revolution since 1945*. New Haven: Yale University Press.

Collins, William. 1998, "Grassroots Civil Society in Cambodia." Center for Advanced Study, Phnom Penh, November. Discussion paper prepared for a workshop organized by Forum Syd and Diakonia in September. http://www.cascambodia.org/file/report/Grassroots%20Civil%20Society%20in%20Cambodia-11-1998.pdf.

Criddle, Joan D., and Teeda Butt Mam. 1987. *To Destroy You Is No Loss: The Odyssey of a Cambodian Family*. New York: Anchor Books.

Davis, Erik. 2011. "Imagined Parasites: Flows of Monies and Spirits." In *Cambodia's Economic Transformation*, edited by Caroline Hughes and Kheang Un, 310–29. Copenhagen: NIAS Press.

———. 2016. *Deathpower: Buddhism's Ritual Imagination in Cambodia*. New York: Columbia University Press.

Delvert, Jean. 1961. *Le paysan cambodgien*. Le Monde d'outre-mer, passé et présent, Première série, Etudes 10. Paris: Mouton.

Derks, Annuska. 2008. *Khmer Women on the Move: Exploring Work and Life in Urban Cambodia*. Honolulu: University of Hawai'i Press.

Ebihara, May M. 1966. "Interrelations between Buddhism and Social Systems in Cambodian Peasant Culture." In Manning Nash et al., *Anthropological Studies in Theravada Buddhism*, Cultural Report Series 13, 175–96. New Haven: Yale University.

——. 1968. "Svay: A Khmer Village in Cambodia." PhD diss., Columbia University.

——. 1973. "Intervillage, Intertown and Village–City Relations in Cambodia." *Annals of the New York Academy of Sciences* 220:358–75.

——. 1974. "Khmer Village Women in Cambodia." in *Many Sisters: Women in Cross-Cultural Perspective*, edited by Carolyn J. Matthiasson, 305–47. New York: Free Press.

——. 1977. "Residence Patterns in a Khmer Village." *Annals of the New York Academy of Sciences* 293:51–68.

——. 1987. "Revolution and Reformulation in Kampuchean Village Culture." In *The Cambodian Agony*, edited by David Ablin and Marlowe Hood, 16–61, Armonk, NY: M. E. Sharpe.

——. 1990. "Return to a Khmer Village." *Cultural Survival Quarterly* 14 (3). https://www.culturalsurvival.org/publications/cultural-survival-quarterly/return-khmer-village.

——. 1993a. "'Beyond Suffering': The Recent History of a Cambodian Village." In *The Challenge of Reform in Indochina*, edited by Börje Ljunggren, 149–66. Cambridge, MA: Harvard Institute for International Development, Harvard University Press.

——. 1993b. "A Cambodian Village under the Khmer Rouge, 1975–1979." In *Genocide and Democracy in Cambodia: The Khmer Rouge, the United Nations and the International Community*, edited by Ben Kiernan, Southeast Asia Studies Monograph 41, 51–63. New Haven: Yale University Southeast Asia Studies.

——. 2002. "Memories of the Pol Pot Era in a Cambodian Village." In *Cambodia Emerges from the Past: Eight Essays*, edited by Judy Ledgerwood, 91–108. DeKalb: Center for Southeast Asian Studies, Northern Illinois University.

Ebihara, May, and Judy Ledgerwood. 2002. "Aftermaths of Genocide: Cambodian Villagers." In *Annihilating Difference: The Anthropology of Genocide*, edited by Alexander L. Hinton, 272–91. Berkeley: University of California Press.

Embree, John F. 1950. "Thailand—A Loosely Structured Social System." *American Anthropologist* 52:181–93.

Evans-Pritchard, E. E. 1950. "Social Anthropology: Past and Present. The Marett Lecture, 1950." *Man* 50:118–24.

Finot, L. 1916. *Notes d'épigraphie indochinoise*. Hanoi: Imprimerie d'Extrême-Orient.

Frings, Viviane. 1997. *Le Socialisme et le paysan cambodgien: La politique agricole de la République populaire du Kampuchea et de l'État du Cambodge*. Paris: L'Harmattan.

Geertz, Clifford. 1973. *The Interpretation of Cultures*. New York: Basic Books, Inc.

Hansen, Anne. 2007. *How to Behave: Buddhism and Modernity in Colonial Cambodia, 1860–1930*. Honolulu: University of Hawai'i Press.

Harris, Ian. 2005. *Cambodian Buddhism: History and Practice*. Honolulu: University of Hawai'i Press.

Heder, Steve. 1997. "Racism, Marxism, Labelling, and Genocide in Ben Kiernan's *The Pol Pot Regime*." *South East Asia Research* 5:101–53.

——. 2004. *Cambodian Communism and the Vietnamese Model*. Vol. 1: *Imitation and Independence, 1930–1975*. Bangkok: White Lotus Press.

Henke, Roger. 2011. "NGOs, People's Movements, and Natural Resource Management." In *Cambodia's Economic Transformation*, edited by Caroline Hughes and Kheang Un, 288–309. Copenhagen: NIAS Press.

Him, Chanrithy. 2001. *When Broken Glass Floats: Growing Up under the Khmer Rouge.* New York: W. W. Norton.

Hinton, Alexander Laban. 2004. *Why Did They Kill? Cambodia in the Shadow of Genocide.* California Series in Public Anthropology 11. Berkeley: University of California Press.

Hughes, Caroline. 2006. "The Politics of Gifts: Tradition and Regimentation in Contemporary Cambodia." *Journal of Southeast Asian Studies* 37:469–89.

Hughes, Caroline, and Kheang Un, eds. 2011. *Cambodia's Economic Transformation.* Copenhagen: NIAS Press.

Human Rights Watch. 2015. "'Work Faster or Get Out:' Human Rights Abuses in Cambodia's Garment Industry." https://www.hrw.org/report/2015/03/11/work-faster-or-get-out/labor-rights-abuses-cambodias-garment-industry.

Jacobsen, Trudy. 2008. *Lost Goddesses: The Denial of Female Power in Cambodian History.* Copenhagen: NIAS Press.

Kalab, Malada. 1968. "Study of a Cambodian Village." *Geographical Journal* 134 (4): 521–37.

———, 1976. "Monastic Education, Social Mobility, and Village Structure in Cambodia." In *Changing Identities in Modern Southeast Asia*, edited by D. J. Banks, 155–69. Paris: Mouton.

Kent, Alexandra, and David Chandler, eds. 2008. *People of Virtue: Reconfiguring Religion, Power and Moral Order in Cambodia Today.* NIAS Studies in Asian Topics 43. Copenhagen: NIAS Press.

Khieu Samphan. 1979. *Cambodia's Economy and Industrial Development.* Data Paper 111. Southeast Asia Program, Department of Asian Studies, Cornell University. Ithaca: Cornell University.

Kiernan, Ben. 2008. *The Pol Pot Regime: Race, Power, and Genocide in Cambodia under the Khmer Rouge, 1975–79.* New Haven: Yale University Press.

Kim Sedara. 2011. "Reciprocity: Informal Patterns of Social Interactions in a Cambodian Village." In *Anthropology and Community in Cambodia: Reflections on the Work of May Ebihara*, edited by John Marston, 153-169. Caulfield: Monash University Press.

Kim Sedara and Joakim Öjendal. 2011. "Accountability and Local Politics in Natural Resource Management." In *Cambodia's Economic Transformation*, edited by Caroline Hughes and Kheang Un, 266–87. Copenhagen: NIAS Press.

Kobayashi Satoru. 2005. "An Ethnographic Study of the Reconstruction of Buddhist Practice in Two Cambodian Temples: With the Special Reference to Buddhist *Samay* and *Boran*." *Tonan Ajia Kenkyu (Southeast Asian Studies)* 42 (4):489–518.

———. 2008. "Reconstructing Buddhist Temple Buildings: An Analysis of Village Buddhism after the Era of Turmoil." In *People of Virtue: Reconfiguring Religion, Power and Moral Order in Cambodia Today*, edited by Alexandra Kent and David Chandler, NIAS Studies in Asian Topics 43, 169–94. Copenhagen: NIAS Press.

Kuipers, Joel, and Ray McDermott, eds. 2007. *Fine Description: Ethnographic and Linguistic Essays by Hal Conklin*, Southeast Asia Series, Monograph 56. New Haven: Yale University Southeast Asia Studies.

Ledgerwood, Judy. 1990. "Changing Khmer Conceptions of Gender: Women, Stories and the Social Order." PhD diss., Cornell University.

———. 1995. "Khmer Kinship: The Matriliny/Matriarchy Myth." *Journal of Anthropological Research* 51:247–62.

———. 1996. *Women in Development: Cambodia.* [Manila]: Asian Development Bank.

———. 2008a. "Buddhist Practice in Rural Kandal Province 1960 and 2003: In Honor of May Ebihara." in *People of Virtue: Reconfiguring Religion, Power and Moral Order in Cambodia Today,* edited by Alexandra Kent and David Chandler, NIAS Studies in Asian Topics 43, 147–68. Copenhagen: NIAS Press.

———. 2011. "A Tale of Two Temples: Communities and their Wats." In *Anthropology and Community in Cambodia: Reflections on the Work of May Ebihara,* edited by John Marston, 105–30. Caulfield: Monash University Press.

———. 2012. "Buddhist Ritual and the Reordering of Social Relations in Cambodia." *South East Asia Research* 20:191–206.

Ledgerwood, Judy, and John Vijghen. 2002. "Decision-Making in Rural Khmer Villages." In *Cambodia Emerges from the Past: Eight Essays,* edited by Judy Ledgerwood, 109–50. DeKalb: Center for Southeast Asian Studies, Northern Illinois University.

LeVine, Peg. 2010. *Love and Dread in Cambodia: Weddings, Births, and Ritual Harm under the Khmer Rouge.* Singapore: National University of Singapore Press.

Marston, John. 2008a. "Reconstructing 'Ancient' Cambodian Buddhism." *Contemporary Buddhism* 9:99–121.

———. 2008b. "Wat Preah Thammalanka and the Legend of Lok Ta Nen." In *People of Virtue: Reconfiguring Religion, Power and Moral Order in Cambodia Today,* edited by Alexandra Kent and David Chandler, NIAS Studies in Asian Topics 43, 85–108. Copenhagen: NIAS Press.

———, ed. 2011a. *Anthropology and Community in Cambodia: Reflections on the Work of May Ebihara.* Caulfield: Monash University Press.

———. 2011b. "An Interview with May Ebihara." In *Anthropology and Community in Cambodia: Reflections on the Work of May Ebihara,* edited by John Marston, 191–212. Caulfield: Monash University Press.

———. 2011c. "Introduction." In *Anthropology and Community in Cambodia: Reflections on the Work of May Ebihara,* edited by John Marston, 5–20. Caulfield: Monash University Press.

Marston, John Amos, and Elizabeth Guthrie, eds. 2004. *History, Buddhism, and New Religious Movements in Cambodia.* Honolulu: University of Hawaii Press.

Martel, Gabrielle. 1975. *Lovea, village des environs d'Angkor: Aspects démographiques, économiques et sociologiques.* Publications de l'École Française d'Extrême-Orient 98. Paris: École Française d'Extrême-Orient.

Mills, Mary Beth. 1999. *Thai Women in the Global Labor Force: Consuming Desires, Contested Selves.* New Brunswick: Rutgers University Press.

Népote, Jacques. 1992. *Parenté et organisation sociale dans le Cambodge moderne et contemporain: Quelques aspects et quelques applications du modèle les régissant.* Paris: Olizane.

Ngor, Haing S., and Roger Warner. 1987. *A Cambodian Odyssey.* New York: MacMillan.

Öjendal, Joakim, and Kim Sedara. 2006. *"Korob, Kaud, Klach*: In Search of Agency in Rural Cambodia." *Journal of Southeast Asian Studies* 37:507–26.

Ong, Aihwa. 2003. *Buddha Is Hiding: Refugees, Citizenship, the New America*. Berkeley: University of California Press.

Ovesen, Jan, Ing-Britt Trankell, and Joakim Öjendal. 1996. *When Every Household Is an Island: Social Organization and Power Structures in Rural Cambodia*. Uppsala: Uppsala University.

Panh, Rithy, and Christophe Bataille. 2013. *The Elimination: A Survivor of the Khmer Rouge Confronts His Past and the Commandant of the Killing Fields*. New York: Other Press.

Parkin, Robert. 1990. "Descent in Old Cambodia: Deconstructing a Matrilineal Hypothesis." *Zeitschrift für Ethnologie* 115:209–27.

Przyluski, J. 1925. "La princess à l'odeur des poisson et la nagi dans les tradition de Asie orientale." In *Etudes Asiatiques*, 2 vols., edited by G. Van Oest, 2:265–84. Paris: École Française d'Extême-Orient.

Smith-Hefner, Nancy. 1999. *Khmer American: Identity and Moral Education in a Diasporic Community*. Berkeley: University of California Press.

Stocking, George W. 1992. *The Ethnographer's Magic and Other Essays in the History of Anthropology*. Madison: University of Wisconsin Press.

Szymusiak, Molyda. 1986. *The Stones Cry Out: A Cambodian Childhood, 1975–1980*. Bloomington: Indiana University Press.

Tanner, Nancy. 1974. "Matrifocality in Indonesia and Africa and among Black Americans." In *Woman, Culture, and Society*, edited by Michelle Zimbalist Rosaldo and Louise Lamphere, 129–56. Stanford: Stanford University Press.

Turner, Victor Witter. 1967. *The Forest of Symbols: Aspects of Ndembu Ritual*. Cornell Paperbacks 101. Ithaca: Cornell University Press.

U Sam Oeur and Ken McCullough. 2005. *Crossing Three Wildernesses: A Memoir*. Minneapolis: Coffee House Press.

Un, Kheang. 2005. "Patronage Politics and Hybrid Democracy: Political Change in Cambodia, 1993–2003." *Asian Perspective* 29 (2): 203–30.

———. 2006. "State, Society, and Democratic Consolidation: The Case of Cambodia." *Pacific Affairs* 79 (2): 225–45.

Ung, Loung. 2012. *First They Killed My Father: A Daughter of Cambodia Remembers*. New York: Random House.

Vickery, Michael. 1984. *Cambodia 1975–1982*. Boston: South End Press.

Vijghen, John, and Sareoun Ly. 1996. *Customs of Patronage and Community Development in a Cambodian Village*. Phnom Penh: Cambodian Researchers for Development.

Yathay, Pin. 2013. *Stay Alive, My Son*. Ithaca: Cornell University Press.

Zucker, Eve. 2008. "The Absence of Elders: Chaos and Moral Order in the Aftermath of the Khmer Rouge." In *People of Virtue: Reconfiguring Religion, Power and Morality in Cambodia Today*, edited by Alexandra Kent and David Chandler, NIAS Studies in Asian Topics 43, 195–212. Copenhagen: NIAS Press.

———. 2013. *Forest of Struggle: Moralities of Remembrance in Upland Cambodia*. Honolulu: University of Hawai'i Press.

# SVAY

## A Khmer Village in Cambodia

*May Mayko Ebihara*

# ACKNOWLEDGMENTS

As I think back to the years during which this research was pursued, a hundred names and faces flow through my mind. It would take many pages to list all of the individuals who aided me in one way or another. I cite only the most important persons below, but I extend public thanks to the numerous others who are not specifically named but whom I remember with gratitude.

I am indebted, first, to the Ford Foundation, without whom this work would not have been written. I am also deeply grateful to my professors at Columbia University, especially Dr. Conrad Arensberg, Dr. Margaret Mead, and Dr. Morton Fried, who provided me with stimulating ideas and valuable advice, and who guided me patiently to the completion of the work. I thank also Dr. Harold Conklin, Professor Georges Condominas, and the late Professor François Martini, who gave me aid and special encouragement through the years, and several French scholars who advised me on research in Cambodia: Professor Georges Coedès, Mme. Eveline Porée-Maspero, M. Charles Archaimbault, and M. Bernard-Philippe Groslier.

Numerous persons in the Cambodian government, the American Foreign Service and the United States Overseas Mission, United Nations organizations, the Asia Foundation, and the Unitarian Service Committee gave me valuable information and aid. In particular, I thank Mr. Gaylord Walker, Mr. William Thomas, Dr. Chris DeYoung, M. Noel Salvarelli, M. Chet Chhem, M. Ho Tong Lyp, M. Or-Kosalak, M. Chet Chhoeur, and Mrs. Tlaing Sambour. I am greatly indebted to the École Française-d'Extrême-Orient for allowing me generous use of their facilities, especially Mlle. Martine Piat. Similarly, Mme. Pich-Sal and other members of the Commission des Moeurs et Coutumes du Cambodge were extremely helpful. Special gratitude is due to my wise and patient tutors in the Khmer language: M. Chea Ton, M. Sok, and Mr. Dale Purtle. I owe particular thanks for warm hospitality and aid to Miss Sandy McCaw, Miss Mary DeForest, Mr. Thomas Weir, Mr. and Mrs. Richard Noss, Miss Dorothy Adams, Miss Doris Crozier, Mr. and Mrs. Brian Heise, and Mr. Gordon Elliot.

Finally, my lasting affection and appreciation go to the villagers of West Hamlet Svay who endured my research with patience and humor, protected me from everything from supposed thieves to leaky roofs, guided me to some understanding of their culture, and provided me with rich friendships and memories. My relationships with these adopted kinsmen and neighbors made field work an intensely moving personal, as well as academic, experience. I dedicate this work to my Khmer "parents," Vireak and Srey, and "grandparents," Kompha and Leak, and to my real parents.

# CHAPTER ONE

# INTRODUCTION

This dissertation presents an ethnological characterization of a Khmer rice-growing village in Cambodia. Rather than focusing upon a particular problem or aspect of Cambodian society and culture, it was thought that an analytic description of the entire round of village life would be worthwhile in view of the unfortunate scarcity of anthropological data on the Khmer, who constitute one of the major ethnic groups in Southeast Asia. At the time this study was conceived and executed (1958–60) there was a fairly voluminous literature on Cambodia, but the greater part of it was outdated, limited to particular topics, or relatively inaccessible to American scholars. This statement is not meant to denigrate the contributions of numerous scholars, primarily French, whose extensive studies and experiences have produced works containing many valuable insights and much information on the Khmer.[1] The writings of Frenchmen such as Aymonier, Leclère, Groslier, Coedès, Maspero, Porée-Maspero, Martini, and others cannot be ignored by any student of Cambodia. However, none of these persons are professional anthropologists, although men like Coedès are renowned scholars in other disciplines while others, such as Leclère, were excellent amateur ethnographers.[2] The bulk of the literature on Cambodia concerned archaeology and history (dealing especially with Angkor), and those works that did contain some ethnological information were either from the nineteenth century or discussed discrete aspects of culture such as ceremonio-religious life, folklore, or formal law (see, for example, the bibliography on Cambodia in Embree and Dotson 1950). Thus, in 1958, our picture of Cambodia had many lacunae from the standpoint of American and British anthropology. In particular, virtually nothing was known about the fundamental structure and functioning of contemporary Khmer culture and society at the level of the village.[3] There was, for example, no data on the scope and significance of kin relations in Cambodian society or precise information on other aspects of social organization such as residence and inheritance patterns. Similarly, there was at that time no clear picture of economic organization, stratification, or the role of religion in village life; the relations between the rural community and the town and city; and many other

---

[1] For brief discussions on French scholarly research in Indochina, see Thompson 1937, 351–52; Thompson and Adloff 1947; Embree 1948; Embree and Dotson 1950, ix–x; Porée-Maspero 1955b; Condominas 1965; Thomas 1955, 38–58; Groslier 1960b. For an assessment of existing ethnological literature on the Khmer, see appendix A.

[2] Apart from this author, the only other trained anthropologists to have conducted research among the Khmer are Eldon Johnson (now director of the Science Museum of the Saint Paul Institute in Minnesota) who worked among Khmer in northeast Thailand, and Mlle. G. Martel who investigated a village in northern Cambodia and is presently completing her thesis at the University of Paris.

[3] Only in 1961 did the first detailed and significant work on Khmer peasantry appear in Jean Delvert's *Le Paysan cambodgien*.

critical questions. Such lacunae impelled and directed my work, and I hope that some are partially filled by the present volume.

My work, then, has a dual purpose. The first and primary purpose is to add an ethnography of one type of Cambodian peasant culture to our reservoir of comparative data. The major portion of the work is, therefore, devoted to a description and analysis of the round of life in Village Svay. Chapter 2 surveys various aspects of the nation as a whole as the context within which the village operates. In chapter 3, after placing Svay in its physical setting, I introduce the villagers themselves in a discussion of social organization. Chapters 4 and 5 discuss village economic life and religious life, the features that, in addition to social organization, seem most critical for perceiving the distinctive cast of the Khmer community. The life cycle (chapter 6) and political structure (chapter 7) are less critical but nonetheless important for a rounded picture. And lest the village seem an altogether self-sufficient unit, chapter 8 emphasizes the relations it maintains with the surrounding countryside and with the city.

In addition to presenting data from my own fieldwork, I have also tried to draw together information on Khmer culture that is scattered in diverse sources and to note—when possible—whether the practices observed in Svay seem to be representative of the culture as a whole, or whether they hold true only for a particular region or segment of the total society. I do so for two reasons: because there are no other published anthropological accounts of a Khmer community, and because some anthropologists have questioned whether the study of one community yields real insight into the total culture (see below). Svay can be seen, therefore, as one example or view of Khmer peasantry.

The second purpose of this dissertation is ethnological and attempts to use the Cambodian data for a higher level of generalizations about the nature of Southeast Asian culture and of peasant societies in general. While I do not wish to burden the body of this work with excessive reference to comparative data from other cultures, certainly the latter are of great importance if this work is to be more than merely idiographic. The concluding chapter will, therefore, be devoted to a discussion of Khmer village society and culture as part of a Southeast Asian culture area and as a type of peasantry.

## SELECTION OF A VILLAGE

My intention was to study a lowland, rice-growing Khmer village because the Khmer comprise the dominant part of the nation's population and rice production occupies the majority of the peasantry. More specifically, on the basis of existing information about the nature of Cambodian villages and my own needs, the initial research proposal called for a community with the following features: (1) a population of no more than several hundred inhabitants (a unit manageable for one researcher) that was primarily Khmer in composition, (2) a village Buddhist temple, (3) location off a main road but with easy accessibility to bus routes, (4) the presence of at least one resident who spoke some French, and (5) villagers amenable to investigation.

The next question was which region of the country to select. Further research, actual surveys of the countryside, and discussions in Cambodia with various persons familiar with the country indicated that the area south of Phnom Penh seemed to be most typically Cambodian in terms of ethnic composition, ecology, and culture (see also Delvert 1961, 542). Other regions or provinces were discarded because they had large minority groups (e.g., Kompong Cham with its Chinese), practiced somewhat atypical economies (e.g., Battambang with its large per capita landholdings and market orientation), were too isolated and sparsely populated (e.g., eastern Cambodia), had been subject to rather unique historical events (e.g., the provinces bordering Vietnam), or were even too conservatively tied to old traditions (e.g., Siem Reap). The search for a suitable community was thus concentrated in the region around Phnom Penh.

One major problem was encountered in the quest. Small villages of several hundred inhabitants were not readily available in accessible regions. After World War II, due to such factors as internecine rebel activity and infiltrations from Vietnam, smaller villages tended to merge with others into larger protective units, either through voluntary choice or through government removal programs (see also Steinberg 1959, 31; Delvert 1961, 207–10). There are still small villages in Cambodia, but they did not fulfill my other requirements. Thus, my choice settled finally upon Village Svay, a community that fulfilled all desiderata except for size, the settlement as a whole having a population of almost eight hundred inhabitants. However, Svay is divided into three hamlets (one of which I had actually mistaken for a small village on my first visit there), and it was decided that the relatively self-contained and isolated West Hamlet would serve as a good approximation of a small community.[4]

I resided in West Hamlet Svay from April 1959 to March 1960. The bulk of my research was concentrated within the hamlet itself. But a census was taken for the entire village; twenty randomly selected families in the rest of Svay (ten in each of the other hamlets) were interviewed in some depth regarding certain points of social and economic organization; and various other data were also checked with villagers in the other hamlets. (See appendix B for other information about the circumstances of the fieldwork.)

A question must inevitably arise as to the "typicality" of Village Svay, a query that raises some important methodological and theoretical issues. Actually, two things are being asked: first, how similar is the community investigated to the other villages in the country; and second, what (or how much) does a description of village life tell you about the culture of the nation (or ethnic group) as a whole. The latter problem in particular has been a topic of some discussion in anthropology (see, for example, Arensberg 1954, 1957, 1961; Steward 1950, 1955, chap. 4; Redfield 1955). In my own mind, one way to view this dilemma of "typicality" was suggested by Kluckhohn, Murray, and Schneider's discussion of personality (1961, 53). To paraphrase their statements by inserting another term in place of the word "man," we may say: "In some ways one village is like *all* other villages; in some ways one villages is like *some* other villages; and in some ways one village is like *no* other village." Each of these points, in reverse order, will be discussed as it applies to Village Svay.

In some respects, Svay is like *no* other village because of its particular concatenation of historical events and individuals, which can be viewed as utterly unique. For

---

[4] There were also two subjective factors that influenced my choice. First, I was immediately attracted to Svay by its pleasant setting, its notably friendly and lively inhabitants who were receptive to study, and the immediate availability of a house and interpreter. Second, in 1959 there were sporadic outbreaks of anti-American sentiment fostered by the Cambodian government that made it desirable to remain fairly close to Phnom Penh. Svay was not only thirty kilometers from the city but near a national teacher training center with a few American advisors, so that aid in event of any trouble would be readily obtainable. The presence of this normal school turned out to be a further advantage in that the villagers were accustomed to foreigners and were sympathetic to the role of student that I assumed.

our purposes, however, these points of uniqueness may be of interest but do not seriously affect the question of Svay as a "sample" of Cambodian culture. Two points, however, should be noted. First, the proximity of Svay to a national teacher-training center (which feature is actually shared with another village) has affected the community in certain ways that will be discussed in relevant sections of subsequent chapters; but it has not seriously disrupted or altered traditional life. Second, the presence of even one anthropologist fostered some unavoidable changes in West Svay (notably in the economies of certain families and in the villagers' awareness of the outside world); again, however, I think that my impact was of minor significance.

In other ways, Svay is like *some* other villages in Cambodia. Regarding this and the next point, it is difficult to itemize exactly the variations in culture that may exist in Cambodia because of the scarcity of comparative data on Khmer peasantry. But from the information that is available (notably in Delvert 1961), it seems that the main differences among Cambodian villages are to be found in their economic basis, ethnic composition, and settlement pattern and size. With this in mind, it can be said, in the most general terms, that Svay is a fair representative of numerous other villages throughout the country that have an economy centered around rice cultivation (as contrasted to those that grow other crops or specialize in crafts or fishing), that have a fairly sizeable dense population, and that are ethnically and culturally Khmer. In more specific terms, Svay's overall economic organization and settlement pattern are especially similar to communities in the general area south of Phnom Penh. The "typicality" or "non-typicality" of Svay in other spheres of culture will be noted throughout the text, where comparative information is available.

Another question is raised by the relative proximity of Svay to Phnom Penh, the nation's capital, that is thirty kilometers distant: namely, whether this closeness to the city means strong urban influences on Svay that make the village "atypical." Svay undoubtedly differs from the remote and inaccessible communities of some parts of Cambodia in certain respects. First, the residents of Svay (as of other villages within about a fifty-kilometer radius of the city) can easily undertake temporary urban employment. Second, it is probable (though there is no information on this point) that Svay villagers are more cognizant of urban affairs and styles than people in the hinterlands. On the other hand, however, it should be emphasized that urbanization, in the sense of the city's impact on the countryside, is still relatively limited; and rural settlements can be found on the very fringes of Phnom Penh. For while villagers may be within close geographical proximity of the city, peasant attitudes, mores, and poverty often create what might be called "social distance" between villager and city such that cognizance of urban life does not necessarily mean adoption of urban ways. In sum, then, it is likely that Svay's nearness to Phnom Penh does not make it significantly less "rural" than most Cambodian villages.

Finally, Svay is probably like *all* other villages in several important respects, as well as exhibiting certain features of the national culture as a whole. As Arensberg (1954, 1957, 1961) has suggested, the question of whether or not any one community can be considered a microcosm involves the problem of separating the general from the specific. In the preceding discussion, attention has been centered on the more specific attributes of Village Svay, elements either unique to itself or shared with some other communities. Our consideration turns now to what I believe to be general features (again with the proviso that comparative data on other villages is limited). First, it is fair to say that the rural population as a whole can be differentiated from the urban segments of Cambodian society by its general mode of life that fulfills the defining characteristics of peasantry (see chapter 9). Second, certain aspects of Cambodian culture seem common to both Khmer peasant and urbanite: in particular, the language; the basic features of the kinship system (including the fundamental bilateral structure, kin terminology, and patterns of residence and inheritance); the religious system composed of both Buddhist and folk elements (with all their attendant rituals, specialists, etc.); and the life cycle (including the general patterns of child rearing and sex roles as well as ceremonial observances). There are indeed variations in these elements according to both region and class (e.g., in the sphere of ceremonio-religious observances, some regions have evidently preserved certain traditional practices that others have discarded, and the aristocracy and other members of the upper strata have life-cycle ceremonies that are much more elaborate and closer to the great tradition than those of the peasantry). But such variations are, I believe, differences of degree (as it were) rather than kind; and the most essential elements of these aspects of culture are ubiquitous among all levels and territorial regions of Khmer society.

It cannot, of course, be claimed that the entire, rich range of Cambodian society and culture is mirrored in Village Svay. As Steward (1950, 1955) and others (e.g., Manners 1957) have discussed, various institutions have national (as well as local) aspects whose nature cannot be clearly discerned by a study of the small community alone. By now it has become virtually a truism that one must have at least a minimal awareness of the larger milieu within which the community operates, particularly for peasant villages that are often characterized as "part-societies with part-cultures" (Kroeber 1948, 284). But an exhaustive examination of the entire national (and even international) context is a taxing chore for the anthropologist whose particular province is, after all, the study of the "grass roots" local culture (Arensberg 1957). And the anthropologist's focus on the village does provide, in the last analysis, a picture of "a full round of life" and a microcosm of at least a sub-culture or certain basic cultural patterns (Redfield 1955; Arensberg 1954, 1955, 1961). It is such a picture that I hope to present in the following discussion of a Khmer community.

## NOTES ON ORTHOGRAPHY, CURRENCY, AND MEASUREMENTS

### ORTHOGRAPHY

I have been somewhat hesitant to introduce a new system of orthography for Cambodian words out of deference to French scholars who have long used certain methods for transcription of Khmer. Yet it seems useful and justifiable to do so for several reasons: (1) because readers of English associate different phonemes with certain alphabetic symbols than do the French; (2) because the French system usually transcribes Khmer words as they are written rather than spoken, and the two often differ from one another; (3) because I myself use the International Phonetic Alphabet (IPA) for transcriptions in the field, and my transcriptions were of spoken rather than written Khmer.

The French orthography has been retained for geographical place names and proper names of famous figures (e.g., kings) in order not to controvert long-standing conventional uses. All other Cambodian words, however, will be transcriptions of spoken Khmer in IPA, with slight changes of symbols due to the limitations of ordinary typewriters. I must emphasize that I am not a trained linguist and cannot vouch for the purity of the transcriptions, especially with regard to aspiration, length of vowels, and exact discrimination among the numerous vowels in Khmer. For more detailed analysis of the Khmer language, consult Maspero 1915; Martini 1942–45, 1955c; Phan and Noss 1958; Cambefort 1950; and Pannetier and Menetrier 1922. (See also the section on language in chapter 2.)

a = as in French "p<u>á</u>s"
æ = as in "h<u>a</u>t"
e = as in "l<u>ay</u>" or French "é"
E = as in "l<u>e</u>t"
ė = as in shw<u>a</u>
i = as in "fl<u>ee</u>t"
I = as in "l<u>i</u>t"
o = as in "d<u>oe</u>"
ȯ = as in "l<u>o</u>ng"
ø = as in French "<u>oe</u>uf"
u = as in "J<u>u</u>ne"
 u̇ = as in "s<u>u</u>n"
y = similar to "i" above, but less pronounced
c = ch (all other consonants are pronounced as in English)
? = glottal stop
<u>h</u> after <u>p</u>, <u>t</u>, and <u>k</u> indicates aspiration
duplication of a vowel indicates length

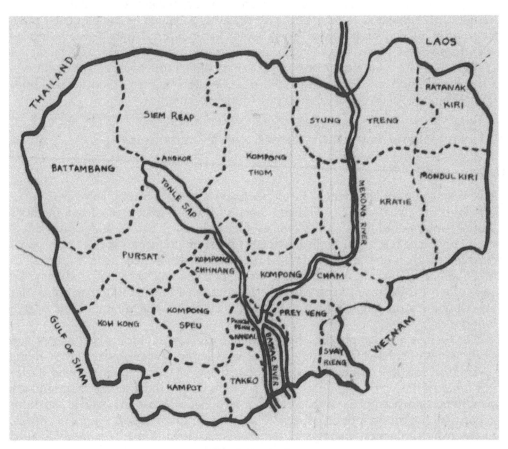

**Map 1** Cambodia

## CURRENCY

The monetary exchange unit in Cambodia is the *rièl* (riel). In 1959, the official exchange rate was about thirty-five riels to one American dollar, the unofficial exchange rate about seventy riels to the dollar. The latter figure is the more realistic one for translating the value of various Khmer goods into terms of our currency.

## MEASUREMENT

Measurements of various items are, for the most part, presented in terms of the metric system that is used in Cambodia. For the benefit of readers, the following table offers American equivalents of various metric units of measure.

1 hectare (ha.) = 100 ares (a.) = 2.47 acres
1 meter (m.) = 3.28 feet
1 kilometer (km.) = 0.6 miles
1 kilogram (kg.) = 2.26 pounds
1 liter (l.) = 1 liquid quart or 0.9 dry quart

# CHAPTER TWO

# CAMBODIA AS A WHOLE

Entering Cambodia by air from the west, the brief flight from Thailand to Phnom Penh offers a capsule view of many historic and contemporary features of the nation. One's first sight of the country is forested mountains that appear deserted and impregnable. Yet in many such regions of Cambodia, especially in the east, live "tribal" peoples who are perhaps descendants of the earliest inhabitants of Southeast Asia. The next significant view is a glimpse of the famous Angkor Wat, once a magnificent complex of structures built during the glory of the ancient Khmer empire and now monumental masses of grey-brown ruins set within the encroaching green of the jungle. The flight continues over Lake Tonle Sap, like a huge inland sea dotted with fish weirs, then along the Tonle Sap River flowing south to meet the Mekong. In the lowlands is a ubiquitous pattern of irregularly shaped rice paddies, their dikes spreading a great web across the countryside, broken by waterways, roads, and clusters of houses in villages and towns. Finally the traveler lands at a small, modern airport in Phnom Penh to be enveloped by warm, moist air. A drive into the city gives a jumbled impression of green palms, black-clothed figures, European villas, pile dwellings, and glaring sun.

## GEOGRAPHY

Cambodia is a rather small country of almost seventy thousand square miles, approximately the size of the state of Missouri, located on the peninsula of mainland Southeast Asia. Open to the Gulf of Siam on the southwest, it is otherwise landlocked: bounded on the west and northwest by Thailand, on the north by Laos, and on the east and southeast by Vietnam (see map 1). The topography is roughly suggestive of a crude bowl. Most of the country's interior is a flat or occasionally rolling lowland plain not far above sea level, but the plain breaks into plateaus and mountains that form some natural as well as national boundaries, although there are lowland passes offering access to neighboring countries. (See Morizon 1936, 15, 34; Zadrozny 1955, 57; Dobby 1960, 300–302; Delvert 1961, 15–21 for details.) Cutting diagonally across this landscape are two major waterways. The Mekong River flows through eastern Cambodia, and the Tonle Sap River in the west originates in the lake of the same name. The two meet at Phnom Penh before becoming separate again (thus the term "quatre bras" that is applied to this confluence); the Tonle Sap becomes the Bassac River and flows more or less parallel with the Mekong into Vietnam. Various other lesser rivers and streams run off these main drainage systems, all of which are important for fishing, sometimes for transportation, and in some regions the provision of alluvial soil through annual flooding. Lake Tonle Sap is also critical for fishing and its floods. (For details, see Morizon 1936, 35–45; Zadrozny 1955, 58; Dobby 1960, 301; Delvert 1961, 55.)

The location of Cambodia between approximately 10 and 14 degrees north of the equator makes it obvious that the climate is tropical: in brief, generally hot and humid.

The climactic year is, however, divided into two important periods that influence the rhythm of life. From approximately November through April (the exact dates vary regionally) is the dry season with winds from the northeast. December and January are relatively fresh and cool, necessitating small fires and shawls to warm the villagers at late night ceremonies or early morning tasks, although the actual temperature does not fall below 65 degrees Fahrenheit and is usually in the 70s during the day. But from February onward, the temperature mounts relentlessly until it is in the 80s and 90s during April and May; the Cambodians themselves become weary with heat, and the land becomes parched. In about May, however, the wind shifts to the southeast and brings the rainy season that will last into November. Although the temperatures remain high, the heat is broken for an hour or more each day by a heavy, benevolent rain that refreshes not only the land but the people. The exact dates of the rainy season and the amount of rainfall vary regionally and annually; but as one example, annual rainfall in Phnom Penh averages 55.8 inches with 121 days of rain (Dobby 1960, 290). (See also Zadrozny 1955, 60–61; Delvert 1961, 35–49, 721.)

Most of Cambodia was originally forested, and nearly half of the country's total area is still covered with dense tropical woods in southwestern highlands and interriverine sections of central Cambodia. One-third of the land is so-called open forest of mixed evergreen and deciduous trees in northern Cambodia. The remainder is covered with short grass and savannah. But much of the open forest and grassland have been cleared for cultivation and are now replaced by rice or vegetable plots and various domesticated flora. (See Zadrozny 1955, 64–65; Delvert 1961, 114–61.)

## HISTORY

Cambodia has a complex history, a detailed description of which is best left to the professional historian. This discussion will present only a general overview of major historical periods and concentrate rather on the nature of sociopolitical organization at various times, insofar as the latter can be reconstructed.

## PREHISTORY

The prehistory of Cambodia and the Khmer is virtually unknown. There can be only conjecture as to the origins and movements of the earliest Khmer who (along with their linguistic relatives, the Mon) evidently moved into peninsular Southeast Asia from somewhere to the north (Chassigneux 1929, 32–33; Olivier 1956, 6; Steinberg 1959, 37). Because of the paucity of prehistoric sites in Cambodia itself,[1] reconstruction of probable early Khmer culture must depend a good deal on inference from remains in other parts of Southeast Asia and suggestion from the life of contemporary tribal peoples. On the basis of such evidence, it has been suggested that protohistoric Khmer (and Southeast Asian) culture at the end of the pre-Christian era, before the impact of Indian and Chinese influences, was of the following nature (viz. Coedès 1948, 25–26; 1953, 370–71; Briggs 1951, 12–16; Linton 1955, 174–76; Giteau 1957,

---

[1] There are three Neolithic sites in Cambodia itself: Samrong Sen and Longprao in Kompong Chhnang province, and Melou Prei in Kompong Thom province; for brief descriptions thereof, see Giteau 1957, 7–10; Briggs 1951, 15–16; Burling 1965a, 35–36.

5–11; Groslier 1957, 14): (a) cultivation of rice[2] and other plants, supplemented by fishing and hunting; domesticated oxen, water buffalo, and perhaps the pig; a technology that included stone, bamboo, and metal implements as well as pottery and basketry; pile dwellings, knowledge of navigation; (b) settlement (primarily in coastal areas or in the hills bordering the river valleys) in villages that were relatively autonomous political entities under village chiefs who may have supervised agricultural labors and officiated religious rites; (c) kinship[3] as a major factor in structuring social relations and providing social cement; endogamous communities; women accorded a respected status; (d) a religious system built around animistic beliefs, ancestor worship, and a god of the soil; location of cult shrines on heights; inhumation of the dead in jars or dolmens; dualism in mythology between mountains and sea, winged and aquatic beings, and people of the coast and the mountains.

## THE ANCIENT KINGDOMS

Subsequent periods of Cambodian history become relatively well illuminated by extensive archaeological remains, Khmer inscriptions, Chinese chronicles, and finally European literature. Because of the nation's diverse and complex background of various kingdoms with shifting boundaries, successive rulers, and numerous events, only a brief account of especially significant points will be presented here.[4]

In the region that is now Cambodia, the earliest known kingdom is Funan, which was evidently founded in the first century AD. Its inhabitants were probably physically, linguistically, and culturally similar to the Khmer, but the Khmer proper seem to have been geographically and politically separate in the early part of the Christian era and more properly identified with the so-called Chenla kingdom to the north of Funan. (At this same time, to the east in what is now Vietnam, were the Chams or Champa kingdom.) Chenla was originally a vassal of Funan, but it rose to ascendancy in the mid-sixth century and moved south to conquer Funan and displace the Chams. At the height of its power, Chenla's empire spread even to the border of what is now China. But in the eighth century it was split by internal conflict and was subsequently conquered by the Indonesian-Malayan Srivijayan empire. However, reunification of the kingdom and reestablishment of indigenous rulers occurred in the ninth century.

Behind these bare historical facts lie some critical cultural developments that are implied by the use of terms such as "kingdom" and "empire." The Funanese and Chenla peoples were originally "tribal" cultures such as described in the preceding section. But during and after the first century, there was a transformation to a monarchic state level of organization, as well as other important changes. The basic stimulus to development was the impact of Indian civilization. The Funan kingdom, according to one account, was founded by the union of an Indian Brahman and a native princess; the Brahman, with supernatural aid, frightened the princess into submission, married

---

[2] Coedès states that wet-rice cultivation was practiced, but Fisher (1964, 81) doubts that it was widespread at this early time.

[3] Coedès feels that the kinship system was matrilineal; cf. Linton who proposes bilaterality.

[4] For detailed accounts of ancient Cambodian history, see in particular Leclère 1914; Coedès 1948; Briggs 1951; Groslier 1957, 1958; Hall 1964. These works have served as the sources for this presentation of history up to the fall of Angkor. For more recent periods, see (among others) Leclère 1914; Robequain 1944; Micaud 1949; Zadrozny 1955; Giteau 1957; Herz 1958; Hall 1964; Cady 1964.

her, and clothed her nakedness. Whether or not this legend is actually rooted in some historical reality, it is important for offering a symbolic representation of one of the most critical aspects of Cambodian history: the influence of India in helping to mold and elaborate early Khmer culture. From about the beginning of the Christian era, Indian merchants, princes, priests, and travelers were drawn to Southeast Asia in search of trade goods, fortune, or adventure. With them came various elements of the Indian great tradition that were transmitted to the native population through inter-marriage, continuous trade relations, Brahmans acting as advisors to native rulers, etc.[5] In addition, Khmer and other Southeast Asians also traveled to India. From such interaction, one of the most important cultural features adopted by the indigenes was the concept of the state or kingdom with a centralized government under a supreme monarch, an administrative corps, and a system of codified law. Coedès (1953, 374) has suggested that the adoption of such a political structure was stimulated by two major factors: first, the execution of certain activities (e.g., the development of irrigation works) required collective effort and central authority going beyond the local villages;[6] and second, once formerly autonomous communities became conscious of a larger unit the role of chief was easily transformed into that of king.

This change in political organization also suggests a critical change in social structure. A monarchic state implies differentiation between rulers and ruled, nobility and commoners, administrative centers and countryside, various non-agricultural specialists and food producers. Thus, if peasantry is considered to be the rural agricultural segment of a nation with important economic, political, and social ties to elite groups in urbanized centers, then a large segment of the population was being transformed into peasants during this same period (cf. Wolf 1966, 11). The Indian tradition of rigid castes never diffused into Khmer culture, but the basically egalitarian social structure of tribal society gave way to a system of more or less well-defined social classes, hierarchical ranking, occupational differentiation, and a distinction between urbanite and rural villager.

Other important cultural traits came from or were stimulated by India during the Funan and subsequent periods, as evidenced in the following examples. The Indian legal system provided a model for the codification of native law. Hinduism (including Sivaism, Vishnuism, and attendant elements of cosmology, mythology, and ceremony) was the official court religion of the early empires and also influenced art, literature, drama, and architecture. The Khmer writing system was originally Indian in origin, and the language had borrowed some vocabulary from Sanskrit and Pali.

One can measure the entire importance of the civilizing action of India by this simple fact of observation: in regard to somatic physical characteristics, a Cambodian peasant hardly differs from a Pnong . . . but the Pnongs . . . have remained in the stage of tribal organization; they settle their disputes following oral custom; they have for religion only a simple animism whose elements vary from one tribe to another; their cosmology is rudimentary; they possess no characters

[5] There are various theories as to the primary means by which Indianization was effected in Southeast Asia; for a review thereof, see Coedès 1953, 372–73; Hall 1964, chap. 2.

[6] Fisher (1964, 93–94) discusses Wittfogel's notions of hydraulic works and oriental despotism with respect to Southeast Asia and concludes that "despotic" features in this area were more a matter of what Wittfogel calls "institutional transfer" from India and China rather than truly indigenous examples of hydraulic despotism.

to write their languages. Whereas the least evolved Cambodian is caught in the machinery of a strongly hierarchical state; he is subject to the jurisdiction of the courts that judge according to written codes; he practices with much fervor a religion that possesses its dogma, cosmology, and . . . coherent views that are those of a great part of Asiatic humanity; finally, he commands a writing system that gives him access to a vast literature and permits communication at a distance with his fellow men. All that he owes to India, and to summarize this statement, in a somewhat gross formula, one can say that the Cambodian is a Hinduized Pnong. (Coedès 1948, 3; my translation)

It must be strongly emphasized, however, that the Khmer did not merely slavishly imitate India. For the most part, India provided frameworks or models that the indigenous culture utilized and developed in its own distinctive ways. The final forms and styles of various aspects of Cambodian culture have a flavor that may be reminiscent of India but are quite unique in themselves.

It might be noted that the early kingdoms also had contact with the other great civilization of the east: China. Chinese travelers, traders, and diplomatic envoys came to this region very early, and a number of Khmer dynasties paid token tribute to Chinese rulers. The impact of Chinese culture on the Khmer was, however, relatively limited as compared to the more overwhelming influence of India. Some details of ceremonials and art, part of the calendrical system, certain aspects of dress, etc., may be traced to China. But Cambodia remains essentially an Indianized rather than Sinicized culture such as Vietnam.

In the ninth century, the Khmer began several centuries of brilliant cultural florescence in the so-called Angkor period (802–1432 AD).[7] Now calling itself Kambujadesa,[8] the Khmer empire as a political entity came eventually to spread over most of the Southeast Asian peninsula, including what is now Cambodia and parts of Thailand, Vietnam, Laos, Burma, and Yunnan. The heights of development and elaboration in other aspects of the culture are still materially evident in the famous ruins of Angkor and its complex of magnificent temples, palaces, libraries, reservoirs and irrigation systems, etc. There is also the chronicle of Chou Ta-kuan, member of a diplomatic mission to Angkor in the late thirteenth century, who describes, among other things, a royal procession replete with soldiers, musicians, hundreds of palace women carrying candles and royal utensils of gold and silver, ministers and princes mounted on elephants and accompanied by gold-ornamented parasols, royal wives and concubines borne in palanquins and carts, and the king himself standing on an elephant whose tusks were sheathed in gold (Pelliot 1951, 34–35).

In brief, the following picture emerges of Angkorean Cambodia. The empire was ruled by a god-king (a concept introduced at the beginning of the Angkor period) who was considered the earthly incarnation of divinity. (This idea was related to the official state religion of worship of a lingam that was considered the seat of the divine essence of kingship; see Heine-Geldern 1956, 6–7.) The monarch had, at least in theory, absolute power over all lands and people. Beneath the king were the aristocracy,

---

[7] The name and dates of this and other periods are taken from Briggs 1951.

[8] The term "Kambuja" derives from the name of Kambu, the presumed founder of the lineage of Khmer kings during the Chenla period. "Kambuja" means "sons of Kambu," and "Kambujadesa" is translated as "country of Kambuja."

priesthood, an administrative hierarchy of various civil and military officials holding different ranks, the common people, and slaves captured in war or from among the tribal groups. There was some tendency to endogamy in royal and priestly lines, but the system of social stratification was essentially one of class rather than caste. There were, however, definite rights and symbols of status associated with particular ranks and strata (e.g., certain kinds of dress and houses were forbidden to the ordinary populace).

It was not uncommon for Khmer kings to build new capitals upon their accession to the throne or to shift the location of the capital for political or military reasons. These capitals may be considered the cities of Khmer antiquity, being large and complex settlements with a diverse population.[9] Angkor Thom and its environs are said to have been larger than any of the European medieval walled cities and could have easily encompassed Nero's Rome (Briggs 1951, 219). The capitals were primarily religious and administrative centers; they served as the symbolic magical center of the empire and a microcosm of the universe with the king's palace or temple as the focus (Heine-Geldern 1956, 3), as the seat of government, and as the place of residence for the nobility and major officials. But their suburbs also encompassed markets and the homes of the ordinary people (artisans, merchants, peasants, etc.). Interesting is the fact that these capitals were located in different parts of the country at different times; thus, peasantry in various regions came into closer or further geographical proximity to urban centers during different periods, which factor may also have affected the intensity of bonds with the elite groups.

Sources for this period do not have a great deal of information on the peasantry per se, but it can be presumed that a substantial proportion of the population was engaged in agriculture and/or fishing (and perhaps the exploitation of forest resources in some cases). There was an impressive and extensive system of irrigation at Angkor that watered the surrounding countryside and was capable of sustaining at least two and even four harvests a year (as well as providing routes of travel) (for details, see especially Groslier 1957, 24–25; 1958, 108–12, plate VII); Chou Ta-kuan also speaks of the use of wet paddies, plows, sickles, and hoes.[10] Moreover, Lake Tonle Sap has always been noted for its abundant supply of fish. The Chinese envoy tells further of a daily market (without established stalls but mats laid on the ground for selling produce) with various media of exchange that included rice and other cereals, cloth, silver, and gold; as well as the existence of some Chinese merchants. One may thus surmise that some agricultural produce was used for trade as well as for subsistence and taxes, though Coe (1961) feels that interregional trade was very limited because of poor transportation facilities and lack of regional diversification of crops (rice being

---

[9] Cf. Coe 1961 who feels that these capitals may be called cult centers but not true cities; also Fisher (1964, 86) who states that the degree of urbanization must not be exaggerated. As Wolf (1966, 11) notes, however, there are different kinds of cities, and the more important point in defining peasantry is the existence of a state with centralized power into which the cultivator is incorporated.

[10] R. L. Pendleton (cited in Fisher 1964, 82) suggests that shifting cultivation was still practiced in the lowlands beyond the reaches of the irrigation works at Angkor. This may be true, but Pendleton perhaps overlooks the possibility of wet-rice agriculture based on rainfall, such as is common throughout contemporary Cambodia. Cf. also Groslier (1958, 118) who suggests that shifting cultivation came after the deterioration of the irrigation system at Angkor.

everywhere the main produce). Foreign export-import trade appears to have dealt mainly in luxury products.

Ordinary people lived in thatch houses (being forbidden to use tiles), either on the periphery of administrative centers or in the hinterlands. Chou Ta-kuan states that a village or villagers were under the jurisdiction of some official, but he does not make clear the exact nature of this position.[11] It is not unlikely that there were village chiefs or councils, and also that communities were under the authority of some noble or official connected with the central administration who acted as protector, judge, tax collector, and levier of corvée labor. There were also numerous villages assigned to the support of temples. Undoubtedly, the peasantry had minimal influence of their own, being largely acted upon from above and contributing food, craft objects, labor, and loyalty to the state and its gods.

With respect to religion, the peasantry had to espouse, at least nominally, whatever system was designated by the rulers as the official state cult. In fact, the masses probably believed in the divinity of the kings, but the more esoteric aspects of Hindu or Mahayana Buddhist doctrine and cosmology were most likely known only to the intelligentsia and elite, and the folk religion was more prominent in the daily lives of the common people (Coedès 1954, 831). However, in the late thirteenth century, Chou Ta-kuan speaks of all the people as being Buddhist (Theravada Buddhist, from his description), so that this particular religion did succeed in penetrating both deeply and widely among the people.[12]

The masses come suddenly into the spotlight when historians speculate on the causes for the rapid decline of the ancient Khmer empire in the fifteenth century. The Thai had become a formidable power and adversary, and their final sack of Angkor in 1430–31 is usually considered to mark the downfall of the Khmer kingdom and glory. But underlying this event were other factors, such as the following cited by various theories. First, several centuries of exaction of corvée labor to build the numerous monumental constructions had exhausted the masses who fell into an apathy that offered little resistance to foreign pressures and a disenchantment with the existing Hindu and Mahayana gods.

> As to the people, nothing proves that they reacted strongly against aggression; perhaps they even saluted it as a deliverance. If one considers the fact that they were constrained not only to furnish the hard labor necessary to these giant constructions . . . but also to assure the service and provisioning of the innumerable sanctuaries sowed on the soil of this Empire which was dressed in a robe of temples, one can scarcely doubt that, after some centuries of this regime, the working population would have been decimated and ruined. It doubtless put little ardor into the defense of the cause of these rapacious gods, proprietors of slaves and collectors of tithes; and it is not impossible that the systematic mutilations practiced in their temples may have been the work of exasperated peasants. (Finot 1908, as quoted in Briggs 1951, 260)

---

[11] In Wolf's terms (1966, 50ff., which terms are evidently derived from Max Weber), this was probably a system of prebendal and/or patrimonial domain.

[12] See Pelliot (1951) for other details of Chou Ta-kuan's description of life in Angkorean Cambodia. Also, Groslier (1957, 163–64) presents a brief (and rather idealized) reconstruction of daily life during this period.

Second, and corollary with the preceding, there had been gradual conversion to Theravada Buddhism that had particular appeal for the common man with its simplicity of doctrine, egalitarian outlook, and priesthood devoted to good works and contact with the people. Third, the loss of certain territories to the Thai had deprived the Khmer of much revenue and labor and had stopped further construction projects. Fourth, when the Thai carried off or killed the elite and intelligentsia of Angkor who were the main bearers of the great tradition and who had promoted the great artistic and intellectual achievements, any further noticeable accomplishments in the arts, architecture, literature, etc. were seriously handicapped. Finally, as central authority weakened, the vast irrigation system deteriorated and the major economic support of the kingdom was destroyed; this was accompanied by a decrease in population (apart from losses in battle or capture by the Thai) and reversion to shifting cultivation that diminished soil fertility.[13] (The preceding is taken mainly from Briggs 1951, 258–60 and Groslier 1958, 108–21.)

PRECONTACT PERIOD

In what might be called a transition period from 1431 to 1864, Cambodia fell into a sort of limbo. Much of the nation's efforts were devoted to the maintenance of a precarious political autonomy. Neighboring Thailand and Annam (South Vietnam) had become aggressive powers who gradually usurped much of what had been Khmer territory, as well as occasionally managing to place their puppets upon the Khmer throne. Europeans began more and more to enter the Southeast Asian scene with trade and colonial interests, and in some instances they were drawn into Cambodia's defensive struggles. The association with France (see the next section) came about in just this manner. Khmer culture in general, however, continued to be visible although there were no further striking cultural elaborations.

Some detailed expositions of Cambodian society and culture were written in the late nineteenth century by French officials with scholarly interests (notably Aymonier 1900 and the various studies of Leclère). Although these works were produced after the French protectorate had already begun, much of the information is applicable to earlier centuries as well; in many instances, the picture does not differ substantially from that given by Chou Ta-kuan for the late thirteenth century. Therefore, a brief summary of Aymonier's description of Khmer social strata in the nineteenth century (see 1900, chaps. 3 and 4 in particular) will be presented here as a supplement to the discussions of Angkorean social organization to provide a more detailed account of native Khmer society before extensive Western contact.

Pre-French sociopolitical structure was divided basically into three broad strata: (1) the royalty, high government officials, and royal priests; (2) the ordinary populace of freemen; and (3) the slaves. The highest class was composed of the following. (a) The king was an absolute monarch, whose authority was sanctioned by the belief in his divine right to his position (either as an incarnation of the god in Hindu doctrine, or as born to the position because of merit in previous lives in Theravada doctrine).

---

[13] Fisher (1964, 115) speculates in a similar vein that shifting cultivation (which he presumes to have been practiced consistently beyond the reaches of Angkor's irrigation works) led to soil erosion and impoverishment, hence a dwindling food supply. He suggests further that soil erosion might have clogged water resources and created swamps that bred malaria in areas that had hitherto been free of it.

## THE FRENCH PROTECTORATE

In 1864 Cambodia became a protectorate of France, giving that country certain rights and powers over domestic and foreign affairs in return for aid in defense against aggression. Cambodia, Laos, and Annam and Tonkin (now South and North Vietnam) came to form what was called French Indochina. During the ensuing eighty-five years of French administration, a number of political, economic, and social changes were introduced. It would seem, however, that much of the culture, particularly that of the peasantry, remained largely and fundamentally unmodified. The similarity between depictions of daily life on the bas reliefs at Angkor and scenes in even contemporary Cambodian villages suggest a great deal of continuity through the centuries; the transformations that did occur would appear to have been more quantitative than qualitative. Various important changes and Westernization of traditional forms and values did take place in the central government and among the elite and intelligentsia. But the peasant probably saw merely some modification in the ruling group that was not unlike a change of dynasties in the ancient kingdoms. The French officials themselves were relatively few in number and remained basically aloof from and usually ignorant of the village populace. There were, however, some innovations (to be outlined below) that could or did have some repercussions at the peasant level.

In the political realm, power shifted from the native monarch to a French resident-general who was under the authority of the French colonial ministry. The king's official functions and powers became minimal, but he retained great symbolic importance and popularity among the people. Among other changes in the central government were some reorganization of the administrative structure, creation of a legislative assembly, revision of the legal codes, and modification of the fiscal system. Much of the basic outline of preexisting native administration and personnel were kept (despite some changes and curtailment of powers), but this was not really a system of indirect rule. Native officials were completely subservient to local French officials who were in turn controlled by the French Ministry of Colonies and the overall central government in France.

So far as the peasant was concerned, the changes in political organization that more or less directly affected him were the following. (a) The district (*srok*) was divided into sub-districts (*khum*) in an attempt to define territorial units more clearly. The *khum*, however, was a largely artificial creation that merely gave the villagers another official with which to deal, albeit one that they were permitted to elect themselves. The village chiefs were also now elected. (b) The abolition of appanages for officials, as well as the institution of the *khum*, was part of the government's attempt to have the peasant look to the central administration rather than to personal protectors. (c) Taxation became more regular, and money now went to the national government in general rather than to the royal treasury or individual officials. Moreover, the tax on rice and produce was changed to a tax on land. (d) Punishments for legal infractions became less severe, and all forms of slavery (which frequently took many peasants) were abolished.

In the economic sphere, the French kept Cambodia a basically agricultural country that could be the source of various natural products. While France assuredly did seek certain improvements in and expansion of the economy (e.g., increase in exports, greatly improved transportation facilities), industrialization was not encouraged since Indochina was to be kept a market for French manufactured goods (Micaud 1949, 224). Thus, the economic system of the peasant remained largely unchanged, although selling crops for domestic or foreign markets became more frequent and possible than formerly.

Some other modifications also touched the villager. (a) The French revoked the ancient tradition that the king was supreme owner of all lands and officially legislated the creation of individual private property. The importance of landownership was further heightened by the previously mentioned shift from a tax on produce to a tax on the land itself, as well as the establishment of a cadastral system to register landholdings (although many farmers still do not admit all their possessions in order to avoid the taxes). (b) A number of services to augment and improve agriculture, forestry, and animal husbandry were created (e.g., an agricultural school and experimental station, veterinary services, forest service), but there seems to have been little actual or widespread effect at the local level. While epidemics of animal diseases were lessened, traditional techniques and crops continued to be used in cultivation. Production of various crops did in fact increase, and in the case of items such as rubber must be attributed to French stimulation. However, in regard to the greater amount of rice harvested per year, part of this increase may be due to population growth and expansion onto hitherto unused land. The government did benefit the *chamkar* cultivators by encouraging the digging of canals that enabled more lands to be utilized (Delvert 1961, 391). Also a credit program was established in 1933 in an attempt to reduce peasant indebtedness to Chinese merchants and moneylenders, but use of government credit facilities does not seem to have become widespread until very recent years. (c) The creation of a School of Fine Arts stimulated the survival or revival of various crafts, which had fallen into listlessness or virtual extinction. Thus, some peasants turned into part- or full-time artisans.

There were some other areas into which the French brought modifications or innovations that variously affected the peasantry. (a) Communication and transportation were greatly improved through construction of roads, a railroad, postal and telegraphic services, etc. This meant greater possibilities for inter-village communication and travel, although such interaction seems to have increased substantially only after World War II. (b) The expansion of educational facilities meant availability of schooling for more people, the opportunity for higher or specialized education in secondary and technical schools, and a broadening of the traditional curriculum. It is uncertain, however, as to whether a very large percentage of the peasantry (especially women) were able to take advantage of the augmentation in education. (c) The improvement in some health facilities (e.g., widespread vaccination) aided the suppression of epidemic diseases and increased longevity among the peasantry.

Native social structure remained essentially the same at the top and bottom levels of society, with the exception of the abolition of slavery. The elite and the peasantry continued to be largely self-contained and self-perpetuating bodies, with no noticeable increase in mobility from one to the other. The upper class was now influenced by what might be called a French great tradition, bringing them certain European values and styles of living. But it still retained its prestige and was basically aloof from the masses, committed to a life either of leisure or of service in the upper echelons of government.

There seems to have been, however, some development of a new middle class. It may have begun to emerge even before the protectorate, but probably it was stimulated to fuller development during the time of colonial administration. Under the French, a number of commercial, professional, and other white-collar positions were either created or multiplied, and these came gradually to form a stratum in themselves (occupied primarily by Chinese and other minorities in the absence of willing or qualified Khmer). The addition of this new level to the system of social stratification did not have much immediate impact on the peasantry, but it did open up new possibilities of mobility. Now, instead of the great leap necessary to bridge the gap between villager and elite, there was a more proximate level into which the peasantry could conceivably move with greater facility. In actuality, at least during the protectorate, very few of the Khmer masses did enter the new stratum, due to still limited opportunities for training and education or to lack of interest. But it is expectable that an increasing number can and will do so in the future. In effect, then, the social structure was somewhat loosened during the colonial period and was to be even further relaxed after independence was gained.

INDEPENDENCE

A gradual breaking away from French rule began during World War II. At that time, Cambodia was technically still under French authority, but it was militarily occupied by the Japanese who encouraged feelings of nationalism and showed that independence was possible. The desire for political autonomy became a major concern of Cambodian leaders during the post-war years, and a series of negotiations with France finally culminated, after various difficulties, in the granting of complete independence in 1954.

Since that time, Cambodia has been under the leadership primarily of the ex-king and sometime prime minister Norodom Sihanouk, who is a vigorous and competent swimmer in the waters of both national and international politics. The nation has earned a reputation for being neutralist, attempting to tread a cautious path between commitment to either the West (the United States and Europe) or East (Russia and Communist China), while accepting aid from both blocs when advantageous. It may perhaps be said fairly that Cambodia's concern above all is to maintain its hard-won independence after years of domination by foreign powers. With respect to domestic affairs, Sihanouk's policy has been one of internal development and amelioration. Immensely popular with the people, he in turn seems to have a genuine concern for their welfare.

CONTEMPORARY CAMBODIA

POPULATION AND DEMOGRAPHY

The total population of Cambodia was estimated at some 4,845,000 inhabitants in 1959 (Delvert 1961, 306).[16] Although there has been a population increase of about 2.5 percent per annum in recent years (Steinberg 1959, 28), the country taken as a whole has been estimated at about sixty-one persons per square kilometer in rural areas (Delvert 1961, 305); and the nutrition density (the ratio of population to cultivated rice lands) is said to be two persons per acre of paddy (Dobby 1960, 306).[17]

---

[16] It must be emphasized that all population figures for Cambodia are only approximations because of limited census techniques and coverage.

[17] For other estimates of population and average density, see Zadrozny 1955, 93, 95; Gourou 1945, 177–80; Ginsburg 1958, 312, 426; Steinberg 1959, 28–30.

Such figures are, however, rather deceptive in obscuring the fact that some regions are totally or virtually uninhabited, while others, especially the riverbanks and the area around Phnom Penh, are thickly settled. A closer examination of the population distribution shows that density may be as low as thirty to forty persons per square kilometer in some provinces, but as high as two hundred to five hundred per square kilometer along the Mekong (Delvert 1958, 102; 1961, chap. 11).[18] In general, however, Cambodia does still retain a good deal of uncleared or sparsely inhabited lands, and it is likely that it can sustain population expansion for some years to come.

### Demography

This total population is composed of diverse ethnic groups: Khmer, Vietnamese, Chinese, Cham-Malays, Eurasians, Indians, etc. The actual numbers of these groups can be only approximated for some groups and is totally unknown for others, but some notion of proportions may be obtained from the following compilation of estimates.

| | |
|---|---|
| Khmer | 3,351,979 in 1950 (Ministère du Plan 1958, 10) |
| Vietnamese | 319,596 in 1950 (ibid.) |
| Chinese | 217,928 in 1950 (ibid.) |
| Cham-Malays | 73,000 in 1955 (Steinberg 1959, 45) |
| Tribal peoples | 54,000 (date?) (ibid., 48) |
| Thai and Laotians | 20,000 (date?) (ibid., 49) |
| Indians | 2,500 (date?) (ibid.) |
| "Europeans" | 4,464 in 1950 (Ministère du Plan 1958, 10)[19] |

(1) The culturally and numerically dominant group is, of course, the Khmer. Comprising some 87 percent of the total population, they form both the peasant base and most of the ruling hierarchy of the nation. The majority of the Khmer occupy the rural lowlands as peasant cultivators and sometimes as fishermen. The urban Khmer are primarily aristocracy, government officials, and religious personnel, with relatively few in commerce.

(2) The Vietnamese are the largest minority group in Cambodia, constituting about 8 percent of the population. Because of the geographical proximity it is not surprising that there has been considerable immigration from Vietnam, stimulated by military or economic pressures, for several centuries. The French imported many Vietnamese into Cambodia to work on plantations and as white-collar or domestic workers. At the present time, they are found as farmers, plantation laborers, or fishermen in rural areas; and as clerks or secretaries in government and business, small merchants, professionals, and domestic servants for Europeans in the cities. The Vietnamese have maintained their ethnic identity and social separateness by living in their own communities and retaining their distinct cultural traditions. Moreover because

---

[18] Delvert's estimates of regional population densities are 30–40/sq.km. in Kompong Speu, Kompong Chhnang, Prey Veng, and Svay Rieng; 100–200/sq. km. in Koh Thom and Takeo; and 200–500 or more/sq.km. along the Mekong from Vietnam to Kratie.

[19] Cf. Delvert (1961, 14, 24, 26) who gives his personal estimate as follows: Khmer, about four million; Chinese, 220,000; Vietnamese, 230,000; and Cham-Malay, 90,000. He notes that the Vietnamese population has decreased because of hostile political relations between Cambodia and Vietnam.

of the ancient and continuing pattern of hostility between Cambodia and what is now Vietnam, the Vietnamese are regarded with enmity and antagonism by both the current government and the common man (see chapter 7).

(3) As in much of Southeast Asia, the Chinese are a significant minority in Cambodia. Historically, they have been in contact with Cambodia since the first century AD when Chinese diplomatic and trading missions were sent to the ancient Khmer kingdoms (which paid tribute to Chinese emperors in return), and contemporary neutralistic Cambodia has amiable relations with Communist China. Chinese immigrants (primarily from the southern provinces) have come continuously through the centuries as contract laborers, merchants, refugees, etc., until they now represent about 5 percent of the population. They occupy mainly commercial roles: large and small businessmen, shopkeepers, rice dealers, bankers, moneylenders, concessionaires in fishing and lumbering, import-exporters, hotel and restaurant owners, etc. Very few engage in agriculture except some pepper cultivators and a few farmers, although the Chinese are ubiquitous in rural life as shopkeepers and small merchants.

In general, the attitude of the Khmer toward the Chinese is somewhat ambivalent, but perhaps more favorable than clearly negative (as toward the Vietnamese). On the one hand, the Chinese presently occupy (albeit largely by default) significant roles in the national economy that the Cambodian government would like its own people to hold; moreover, they are an alien cultural enclave within the nation with distinct traditions, communities, schools, temples, associations, etc. On the other hand, however, there has not been a deep-rooted hostility toward the Chinese as toward the Vietnamese, and, in fact, there is sometimes open or grudging admiration for Chinese commercial ability and financial success. Considerable Chinese-Khmer intermarriage has occurred through the years, and the number of Sino-Cambodians is probably considerable although exact figures are impossible to obtain because the offspring are absorbed into one or the other parent group.

(4) Cham-Malays (or Khmer Islam as they are designated by the Cambodian government) are a mixture of immigrants from Malaya and sometimes Indonesia, and the descendants of the ancient kingdom of Champa that was located in what is now South Vietnam. These people, who comprise about 1 percent of the population, are basically similar to the Khmer in both physical type and culture. But they are differentiated in one major respect: the Cham-Malay are Muslims rather than Buddhists, so that various aspects of their life assume a different cast from that of the Khmer. They live in separate communities (concentrated in the provinces of Kompong Cham and Kampot) and work as cattle breeders, traders, butchers, fisherman, cultivators, dealers in wood, transporters, and traders. The Cambodian government has traditionally been tolerant toward the Cham-Malays who have full citizenship and are allowed to have their own leaders equal in rank to Khmer royalty.

(5) The so-called tribal peoples, concentrated mainly in the more isolated highland regions of eastern Cambodia, are a small but ethnologically significant part of the population. The Khmer refer to them collectively and often disparagingly as Phnong or "savages." But they are actually divided into a number of groups with distinct cultures: for example, the Rhadé and Jarai are matrilineal and speak a Malayo-Polynesian language, while the Stieng, Kuoy, and Pear are patrilineal and speak a Mon-Khmer language. As contrasted to the Khmer, the tribal groups were relatively untouched by influences from the great traditions of India and China. They maintain a social organization in which the village and kin groups are primary, and their subsistence is based on slash-and-burn cultivation. For those groups that have not been virtually

extinguished by disease and assimilation, there is some interaction with the larger society through intermarriage, trade, and employment as soldiers, laborers, etc. But many groups retain their autonomy to a great extent by virtue of geographical and social isolation.

(6) There are also a number of other ethnic minorities of very limited size. Laotians and Thai live mainly in northwestern Cambodia as peasant farmers. Burmese work as prospectors, cutters, and dealers in jewels. Indians are present in business (e.g., cloth merchants) and government. The European population is composed primarily of Frenchmen and members of diplomatic missions from various nations.[20]

## Settlement Patterns

Types of settlements in Cambodia might be crudely classified into three rudimentary categories: cities, towns, and villages. The city can, for our purposes, be characterized as a large and complex settlement with a population composed of different ethnic groups, classes, and occupations; diverse, complex activities and functions performed not only for itself but for the surrounding region (and perhaps the nation as a whole); and differentiated structures and districts (business, residential, etc.). Perhaps only Phnom Penh, the capital, truly deserves to be called a city. But some of the provincial capitals might be considered embryonic cities on account of their diversity of population and structures as well as the functions they perform for their respective provinces, though they are but feeble likenesses of Phnom Penh.

The town may be described as having much the same attributes as a city but on a much more limited scale. Usually a town is located on a major thoroughfare, has a population of over a thousand inhabitants of more than one ethnic group (usually Chinese or Sino-Cambodian in addition to Khmer), and the presence of specialized installations such as a market, school, government offices, etc. It thus functions as political, economic, and often educational center for the immediately surrounding countryside.[21]

The village may be defined as a cluster of households that is recognized subjectively by the inhabitants and/or objectively by the government as belonging together in one named unit.[22] More specifically, in contrast to the town and city, the village has a population that generally averages several hundred individuals of predominantly or wholly one ethnic group, an economy with one major focus and little or no occupational diversification beyond part-time specializations, no internal distinctions of class, and little or no significant differentiation of structures except for the possible presence of a Buddhist temple.

Except for certain regions along major rivers where high population density and necessities of land usage make for settlements that appear to merge into one another

---

[20] For further or more detailed discussions of minority groups in Cambodia, see Leclère 1890, 36–44; Morizon 1936, 62–91; Zadrozny 1955, 95–100, chap. 13, 319–21; Steinberg 1959, 33–53; Thompson and Adloff 1955. For other sources on the diverse tribal groups the reader is best referred to Embree and Dotson 1950 and LeBar, Hickey, and Musgrave 1964. Further data on population and demography in general maybe found in Zadrozny 1955, 89–95, 100–105 and especially Delvert 1961, chaps.11, 14.

[21] On the city and town, cf. Zadrozny 1955, 95; Delvert 1961, 217–18; Ginsburg 1955. Delvert's "market-village" is essentially the same as what I chose to call a town.

[22] For further discussion on this point, see the next chapter.

without a break, most villages have more or less clearly defined spatial boundaries. There appear to be three basic patterns of village layout: (1) linear, with houses in relatively close proximity to one another and spread out along a road or waterway; (2) compact, with houses clustered together in a roughly circular or rectangular community surrounded by open land; and (3) dispersed, with houses scattered at some distance from one another in a rather irregular manner, interspersed with land. The type of settlement pattern for any one community will be determined mainly by environmental setting (e.g., linear villages are typical along the rivers) and population density (e.g., dispersed villages are found in regions of low density).[23]

In earlier periods, the pattern over much of Cambodia, especially in the rice-growing areas, seems to have been either scattered or isolated homes and small villages. This is consonant with the gradual population expansion that occurred in the past; individuals would go out to clear hitherto uncultivated lands, children would marry and settle near the parental home, and the germ of a village would be created (Delvert 1961, 204). Old traditions state that misfortune befalls villages that grow too large, and nineteenth-century law codes seem to discourage building houses in very close proximity to one another (Leclère 1898, 382, 404). This pattern is, however, relatively rare at the present time for two reasons. First, incursions of Vietminh from Vietnam during 1947–54 led the government and the population to "regroup" into larger, more concentrated, and accessible communities for purposes of defense and safety. Various relocation programs were carried out in all the southerly provinces, consolidating smaller villages into larger units, moving isolated families into settlements, and locating communities on routes of communication (Delvert 1961, 207–8; Steinberg 1959, 31). Second, even villages in undisturbed areas have also grown due to the natural increase of population that is not substantially drained off by emigration to the city or other regions. Strong ties to one's own land and village, lack of significantly better economic opportunities for the unskilled outside the village, and a basic provincialism keep a good proportion of each successive generation within their natal or neighboring communities. Although no exact figures are available, it would seem that the majority of Cambodian villages at the present time have at least several hundred (300–400?) and often many more (sometimes close to a thousand?) inhabitants.

## NATIONAL AND SOCIOPOLITICAL STRUCTURE

### Organization of the Government

Cambodia's government is technically a constitutional monarchy not unlike that of various European countries. At the apex is the king, a hereditary position that now has few important functions and almost no real power, except insofar as it retains a great symbolic significance and commands much respect and loyalty from the populace. The king is assisted and advised by the Royal Family Council (male members of his immediate family) and the Crown Council (composed of the president of the Royal Family Council, the prime minister, the presidents of the two legislative bodies and High Court of Justice, and the heads of the two Buddhist orders). Actual authority has come to be wielded by the prime minister who attains his post by leadership of the

---

[23] See Delvert 1961, 204–18 and Gourou 1945, 181 for detailed discussions of settlement patterns. Also, the CMCC category #49 contains numerous descriptions of different villages that often include a brief account on layout (as well as number of inhabitants, etc.).

majority party in the National Assembly. (In the hands of Norodom Sihanouk, a former king who voluntarily renounced the throne to become prime minister, this office has become extremely powerful and draws tremendous popular support.) The prime minister selects a cabinet of twelve ministers who oversee various departments such as the Ministries of the Interior, Foreign Affairs, Justice, Defense, Agriculture, Public Works, Education, etc. The prime minister and cabinet are critical in molding national policies and executing legislative decrees. Completing the core of the central government is the legislature that is composed of two branches. The upper house of the legislature is the Council of the Kingdom, whose members are appointed by the king or elected by other governmental officials and by professional and trade organizations. It has no formal right to legislate but may exercise considerable influence through its advisory capacity. The National Assembly is composed of members selected for four-year terms by the populace, with one representative for every thirty thousand voters. It normally meets twice a year and has the sole authority to make laws.

This hierarchy then broadens at the base to include various lesser officials and the heads of the territorial political divisions: that is, provincial governors, district (*srok*) chiefs, sub-district (*khum*) chiefs, and finally the village headmen. All but the latter two posts are filled by appointment by the Ministry of the Interior from their ranks of civil servants.[24]

### Social Stratification

With respect to social stratification, Cambodia may be said to have a class structure if we use the term "class" to refer to groups of individuals that are differentiated subjectively and objectively on the basis of differential wealth, power, prestige, and occupation. An observer might crudely delineate three broad strata within the society as a whole, although perhaps only the top and bottom can be defined with any clarity and are clearly recognized by the people themselves. (a) The elite group centers around the royal family and related aristocracy. It also includes the high-ranking officials in governmental and religious organization, and possibly very wealthy Khmer or Sino-Cambodian businessmen or professionals. (b) The lowest group is composed of the rural peasantry, craftsmen, fishermen, etc., as well as unskilled laborers in the city, who are often little removed from their rural origins. (c) What might be called an "intermediate" group is a somewhat residual category for those individuals who fall between the two obvious ends of the social scale. This stratum would include such individuals as businessmen and merchants, professionals (teachers, doctors, etc.), the middle and lower ranks of government bureaucracy, white-collar workers in commercial offices, etc. At the present time, this level is an ethnic mixture of Chinese, Vietnamese, and Khmer.

While the top and bottom strata tend to be self-perpetuating to a great extent, some social mobility is possible. Those in high positions can fall from grace through political or financial reverses, and conversely, the child of a peasant farmer might rise to a high position with enough motivation, education, and good luck. Such cases are, however, relatively rare.[25]

---

[24] For details of political organization, see Zadrozny 1955, chaps. 8–9; Steinberg 1959, chaps. 8–11; Smith 1964.

[25] On social stratification, see Steinberg 1959, chap. 7; Du Bois 1949, chap. 2.

ECONOMIC BASES OF THE COUNTRY

Cambodia has a dominantly rural economy. Two major types of agriculture can be distinguished (and are differentiated by the people themselves) on the basis of emphasis on certain crops. First and foremost, rice production occupies about 80 percent of all cultivated lands, grown primarily in wet paddies in the lowlands (though there is also some dry-field cultivation). It seems that the majority of rice farmers grow their crop mainly for family consumption with only occasional or limited surplus sold on the market because of relatively small landholdings and limited yield. But certain regions (with relatively low population density and large per capita landholdings) do produce substantial amounts of rice for both regional and international trade, thus earning Cambodia's reputation as one of the rice baskets of Southeast Asia. Second, the so-called *chamkar* cultivation along the riverbanks (mainly the Mekong, Bassac, and Tonle Sap Rivers) focuses rather on vegetable, fruit, and fiber crops such as maize, beans, peanuts, sugarcane, soybeans, bananas, coconuts, cotton, tobacco, ramie, kapok, etc. Any one community or household is likely to grow a variety of such crops (as well as limited amounts of rice) in different seasons and on different fields throughout the year, using (as do the rice cultivators) mainly family labor. In contrast to rice agriculture, however, *chamkar* cultivation (especially of non-comestibles) is very much geared toward the market. The general economic organization of *chamkar* villages thus differs from that of rice-growing villages in a variety of respects: the annual work cycle, the layout of fields, the maintenance of water control and distribution systems, the close articulation with the market, the higher average annual incomes, etc. (for details of *chamkar* economy, see especially Delvert 1961, chap. 13). Finally, in addition to the preceding, there is actually a third type of cultivation activity: the large-scale production of plantations of pepper and rubber. These plantations are, however, owned or operated by French or Chinese concerns and utilize mostly Vietnamese contract labor.

Every Cambodian farmer fishes to a limited extent in his paddies or nearby water holes or streams for family subsistence. Those who live along Lake Tonle Sap, rivers, or on the coast may be exclusively fishermen, but these tend to be Vietnamese rather than Khmer. Fishing as an organized commercial activity is controlled largely by Chinese concessionaires who lease rights to fishing grounds on the Tonle Sap or Gulf of Siam from the government. The total national yield is quite large and is marketed fresh, dried, or as fish paste or oil; about one-third to one-quarter of the catch is exported.

Other economic pursuits of lesser significance include the following. (a) Timber and other forest products (resins, oils, etc.) are an important export.[26] Exploitation of these resources is handled mainly by Chinese and Vietnamese concessionaires. (b) Almost every agricultural community has a few individuals who practice some craft skill on a part-time basis. In some instances, however, entire villages may devote themselves more or less full-time to some handicraft such as weaving, basketry and the making of mats, pottery, work in metals (bronze, silver, gold), woodwork, etc. Indeed, some regions have traditionally specialized in certain crafts. The products of these cottage industries are disseminated in both local and interregional trade.

---

[26] The major exports of Cambodia are rice, maize, timber, rubber, and fish, of which items are sent mainly to France and its affiliates, some other Southeast Asian countries (e.g., Malaya and formerly South Vietnam), Hong Kong, the United States, and the Philippines (Ministère du Plan 1958; Steinberg 1959, 229).

Large-scale manufacturing and industry are still embryonic. Processing of raw materials (e.g., rice mills, alcohol distilleries, sawmills) is primary, but there is also some production of items such as bricks and cigarettes. This is a sphere of the economy that the government is particularly anxious to develop. (c) Animal husbandry as a commercial venture is practiced mainly by Cham-Malay cattle breeders in a few provinces. On a much smaller scale, individual Khmer families may raise a few pigs and chickens for sale. Cattle and pigs form some proportion of the nation's export.

In sum, Cambodia has what is sometimes called a dual economy, though the two parts are not evenly balanced. The agricultural sector remains dominant, while the "Westernized" sector (e.g., manufacturing) is still nascent at best. Furthermore, the bulk of the Khmer remain peasant cultivators while the marketing and other commercial aspects of the economy are handled primarily by the Chinese. The Cambodian government has high aspirations for developing many parts of the national economy, such as expansion of industry, further development of natural resources, movement of more and more Khmer into technical and commercial positions, a rise in peasant standards of living, etc. And it has actively attempted to realize such goals by encouraging foreign aid, investment, and technical assistance, signing trade agreements with various countries, increasing the extension of agricultural credit and development of cooperatives, etc. Thus far, however, economic growth and modernization have been rather slow and uneven.[27]

## RELIGION

During their early history the Khmers received and adopted several alien religious traditions, as well as maintaining an indigenous religious system throughout the centuries. Hinduism (or more specifically, Sivaism and Vishnuism) and Mahayana Buddhism were espoused by various rulers during the ancient kingdoms, either simultaneously or at different times. Hinduism and its associated ideology and cosmology were of special importance in shaping early Khmer culture, but as an organized religious system it has since subsided largely to a mere memory. Only discrete elements of it remain in varying aspects of contemporary life, such as court rituals with Brahmanic priests, literature, drama, details of life-cycle and other ceremonies, and recognition of certain deities that are Hindu in origin.

The last and ultimately most important religion to penetrate Cambodia was Theravada Buddhism. The Sinhalese form of Theravada began to filter into Cambodia probably during the thirteenth century, coming from Burma and perhaps to a lesser extent from the encroaching Thai. The historical records are not altogether clear as to the exact chronology or processes involved in Theravada's gradual supplanting of Mahayana and Hinduism, but by the mid-fourteenth century, Cambodia had been converted to Theravada and was even proselytizing neighboring Laos.

Theravada is now the official national religion of Cambodia. At the national level, the king is symbolic leader of Buddhists and includes the heads of the two Buddhist

---

[27] For more details on the economy, see Morizon 1936, parts 3–4; Robequain 1944; Gourou 1945; Du Bois 1949, 37–42; Zadrozny 1955, chaps. 10–11; Ginsburg 1958, 414; Ministère du Plan 1958; Steinberg 1959, chaps. 12–17; Dobby 1960, 19–20; Delvert 1961, especially chaps. 9, 12, 13, 17; CMCC 40.010. Also, various points of economic organization will be discussed further in chapter 4.

orders (Mohanikay and Thommayut)[28] in his advisory Crown Council; there is also a Ministry of Religion (Cults) that oversees religious activities and institutions, including a Buddhist Institute and Higher School of Pali. At the local level, Buddhist precepts and practices pervade the values and behavior of the populace who accept this religion sincerely and devoutly. In the mid-1950s there were over 2,500 Buddhist temples throughout the country, serving as religious, educational, and social centers for their congregations, as well as more than 37,500 monks who act as teachers and exemplars of Buddhist doctrine.

While Buddhism is the official and dominant religion, it coexists and is intertwined with a folk religion that is also of considerable significance in Khmer culture. This old and native religious system is based on belief in a variety of animistic, ancestral, guardian, ghostly, or demon-like spirits, and it has its own rituals and specialists.

There have been attempts to introduce different versions of Christianity into Cambodia but without notable success at conversion of the Khmers. There are a number of Roman Catholic churches in the country, but their congregations are almost wholly Vietnamese or European. A few Protestant missions exist and have managed to make some converts among certain tribal groups.[29]

## LANGUAGE

The Khmer language is linguistically classified as part of the Austro-Asiatic stock and the Mon-Khmer family that also includes the speech of the Mons of Burma and various tribal groups scattered over Southeast Asia (e.g., the Sedang, Mnong-Gar, Rhadé, Jarai, etc.) (P. Benedict 1947). A complete description of Khmer is best left to professional linguists,[30] but a few of its features will be noted. Briefly, Khmer is a non-tonal language with a relatively complex phonemic system that includes some thirty vowels and twenty-one consonants. Apart from infixing, the morphology is fairly simple and lacks the complications of verb tenses and conjugations, articles, and gender. Syntax is not vastly different from English word order. Vocabulary is simple in some respects and complicated in others. Some words have a variety of meanings depending on the context; in other instances, however, one action, thing, or concept may have a host of different words appropriate for certain situations (e.g., the verb "to carry" has various forms depending on what is being carried or how it is carried; the verb "to eat" also differs according to whether an animal, a monk, an aristocrat, an ordinary person, etc. is the actor, or whether one is speaking formally or casually). The vocabulary includes derivations from Sanskrit (especially in the realms of government, literature, and honorific titles), Pali (particularly in religion), and to a limited extent from French, Portuguese, Malay, and Thai.[31]

---

[28] For discussion of these two Buddhist orders, see chapter 5.

[29] For details regarding religion in the ancient kingdoms, see Briggs 1951; Coedès 1948. On other aspects of religion discussed above, see Aymonier 1900, chap. 3; Martini 1955a, 1955b; Zadrozny 1955, chaps. 7, 12; Steinberg 1959, chap. 5, 125, 255. Other details and references will be found in chapter 5.

[30] See in particular Maspero 1915; Martini 1942–45, 1955c; Phan and Noss 1958; Cambefort 1950; Pannetier and Menetrier 1922. A major Cambodian–French dictionary is Guesdon 1930.

[31] Martini has suggested that early Khmer was suited to a fairly simple "prehistoric" culture, but the elaborations introduced from India required borrowing from Sanskrit and Pali (1955c, 428). This process continues to the present time with a special commission at the Higher

A complication on another level arises from the existence of several different systems of vocabulary that are to be used in speaking to or about individuals in certain statuses. These various forms of Khmer are (1) words used in speaking to or about royalty, (2) words used in speaking to or about Buddhist monks, and (3) words used in common discourse among ordinary people. These systems are clearly defined and consciously recognized by the people; and although the ordinary villager usually knows only a smattering of the royal language, he does know and judiciously uses the language for monks. Within the third system, that of ordinary discourse, a distinction might also be made between what I call "formal" and "colloquial" Khmer. The former is what could be termed textbook Khmer: that is, proper, polite, with pronunciation of words that closely follows the written form, and vocabulary that includes many Sanskrit- or Pali-derived words unfamiliar to the untutored; this is used by educated people (mainly urbanites), particularly in formal situations, and peasants will use as "proper" a language as their level of education permits when speaking to those of superior rank (e.g., a government official). "Colloquial" Khmer is especially distinguished by the different pronunciation of many words (in particular, *r*'s are dropped or change to other phonemes, and terminal phonemes often lapse),[32] and words or expressions not used in polite conversation are frequent; this type of speech is used among villagers and even among educated urbanites when among family or friends or engaged in casual conversation. Such a distinction between "formal" and "colloquial" speech is, of course, not unique. But the difference between the two in Khmer can be so great that, for example, villagers often cannot comprehend radio broadcasts in informal Khmer;[33] and Sihanouk, in his speeches to the populace, customarily breaks into "colloquial" Khmer midway through his talk to make certain he is being understood by the common man.

Khmer is written in a script derived from southern India in the sixth century. There are two types of writing: *chrieng* used for most everyday purposes in government, literature, etc., and *mŭl* for religious texts, inscriptions, Pali, or for emphasis (see Martini 1955c, 427). Some attempts have been made to evolve a Romanized script for Khmer, but these have been largely unsuccessful.

French is the main European or "second" language in Cambodia. It has been estimated that 10 percent of the Khmer population are bilingual (Zadrozny 1955, 108), but this figure is probably inflated. While many of the upper class and intelligentsia are indeed adept speakers of French, fluency declines to a minimal level as one moves from the white-collar to the peasant stratum. Bilingualism may, however, increase with the recent expansion of education, for French is begun in the third year of primary school.[34]

---

School of Pali in Phnom Penh charged with the innovation of new Khmer words, based usually on Pali or Sanskrit, as the need arises (especially in science and technology).

[32] For example, compare the following examples of pronunciation of words in "formal" and "colloquial" Khmer respectively: *pram* (five)—*peam*, *rotiĕ* (cart)—*atiĕ*, *rovŭl* (busy)—*lovŭl*, *roo* (look for)—*hoo*, *maok* (come)—*mao*, *Angkor*—*ankoo*; also initial *ch* sometimes becomes *s*, as in *cmŏŏp* (midwife)—*smŏŏp*, *cmaa* (cat)—*smaa*.

[33] In the reverse situation, after having been instructed in "formal" Khmer it took me over a month of adjustment to become accustomed to the "colloquial" Khmer spoken in the village, particularly in the recognition of words pronounced differently.

[34] For example, the entire village of Svay had only one resident moderately fluent in French when I arrived. But a number of boys and girls in West Hamlet alone have now begun learning French in school.

Members of various ethnic minority groups, such as the Chinese and Vietnamese, are usually bilingual or even multilingual in their own language, Khmer, and French. Some Khmer, even peasants, may acquire a minimal knowledge of Vietnamese or Chinese through varied contacts with these groups, though they often know no more than a few simple phrases or words.[35]

---

[35] Steinberg (1959, 33) states that "Vietnamese and, to a lesser extent, Chinese are the lingua franca of the marketplace. Cambodians hold their own language aloof from such unsavory and boisterous demonstrations as bargaining, using Vietnamese when haggling . . . with the Vietnamese and Chinese merchants." This was assuredly not the case in any markets I saw where very vigorous bargaining was conducted in Khmer by Khmer with Chinese, Vietnamese, or Sino-Cambodian dealers. For Khmer, especially villagers, may not know enough of another language to conduct the sort of skilled bargaining upon which they pride themselves, while all merchants know enough Khmer to deal with their customers.

# CHAPTER THREE

# VILLAGE SVAY: THE SETTING AND SOCIAL STRUCTURE

Near the central food market in Phnom Penh is a line of buses painted in flamboyant colors as if to give moral support to their rattletrap bodies. Boarding the one that goes to Kompong Tuol the traveler begins his journey to Svay. By regular car the trip takes about half an hour, but the bus rides last an hour or longer because of numerous stops along the way to discharge some passengers and pick up others, or to satisfy the driver's whim to stop for a snack. Leaving Phnom Penh, one passes by large apartment buildings, stucco villas, and the airport that speak of modernity. Then one enters the quiet countryside: miles of palms and rice fields, brilliant green in the rainy season and sere brown in the dry months, interrupted periodically by clusters of houses and shops, paths leading to distant villages, and serene Buddhist temples. Finally the bus coasts into the marketplace of Kompong Tuol, the town nearest to Svay. The traveler now hails a remorque, a rural bicycle cab, for the three-kilometer ride to Svay (often sharing a cab with other people who are returning home after marketing or a trip to the city). Going quickly past the shops lining the road through town, then the primary school, a temple, a village, and the inevitable rice paddies and palms, the remorque arrives at the path leading from the highway to West Hamlet Svay. Gathering one's bundles, one starts the short walk down the path that covers one's legs with mud in the rainy season and with dust in the dry season. If one has not already encountered villagers who are taking cattle to pasture or rice to the millers or going elsewhere, one is almost certain to see people fishing, wading, or bathing oxen at the huge water hole along the path. The village is almost invisible behind the verdant growth of trees and bushes that encircle the hamlet, but one finally passes through a rude gate marking the entrance to West Svay. As one weaves among the thatch and wooden houses, people call out their usual greeting: "Where are you coming from?" "What do you have?" as they look up from their tasks or as they sit chatting at one another's homes. Children come running; the dogs set up a fearful clamor. One has arrived in Svay.

## VILLAGE SVAY: THE SETTING

Svay is located about thirty kilometers southwest of Phnom Penh in Kandal province, the district (*srok*) of Koh Thom, sub-district (*khum*) Treang. It spreads out for more than a kilometer along a minor highway that connects Svay with the market town of Kampong Tuol, a Buddhist temple (Wat Samnang), and the neighboring villages of Ta Chas and Sandan; also in the vicinity is the national normal school, the Centre Pedagogique de Kompong Tuol. Almost all of Svay's houses are situated south of this road, usually several hundred feet or yards inland from the thoroughfare (although a few front directly on the highway). At the eastern end of the community is another Buddhist temple, Wat Svay, and across the road is a small Chinese shop. Taken as a whole, the village is basically linear in its settlement pattern, but the inhabited area forms, in some sections, quite a broad strip that can be more than a dozen houses wide. In all, there are about 168 houses with approximately 790 inhabitants.[1] The rice fields belonging to Svay's residents are located on all sides of the village, but most of them stretch to the south for more than a kilometer until they meet the paddies owned by the inhabitants of other communities.

The inhabitants of Svay distinguish three parts of the village: "East *phum*" (*phum kaüt*), "Middle *phum*" (*phum kandal*), and "West *phum*" (*phum layt*).[2] These are residential sections that I have chosen to designate as hamlets. They are spatially demarcated in a more or less clear manner: West Hamlet is clearly set apart from the others by a swathe of uncleared land, but East and Middle Hamlets are differentiated only by a small bridge over a dry streambed that runs between them.[3] The hamlet can be an important social unit (see below), but the village as a whole constitutes a distinct entity in several respects. First, it is a territorial entity in the sense that the village is spatially separated from other communities. It has few fences or other explicit boundary markers, but there is land cultivated or uncleared that sets the inhabited part of Svay apart from other villages. Second, in the eyes of the government, Svay compromises one administrative unit under the jurisdiction of one village chief as well as other particular officials. Finally, Svay is a clear entity to those who name it as their place of residence. Although there are relatively few community endeavors and no communal lands, the inhabitants nonetheless feel a loyalty to and identification with their village as opposed to other settlements, as well as deep attachment to the place where their kinsmen and friends reside and where their property is located.[4]

**Brief History.** There are no special legends or stories about the founding of the village, except that it was presumably named by some ancient king who was traveling through the area and called the community "Svay Domnak," "to stay awhile [where there are] mangoes" because of the numerous fruit trees.[5] The name of this ruler is lost to memory, as is the age of the village. The inhabitants say simply that Svay has

---

[1] This figure is only an approximation as of May 1959, because there are continual variations in population. See also appendix C.

[2] The term *phum* has several connotations, as discussed by Delvert 1961, 201–3. It is most commonly translated as "village" (as in Phum Svay = Village Svay). But it may also, as in this case, refer to a hamlet or section within a village. And according to one source, the word is used to designate any inhabited place even if there is only one house (Porée-Maspero cited in Delvert 1961, 202).

[3] There was once a fourth hamlet situated to the southeast of West Hamlet, but it was abandoned several years ago because its location across a swampy stream made access to it difficult. Its inhabitants relocated to other parts of Svay.

[4] Although Svay is probably not remarkable in being delineated in these respects, Delvert (1961, 201–4, 214) points out that there are other villages that are harder to define. In some instances the boundaries of villages are hard to demarcate, and sometimes the government's definition of an administrative unit called a *phum* may or may not coincide with what the people considered to be a *phum*.

[5] "Svay" (mango) is a very common village name throughout Cambodia where villages are named after trees, features of the landscape, etc. (see Delvert 1961, 203 on the names of communities). In fact, Svay has relatively few mango trees at the present time, although older inhabitants report that they were once more numerous.

existed for "a very long, long time," and I found no official records to clarify the mystery of the date or circumstances of Svay's origin.

There is other historical evidence that the general area in which Svay is located has been inhabited for many centuries, although the exact distribution and density of the population undoubtedly varied through the ages. The river banks and their environs in southern Cambodia were one of the centers of population concentration during the earliest known kingdom of Funan (Briggs 1951, 13), and several ancient ruins not far from Svay are testimony to further habitation in succeeding kingdoms as well.[6] While the focus of government, and probably settlement, shifted to northern Cambodia during the Angkor period, Phnom Penh and its environs became the locus of Khmer capitals after the mid-fifteenth century and the abandonment of Angkor (Coedès 1948, 394; Giteau 1957, 123, 166). By the late nineteenth century, the districts of Koh Thom and neighboring Bati together constituted the most populous region in the nation (Delvert 1961, 429–30). Aymonier (1900, 206) offers a description of Koh Thom district at this time.

> [Koh Thom] is, in effect, a small piece of land ["Mésopotamie"] between Prek Tauch [River] to the south and Prek Tenot [River] to the north. The land . . . is . . . in the entire center of the province sometimes covered with veritable forests [and] sugar palms, sometimes cultivated in vast plains of rice fields where all the land is utilized. Not having pastures, the inhabitants have few beasts and often leave their buffaloes or oxen to pasture on the banks of rice fields. . . . The very industrious inhabitants make palm sugar during the dry season, help each other in agricultural work, hastening en masse to work awhile at one's home, a while at another's home, then all being fed by the proprietor. Abstaining from strong liquor and reprehensible acts, observing generally the precepts of the religious lay that concerns the laity, they surpass all their neighbors by their spirit of . . . Buddhist piety. [my translation]

Thus, it is not unlikely that the environs of Svay have been inhabited for a considerable length of time, although the village as it is known today probably did not exist until the nineteenth century. Toward the end of that century, Svay had a Buddhist temple of its own (Wat Svay), so one may infer that by that time the community had become a distinct named entity and was large enough to build and support such an establishment. According to the estimates of the older inhabitants, the population of the village about fifty years ago was probably half or less of what it is now. The proliferation of houses and people was commented upon by many old people:

> When I was young, the village was big [in the area of land covered]. But there weren't so many houses; they were scattered around. But, then, one child builds

---

[6] Angkor Borei, about fifty kilometers southeast of Svay, is thought by some to have been the capital of Funan and the occasional capital of the Chenla kingdom during the sixth to eighth centuries (Briggs 1951, 13, 34–35, 48, 52; Coedès 1948, 117, 124). In the neighboring district of Bati are Phnom Chisor (about twenty-five kilometers south of Svay) with a temple attributed to Suryavarman I of the eleventh century and a rest home built by Jayavarman VII in the twelfth to thirteenth centuries, as well as Ta Prohm with a sixth-century inscription (see Coedès 1948, 105, 230, 274, 296–97; Briggs 1951, 31, 149, 193, 214). There are also thirteenth-century ruins at Tonle Bati (Delvert 1961, 538), which is less than ten kilometers from Svay. See also Delvert 1961, 537 who suggests that the "human occupation seems to have been almost continuous" in the districts of Bati and Kandal Stung.

a house, another child builds a house, and grandchildren build houses, and now there are many houses. I can remember when there was empty land in many places.[7]

The coming of the French protectorate is not within the memory of any inhabitant and evidently had no special impact on Svay itself. Neither did World War II and the Japanese occupation disturb the villagers (several men worked for the Japanese in menial jobs and had amiable relations with their employers). The most notable event in the recent memories of the villagers, and one that is often resurrected in discussions, was a time of turmoil following the war. After World War II when Cambodia was seeking independence from the French, the so-called Khmer Issarak (Free Khmer) nationalist movement commanded the loyalties of some Svay villagers and created some violent eddies in the normally placid flow of village life (see chapter 7).

Apart from the Issaraks, the only other unusual event in Svay's recent history was the building of a teacher training center (Centre Pedagogique de Kompong Tuol) in the immediate vicinity of the community. This normal school was opened in March 1958, and its effect on the village was (is) primarily an economic one. Some villagers in West Hamlet had to sell rice fields and palm trees that were on the school's site and felt some bitterness because of what they considered to be insufficient recompense for their losses. But the villagers have now assumed an approving, or at least neutral, attitude toward the school. It offers opportunities for temporary or permanent employment, entertainment (villagers go as uninvited but accepted spectators to school events), a chance for sociability and gossip with and about the students, and, not the least, exposure to the idea that education is an important channel for social mobility.

## WEST HAMLET SVAY

If a stranger were to walk into Svay at any one place and ask where he was, an inhabitant would reply "*phum* Svay." Certainly there is some identification with and loyalty to the village as a whole. But in conversation with persons familiar with the community, the more common practice is to refer to the intra-village divisions ("There will be a wedding in East Hamlet next week," "Sok in Middle Hamlet has gone to Phnom Penh," etc.). Moreover, the bulk of daily interaction usually occurs with kinsmen and neighbors within one's own hamlet. This is especially true for the residents of West Hamlet who are geographically separated from the rest of the village by a considerable expanse of uncultivated and uninhabited land. While the inhabitants of East and Middle Svay (particularly those who live on the rather nebulous border between

---

[7] Delvert (1961, 207, citing Bellan) states that this is the usual manner in which "hamlets" (in his sense, small clusters of dwellings or small villages) are formed: offspring build new houses near the parental home, and after several generations one finds small hamlets scattered over an area (thus, he notes, it is common for the residents of small *phum*, and even many larger ones, to be kinsmen). With respect to Svay, one is tempted to relate the presence of separate hamlets to the growth of the village. It is possible that East Hamlet, which is the most densely populated and the site of the village temple, is the oldest part of the village, and that the increasing population fissioned off into Middle and finally West Hamlets (the latter is the smallest). But this is mere speculation. The villagers stated definitely that no one hamlet was older than another, and all three existed for at least the past seventy-five years. Moreover, Delvert (1961, 539) notes that the hamlet pattern is common in this area.

these two hamlets) may see one another frequently, those in West Svay must make some effort to visit people in other parts of the community (although such efforts are made). In many respects, West Svay is very much like a small village in itself and has strong hamlet identification ("We in West Hamlet . . . ," "Our West Hamlet . . ."). And it is primarily with West Hamlet Svay that this study will be concerned.

**The Setting.** West Hamlet is situated several hundred feet from the highway, separated from the road by rice paddies and a few small buildings at the normal school, and largely invisible from the highway because of sheltering trees and shrubbery. A few minutes' walk along a winding footpath, or a shortcut along a paddy dike, offers access to the hamlet from the road. About a hundred feet from the westernmost houses, along the footpath, is a large water hole used for fishing, bathing, swimming, and washing cattle. Two lesser holes offer more water during the rainy season (and there are three wells within the hamlet for drinking, cooking, and bathing water). Aerial photographs reveal that a fairly sizeable stream once ran along the southern border of the inhabited area, but the streambed is now mostly rice paddies except for a swampy, overgrown area at the eastern end of the hamlet (see maps 2 and 3).

The homes of West Hamlet cover a roughly rectangular plot of ground whose length runs east–west for the equivalent of several city blocks and whose width is only about one city block. The gable-roofed dwellings, raised on wooden or concrete piles that vary in height from about two to eight or more feet, are usually made entirely of sugar palm thatch for poor families, of wood and thatch for those of average means, and wood with tile roofs for the wealthy. Of square or rectangular form, the houses range in size from about twelve by twenty feet to twenty by thirty feet (for further details of construction, see Delvert 1961, 180–98, figs. 31–33; Bitard 1955). The homes of wealthy people may have several rooms. But the interior of most houses is essentially one large room that may have a few scattered, flimsy partitions of cloth, thatch, or wood to give some privacy to certain members of the family at night. Sometimes there is a kitchen area or partial room within the house itself, but many people cook outside, beneath or beside the house. Most homes are quite bare, with only a trunk or armoire to store clothes, mats that are unrolled only for sleeping or to seat guests, a picture of Buddha with a small altar before it, and miscellaneous household goods such as tiny kerosene lamps or kitchen equipment. (Tables, chairs, and Western-style beds are only for rich villagers.) The space beneath the house is also an integral part of life and is used in many ways: to cook and eat meals, to store rice, to keep large objects such as plows, to stable animals, and not the least, to provide a cool place to relax during the heat of the day.

The houses are situated sometimes very close together (separated by only a few feet) and sometimes in relative isolation, depending on what land is available to the builder and his personal preferences.[8] Scattered among the dwellings are trees, bushes, and small garden plots of herbs and vegetables. Occasionally a crude fence or row of trees will demarcate one family's property from that of another (for every bit of land within the settlement has an owner). As a sort of natural enclosure for the

---

[8] Even those houses that are relatively separated from the other homes are still within easy reach, for it is considered preferable to live near others to be safe and to avoid loneliness and boredom. Cf. Delvert (1961, 205) who feels that the Khmer peasant prefers isolated homes, and an old legal code (in Leclère 1898, 2:404–5) that states that anyone building too close to the property of another must pay a fine if misfortune befalls the latter. See Leclère 1898, 1:382–85, 2:360, 404–8 for other statutes concerning house sites and other land.

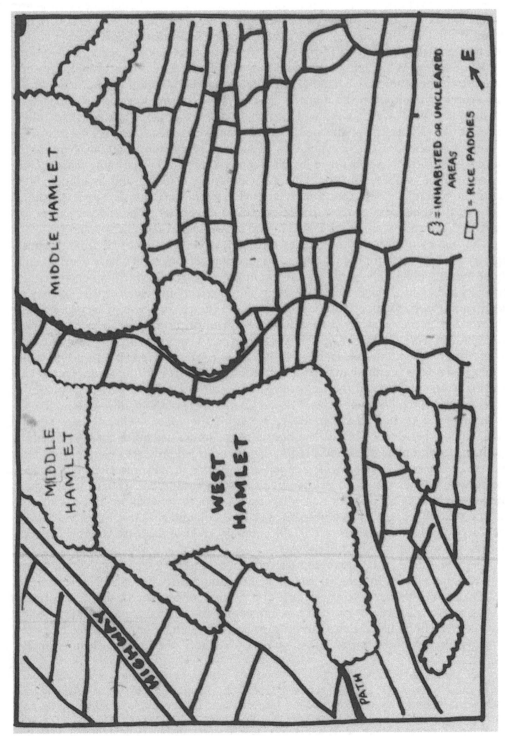

**Map 2** West and middle hamlets and rice paddies (from an aerial photograph)

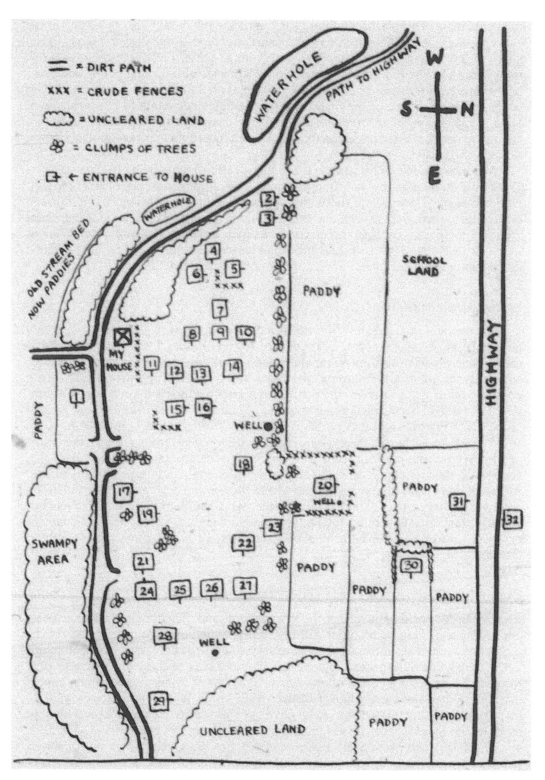

**Map 3** West Hamlet Svay (not to scale)

hamlet, a mass of abundant wild flora surrounds the inhabited area, especially to the east and west where there are often extensive stretches of uncultivated land. To the south of the hamlet stretches an irregularly quilted pattern of rice paddies as far as the eye can see, the flat expanse punctuated by thrusts of tall sugar palms and other bushes and trees growing on the dikes. Other fields are located to the north, including some on the other side of the highway. The rice fields belonging to the residents of West Hamlet cover, in all, some twenty-eight hectares. But these paddies are not all contiguous and are interspersed with fields owned by people in other hamlets or even neighboring villages.

West Hamlet had, in December 1959, about 160 residents living in thirty houses. The actual number at any one time fluctuates several persons more or less, for even within this small population there are constant additions and subtractions through births, deaths, marriages, divorces, and the taking in of kinsmen. In addition, there are more temporary changes in population as men leave for temporary employment in the city, visitors come to stay for indefinite periods of time, etc. (For more detailed demographic analysis of West Svay's population, see appendix C.)

## SOCIAL ORGANIZATION

The overall social organization of West Svay is difficult to delineate in any tidy fashion because it has no neat, clear-cut architecture. Rather, like village houses that can be constructed of various materials in different shapes and sizes, the social bonds among the community's residents are diverse and relatively unstructured. There are no well-defined groups beyond the family and household, no clear-cut social stratification, and no rigid norms dictating interaction. But just as the houses are built according to some basic design, it is possible to discern some form and patterns in village social structure. Although there are no significant formal groups apart from the family and household, the latter do constitute the basic socioeconomic unit of village life, and ties of kinship may have explicit or subtle influences on interpersonal relations. Although there is no rigid stratification within the community, certain individuals are accorded greater respect of higher rank than others. Although there are relatively few powerful sanctions governing interaction, there are certain norms that exert greater or lesser control over behavior. The following sections will explore these points in greater detail.

## FAMILY AND KINSHIP ORGANIZATION

Kinship is not as critical for the organization and functioning of Khmer peasant society as it is in some other cultures, but it nonetheless constitutes one of the more important bases for interpersonal relations in village life. Many rural communities probably had their genesis in a cluster of households of close kinsmen, and grew through the constant addition of new homes established by successive generations of married children and other relatives (Delvert 1961, 207). Thus, it is not uncommon for many or most of the residents of a Khmer village to be related to one another, whether by blood or by marriage, close kin or remote (Delvert 1961, 207; CMCC 49.002, 49.017, 49.023). In West Svay, a variety of kin ties links twenty-two out of thirty-two households, while the remaining families are related to at least one or two other households in the hamlet (see chart 1). Such a situation may not exist in all Khmer villages (see Zadrozny 1955, 313 who suggests that communities are composed largely of non-kinsmen), for there is neither a legal bar to individuals of reputable character establishing residence in any village, nor the deliberate exclusion of outsiders that is characteristic of what Wolf (1955, 1957) calls "closed" peasant communities. But since villagers generally distrust and fear any place where they have no kinsmen or friends (see chapter 7; Pym 1959, 164), it is highly unlikely that a person would move into a community unless he were marrying, already related to, or at least acquainted with some indigenous family.[9] (All the residents of West Svay who were not actually born in the hamlet came to the community in marriage, or because they had close kinsmen here, or because they had inherited land in the village from a peasant who was native to the village.) The web of kinship extends beyond the village as well.

Khmer kinship is basically bilateral (cognatic). The paternal or maternal line may be emphasized in certain respects: for example, personal surnames (instituted by legal decree in 1910 [Steinberg 1959, 78] although rarely used except for legal and administrative concerns) come from the father; membership in the Baku, the official priests of the royal family, is handed down through males (Aymonier 1900, 63); and there is some emphasis upon the female line in residence patterns and parts of the kin terminological system that (along with other practices) are thought by many writers to be survivals of matrilineal descent among ancient Khmer (see, e.g. Coedès 1953; Condominas 1953, 602; Thierry 1955; Groslier 1957, 14; O'Sullivan 1962).[10] In general, however, there is no significant weighting of either the male or female lines with respect to property ownership and inheritance, kin terminology and residence patterns in general, and recognition of and behavior toward kinsmen. Any skewing toward one side or another is usually due to certain circumstances rather than to absolute rules, for in this as in many bilateral systems there is considerable flexibility.

The general features of Khmer kinship are consistent with Murdock's characterization of the bilateral or Eskimo type of cognatic social organization that is widespread throughout Southeast Asia (see Murdock 1960a, 6, 14).

(1)   The primary kin unit is the small domestic unit of a nuclear family or some sort of extended family.[11]
(2)   Monogamy is predominant; polygyny is legally permitted but actually rare.
(3)   Marriage with any degree of cousin is permitted.
(4)   Residence is neolocal or (in Murdock's terms) ambilocal; there is a strong tendency toward, but no firm rule dictating, uxorilocality.
(5)   There are no rules concerning community exogamy or endogamy.

---

[9] Cf. Delvert (1961, 198–99) who comments on the ease with which Cambodian peasants change residence (see also Gourou 1945, 380). This may be true in some areas, especially sparsely populated regions where land is readily available for fields or house sites. But it is certainly not typical of Svay villagers who move only in post-marital residence to the communities of their spouses, or to assume employment elsewhere.

[10] The question of possible matrilineality among the ancient Khmer is too complex a problem to be discussed at length here. In general, I would agree with O'Sullivan who argues that, in the time of the ancient kingdoms, "matrilineal descent . . . was an ideal to which the society 'ought' to adhere, and in fact did adhere in certain sacred and ritual situations, while the bilateral organization of kinship was in general effective and has since become almost totally effective" (1962, 94). If his analysis is correct, the ancient Khmer could fall within Type IV of Befu's (1963a) unilineal-bilateral societies.

[11] N.B. I do not use the term "extended family" in the same way that Murdock does.

(6) Beyond the family there is only a bilaterally extended "personal kindred."
(7) Cousin terminology is Eskimo in terms of reference (although Hawaiian in terms of address), and avuncular terminology is lineal (see appendix E).

These points will be discussed in detail below.

### Marriage Rules, Preferences, and Patterns

Various aspects of marriage—certain factors in the selection of a spouse, polygamy and monogamy, and wedding rituals—will be discussed in chapter 6. But two points regarding marriage rules and patterns will be explored here: incest prohibitions and patterns of community exogamy and endogamy.

**Incest.** The only incontrovertible norms that restrict the choice of a marriage partner are the prohibitions against incest. Both the modern and especially the ancient legal codes explicitly interdict(ed) marriage or fornication between certain relatives.[12] The villagers themselves regard sexual relations or marriage with certain kinsmen as unthinkable; specifically: parents, children, siblings, grandparents, grandchildren, aunts and uncles, and nephews and nieces, whether the relationship is natural or adoptive (relatives by marriage, e.g., wife's niece, are also considered somewhat askance) (see also CMCC 42.003, 42.004). My stories of, for example, brother–sister incest[13] in other societies were received with amazement and disgust: "If one did that sort of thing here, one would be thrown out of the village . . . there are laws against that." (One villager did whisper that a former king had taken an aunt "as a wife," but this was excused as a prerogative of royalty.)

But marriage with other kinsmen, including cousins of any degree, is permissible and not uncommon (e.g., Rith and Nara [House 20] are first cousins).[14] The sororate

---

[12] The modern civil code (see Clairon n.d., 57–58) absolutely forbids marriages between natural and adopted members of the nuclear family, while unions between aunt/uncles and nephews/nieces are permitted only after an appeal to the Ministry of Justice, consideration by a council or ministers, and authorization by the king. Royalty, however, are permitted to marry half siblings, parents' siblings, or siblings' children if approval is obtained from the king (Aymonier 1900, 62; Steinberg 1959, 84; Clairon n.d., 58). The law also states that any children born of incestuous relations will not be legally recognized for "moral and physiological reasons" (Clairon n.d., 79).

The older legal codes gave very detailed specifications concerning different kinds of incest and various punishments for breaking the rules. In the category of intolerable incest that was severely punished (with heavy fines, confiscation of property, and annulment of marriage) were relations between members of the nuclear family, grandparents and grandchildren, and certain other alliances (such as polygyny with two women related to one another). Marriages to certain other relatives (ranging from an aunt to an ElSiHuSi to the ex-wife of anyone of the fifth degree of kinship) were considered incestuous but permitted to stand after payment of a fine. Certain incest prohibitions also applied to persons who assumed a fictive kin relationship to one another, and to a former monk and the individual who conferred his religious orders, habitually gave him alms, or lived near the monastery in which he took his vows. For details on the above, see Leclère 1894, 395–404; 1898, 1:290–94, 324–25; Daguin n.d., 23–26; Aymonier 1900, 62–63.

[13] See CMCC 41.001 for a Khmer tale of a royal brother and sister who were ordered to marry because mates of suitably high rank could not be found for them; the siblings, however, could not bring themselves to consummate the marriage until love potions were administered to them.

[14] Cf. CMCC 42.003, which states that one cannot wed first cousins although more remote cousins are acceptable spouses; and Daguin n.d., 24, who says that first cousin marriage is permissible only if the man's parents are older than the woman's.

is also possible (e.g., Kim is married to his deceased wife's sister),[15] as are marriage in which two brothers marry two sisters (although in such cases the elder of the two brothers should wed the elder of the two sisters).

**Community Endogamy and Exogamy.** There are no rules concerning village endogamy and exogamy. Some people assert that endogamy is best because potential spouses (and their families) know one another well and can accurately assess each other's virtues and faults before marriage. Other villagers, however, say that neither exogamy nor endogamy is preferable and that other concerns, such as the character of a possible mate, are paramount.

In fact, there is a decided preponderance of hamlet and village exogamy: some three-quarters of all the marriages in West Svay within the past seventy-odd years are exogamous to the village and some 90 percent exogamous to the hamlet (see table 3.1).[16] Because there is no definite preference for community exogamy, the reasons for its high incidence in West Hamlet are not completely certain but may be due to several factors. First, the population of West Hamlet is small and does not offer a large selection of individuals from which to choose mates. This may help to explain hamlet exogamy but not village exogamy because Svay as a whole is quite populous and, at present, the sex ratio is about even for adolescents and young adults.

**Table 3.1. Community exogamy and endogamy in marriages of the past seventy years**

| Total number of hamlet exogamous marriages: 96 (90.6%) | Hamlet endogamous marriages: | 10 (9.4%)[a] | Total number of village endogamous marriages: 23 (21.7%) |
|---|---|---|---|
| | Hamlet exogamous–Village endogamous marriages: | 13 (12.3%) | |
| | Village exogamous marriages: | 83 (78.3%) | |
| | Total number of marriages: | 106 (100%) | |

*Note:* The total number of marriages includes those of the present inhabitants of West Svay as well as those of their parents, siblings, and children who were born in the hamlet (although some of these may now be deceased or moved away). Not included are three marriages that ended in divorce and nine marriages where the facts were unclear or unrecorded.

[a] The percentage figures presented here and elsewhere are not meant to indicate statistical significance but only to present crude proportions for the benefit of the reader.

A second and more important point, especially regarding hamlet exogamy, is that, so far as young people in West Svay are concerned, the boy or girl next door has been known too long and too intimately to become an object of romantic interest. When adolescents discuss marriage and desirable spouses, they may acknowledge the physical or personal attractiveness of certain fellow residents of the hamlet. But they are usually dismissed as possible mates because they are like siblings or old shoe friends. By contrast, an unknown beauty glimpsed at a Buddhist festival, or an engaging friend of a friend visiting from another community, is much more intriguing. This is not to

---

[15] According to Daguin n.d., 25, and Steinberg 1959, 84, legal authorization must be obtained for sororate marriages. Older legal codes punished sororate and levirate marriages if there were children born of the first marriage (Leclère 1894, 397; 1898, 1:292).

[16] I have no information as to whether community exogamy is common in other Khmer villages.

### Table 3.2. Communities in which exogamous marriages occur

| Number of marriages of an individual from West Svay with a person from: | |
| --- | --- |
| Another hamlet of Svay: | 12 (18.0%) |
| Another village within a 5 km radius: | 33 (49.3%) |
| Another community more than 5 but less than 30 km distant: | 11 (16.4%) |
| Phnom Penh: | 3 (4.5%) |
| Another community more than 30 km distant: | 8 (12.0%) |
| Total: | 67 (100%) |

*Note:* This table does not include a number of exogamous marriages for which the exact natal villages of the spouses was not recorded.

suggest that all marriages are based on romantic attraction because they are not. But a relatively unknown suitor or possible fiancée whose virtues are glorified and whose faults are concealed or minimized may seem a more attractive spouse than a neighbor whose defects are known all too well. Third, pragmatic economic considerations can sometimes be of primary concern. The amount of rice paddy land owned by a West Svay family is, on the average, very small because of parcelization that becomes more acute with each generation (see chapter 4). Thus, those families who already have little land and/or many offspring may encourage their children to make exogamous matches with individuals in other communities who have more favorable property holdings or who may have non-agricultural employment with regular wages, and such children will often emigrate from the hamlet or village upon marriage.[17] Therefore, exogamous marriages that are economically advantageous and/or emotionally satisfying may serve another function in draining off individuals from a community that does not have enough land to adequately support all the offspring of each new generation.

This last point warrants further comment. Given overpopulation and limited land resources, it seems surprising that, within the past seventy-odd years, the number of people who have moved into the hamlet through marriage is slightly more than the number who have moved away. But there are several factors that must be considered. First, the ratio of emigrants to immigrants has varied through time. Fifty to seventy years ago, when the hamlet's population was relatively small and could easily absorb more residents, the number of people who married into the hamlet outnumbered those who moved away. Within the past few decades, however, the proportion of emigrants and immigrants has been roughly equal. Second, certain households in West Svay had or still have more rice fields than some families in other villages, particularly within the immediate area, which is overpopulated in general. There are many

---

[17] While I shall not cite figures, an examination of genealogies reveals that in all families that had/have more than three children, at least one of the offspring married exogamously and moved from the hamlet, and that when there are five or more children, a majority of the offspring emigrate upon marriage. To take one example, Heng and Seang have about one hectare of rice fields and eight children. Of the six children who are already married, all married exogamously and all but one left Svay and inherited no fields. The married daughter who remains in the hamlet shares her parents' fields, and her husband has some land in a nearby village that he continues to work.

examples of persons such as Kouch who came from a very poor family with seven children in a nearby village to marry Thida who stands to inherit almost a hectare of land and the parental home.[18] Thus, it seems that exogamous marriages, and the establishment of post-marital residence in the community of whichever spouse is better off, help to shift about and distribute the population in a pattern consistent with available land resources.[19] Third, immigration through marriage persists because of the high incidence of uxorilocal residence. Women are generally more reluctant than men to leave their natal homes, especially when it involves moving to another community. Therefore, in exogamous marriages it is likely that the male will move to his wife's community.[20]

To introduce another point of interest: some three-quarters of the exogamous marriages in West Svay involve persons from the other hamlets of Svay or communities within a fifteen-kilometer radius; in particular, half of the marriages involve spouses from villages within a five-kilometer radius (see table 3.2). Again, there are neither rules nor firm traditions that one should wed someone from a nearby community. But that many such marriages occur may be explained by several factors. Villagers are generally deeply suspicious of strangers and unknown regions (see chapter 8), but the immediately neighboring villages are linked to Svay by a network of kinship and friendship bonds resulting from generations of intermarriage among these communities. An individual from one of these villages makes an attractive spouse on several counts. First, he (or she) is likely to be sufficiently unknown to arouse more interest than would a fellow resident of the hamlet, yet his (or her) assets and liabilities can be well evaluated by the relatives or friends that one probably has in a nearby community. (In fact, such kinsmen and friends in other villages often promote exogamous marriages by suggesting one of their younger relatives or acquaintances as a possible spouse for someone in Svay.) Second, should one move to the community of one's spouse, it is still possible to return home quickly and easily to visit family and old friends. (Indeed, frequent exchange of visits among close kinsmen in Svay and its adjacent communities is very common.) Moreover, it is not unlikely that a person who assumes post-marital residence in another but nearby community will already have some kinsmen there; for example, when Sok came from Ta Chas to marry Sreypich in House 26, he had a first cousin living practically next door (Heng in House 21). Third, if one marries an individual from and moves to a distant community, it is highly probable that one will not inherit any rice fields in Svay. But if post-marital residence is assumed in a nearby village, one may well receive some paddies because they will be close enough to be worked without difficulty. In fact, a number of households in West Svay own fields that are located in the vicinity of neighboring communities, just as some of the paddies in the immediate environs of Svay belong actually to people in other hamlets or villages.

---

[18] Of twenty persons who married into West Svay for whom I have genealogical data, thirteen came from families with from five to nine offspring.

[19] Without citing the exact figures, I might note that in exogamous marriages of West Svay residents with persons from communities within a five-kilometer radius, the number of couples who assumed post-marital residence in Svay is greater than those who went to the natal community of the non-Svay spouse. But when exogamous marriages involved persons from other regions, especially areas more than thirty kilometers away that are less densely populated, the number of Svay residents who emigrated to their spouses' communities is twice as large as the number of people who married into the hamlet from these distant communities.

[20] For example, in one sample of fifty persons who moved into West Svay through marriage, thirty-two were males and eighteen were females; of forty-four persons who emigrated from the village through marriage, thirty-three were males and eleven were females.

## Residence Patterns and the Family and Household

The basic local kin group among the Khmer is the household (i.e., those persons living in one house). The composition of households in Svay is quite varied (see table 3.3), reflecting different patterns of post-marital residence and different circumstances that bring various kinsmen under one roof. But most common are nuclear

### Table 3.3. Household composition in Svay

|  | West Svay | Other hamlets | Totals |
|---|---|---|---|
| I. Nuclear families | 18 (56.3%) | 61 (48.4%) | 79 (50.0%) |
| (a) couples + unmarried children | 17 | 54 | 71 |
| (b) widow(er) or divorcé(e) + unmarried children | 1 | 7 | 8 |
| II. Extended families |  |  |  |
| 1. Stem families | 8 (25.0%) | 31 (24.6%) | 39 (24.7%) |
| a. Parent(s) ± unmarried children + married child+ latter's spouse ± children[a] | 7 | 29 | 36 |
| b. Spinster + married niece + latter's spouse ± children | 1 | 2 | 3 |
| 2. Other kinds of extended families | 3 (9.4%) | 26 (20.6%) | 29 (18.4%) |
| a. Parent(s) ± unmarried children + widowed or divorced child + latter's children | 0 | 9 | 9 |
| b. Widow(er), divorcé(e), nuclear family, or stem family with core individual or couple's sibling(s) ± latter's spouse + children | 2 | 10 | 12 |
| c. Same as above with niece or nephew ± latter's spouse ± children | 1 | 4 | 5 |
| d. Same as above with grandmother or grandchildren | 0 | 2 | 2 |
| e. A couple with some other combination of kinsmen | 0 | 1 | 1 |
| III. Married couples alone | 2 (6.3%) | 3 (2.4%) | 5 (3.2%) |
| IV. Single persons | 1 (3.1%) | 2 (1.6%) | 3 (1.9%) |
| V. Other[b] | 0 | 3 (2.4%) | 3 (1.9%) |
| Totals: | 32 (100%) | 126 (100%) | 158 (100%) |

*Note:* These figures are for December 1959; as noted in the text, household composition can vary through time.

[a] This type has been put into the category of stem family because, for all intents and purposes, it is functionally equivalent to a stem family.

[b] This category includes two households in which two unmarried sisters live together, and one household with two unmarried females living together.

families and stem families, which together account for 75 percent of all households in Svay. These and other points are explored below.[21]

Before proceeding further, a word must be said about the terminology to be used, because there has not always been agreement on the precise meanings of terms for different types of residence or families (see, e.g., Adam 1948; Goodenough 1956; Fischer 1958; Bohannan 1957; Ayoub and Lieberman 1962; Murdock 1949). I will, therefore, state exactly how I shall use certain terms that have been adopted or adapted from Murdock (1949), Fischer (1958), Adam (1948), and Bohannan (1963).

## Residence Patterns

(a) Neolocality: a couple establishes a new home separate from the families of either spouse.

(b) Uxorilocality: a couple lives with the wife's family. (Village-uxorilocality: a couple resides within the wife's village but not actually in her family's house.)

(c) Virilocality: a couple lives with the husband's family. (Village-virilocality: a couple resides in the husband's village but not actually in his family's house.)

(d) Amitalocality: a couple lives with an aunt of either the husband or wife.

(e) Fratrilocality: a couple lives with a brother of either the husband or wife; sororilocality: residence with a sister of either spouse.

## Types of Families

(a) Nuclear family: a two-generational unit consisting of parents and unmarried children.

(b) Stem family: a two- or three-generational unit consisting of parents, perhaps still unmarried children, and a married child plus his/her spouse and possibly the latter's children.

(c) Extended family: any familial grouping that is larger than a nuclear family, that is, a unit that incorporates kinsmen other than parents and unmarried children. (The stem family can be considered one type of extended family.)[22]

**Residence Norms and Patterns.** There are no definite norms and no consensus in Svay as to what constitutes ideal post-marital residence. Attitudes about preferred residence patterns vary according to circumstances and can change with age. A number of couples, particularly the younger ones, feel that a nuclear family living in neolocality is ideal. "One has more room. . . . One does not quarrel with other relatives in the house. . . . One can do as one pleases. . . . One feels good in a house of one's

---

[21] In the following discussion I shall draw upon comments from Goodenough 1956, Fischer 1958, Barnes 1960, and others who have refined the investigation and analysis of residence patterns.

[22] Lévi-Strauss 1960 and Wolf 1966 also use the term "extended family" in this way, although Murdock (1949, 1957) does not. The Khmer themselves do not have separate terms for the different types of families.

own . . . etc." (see also Aymonier 1900, 34). But other couples may feel that residence with one of the spouse's parents (or other kinsmen) has advantages and is preferable to neolocality. Many who live in extended families assert that they are quite content (although in some cases they may be rationalizing conditions that stem from necessity rather than choice): "It is pleasant to have company in the house. . . . My mother helps me with cooking and caring for the children. . . . We have more people to tend the fields. . . . One should support one's parents when they get old . . . etc." And old couples who are approaching or past the age of active labor feel that uxori- or virilocality is admirable because "it is good to have a married child come to live in one's home, to help keep house and work the paddies, and to have the pleasure of grandchildren playing about the house." In sum, then, there are really two basic ideals of post-marital residence: either neolocality or residence with one of the spouse's parents. There is perhaps a stronger preference for neolocality, but it cannot be considered a truly dominant norm (cf. Zadrozny 1955, 313; Murdock 1957, 680; Condominas 1953, 589).

Actual instances of post-marital residence reflect these attitudes. Approximately half the couples in West Svay live neolocally, while others have assumed various other kinds of residence. To take for the moment a static picture of West Svay in 1959, the following types of patterns were present.[23]

| | | |
|---|---|---|
| Neolocal residence | 17 couples | 47.2% |
| Uxorilocal residence | 11 couples | 30.6% |
| Virilocal residence | 5 couples | 13.8% |
| Amitalocal residence | 2 couples | 5.6% |
| Sororilocal residence | 1 couple | 2.8% |

**The Nuclear Family.** A nuclear family household may come into being either through neolocal residence or because the older set of parents has died in what was originally a stem family. In any event, the nuclear family can be considered the most fundamental social group in Khmer society, bound together by a variety of affective, economic, moral, and legal ties. The strongest and most enduring relationships in village life are found in the bonds between husband and wife, sibling and sibling, and especially parent and child. Even after a family or orientation has split into the various families of procreation of the different offspring, members of the former often retain deep affection for and frequent contact with one another. According to both legal codes and cultural norms, family members should (and usually do) offer one another daily support, loyalty, and consideration, as well as special assistance in time of trouble. In addition, the nuclear family is often the basic economic unit of production and consumption, which cooperates in subsistence activities and shares produce, income, and property (see chapter 4). It also frequently acts as (and is considered by others to be) a single social unit in other endeavors; for example, in cooperative labor exchange the quid pro quo is calculated basically in terms of the amount of work owed by one

---

[23] Note the following: (a) Some of the "couples" designated below may, at present, be reduced to a widow or widower. (b) Some of the couples designated uxori- or virilocal may appear to be living neolocally. But in fact they had moved in with one of the spouse's parents when they were first married; these parents subsequently died, leaving the couple with the house to themselves. In such cases, residence is classified according to the situation at the outset of the couple's marriage. (c) Two couples in West Svay are not included in the table because of problems as to how they should be classified.

family (or household) to another rather than by one particular individual to another; in contributions to Buddhist or life-cycle ceremonies, a gift is often meant to come from the family as a whole; and in community activities each family or household gives a certain amount of money or labor. Finally, it is a residential and commensal unit whose members ordinarily live under one roof and eat, sleep, and work together.

The rights and obligations of family members toward one another and the nature of the relations that should obtain among them are defined and sanctioned in several ways: by legal statutes in the civil code, by Buddhist precepts and teachings, by belief in ancestral spirits (*meba*) who oversee their descendants' conduct, and by general cultural norms regarding proper behavior within the family.[24] Real behavior does not, of course, always approximate ideal standards, particularly when Khmer culture does not in general demand rigid adherence to norms. But relations within the nuclear family do not allow the same degree of latitude and personal choice that is evident in an individual's relations with more remote kinsmen.

(a) Husband and wife. The emotional content of the relation between spouses naturally varies from couple to couple. For some, marriage seems to be primarily a matter of necessity or convenience, and the spouses work and live together harmoniously but impassively. Other couples, despite the fact that public displays of affection between spouses are not customary, clearly reveal a deep mutual sentiment and regard: a man will grieve over his wife's illness; a woman will eulogize her husband's character and skills; spouses may give one another playful nicknames; etc. Naturally, even the most loving couples occasionally squabble. But since deep-rooted disagreements or prolonged and obvious incompatibility usually lead to divorce, there is at the least mutual tolerance and at the best mutual love between spouses.

According to the legal code, the man is "chef de famille" with almost absolute powers over his wife, children, and household matters, and he possesses certain prerogatives denied to women (see, e.g., Clairon n.d., 65–67). Buddhist doctrine also assigns a superior position to the male (see chapter 5). But closer inspection of both the law and religious teachings reveals that the woman, while owing fidelity and obedience to her husband and possessing minimal legal capacity, is granted a number of rights and privileges (e.g., a woman can initiate divorce proceedings; a man must obtain his wife's consent to enter the monastery or take another spouse; a man owes his wife food, shelter, "material and moral aid" according to law, and respect and consideration according to Buddhist norms [Clairon n.d., 64–65; Burtt 1955, 110]). And in village life, the relative positions of male and female, husband and wife, are virtually equal. The husband is technically the supreme authority who is owed deference, respect, and obedience by his family. But the peasant wife is by no means a totally docile and submissive creature. Her role in the maintenance of the family is critical, and her activities are varied: she has primary responsibility for the care of the children and household; she is coworker in the fields; she oversees and keeps the family budget; she shrewdly handles many financial transactions and often undertakes her own commercial ventures to earn money; she owns and can dispose of property in her own right;[25] she assumes explicit legal authority over the household when her husband is

---

[24] On legal codes and Buddhist precepts, see, e.g., Daguin n.d.; Leclère 1890, 1898, 1899; Lingat 1952–55; Thierry 1955; Clairon n.d.; Burtt 1955.

[25] Indeed, in certain cases of uxorilocal residence, especially those in which the husband comes from another village, the woman may hold all the major property used by the family.

dead, absent, incapacitated, etc. As a result, the wife and mother exerts considerable authority, both overt and covert, within her family. (On the position of women, see also chapters 4, 5, 6, and especially Thierry 1955, as well as Aymonier 1900, 34–35; LeGallen 1929, 221; Monod 1931, 31; Steinberg 1959, 78; Ward 1963, 65–70, 479).

(b) Parents and children. The legal code contains a number of articles concerning the relation between parents and children with respect to types of filiation (legitimate, illegitimate, or adoptive), parental authority, and emancipation of children from familiar control (see Clairon n.d., 75–79, 87–90, 104–5, 111–13; LeGallen 1929, 220; Aymonier 1900, 34; Leclère 1890, 65). In general, parents are given strong powers "to protect minor children from the dangers to which their youth exposes them" (Clairon n.d., 87), including the rights to exact obedience and respect, to discipline and punish by physical and other (but not excessive) means, to administer and use a child's property, to consent to or veto a child's marriage, etc. The parents are also legally obligated to educate, "nourish, maintain and raise the child (Clairon, n.d., 87–88). And, according to religious precepts and cultural norms, they must also act as moral guides, oversee the making of suitable marriages, and provide (through inheritance) for the future welfare of their offspring. The latter, in turn, owe their parents honor, deference, support in old age, and a proper funeral (see also Burtt 1955, 110; Aymonier 1900, 85; CMCC 42.003).

In the reality of village life, the parent–child relation is more informal and indulgent than the legal and religious codes suggest. Parents derive great pleasure and entertainment from children who are generally treated with considerable permissiveness and given much affection (see chapter 6). Concern for offspring is manifest in a variety of ways: parents give their children the best of whatever food or clothing are within their means (as well as occasional treats that they can sometimes ill afford), worry about their children obtaining an adequate education and making favorable marriages (and, in most cases, the child's own inclinations and desires are taken into consideration and he/she is not forced into doing something distasteful), make decisions concerning residence and inheritance that generally attempt to treat all offspring equitably and provide for their future well-being, accept widowed or divorced children back into the family fold, etc.

In return, parents generally receive obedience, deference, and devotion from their children. Although youngsters are sometimes defiant and insolent to their parents, as children grow older they show increasing respect for and submission to parental judgment and authority, as well as heightened solicitude for the welfare not only of parents but of other members of the family as well.[26] For example, adolescent or young adult offspring often take temporary jobs to help supplement family income; when males become monks, they earn merit for both their parents and themselves; individuals rarely marry without parental approval and, in fact, often allow parents to arrange marriages for them despite the ideal that young men and women can wed as they please (see chapter 6); and there is a very strong feeling of obligation to help support parents in their old age (whether by remaining in residence with them, by

---

[26] See Leclère 1899, 531–32 for his interesting hypothesis that the Buddhist doctrine of reincarnation creates tight familial bonds because "a Christian child [does not know] why he was born into one family rather than another. The Buddhist knows that he deserves to be the son of his parents and the father of his children, and that his parents have deserved to have him as their son."

taking them into one's own home, or by sending contributions for their maintenance if one lives separate from them) and to give them proper funerals upon their deaths.[27]

Of the two parents, children have more frequent interaction and deeper emotional ties with the mother who is the major source of sustenance and love. A father can also be affectionate, but usually he is openly loving to his children only during their earliest years and grows more authoritarian as they grow older. While neither parent is overly strict, the father tends to be less patient and tolerant, more demanding of immediate obedience, and quicker to chastise than the mother. Relations between fathers and sons can become closer as boys begin to accompany their fathers in various tasks, but sons will always view their mothers as the warm and protective figure. Similarly, the bond between mothers and daughters deepens in the latters' adolescence as the two cooperate in household and other chores; and, especially when the mother is relatively young, there can be great informality between the two that is more like a relation between peers than between parent and child (cf. Nash 1965, 151ff. for a similar situation among the Burmese). The intensity of the mother–daughter relation is further evidenced by the high incidence of uxorilocality explained by the villagers as the result of a girl's reluctance to leave home and her mother. And the bond between mothers and children in general is shown in the fact that children almost always chose to go with their mothers in the event of divorce, and by sayings such as "Better to be deprived of a father than a mother, better to drown than to be burned" (CMCC 42.003) or "A father is worth a thousand friends and a mother worth a thousand fathers" (Leclère 1899, 352).

Disruptions of the parent–child relation can occur. For example, the father of Vireak deserted his family when the latter was a boy, and there have been other instances of fathers who abandoned their homes or were drunkards, wastrels, or persons of "bad character" and who are spoken of by their children with bitterness and sorrow.[28]

Conversely, parents have the legal right to disown or disinherit a child who has offended them or has been guilty of grave misconduct, although, in fact, absolute repudiation of offspring seems to be extremely rare. In general, however, the bond between parents and children is perhaps the strongest and most enduring relationship in village life.[29] Even when an individual marries and establishes a family of procreation that comes to take precedence over the family of orientation, deep-rooted sentiments and feelings of obligation persist toward parents and are manifest in mutual visiting, aid in times of need, and abiding concern.

(c) Siblings. Ideally, the relation between siblings should be one of loving harmony, generosity, mutual aid, and concern. Older offspring should help parents in providing

---

[27] In fact, both ancient and modern law specify that children who do not care for their parents in the latter's "last illness" or attend the funeral would be disinherited (see Clairon n.d., 123–24; Leclère 1898, 1:348–51, 355).

[28] There is often, however, a willingness to forgive and forget transgressions that is typical of the culture in general (see infra). For example, when Vireak grew up, he set out on a journey of almost a thousand miles in search of his lost father.

[29] Note also that ancient legal codes specified parricide and infanticide, especially the former, as the most heinous, inexcusable, and rare of crimes. A parricide would not only be executed and tormented by "spirits and demons from 10,000 worlds," but "the greatest misfortune would come to the family and the kingdom: cholera, smallpox and fever would kill many people and all the buffaloes" (Leclère 1894, 352).

moral guidance, material support, and protection for their younger brothers and sisters; while the latter owe respect and deference to their elder siblings.[30] Such norms are nurtured from an early age when babies and youngsters are frequently placed in the care of older siblings who become virtual parental surrogates with authority over and responsibility for their charges. Affection and loyalty among siblings are encouraged, and serious discord among family members (both siblings and parents and children) is thought to be punished by ancestral spirits.

In fact, the bond between siblings can be, at its best, extremely close-knit and long-lasting. In West Svay there are several examples of siblings who constantly visit one another's houses to gossip, joke, and exchange confidences, and they help one another in the fields or at various other tasks. Sentiment and feelings of obligation between siblings are also expressed in other ways. Siblings who live in different communities will make efforts to see one another frequently or periodically, depending on their geographical proximity and fondness for one another. Siblings may help support one another: for example, older children contribute to the sustenance of younger siblings by working in the fields or at temporary jobs; and individuals sometimes take into their households a sibling who is destitute or orphaned. Siblings also aid one another in times of special need: for example, by lending one another money (usually at no interest)[31], by caring for one another's children if the latter are ill, poor, orphaned, or otherwise in want, and by proffering assistance during especially busy times (such as labor for certain stages of rice cultivation or for the preparation of life-cycle ceremonials). Finally, siblings may act as moral guides and arbiters for one another, especially when the parents have died; for example, an individual may try to conciliate quarrels between his siblings, or harangue and plead with a wayward sibling to mend his ways.

The warmest sibling relations are between those who are of the same sex[32] and close in age. There may also be firm ties between brothers and sisters as well. But the similarity of interests and activities among those of one's own sex make for closer bonds between sisters and between brothers.

There are many instances of siblings who fulfill the norm of loving harmony between brothers and sisters. But the sibling tie can also be one of indifference (in which siblings do not actively dislike one another but have relatively little interaction with and sentiment for each other) or, at the worst, liable to outright fracture. In childhood and adolescence, squabbles between siblings are common but are usually temporary altercations to be expected among youngsters. Disputes between adult siblings, however, are much more serious and can lead to long-standing or even permanent antagonism. For example, Rouen (House 9) and Vireak (House 1) have not spoken to each other for years because of a fistfight between their sons; each one felt

---

[30] Viz., precolonial law and tradition that gave a double share of inheritance "to the eldest [child] who had to support all his younger brothers" (Aymonier 1900, 85), and part of the wedding ritual in which three stalks of coconut flower represent the father, mother, and eldest sister who are important in raising children (Porée-Maspero et al. 1958, 56, 61).

[31] In nineteenth-century laws, no interest could be charged on loans between members of the same nuclear family (see Leclère 1898, 1:458–62; Aymonier 1900, 86). Note that among the various debts of West Svay villagers that are discussed in chapter 4, many involved loans between siblings.

[32] Cf. Zadrozny 1955, 315 who suggests that the bond between brothers and sisters may be stronger because their relation is "complementary" rather than "competitive" in terms of sex roles and inheritance.

that the other's child was at fault and demanded apologies that were never given. As a result, not only Rouen and Vireak but their entire families have studiously avoided any contact ever since. Such enduring estrangement is somewhat unusual because disputing siblings are usually reconciled by the admonishments and mediation of other members of the family, by submission to public opinion that does not condone such quarrels, or by the fear of offending the ancestral spirits. But, according to villagers, bitter clashes between mature siblings, provoked by any of a number of reasons (disputes over inheritance, altercations over one's children, quarrels over presumed selfishness or thoughtlessness), are not at all uncommon. In general, the relation between siblings is similar to that described by Firth (1956, 63) for British kinship: there is stronger affect, either positive or negative, between siblings than between more remote kin; and while siblings may be ignored, they are more often "a locus for emotional attitudes of some intensity and an important field for social relations."

**The Stem Family.** Stem families account for some 25 percent of all households in Svay. They occur for two major reasons: first, many couples must forego or postpone neolocal residence because of the expense of building a new house; and second, aging parents want one married child to remain at home to provide labor and support in their dotage.

With respect to the first point, an old Khmer tradition holds that a man who is about to be married should build a new house for himself and his bride (which home might shelter his parents-in-law as well).[33] But, villagers say, this custom is nowadays rarely followed because the cost of house construction has become too great. Actually, it appears that the financial burden of erecting a new home has always been more than most young men could afford and that the tradition has long been more an ideal than real procedure because only three couples presently living in Svay had established immediate neolocality upon marriage. But it is undeniable that within the past few decades, building an entirely new house has become extremely expensive: even a miniscule house made entirely of thatch would cost about 500 riels, while one of average size with wooden walls (and thatch or tile roof) can range anywhere from 10,000 to 50,000 riels (see also Delvert 1961, 193, on the cost of building houses).[34] Moreover, if one has not inherited land within the village upon which to build a dwelling, the need to purchase a house site would be an additional expense. Thus, in almost all cases nowadays, the fiancé does not build a new house, but instead gives a monetary

---

[33] Svay villagers spoke of this house as intended primarily to furnish a home for the newlyweds. But various sources (Thierry 1955, 148–54; Lingat 1952–55, 2:48–49, Clairon n.d., 119–20) discuss the ambiguities regarding the ownership and usufruct of what they call the "matrimonial house." According to these writers, the fiancé traditionally offers the house to his future parents-in-law. Court decisions prior to 1944 ruled that the house was actually the property of the girl's parents and meant to insure them a home in their old age (although the young couple had a definite right to reside there as well). Upon their death the house passed to the daughter (or, upon her death, to other heirs and not to the son-in-law). Subsequently, however, this view changed to give ownership of the house to the young couple and was considered to be their communal property, although the wife's parents retain a clear and lifelong right of habitation in the house: "the house . . . is destined to shelter the generation that comes and that which goes" (Thierry 1955, 153). Note that this custom of the "matrimonial house" is also present (although evidently declining) in Thailand, according to Lingat (1952, 1:48).

[34] Contrary to Zadrozny 1953, 313, which states that neolocality is universal in urban areas, the problem of house building is even more acute in Phnom Penh where materials, labor, and dwelling sites are even more expensive (not to mention the cost of apartments). Thus, according to several urban informants, uxorilocality or virilocality is very common in the city.

gift symbolically called "the worth of a house" (*tlay ptea*) to the girl's family.[35] And should a new house be built, either before or sometime during a couple's marriage, it is highly likely, contrary to the tradition, that the woman's family will give financial aid in its construction.

With regard to the second factor, no explicit norm demands that one married offspring must remain in the parental home,[36] but it is exceedingly common; in the entire village only three old couples and two widowed persons live by themselves. Continued residence of a married child is especially likely when a parent has been widowed and needs a younger person of the opposite sex to handle normally masculine or feminine chores; but it also occurs when both parents are alive.

It is not clearly predictable which child will stay. It is likely to be a daughter but may be a son; and it can be the eldest, youngest, or one intermediate in the birth order. Rather, the question of who will remain is decided according to particular circumstances; one child may be more devoted to or doted upon by the parents than are his siblings, or may have married someone with little or no resources, or may have been too thoroughly settled at home to leave when younger siblings married, or may simply have been the last one to get married and stayed home by default. Whatever the reason, whoever remains has the extra burden of caring for aged parents, but he (or she) is compensated by the prospect of inheriting, upon the parents' death, the family home and whatever rice fields the latter had retained for their own use.

When a couple must choose to live with either the wife's or the husband's family, the decision is determined not by any formal norms but by particular circumstances: which of the two homes has more room, which spouse has received or will inherit any (or a greater amount of) land or other property, which set of parents has a stronger desire or need for a married child to remain in residence, etc. There is, however, a decided tendency toward uxorilocality.[37]

Many sources have spoken of temporary or permanent uxorilocality, residence either with or near the wife's family, as traditional practice in Cambodia (Aymonier 1900, 34, 215; Lingat 1952–55, 2:48–49; Zadrozny 1955, 317; Thierry 1955, 123; Murdock 1957, 680; CMCC 42.004; the discussions of the "matrimonial house" also imply uxorilocality). If West Svay is any example, there is indeed a high incidence of uxorilocal residence among Khmer villagers. Of thirty-eight couples in the hamlet, eleven are presently living with the wife's family; another eight lived uxorilocally for a period of time before establishing another form of residence; and seven more couples are classified as neolocal but are exogamous marriages in which the husband has come to the wife's community. Thus, almost 70 percent of the couples in West Svay had been or are living uxorilocally in the broad sense (with or near the wife's family), of which 50 percent actually live or lived in the wife's household.

Villagers note the frequency of uxorilocality but clearly state that there has never been a firm rule or even clear preference for it. Rather, they feel that it is common

---

[35] Actually, this money is used to finance various wedding expenses (see chapter 6).

[36] It is also possible but relatively rare to have more than one married offspring in residence. One household in another hamlet of Svay has two married daughters at home. In West Svay, two households had two married children in residence for a period of several years in the past.

[37] According to Thierry (1955, 98–99 citing Leclère), the old legal codes stated that the husband is head of the family and thus decided the place of residence. It is probable, however, that the wife had then, as she does now, a definite say in the matter. For example, in East Svay, a young woman divorced her husband because he wanted them to live with his parents instead of remaining with hers.

simply because women are more reluctant than men to leave the security of their homes.[38] Their explanation seems reasonable because villagers speak of their special concern for daughters. Sons are not necessarily regarded with less affection, but girls are thought to need more protection and surveillance. From the time of adolescence, females are constantly warned not to stray from the security of the village or to go anywhere without escort; they thus develop a certain timidity that is reinforced by the generally insular outlook of villagers (see chapter 8). Adolescent girls are often apprehensive about the possibility of having to leave the comfortable warmth of home and community, where family (especially the mother) and friends are ever present and can be readily called upon for aid, when they marry.[39] Correspondingly, parents are reluctant to see a daughter move away, especially if she marries young. Males, on the other hand, are given much more freedom to do as and go where they please, and they are much more adventuresome and self-assured in dealing with new persons and places.

Virilocality is the third most common type of residence in West Svay, although it is much less frequent than uxorilocality.[40] For purposes of comparison, the relative incidence of the two in West Svay is presented in table 3.4.

**Table 3.4. Uxorilocality and virilocality in West Svay**

|  | Uxorilocal | Virilocal |
|---|---|---|
| Number of couples in permanent uxori- or virilocality | 11 | 4 |
| Number of couples who lived in temporary uxori- or virilocality and have since changed residence | 8 | 4 |
| Number of couples who are classified as neolocal but are exogamous marriages that can also be considered as village-uxorilocal or village-virilocal residence | 7 | 6 |
| Totals: | 26 | 14 |

When virilocality does occur, it is due to circumstances such as found in House 20. Rith and his wife live with his parents because they are old and need help, because his brother (the only other child) works and lives in Phnom Penh, and because he stands to inherit the parental home and other property. (Moreover, uxorilocal residence was not feasible in this case because Rith's wife comes from a family of eight children, four of whom still reside in the village or at home, making it unlikely that she would inherit any substantial amount of land or find comfortable living conditions in her household.)

---

[38] Some writers (e.g., Aymonier 1900, 34; Thierry 1955, 123; CMCC 42.004) have suggested that uxorilocality is a natural outgrowth of an old tradition of bride service whereby the fiancé comes to work and sometimes to live at his future parents-in-law's home before marriage (see chapter 6).

[39] Temporary or permanent uxorilocality is also common, often for similar reasons, in Burma, Thailand, Laos, Malaya, and Java (see, e.g., Nash 1965, 51–52; DeYoung 1955, 23–24; Kaufman 1960, 29; 1961, 21; Ayabe 1961, 13; Djamour 1959, 80; Koentjaraningrat 1960, 102), although all of these groups also show the same variety of residence patterns as do the Khmer.

[40] CMCC 42.004 implies that it is customary for one year of virilocal residence to follow one year of uxorilocality, but this has not been substantiated in any other sources or in my research.

One informant suggested that "rice cultivators usually go to live with the wife's side, but people with occupations go to live with the husband's side." There is some truth in this observation, for when the man has some non-agricultural employment or profession (e.g., a soldier, mechanic, or teacher) the wife must reside where her husband works. Sometimes this involves completely neolocal residence, but a couple may also live virilocally if a young woman marries an urbanite who is likely not to be able to afford a separate residence in the city.

Within the stem family, the resident son- or daughter-in-law usually comes to feel and to be accepted much as a natural child when he/she makes an effort to be respectful and diligent, and is treated by the parents-in-law with affection and consideration. In certain cases there can be some tension: for example, a woman in virilocal residence may be lonely for her family and friends elsewhere during the first years of marriage; or a young couple may chafe at having to live with parents rather than in their own house. In general, however, serious strife in a stem family is minimal or muted because the household can and probably would split apart if the friction became unbearable.

A stem family may operate as two units or one, depending on its composition and particular circumstances. When both parents are alive and vigorous (e.g., House 20) or a widowed parent is active and still has some unmarried offspring at home (e.g., Houses 7 and 17), there is a distinct and viable remnant of the original family of orientation that can maintain some sort of separate existence. In such cases, the stem family does not always operate as a solidary unit. So far as rice cultivation is concerned, the entire household has usufruct of the family's fields (that may technically belong to either the parents or to the married child) and all able-bodied members cooperate in working the paddies. But the two nuclear units within the stem family have different granaries, eat separately, maintain distinct budgets, and act separately in other ways despite residence under one roof and cooperation or sharing in certain endeavors.

A stem family will, however, form a single social, economic, and commensal unit when there is a widowed parent and only one married child remaining in the household (e.g., House 26), or when one or both of the parents is/are physically incapacitated with illness or old age (e.g., Houses 10 and 12) and there are no other unmarried children at home. In such cases, the entire household keeps a common granary, eats together, shares all produce and income, and contributes as one unit to ceremonies and the like, because it is senseless or impossible to maintain separate meals, budgets, etc. The younger couple supports and nourishes the elderly parents much as if the latter were children.

It should be noted here that a veritable stem family can arise also through amitalocality. Although amitalocality does not occur with any great frequency, it should be recognized as an acceptable pattern. In the entire village of Svay there are four examples (two in West Hamlet itself) of a married couple residing with an aunt; in all cases this aunt is the wife's mother's sister who is also, in all but one instance, a spinster. There are two points to note. First, a maternal aunt frequently becomes a mother surrogate by collateral extension of filial sentiment along the female line. Warm affection between aunts and nieces is evident in daily interaction within the hamlet, and it is not uncommon for a woman to take a sister's child (or children) in temporary or permanent residence. Second, a spinster can have, in effect, a ready-made family by having a niece assume the role of daughter and come to live with her upon marriage. This provides an excellent solution to the problem of her support in old age if she has no alternative recourse,[41] and the situation is also advantageous for a young couple who may be orphans or from a poor family.

There can also be more complicated factors involved in amitalocal residence if the two cases in West Svay are any example. In House 13, spinster Vanna was one of four children; two brothers moved away upon marriage, and her sister (who lived in House 16 but is now in Phnom Penh) has a hushed and lurid past of illicit sexual relations and illegitimate children. Vanna inherited the parental home and some rice fields and, having no children of her own, took in one of her sister's illegitimate daughters and the latter's husband (an orphan). Both of them call her "mother" and for all intents and purposes consider her as such (just as the niece's children think of Vanna as their grandmother). In form and function, this household is really indistinguishable from a true stem family. House 25 presents a different situation: here a couple resides with the wife's maternal aunt (who is a divorcée rather than spinster) because they are poverty stricken and have nowhere else to go. Unlike House 13, this household really has two separate families (the divorcée and her children, the couple and their children) who were thrown together by chance and necessity rather than choice.

There are also cases in which a couple (or widowed person) goes to live in the household of a married son or daughter. This obviously occurs late in life rather than during the initial periods of a couple's marriage. There are no examples of this pattern in West Svay, but it is not unlikely that some of the stem families in the other hamlets involve parents coming to reside with a married child rather than vice versa (there are four known instances of elderly widows who have moved into a married daughter's household). In general, however, it seems that this sort of residence is relatively infrequent because most old couples (or widowed individuals) have either arranged to have a married child remain at home or have decided to live alone.

**Other Kinds of Extended Families.** One-fifth of the households in Svay contain extended families of varied composition (see table 3.1). These are formed when a widow(er), couple, nuclear family, or stem family takes some relative(s) more or less permanently into the household. According to law, one is obligated to provide food, shelter, and other necessities to grandparents, parents, siblings, a child's spouse (while the child is living), and grandchildren if they are in obvious need, and if one can provide a home or financial aid (Clairon n.d., 112–14). Legal code aside, villagers consider it a moral duty to help a close relative who requires shelter and sustenance.

Most frequently taken into residence are siblings, nieces or nephews, and grandparents or grandchildren of the individual or couple who heads the household. When the kinsman is young and/or unmarried, he (she) comes from an impoverished family that cannot adequately support all its offspring, or is an orphan. (E.g., House 6 took in a wife's younger brother who, although an adult, is a deaf-mute thought to be incapable of self-support after their mother died.) Even a married kinsman, along with spouse and children, are given shelter if they are destitute and have no other recourse. (E.g., House 11 took in the wife's younger sister and husband because the latter barely earns a living as an occasional pedicab driver in the city.) Some families even have two or more different kinds of kinsmen in residence (e.g., one family in East Svay is composed of a man, his wife, and the latter's younger brother, younger sister, and nephew).

---

[41] There are six spinsters over forty years of age in all of Svay, and three have a married niece in residence. Of the other three, one lives with an older brother, while two others live together in what may or may not be a sort of lesbian relationship.

It is interesting that the "sponsor" (Fischer 1958) who introduces a relative into the household is almost always a woman.[42] She is usually the elder sister or the mother's sister of the kinsman taken into residence, for it is not surprising that an individual in need would seek out or be rescued by the closest substitute for a mother. If a maternal substitute does not exist or cannot afford aid, then a father surrogate (elder brother or uncle) may be chosen. Although grandparents are loving figures and preferred guardians for orphans according to the legal code (Clairon n.d., 93), they are less frequently sponsors because they are likely to be old and unable to assume extra responsibilities.

The duration of a kinsman's residence is hard to predict because it varies with circumstances. An orphan is usually adopted[43] by some relative and is likely to remain in the latter's household until marriage or even afterwards if the guardian is childless, or if his own offspring have married and moved away. A widowed or divorced person will probably stay for a few years until remarriage occurs (as it usually does). When a married couple establishes sororilocal residence, it is usually a temporary arrangement that will last until the pair can fend for itself (although this may be a matter of years).[44] Finally, a spinster or old bachelor may spend the remainder of his/her life in a relative's household.

---

[42] Out of eighteen instances where kinsmen other than grandchildren were taken into a family, sixteen involved female "sponsors." Comparable situations are found among the Malays, Javanese, and Burmese; see Djamour 1959, 63–64; H. Geertz 1961, 34, 41–46; Nash 1965, 153.

[43] Not only orphans, but children who are abandoned, illegitimate, or willingly relinquished by their parents may be adopted. Such adoption can be of two sorts. (1) In formal adoption, the adopter must meet certain legal requirements and sign an official certificate of adoption (see Clairon n.d., 85–86). The adopted children then assume all the rights and obligations of a legitimate child. (See also Leclère 1890, 59; 1898, 2:571–73 for older statutes on adoption.) (2) Also common is what might be called informal adoption in which the legal amenities are not fulfilled, but there is social recognition that an individual has assumed the status of a natural or legitimate child in some family or to some person. Sometimes the adopter may hold a small ceremony to make a public declaration of adoption to kinsmen and friends (see Leclère 1898, 2:35; Aymonier 1900, 84), but there may be no fanfare whatsoever.

The most common circumstances in which adoption occurs are (1) when a sterile couple adopts a child, (2) when a spinster "adopts" a niece, and (3) when one adopts an orphaned kinsman. If legal adoption has occurred, the child has full rights of inheritance from his adoptive parents (as well as from his natural parents unless the latter specifically disinherit him). But in "informal" adoption, inheritance depends upon the largesse of the adopters and particular circumstances.

Note that adoption in the strict sense is to be distinguished from several other situations in which individuals reside in households other than their families of orientation. First, someone who is orphaned or otherwise in need may go to live more or less permanently with a kinsman, but does not assume the status of an adopted child within the household. Such cases might more properly be considered instances of guardianship rather than adoption. (See Clairon n.d., 92–100, for details of law codes dealing with the nature and exercise of guardianship.) Second, children are sometimes sent to live for long periods of time with a kinsman who is affluent or lonely; but such cases are more in the nature of "lending" or "borrowing" a child rather than adoption, because the child never breaks his ties with his natural family. Finally, there is the *towaa* relation in which individuals assume a fictive kin relationship; this is discussed elsewhere.

[44] The rarity of permanent joint families composed of married siblings and their families may be due to the facts that (1) most houses are not large enough to contain two fertile couples and their offspring; and (2) sibling ties can be close, but they are less firmly knit and more likely to break under stress than the parent–child relation that binds a stem family. There are, however, two examples in Svay of joint families that endured for ten years or more. Cf. Murdock (1960a, 4, 14) who states that extended families of two or more married siblings in the senior generation are "invariably absent" among "bilateral Eskimo" type societies such as the Khmer.

With such diverse compositions and circumstances, it is difficult to generalize about the operation of extended family households in comparison to nuclear and stem families. In general, however, it is probably fair to say that when the resident kinsman is single, widowed, or divorced, he/she is likely to be treated as an unmarried offspring and incorporated into the family. But when the resident kinsman is married and brings along his/her family of procreation, the different nuclear units within the household may act separately as they do in some stem families.

**Other Kinds of Households.** In addition to nuclear, stem, or extended families, there can also be households composed of a married couple living by themselves, a single individual, or two (or possibly more) persons who may be kin or non-kin. All of these occur infrequently in Svay (see table 3.1). Single-person households are rare (there are only three cases in the entire village, all of which are widowed or divorced individuals) for two reasons. First, it is difficult for one person to handle all household tasks and cultivation of the fields. A person living alone must either rely heavily on aid from neighboring kinsmen and friends (e.g., Sareth in West Svay cultivated only a few rice paddies and worked at odd jobs to support himself, and frequently cadged meals from brothers and friends in the hamlet) or resort to hired labor and sharecropping. Second, it is considered extremely "lonely," "unhappy," and somehow unnatural for an individual to live by himself. Thus, people who are reduced to a single state will usually join the household of a kinsman. But some may remain alone, because of a streak of independence or because they have no relative to take them in.

Two-person households, composed either of a lone married couple or two persons who are usually kinsmen,[45] face similar problems. They have an easier time managing household chores than does a single individual, but such households (if the couple is elderly or the individuals are both female) must also rely on outside help to work the fields.

**The Developmental Cycle and Other Changes in Households.** A significant feature of household composition is the fact that it is highly changeable through time. Some of the changes are natural and expectable sequences in the developmental cycle of the family (Goody 1958). But a household can undergo more unpredictable or temporary alterations when kinsmen are sheltered for short or long periods of time.

Examination of residential histories reveals that there are three main patterns of residence and, resulting from these, two main types of families in the developmental cycle of households. The major alternatives open to a couple are as follows.

(1) A young couple may establish immediate neolocality at the outset of marriage; the family of procreation thus lives separate from the spouses' families of orientation throughout the marriage. This occurred among only seven out of thirty-eight couples in West Svay.

(2) A young couple may live in temporary uxorilocality or virilocality for a number of years and then eventually move into a separate home. Ten couples, or more than half of those that now reside neolocally, had originally lived with one of the spouse's parents for some period of time that ranged from one to twenty-five years (the average length of time being ten years).

One or more factors may impel a couple to move out of a parental home and establish a separate residence: for example, the parental home may become increasingly crowded as the couple bears its own children, especially if the parents still have

---

[45] In Svay as a whole, there are two cases of two sisters living together and one instance of two spinster friends sharing a house. There are also three households composed of a widow(er) and one child.

# Kinship among some residents of West Svay

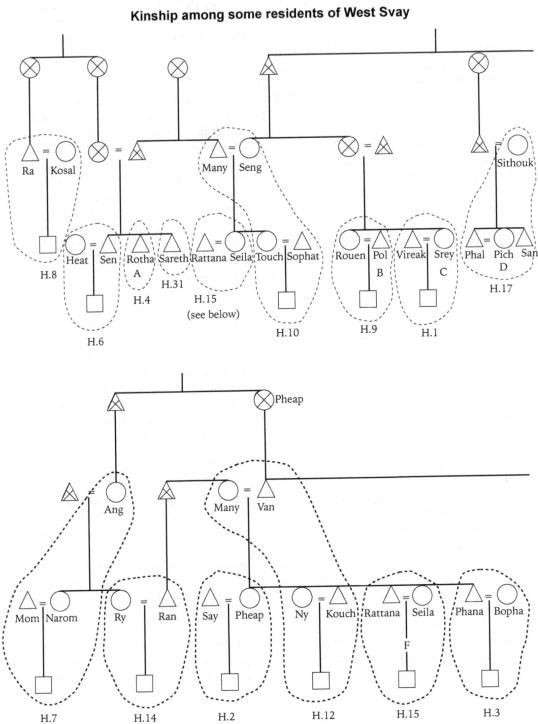

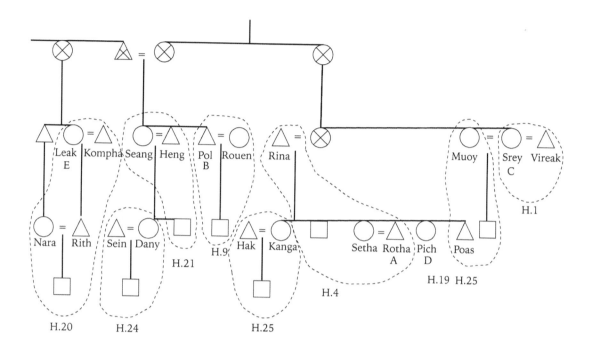

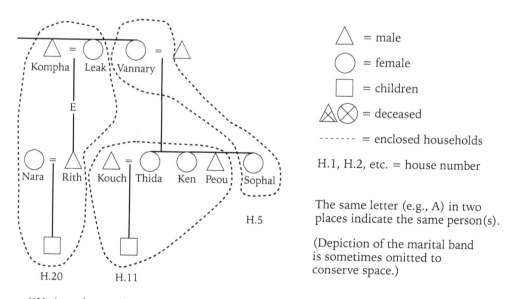

△ = male

○ = female

□ = children

⧄ ⊗ = deceased

------ = enclosed households

H.1, H.2, etc. = house number

The same letter (e.g., A) in two places indicate the same person(s).

(Depiction of the marital band is sometimes omitted to conserve space.)

(*Various deceased persons and non-residents of Svay are omitted from the genealogies.)

unmarried offspring at home; the couple may be displaced by a sibling who marries and needs or wants to remain at home; the couple may eventually accumulate enough money to build their own house; the wife, after several years of marriage, may feel more confident about living apart from her parents; etc.

(3) A young couple may live uxorilocally or virilocally from the outset of their marriage and intend to remain so permanently, with the expectation that they will have the house to themselves after the parents die. Fifteen couples followed this pattern, and nine of them do indeed now have the parental home to themselves.

In turn, then, when the next generation marries, most of the children will follow patterns 1 or 2 of immediate or eventual neolocality. And almost always, one child in each household will follow pattern 3 of permanent residence at home.[46] Thus, the cycle of residence repeats itself through time and can be readily traced in the continued existence of certain old houses and the proliferation of new homes in the hamlet. Around the turn of the century, there were about sixteen houses in West Svay, and all but a few still exist (although many have been rebuilt in whole or part). Now there are thirty-two houses in all, about half of which have been erected within the past decade as eleven couples established neolocality after initial uxorilocality or virilocality; two widows built entirely new houses in order to give their former homes to married children; and one divorcé constructed a new house for himself.

These abstract statements about choices and patterns of residence, developmental cycles, and growth of the village can be given a concrete illustration in the chart "Kinship among some residents of West Svay."

In Generation I, Pheap, a resident of West Svay, married a man from a neighboring village and established neolocal residence in House 12. She and her husband had three children: Van, Kompha, and Vannary. In Generation II, when Van married in about 1907,[47] he and his wife (from another village) established virilocal residence with his parents (and his two as yet unmarried siblings) in House 12. Kompha married in 1915 and decided to establish immediate neolocal residence because a good deal of land was available to him, so he built a house on the site of his present home (House 20). Vannary was the last to marry in 1921, and since her eldest brother was firmly ensconced at home, she and her husband built House 11 next to her parents' home.

In Generation III, the three main households underwent varied changes in composition and generated other families and homes. In House 12 (which was rebuilt about twenty years ago), Van and his wife bore seven children. The three oldest married exogamously and moved out of the hamlet. Pheap married in 1935, and she and her husband lived uxorilocally because her parents were approaching middle age and needed aid. (There were also, at that time, three younger children at home.) Rattana was the next to marry (in 1944) and, since Pheap was living at home, went to reside with his wife's parents in House 10. Phana married in 1951 and remained at home because he had no financial resources and his wife's house was too small to take them in. So from about 1951 to 1955, House 12 was rather crowded with Van and his wife, Pheap and her husband and five children, Phana and his wife, and another still unmarried daughter. Phana eventually moved out when he had accumulated enough

---

[46] Exceptions to these basic patterns were noted in previous sections, e.g., amitalocality, or the possibility that a couple may have all of its offspring move away.

[47] These and other dates are approximate.

money to construct a separate residence (House 3). Pheap and her husband remained in House 12 to aid her now quite aged parents until her younger sister, Ny, finally married in 1957. Because Ny's husband came from a poor family with numerous offspring in another village, it was decided that she would remain at home and assume the support of the parents; while Pheap and her family, after some twenty-odd years of uxorilocality, would move out and build their own home (House 2). (In the meanwhile, Rattana had left his parents-in-law's home and assumed neolocal residence in House 15 near his parent's dwelling.) At present, then, House 12 contains Van and his wife, and Ny and her husband and newborn child; while Houses 2, 3, and 15 have been established by Van's other offspring. House 12 will undoubtedly be inherited and maintained by Ny after her parents' deaths.

The situation was much simpler in House 20 where Kompha and his wife bore two sons. The eldest son, Rith, remained at home when he married because the house was spacious, because his mother wished to have a younger female aid her in various activities, and because uxorilocal residence was not feasible (not only was his wife's house crowded with her numerous siblings, but she stood to inherit little or no property). The younger son emigrated to Phnom Penh, so Rith and his family are still in House 20 and will eventually inherit the home.

In House 11, Vannary and her husband had five children. The eldest daughter, Thida, married in 1940 and remained in uxorilocal residence with her parents (and four as yet unmarried siblings). A few years later, two sons married exogamously and went to live with their wives in other villages. Another daughter, Ken, was married in 1956 and lived for about a year with her mother (by then widowed) and elder sister until her husband was killed in an accident; she then remarried and went to Phnom Penh for a while. House 11 became rather cramped with Vannary, an unmarried daughter (Sophal), and Thida, her husband, and four children. So in 1958 Vannary decided to move out and give the house to Thida, and built a smaller, separate home (House 5) for herself and Sophal. (Later, Ken returned to Svay and, being poor, moved into House 11 with her sister rather than staying with her mother, because the latter's house is small and because Sophal expected to be married soon and would probably reside uxorilocally in House 5.)

Thus, the original couple in House 12 eventually gave genesis to six other households. And the various processes just described for one family's descendants—decisions about where to live, shifts of residence through time, changes in family composition, and the establishment of new homes—are replicated in numerous other village households.

Unforeseen changes in household composition, when relatives are taken in for various reasons, have already been discussed. In addition to these cases, there are others mentioned in passing that should be noted more fully.

First, it is usual for a widow or divorcée of relatively young age to return to (or, in the case of uxorilocal residence, remain with) her family of orientation for shelter, sustenance, and security (see also chapter 6).[48] (In some cases she may go instead to an aunt or sibling if the parents are dead or unable to take her in.) This pattern is much less common among widowers and divorced men because males are generally more self-sufficient and better able to support themselves until they remarry.

---

[48] This is also common among the Javanese (H. Geertz 1961, 34) and Malays (Djamour 1959, 128).

Second, another common practice is that of sending children to live with relatives (usually grandparents or a mother's sister) for extended periods of time—either because the family is poor and cannot adequately support all its offspring, or because one's kinsman is "lonely" and asks for a child to keep her company. For example, one of the daughters in House 1 lives for about nine months out of the year with a maternal aunt in another province because her own family has six other offspring to maintain; and some children of Muoy (House 25) alternate between living with their mother and an older sister elsewhere.

Third, families also experience losses or additions that are obviously temporary, but the duration of the change may be as long as several months or as short as a few days or weeks. A family may have its children go away to school; elderly parents in stem families may leave on extended visits to other married children; a father or sons may be absent while temporarily employed in the city. Conversely, a family may receive kinsmen who come to convalesce from illness, attend life-cycle ceremonies or celebrate Buddhist holidays, lend a hand during the busiest seasons of cultivation, or simply come for the pleasure of visiting.

Thus, within a year's time in West Svay, numerous households changed in size or composition. Apart from a few that had births, deaths, or marriages, many other households had either extended visits from kinsmen or temporary losses, while three nuclear families took in siblings for indefinite but seemingly prolonged stays, thus becoming extended families. Even more striking are the changes that occurred among twenty sample families in Middle and East Hamlets: four nuclear families had various kinsmen moving in for indefinite stays; two extended families lost a kinsman who had been in residence; two stem families lost a married daughter (and her family of procreation) who had been in uxorilocal residence; and one stem family lost a son-in-law when the daughter was divorced.

### Kinsmen beyond the Family and Household

In village society there are no larger, organized kin groups beyond the family or household.[49] Although distinct groupings of kinsmen descended from common pro-

---

[49] Note, however, that the royal family, individuals who were once royalty, and the royal priests (Baku), as described in the late nineteenth century by Aymonier (1900, 57, 61–65), appeared to have more clear-cut kin grouping. First, the royal family had some, if not all, of the qualities of a non-unilinealnon-unilineal descent group (as conceptualized by Goodenough 1955; Davenport 1959; Firth 1959): it was a named group (Brahman Vansa) composed of all persons who were within the fifth degree of kinship to the reigning monarch and who had been consecrated as royalty at a puberty ceremony. Although the group as such had no collective ownership of land or property, its leader (the king) had ultimate title to all lands, and both he and his kinsmen were supported by the products of land in royal domain. The group in effect controlled a certain domain of power in that the title of monarch was usually passed on to one of its members; and the group also possessed certain privileges such as exemption from taxes. In another sense, however, the Brahman Vansa was more like a bounded personal kindred of the king, and it may have been delineated mainly for the purposes of defining a group from which an heir to the throne could be picked (cf. Firth 1959).

Second, individuals beyond the fifth degree of kinship but related patrilineally to the king also formed a named group (Brahman Van) that had its own chiefs and whose members possessed certain prerogatives such as exemption from taxes, honorary titles, etc. Third, the Baku or royal priests (considered to be descendants of ancient Indian Brahmans) formed a named group in which membership passed "through the males" (Aymonier 1900, 63). The Baku also

genitors can be abstracted from the villagers' genealogies, these are not corporate bodies or non-unilineal descent groups: there is no property held in common, no continuity through time as a distinct unit, no real remembrance of common ancestors, and no union as a group except in what Firth (1956, 14) and Mitchell (1965, 981) call occasional, partial, "ad hoc assemblages." Rather, there is only what has sometimes been called the "personal kindred" (Leach 1950, 62), that is, those individuals considered to be related bilaterally to an Ego (cf. Murdock 1949, 1960a; Goodenough 1955, 1961, 1962; Davenport 1959; Mitchell 1963).[50] This kindred is not an organized group with clear-cut boundaries, membership, or functions; it might be better considered as a "field of association" (Geddes 1954, 47) whose exact nature varies from person to person.

An initial question to consider is this: What individuals are considered to be kinsmen? There are two dimensions to this query: legal definitions of kin and commonplace notions of who is or is not a relative (including the designation of relatives in the kin terminological system). With respect to the first point, Leclère, in a discussion of law (1890, 57–64) outlined the basic kinds of relationships recognized in Khmer kinship. These are (1) consanguineal kinship (*parenté naturelle*) composed of lineal relations (*parenté directe*) or "the bond existing between persons born one from the other," and collateral relations (*parenté collaterale*) or "the bond existing between persons coming from the same 'souche' but not descended one from the other" (57, 58); (2) affinal kinship (*parente par affinité civile* or *par alliance*), which comprises the links with the consanguineal relatives of one's spouse and with the spouses of one's consanguineal kinsmen (61); and finally, (3) kinship by adoption (*parenté par suite d'affiliation*), the bonds forged when an individual is formally or informally adopted into a family, or when two persons adopt one another as fictive kin.[51] He goes on to note:

> The Cambodian legislator has not defined kinship, but when, in regard to inheritance and marriage, he is led to speak of related rightful heirs or kin who cannot marry, he seems to recognize, in the collateral line, only kin on this side of the fourth degree. Beyond first cousins, who can inherit one-tenth from one another, it seems there are no more relatives.[52] (Leclère 1890, 58; my translation)

In fact, however, certain ancient statutes, such as those pertaining to incest or insult and injury to kin, speak of kinsmen of the "fifth" or even "sixth" degree (e.g., see Leclère 1890, 63; 1898, 1:293, 299–300, 320) and mention individuals such as the

---

had special chiefs and privileges, as well as ceremonial duties at the royal palace, distinctive hair style, and certain traditional observances within the home.

It is unclear whether these groups still function as was described by Aymonier. Steinberg (1959, 88) suggests that the Baku do; but it is uncertain whether his description was simply taken from Aymonier and other older sources without updating.

[50] I do not wish here to enter into a prolonged consideration of what a kindred is or is not, a subject that has provoked considerable discussion (see, e.g., in addition to the references cited above, Freeman 1961; Befu 1963a; Murdock 1964; Mitchell 1965; Appell 1967). For my immediate purposes, the kindred is best viewed as defined above.

[51] Leclère also listed a sort of kinship *par affinité spirituelle* that exists between a monk and whoever conferred the orders upon him or whoever habitually gives him alms (1890, 62–63). According to Leclère, upon the monk's return to lay life, he must observe incest taboos toward all female kinsmen of these persons. I do not know if this custom is still in practice.

[52] The same is true also of the modern civil code.

parents of parents-in-law, cousin's husband, or elder sister's husband's sister as within the category of relatives.[53]

Leclère continues further, saying:

> In fact, the idea of kinship extends further among the Cambodians, and it is not unusual to hear said to a Cambodian: "This man is my relative, but eight times further than a first cousin." The memory of alliances formerly contracted persists for a long time, but often without any sort of interest or motive attached to it. On the other hand, women and men always marry young; they are grandparents at forty and great-grandparents at sixty; in this case, as one has known the children of the grandfather's brother, those of the uncle, etc.; as one has seen the marriage, birth, and growth of children of first cousins, it is easy to keep the memory of it and recall collateral relatives, even distant ones. In summary, collateral kinship is recognized by the law only to the fourth degree inclusively; the custom is to know it beyond that, and as far as possible. Legal kinship is effective; kinship beyond that is without legal effect. (Leclère 1890, 58–59; my translation)

Leclère exaggerates the kinship recall of the average Khmer, at least villagers in West Svay. But his general point is well taken: that is, collateral relatives who are beyond the range of legal effectiveness or who lack distinct kin terms are nonetheless considered to be kinsmen, often even when the exact lines cannot be articulated.

Theoretically, a Cambodian would recognize as a kinsman (*bòng pʔon*)[54] anyone who is known to share a lineal ancestor with him. In village practice, however, no attention is paid to the remembrance or tracing of common ancestors or extended linkages, although there are kinship terms extending lineally to the fifth ascending and descending generations and collaterally to fourth cousins (see appendix E for full details of the terminological system).[55] The genealogies of villagers generally have a narrow range that covers only one or two ascending and descending generations; most persons cannot remember their grandparents' names or the latter's siblings, much less more remote ancestors. Sometimes even parent's siblings are vague because "They died when I was young," "They lived far away," or "It's too long ago to remember," although aunts and uncles are usually known with some clarity. On Ego's generation, villagers become uncertain about the precise manner in which they are linked to per-

---

[53] The modern civil code defines degrees of kinship as follows: (a) lineal relations—parents and children are first degree, grandparents and grandchildren are second degree; great-grandparents and great-grandchildren are third degree; (b) collateral relations—brothers are second degree, uncles/aunts and nephews/nieces are third degree, first cousins are fourth degree (see Clairon n.d., 91). What Leclère means by fifth or sixth degree of kinship is unclear but may refer to Ego vis-à-vis children of first cousins and second cousins (cf. Webster 1951, 176 on degrees of consanguinity in canon and civil law; also cf. Leclère 1898, 2:480).

[54] The term *bòng pʔon* (literally "elder-younger") has varied meanings (see appendix E), one of which is "kinsman" or "kinsmen." The term *ñilt* is also sometimes used to mean "relatives."

[55] CMCC 42.003 and Aymonier 1900, 83 state that all descendants of an ancestor on the seventh ascending generation are kinsmen to one another. In practice, however, such extensive genealogies are never remembered (except perhaps among royalty). For example, even though the kin terms for cousins explicitly cite the existence of a common ancestor (first cousin = "same grandmother," second cousin = "same, one great-grandparent," etc.), villagers who can name second cousins are most likely to remember their relationship in terms of their parents having been first cousins to one another, rather than by reference to a common great-grandparent.

sons beyond the range of first cousins and fall back on saying simply, "We are *bòng p?on* [though I'm not sure exactly how]." Indeed, as in our own society, there is some confusion about what constitutes a second cousin (*cituèt muy*) link; some persons explain it as the relationship between two persons whose parents are first cousins to one another, while others apply the term to their own first cousins' children. By the time third cousins are involved, a villager will either have forgotten that a relationship exists at all, or know only that some sort of vague kinship tie is present. When asked about relatives beyond the first cousin range, villagers frequently reply: "They are so distant . . . we have stopped knowing them."

An adult's knowledge of descending generations is likely to be more extensive and exact in collateral as well as lineal lines; a number of villagers can cite, for example, cousins' children, siblings' grandchildren, or even cousins' grandchildren. It is not surprising that kinsmen on descending generations are better known than ascendants because the latter often die before an individual has clear familiarity with them. But, as Leclère suggested, an adult memory can and generally does keep good track of the offspring of his siblings and other collaterals (although the elderly often falter at the task of remembering exact names and numbers of collateral descendants, especially if the latter live elsewhere). But the older people do not pass on their knowledge of kinship links to the younger generations so that, for example, while Grandmother Vannary's genealogy shows that Sreymom and Chenda are third cousins, the latter themselves know only that they are "kinsmen" of some unspecified sort. Indeed, even Grandmother Vannary herself, like most villagers, would not be able to articulate the fact that the youngsters are third cousins, and would throw up her hands in despair at any attempt to follow an ethnologist's explanation of the linkages involved in such a category of relationship.

Leclère stated that affinal relations were an important part of Khmer kinship. The strongest bonds and moral obligations exist between consanguineal kin, but it is important to note that in village life the spouses of kinsmen and the relatives of one's spouse are often considered in the same light as consanguineals. This is particularly true for the spouses of parents' siblings (who are not terminologically distinguished from consanguineal aunt and uncle) and for one's parents- and siblings-in-law, toward whom one usually has (or is supposed to have) loyal affection, respect, and certain obligations.[56] Depending on geographical proximity and personal factors, close ties and sentiments may also be extended to even more remote affinal kinsmen such as cousin's spouse, wife's sister's husband, niece's husband's mother, or even sister's husband's brother's wife, who may well be considered to be "kinsmen" and who may come to assume as much importance as consanguineal relatives.[57]

[56] Certain ancient law codes punished insult or injury to affinals such as parents-in-law or cousin's spouse as severely as maltreatment of consanguineal relatives (see Leclère 1894, 155, 205; 1898, 1:298–99, 320–21, 324) and extended the incest taboo to affinals as remote as elder sister's husband's sister or the ex-wife of anyone in the "fifth degree" of kinship (see previous section on incest). See also Leclère 1898, 2:91–92 for his further comments on affinals in Cambodian kinship.

[57] Schneider, in his discussion of Yankee kinship terminology (1965, 294–95) notes that in America, various kinds of affinals (such as the ones mentioned above) may flesh out a "skinny kindred" or be drawn into one's kin network more often than distant collateral consanguineal relatives. The same is certainly true among the Khmer, depending on individual circumstances and sentiments, particularly when the Khmer often loses track of distant collateral consanguineal kin ties but can more readily trace connections such as sister's husband's brother. Schneider

**Behavior toward Kin.** There are no rigidly defined, obligatory rules of behavior toward kinsmen. Villagers will make statements such as "One should be friendly to younger kinsmen and respectful to older ones" and "One should help relatives in many ways." But it is clear that such assertions are often ideal expectations rather than real practice. An individual has considerable freedom to act as he pleases toward kinsmen, and the quality of his interaction with particular relatives depends in large part upon personal inclinations (to be discussed in more detail below). Nonetheless, kinsmen do form a social category (if not an organized group), in contrast to non-kinsmen, and there are strong moral (and sometimes legal) obligations or rights that obtain among relatives. Among these are the following.

(1) Affection and respect. The existence of affection and respect among kinsmen, or at least the absence of serious quarreling and rupture, is sanctioned by both secular and religious norms. Villagers are discomfited by quarreling in general, but squabbles between relatives are viewed with special distaste because they contravene the norm of harmonious relations among kin that is upheld both by Buddhist teachings and by the ancestral spirits (*meba*) of the folk religion. The latter have a particularly powerful force in conciliating disputes between relatives because it is believed that the *meba* punish discord by inflicting illness upon some innocent member of the family or kindred rather than upon the disputants themselves (see also CMCC 59.007 and 42.004). In addition to such sanctions, legal codes in ancient times also exacted various forms of punishment for different kinds of "insult or injury" (such as slander, threats, curses, blows, and accusations in court) to kinsmen as remote as granduncle's daughter's husband (for details, see Leclère 1894, 155–56, 203–6, 208–10, 216, 219, 298–300, 320–21, 324; Aymonier 1900, 83).[58]

Certainly disputes or ill feelings between kinsmen do occur despite sanctions to the contrary. For example, Neary and San, first cousins, quarreled over a trivial incident and did not speak to one another for several months despite disapprobation by many villagers and attempts by other kinsmen to conciliate them. (They finally did reach a grudging truce, mainly because they feared retribution from ancestral spirits.) But, generally speaking, amiable relations seem to be more usual than dissensions. Depending on personal inclinations, this amiability may range from token cordiality to the deepest affection. In general, the warmest bonds beyond the nuclear family exist between grandparents and grandchildren, aunts/uncles and nephews/nieces, and between first cousins. The relation between grandparents and grandchildren is almost always one of gentle, indulgent concern and abiding love, and when the two live in different communities, special efforts are made to maintain contact. Aunts and uncles, if they are older than one's parents, are supposed to be treated with respect. But frequently they, and the younger siblings of parents, often have a sort of joking

---

raises the question as to whether such affinals are "really kinsmen," and there has been some dispute as to whether affinals should be included in definitions of kindred (see, e.g., Mitchell 1963, 351; 1965, 984; cf. Freeman 1960, 71). So far as the Khmer villagers are concerned, affinals must certainly be considered as part of many people's personal kindreds and "intimate" kin.

[58] Accusing a kinsman of a crime in court was punished only if the accusee was a close relative (parent, grandparent, parent's sibling, elder siding, spouse, or parent-in-law). But other kinds of "insult or injury" were punished if they involved kinsmen as remote as "sixth degree" collaterals. The nature and severity of the punishment varied according to the degree of relationship between the parties concerned, and ranged from monetary fines to different kinds of corporal punishment or public exhibition.

relation with nieces and nephews in which affection is enlivened by physical or verbal horseplay. Moreover, as noted previously, a parent's sibling, especially the mother's sister, may assume the role of a surrogate parent. First cousins, particularly if they have grown up together, are often extremely close friends.

That a kin relationship implies a tie of special affection is indicated by the fact that a villager will often refer to a particularly close friend by a kin term even though the two are not in fact related (or only remotely so). Thus, Sok fondly refers to a next-door neighbor as "my niece," or Vireak will refer to a special comrade as "my younger brother" to express bonds of special friendship (see also appendix E).

(2) Assistance in times of need. Kinsmen are almost always the first persons to be called upon in times of various need. Villagers tend to turn initially to parents, siblings, or children for aid. But they frequently rely upon more distant relatives as well, whether because their immediate families are unable to give aid or because an individual feels more intimate with some other kinsman. The kinds of aid that may be sought are varied. (a) Labor or other types of assistance may be needed for activities such as rice cultivation,[59] the preparation of life-cycle ceremonies, and house building, or in times of trouble such as illness. (b) Lending and borrowing are frequently necessary in a society where goods and money are in short supply. Items such as clothes or equipment, or foodstuffs such as fruit and fish, are usually generously loaned to or shared with kinsmen (often non-kinsmen as well). Villagers are more chary about money because most people have little cash to dispose of and one is uncertain about the promptness of repayment. But borrowing and lending of money among kinsmen does occur with some frequency and is considered to be in the nature of "sharing" rather than the sort of business arrangement that involves a moneylender. No interest is charged unless the kinsman is a hard dealer, and the time of repayment is usually left unspecified.[60] An individual generally prefers to borrow from someone in his own or his spouse's family of orientation, but a more distant and affluent relative, such as a cousin, may also be petitioned. (c) Finally, food and shelter are given to kinsmen who are in need. In times of stress the needy villager tends to turn first to members of his family of orientation. But if help is not available from the latter, an individual may well turn to other relatives. Such is the case with orphans who are taken in by aunts or uncles, or widowed persons who may live with parents-in-law rather than someone in their own families.[61]

---

[59] The cooperative groups that form for rice cultivation are varied in size and composition. When the groups are large, they contain both kin and non-kin (see chapter 4). But small cooperative groups (that involve persons outside the household) are usually composed of close relatives. (E.g., one female group that often worked together was composed of two sisters, their daughters, their niece, and the niece's mother-in-law.) Moreover, if one should see someone in a work group who does not reside in the hamlet, that person is almost always a kinsman of the field's owner. See also Delvert 1961, 219 who notes that mutual aid is usually exchanged between kinsmen.

[60] See Leclère 1898, 1:458–62 and Aymonier 1900, 86 for old law codes dealing with borrowing and lending money among kinsmen. No interest could be charged in loans between members of the same nuclear family; interest in loans between other kinsmen varied in proportion to the degree of relationship. See also chapter 4 on credit and debt.

[61] The court can order someone to support any category of kinsman if the latter has no other sources of aid (Clairon n.d., 113–14). See Clairon n.d., 94–96, also on "family councils" for orphans, which may include collateral relatives or affines.

(3) Participation in life-cycle and other ceremonies. One of the most important obligations of kinsmen is to attend and aid in the preparation of one another's life-cycle ceremonies, especially weddings and funerals. Such occasions are also one of the few times when a large segment of an individual's personal kindred is actually gathered together in one place at one moment. The marriage and death rituals command the presence of a great number of kinfolk, including close relatives who will make long journeys for such events, and remote kinsmen from nearby areas.[62] Sometimes certain kinsmen are assigned definite ceremonial roles: for example, the ritual go-between at betrothals and weddings is often a relative; attendants for the bride and groom are usually siblings or first cousins; and close relatives are expected to keep vigil over a deceased kinsman's corpse until cremation. Most kin, however, provide non-ceremonial but nonetheless important assistance by performing the numerous chores that a major ceremony entails and by giving monetary gifts that play a substantial part in the financing of such rituals.

Other events that may draw together a substantial number of kinsmen are the annual holidays of the New Year and the Pchum Festival for the Dead. At these times it is traditional and common for émigrés to return to their natal homes and villages, or for individuals to make special visits to close kinsmen living elsewhere. In the main, these reunions bring together the often scattered members of families of orientation and procreation, but in doing so they also provide contact between various collateral relatives such as parents' siblings and siblings' children, and first cousins who may see little of one another during the rest of the year.

(4) Responsibility for one another's actions. The larger circle of kinsmen has no explicit or definite commitment to account for one another's actions in that there is no institution of wergild or vendetta that extends to the personal kindred. In one sense, however, a person must take account of his kinsmen if he is guilty of misconduct because, as noted previously, the ancestral spirits punish not only quarrels between kinsmen but individual acts of misbehavior[63] by visiting illness upon some other member of the family or kin circle. (For example, Leclère 1898, 1:156, cites a case in which an adulterous woman's brother-in-law fell ill because of her transgression; see also CMCC 42.004, 59.107.) Thus, a person has some obligation to observe certain norms of behavior lest he be responsible for the sickness (and possibly even death) of a kinsman. And should a relative become ill, a wrongdoer is morally obligated to confess his guilt and make offerings to the ancestral spirits to cure the relative's malady; for if the latter dies, the transgressor would be considered tantamount to a murderer. It should be stated that fear of the ancestral spirits does not by any means prevent all discord among kin or grave misconduct, but it has conciliated many quarrels and acted as some deterrent to transgression.

(5) The right to inheritance. In village life, virtually all property is divided among offspring (see chapter 4). But kinsmen beyond the families of orientation and procreation may have legal claims upon a deceased relative's property if the latter had no children or surviving parents, grandparents, siblings, or spouse. In such instances, according to the civil code, aunts, uncles, or first cousins may become heirs (Clairon

---

[62] For example, San's wedding brought aunts, uncles, and cousins from several distant provinces. And Srey and Muoy from West Svay rushed to "help" at the funeral of an old lady in East Svay who was considered to be an affinal relative (*bóng tlay*) because her deceased son had been the first husband of one of Srey and Muoy's sisters.

[63] Such acts are usually fornication (e.g., adultery, premarital sexual relations), or a situation in which parents do not permit a child to marry someone he/she loves.

n.d., 125–26).[64] Such situations occur rarely in village existence, but occasionally a spinster may cede property to a niece (usually a sister's daughter) who has shared her home and become a virtual daughter.

**Interaction with Kin.** The average villager in West Svay can cite the existence, and usually the names and residences as well, of more than fifty consanguineal kinsmen (and their spouses) beyond the families of orientation and procreation.[65] Many persons have a great number of both close and distant relatives within the hamlet itself whom they see daily, and others within the immediate area with whom fairly frequent contact is maintained. But the mere facts of kinship and geographical proximity do not by themselves ensure deep emotional attachment and intimate contacts that go beyond surface amiability and an exchange of pleasantries. One of the most important points to consider in discussing an individual's interaction with his kinsmen is the fact that one is free to have deep sentiments for and significant contacts with some kinsmen and not others. This "personal selectivity" (Firth 1956, 44) among kinsmen is based upon various factors, such that it is difficult to predict who will be counted among any one individual's "intimate" kin. The various obligations toward kinsmen that were enumerated in the preceding section, especially the one regarding affectionate feelings, apply most strongly to grandparents and grandchildren, aunts and uncles, nephews and nieces, first cousins, and the immediate family of one's spouse. But beyond this range, and sometimes even within it, an individual's feelings of sentiment and duty will vary greatly.[66] To take but a few of numerous examples: Vireak counts Rina, an "affinal relative" (*bòng tlay*) because he is a deceased sister-in-law's husband, as one of his most beloved kinsmen; he dislikes another sister-in-law and niece to whom he speaks only when necessary; and he completely avoids his sister and her husband. Rattana is seen in frequent visits to and cooperative labor with his wife's sister's husband rather than his own brothers or brothers-in-law; and Srey is more intimate with her husband's mother's first cousin's wife than with most of her own first cousins.

Among the factors that influence this personal selectivity among kin, the most important is, quite simply, likes and dislikes stemming from personal experiences and from comparability of personality. Vireak, for example, dislikes one sister-in-law because he feels that she has not been grateful for favors he has tendered her over the years, and further dislikes her daughter, his niece, because she is rude and aggressive to his children. On the other hand, he is devoted to another sister-in-law and her husband whom he characterizes as generous and sympathetic persons, and has

---

[64] See also Leclère 1898, 2:480 for old law codes that specify nieces or first, second, third, and fourth cousins as possible heirs.

[65] The largest number of kinsmen (exclusive of families of orientation and procreation) given on a genealogy was 163; the smallest, only one relative. Villagers averaged about fifty kinsmen on a genealogy, but note that genealogies did not include knowledge of spouse's kindred nor relatives such as sibling's in-laws, whom many villagers do in fact know. Moreover, a villager often recognizes as kinsmen many persons who do not appear on his genealogical chart because the exact linkage is unknown.

[66] Similar institutions of selectivity among kin exist among other bilateral groups in Southeast Asia and elsewhere. See, for example, H. Geertz 1961, 2 and Koentjaraningrat 1960, 114 on the Javanese; Djamour 1959, 31–34 on the Malays; Geddes 1954, 43, 47 on the Land Dayak; Nash 1965, 68–69 and Mi Mi Khaing in Ward 1963, 105, 108 on the Burmese; Hanks in Ward 1963, 434 on the Thai; Fox in Ward 1963, 348 on the Filipinos; Johnson 1964, 841 on the Japanese; and Firth 1956, 16, 44, 62–63 and Bott 1957, 222 on the English. See also discussions by Mitchell 1963, 350; 1965, 983; Leach 1950, 61; Goodenough 1961, 1345–46; and Leichter 1958.

the deepest affection for Rina who he finds to be congenial and admirable. In many instances an individual feels guilty about having ambivalent or negative sentiments toward certain kinsmen and rarely expresses them overtly. And so long as an outward appearance of civility is maintained, one is free to think and feel as one wishes.

Geographical proximity can be another factor in determining intimacy with particular kinsmen. Obviously it is easier to have frequent contact with relatives who live in the same or a nearby community, and such recurrent interaction may well lead to or reinforce deep sentiment (viz. Homans 1950) between persons who are predisposed to like one another. Correspondingly, it is harder to forge strong bonds with relatives who live far away and are rarely seen. While many villagers know a surprising amount about collateral relatives who live elsewhere, there are others who completely lose track of kinsmen in other locales (even close relatives such as parent's siblings or first cousins may be vague because "they live far away and I do not know them"). In some situations, too, distant kin who live nearby (especially in the same hamlet) will come to have more importance for an individual than close kin who live elsewhere (cf. Goodenough 1962, 9).

On the other hand, contact can reinforce negative as well as positive sentiments. Thus, the mere fact of closeness of residence does not necessarily imply emotional intimacy. Even within a small hamlet, it is possible to avoid people. It is also possible and not uncommon for a villager to have deep sentimental ties with relatives who live some distance away. Although they may be seen relatively infrequently, some contact can be maintained through visits, reunions at various ceremonies or holidays, and sometimes letters. Thus, Vireak has nothing to do with a sister and brother-in-law who live about a hundred yards away, while expressing profound affection for a sister-in-law in Phnom Penh whom he sees perhaps four or five times a year.

Some other factors of lesser significance are the following. First, as noted previously, mother's kinsmen (especially the mother's sister) are often felt to be more receptive and kindly, and closer ties may be forged with maternal relatives. Second, strong differences of social status may affect relations between kin. Occasionally, someone born in the village manages to become an urbanite with distinctly high social status. In such situations, that individual's ties to his family of orientation usually remain strong. But ties to other village relatives (such as cousins) may become attenuated, although overt snobbery toward or disavowal of rural kinsmen is not condoned. (In fact, some urbanites feel a special nostalgia and sentiment for village relatives and may aid them in times of need or in achieving social mobility.) The villagers on their part have varied feelings about such successful relatives; some care nothing about status differences (especially if one is older in terms of relative age), some are made uncomfortable by them, while others may look upon a wealthy urban kinsman in a mercenary light. But social and geographical distance may well hinder the development of the strong bonds that are more easily forged between social equals who interact frequently.

Each individual, then, has a different "personal kindred," not only in terms of its component members but with respect to the different kinds of sentiment and interaction he has with specific kinsmen. Following and enlarging upon Firth (1956, 45) and Mitchell (1965, 983),[67] there are "peripheral kin" with whom social contact is "distant

---

[67] Firth and Mitchell speak primarily in terms of frequency of contact, with the implication that frequency varies with affect. But in the case of West Svay villagers, unlike the urban settings that Firth and Mitchell have described, one can have daily contact with kinsmen who live in the same small community. But such interaction may be very superficial and does not necessarily connote emotional attachment as well. On the other hand, as noted above, one can also have great affection for relatives who are seen infrequently.

or sporadic" and toward whom sentiment is neutral or negative, "effective kin" with whom occasional social contact is maintained and toward whom sentiment is positive but not profound, and "intimate kin" with whom contact is "purposeful, close, and frequent" and toward whom sentiment is profound. Those persons considered by one another to be "intimate kin" see one another constantly if they live in the same community: they work together in the fields during busy seasons; sit at one another's homes to exchange confidences, gossip, and jokes in leisure moments; quickly lend one another goods or assistance, whether it be some extra food or aid in childbirth; travel together to temple festivals or to places such as Phnom Penh; etc. But it is hard to predict who will be counted among any one person's intimate relatives. Using the analogy of a net or network that is so common in discussions of bilateral systems (see. e.g., Pehrson 1957; Bott 1957; Barnes 1960; Befu 1963a; Mitchell 1965), a Khmer villager's net has at its center the families of orientation and procreation that bind him closely in terms of emotional bonds and moral obligations. But the rest of his net, his other kinsmen, lies loosely, and the individual is free to pull in whatever parts he wishes. And while he is likely to draw in portions of the net immediately around the center—close relatives such as grandparents, parents' siblings, and first cousins—he is free to and frequently does gather in persons from the furthest reaches of the net.

In sum, among the Khmer the "personal kindred" is not a very tangible phenomenon: it is not clearly bounded; it has no formal organization; it does not crystallize as a group except in periodic "assemblages ad hoc" of only part of its total possible membership. Nonetheless, it should be emphasized that kinsmen do play an important role in the life of a villager. First, they provide a pool of persons, much more extensive than the immediate family, upon which an individual can draw when he requires aid of any sort. A villager can and does call also upon neighbors and friends who are not kin, but the latter do not have as strong a moral obligation to respond as do relatives. And the fact that kinsmen do constitute a group of "potential mobilization" (Firth 1956, 13) is especially important in a society that lacks other sorts of associations or formalized means of cooperation that would ensure aid for various economic, social, and ceremonial activities (cf. also Geddes 1954, 73; Freeman 1960, 73; Befu 1963b, 1332; Johnson 1964; Murdock 1964, 130). Second, the circle of kinsmen provides an individual with a certain sense of security and safety. The villager is a rather gregarious person who dislikes being alone, is happiest in the constant company of familiar faces, and feels threatened by people he does not know. The immediate family, of course, provides a person with the strongest feeling of security and of belonging to a unit. But this sense of security is widened by the knowledge that there is a larger circle of (presumably) warm and protective individuals from at least some of whom one can expect aid, affection, and protection. It is significant that individuals rarely venture into unknown regions unless they have kinsmen there,[68] and that a villager who is forced to travel or stay in strange areas will usually establish a fictive kin (*towaa*) relationship with someone. Finally, it would seem that, similar to some other bilateral societies (see, e.g., Geddes 1954, 15; Kaufman 1960, 26; Eggan 1960, 45), the overlapping personal kindreds within a community help to give it a certain cohesion. There are relatively few norms or activities that weld the inhabitants of a community together, and a great deal of whatever solidarity exists in a hamlet or village comes from the fact that it is a collection of kinsmen (and the relatives and friends of

---

[68] A similar situation is reported for Thailand by Kaufman (1960, 25), leading him to suggest that distant kin function primarily to link people in different communities.

kinsmen), just as a villager's loyalty to his community is based primarily on his ties to these kinsmen and friends who are his fellow residents.

## Non-kinsmen Neighbors and Friends

Although many residents of West Svay are ultimately related (albeit sometimes tenuously) to one another, non-kin neighbors and friends are also an important part of a villager's social universe. The preceding section noted that an individual is not compelled to interact with kinsmen in general, but may have close ties with some relatives and ignore others. As an extension of this point, a villager also has the freedom to select non-kinsmen as objects of special affection and interaction.[69]

Ideally a villager has some special feeling for the non-kinsmen who are fellow residents of his community. Like the ideal norms of sentiment and interaction among kinsmen, there is the feeling that villagers should like and help one another,[70] and that co-residents are trustworthy and "good" people as contrasted to "bad" strangers. In practice, of course, individual predilections hold sway. Even in a small community, such as West Svay, one can have only nominal relations with the family next door while feeling special affection for someone on the other side of the hamlet, and frictions of one sort or another periodically arise between neighbors.

Close friendships may occur in dyads or in larger groupings of half a dozen or more people (kinsmen and/or non-kinsmen) who are seen habitually visiting at one another's homes, working together, or exchanging favors. Some of the friendship circles have fairly well-defined boundaries and "memberships," while others are more vague and varying in composition. In both instances, constellations may change through time because of quarrels, emigration, etc., but the circles or pairs are generally composed of persons of the same sex, approximate age, and compatible temperaments.

The primary ostensible function of such friendships is pure sociability and the pleasure of good company. One friendship clique of five adolescent girls engages in gay conversation about clothes and the opposite sex; a group of five young men with a special interest in music gathers almost every evening for an impromptu jam session; and another clique of four married women continually gossips at one another's homes during leisure moments. But friends are not simply pleasant company; they are also sources of various kinds of aid. Members of friendship dyads or circles are also commonly seen helping one another and exchanging favors in many ways: laboring on one another's fields, helping in one another's life-cycle ceremonies, giving assistance in times of crisis such as illness and births, lending one another things,[71] arranging marriages for one another's children, staying together when working in the city, etc. Thus, close friends constitute another reservoir of persons who can be called upon for assistance in times of need, and this is especially important in a society where there is

---

[69] Zadrozny 1955, 313 states that "a large part of social interaction beyond the family level seems to be with neighbors, not kin," which statement is based on the assumption that there are few related families within a Khmer village. But communities vary as to whether many or most of their residents are related.

[70] In the late nineteenth century when, according to Leclère (1898, 2:187–90, 308–19), police were corrupt and negligent, neighbors within a radius of 123 meters had to come to one's aid in case of fire, theft, or other difficulties, or face punishment if they did not.

[71] Note, however, that= it is relatively rare for non-kinsman friends to borrow money from one another.

an ideal that kinsmen and neighbors will help one another, but no compelling sanctions that will actually force them to do so if they do not so desire.[72] One can count on friends because sentiment rather than sanctions will move them to lend a hand. But, as Foster has noted: "Friendship differs from other systems in that a long-enduring gap between ideal and real behavior can hardly exist: when friends cease to be friendly, the institution dissolves" (1961b, 1184). Thus, for the West Svay villagers, friends are indeed an important source of assistance, but only while relations are intimate and cordial.

The role of non-kin in performing some of the functions that, ideally, kinsmen should or would fulfill is formalized in an institution known as the *towaa* relationship.[73] In this practice, friends informally "adopt" one another and assume a fictive kinship relationship approximating that of parent and child or siblings. Such *towaa* arrangements can come about in several ways. First, two persons may become very fond of one another and wish to make their relationship more than one of mere friendship. If there is a significant age difference between the two, the younger asks the older (or possibly vice versa, although this is more unusual) to become his *towaa* parent (or child).[74] Or, if the friends' ages are approximately the same, one of them can ask the parents of the other to be his *towaa* parent and thereby become a *towaa* sibling to his friend. Second, an individual who is traveling or temporarily residing away from home may be befriended by, or will seek out, someone whom he will ask to be his *towaa* parent.[75] In this way, he will be assured of trustworthy friends and a safe haven where he can find shelter, company, and protection while in an unfamiliar region. Third, an individual who is orphaned or who has lost one parent may seek a surrogate parental figure, whether he is at home or away. (Note that it is possible to have *towaa* parents even though one's true parents are alive.)

A number of West Svay villagers have had or do have *towaa* relationships. To cite some examples, Vireak has had two *towaa* parents: one was an older man in the neighboring village of Ta Chas who was a source of fatherly comradeship and advice for many years, and the other was a woman in a distant province who took Vireak into her home when he fell ill while traveling through the area. Grandmother Leak (House 20) has had about ten *towaa* sons, most of them young men from other regions who had come to be monks at nearby temples. Grandmother Sithouk (House 17) has two *towaa* sons. One of them was originally a close friend of one of her real sons; he is an orphan

---

[72] Foster (1961b), Fitchen (1961), and Wolf (1966) have suggested that "voluntary" "contractual," and basically "temporary" relations between individuals or households are common in peasant societies. This is essentially true for West Svay, although Wolf's discussion of the formation of temporary "coalitions" for "short-range ends" (1966, 80, 91) is true primarily of cooperative labor groups and certain *towaa* (see below) relationships. Otherwise, friendships (with their attendant exchange of favors and aid) in West Svay seem to occur more as a matter of sentiment than the deliberate calculation that Wolf implies.

[73] Leclère 1890, 59–60 speaks of "amiable unions" or "a sort of kinship by adoption" called *klo* that sounds very much like the *towaa* relation. Note that Guesdon 1930, 1:850, also 42, 137, 1388 speaks of *thor* (which appears to be his transcription of the written form of the word *towaa*) as implying legal or *sacré* adoption; e.g. *aupok thor* = adoptive father or godfather.

[74] *Towaa* parents are designated as *mday towaa* = *towaa* mother and *aupok towaa* = *towaa* father. In actual address, however, a *towaa* parent may be called "mother," "father," or some other kin term such as "aunt," "uncle," or "elder sibling" appropriate to his/her age relative to the "*towaa* child."

[75] For a similar practice in Malaya, see Djamour 1959, 31. The Meso-American *compadrazgo* relation, as described by Foster 1961a, is also sometimes made under these circumstances.

who resides part of the year with relatives in Phnom Penh and the rest of the time with Sithouk's household where he is virtually a full-fledged member of the family. Another young man became Sithouk's *towaa* son while he was a student at the nearby normal school; he now lives in another province but visits Sithouk from time to time.

The *towaa* relationship has a number of features, some of which are evident from the preceding examples. (1) The *towaa* relation attempts to duplicate, albeit in a somewhat attenuated and usually temporary manner, the warmth, security, and nurture that is present between true parents and children. The *towaa* parents constitute a second home in which the *towaa* "child" can receive shelter, food, companionship, advice, and perhaps even material gifts such as clothing or other goods. In return, the *towaa* child usually gives gifts of money, food, or other items to his fictive parents and may also contribute labor to household activities. (2) The intensity, degree of interaction in, and duration of a *towaa* relationship depends upon individual circumstances. Sometimes it is relatively casual and fleeting, as in the case of Grandmother Leak and her numerous monk "*towaa* children" (*kon towaa*), most of whom she usually saw for only a few hours or few days at a time when they came to eat, talk, and sleep at her home, and with whom she subsequently lost touch after they returned to their own villages.[76] In other instances, the relationship can last for long periods of time and bonds can become deep, as in the case of Sithouk and her *towaa* son who is part of the family for much of the year. The *towaa* relation is necessarily short-lived when the arrangement is made while one is traveling or temporarily residing elsewhere, but *towaa* parents and children always remember one another fondly and will often attempt to maintain contact if they do not live too far apart. (3) An individual may have more than one *towaa* parent and more than one *towaa* child. Furthermore, men are more likely to become *towaa* children because they have more occasion to travel or reside elsewhere and thus have need of *towaa* parents. On the other hand, women are more often asked to become *towaa* parents because their natures are thought to be warmer, more nurturing, and more sympathetic than men's.[77]

## "GROUPINGS"

A striking feature of Khmer village life is the lack of indigenous, traditional, organized associations, clubs, factions, or other groups that are formed on non-kin principles. The only thing that approaches a formal organization in West Svay is the local militia composed of able-bodied men between the ages of twenty and fifty (see chapter 7), and this was initiated by the central government rather than by the villagers themselves.[78] Otherwise, the only "groupings" found in the hamlet are the friendship

[76] Leak recalls, however, that one of her monk *towaa* sons specifically sent for her to come and see him when he thought he was dying.

[77] A *towaa* mother's husband technically becomes a *towaa* father. But it is the woman who is usually approached first by a prospective *towaa* child and who will be the main source of affection and care.

[78] A few West Svay children belong to a youth organization that is comparable to Boy and Girl Scouts, but this is based in the local school rather than the village. The *chamkar* or fruit and vegetable cultivators evidently have associations concerned with irrigation (see Delvert 1961). But otherwise, Khmer villages have none of the associations found in certain other Southeast Asian peasant societies such as mutual loan and aid societies, clubs organized by the Buddhist temple, or political party associations.

circles mentioned in the previous section, cooperative work parties that are convened for particular purposes and change composition through time, and occasional displays of short-lived factionalism.

(1) Cooperative work teams are organized primarily for agricultural labor at certain stages of the rice-cultivation cycle when the household alone cannot supply enough manpower. Work parties may also be formed for other purposes such as house building or the construction of a communal well.

The agricultural work groups for plowing, transplanting, harvesting, and thresh-ing are of varied size and composition. When the groups are small, its members are usually kinsmen and close friends who form a friendship clique and customarily coop-erate with one another throughout the year and from year to year. The composition of large work teams, however, is quite variable because they are generally composed of whoever happens to be available for a certain task at a certain time, and are thus likely to include people who are not intimate kinsmen or close friends. All of these teams operate on the principle of quid pro quo exchange labor.[79] (For further discussion of cooperative labor in cultivation, see chapter 4.)

For activities such as house construction, the bulk of aid will likely be provided by close kinsmen and friends of the household, but others will often give some minimal assistance. Such services are reciprocated by the provision of meals and by the implicit expectation that the recipients of such aid will have some future occasion to return the favor.

(2) Factionalism is rare in Village Svay, and when it does occur the grouping of indi-viduals into opposing forces is likely to be temporary and rather vague. There are only two instances of factionalism in the recent history of the village. The most clear-cut and important example of factions occurred at the time of Issarak rebel activity after World War II. Some (seemingly a minority) of Svay residents were sympathetic to the Issarak cause, and a number of men actually joined the rebel forces, but others were neutral or even anti-Issarak in their sentiments. It should be noted, however, that the Issarak and non-Issarak were not two clearly defined camps that fought one another. While the men who joined the rebel forces did form an identifiable group, the non- or anti-Issarak villagers were not comparably organized and carried on their usual lives as best they could. Certain individual Issaraks occasionally terrorized their non-Issarak neighbors, but there was no general persecution of those who were not sympathetic to the rebel cause. In fact, it seems that the Issaraks and non-Issaraks managed to coexist relatively peacefully within the same community for most of the time. By now the Issarak move-ment is only a memory, and whatever factionalism existed has disappeared.

The only other instance of factionalism offers a clearer example of confrontation between sides, but again, the factions had no definite organization and the conflict was very short-lived. West Svay villagers attend two Buddhist temples that belong to two different religious orders: the Mohanikay and Thommayut. Half the households in the hamlet attend both temples equally often, but some families are either loyal Thomma-yuts or devoted Mohanikays (see chapter 5). Villagers recognize this divided allegiance, but ordinarily it is relatively meaningless because the differences between the two orders are so minor. In 1959, however, there was a brief flare of factionalism along religious

---

[79] There is also a vestige of corvée labor in that all able-bodied adult males can be called up for work crews to labor on government projects (see chapter 7), but this situation is different from the ones being discussed here. Also, a Buddhist temple may send out a request for volunteer laborers to work on temple construction activities.

lines. It is customary for the hamlet to sponsor an annual post-harvest festival to which monks from the two temples are invited to feast. But in this particular year the harvest was meager, and villagers felt that they could contribute money for only one meal for one group of monks, instead of the usual procedure of having two separate feasts for the monks of both temples. Mohanikay adherents were unwilling to contribute money if only Thommayut monks were to be invited, and the Thommayut followers were opposed to inviting only Mohanikay monks. Neither side capitulated, and the post-harvest festival was never held. But once the season for the post-harvest festival had passed, the matter was forgotten and neither faction seemed to hold a grudge against the other.

The reasons for this relative lack of factionalism are not certain, but some clue may be found in the nature of general interpersonal relations within the community. Certainly village life is not altogether harmonious, and disputes between individuals do occur. Apart from minor quarrels between children, young siblings, and spouses, which are expectable, clashes between adults also erupt from time to time for a variety of reasons: quarrels over water in the rice paddies (see chapter 4), over the disposition of inheritance, over the conduct of one another's children, etc. But, in the first place, such quarrels seem to be relatively infrequent (during my residence in West Svay there were only three obvious disputes between adults although I heard of others that had occurred in the past). There is, on the whole, almost none of the constant bickering and backbiting that is said to exist in some peasant groups (see, e.g., Foster 1961a and 1961b on Meso-America). Second, the pattern of conduct in such quarrels is usually not a direct confrontation between the persons involved. Rather, one of the individuals shouts out his grievances in an angry monologue that is apparently directed to no one in particular but is loud enough to be heard by the entire hamlet (including the offending party).[80] This is coupled with absolute avoidance of the person with whom one is quarreling, and sometimes disputants will not speak to one another for weeks, months, or even years. Some people may attempt to mediate such quarrels (especially if they occur between kinsmen), and a few persons may take sides with one or the other disputant. More typically, however, onlookers will remain simply observers who refuse to become entangled in the fracas This holding aloof from other people's quarrels is due partly to the feeling that fighting is an affront to Buddhist precepts of harmony and partly to a distaste for becoming unnecessarily involved in unpleasant situations. Given, then, this dislike of open confrontations and uncomfortable situations, plus a certain tendency toward individualistic behavior (see infra), it is not too surprising that full-fledged factionalism is uncommon.

In sum, then, the family and household are the only enduring and clearly defined units in West Svay. There are no larger organized kin groups and no formal associations or clubs, while groupings such as friendship cliques, work parties, or factions tend to have shifting or ill-defined membership and to be temporary coalescences.[81]

---

[80] A similar practice is described for Burmese and Thai peasantry; see Nash 1965, 81–84 and Phillips 1965.

[81] Foster (1961b, 1177, 1180) speaks of a Meso-American village in which, like Svay, the family and household are the only enduring, well-delineated groups. He suggests that the lack of other organized groups or associations (especially larger kin groups) may be due to the fact that there is no economic need for larger groups, and that political structure, religion, and law are organized by a larger outside hierarchy not indigenous to the community. The same is largely true for Svay (although there is some economic need for large work parties, it is only at certain times of the year).

SOCIAL STATUS

From one point of view West Svay is a homogeneous community whose inhabitants duplicate one another like Durkheim's (1947) "social molecules." All of the hamlet's residents are ethnically and culturally Khmer; the great majority are rice cultivators and even those who have other occupations are basically rural peasants; all are Buddhists; there are no enduring, well-defined groups beyond the family or household that differentiate individuals; and status differences within the community are not extreme. Such homogeneity, in addition to Buddhist ideas stressing the essential equality of men, helps to foster a basic egalitarianism in behavior and attitudes. Although there are some people who receive more respect and exert more influence than others, their authority is not overwhelming, and no great gulf divides them from their neighbors. As the villagers themselves say, "We are all people of the rice fields," "We are all poor," "We are all just the same." Fellow villagers treat one another without special formality or etiquette (except for the deference that is accorded to old people). Conversations between social equals have a free and easy, sometimes almost rough and tumble tone full of joshing, teasing, mock anger, and loud voices that is a striking contrast to the subdued, humble, hat-in-hand manner that villagers assume toward government officials, monks, or other social superiors, or to the subtle condescension that is sometimes displayed toward Chinese or Vietnamese. Buddhist teachings emphasize that worldly possessions and power are not as important as spiritual worth, and while nowadays there is some desire to achieve higher socioeconomic status, one seeks to achieve this goal outside rather than within the village. Villagers do not care about jockeying for positions of high status within their own community.[82] Moreover, those who may have wealth or power are most respected if they show generosity and selfless concern for their neighbors. Such benevolence and aid to others are prime virtues that are often manifest not only in time of crisis but in ordinary daily routine, and not only by the "haves" but by the "have-nots" as well: numerous items ranging from lengths of rope to jewelry are freely lent and borrowed; a woman who has just cooked a batch of sweets will cheerfully give one to any child who asks for one even though her own family can rarely afford such treats; friends are unhesitatingly asked to share one's meal if they happen to call when food is being served; etc.

Neither do those with riches or authority flaunt their assets. A man of informal power exerts his influence only in times of need or when he is called upon by others to do so, not for his own self-aggrandizement. And there is no flamboyant conspicuous consumption. Apart from noticing that some homes are clearly larger, better constructed, and better furnished than others, and that some people have more jewelry or holiday clothes than others, a casual observer would be hard put to tell who was rich or poor. Even at House 27, the richest couple in the entire village, Grandfather Map can be seen sewing his own thatch, while Grandmother Sethol wears a torn and shabby blouse. This does not imply the existence of a real "cult of poverty" (Wolf 1955, 1957) in which wealth is frowned upon and poverty idealized. Indeed, the possession of wealth is looked upon with some envy, and many people (especially the young) dream of having riches (see also Steinberg 1959, 28, 272). But at the same time, villagers who are relatively well off neither put on airs nor receive any special accord simply because of their affluence.

---

[82] Cf. status relationships in Wolf's "open" type of peasant community (1955).

But despite this fundamental egalitarianism in outlook, a balanced picture of village life should note that differences of status do exist and that villagers are, of course, distinguished from one another by a variety of features. Any one person's status (or "role set" in Merton's terms [1957, 369]) is a mosaic of elements that influences the way he behaves and the way others act toward him. Some of these features are of relatively minor significance and serve mainly to guide proper forms of behavior among equals. But certain combinations of features may also make some persons achieve special distinction among their fellows and become first among equals. The major components of a villager's role set are briefly outlined below.

(1) Sex. Khmer villagers do not have as rigid a sexual division of labor and behavior patterns as in some societies. Many activities can be performed by either or both sexes, and in many instances a man can occasionally execute what is normally a woman's task, or vice versa, without incurring derision or embarrassment. But certain activities may be strictly restricted to a particular sex (e.g., only males can become monks), or are considered to be more appropriate to one sex (e.g., men plow the rice fields, women care for the household), or are more typical of one sex (e.g., females are usually more consistently devoted to religious activities throughout their lifetimes than are males). In general, men occupy a superior social status according to both the secular legal code and Buddhist theology. Women do in fact possess a considerable degree of equality, voice, and independence in village life. But it is also true that females generally defer to males, that they generally possess less freedom of action and mobility than do men, and that although they may wield great authority within the family, they do not obtain offices of formal power within the community as a whole. Sex also affects patterns of interaction in that, outside of the family, individuals associate more with persons of their own sex than with those of the opposite sex. This is evident not only in work groups that are largely defined by the sexual division of labor (e.g., male plowing teams and female transplanting crews) but in friendship circles and even more casual daily interaction within the village.

(2) Age. The term *bòng pʔon* or "elder-younger" is important in kinship terminology, but it has a significance beyond that of differentiating various relatives. The principle of relative age influences behavior in general: ideally, anyone older than oneself should be treated with deference and respect. As a corollary of this notion, those of chronological old age (i.e., people in their fifties and older) should receive special courtesy and esteem from younger people. These norms are usually well observed when one interacts with persons of the parental or grandparental generation. But quite often, no special deference is given to someone who is slightly older than oneself.

Just as one tends to associate most with those of one's own sex, so does one tend to interact more frequently and form the closest friendships with persons of approximately the same age. This tendency is strongest among children, adolescents, and the elderly. But friendship and work groups among young adults and the middle-aged often include persons of various ages.

(3) Occupation or specializations. Occupation is not a very significant feature for distinguishing among fellow villagers when almost everyone in the community is a cultivator. Even those villagers who happen to earn the major or the entire part of their living by non-agricultural occupations (see chapter 4) are given neither special approbation nor disapproval because their styles of life and behavior are fundamentally similar to that of their neighbors. But if a villager encounters someone with an occupation that puts the latter in a clearly higher socioeconomic level (e.g., a schoolteacher or minor bureaucrat), he assumes the restrained decorum that obtains between social inferiors and superiors.

A villager might obtain some repute as a particularly skilled craftsman, for example, as an especially accomplished weaver or expert carpenter, but such abilities are important only if, for example, one wishes to purchase a sarong or build a house. Of greater importance where specializations are concerned are the part-time lay priests (*achaa*) and magical practitioners (*kru*) who often receive special prestige and respect. Certain lay priests, who are considered to be particularly knowledgeable and adept, gain far-flung reputations and are called upon by persons from neighboring villages as well as their own. Such repute may also be gained by skilled magical practitioners, for whom respect is sometimes tinged with fear.

(4) Official position. Certain political offices, namely the positions of sub-district chief, village chief, and leader of the rural militia, are held by villagers rather than by professional civil servants (see chapter 7). But if Svay is any example, it seems that such an office does not automatically confer prestige unless its incumbent is a man of some forcefulness. The village headman of Svay is a non-entity whom the villagers constantly bypass to go directly to the sub-district chief, a man who does receive substantial respect by virtue of both his position and a reputation for energetic pursuit of his duties. In West Svay, the leader of the local militia does command respect, although his powers and duties are in fact minimal, because he also happens to be a sociometric center for the young men of the hamlet. But otherwise, the main authority in West Hamlet is actually wielded by a man who holds no official position but is simply an informal leader (see below). Political office is, however, of great importance above the sub-district level. Such positions are held by bureaucrats from the central government to whom the villagers automatically accord deference.

(5) Wealth. From both subjective and objective viewpoints, there are some variations in wealth among the villagers. They themselves categorize such differences as follows. (a) *Neak miln* ("people who have"): rich persons with "many rice fields, money, jewelry, a nice house, good clothes, and other things." (b) *Neak kuĕsŏm* ("people [who have] enough"): persons who are relatively well off with "enough rice fields, enough to eat through the year." (c) *Neak krŏŏ*: the "poor people" who "may have to buy food to eat by the end of the year [before the next harvest]." (d) *Neak toal*: people who are "poorer than poor" who have no fields or only miniscule plots and are hard put to provide for daily subsistence.

In village society the main criterion for evaluating wealth is the amount of rice fields one possesses.[83] For the produce of these paddies yields not only the staple food but surplus rice to sell for cash that provides other amenities (and manifestations of wealth) such as a fine house, more and better clothing, jewelry, abundant and varied food, household luxuries, secondary education for one's children, frequent trips to the city, etc.

The residents of West Svay categorize one another as follows:

(a) Map and Sethol in House 27 are universally acknowledged to be the richest people in the entire village. They own four hectares of rice fields, one hundred sugar palms, and the largest house in West Hamlet constructed of wood and

---

[83] Rich persons also tend to own a large number of sugar palms, but the trees actually yield little income (one can rent them out for tapping, but the rent charged is little and tapping itself is done only by poor men; see chapter 4). Ownership of many oxen may also indicate wealth because cattle cost money, but in and of itself it is no clear criterion of affluence because older people may not keep animals for religious reasons.

tile and outfitted with various furniture. Their son became a medical technician in Phnom Penh.

(b)  Four or five households are said to be "people with enough." All but one own
about two hectares of paddies (the exception derives additional income from
his specialty as a magical practitioner), and several also have a considerable
number of palms. Most live in houses that are larger than ordinary, usually of
wood and tile, and have more than two oxen.

(c)  The majority of households are considered to be "poor people," with holdings ranging from about one-half to one hectare of fields, a varied number of
palms and oxen, and different kinds and sizes of dwellings (usually of wood
and thatch or entirely of thatch).

(d)  About half a dozen families or couples are said to be "poorer than poor." In
three cases, the families had no fields whatsoever, while the others owned a
minimal amount of paddies (e.g., six ares, twenty ares). They live in houses
made entirely of thatch.

But despite these recognized variations in wealth, relative affluence has no significant influence on daily interaction within the community. Someone who is "poorer
than poor" is not scorned (rather, one tends to sympathize with or pity them unless
they are lazy slackers who make no effort to earn a living), and neither is a "rich
person" automatically accorded prestige on the basis of wealth alone. In fact, the villagers tend to regard themselves as all being poor (even those who are relatively well
off will claim that they are "poor people"), and indeed, the variation of wealth within
the village is relatively small when contrasted to the difference between villagers and
affluent urbanites.

(6) Individual character and personality. A villager's character and personality
may be a significant component of his status and can affect the manner in which he is
viewed by his fellows. Certain traits of personality, such as forcefulness or a reputation for wit and good humor, may set one apart. But more important is the assessment
of an individual's personal character that figures in the various situations such as
the selection of a marriage partner, election of local officials, the formation of fictive
kin relationships, the acceptance of newcomers into the community, etc. The phrases
that are most often heard in evaluation of character are: *cEt l?ŏŏ* ("good character")
and *cEt akrowak* ("bad character").[84] The major characteristics of "good character"
are generosity and selfless concern for others; warmth and good-natured tempera-
ment; abhorrence of fighting, drinking, fornication, and other sins; devotion to family;
industriousness; religious devotion; and honesty.[85] The reverse of such qualities—
selfishness, bad temper, quarrelsomeness, drunkenness or even worse sins such as
thievery, the breaking of Buddhist norms of conduct, disregard of familial obligations,
dishonesty, etc.—constitute bad character.[86]

---

[84] The term *cEt* refers to what might be called a center of feeling, comparable to our usage of
the terms "soul" or "heart" in phrases such as "he has an evil soul" or "she has a good heart."

[85] Cf. the qualities used by Thai villagers in rating one another's prestige as listed in Sharp
et al. 1953, 108–9.

[86] A distinction should be made between those persons who have only some of the milder
characteristics of "bad character" (such as laziness or addiction to drink) and who are held in
low esteem but not utter disrepute, and those who break the strongest norms of conduct (e.g.,
murderers) and incur utter ignominy. For example, the only real ne'er-do-well in West Svay

Individuals who manifest notably "good character" are sought after as desirable mates, friends, adoptive kin, and go-betweens, and may well become figures of informal authority as well as objects of special affection and respect (see also Steinberg 1959, 277–78). Conversely, those who evidence traits of "bad character" are undesirable: they may be upbraided by their families and subject to critical gossip; men who are known to be lazy or drunkards are rejected as suitors for marriage; individuals of attested "bad character" are denied candidacy for political office or permission to move into a village; certain legal statutes deny rights to known criminals, drunkards, etc.; and someone with extremely bad character may actually be ostracized from the community.

**High Status.** While the villagers clearly form a distinct socioeconomic stratum within the nation as a whole, there are no social classes within the community itself. But certain individuals can occupy positions of higher prestige than others. The features enumerated in the preceding section differentiate people in various ways. Some of these attributes are more important than others, and certain combinations of them are likely to promote high standing within the community. The most significant qualities appear to be the following (not necessarily in order of importance): age, "good character," religious devoutness, and an energetic and forceful (but not aggressive) personality. Of lesser but possible importance are wealth and the possession of an official post. The particular combinations of qualities that are found in individuals of high status may vary from community to community or even within one village.[87] In West Svay there are several people who receive special respect. Each has somewhat different attributes, and a brief description of these villagers may give some idea of the sorts of persons who hold high rank and what influence they wield.

(1) Kompha. The "most important person" in West Svay, according to general consensus, is Grandfather Kompha. Although he holds no official position, he is the true leader of the hamlet and possesses considerable informal authority. Age sixty-six, he had once been a monk for seven years and is a devoted supporter of religious activities, as well as being a lay priest (*achaa*) much in demand for healing and for conducting life-cycle and other private ceremonies. He is also fairly well-off (a *neak kuèsòm*), and his gentle yet vigorous and commanding personality enables him to organize and direct activities in a

---

would periodically exasperate his brother and friends for his drinking, gambling, and general improvidence. But otherwise, he was tolerated and even loved. At the other extreme, one ex-villager was "thrown out" of the community for having committed theft and even murder as an Issarak rebel.

[87] The only comparative data available is from a rice-cultivating village in Siem Reap province as reported in CMCC 49.002. According to the author, the residents of this community went for advice, adjudication of quarrels, etc., to a man who was old, a "grand lai'que" who spent much money to maintain a temple and was himself a monk for twelve years before his death, the wealthiest man in the area who possessed "good character" and was a kinsman of almost all the inhabitants. There were also two other "Vénérables viellards" but they were not as rich or of such good character and were thus less respected. (Certain other residents are also mentioned as having reputations as magical practitioners, good cooks, skilled artisans, or poets and wits.) In sum, the writer emphasizes age, good character, religious devotion, and wealth ("to have wealth is to have authority") as the important qualities for high prestige. I think that he overemphasizes wealth, but it is true that although wealth in and of itself does not automatically bring prestige, it can enable one to pursue prestigeful activities such as devoting a great deal of time and money to religious endeavors or running for public office.

competent manner. And, perhaps most important of all, Kompha possesses exceptional "good character" that is widely admired (see also Ebihara 1966).

Kompha commands both considerable respect and a certain power. No important community matter proceeds without his consent (e.g., the planning of the hamlet's post-harvest festival was delayed several weeks because Kompha was away in Phnom Penh). He supervises and assists in numerous problems or crises of the hamlet's residents (e.g., in times of critical illness or death it is usually Kompha—regardless of whether he is a close kinsman of the family or not—who takes charge and dispatches messengers to fetch a physician or absent members of the household and begins to organize the proper ceremonies). His advice and opinions are well heeded (e.g., when I first moved into the village, it was primarily Kompha's admonitions to give me a chance that kept the villagers from asking me to leave immediately). His household constantly receives visits and small gifts from other residents. And he can make not only expectable but unusual demands on his fellows (e.g., a number of men have been awakened in the middle of the night by Kompha and told to go fetch an ill or dying neighbor's kinsmen in other communities, as well as being commandeered to go help build a house for Kompha's son in Phnom Penh). As one man noted with a smile, "If Kompha tells you to do something, you do it!"

(2) Map. At first glance, Grandfather Map seems the likeliest candidate for having the most prestige in West Svay. He is the oldest man in the hamlet, the wealthiest person in the entire village, an extremely devout Buddhist, and he was a sub-district chief for twenty-four years. Map is indeed highly respected: many villagers append an honorific "sir" to the kin term by which they address him; he, along with Kompha, is consulted about community undertakings, and his opinions carry weight; and villagers agree that he is certainly a venerable old man to be honored. Yet he takes second place to Kompha in authority and affection, probably for two reasons. Although Map certainly has "good character," he lacks one important quality that Kompha has: generous concern for others that is manifest in warmth and quickness to help anyone in need. Map is and always has been remote and aloof; at present this is due in large part to his advanced age (although not at all senile, he can hardly keep track of all the young villagers) and to his preoccupation with otherworldly religious concerns; and in the past, his duties as sub-district chief kept him from deep involvement with the personal lives of individual villagers although he was concerned with the general welfare of the community.

(3) Phana. In contrast to the preceding men, Phana is young (age thirty), rather poor, and has a shady past. But he is the locus of both limited formal and informal authority. As head of the hamlet's rural militia, he acts as the local representative of the village and sub-district chiefs and is often delegated to take charge of communal activities that are initiated by the government. In addition, he is a hub for the younger married men of West Svay who often gather at his house for conversation. Phana is outgoing, energetic, cheerful, and, like Kompha, evidences ability to command and organize people. He is well liked and his opinions respected by the younger men. But he is also regarded with some ambivalence or even distaste by other villagers (especially the older ones) because of his activities as an Issarak rebel in the past. Some hint that he was guilty of evil deeds during the time of the Issarak

movement, but he has since led a respectable life and is an accepted member of the community.

In general, then, so far as West Svay is concerned, age, "good character," religious piety, and ability to assume leadership seem to be the most important characteristics of men with high prestige. But the case of Phana shows, first, that younger men may be able to achieve limited respect and authority within a segment of the community and, second, that individuals with checkered pasts can, if they reform their ways, become respectable and even reputable figures.[88] This latter point is part of a more general feature of Khmer society:

the ability and freedom to shift status, within certain limits, at will and to make a clean break with the past is highly prized. (Steinberg 1959, 276–77)

[The] shift in status must be clear and abrupt . . . and must be publicly announced. . . . Once a person has made such a shift, he does not wish to be held to the obligations and responsibilities of his former roles or to be considered liable for the policies and actions which he then advocated. (273)[89]

The story of Phana's shift from a rebel against the government to an officially appointed occupant of a governmental position (albeit a minor one) is not at all unusual; similar situations have occurred in the highest levels of society with rebel leaders who shifted allegiance and were reaccepted as loyal officials of the central government (see Steinberg 1959, 274), or the opposite instances of distinguished individuals falling from grace. In a somewhat different vein, an abrupt change in status is also involved in the transition from layman to monk (and usually back to layman again) that many Khmer men experience.

### INDIVIDUALISM AND THE COMMUNITY

**Individualism.** Several anthropologists have noted a marked tendency toward individualistic behavior in some of the Southeast Asian cultures that neighbor and resemble the Khmer (see, e.g., Nash 1965, 161 on the Burmese; Embree 1950; Sharp et al. 1953, 26; Benedict 1952; Phillips 1965 on the Thai; Fraser 1960, 122, 219–23 on the Malay), and individualism is said to be characteristic of the Khmer as well (Steinberg 1959, 272, 276–77). This "individualism" has two facets: first, individualism in the sense of stress upon the individual rather than upon a larger unit; and second, individualism in the sense of social tolerance for individual variations in behavior.

Some authors have suggested that the emphasis upon the individual is due in large part to the Buddhist doctrine that each person accumulates his own tally of meritorious and sinful deeds that determine his fate in successive reincarnations; thus, everyone is ultimately responsible to and for himself alone.[90] Buddhism is undeniably

---

[88] Such an idea is consistent, too, with the Buddhist notion that merits accumulated in later life can make up for or outweigh sinful acts in one's past.

[89] Such changes are also common in Thai society, according to L. Hanks 1962.

[90] Nash (1965, 161) in speaking of Burmese peasantry, also states that Buddhist individualism inhibits "The formation of groups above the domestic level of organization . . . group effort, and cooperation." (Embree [1950, 188] also sees it as a factor in the "less, closely woven pattern

influential, but since the Muslim Malays are also said to have an individualistic orientation (see Fraser 1960), other cultural features are also significant. For example, among the Khmer at least, individualism is further encouraged and supported by factors such as individual ownership of property, the lack of larger organized groups beyond the family and household, subsistence activities that can be performed by single persons or family units except at certain times of the year, the relative independence and voice that is granted within the family to women and children despite the theoretical dominance accorded to males and elders, etc.

Corollary to the stress upon the individual is a permissive attitude toward variations in behavior. The Khmer bear a marked resemblance to what Embree (1950) called a "loosely structured social system" in speaking of the Thai. Various kinds of ideal, correct, or customary behavior are spelled out by the Cambodian legal code, Buddhist precepts and teachings, and less formalized but nonetheless firm traditions or norms of conduct. But at the same time there is considerable tolerance for variation in adherence to norms: some can be bent or ignored according to particular circumstances; while others, even powerful ones, are sometimes flagrantly broken. There are numerous examples of such behavior that have already been mentioned or will be noted in subsequent chapters: for example, one treats relatives according to personal likes and dislikes despite the ideal of affection for all kinsmen; inheritance is often unevenly divided despite the ideal of equal partition among all heirs; brides are sometimes pregnant despite the moral code of premarital chastity; etc. A lack of perfect congruence between the real behavior and the ideal norms is, of course, commonplace in all cultures, not just among the Khmer. But Khmer village society (like the Thai) does seem to have less rigid controls and more tolerance for variation than some groups. Adherence to most cultural norms depends primarily upon individual conscience, sensitivity to public opinion, or the desire to avoid trouble (see also Steinberg 1959, 277). Obviously the strength of such constraints will vary according to the person or to circumstances. Some people are extremely pious and scrupulously observe religious precepts, or are highly sensitive to the possibility of "shame," or fear the retribution of ancestral spirits for misdeeds; while others are more indifferent or nonchalant about such matters, either in particular situations or in general. For example, most men feel that drinking a bit of liquor at weddings or holidays is not really a grave offense despite the Buddhist injunction against alcoholic beverages, but some devout persons forswear liquor altogether, while a few others drink to excess.

It must be said, moreover, that external constraints on behavior are relatively weak. Certain acts, especially crimes against one's fellows such as rape or murder, are punished by criminal law if the offender is actually apprehended, accused, tried, and convicted (which may or may not happen)[91], or are grave enough offenses to arouse extreme condemnation and ostracism by one's neighbors. (For example, the ex-husband of one villager was "thrown out" of West Hamlet for committing theft and murder during the Issarak rebellion.) But otherwise, deviant behavior that does not seriously rend the social fabric usually brings down only adverse public opinion. And

---

of cooperative organization for agriculture" in Thailand as contrasted to Japan.) See, however, chapter 5 for a discussion of some of the ways in which Buddhism also encourages group action and integration as well as individualism.

[91] Several incidents suggest that individuals who are suspected, or even are known, to have committed criminal acts (such as theft) are not reported to officials because no one wishes to be put in the uncomfortable position of making a formal accusation.

typically, such disapproval and criticism is voiced behind an offender's back but not directly to his face, because villagers are wary of becoming unnecessarily involved in an unpleasant situation with unpleasant people, and because of the feeling that they are not their brother's keepers.[92] Most villagers are, in fact, quick to feel and respond to the possibility of censorious gossip about themselves; they often speak of the fear of incurring "shame," even with respect to trivial matters such as a girl worrying about whether she has on too much makeup. In this respect, public opinion is indeed a powerful force, particularly in a small community where it is difficult to keep any-thing unremarked or a secret. But a thick-skinned person may go his own way with-out acknowledging that any misdeed has been committed, and his neighbors may do nothing about the situation except talk among themselves. An example of this is one striking and high-spirited young girl who, according to all evidence, is the mistress of a man from Phnom Penh. Villagers murmured among themselves that this was a shocking state of affairs. But no one would openly denounce or rebuke the girl or her family for fear of being accused of slander; and she (who never explicitly stated that she was anyone's mistress) simply kept on appearing with new clothes and other gifts that she got from "a friend." Even more serious is the case of one old lady who, in her youth, had several adulterous affairs, bore and raised three illegitimate children, and is suspected of having committed abortion or infanticide on another illegitimate child. This indomitable woman thus defied convention repeatedly, and while she was subject to extreme disapproval by her neighbors, no one stopped her or even brought charges of suspected abortion or infanticide, which are grave offenses against moral and (in the case of the latter) legal codes.

Finally, it can also be said that while villagers may initially show disapproval of some deviance from strong norms, after a lapse of time they are often willing to for-give and forget. This is evident in the case of Phana, who was discussed in a previous section. It is manifest, too, in the instance of the man (also mentioned earlier) who was ostracized from the hamlet for extreme misconduct. His divorced wife and daugh-ter continued to reside in West Svay and, upon the occasion of the latter's marriage, the villagers decided that they would relent enough to invite him to the wedding (in fact, he refused the invitation because he was afraid to face his former neighbors). It must be said, moreover, that the transgressor himself has an "out" for deviant behav-ior by resorting to a sudden shift of status such as discussed earlier, or by the thought that he will make up for present sins by accumulating a large amount of religious merit in later life.

To balance the picture, it must be emphasized that this discussion of tolerance for variations in behavior is not meant to suggest that Khmer village society is atomistic or anarchic. It is important to recognize that there is "loose structure" in the sense that some aspects of life have ill-defined rules of conduct, while other areas may have definite norms but allow for variation or even transgression without incurring strong negative sanctions. But village life in general is both orderly and relatively harmoni-ous, implying that even a "loosely structured system" does have *some* structure. The cases of extreme deviance that have been described are relatively rare, and the major-ity of villagers are "good people" who commit only minor peccadilloes, such as getting

---

[92] Sometimes, if an errant person is in fact a brother or some other close relative (especially a child), one may well admonish and chastise him. But even close kin may avoid involvement or a confrontation. Such action is similar to the behavior typical of quarrels in which the disputants rarely confront one another directly but instead voice their discontent to other people.

tipsy at a wedding or quarreling with a sibling, that may affect their personal lives but do not seriously disturb the social order. The major Buddhist precepts are important guideposts for behavior (see chapter 5), and fear of ancestral spirits or public opinion does in fact keep most people in line most of the time.

**Community.** The extent to which community cohesion and solidarity exist is a rather moot point. Delvert, who surveyed numerous villages in his study of Khmer peasant economy, states the following:

> Whether *phum* [villages or hamlets] are small or whether they have several hundred houses, one fact appears certain: the absence of a rural community. No communal house. No communal property. The Cambodian peasant is, however, not jealously individualistic. Forms of mutual aid are very frequent. . . . But these always involve, except for the particular case of [riverbank irrigation associations], mutual aid agreements between neighbors and generally kinsmen. There are no practices made obligatory by the collectivity. This mutual aid is bounded by the *phum* when the latter is small, set apart, or a hamlet; when a large village is concerned, mutual aid applies only between neighboring families. . . . But there is no *communauté villageoise*, whatever the type of settlement. (Delvert 1961, 218–19; my translation)

In general, Delvert's points (except the last statement, which will be discussed later) are applicable to Svay, particularly the village as a whole whose large size would make it difficult to have overall community cohesiveness or communal endeavors. Moreover, although Svay appears to be a natural entity and not an administrative creation as are some *phum*, village political organization is weakly developed; and although there is a village temple that the community is responsible for maintaining, many residents (especially in West Hamlet) actually give equal or more support to a temple elsewhere (see chapter 5).

Even on the smaller scale of the hamlet, particularly West Svay, which is set apart from the rest of the village and forms a virtual small community in itself, there are relatively few activities that involve the hamlet as a whole. The only communal endeavors are (1) the local militia, composed of all able-bodied men, which is responsible for maintaining the security of the hamlet; (2) occasional public works, such as the building of a well, to which all families contribute either money and/or labor; (3) the sponsorship of occasional temple ceremonies; (4) the giving of an annual post-harvest festival (*daè phum*) for which all residents contribute money and act as collective host to monks and other guests; and (5) during times of drought, epidemic, or other calamities, the community may hold a ceremony to propitiate both Buddha and folk spirits.[93] One notes, however, that the local militia and many public works are fostered by the central government, and that community efforts for Buddhist ceremonies are prompted by the temple. Only the post-harvest festival and ceremonies in times of crises are stimulated from within the community itself.

---

[93] In other communities there may be other kinds of communal activity such as group fishing, building dams, or construction of boats to participate in the annual water festival in Phnom Penh. Delvert notes that riverbank villages with irrigation works have a more organized communal life than other villages, but that even here "collective life" is not very developed (1961, 216–17).

But despite the paucity of communal endeavors and the absence of strong community organization, West Svay residents do have a definite sense of loyalty and attachment to their village in general and to their hamlet in particular. The community in which one was born, or in which one assumes post-marital residence, is, first of all, where one's family, kinsmen, and friends are found. Villagers feel both physical and emotional security within its confines and are often uneasy about venturing beyond its borders to unknown territory (see chapter 8). One's fellow residents are characterized as "good people" in contrast to "bad people" in other villagers. Girls are frequently reluctant to assume post-marital residence in another locale, and even hardy men journey to distant regions with some wariness and trepidation. Attachment to the community is further strengthened by the villager's tie to his lands, which are located in and around the settlement. Land as the primary means of livelihood is an extremely precious possession, particularly in this area where it is difficult to obtain except through inheritance, and one does not easily relinquish or move away from it. But land is not the primary attachment, for there are examples of persons such as Sam who had emigrated from Svay to earn a living elsewhere, but who ultimately returned to the hamlet—even though he had to buy land on which to live and ekes out the barest subsistence because he has no rice fields—because he feels most "happy" and "comfortable" in his natal village.

Villagers themselves conceive of the hamlet or village as a unit and identify with it when they distinguish between "we" and "they," "our *phum*" and "that other *phum*," "good people" and "bad people." And the village is indeed something more than a mere conglomeration of households within a certain territory. For the village (or hamlet) forms, as Delvert says, a "cadre" or framework within which most activity occurs, and special bonds are forged among the people who interact with one another daily, annually, and sometimes for an entire lifetime. It cannot be said that the village or hamlet is tightly cohesive or that there are strong pressures for community solidarity. But both the web of kinship and the bonds of close friendship weave throughout the community, and loose, flexible, and rambling as this network may be, it nonetheless binds the inhabitants together.

A village may also form a religious as well as secular community. This is not so evident in West Svay because the hamlet's inhabitants have divided loyalties to two Buddhist temples. But in a community that supports only one temple, the residents constitute a congregation and may be called upon to cooperate as a unit for various religious endeavors. In such instances it is especially true that, as Delvert (1961, 220) says, "the temple . . . is a place of retreat, a place of gathering, a place of assembly: it is a true communal house." Some villages, too, have a community guardian spirit for whom periodic or annual communal rituals may be held (see Porée and Maspero 1938, 227; Porée-Maspero et al. 1950, 27–31). Svay does not have such a village guardian spirit, but there is one particular *neak taa* spirit (see chapter 5) that the villagers customarily propitiate, either as individuals in the case of personal troubles or as a community in the event of widespread calamity, such as drought.

In general, then, I would dispute what Delvert has implied about Khmer peasantry in his statement "il n'y a pas de communauté villageoise, quelle que soit la forme de l'habitat" (1961, 219). In West Svay, at least, it seems fair to say that the villagers do have a sense of community, and that they are bound together by diverse social, economic, political, and religious ties that form a loosely knit but nonetheless true community.

# CHAPTER FOUR

# ECONOMIC ORGANIZATION

The economy of West Svay and much of the rhythm of its annual life are based upon the cultivation of wet rice. Because it is a region of small landholdings and there is only one crop a year, the rice is grown primarily for subsistence rather than for the market. Food resources are supplemented by small kitchen gardens, fishing, and limited gathering of plants. Cash income, necessary to purchase items not produced at home, must also be augmented by various non-agricultural activities such as making palm sugar, raising pigs and chickens for sale, or finding temporary employment of different kinds. For most of West Svay's villagers, subsistence involves worry and effort to make ends meet, and a surplus of food or money is by no means assured. The following account of economic activities in West Svay is representative of numerous other rice-growing villages in the region to the south and west of Phnom Penh (cf. Delvert 1961, 449–52, 537–44).

## RICE CULTIVATION

As in most of Southeast Asia, rice agriculture has great significance in Cambodian life. It is "not only the principal activity, but equally, the most ancient, traditional activity" (Delvert 1961, 323). Rice is the staple food; the term for eating a meal is, literally, "to eat rice," and hunger is expressed as "to be hungry for rice." Rice is also an essential component of many ceremonials although West Svay villagers do not invest rice with a sacred quality[1] such as it possesses in some cultures (e.g., see J. Hanks 1960 on Thailand).

There are three basic types of rice agriculture in Cambodia: (1) rice grown during the rainy season that depends primarily on rainfall for water; (2) "floating rice" cultivated in fields inundated by flood waters from rivers, streams, etc.; and (3) rice grown during the dry season. In some regions, two (or even three) of these methods of cultivation may be used to yield more than one crop per year. But the more common pattern is cultivation of only rainy season rice with a single annual crop, such as is practiced in Svay and its environs (Delvert 1961, 324, 329–32, 358–65; see also Gourou 1945, 253–55, 387–88). From the descriptions of Cambodian rice agriculture in various sources, it is evident that the techniques and other aspects of cultivation in West Svay are virtually identical to those practiced by the majority of other Khmer villagers who grow "rainy season rice" (*sray vosa*), as well as essentially similar to the

---

[1] Cf., however, an article in the nineteenth-century *Codes Cambodgiens* that mentions "the holy mother of rice" (Leclère 1898, 2:361), and Delvert (1961, 343) notes an animistic ceremony during rice cultivation for the purpose of "giving soul to the rice." Aymonier (1900, 37) states that in legal and intellectual writings, rice is given a name that is a corruption of the name of a Hindu god of wealth, which leads Gourou (1945, 255) to say that rice has a sort of sacred value for the Khmer. Porée-Maspero (1962a, 20–21) also speaks of the soul or spirit of rice.

methods of wet-rice agriculture in other Southeast Asian societies.[2] Certain features of rice agriculture in Svay are, however, conditioned by particular circumstances that are typical of the region in which the village is located but cannot be generalized to the country as a whole.

## LANDHOLDINGS

The rice fields cultivated by West Svay's residents cover a total of about twenty-eight hectares and stretch mainly to the south, north, and west of the village (though a few plots are located in other communities). Each field is owned individually (except in the few cases where a couple may have jointly purchased a paddy) although it is shared and worked by the entire family or household. The primary means of acquiring a field is through inheritance, with parents passing on land to both sons and daughters. It is also possible to buy fields from fellow villagers or, more occasionally, from persons in neighboring communities if the fields are nearby; but such purchases are relatively infrequent because few persons can afford the cost. (For further details, see the section below on "Property and Inheritance.") Legally, land may also be obtained through the clearing and/or utilization of any unoccupied, unowned land for five consecutive years (Clairon n.d., 183; Delvert 1961, 490–91). In Svay, however, there is no such land for expansion.

In the late nineteenth century, the French instituted a policy of land registration and certification of ownership that continues to the present time (see Steinberg 1959, 206; Delvert 1961, 490). Every district office has an Office of Lands (Bureau Foncier) under the aegis of a national Board of Surveys (the Cadastre). Technically, every landowner must have a "Certificat d'Immactriculation Foncière" (called a *plan* by the villagers) for each field as evidence of true ownership. In actuality, however, villagers often do not register all of their lands, either because of the bother involved or because they wish to avoid paying taxes on the field.[3]

Money rental of land does not occur in Svay. But there is a traditional form of sharecropping called *provas sray* that is common throughout Cambodia (see Delvert 1961, 503–4). Persons who cannot or do not wish to work some or all of their fields (e.g., aged couples, families with sizeable holdings, or persons who have emigrated from the village but retain land there) will grant usufruct of land to someone else. In West Svay, the usual payment for rights of usage is half of the harvest, or more rarely, a certain proportion of the produce equal to some sum of money. In West Svay in 1959, *provas sray* arrangements were made in the following situations: (a) Map and Sethol (House 27), an old couple with considerable holdings of four hectares, made *provas* arrangements with eleven households (in West Svay and the other hamlets),

---

[2] On Cambodian rice cultivation, see in particular Delvert 1961; also Gourou 1945; Morizon 1936; Porée-Maspero 1962a, 32–38; Aymonier 1900, 36–37; CMCC 21.023, 21.066. For rice agriculture elsewhere in Southeast Asia, see, among others, Dobby 1960, 178–79; Fisher 1964, 75; Rajadhon 1961 and Kaufman 1960, 41–47 on Thailand; Swift 1965 and Cooke 1961 on Malaya; Kaufman 1961 on Laos; and Hickey 1964, 135–48 on Vietnam.

[3] In precolonial times, when the produce and not the land was taxed, villagers often endeavored to hide part of their harvest (Kleinpeter 1937, 97). The colonial administration thought that taxes on land rather than produce would mitigate such evasions (Kleinpeter 1937, 98), though in fact it has not. Delvert (1961, 490) also notes that land registration has not been totally successful.

all of whom had little or no land of their own; (b) Rith (House 20) worked some land belonging to his brother who emigrated to Phnom Penh.

The landholdings in West Svay are quite small, averaging somewhat less than one hectare (specifically eighty-eight ares) of rice fields per household, with a range from six ares to four hectares per family.[4] The rough distribution of holdings is as follows (for details, see appendix G).

| | |
|---|---|
| Less than one hectare | 14 families |
| One to two hectares | 10 families |
| Two hectares | 4 families |
| Four hectares | 1 family |

Four families have no rice fields. Of the families with less than one hectare, four have less than 50 ares; three have 50+ ares; three have 60+ ares; and four have 80+ ares.

The average holding in West Svay is lower than the national average of 2.2 hectares of rice fields per *ménage* among rice cultivators in Cambodia as a whole, though it should be noted that the size of holdings varies regionally from as high as five to ten hectares in some areas to as little as half a hectare in others. (Delvert 1961, 470–74; see also Gourou 1945, 383, 385; and Steinberg 1959, 298). But the figures for West Svay are not at all exceptional when compared to neighboring villages; for example, in the adjacent sub-district of Bakou, 83 percent of landholders had less than one hectare of rice fields (Delvert 1961, 684). Even taking the country as a whole, a 1956 census indicates that 55 percent of landowners had less than one hectare of fields, and central Cambodia in particular averages less than two hectares per household (Delvert 1961, 491, 495–96).[5]

The holdings in Svay are not only small but are heavily parceled as well. The twenty-eight hectares cultivated by West Hamlet villagers are divided into about 146 separate parcels. The average number of plots held by a household is five, ranging from one plot to as many as twenty in the case of the largest landowners. Furthermore, it is likely that not all of a household's fields will be contiguous, but rather will be scattered over the countryside in different locations that may be as close to home as a hundred feet or as distant as a kilometer or more. As the result of bilateral inheritance by both spouses and of hamlet or village exogamy, a number of villagers have fields in the vicinity of other hamlets or neighboring communities. Correspondingly, a number of paddies in the immediate vicinity of West Svay belong to persons from the other hamlets or to individuals from adjacent villages (see map 4A for schematic diagram of layout of fields; also map 3).

---

[4] Note that the villagers' reports of their holdings may be underestimated in some instances, either because of uncertainty as to exact hectarage or because of fear that government officials might learn of lands that are not registered. The average size holding may therefore be closer to one hectare in West Svay.

[5] Delvert (1961, 496) notes that in Kandal province, 100 percent of peasant landholders have less than five hectares of fields. Even in Cambodia as a whole, holdings of more than ten hectares (owned usually by temples, royalty, former officials, or wealthy merchants) constitute only about 1 percent of the total number of holdings (Delvert 1961, 195–500). The exact number of landless peasants is unknown but is evidently quite small. A system of absentee or local landlords using tenant farmers or hired labor is important in some regions but insignificant in the country as a whole where 90–100 percent of the peasants in the most populated provinces own their own land (for details, see Delvert 1961, 500–509).

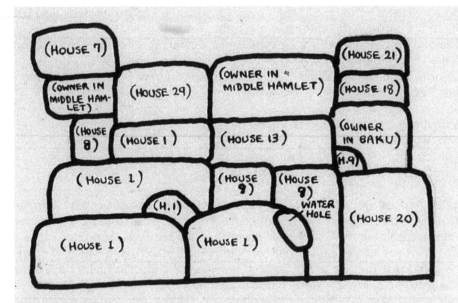

A. Schematic map of some rice fields south of West Svay showing parcellization and ownership. (Household owning field is indicated in parentheses.)

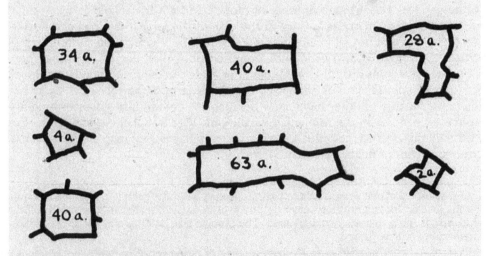

B. Actual shapes and sizes of some paddies (taken from a Certificat of Ownership)

**Map 4** Rice paddies

Both the parceling and the smallholdings in general are characteristic of the region south of Phnom Penh and are the result of several interrelated factors. (1) The provinces around Phnom Penh (especially Koh Thom and Takeo) have been inhabited since antiquity and have been relatively densely populated since the last century. (At present the district of Koh Thom has about 170–90 persons per square kilometer: Delvert 1961, 435, 447, 449, 492, 542.) (2) Because of the dense settlement, there is no opportunity to expand holdings except through purchase of land, which few villagers can afford.[6] (3) Bilateral inheritance and the ideal (if not always the real) practice of equal inheritance for all children means that the land has been and is subject to extensive sub-division through the generations.

The parceled rice fields in Svay are in the form of contiguous, flat paddies separated by earthen dikes.[7] The fields are not terraced, but since they follow the general curvature of the land, some paddies may be a foot or so higher than others in some places. The plots are of various shapes (see map 4B) and various sizes, ranging from about one are to eighty ares in West Svay, or anywhere from about eight by ten meters to as large as eighty-five by one hundred meters.[8] The dikes may be a foot or more in height, and the width is often greater because they frequently serve as footpaths for men and cattle as well as support for a variety of flora including huge sugar palms and other trees, bushes, grasses, and clover. These flora are sometimes planted but are more often wild growths or the remnants of vegetation that grew on the land before it was cleared. These trees and bushes are a nuisance in that they waste land, cast a shade on the rice, and may cause trouble with their roots. But on the other hand, they also provide cool shade for workers and cattle resting from their labors, serve as boundary markers, and in some instances give fruits or other products to be used as food, medicines, etc. (see also Delvert 1961, 326–27).

The villagers categorize the paddies (*sray*) into several types on the basis of location and/or the amount of water they receive. These are as follows: (a) *oo*: fields with a great deal of water; in West Svay, the paddies directly south of the hamlet and close to a streambed that sometimes fills up during the rainy season and provides the plots with abundant water; (b) *tropeang*: paddies more distant from the village that receive good amounts of water (West Svay does not have many of these); (c) *biè*: fields with an extreme abundance of water, often so much that rice cannot be planted at all and the plot is left for fishing or perhaps growing lotus; (d) *sray*: while this is a general term for rice field, it is also sometimes used to designate any paddy with a moderate amount of water; most of West Svay's fields fall into this category. In addition, different paddies are sometimes given specific names, such as "old field," to distinguish among one's various holdings.

---

[6] Actually, there are some tracts of overgrown land around West Svay that could conceivably be used for rice paddies. But the villagers assert that these would not be suitable for cultivation because they are difficult to clear and water is lacking. Also, most of this land belongs to persons who already have satisfactory returns from existing rice paddies. Too, this uncleared land serves some useful purpose as pasturage and as a source of firewood and useful plants.

[7] Cf. the picture of non-contiguous paddies separated by unused land in Gourou 1945, 380 and Ginsburg 1958, 428. Though Gourou says his map is taken from an aerial photograph of one of the most actively cultivated regions of Cambodia, this type of parceling is certainly not characteristic of the Svay region.

[8] See Delvert 1961, 328–29, 676–77 for the kinds and sizes of parcels elsewhere in Cambodia.

The villagers in West Svay differentiate further between two basic types of soil in their fields: *dey ksayt* or sandy soil, and *dey kondeng* or clayey soil (also known as *sèŭt* or *lbŏb* when it is very muddy and thick) that is overlain by a layer of soft, light soil. According to the villagers, most of the fields around the hamlet are *kondeng* although some *ksayt* is also said to be present.[9] Plowing and transplanting procedures must be varied somewhat according to the type of soil, but both varieties have low to mediocre fertility.[10]

## The Cycle of Cultivation

The rainy season in this part of Cambodia begins in May or early June. In striking and welcome contrast to the brilliantly sunlit and clear skies of the dry season, clouds now appear. At least once almost each day, the sky darkens and the atmosphere becomes stiflingly oppressive, ants are seen scurrying for shelter, a great wind suddenly rushes through the trees, and a torrent of rainfall begins to fall for an hour or more. Children often splash and play in the rain; girls may wash their hair in the water cascading from the eaves of the houses; and people sit chatting under their houses, refreshed by the cool air brought with the shower. The rains replenish the water holes and water jars and drench the desiccated soil. When the earth becomes soft enough to be worked, the annual cycle of rice cultivation begins. Its stages determine much of the rhythm of village life for the ensuing eight or nine months until the harvest is finally stored in the granaries in December and January (see also appendix I on the annual cycle).

### (I) Preparation of the Fields

In May, when the first tentative and occasional showers signal the beginning of the rainy season, the villagers begin to prepare their fields for plowing and planting. A simple hoe, a sort of spade, and a machete are used to repair and build up the dikes, clear them of extraneous overgrowth, cut channels that will later be used to drain off water or hold fish traps, and build fences of brush and branches to keep out wandering cattle. Sometimes a field is set afire to clear the stubble of the last year's crop, but more frequently the dried stumps are left to be plowed under. Some attempts at fertilization may be made by piling up and burning small heaps of brush and straw at various spots in the field, by placing clumps of fresh or dried cow dung here and there, or occasionally by applying coarse salt all over the field.

The first plots to be prepared are the nursery beds that will nurture the seedlings later transplanted to other fields. These nurseries are usually small paddies that

---

[9] A soil sample taken about one hundred yards west of the inhabited section of West Svay was given a crude analysis by Mr. W. Compy (of the Agricultural Division of the United States Overseas Mission in Phnom Penh) who characterized it as alluvial soil of low fertility, mildly acid, and affording poor drainage. For further discussion of soil types, see Delvert 1961, 90–97, 354–55; Zadrozny 1955, 63–64; Gourou 1945, 64–65; Dobby 1960, 300–5 and chap. 5.

[10] The mediocrity of the soils around West Svay is also indicated in the taxes assessed on the rice paddies. Taxes vary according to the crop-growing value of the land, for which the government has ten numbered categories ranging from Class #1 for rich riverbank lands to Class #10 for uncultivated, uncleared land (Gaylord Walker, Agricultural Division, United States Overseas Mission, Phnom Penh, pers. comm.). The fields around Svay are classified mostly as Classes #6 and #5, i.e., lands of medium quality.

are relatively assured of receiving a good amount of water and preferably are located near the village. Once these beds are readied, then the other fields may be similarly prepared.

## (II) Plowing and Harrowing

According to ancient tradition, plowing of the fields could not begin until after the Royal Ceremony of the Sacred Plow, on the fourth day of the waning moon of the month of *Visak* (sometime in May). In this Hinduistic-animistic ritual, the king (nowadays his surrogates) goes through the motions of plowing a paddy, offerings are made to the Master of the Soil and other deities, and prognostications are made as to the future harvest and well-being of the kingdom.[11] The villagers in West Svay, however, take no note of this symbolic ceremony; rather, the inception of their labors is prompted by climatic rather than ritual considerations. The beginning of the monsoon season is characterized by irregular and only moderate rainfall; so whenever sufficient rain has fallen to make the ground soft and workable, the villagers seize the opportunity to plow lest a subsequent dry spell harden the soil again.

The Cambodian plow (*ngwal*) is made of wood, has a plowshare tipped with metal, and is light enough to be carried easily on a man's shoulder (obviously an advantage when one's paddies are likely to be scattered in different locations and sometimes a fair distance from home).[12] The plow is drawn by a pair of oxen and digs only several inches deep, but this is enough to break the ground and help distribute water evenly over the field. Furthermore, the very shallowness of the furrows is an advantage in clayey soils because the surface layer of light soil is usually very thin, and a heavier plow would churn up the infertile, compact clay underneath (Delvert 1961, 223). The field is plowed over two or three times in various patterns.[13] It might be noted that the habit of rounding corners for ease in plowing, plus the irregular shapes of the fields and their large dikes, leads to some wastage of arable land (Delvert 1961, 341; Gourou 1945, 380; Ginsburg 1958, 427).

After plowing, the field must also be harrowed—either immediately afterwards, later the same day, or the next day, depending on the size of the field and the time, energy, and labor power available to the worker. The harrow (*rowaa* or *howaa*) is like a huge rake on a long pole. It is even lighter than the plow, and a man often stands on the bar to make the harrow bite the soil more effectively. Tracing the same sorts of patterns as in plowing, the harrow's teeth break up the ground a bit more finely. To complete the job, the bar of the harrow is turned over so that the flat side is down to smooth out the rough spots and make a relatively level surface for the water to glide evenly over the paddy. If a nursery bed is being harrowed, during the last round, a bunch of leaves is tied on the bar to trail in the soft mud and define furrows for sowing seed.

---

[11] For details of the royal plowing ceremony, see Porée and Maspero 1938, 155–56 and Porée-Maspero et al. 1950, 33–36; Aymonier (1900, 46). Cf. a "first plowing" ceremony among Thai villagers (Kaufman 1960, 201), parts of which are similar to the Khmer ritual.

[12] For details of the construction of a plow, see Delvert 1961, 221–23; Porée-Maspero 1962a, 30. This kind of plow has diffused to Vietnam (Hickey 1964, 136) and is also similar to those used in Thailand (Rajadhon 1961, picture following 57).

[13] The plowing patterns observed in West Svay are similar to those noted by Delvert (1961, 339, 341) who also discusses other aspects of plowing.

Plowing and harrowing efforts take place in what are essentially two phases. First, the nursery beds are worked at various times throughout the latter part of May and early June. This is a relatively easy task, although the plots must be plowed and harrowed twice (usually with a few days' interval in between), because each household usually needs only one or two nursery beds. Subsequently, however, in late June and July as the seedlings in the nurseries become ready for transplanting, all the other fields must be plowed and harrowed in preparation for transplanting. This second phase is a time of intense and arduous activity for the males of the village (see infra).

### (III) Sowing Seed

Rice for sowing (*srau puit*) is saved from each year's harvest, though a family may have to borrow or purchase seed if they have been driven to eat the rice in the intervening time. Villagers estimated that about four *tang*[14] (about five bushels or eighty-eight kilograms) of rice are needed to provide enough seedlings for one hectare of land (cf. Delvert 1961, 340).

Sowing takes place at various times from mid-May through June, depending upon when the nursery plot could be prepared and upon the type of rice sown. The unhulled rice is prepared for sowing by, first, a brief drying in the sun, then soaking in water for a day and night to soften the seed and begin germination, and finally leaving the seed to germinate further and dry for two days (cf. Delvert 1961, 340; CMCC 21.023, 21.066). The actual sowing is done by one or two women of the household who throw out handfuls of seed along the furrows. The rice takes root better if left without too much water for a few days, so most of the water is drained out of the field, either by cutting a channel in the dike to let it flow into an adjacent plot, or by using a water scoop to throw out the water.[15] Subsequently, however, the seedlings need moist earth (if not an excess of water) so some water is put back into the field if possible (by reversing the procedure just described), or one hopes for adequate rainfall. Within a week's time after sowing, the fields change from the dreary brown of sunbaked earth to a delicate, pale green. By the end of several weeks, if all has gone well, the plants will be a foot or more in height and a healthy dark green.

It might be mentioned here that there is one kind of rice cultivation that does not involve deliberate sowing of seed. In certain fields, rice that falls on the ground from one year's crop will germinate and grow by itself when the next rainy season comes; this is called *muė*. The plants can later be pulled out and transplanted in orderly fashion, or the rice can be left to grow as it comes up. There were only a few paddies with *muė* in West Svay.

---

[14] Unmilled rice (*srau*) is measured in *tau* and *tang*, with two *tau* making one *tang*. A *tang* is calculated as 20–22 kilograms by Delvert (1961, 12, 340); while its capacity is given as 30 liters by the Institut d'Emission des Etats du Cambodge, Laos, et Vietnam, Annexe II, 1959, and as 40 liters by Delvert (1961, 12). If 1 kilogram = 2.2 pounds avoirdupois and 1 liter = 0.02837 bushels (*Heath's New French Dictionary* 1932, 582), then: 1 *tang* = 20–22 kilograms = 48.4 pounds = 30–40 liters = 0.851–1.135 bushels. (Milled rice has different units of measurement; see infra.)

[15] The water scoop (*snayt*) is either a wooden box with the top and one end missing, or a large metal can that has been cut in half horizontally with the end taken out. It is hung on a tripod by ropes, and a man pushes or pulls a handle attached to the box or can opposite the open end, swinging it into and out of the water. Delvert (1961, 224, 340–41) says the scoop is the most commonly used instrument of irrigation in Cambodia.

West Svay villagers can list more than twenty-five varieties of rice, each with certain distinctions of form (e.g., length, shape), color (white or dark), taste, or other attributes.[16] Each also has a particular name that may reflect its physical qualities (e.g., *pong tiè* or "duck egg"), or be poetic (e.g., *nièng sèaat* or "trim maiden"), or both (e.g., *cmaa sòò* or "white cat"). All of these fall into two major classifications. First, there is a distinction between (a) "rice for ordinary eating," *srau ksay*, which is *Oryza sativa* and has about eighteen varieties in West Svay; and (b) "rice for making sweets," *srau domnap* (or *srau tnap*), which is Oryza *[sativa var.] glutinosa* and has about eight varieties. Each household plants both; the ordinary rice makes up the bulk of the harvest, but at least a small amount of the latter is considered a virtual necessity to make delicacies for temple festivals, life-cycle events, or simply occasional treats for the family. Second, and more important for the timing of the agricultural cycle, there is a differentiation between (a) "light rice," *srau sral* (or *srau seal*), of which there are about five varieties in West Svay (apart from the different kinds of glutinous rice that are categorized as "light" in Svay); and (b) "heavy rice," *srau tungun*, with about twelve varieties.[17] The main difference between the two, apart from weight ("heavy" rice is indeed heavier than "light" rice), is the growth period. Light rice has a short growth period from five to six months; the varieties in West Svay that are planted from mid-May to mid-June are harvested in late October and November. Heavy rice, on the other hand, requires six to seven months to mature and is reaped through December. Also, light rice requires less water during its growth, but heavy rice gives a greater yield. Most families try to sow both. Light rice is usually planted in less quantity, but it is critical in providing food at a time when the last year's crop has been nearly or completely devoured and most of the present crop has not yet fully ripened. But sometimes a family may plant only light rice if they need an early harvest because of a fast diminishing granary, or only heavy rice if they think they can wait until December. Another consideration can be the type of paddies one owns: light rice is not planted in paddies with a great abundance of water because it ripens quickly and will spoil if dampened by water remaining in the paddy at the end of the season; heavy rice, by contrast, needs just such paddies to sustain it through its slower maturation period (see also Delvert 1961, 335).

As for the selection of particular varieties of light or heavy rice, the villagers are guided in their decisions by considerations of taste, texture, and ease of cooking. Also, sometimes one may have to buy or borrow varieties other than the kinds one had intended to plant, if the seed has been eaten during the year. Any one household may plant as little as two varieties of rice (one ordinary and one glutinous), or as many as five or six if they have many parcels and/or relatively large landholdings. In both the planting of the nursery bed and in transplanting, the villagers try to keep the varieties of rice separate by placing them in different paddies or in different sections of the same field (though the different kinds sometimes get mixed up in the process of pulling seedlings and transplanting.

---

[16] This abundance of varieties of rice is common throughout Cambodia, though there are regional differences in the names and number recognized (see Delvert 1961, 332–38; Porée-Maspero 1962a, 26–27; also Morizon 1936, 98–99). Delvert (1961, 352) says that the selection of variegated types gives the peasant the maximum chance of success in view of the unpredictable rainfall and the varying quality of the soil.

[17] Cf. the threefold classification of rice given by Delvert 1961, 333.

### (IV) Preparations and Transplanting

The seedlings are left to grow in the nursery beds for about four weeks if the rice is light and six weeks if it is heavy. As the plants become ready for transplanting, the work force of the village is thrown into a flurry of intense activity that lasts for over a month. There are two essential tasks: the men must plow and harrow the fields that are to receive the seedlings, and the women must pull up the rice for transplanting. The demands of cultivation require considerable haste and coordination: as seedlings are pulled out, the men must plow some fields; and while these plots are transplanted, still other paddies must be readied for more transplanting. This procedure is repeated endlessly until, finally, all the fields have been filled with green. In all, the months of June and July, including the process of transplanting itself, constitutes the busiest part of the cultivation cycle.

A. Plowing the Fields. At this time, the adult and adolescent males of the village must hasten to prepare the remainder of their households' fields, and sometimes another's lands as well if they are sharecroppers or have been hired to plow by someone without oxen. Depending on the nature of the soil, each plot must be plowed and harrowed at least once if the earth is clayey and sometimes twice if it is sandy.

Several factors condition the pace at which this work proceeds. Plowing must be done during hot and humid weather. Thus, most work is done only in the cool of the morning hours from daybreak to midmorning, and it is mandatory for both the men and the oxen to rest from the blazing afternoon sun. Then, depending on energy and inclination, further plowing and harrowing may be done in the late afternoon until twilight. Delvert (1961, 234–35) estimates that, working an eight-hour day in such a split shift, a pair of oxen can plow only twenty ares a day (though they can harrow sixty-six ares per day). Thus, a man with one hectare of fields would work about five days on plowing and about one and a half days on harrowing (slightly more if there is parceling, and double this number of days if the fields are sandy soil that requires two workings) (Delvert 1961, 347).[18] Though this may seem a relatively limited amount of effort, it should be noted that the work is not spread evenly through time for two reasons. First, one cannot be assured of how much and when rain will fall during June and July. June is still the beginning of the rainy season with irregular, light rainfall. July is part of a "little dry season" (that runs through August) when rainfall is apt to be even lighter than the two previous months. Prolonged dry periods can occur throughout Cambodia and are especially common in the Svay area (Delvert 1961, 45). Thus, a man may have to plow as much as possible in a period when the rains have been sufficient to make the ground workable or run the risk of suffering an extended dry spell during which he can do nothing. Second, the plowing of the fields must be coordinated with the time at which the rice seedlings become ready for transplanting, because transplanting is done immediately after the final plowing and harrowing if the soil is sandy, or at the most several days afterwards if the soil is clayey. Therefore, plowing may again be compressed into a relatively short period, even allowing for the fact that the various nursery beds have been planted at slightly different times from mid-May to mid-June and thus come to maturity for transplanting at different dates.

---

[18] Because of the limited amount of work that oxen can execute in one day, and because of the climatic conditions and the requirements of the growth cycle of rice, Delvert (citing Jacques Marinet) feels that four hectares is the maximum amount of land that could be cultivated with one pair of oxen or buffalo (Delvert 1961, 235, 342).

Because of these considerations, and depending on the size of one's holdings as well as the necessity or desire for quicker and easier completion of the job, men often resort to cooperative plowing and harrowing arrangements. Anywhere from two to six (or conceivably more) men agree to work as a group in tilling one another's fields in tandem; such plowing teams may be composed of kinsmen, close friends, or neighbors, usually from one's own hamlet but sometimes from other hamlets as well.[19] The quid pro quo is calculated roughly in terms of hours of work owed one another. In addition, the owner of whatever field is being plowed is expected to provide a small meal and cigarettes for his coworkers.[20] Such cooperative efforts do greatly decrease the amount of time required to prepare a field; for example, a plot of approximately eighty ares belonging to Peng was harrowed by six men in about one hour, when it would have taken him over a day's labor to have done it alone. Thus, during the busy period of plowing, a frequent and handsome sight in the countryside is groups of men and their gracefully curved plows trailing one another through a field, gliding like ships as the soil is flattened and the water spreads over the field. At the end of the harrowing, the pleasure of completing the task often makes high-spirited men race their oxen at a gallop around the paddy, whooping exuberantly and creating great splashes of water.

It might be noted here that one-third of the households in West Svay own land but either no oxen or only one ox, when a pair of oxen are essential for the plowing without which no cultivation could proceed. Such families must, therefore, make some arrangements to have their fields plowed, and several alternatives exist. (1) *Provas sray*, or sharecropping, gives complete usufruct and responsibility for cultivation of one's fields to someone else. (2) Another kind of *provas*, called *provas stung*, is more in the nature of mutual aid in different activities. As an example, Grandmother Vannary, who has no oxen, asked Sophat to plow her fields; in return, Vannary had to transplant (*stung*) Sophat's fields and helped him at harvest time as well. (3) A family without oxen can also hire someone (most frequently a neighbor or kinsman) to plow and harrow for the usual wage of twenty-five to thirty riels for one morning's work. (E.g., House 11 hired a brother-in-law from the neighboring village of Ta Chas for 280 riels.) It is also possible but more expensive and rarely practiced, to rent a pair of oxen for 700 to 800 riels for the entire cultivation season from "*chamkar* farmers who have no need for them during the rainy season." (4) An individual with only one ox will usually make an exchange labor agreement with someone who is similarly handicapped; by working together they form a full team and plow one another's fields in turn. Such was the arrangement between the brothers-in-law Sophat and Rattana who habitually plow together. (5) On occasion, a man may also attempt to float a loan

---

[19] Such groups may become organized in different ways. Either a man will go out and deliberately seek plowing partners, enlisting the aid of anyone who is amenable; or agreement to plow together may arise more informally and spontaneously between (or among) friends, kinsmen, or neighbors: e.g., in the course of casual conversation about the progress of one's plowing efforts, someone may suggest that they band together to make the work go more quickly.

[20] Such meals may include rice, rice gruel, soup, various dishes, and sometimes even wine. In 1959, the villagers of West Svay had agreed among themselves that only rice gruel and dried fish need be provided in cooperative plowing exchanges because the cost of additional food was too great an expense for many families. But actually, in many instances, especially if the coworkers were relatives or good friends, a small amount of rice continued to be part of the meal. Evidently the inhabitants of the other hamlets of Svay continued to offer more elaborate meals.

for money to buy an ox for the cultivation season and plan to sell it after the harvest for approximately the same price.

B. Pulling the seedlings (*dŏk samnap*). While the men are occupied with plowing, women have the main responsibility for the pulling and transplanting of the rice. Handfuls of seedlings (*samnap*) are pulled out from the nursery beds and tied into bundles. Several inches are cut off the tops of the seedlings so that they will not be blown over by winds or beaten down by heavy rainfall once they are transplanted (moreover, the green leaves provide food for oxen at a time when it is needed). The bundles are left to stand overnight in water, then allowed to dry on the dikes over another night so that the roots will become firm for transplanting (see also Delvert 1961, 342; CMCC 21.023). They are then transported from the nursery beds to other paddies by shoulder poles.

### (V) Transplanting (*stung*)

In West Svay, transplanting reaches its peak in July, especially in the latter half of the month, though some sporadic transplanting may continue well into August if insufficient or sporadic rainfall has delayed plowing and caused an inadequate accumulation of water in the paddies. Fields with sandy soil must be transplanted immediately because, say the villagers, the earth "hardens" quickly, while plots with clayey soil must be transplanted within several days after plowing. Ideally, a field is plowed in the early morning and transplanted in the afternoon, though it is common to plow one day and transplant the next.

Transplanting is done primarily by the adult and adolescent women, though they are sometimes aided by a few adolescent boys or an occasional adult male who has energy to spare. It is common throughout Cambodia for this task to be performed by large cooperative work groups because of the large number of paddies that must be hastily transplanted within a short period of time. The village becomes strangely silent during the peak of the transplanting season as all able females spend most of the day in the fields. Holding bundles of rice in one arm, a woman bends, stands, and steps backward in an even, graceful rhythm as she plunges small bunches of seedlings into the mud. (A hole is usually made with a finger but sometimes with a small wooden dibble if the ground has hardened.) Each woman begins at one end of the field and plants a strip about four or five bunches wide, with the seedlings placed about six inches apart.[21] The older women, made skillful by years of practice, race ahead of the adolescent girls who are just learning to *stung*, and tease the latter about their slowness. Despite the heat and arduous work, the women (and occasional males) chat, the girls may sing, and there is frequent laughter at jokes or as someone breaks into a mock dance. The workers also take numerous breaks (especially when the field is not one's own) to rest in the shade on the dikes and have some water, betel, or cigarettes supplied by the owner of the field; occasionally, some rice gruel may also be provided as a snack if the group is not too large.

---

[21] Cf. Delvert 1961, 344; Morizon 1936, 100; and CMCC 21.023. West Svay villagers say that if the plants are put too close together, one obtains a lot of leaves but not too much grain, while placing them too far apart wastes land. On occasion, however, rice may be planted thickly and close together but will later be pulled out and retransplanted into other parts of the field that are more sparsely planted.

The size and composition of these transplanting groups are variable, depending on the dimensions of the field to be worked and/or the time of transplanting. At the beginning and end of the transplanting period when pressure is not too great, a household may have enough females to handle small- or medium-sized paddies by itself, or with the aid of a few kinsmen or close friends, in little groups of about two to four persons. But during the peak of the transplanting season when the villagers are confronted with a great number of paddies that must be transplanted quickly, teams ranging in size from about six to twenty women are common. At this time, all the able-bodied females (from about the age of fourteen and up) in the hamlet are called into action each day and split up into groups of different size and composition that fan out to transplant whoever's fields are ready.[22] As in the cooperative plowing groups, the women attempt to calculate the amount of labor owed to one another's household on a quid pro quo basis: "If you help me in my field, I or someone in my family must help you on yours" (a common phrase used is *tøu ving tøu mao*, literally "to go and come," figuratively "give and take"). But strict accounting of reciprocity seems to break down during the busiest weeks of transplanting; rather, the women appear to form a vast labor pool from which teams are sent wherever necessary, with reciprocal obligations evening out in the end.

Occasionally, a more affluent household, or one that cannot or will not participate in cooperative exchange labor, will hire workers for transplanting (and/or harvesting).[23] These hired laborers are usually women from other villages, generally persons from poor families with small holdings who can hire themselves out after their own fields have been readied, or young women and girls who wish to earn some extra cash for feminine luxuries (see also Delvert 1961, 485; Gourou 1945, 384). It is common for anywhere from half a dozen to fifteen or more women to band together and travel from village to village until they find work. The laborers are usually paid according to the number of plants they transplant or harvest, with the exact rate depending on whether or not lodging and meals are to be provided and, of course, on the bargaining prowess of the employer and workers. Peng paid 200 riels to fifteen girls and women from nearby Village Chey to pull seedlings and transplant a little less than one *slùk* of rice for two fields;[24] he also provided a noon meal, but supper and housing were

---

[22] I was never able to figure out exactly how the women organized themselves into groups of different size and composition. They have no one leader or supervisor for transplanting teams. Rather, it was simply known from day to day whose fields had been plowed and were ready for transplanting, and these paddies were then transplanted by a group of appropriate size composed of those who owed labor to the field's proprietors or who were willing to help with the expectation of reciprocal aid in return. A woman usually knew what fields she would work on the next day, and sometimes several days in advance. [In the 1990s the villagers told Ebihara that they kept count of the number of bundles of seedlings they did for each other and thus kept a stricter accounting of the exchange than she was able to ascertain at the time.]

[23] The only persons who hired labor in 1959 were Peng (House 30) and Sao (House 29). Peng hired both transplanters and harvesters and evidently does so annually. He has large holdings (two hectares) and is considered to be moderately well off; also, his wife is sickly and there are only two sons to provide other labor power. Sao has about one hectare of land and is of average means; but his wife was very ill in 1959, and he has only one adolescent daughter to work the fields (also, this family has no close kinsmen or even especially close friends in the hamlet). Cf. Delvert (1961, 487) who says that hiring help is not so much a function of large landholdings as of the lack of sufficient labor power in times when work must be completed quickly.

[24] A *slùk* is a sheaf of rice containing a certain number of stalks; see Delvert 1961, 12, 344.

unnecessary because the women returned home after their labors (cf. Delvert 1961, 486 on types of payment for hired labor).

Delvert (1961, 347) estimates that one hectare of land requires fifteen days for transplanting as well as three days for the pulling and transporting of seedlings. It is unclear, however, how large a work force Delvert has in mind in making his estimate.

### (VI) The Period between Transplanting and Harvest

Once the seedlings are transplanted, the villagers enjoy a period of relative leisure until the major harvest in late November and December. Some men now leave the village for weeks at a time to take temporary jobs in Phnom Penh and elsewhere for money to tide their families over until harvest. Other people journey to visit kinsmen in other communities. Weddings, annual holidays, and Buddhist festivals occur during October and November (see appendix I), making this a period of happy conviviality.

In the rice fields there are several tasks that must be pursued, particularly while the plants are relatively young, but none are arduous or time-consuming. (1) Small crabs that infest the paddies must be caught because they cut the stalks of (and thus kill) the tender young seedlings (see also Delvert 1961, 356; Gourou 1945, 410; CMCC 21.066). The damage wrought by these pests is repaired by setting in new plants taken either from another part of the paddy that has thick growth or from spare bunches of seedlings left over from transplanting. Later on, the crabs become less of a menace because the rice stalks harden as they mature.[25] (2) There is some weeding of grasses and weeds that would stifle the young plants. But this is usually done in a rather desultory manner. (3) The dikes must be kept in proper repair. (4) The water level in the paddies is controlled and equalized, either by cutting channels in the dikes to let water run from a field with an abundance of it to one that has less (assuming that one's paddies are contiguous), or by using the water scoop.

From August to November the countryside has a splendid beauty. In contrast to the drab grey-browns of the dry season, the fields have become a sea of greens ranging from the chartreuse of the youngest plants to the vibrant green of the more mature leaves, the stalks undulating in any breeze. The varying quality of the growing rice is pointed out by a villager as he walks along the dikes. At a paddy where the plants are tall and have thickly abundant leaves of a deep green color, he will exclaim "Very good." In another plot where some plants are scraggly, small, and colored a sickly yellow-green, while others are withered brown and dead or dying, he shakes his head and says "Not good." The two major factors that create a good crop, as stressed repeatedly by the villagers, are (1) sufficient water to nourish the growing rice, and (2) fertilization. Their discernment is accurate, for these are two of the principal problems of rice cultivation in Cambodia that are noted also by the economic geographer Delvert (1961, 352ff).[26]

The villagers can exercise some control over the latter of these two factors, fertilization. Ash, dung, or salt is put in the fields before plowing and sometimes afterwards.

---

[25] Delvert (1961, 356–57) speaks also of caterpillars, grasshoppers that come in seven- to eight-year cycles, and birds as other menaces to the growing rice. West Svay villagers, however, spoke only of the crab as a threat.

[26] Delvert (1961, 352–58) feels that the major unsolved problems of Cambodian rice cultivation are (1) water, (2) mediocre or poor soils that need enrichment, (3) pests such as crabs, insects, etc., and (4) mediocre yield.

Further fertilization is provided during the plowing itself as the oxen drop fresh dung, and grasses and old rice stalks are plowed under. There is a final application of fertilizers to the fields after the harvest.[27] But the villagers may not fertilize all their paddies equally well (the seed beds receive the greatest attention), and even within one field the fertilizer is not distributed evenly through the plot. One frequently notices distinct patches in a paddy where the plants are thicker and greener than the others, indicating the places where fertilizer was placed in a heap.

(It might be noted here that in West Svay there is no deliberate fallowing of fields to restore fertility,[28] which is not too surprising in view of the small average landholdings per household. In 1959, several families did leave one or two of their paddies uncultivated; but this was either because the plots were small ones that were deemed not worth the trouble of labor, or because their owners had run out of time and energy to work them. Actually these overgrown paddies had utility as miniature pastures for oxen at a time when food for them is scarce and hard to obtain.)

The problem of water is more difficult for the villagers because they have no control over the main source of water: rainfall. The question of whether or not there will be sufficient rains is a constant worry, particularly since Svay is in a region that experiences not only an aggravated "little dry season" in July and August, but is near the driest rain station in Cambodia.[29]

The rains of August through the first part of November are especially important for the growth of the rice. According to rain charts, August has limited rains in this area south of Phnom Penh, and in 1959 this month was considered even drier and hotter than usual in Svay. The September and October rains, however, are always more abundant everywhere in Cambodia. In some years the streambed and water hole to the south and southwest of West Svay have overflowed into adjacent parts of the hamlet, and in 1959 the path in back of my house was flooded for a couple of weeks in mid-October.

It is not merely the sheer amount of rainfall that is important, but also its timing relative to the different stages of rice cultivation (Gourou 1945, 75; Delvert 1961, 353; Dobby 1960, 291). Rain must be sufficient at certain times to allow such activities as plowing and to nourish the plants to a certain point of maturity, while dry spells can seriously disrupt the agricultural cycle and damage the crop. Prolonged periods of drought during the rainy season create great anguish among the villagers who may appeal to supernatural powers for deliverance. On the other hand, rain can also be detrimental: an overabundance of rain can cause floods in some areas and is especially

---

[27] In other areas, fertilization may be provided by balls of unmilled rice, oil cakes, and mud from ponds (Delvert 1961, 335; Zadrozny 1955, 298–99). Chemical fertilizers have been used only since 1951 in a few areas by relatively wealthy people (Delvert 1961, 335). Night soil is never utilized by the Khmer.

[28] Cf. Delvert (1961, 355) who says that fallowing is widely practiced in Cambodia.

[29] According to Delvert (1961, 45–49, 352–53, 539) the major handicap to rice cultivation in Cambodia is rainfall that is insufficient for the demands of rice agriculture: the rains begin late, are often irregular and not abundant, diminish during the "little dry season," and sometimes end too soon or go on too long. These problems are especially evident in the area south of Phnom Penh, and particularly in Kompong Tuol (a few kilometers from Svay), which is the driest rain station in the country (see Delvert 1961, 721, fig. 3). Dobby (1960, 265–67, 270, 290–91) notes that inadequate and/or unpredictable rain constitutes a problem for rice cultivation also in central Thailand and other Indochinese states. See also Wolf 1966, 27.

serious immediately after transplanting because short seedlings can drown; and rain is greeted not with pleasure but with anxiety during the harvest season.

Even assuming that rain has fallen properly, there is little control over the distribution of its waters. Irrigation techniques in West Svay, as throughout Cambodia, are extremely simple and limited.[30] A few persons have access to extra water because their paddies border on a water hole or the streambed that sometimes fills up during the rainy season; from these sources, water can be scooped into some fields and made to flow into adjacent ones by cutting channels in the dikes. But water from these sources cannot be distributed very far because the land rises to a slightly higher elevation at certain points south of the hamlet. Other persons must depend solely on rainfall to obtain water and can only try to equalize the water level in different paddies by scooping from one field to another or letting water run through channels in the dikes. However, such procedures can be followed only if one owns paddies contiguous to one another, or if one has gotten permission from the owner of an adjacent plot to have water taken out of or put into it. There are often quarrels over failure to obtain such permission and acts of negligence that damage another's fields; the sub-district chief states that, of the various cases brought to him for adjudication, disputes involving water are the most frequent.[31] Deliberate theft of water from someone else's paddy (by surreptitious cutting of channels or scooping) is relatively rare. But a common offense is cutting a channel for a fish trap in a dike between one's own field and another's plot that causes water to escape from the latter. Another and different example of negligent acts was the thoughtless behavior of one West Svay villager who, in preparation for harvesting, drained the water from his plot into an adjacent field belonging to someone else where bundles of already harvested rice became completely soaked.

As a parenthetical but not unimportant point on another topic, it might be noted that there are very few magico-religious observances connected with rice cultivation in West Svay.[32] In previous years at the time of the Buddhist Pchum Festival, objects called *cróm* were placed in the rice fields to obtain a good harvest. These *cróm* were bamboo poles with a sort of woven basket at the top that was encircled with chicken heads and filled with cakes and rice.[33] But this practice was discontinued about seven

---

[30] The rudimentary irrigation techniques in contemporary Cambodia are in marked contrast to the impressive hydraulic system of ancient Angkor (see Groslier 1957, 24–25, 40–41; 1958, 108–12; Delvert 1961, 224). At the present time, the Khmer peasant drains or fills the fields by means of the water scoop (as in Svay), in some areas the water wheel, and in a few regions simple canals (see Delvert 1961, 224–26, 354). Irrigation techniques are, however, more developed among the *chamkar* cultivators of the riverbanks (see Delvert 1961, 389–94).

[31] In cases where the plaintiff is extremely angry or the damage is great, the chief orders the offender to pay the plaintiff a sum of money requested by the latter. But if neither anger nor damage is great, the chief will try simply to mollify the plaintiff and chastise the offender. See also nineteenth-century law codes (in Leclère 1898, 1:370, 397, 400) in which inadvertent or deliberate theft of water from someone else's field, or allowing water to enter another's paddy without permission, was punished by various fines.

[32] I do not know how exceptional West Svay is in this respect. Porée-Maspero et al. 1950, Delvert 1961, and especially Porée-Maspero 1962a note a variety of observances and rituals associated with rice cultivation. It is not altogether certain, however, how many and to what extent the practices discussed by Mme. Porée-Maspero in her extensive study of "rites agraires" (1962a) are actually observed by contemporary Khmer villagers.

[33] A similar custom is noted by Porée-Maspero et al. 1950, 56 and Delvert 1961, 343; the latter speaks of this practice as giving "soul to the rice."

years ago because it necessitated killing chickens (whose entrails were examined for omens of the coming year), which is a sin in Buddhist teaching, and because the practice was also expensive. At the present time there are only two magico-religious procedures in West Svay. First, there is a belief that *neak taa* spirits (see chapter 5) inhabit the rice fields, and these are sometimes enjoined to prevent crabs from cutting the stalks of young rice seedlings (see also Delvert 1961, 357). Second, in the event of prolonged drought, the villagers may hold a ceremony in which monks from a nearby temple are invited to a meal and requested to pray to the Buddha for relief. Also, offerings of fruit and incense are taken to the shrine of a local *neak taa* spirit who is asked for aid. It is not altogether clear exactly why cultivation in West Svay is evidently more "secular" than in other areas. Some traditional practices (e.g., the *cròm*) have been dropped for one reason or another. But another important point seems to be that, for all their assorted worries, West Svay inhabitants are fundamentally optimistic about their crop. For when they are questioned about certain ritual observances in other areas, the villagers reply that such things are done in regions of very poor soil where there is cause for real uncertainty about an adequate crop, or when other circumstances endanger the rice, but that in West Svay one could be generally assured of a sufficient harvest.

It might also be mentioned that two other important activities take place in the rice fields between transplanting and harvest, though they do not involve cultivation. The first is fishing in the rice paddies, and the second is cutting grasses on the dikes to take home as fodder for cattle (see sections below on "Fishing" and on "Animal Husbandry").

## (VII) Harvesting (*cruut*)

By the first of December the fields have changed color again from the radiant deep greens of growing rice to the dusty, yellowish-green brown of mature rice. The rainy season draws to a close at this time. There are still rains (usually at night) in the first half of November, but they become infrequent by the end of the month. The rains of early November are necessary for a good crop, but late showers can be hazardous to the rice and create dismay for the farmer. Not only do the night rains dampen the open grain buds and wash away the pollen (Delvert 1961, 47), but they may also beat the heavy, ripe grain heads on their slender stalks into the water (such soaked grain breaks easily when milled and is "not tasty" though edible). Rain is a nuisance immediately after harvest as well because sheaves of rice left in the fields for threshing will become dampened and must be dried out before threshing can take place.

Harvesting in West Svay proceeds at a leisurely pace from November through the beginning of January, with the bulk of the crop reaped during December (cf. Delvert 1961, 347). In preparation for harvesting, a field is often (but not always) drained of water (if the water has not disappeared naturally), because it makes the work easier. Also, a long bamboo pole is usually swept through the rice so that the stalks are shoved over to lie at an angle to the ground and facilitate harvesting, though sometimes the rice is left standing straight. The actual reaping is done by a sickle (*kandiu* or *kdiu*), which in Svay is usually a graceful wooden implement in the shape of an S that has a short, serrated metal blade set into one of the curves that serves as a handle (see also Delvert 1961, 226–337; Porée-Maspero 1962a, 29, 31–32). Holding the sickle in the right hand, the top curve of the S is used to gather or pull up a bunch of plants that is grasped with the left hand; the sickle is then skillfully flipped over so that the blade can be pulled toward the body to sever the stalks. (A good length of stalk is left attached to the grain head because of the nature of the threshing process—see below). The rice is then tied into loose sheaves that are usually left lying in the fields if the ground is dry, or brought home.

Reaping is done by both males and females, but more usually women since men do most of the threshing. Large cooperative work groups for harvesting are common in other communities (see Delvert 1961, 344) and were seen occasionally in the other hamlets of Svay. But harvesting can proceed at a more gradual pace than transplanting because the grain ripens at different times in different fields, and, once matured, can be left standing for at least a while (though there is the problem of ripe grains coming loose and falling to the ground). Thus, in West Svay, there are some small cooperative work groups made up of friends and kinsmen (usually no more than half a dozen people), but harvesting is more commonly done by household labor alone. The women in a family often go off to the fields in the morning with mats and food and work there until suppertime, the children playing while the adult and adolescent females harvest. Delvert (1961, 345) estimates that, using only family labor, about ten days are needed to harvest one hectare of land.

If one's holdings are large or adequate labor power is not available, harvesters may be hired from other villages. The wages are calculated in terms of the number of sheaves harvested, whether or not the field is dry or still wet, and if the workers need to be fed and housed. The usual rate is twenty-five riels per *slŭk* for harvesting a dry field and sixty riels per *slŭk* for a wet field (which is harder to work in), without food or lodgings; if the latter are provided, the rate is less (see also Delvert 1961, 486).

### (VIII) Threshing

If the rice is dry, threshing can proceed at once. If, however, the grain has been harvested from wet fields or has been dampened by rain, it must be dried out for one or two days before threshing. The ideal pattern is, if possible, to harvest during the earlier part of the day and thresh in the late afternoon or cool of the night. But actually, threshing goes on at any time that is convenient: a family may take food to the fields and thresh throughout the day; or a villager may thresh when any free moment is available. The threshing is generally done in the fields (on dry ground), though it may also be carried on at one's house. This work is mainly the task of the adult and adolescent males, but it is not unusual to see females threshing if their husbands or brothers are tired or occupied with other chores. There is a moderate amount of cooperative labor exchange for threshing with groups of from two to half a dozen or more persons aiding one another in turn (the owner of the rice being threshed provides his helpers with cigarettes and food). But much of the work is done by household labor alone, especially when the holdings are not extensive.

In West Svay the method of threshing is *bauk srau* in which the rice is flailed against a wooden board.[34] This board (*kdaa bauk*), measuring about twenty by forty inches, is set up at about a 45-degree angle to the ground (resting on a leg that holds

---

[34] Delvert (1961, 345) indicates that this method of threshing is predominant in the region southwest of Phnom Penh and is related to smallholdings that average less than two hectares per household. Another means of threshing that is common throughout Cambodia (but not used in Svay) is trampling by cattle (see Delvert 1961, 345–46 for details). It is interesting that one oxen trampling the rice evidently does not thresh any greater quantity of grain than does one man using the *bauk srau* method (ibid.).

it at a slant). A sheaf of rice is gripped in an object called a *dombièt*: two cylindrical handles of wood or bamboo held together by a length of palm fiber rope that is twisted tightly around the end of a bunch of rice stalks. The sheaf is raised over the head and slammed down repeatedly against the board until the kernels fall off onto mats that have been laid down on flat ground. The denuded sheaves are thrown to the side, later to be used as fodder for cattle. The rice that accumulates on the mat is swept up by women into a pile; bits of straw in the rice are picked out and shaken or rubbed to make certain that all the grain has come off them. The rice is then carried home in baskets for drying, winnowing, and storage. Delvert (1961, 345–46) states that this method of threshing can yield 150–250 kilograms of rice per day, and that threshing and transporting the grain from one hectare of land takes about eight days (using only family labor).

Another means of separating grain from the stalk is used at the beginning of the harvest season when only part of the crop is ripe and a few bunches of rice are brought home at a time. The plants are laid on a mat and kneaded with one's feet to remove the kernels. This procedure, called *bain srau* is obviously practicable only for threshing small amounts of rice (see also Delvert 1961, 345–46).

### (IX) Winnowing, Storage, and Milling

A. Winnowing (*roy*). In West Svay there are several means of winnowing (done by the women).[35] (1) A basket of grain is held over one's head and the rice poured to the ground so that wind can blow away the chaff. (2) A round, flat, woven tray is filled with grain and shaken so that the rice is thrown up, down, and around to catch the wind that carries off the chaff. (3) There is a simple but effective winnowing machine, called a *tbal bok*.[36] This device consists of what is essentially a large, rectangular, wooden box; it is open at one end and has a paddle-wheel arrangement at the other end that is turned by a crank to create, in effect, a miniature wind tunnel. While one person pours rice into a funnel at the top of the box, another person (often a man) turns the crank to produce the artificial wind that blows the chaff out the open end; the grain then falls through slots in the bottom of the box onto a mat underneath the machine. Two families in West Svay own a *tbal bok*, and both freely and frequently lend their machines to other villagers.

B. Storage. Once winnowed, the rice is ready for storage in individual household granaries: either large woven containers or holds constructed of mats tied together. They are usually placed underneath the house (raised on small platforms), though sometimes rice is kept within the house itself or, more rarely, in a separate shed. Smaller bins and baskets are also used to keep different kinds of rice separate, and sometimes each of the different nuclear family units within an extended family

---

[35] The first two of these methods are common throughout Cambodia (Delvert 1961, 346). Delvert does not, however, mention the winnowing machine, so I am uncertain how widespread its use is.

[36] The *tbal bok* first came to West Svay villagers' attention about twenty years ago. A "rotary winnowing machine with crank handle" is said to have been known in China as early as 40 BC, while it did not reach Europe until about fourteen centuries later (Singer, Holmyard, and Hall 1956, 98, 770), so this device may have been introduced to Cambodia by Chinese immigrants. A picture of an English winnowing machine in Singer, Holmyard, and Hall 1958, 10, fig. 8, is very similar to the Khmer winnower.

household will store its rice in separate containers. Also, seed for the next year's crop is usually put aside separately. Although the villagers attempt to construct fairly sturdy granaries, during the storage period there is some small loss of rice due to depredations of ants, rats (though the cats in the hamlet seem to keep the rodent population at a low level), and chickens.

Delvert (1961, 346) calculates that three days are needed for drying and storing the rice from one hectare of land (this presumably includes the process of winnowing as well).

C. Milling. As the need arises, small amounts of rice for eating are taken from the granary and spread out on mats to dry for four or five hours before it is dehusked (*kŭn srau*). Nowadays in West Svay the milling process is accomplished by no more effort than carrying the rice several hundred yards down the road to Ta Chas where some Chinese operate a motor-driven milling machine; the millers exact no payment for their service because they keep the rice husks to sell as food for pigs.[37]

More traditional implements for dehusking and polishing rice are still extant in the village though they are rarely used anymore. These are (1) a large wooden mortar and pestle (*tbal bok*), (2) the *tbal kŭn*, a hand-operated device that scrapes the paddy between two flat cylinders with corrugated surfaces, and (3) the *tbal cŭen*, a sort of gigantic mortar and pestle in which the pestle is set into one end of a huge trunk of wood that is balanced as a lever; when one steps on and off the end of this trunk, the pestle is pounded into a cement- and pebble-lined hole in the ground. There is also the *tbal kŭn msau* that makes rice flour by pounding the grain between two heavy stone slabs.[38] (See Delvert 1961, 228–29 for details of the construction of these devices.)

### (X) Bringing in the Hay and Application of Fertilizer

Two final tasks remain to complete the annual cycle of cultivation. First, the great quantity of dried rice stalks (*cambaung*) left piled in the fields after threshing must be brought home to use as fodder for cattle. The fields become worn with ruts and the dikes are broken through as carts bring back tremendous loads of hay that are stacked in enormous banks near each house.

Second, with the fields now cleared and returned to dry stubble, some fertilizers are put out (especially on those fields that do not receive much water). At this time of year the common fertilizers are cow dung (collected from wherever the animals are pastured or tethered); the heads, tails, and bones of fish that are now plentiful; and rice husks.

With these chores disposed of, the work of rice cultivation is completed for the year. (In 1959 in West Svay, everything was finished by the end of January). The next few months are usually a time of relative leisure for the villagers. There are always other tasks to be done: making fish paste, sewing fresh thatch to repair houses, going to cut grass for oxen, making palm sugar, etc. But the village has a relaxed air, and this is also a period of pleasures: trips to visit relatives, weddings, the traveling theater, spirit possession ceremonies, and not the least, the joyous celebration of the

[37] Delvert (1961, 229, 338, 347) notes that mechanical huskers and "rizeries" have multiplied in the countryside since 1954 and that the peasants are making increasing use of them.

[38] These implements are virtually identical to ones used in Thailand; see Kaufman 1960, appendix; Rajadhon 1961, appendix following chap. 1; pics. nos. 39–41, 47.

Cambodian New Year in April. The weather changes as well. In January and February the afternoons can still be warm, but in the early morning hours the villagers shiver around small fires and wrap their thin cotton scarves around them. But in March and April, the weather again grows hot and muggy. And in May, with the first tentative rains, the annual cycle of rice cultivation begins again.

According to various estimates, the various activities of the agricultural cycle just described require from sixty to more than eighty days of work to farm one hectare of land, using family labor and two oxen.[39] To summarize the figures mentioned previously:

|  | Delvert's estimate[a] | Baudoin's estimate[b] |
|---|---|---|
| Two plowings | 10 days | 16 days |
| Two harrowings | 3 days | 8 days |
| Preparation of nursery bed, sowing, and maintenance | 8 days | 2 days |
| Pulling seedlings, transporting plants | 3 days | 20 days |
| Transplanting | 15 days | |
| Harvesting | 10 days | 20 days |
| Threshing, transporting grain | 8 days | 16 days |
| Drying rice and storing it in granaries | 3 days | [no figure] |
| Total | 60 days | 82 days |

[a] Delvert 1961, 347.

[b] M. F. Baudoin, *La Culture du Riz au Cambodge* (no date or publisher is given), cited in Delvert 1961, 348, and passim. Delvert (ibid.) notes another estimate of seventy days given by M. Robbe, head of the Mission Française d'Aide Economique in Cambodia. (See also Wolf 1966, 28, for figures on cultivation in Japan and China.)

Two points should be noted regarding these estimates. First, Delvert states that Baudoin's figures (and by implication, his own) hold true only for "exploitations groupées" and must be increased when the fields are parceled. Second, Delvert's (and perhaps Baudoin's) estimates do not take account of cooperative labor exchanges. Perhaps, however, whatever amount of time is saved by having help is used in returning such aid, the main object of such mutual cooperation being to accomplish certain tasks (especially plowing and transplanting) as quickly as possible within a certain space of time.

Even if one takes the higher estimate of days for cultivating one hectare of land, and if one notes that many villagers in West Svay have less than this amount of land (and hence less work), the total number of days expended on rice cultivation seems like a small proportion of the entire year. (Hence lending apparent credence

---

[39] By "days" Delvert implies a work day of about eight hours. The number of members in the "family labor" force is not specified.

to frequent naive comments about the indolence of the Khmer peasantry.) It must be remembered, however, that much of the work is extremely arduous (often almost literally backbreaking) in view of the simple technology, and also that certain stages of cultivation (e.g., transplanting) require tremendous expenditure of effort within a brief period of time, such that subsequent respite is both needed and deserved. Furthermore, West Svay and numerous other villages in the "central provinces" cannot depend on rice cultivation alone for subsistence but must use periods of relative leisure (before and after harvest) for other activities that earn needed cash income or procure other food (e.g., temporary urban employment, gardening, fishing, etc.). Obviously, too, time is needed for other necessary chores such as house repairs, obtaining food for cattle, and the like.

### YIELD AND USES OF RICE

Villagers estimate that their yield per hectare is about forty *tang* (880 kilograms or 34 bushels) in an average year, about fifty *tang* (1,100 kilograms or 47.5 bushels) in a good year, and about sixty *tang* (1,320 kilograms or 51 bushels) in an excellent year.[40] But the 1959 harvest in West Svay was considered by almost all the inhabitants to be only a fair crop with the blame placed on inadequate rainfall. This particular year's yield averaged about thirty-one *tang* (682 kilograms or 26 bushels) per hectare, about two-thirds the crop of an ordinary to good year, and one-half that of a superior harvest.[41] Given, then, the average size landholding in West Svay of 0.88 hectares per household, the hypothetical average family had twenty-seven *tang* (594 kilograms, 23 bushels) of rice to store in its granaries in 1959. Such an average can be misleading, however, and it must be emphasized that it is deduced from a wide spectrum of yields ranging from a meager fifteen *tang* harvested by several households with smallholdings to about two hundred *tang* gathered from the four hectares belonging to House 27 (of which one-half was kept by various sharecroppers). The varying amounts of rice garnered by each family depends on the size of its holdings, the quality of the soil, the type of rice planted, and the amount of water and fertilizer that nourished the crop.

This harvest was by no means the worst that West Svay had ever experienced, but there were memories of some other years when there had been enough rice for a number of households to sell part of their crop. In 1959 the general mood of the villagers was rather heavy-hearted. Some residents shook their heads and said, "There will be

---

[40] The villagers' calculation seems fairly accurate in view of Delvert's (1961, 357–58) statement that the national average yield is about 1,000 kilograms per hectare, with annual yields varying from about 450 to 2,000 kilograms per hectare, depending on the soil in different regions of the country (see also 674–75). Ginsburg 1958, 314; Zadrozny 1955, 264; Morizon 1936, 101; and Baker 1958, 9 also give similar estimates (cf. Steinberg 1959, 199 who gives half a ton). The Cambodian yield is roughly similar to that of other Southeast Asian nations, though much less than that of Japan (see table in Fisher 1964, 73, based on a United Nations economic survey; N.B., however, that the figure given for Cambodia in this table is very misleading because the particular year noted, 1954–55, had an unusually bad harvest due to poor rainfall [Steinberg 1959, 198]).

[41] According to persons in the Agricultural Division of the United States Overseas Mission (Gaylord Walker, pers. comm.) and the Economic Division of the United States Embassy (William Thomas, pers. comm.) in Phnom Penh, in 1959 the rainfall was generally normal and the crop was average to good in Cambodia as a whole, except parts of Kandal, Kompong Speu, and Pursat provinces.

just enough rice to eat and to save for next year's planting." For other families, it was clear that their granaries would be exhausted in short order. West Svay has, then, basically a subsistence rather than market economy; the rice is grown primarily for direct consumption by the family and is sold only occasionally or in small amounts by relatively few households.[42] Rice also serves purposes other than food alone, making it further unlikely that most families will have enough surplus to put on the market. An examination of the different uses to which rice is put will make clear why West Svay has largely a subsistence economy.

(1) Rice for food. Rice is the staple of the Cambodian diet and the basic component of every meal: in West Svay, rice gruel (*bóbóó*) is served at breakfast and the midday meal as well among poorer families, while boiled rice (*bay*)[43] is eaten at the evening meal and sometimes as a replacement for gruel at the midday meal if one can afford it; the hard, burned crust left in a pot after cooking rice is often munched on as a snack; and a variety of sweets and cakes made from glutinous rice for special events or simply as an occasional treat are always eagerly devoured when available.

Estimates of rice consumption given by the villagers indicate that an adult eats about one to one and a half *tau* (about 15–22.5 kilograms) of milled rice per month, or about 180–270 kilograms per year.[44] This is substantially in accord with Delvert's (1961, 154) estimate of rice consumption in Cambodia of 600–700 grams per person per day or about 220 kilograms per year (see also Clark and Haswell 1964, 79). The consumption per household is more difficult to average because of the variables involved. The amount of rice eaten will vary according to (a) family size and age/sex composition (e.g., the very young and old usually eat less than able adults, and men probably eat more than women), and (b) the size of the crop relative to the number of mouths to feed: those families who have smallholdings, many persons to nourish, or have suffered a bad harvest will eat more sparingly than those who are more fortunate, or than in a year of abundant harvest. But in broad terms, rice consumption in West Svay ranges from a low of thirty-six *tau* (540 kilograms) per year in the smallest households of two to three adults, to a high of seventy-two or more *tau* (1,080 kilograms) per year for the largest families of two adults and five or six children (cf. Delvert 1961, 346, 360 who gives a higher estimate of household consumption). Thus, given the small landholdings, most West Svay families produce barely enough rice to eat in normal years, while some never do (and must therefore earn cash income by various means in order to buy rice for food). And in a year such as 1959 with a less than normal crop, the majority of households would undoubtedly eat up their entire supply of rice before the next annual harvest was ready.

---

[42] This is evidently true for the majority of Cambodian rice cultivators. The bulk of the total amount of rice grown in Cambodia is for family consumption (and other needs). Most of the grain that is marketed and exported comes from certain regions (Zadrozny 1955, 256, 264; Steinberg 1959, 198; Delvert 1961, 329, 360; Dobby 1960, 314). Subsistence agriculture is also the rule for about two-thirds of Southeast Asia as a whole, according to Dobby (1960, 349–50).

[43] Rice has several terms depending on its condition: growing rice or unhusked rice is *srau*; rice that has been milled but is uncooked is *ónkóó*; and ordinary cooked rice is *bay*. (See also Porée-Maspero 1962a, 18–19, 26–27.)

[44] Milled rice (*ónkóó*) has terms of measurement different from those for unhusked rice (*srau*). The former is calculated in terms of *tau*, which Delvert (1961, 12) says is approximately fifteen kilograms. Villagers say that two *tau* of *srau* (unhusked rice) are equivalent to one *tau* of milled rice.

(2) Rice for seed. As indicated previously, a certain amount of rice is set aside after each harvest for the next year's sowing (though it may well be eaten before then). From three to five *tang* (66–110 kilograms) are needed to provide seedlings for a hectare of land.

(3) Rice for religious contributions and ceremonials. It is highly likely that at some time(s) during the year, a family will use some of its rice for religious or ceremonial purposes. Only two or three households give daily alms of a few spoonfuls of cooked rice to mendicant monks from Wat Svay. But on various Buddhist holidays when virtually all families take special foods to the monks, the dish prepared is frequently a glutinous rice delicacy. Also, after the harvest there is the Ceremony to Make a Mountain of Rice (held annually by Wat Svay and occasionally by Wat Samnang) in which many West Svay villagers contribute whatever paddy they can afford (ranging from a few handfuls to a basket or more) to the temple, which then sells the rice to obtain money for its building fund.

Apart from these contributions to gain religious merit, a family may have occasion to sponsor some private ceremony, such as a life-cycle celebration or a ceremony to cure illness. Such events necessitate a large or small expenditure of rice: to feed guests, to give offerings to spirits, or to fulfill certain ceremonial procedures that require, for example, ritual bowls of rice.

(4) Rice as a money substitute. Because most village families rarely have much ready cash on hand, rice is often used as a substitute for money in both purchases and the payment of debts. Payment by rice rather than currency, which is called *doo*, is used mainly for relatively small purchases. When such "barter" is used, the rice is measured out by any of a variety of objects ranging from tin cans to certain kinds of baskets; each of these is a standardized proportion of a *tau* of paddy, with the *tau* evaluated at twenty-five riels in 1959. Sometimes, too, the vendor may set up certain equivalences, such as asking for one basket of rice in return for two (of the same size) baskets of fish (see also Delvert 1961, 171). Rice is also commonly used in repaying debts and their interest, whether one has borrowed rice or money. Although large-scale indebtedness is not widespread in West Svay, it does happen that most or virtually all of an unfortunate household's crop is carted away immediately after harvest by creditors.

(5) Rice for sale. Only one household in West Svay, the aged couple in House 27 with their four hectares of fields, can expect to sell a sizable quantity of rice every year. Among the other residents of the hamlet, the sale of rice is only occasional or limited for some families and a distinct impossibility for others. Those with a hectare or more of land might be able to sell very small amounts (several *tang*) of rice in an average year, or somewhat larger quantities if the crop has been abundant; while those with two hectares of land can expect to market more frequently and in greater quantity. For example, House 1 with one hectare of land sold about one-third of their crop (approximately twenty *tang*) for 1,000 riels in 1957; and House 9 with two hectares of land sold almost half their harvest (about forty *tang*) for 2,000 riels in 1958 (both years had relatively good yields). But neither one of these households nor anyone else in the hamlet sold any rice in 1959, except land-rich House 27, which sold about forty *tang* of rice for over 2,000 riels shortly after harvest and would probably sell additional small amounts to fellow villagers in the course of the coming year.

Rice may be sold to fellow villagers (usually in small quantities), or more commonly to Sino-Cambodian merchants from the neighboring village of Sandan, or sometimes to Khmer rice brokers who come from other regions.[45] (In previous years, villagers sometimes took rice directly to Phnom Penh to market it, thus eliminating the middleman; but in 1959 a new ordinance prohibited carts from entering the city so that transport became somewhat of a problem although buses are available.)[46] The price of rice is dependent, of course, on several factors: the international rice market, the nature of the harvest in the country as a whole, the type and quality of rice (glutinous rice and certain varieties of ordinary rice are more expensive), and the time of selling (rice is cheapest at harvest time). In 1959, the merchants from Sandan were paying 1,000 riels for nineteen *tang* of average quality, ordinary rice in the month after harvest.[47] (By way of comparison, twenty *tang* of rice sold for 1,000 riels in the previous year, and only ten *tang* commanded the same price about four years ago when the crop was extremely poor throughout Cambodia.) The villagers calculate that, on the average, one *tang* of paddy is worth about fifty riels (cf. Delvert 1961, 360, 517, passim, who usually values a *tang* at forty riels). If a villager sells rice later on in the year, he will obtain a higher price: for example, one might get 100 riels for two *tang* of rice right after the harvest, but the same sum for only one and a half *tang* if he waits until May. But most people sell immediately after the harvest because they have limited storage capacity and because they fear that their store of rice will be somehow depleted (e.g., from profligate eating or from pillage by insects, chickens, and rats) if it is not marketed at once. As Delvert points out, the villagers sell their rice under the worst conditions: (1) they sell at harvest time when prices are lowest (and for other regions where the harvest is late, in February or March, the situation is even worse because the international market is saturated with rice at this time); (2) they sell to local merchants because they lack means of transporting great quantities of rice elsewhere; and (3) the price is fixed by the merchant or broker, and "the pressed and ignorant peasant can scarcely debate it" (1961, 512).[48]

To mitigate such problems, the Royal Office of Cooperation (concerned with providing fair credit and cooperatives for the peasantry and small-scale artisans) has been interested in building cooperatives at which the farmer could get equitable returns for his crop; but as of 1955 there were only three rice cooperatives in the country (for further details, see Steinberg 1959, 191–93, 207–9). Shortly before my departure from

---

[45] Heng (House 21) was a small-scale rice broker in his younger days. Traveling to neighboring districts and provinces (such as Tonle Bati and Kompong Speu), he would go to villagers in October and November to lend money to whoever needed it and return in January for payment of the debt (and interest) in rice. He would then either use the rice for family consumption or sell it in Svay and neighboring villages (but not in Phnom Penh). He dealt in very limited amounts of rice, perhaps only fifteen to twenty *tang* a year, but he claims he made almost a 100 percent profit on his small ventures. For discussion of Chinese and Sino-Cambodian merchants and rice brokers, and some of the operations of marketing rice, see Delvert 1961, 510–14.

[46] According to Delvert (1961, 515), in recent years peasants living in the regions near the capital city have begun to sell their rice directly to Phnom Penh, thanks to the increased means of transportation and the increased tendency for villagers to live directly on and near roadways.

[47] These merchants expected to sell milled rice in Phnom Penh for fifty-eight to fifty-nine riels a *tau*. Since nineteen *tang* of paddy is equivalent to nineteen *tau* of milled rice, this meant that they would make a profit of 102–21 riels on the rice they bought from House 27 if they sold immediately. (For listing of wholesale and retail prices of rice in Phnom Penh in 1959–60 and earlier years, see Ministère du Plan 1961, 82–83; 1958, 100, 102.)

[48] Such problems of marketing produce are common among peasantry in general; see Wolf 1966, 45.

Svay in early 1960, there was talk that a building being constructed near Wat Samnang was to be a rice cooperative where villagers could sell their rice for good prices, but I do not know if this cooperative ever went into operation.

## OTHER SOURCES OF FOOD

### GARDENS AND TREES

Apart from rice, the only other agricultural activity in West Svay is the cultivation of kitchen gardens and fruit (and other) trees that are a limited but important source of food and other products for the villagers. All except five families have a garden plot (or plots) near the house that, depending upon the amount of village land owned by a household and upon its interest in gardening, range in size from the tiniest patches of only a few square feet to extensive plots that grow a variety of flora. Fruit and other trees are usually located near the house, but they are also scattered in random profusion that gives the village a refreshing verdant appearance and provides welcome shade. Several of these trees (especially the palms) are also found on the dikes of the rice fields and in the uncleared land bordering the hamlet.

In contrast to (or perhaps because of) the arduous labor and concern devoted to rice cultivation, minimal effort is given to the growing of fruits and vegetables. The trees are all relatively mature and well established; they get no attention whatever except that small, wicker baskets are sometimes tied over the fruits of certain trees to prevent depredations by birds. Gardens do require some toil: the ground is broken with hoes and spades; seeds or shoots are planted at the proper times if necessary; cow dung fertilizer is sometimes applied; some minimal weeding may be done; and the plants are watered during the dry season.

From these gardens and trees, the villagers obtain a variety of herbs (e.g., basil, mint, peppers), vegetables (e.g., potatoes, gourds, beans, cucumbers), and especially fruits (e.g., mangoes, bananas, papayas, guavas, oranges) (see appendix F). All are welcome additions to the diet, whether used as flavoring or condiments, eaten in pristine state or mixed into various dishes. The sugar palm and coconut also provide liquid that can be drunk fresh, fermented or boiled into sugar in the case of the sugar palm, or used in cooking certain dishes. Some serve additional purposes as well. Several flora are used for medicines as well as food.[49] The sugar palm provides leaves for house thatch, mats, and containers of all sorts, as well as fiber for rope and brooms. Empty coconut husks are handy kitchen utensils, used as scoops, dishes, and spoons. Banana leaves wrap foodstuffs for carrying or cooking, substitute for cigarette paper, and decorate ceremonial objects; the trunks are also fed to pigs and used to fashion items used in rituals (see Porée-Maspero et al. 1950, 11–12; 1958, 16 for details of the latter).

Several non-edible flora are also grown in the village: betel (and some areca), bamboo, kapok, and *makløė*. The latter is a tree with berries that, when mashed and soaked in water, produce a blue-black dye for clothes (see also Delvert 1961, 145–47). Kapok is often left unharvested and used simply as kindling. Bamboo is one of the most important components of village material culture: it provides fences, flooring,

---

[49] E.g., mint and basil mixed with other ingredients are pounded and boiled in water for a "hot body"; guava is cooked and the liquid drunk for stomachaches; sweet sop bark is pounded, mixed with liquid, and drunk for diarrhea.

buckets, poles and frames for carrying baskets, fish traps and poles, filters, handles of tools, "threads" to sew thatch together, woven containers, etc. The young shoots may also be eaten but are more often left to grow because the mature plant is so valuable for uses other than food. Rather, it is common for groups of people to travel six or seven kilometers to gather young shoots from bamboo growing wild in an uninhabited area.

Obviously not every household cultivates all these flora. But the products of any one family are often generously shared with kinsmen and neighbors (given especially to small children who inevitably congregate wherever fruit is being gathered), or sometimes sold in small quantities to fellow villagers. Occasionally, if a surplus occurs, it may be taken to be sold at the market in Kompong Tuol; but, in general, the harvest from garden and trees is for family and local consumption.[50]

It should be noted that, in addition to cultivated plants and trees, there is a great profusion of wild flora that grow unattended. These grasses, vines, cacti, ferns, bushes, and trees are found primarily in a tangled growth covering the uncleared land to the east and west of the hamlet; but some also grow on the dikes of the rice paddies (or even in the fields themselves during the dry season). Some of these flora are utilized: the various grasses serve as pasture for cattle; a number of plants or trees are components of medicinal potions or dressings; certain woods are suitable for making various objects; and some plants or tree fruits are edible.

## Fishing

Next to rice, fish (*trèy*) is the second most important ingredient of the villagers' diet, eaten in a variety of ways: fresh, dried, or smoked; grilled, stewed, or boiled in soup; mashed into a paste or refined into oil. Delvert (1961, 155) estimates the annual consumption of fish at about twenty kilograms per person (as contrasted to perhaps less than half that amount of meat). Because it is eaten the year round and at almost every meal in one form or another, fish must often be purchased at the Chinese shop, the market in town, or from traveling vendors. But from about August, fish can be caught in the flooded rice fields until the harvest or in any of three water holes bordering the hamlet until about February.[51]

Several fishing techniques are used in West Svay. (1) Line-and-hook fishing (*santut* or *stuut trèy*) is the simplest and one of the most frequently utilized methods because it can be practiced by children as well as adults, and because it is a pleasant as well as profitable way to while away a hot afternoon or enjoy the cool evening. The equipment is rudimentary: a bamboo pole or any suitable piece of wood, string, a floater made from a piece of a plant, a metal hook (either made from a scrap of wire or a manufactured hook purchased at the market), and bait of fish paste, rice, or sometimes a frog. (2) The *truu* (or *tuu*) is a long, cylindrical fish trap made of bamboo with a funnel-shaped entrance for the fish, and its use is widespread. It is placed in a channel cut in the dike of a rice paddy and left overnight or throughout the day. (As noted in a previous section, the setting of such traps often leads to quarrels when they cause

---

[50] In the neighboring village of Ta Chas, some rice farmers also cultivate a fairly large quantity of maize that is destined primarily for the market. See Delvert 1961, 365–70 for kinds of secondary cultivations (apart from kitchen gardens) practiced by rice farmers elsewhere in Cambodia.

[51] I do not know the scientific names of the fish caught in Svay, but see Delvert 1961, 150 for some of the common species of fish in Cambodia.

water to drain out from someone else's paddy.) (3) The *ȯnrut* (or *ėnwhut*) is another type of fish trap, shaped rather like a rounded lampshade made of bamboo, with the top and bottom open.[52] The *ȯnrut* is plunged into the water to catch a fish within the wicker enclosure, and the creature is seized by hand through the opening in the top. (4) The large tray-shaped wicker filters that are used in processing palm sugar can also be utilized for scooping up small fish while wading in shallow water. (5) Though there are no special fishing nets in Svay, some resourceful villagers have been known to use old mosquito nets to catch fish. (6) Finally, the two small water holes directly south of the hamlet are usually drained in January or February to make certain that most of the fish (especially the large ones) are caught. The water is scooped out by a large bucket or gasoline drum suspended at the end of two long ropes by two men. When the water hole is almost completely dry, any remaining fish are caught by hand. After Nen's (House 23) water hole was drained, men, women, and children from the hamlet swarmed into the mud in a wild scramble after the fish, and a family was allowed to keep all small fish and one of any large fish they captured. All other good-sized fish, however, were turned over to Nen who gave generously of them to four men who helped him drain the hole; he himself ended with about half a gasoline drum full of fish. (Water was then made to flow back into the hole because it is used frequently for washing cattle and bathing, as well as fishing again the next year.)

If not consumed immediately in various dishes, most of the fish thus caught (especially the small ones) are made into *prahuėk* (commonly transcribed as *prahoc* in the French literature). This is a salted, fermented fish paste that is one of the essential ingredients of Cambodian cuisine, whether eaten plain or used as a component of various dishes and soups. (It also has excellent nutritional value since it is a fine source of protein, calcium, iodine, and has greater nitrogen and phosphoric acid content than does fresh meat or dried fish [Zadrozny 1955, 232; Delvert 1961, 151]). Because a supply of *prahuėk* is a necessity for every household, many families also purchase fresh fish for this purpose, usually from Chinese or Vietnamese (sometimes Cham or Khmer) vendors who travel from village to village in January with truckloads of fish.[53] About two containers of fresh fish are required to make one container of paste. The little fish are cut into small pieces, mixed with water, mashed and kneaded by hand, heavily salted, spread out to dry in the sun for a day, pounded in a mortar with more salt, and packed into earthenware jars that are left to dry again in the sun for about two days (cf. also Delvert 1961, 150–51 and Gourou 1945, 407–8 on making paste). When the fish have been thus treated and put into containers, fermentation occurs and allows the paste to be kept as long as a year or more (though a family's supply is usually exhausted before that time elapses). There is also a liquid (*tůk trėy*), the

---

[52] For details of the construction of both the *ȯnrut* and *truu*, see Delvert 1961, 164–65, and figs. 24 and 26 in the appendix. Both are common throughout Cambodia for subsistence fishing.

[53] In some regions (but not Svay), many villagers journey to the rivers in great caravans during December, January, and February, to buy, barter, or catch their supply of fish for *prahuėk*. On a trip along the Tonle Sap and Mekong rivers in January, I saw great hordes of people along the banks at various points and various stages of *prahuėk* preparation. See also Delvert 1961, 169–71 for a discussion of such fishing expeditions. He does note that such caravans are nowadays less frequent because, among other things, trucks readily transport fish to rural markets, and Vietnamese and Cham fishermen often bring their catches to the peasants. The vendors who came to West Svay were from a region northwest of Phnom Penh on the Tonle Sap River.

Cambodian equivalent of the Vietnamese *nuk-mam,* that collects above the paste and is an important seasoning (fish oil is also often purchased in bottles).

It might be noted here than aquatic fauna other than fish are also sources of food. Primary among them is a small crab that is caught throughout the rainy season in the flooded rice fields by making them clamp onto twigs, by digging where there are evidences of crab holes and tunnels in the mud, or snared in traps set out for fish. The crabs are used to make soups. In the fields and the swampy area south of the hamlet are snails (for soups), frogs (eaten boiled, roasted, or in soups), and snakes (eaten boiled and considered to be tastier than chicken). These latter creatures do not, however, constitute a regular part of the diet and are only occasionally hunted in a deliberate manner (by a poor family or by men and boys as a sort of lark); more often, they are caught simply if one happens to chance upon them.

## OTHER SOURCES OF INCOME: NON-AGRICULTURAL PURSUITS

A village family is self-sufficient to some degree. Rice cultivation, kitchen gardens, fruit trees, and local fishing can provide a fair proportion of a family's food. Numerous implements, tools, house parts, and other material objects are still fabricated by the villagers themselves. But the fruits of the land and the water cannot provide the whole of a family's nourishment; it must buy certain foodstuffs that are not cultivated or not available in sufficient quantity in the hamlet. There is also increasing reliance on manufactured items from the marketplace. In addition, every household has some special needs at certain times, such as the financing of a life-cycle ceremony or the purchase of an ox. The villager therefore has need for some cash. And because the majority of West Svay residents cannot depend on selling a consistent or sizable surplus of rice, they—like numerous other villagers in this region—turn to various part-time or temporary occupations or employment to earn money.[54] This section will discuss various ways of acquiring money: the making of palm sugar, crafts and other specializations, temporary employment in Phnom Penh or elsewhere, and sale of small food items (on the raising of pigs and chickens for sale, see the section below on "Animal Husbandry"), as well as the few full-time non-agricultural occupations held by some men in the village (see also appendix G).

## SUGAR PALM AND FABRICATION OF PALM SUGAR

The lontar or sugar palm (*dam tnaot*) is a characteristic and virtually ubiquitous part of Cambodia's landscape. The tall, slender trunks topped with a burst of long, narrow leaves are seen everywhere around Svay, growing both in and around the village proper and on the dikes of the rice fields where they break the flat monotony of the fields. Each tree is owned individually and transmitted through inheritance or sale. Twenty-five inhabitants (in nineteen households) own a total of about four hundred palms (see appendix G).

When asked what was the most important possession one could have, one villager replied: "The sugar palm. For rice gives only one crop a year; but the *dam tnaot* gives many different things, both to eat and to use, all year around." The sugar palm is

---

[54] Part-time non-agricultural activities to earn money are also common among other Southeast Asian villagers (see, for example, Kaufman 1960, 54–66 on a Thai village, Nash 1965, 214–23 on a Burmese village), as well as among peasantry in general (see Wolf 1966, 45).

indeed one of the richest sources of various products and materials in village life. The leaves are sewn together to make thatching for house walls and roofs, or are woven into mats, bins, boxes, and baskets; the leaf stems yield a fiber that is twisted into rope; dried leaves and stalks are used as fuel (the trees are virtually denuded for this purpose at the end of their annual season); if a tree is cut down, the trunk is sawed into lumber for construction (or sometimes hollowed out into boats in some areas), and the pulp can be fed to livestock. There is also the fruit that is available from late February through May. When hacked open, there are small pulpy sections containing a small amount of liquid that can be eaten or drunk fresh or mixed into various dishes; the seeds are heaped in piles, allowed to germinate for several months, and broken open to eat a soft, sweet meat; and the remainder of the fruit can be fed to livestock. Finally, rootlike structures at the top of the tree give off a juice that can be drunk fresh, fermented into wine, or boiled into palm sugar (see also Vialard-Goudou 1959, 42, and Delvert 1961, chap. 10).

The making of palm sugar (*skòò tnaot*) was in the past, and still is to some extent, a major means of earning income in this region to the south and west of Phnom Penh.[55] Exploitation of the lontar for sugar may have begun shortly after the turn of the century because this area was already densely populated in the late nineteenth century and resources other than rice cultivation were probably sought (Delvert 1961, 301). Some 60 percent of all married men in West Svay have pursued this occupation at some point in their lives. Sugar-palming has become less important in West Svay in recent years for two major reasons: (1) the increasing availability of temporary urban or other employment that is less dangerous if perhaps equally arduous; and (2) a frightening accident several years ago in which a West Svay villager was killed by falling from the top of a tree that he was tapping. (Indeed, in old law codes, any man who worked the sugar palms was exempt from taxes because he was considered virtually dead [Delvert 1961, 292]). In 1959, only four men in the hamlet (all of them poor) were making palm sugar, while in early 1960 no one pursued it because other kinds of temporary employment were available.[56] But it remains a possible source of income for men who are in need and are hardy enough to withstand the labor it requires (see also Delvert 1961, 293, 301).

The season for making palm sugar runs from late October or November through May (approximating the dry season), though a man may not begin collecting sap until January when the rice harvest is over. If a household does not own enough palms of its own to collect sufficient sap, a man may rent palms from other persons for ten riels per tree for the season (for rental fees in other regions, see Delvert 1961, 298; 1958, 102). The trees are climbed by means of long bamboo poles, with small projections at the side, that are lashed to the palm trunk. At the top of the palm are slender, rootlike

---

[55] Also, villagers sometimes sell surplus fruit, germinated seed, or fresh juice to fellow residents, the roadside restaurant operated by House 32, students at the normal school, or in the market at Phnom Penh. Such sales, however, usually net very small amounts of money (e.g., six seeds sell for one riel, a container of juice for eight riels).

[56] Delvert (1961, 299–301) states that sugar palm exploitation is being abandoned throughout Cambodia in favor of other pursuits, especially cottage industries such as weaving and temporary employment in Phnom Penh for the villagers in Kandal province. He feels that the major reason for this decline is the lack of firewood necessary to boil sap into sugar. But in West Svay there did not seem to be a noticeable scarcity of fuel because of the abundant wild flora near the village.

projections that are slashed at the tip to drip juice into hollowed bamboo containers. This occupation is extremely arduous because a man may exploit anywhere from about fifteen to twenty-five trees that are usually scattered in different and sometimes quite distant places, and each tree, which may be thirty to sixty feet high, must be climbed once or twice a day to exchange full containers for empty ones. (On one trip, a man took about an hour and a half to tap seven trees that were about an eight-minute walk from the hamlet.) The juice is brought home and boiled for four to five hours in a huge cast-iron basin (over an earthen stove) until the milky liquid turns into a thick, brown syrup rather like molasses. It is then stirred briskly with a wooden paddle (set into a frame and whirled by ropes wound around its stem) until it becomes somewhat like taffy. Finally, it is scooped into pottery jars where it either solidifies or remains in a semisoft state.

The villagers cannot specify exactly how much liquid one tree produces, the amount of trees and effort required to produce one jar of sugar, the precise number of jars produced per season, or the total sum of money earned from sales, because a man is accustomed to gathering a bit each day from many trees, gradually filling a jar of sugar, and selling one or several jars at a time over a period of months. For example, Cheang can say only that he usually exploits from eighteen to twenty trees a year (usually only from January through May), makes one jar of sugar every three or four days, and produces about fifty or more jars per season.[57] (In some years he produces ninety to one hundred jars a season, but this means tapping must be started in November or December and exhausting effort.) In May 1959, the Chinese merchants in the area paid seventy riels per *pièng* (36 kilograms) of palm sugar.[58] About three of Cheang's jars equal one *pièng*, so on fifty jars he earns about 1,190 riels, minus the expense of fifty riels for renting five trees. Actually, Cheang's rough estimates are substantially in accord with Delvert's calculations of the amount of sugar that one tree can produce (1961, 293–94; see also 296, 298–99 on income and expenditures in making palm sugar).

It is interesting that in January 1960 the Cambodian government took a census of the number of palms owned by families in Svay and other villages in the region, in connection with a plan to begin buying and processing palm sugar itself. At about the same time, the United States Overseas Mission was exploring the possibility of establishing sugar palm cooperatives; and the Fundamental Education project held a meeting for villagers in this area to discuss means of increasing the yield from sugar palms. All these may be attempts to revitalize the exploitation of the sugar palm, a pursuit that is becoming increasingly neglected in Svay and other villages.

## CRAFTS AND OTHER SPECIALIZATIONS

Some villagers are able to earn extra income as craftsmen or practitioners of other skills that require special training or talents. Such specializations, which may be

---

[57] For further details on tapping and the processing of palm sugar, see Delvert 1961, chap. 10; Monod 1931, 47–48; Porée and Maspero 1938, 236–37; Aymonier 1900, 37.

[58] Once sold, the sugar from Svay may go to the market in Kompong Tuol but more likely to Phnom Penh where it may be sold as is for more than 100 riels, or refined further. Refining palm sugar is one of the country's newest industries with the single largest factory in Cambodia employing more than five hundred workers (Steinberg 1959, 214). Much sugar is consumed within the country itself, though in the past a good deal was exported to Vietnam (Ministère du Plan 1958, 124).

acquired through either formal apprenticeship and study or more informally through the instruction of parents and friends, are generally pursued on a part-time basis, for example, during the dry season, other periods when the rice does not need tending, or whenever services are required.

(1) Crafts. The following craftsmen are present in West Svay.

(a) Carpenters (*cièng cun, cièng ptea*). Almost all adult males in the village have at least an elementary and sometimes considerable ability in carpentry. But Daen (House 28) and Rina (House 4) are recognized as professional carpenters with detailed knowledge and skills in the construction of houses (*ptea*) and furniture (*cuun*). Rina considers himself a full-time carpenter. Neither one, however, can derive an assured income from his craft because requests for services are few and far between. Daen fortunately has a wife with considerable land, but Rina (who has no land) leads a penurious existence and is supported partly by a resident son-in-law. (There are also several carpenters in the other hamlets of Svay, including one who earns a steadier income by making rice sickles for local trade and miniature plows for the tourist trade in Phnom Penh.)

(b) Weavers (*neak lèbaing*). Nara (House 20) is the only weaver in West Svay, although there are about half a dozen others in the other hamlets.[59] This is a woman's craft, passed on usually from mothers to daughters. Weaving is done primarily during the dry season (occasionally on spare days during the cultivation season as well), and then for only a few hours a day in Nara's case since she has no pressing need for money. Using a large, rectangular standing loom (see Delvert 1961, 276 for details of the construction), Nara weaves a variety of things: cotton scarves (*kroma*) and several kinds of silk sarongs (including the black *sampot* and the heavy *pramøèng* in rich solid colors). Working at her leisurely pace, it takes Nara about a month to do a scarf, two months for a *sampot*, and several months for a *pramøèng*. Many of her products are made for members of her family, but she occasionally sells to fellow villagers. Her prices are ordinarily about one-third more than the cost of materials: a scarf sells for about 30 riels, a *sampot* for about 200 riels, and a *pramøèng* for about 450 riels (the prices of the latter two vary somewhat according to the cost of silk thread). In 1960 Nara temporarily ceased weaving because she prefers silk to cotton, and silk thread was not available in Phnom Penh.

(The only other kind of home industry present in Svay are a few families in the other hamlets who make a special sort of cow collar: lengths of rope are covered with lacquer and decorated with pieces of different colored metals. These collars are vended [sold for six or ten riels depending on the width of the collar] throughout southwestern Cambodia.)[60]

(2) Other specializations. (a) Religious specialists. Kompha (House 20) and Samnang (House 22) are *achaa*, a sort of lay priest, and Kosal (House 8) is a *kru* or magical practitioner. All have specialized knowledge and skills and are consulted for

---

[59] The region south of Phnom Penh is noted for weaving, especially of silk in Koh Thom and other districts. This activity is, however, evidently on the decline due to the soaring prices of silk thread in recent years. See Delvert 1961, 276–86 for details on this and other aspects of weaving.

[60] Of the twenty families surveyed in the other hamlets of Svay, eleven pursue various kinds of activities just described. Two families make cow collars, one family vends cow collars; four households fabricate palm sugar; two households weave. Also, one family vends miscellaneous items, and a man in another family finds odd jobs as a mechanic.

various purposes or asked to conduct ceremonies with varying frequency, depending on their popularity and talents. One does not become an *achaa* or *kru* specifically to earn money, but their practices do nonetheless procure some extra though usually minimal income. They are paid varying amounts of money and kind (fruits, rice, etc.) depending on the services rendered and the resources of the donor (e.g., for officiating at a wedding, Kompha receives 50–100 riels, two bunches of bananas, sixteen cakes, two coconuts, and five kilograms of candles).

(b) Musicians (*neak leng pleng*). Six men in the hamlet can play one or several musical instruments. Only one is considered to be a full-fledged professional musician: Hak (House 25) whose entire income is earned from playing music, making and selling musical instruments, and miscellaneous odd jobs. Music is primarily a pleasant avocation for the other men, but all are occasionally hired to play at weddings or other events for 100–200 riels each (though they also often donate their services free for friends).

(Two other specialists of different kinds, living in neighboring villages, are a treecutter in Ta Chas and a midwife in Sandan. The former receives fifty riels for felling a tree and cutting it into lumber; the latter receives about the same sum [more if the family can afford it] for delivering a baby, in addition to traditional gifts such as betel, candles, and foodstuffs.)

## TEMPORARY EMPLOYMENT

(1) Driving bicycle cabs (*twèr "cyclo"*). Because Phnom Penh is relatively close by and has become accessible in recent years by buses, driving bicycle cabs is a source of temporary urban employment. A number of men from West Svay and other villages in this region journey to the capital city during the dry season or the period between transplanting and harvest to become "cyclo" (bicycle cab) drivers for several weeks or months at a time.[61] Nine men in the hamlet have pedaled cyclos at one time or another, all of them from relatively poor households (see appendix G).[62]

Cyclo driving requires, above all, stamina and sturdy legs to pedal the vehicle that consists of a small passenger seat (also capable of carrying loads) mounted on what is essentially a large tricycle, except that there are two wheels in front and one in the back. The procedure for becoming a cyclo driver sounds relatively simple: one first obtains a police license to work and then rents a cab from one of several companies in Phnom Penh. But because there are often a greater number of aspiring drivers than there are cabs, a man often cannot find one to rent or must offer a bribe to get one, and sometimes the police become difficult about granting licenses unless every bureaucratic regulation is properly fulfilled. Ordinarily a cyclo rents for thirty to forty riels per day, plus a payment of about 100 riels in advance to be applied against future rental fees (cf. Delvert 1961, 450). Having gotten his cab, a man often works ten to fifteen hours a day cruising the streets in search of passengers. The usual fee ranges

---

[61] Delvert (1961, 450) notes that peasants from Koh Thom district and the neighboring district of Bati provide most of the cyclo drivers, water-barrel pullers, and dockhands in Phnom Penh during the dry season. For a comparative study of pedicab drivers in Bangkok, Thailand, see Textor 1961.

[62] Sam (House 19) was a full-time cyclo driver for four years before he moved back to West Svay. Kouch and Peou (both in House 11) are almost full-time drivers who spend as much or more time in Phnom Penh as they do in the village.

from two to ten riels (usually with no tips) depending on the length of the ride and the bargaining prowess of driver and passenger. A man may make anywhere from ten to seventy riels net profit (after paying the rental fee) per day depending on his energy and luck; the monthly earnings can range from 800 to 1,500 riels, averaging about 1,000 riels. (Cf. Delvert 1961, 450–51, who estimates earnings at about forty to fifty riels a day, minus rental fee and about ten riels for food.) Some of the gains may be depleted by expenses of meals, snacks, succumbing to some of the temptations of city life (movies, women, etc.), bus fares to and from the city (men usually return home once every week or two weeks to bring their wages), and paying fines for traffic violations. (Fortunately, West Svay men have no problem of housing because they always lodge with relatives or friends in the city.) But a man can nonetheless earn a good amount of money in a relatively brief amount of time: for example, in 1959 Vireak (House 1) netted about 1,200 riels for four weeks of driving; Chea (House 18) had 1,500 riels after five weeks of work; and Sareth (House 31) earned 1,000 riels for five weeks.

In rural areas, the remorque (*rèmak* or *lèmak*) replaces the cyclo for traveling short distances. This is an open cab, capable of carrying several passengers and/or loads, pulled by an ordinary or motorized bicycle. It is possible to rent a remorque from a man in Kompong Tuol for fifteen riels a day for one with a simple bicycle, or forty riels per day for one with a motorbike. Driving a remorque is easier than a cyclo in that one may have a motorized bicycle; one can wait for passengers at the marketplace or bus stop in Kompong Tuol as well as cruising the highway; and one can return home for meals. But at the usual fare of about two riels per kilometer per person, and the large number of remorques in Kompong Tuol that vie for passengers, the monetary returns are generally not as great as what one earns from pedaling a cyclo. Sein (House 24), the only man in West Svay who has tried driving a remorque, netted about 700 riels for four weeks' work. (Cf. Delvert 1961, 516, who says that a remorque driver can earn about 1,200 riels a year by working "between labors in the field.")

(2) "Coolie" labor. "To work as a coolie" (*twèr kuli*) means almost any sort of manual (usually unskilled) labor, whether it be digging ditches, building a road, carting building materials, laying bricks, twisting pipe, etc. Such jobs, usually on construction of buildings, are available in several places: Phnom Penh, the nearby normal school, and occasionally a temple. Both males and females may seek such employment during the periods when rice cultivation does not demand their efforts. (Six men have worked as coolies in Phnom Penh; two young women who used to reside in House 16 are now supporting their mother by coolie labor in the city; about a dozen young men and women have worked occasionally at the normal school; and one youth has worked for wages at Wat Samnang.) The wages vary, depending on the exact nature of the work, but daily pay ranges from about twenty to twenty-five riels in Phnom Penh, fifteen to twenty riels at the school, and thirty-five riels at the temple.

(3) Hauling dirt (*dùk dèy*). The residents of Svay and neighboring villages had a special opportunity for temporary employment in the digging and hauling of cart-loads of dirt to be used as fill in constructing buildings at the normal school. About ten households worked at this task for brief periods in June, September, and October 1959. Later, from mid-December through early January 1960 (when the rice was almost completely harvested), an extensive building project at the school occupied all but five households in West Svay, as well as attracting workers from villages for miles around. (A veritable colony of temporary shacks sprang up around the hamlet, and

competition for employment became intense.) The villagers thought that dirt-hauling would earn several hundred riels a day, and several families went into debt to purchase oxen or build special oxcarts so they could participate.

In reality, a household was able to earn about sixty-five to seventy-five riels a day (being paid four riels for one cartload of dirt). About ten hardy families worked a total of thirty days for gross wages of about 2,000 riels; others earned anywhere from 1,000 to 1,500 riels. In a few cases, the gains were virtually depleted because of debts incurred to buy cattle or construct carts; for others, lesser amounts were eaten away by the need to buy food for cattle, payments to hired helpers, or rental fees for digging sites (if one did not own a plot of land from which dirt could be dug, one paid ten riels a day for the right to dig on someone else's site). But the majority of households were able to realize greater or lesser amounts of profit from this employment.[63] (And several made a few more riels profit by selling food and drink to the "strangers" who had come to haul dirt.)

## SALE OF SMALL ITEMS

It has been noted that there is occasional selling of small surpluses to other villagers, whether it be rice, fruit, betel, chickens, fish, etc. In addition, it is common for a few families to prepare various snacks (cooked dishes, cakes, sugar palm seeds, dried fish, etc.) from time to time that can be vended mainly to students at the normal school and secondarily to fellow villagers in Svay or a neighboring community. (Individuals in other villages do this as well and often come to Svay with their snacks.) Such foods are sold cheaply (e.g., one or two riels for a cake, one riel for five small dried fish) and net little profit. No family makes a regular practice of vending snacks but does so only when resources and time are available or when a bit of pin money is needed. Occasionally, too, women from other hamlets or villages come to West Svay selling sarongs or blouses that they had either bought outright and were now selling for a slight profit, or that they were vending on a commission basis.

## FULL-TIME NON-AGRICULTURAL EMPLOYMENT

Several men in West Svay have some sort of full-time non-agricultural occupation, either through necessity or choice. (a) Sok (House 26) works as a chauffeur at the normal school for about 2,000 riels a month. Though his wife owns rice fields, he is not and never has been a cultivator (the paddies are worked by hired labor). Sok is notable for his unusual history of varied occupations, as coal seller, cyclo driver, ice vendor, coolie, and hospital attendant. (b) Sen (House 6), who recently returned to his natal community of West Svay but had inherited no rice fields here, also works at the school as a cook and kitchen helper for about 1,200 riels a month. He, too, has never been a farmer and is actually a trained gold artisan, though he has now given up his craft in preference to the steady income of a regular job to support his large family.

---

[63] Note that though Svay and the neighboring communities are unusual in having special opportunities for temporary employment at the normal school, the general pattern of seeking non-agricultural work and additional sources of income is common throughout this entire region where landholdings are limited (see Delvert 1961, 300–301, 450–51, etc.) If the school were not present, it is reasonable to expect that West Svay residents would simply turn to other means of earning money.

(c) Hak (House 25) is a professional musician, having studied music at a school in Phnom Penh for several years (prior to which he worked as a clerk in the railroad station in the capital). Neither he nor his wife have any fields, and Hak ekes out a penurious existence by playing any of a variety of instruments at weddings and other festivities for 200 riels a day, occasionally making and selling musical instruments (at a profit or 100–300 riels per instrument), and sometimes working as a barber. He is considered to be extremely poor and is looked at askance by some villagers for not exerting effort to find steadier or more profitable employment. (d) Sam (House 19) also has no rice fields and worked for a number of years as a coolie and cyclo driver in Phnom Penh. Having no special skills or talents, he finds odd jobs as coolie laborer at the normal school and is virtually poverty stricken. (e) Bros and Noch (House 32) own some rice fields and were formerly cultivators, but four years ago they decided to open a roadside snack stand across the highway from West Svay. (They also continue to grow rice, using hired labor or sharecropping with Noch's brother in House 30.) Catering to villagers, persons who work at the normal school, students, and travelers, the stand offers a noodle soup, fruits, sweets, and beverages, as well as a convenient place to relax on a hot afternoon or in the cool of night. The owners estimate that they earn approximately 500 riels a month from their stand; evidently they have done fairly well because they recently built a good-sized wooden structure with tables and chairs to replace their former thatch stand. (Another villager, Sareth [House 31] had planned to open another roadside stand selling soft drinks and sweets. But being rather a wastrel, he never managed to accumulate enough capital to buy provisions for the stand he built.)

It should be noted also that many other men in West Svay have held full-time, non-agricultural occupations for greater or lesser amounts of time in the past. Among these occupations were soldier, metalworker, gold artisans (two men, in addition to Sen), work on an experimental pepper plant station maintained by the School of Agriculture in Phnom Penh, rice broker, and printer. (Moreover, a number of persons who have emigrated from West Svay have assumed or married someone with a non-agricultural occupation: laboratory technician, protocol officer at the palace in Phnom Penh, caretaker at a school, soldier, bus driver, coolie, mechanic, bus boy at a hotel, etc. It is likely that such movement from the village and into blue-collar and white-collar jobs will increase in the future.)

## ANIMAL HUSBANDRY

One of the villager's most important possessions is oxen (*koo*), used as draft animals for the plowing and harrowing essential to rice cultivation and for pulling oxcarts. In May 1959, the hamlet had a total of forty-five oxen distributed among twenty-one households (see also appendix G). The average number of cattle per household is two, which constitutes the necessary team for pulling a plow or cart. There were also eleven households without any oxen whatever, due to one or several factors: (1) some lack money to buy cattle; (2) old people who adhere strictly to Buddhist precepts do not wish to keep animals because the beasts require attention that might better be spent on religious efforts and because the animals will usually eventually be slaughtered; (3) some households have no land, or non-agricultural occupations, such that they either do not need cattle or can hire labor to work the fields; (4) a family may prefer to rely on the labor of brothers or sons-in-law in other households who do own cattle rather than acquiring some of its own.

The cattle in West Svay and neighboring villages are of the *Bos taurus* variety or crossbreeds of the latter and zebu (with the exception of occasional full-fledged zebu). (Water buffalo are also common in Cambodia but are utilized more by *chamkar* villagers.) They receive better care than any other domestic animals—partly because of religious sanctions (both Buddhist teachings about the sanctity of all living creatures, and a belief in a guardian spirit of animals that punishes anyone who mistreats them), but mostly because the villager realizes that oxen are essential to certain tasks and must be in good physical condition to perform them. The general welfare of cattle is of constant concern to their owners who worry when the oxen are undernourished or show signs of overwork or illness. They are carefully guarded when at pasture and tethered at home. During the plowing season the oxen are worked for only several hours at a time and are always thoroughly bathed and rubbed down after any labors or on a hot day.

Feeding cattle is a major task and problem.[64] At the start of the rainy season before cultivation begins, cattle can pasture in the fields on the grasses that spring up in the paddies and on the dikes. But once cultivation starts, feeding becomes difficult. West Svay residents are given rights to pasture on a plot of grassy land now belonging to the normal school, but this area is too small to sustain all of the hamlet's cattle. Thus, villagers must often expend great effort to obtain grasses and other greens because they feel that hay alone does not provide adequate nourishment. Groups of people often take exhausting day-long journeys to marshlands ten or twenty kilometers distant to bring back cartloads of grasses and plants; greens are cut daily from the dikes of rice paddies and carried home to the oxen (during the cultivation season, markers of straw are placed on the dikes of certain paddies to indicate that no one but the field's owner can cut grasses there); or, as a last resort, greens must be purchased. All in all, villagers go to considerable trouble to sustain the cattle that are actually utilized for only part of the year (mainly for cultivation now that oxcarts have been largely replaced by remorques and buses for travel).[65]

The age, size, strength, and sometimes color of different oxen are always the objects of lively conversation among men and of considerable debate in the buying, selling, and trading of cattle. Such transactions are common. In the course of a year, five households bought new oxen, while five other families had replaced one or more of their cattle. Rather like the American custom of trading in old automobiles for better models, an ox would be sold and the money applied to the purchase of another. There were more than the usual number of such purchases and "trade-ins" in 1959–60 because many villagers acquired hardy oxen for dirt hauling. But even in ordinary years there is always a turnover and fluctuation in the number of cattle: a villager may be forced to sell cattle because he needs money; another may have accumulated

---

[64] See Delvert 1961, 233–61 for further details on this and other aspects of animal husbandry in Cambodia; also Steinberg 1959, 200; Gourou 1945, 247. Leclère 1898, 2:357–78, 385–95, 419–21 gives ancient law codes concerning the treatment of animals, strays, theft, damages caused by cattle, etc.

[65] Delvert (1961, 245, 255) states that it is not uncommon for villagers in some areas to sell oxen at the end of the rice-cultivation season so they will not have the bother of feeding them during the dry season; they then purchase cattle when cultivation begins again. This occurs also in the lower Tonkin Delta (Gourou 1945, 241). In West Svay, however, villagers preferred to keep their cattle the year round, despite the trouble of feeding, unless they were in dire need of money.

enough cash to buy one; an animal may become old and have to be replaced with a younger and stronger beast; and sometimes (again as with automobiles) there is simply the pleasure of acquiring a different "model." The price of oxen varies from about 2,000–7,000 riels for a mature animal, depending on its general condition (age, sex, size, musculature, etc.); West Svay villagers usually pay or receive from 2,500–4,500 riels for a healthy mature ox. Such sales and purchases are made sometimes within the village itself but more often with persons in other communities (sometimes quite distant) or in Phnom Penh.[66]

Old cattle are sold cheaply (for about 1,000–1,500 riels) to be butchered for beef, but there is absolutely no slaughtering of cattle by the villagers themselves because of the strong Buddhist injunction against killing. Muslim Chams serve as cattle butchers throughout Cambodia, and there is one of them living in Kompong Tuol. Only if death is the result of old age or an accident (e.g., being hit by a car) would a village ox be butchered and eaten; otherwise, all beef for eating is purchased at the market (and relatively rarely at that, because of its expense).

Second in importance among domestic animals are pigs and chickens, both of which are kept mainly as sources of cash income rather than as food. With a few exceptions, these animals are raised only by poor families who are in need of money and willing to ignore Buddhist precepts that frown upon nurturing creatures that will eventually be killed.[67] (It is, moreover, interesting that both swine and poultry are cared for by women rather than men. While this may be a matter of pure expediency in the sexual division of labor, one wonders whether a religious factor might not be operative in assigning this religiously suspect task to females who occupy a lower status than males in Buddhist ideology.)

The Cambodian pig (*cruuk*) is a unique-looking animal characterized by an elongated body and a pronounced swayback. Between May 1959 and March 1960 eight to ten families maintained from twelve to nineteen pigs; with one exception, all of these households were poor.[68] The pigs are occasionally kept within a rude fenced enclosure near the house, but more usually they are left free to roam about the village foraging on flora and loose garbage. Apart from what the animal can find on its own, the pig is fed leftovers, various fruits, banana stalks and trunks, or a gruel of rice husks and water. Except for feedings and guarding against straying, the pig receives no special attention or affection such as cattle get. (Curiously, pigs and chickens do not fall under the protection of the guardian spirit of animals as do oxen.)

The villager does not breed pigs himself; rather, they are purchased from (and sold back to) Chinese merchants in Kompong Tuol or Chinese vendors from Phnom

---

[66] The problem of buying cattle when one has limited funds is illustrated in the account of Vireak's purchase of an ox. At the beginning of the cultivation season he had only one ox and needed another to form a full team. Having accumulated some money, and not wanting to waste any of it on bus fares, he walked a total of 140 kilometers to Phnom Penh and other areas in search of an ox he could afford.

[67] See also Delvert 1961, 156, who states that Buddhist prohibition against slaughter is the main reason for the feeble importance of "petit betail" in Cambodia; he says also that "everywhere religious observance is fervent, there is a clear tendency to abandon pig raising in the face of criticisms from the faithful and the monks." See also Pfanner and Ingersoll 1962, 345; Pfanner notes that the attempt to introduce poultry and swine raising into villages of lower Burma has failed because "raising of livestock, even for sale, is considered a sinful occupation."

[68] Throughout Cambodia, pigs are kept by poor Khmer peasants or by Chinese (Delvert 1961, 158). For further discussion of pig raising, see Delvert 1961, 156–59 and Zadrozny 1955, 291.

Penh who travel from village to village with a truckload of swine. The villager buys a piglet or young pig at a cost ranging from 200 to 600 riels depending on its age and size. After a period of anywhere from about three to seven months when the animal has matured and fattened, it is sold back to the Chinese for prices ranging from 500 to 1,500 riels; in 1959 one got 1,000 riels for a pig weighing one hap (sixty kilograms). A good profit can sometimes be realized; for example, House 15 purchased a small pig for 300 riels and sold it later for 1,500 riels.[69] One must, of course, take into account the fact that the pig had to be nourished for about six months, but most of its food was available at no cost. There is some risk that a pig may die of accident or disease, but if the former, a family can recoup some of its loss by consuming or selling the meat. (Actual slaughter of pigs is always done by Chinese, and pork for food is otherwise always purchased at the market.)

The hamlet's chicken (*mwan*) population fluctuates widely with births and losses of chicks, as well as sales or acquisitions of mature fowl; but in June 1959 there were thirty-six chickens (mostly chicks and more hens than roosters) distributed among eight households.[70] They are kept sometimes in small wickerwork enclosures under the house, but more frequently they, too, are left to forage about the hamlet for insects, scraps, plants, and bits of grain that may fall from a granary or a meal eaten outdoors. Occasionally they are fed uncooked rice, but the latter is usually too precious to be spared in any quantity. When eggs are laid, they are not eaten but kept to be hatched (although mortality is high among baby chicks who are often devoured by predatory cats or dogs or lost to some unknown sickness).

Chickens are rarely consumed by their owners. More usually, they are sold to fellow villagers who plan to raise chickens themselves or who wish to prepare a fine dish for a special occasion. The price varies from sixteen to twenty riels for a small or young chicken, twenty-five to forty riels for a medium-sized mature fowl, and eighty-nine to ninety riels for a fine, large specimen. If one wishes to buy a chicken for food, it is considered preferable to get live fowl, rather than one already dressed at the market, the make certain that it is truly fresh. However, this raises the problem of how the chicken is to be killed when slaughter is a sin in Buddhist ideology. A meticulous person may ask the Chinese in the shop across the road or in Kompong Tuol to perform this task. But more usually, the Buddhist precept is circumvented in an interesting manner: the chicken is given to children to be killed, on the assumption that they are too young to be completely subject to Buddhist injunctions and are not yet fully responsible for their sins.

The only other domestic animals in the village are dogs and cats kept as pets. Their numbers vary through time as litters are born and others die naturally or are killed by cars on the road, but at any one time there are about a dozen dogs and as many cats belonging to various households. The dogs are gaunt, battle-scarred creatures that are given no affection or care. They eat, in the words of one villager, "anything and everything," living on leftovers and whatever else they can find or kill. The dogs are kept

[69] Delvert (1961, 158) implies that the average profit per pig is about 800 riels, with piglets costing about 100 riels and a seventy kilogram pig being sold for 940 riels. The merchants dealing with West Svay seemed to give better prices for mature pigs but asked more for young ones.

[70] Cf. Delvert (1961, 159) who implies that virtually every peasant family has one or two chickens, not for sale or consumption but just to keep on hand for ceremonies. This is not the case in West Svay. (Some Khmer villagers also raise ducks, but these are more generally kept by Vietnamese and Chinese [Delvert 1961, 156, 160].)

mainly as watchdogs, and they perform that purpose admirably by setting up a fearful racket whenever any stranger enters the hamlet. Cats are much less mistreated and sometimes better fed on table scraps, though they, too, must forage on their own and are sometimes guilty of pouncing on stray chicks or stealing a fish from someone's kitchen. Cats also serve a useful function by catching rats that may prey on the rice granaries and are successful in keeping the rodent population down to a low level.

## FINANCES

In general, the nuclear family is the basic economic unit of production and consumption in village life: its members cooperate to work the rice fields and pursue other activities that supplement food or income, and the proceeds of such efforts are shared by and used to support the entire group. This generalization has, however, two qualifications that should be noted. (1) In some extended or stem families, the entire household may cooperate in rice cultivation and other endeavors, but the nuclear family units within the larger family will maintain separate granaries and budgets. But in other such stem or extended families, particularly when they are headed by an elderly couple incapable of hard labor or by a widowed parent, the entire household maintains a common budget and granary. (2) A resident minor or unmarried child who finds occasional employment may be allowed to keep a proportion of his/her wages for him/herself, no matter how poor the family. But that child always voluntarily contributes a greater or lesser amount of money (sometimes all of it) for the support of the family as a whole.

Within the family, the wife and mother is the treasurer. Money earned by the husband or children is given to her for safekeeping and apportionment, and angry tirades befall anyone who takes even a few riels from the family kitty without telling her beforehand. Since ancient times the Cambodian woman has also been active in other financial activities.[71] Except for the buying and selling of cattle, chickens, sometimes rice fields, the husband's personal property, or implements habitually used by males, the woman handles all other purchases and sales.

While small sums of money must be kept at home to purchase essentials, the villager dislikes having large amounts of cash at home for fear of theft. There are several large banks in Phnom Penh, but the villager never uses them because of unfamiliarity with banking procedures and the distance to the city. Instead, the common method of "depositing" money, as it were, is to purchase gold jewelry: rings, necklaces, pendants, bracelets, earrings, etc. (which are sometimes set with semiprecious or precious gems).[72] The jewelry is expensive, the price depending on the amount of gold a piece contains (one *chi* or 3.75 grams of gold was evaluated at 400 riels in 1959); a

---

[71] The chronicles of Chou Ta-kuan states that in thirteenth-century Cambodia "it is the women who attend to commerce" and were married by Chinese immigrants for their "commercial aptitudes" (Pelliot 1951, 27; see also Thierry 1955, 27). The woman as treasurer and marketer is also common in other parts of Southeast Asia; see, for example, Ward 1963, 128 (Burma), 246 (Laos); Djamour 1959, 42 (Malaysia); H. Geertz 1961, 123–25 (Java).

[72] Such buying of jewelry is common elsewhere in Southeast Asia as well; see, for example, Firth 1964, 23–24; Halpern 1964a, 97, on Laos; Swift 1964, 136–37 on Malaya.

simple bracelet of gold links costs about 600 riels at minimum, and a long gold neck-lace can go as high as 3,000 riels. But jewelry is, in fact, a sensible investment: it can be readily pawned or sold in case of need, and it is rarely stolen because it is worn constantly (usually by the unmarried girls in the family, though men may also wear rings or necklaces). All but the poorest families manage to have at least one or two pieces of jewelry in their possession.

## INCOME AND EXPENDITURES

(1) Income. It was noted previously that although a good proportion of food and other essentials are obtained or produced at home, there are still a number of items that must be purchased or exigencies that must be met, such that cash is a critical necessity. Various sources of cash income have already been mentioned in preceding sections, but it may be useful to recapitulate the various means of acquiring money. Among these are occasional and/or limited sale of surplus rice; sale of surplus gar-den or fruit tree produce; sale of pigs and chickens; sale of craft items, special labor skills, or talents; sale of palm sugar; cyclo driving in Phnom Penh or remorque driv-ing; dirt hauling; occasional sale of prepared foods; hired agricultural labor for other households; rental of sugar palms; and finally, the sale of oxen, house materials, land, jewelry, or other property in an emergency. Obviously no one household pursues all these possibilities in any one year; but those without much land or with a large family to support are generally very energetic in their attempts to earn money. For example, House 2, which has a miniscule amount of land to support a large family, has at one time or another engaged in the making of palm sugar, pig raising, driving cyclos (both father and son), occasional jobs in Kompong Tuol, and dirt hauling. And it is not unusual for other families, even some considered to be well-off, to have anywhere from one to several sources of supplementary income in any given year, depending on their needs and available manpower (see appendix G). Only House 27 with its four hectares of rice fields and annual sale of rice has never needed to seek other income-producing activities.

This diversity of activities in addition to rice cultivation is not unique to West Svay. Delvert (1961, 449–52, 522, 540–42) notes that the same situation obtains throughout the region south of Phnom Penh where population is dense and landhold-ings are small. Indeed, non-agricultural pursuits (most commonly the making of palm sugar, crafts, temporary urban employment, and raising pigs for sale) may account for more than one-quarter of total income of peasant families in this area. Even in house-holds that have two to three hectares of land (which by Svay's standards would make one quite prosperous), it is often necessary to have extra means of income to make ends meet (see Delvert 1961, 528–31).

It is difficult to give accurate figures for the total annual income of families in West Svay without detailed records of daily earnings and expenditures (which, unfor-tunately, I did not collect systematically). The villagers themselves have no precise idea of annual income because "as soon as money comes in, it is spent for something." But they estimate that actual cash income varies from about 1,000 to 4,000 riels per year for most families, depending on the various resources available to them (the amount of rice land and supplementary activities). This estimate is probably not too far wrong for those households that do not sell rice, engage in a limited number of activities to earn money, and do not have recourse—as they did in 1959—to extended employment as dirt haulers.[73]

Another estimate by the Cambodian government gives the average annual income in Cambodia as about US$90.00 per household (William Thomas, former economist with the American Embassy in Phnom Penh, pers. comm.), or about 3,150 riels (at the official exchange rate in 1959). Another figure is given by Delvert (1961, 524) who calculates that the average annual income from agriculture is 1,700 riels per person, or about 8,619 riels per family (see also Delvert 1961, 531–32 and appendix X). This is obviously much higher than the estimated incomes of West Svay families, but it must be noted that Delvert's calculations of income include the monetary value of such things as the total amount of rice produced by the family (whether it is consumed or not), the amount of fish caught for consumption, chickens raised for food, etc. (see the family budgets in Delvert 1961, 524–31). If such items are not taken into account, the incomes of the families he describes become more similar to those in Svay. Delvert (1961, 532) also notes that there are regional variations in income: *chamkar* cultivators earn significantly more than rice farmers (a fact also remarked upon by Svay villagers); income is low among rice cultivators south of Phnom Penh who must pursue other activities to make ends meet; but income is lowest where rice cultivation is the only resource (see also Gourou 1945, 532–33).

(2) Expenditures. If villagers have no exact notion of their annual incomes, they have even less idea of how much they spend in any one year—again, because of the habit of spending money as soon as any is acquired. One can, however, review the major categories of expenditures. (a) Food is usually the most essential item in a family's budget. As one housewife stated: "One buys clothing and other things only once in a while, but one eats food every day." Although some proportion of villagers' diet is obtained at home, there are still a number of foodstuffs that must be purchased because they are locally available in insufficient quantity or not at all. Villagers estimate that food accounts for one-third to one-half, sometimes more, of their total expenditures,[74] depending on particular situations (the amount of rice produced and consumed, the amount and variety of vegetables and fruits grown at home), and the general financial resources of a family that will determine whether it can afford only the bare essentials (eaten in meager quantity) or if it can buy "luxury" foods such as meat and tea with any frequency. The most common and necessary food items purchased are fish in various forms (including paste and oil), seasonings (e.g., salt,

---

[73] For example, crude calculations of cash income for two families in West Svay of average-to-poor means from March 1959 to March 1960 are as follows:

| House 1 | | House 15 | |
|---|---|---|---|
| sale of palm sugar | ca. 700 riels | sale of a pig | ca. 1,200 riels |
| cyclo driving | ca. 2,500 riels | coolie labor | ca. 250 riels |
| dirt hauling | ca. 2,000 riels | dirt hauling | ca. 1,800 riels |
| Total: | ca. 5,200 riels[a] | Total: | ca. 3,250 riels[b] |

[a] If there had been no dirt hauling, the total would be 3,200 riels.

[b] If there had been no dirt hauling, the total would be 1,450 riels.

[74] Cf. the proportion of income spent on food and other items by the families in the budgets cited by Delvert 1961, 524–32.

vinegar, also cooking oil or fat), some vegetables (e.g., onions, corn), and snacks from traveling vendors. One may also buy other vegetables and fruits (e.g., durian, pineapple), additional seasonings (e.g., soy sauce, garlic, curry ingredients), manufactured items such as noodles and flour, meat, various sweet confections, and tea or wine. But these latter foodstuffs are usually purchased only occasionally by most families, for special events such as the preparation of dishes to take to temple festivals, annual holidays, life-cycle ceremonies, etc. Delvert (1961, 532, 154–55) estimates that a poor peasant family in the region south of Phnom Penh consumes per year (apart from rice) fifteen to thirty kilograms of fish, two to four kilograms of pork, two to four kilograms of chicken, and one to two kilograms of beef, which figures are probably applicable to the majority of West Svay residents.

(b) Another indispensable purchase is clothing, which may account for an estimated one-third to one-fourth of expenditures. The amount spent by any one family varies, again, with its relative affluence and the number of persons. Daily wear (sarongs and blouses for women, shorts and shirts or underwear for men and the ubiquitous *kroma* scarf) have a life span of about one year when worn, as they are, with great frequency. In addition, children must have neat outfits for school, and every family has a few dressy clothes. One might also include in the category of clothing the beauty salon permanents that are considered a necessity for adolescent girls.

(c) Taxes are unavoidable, although the villagers may neglect to report all their taxable property and may pay annually whenever they have accumulated enough money. The following items were taxed in 1959, land (usually at thirty riels per hectare), oxen (ten riels per pair), oxcarts (six riels), bicycles (six riels), and betel plants (one riel).

(d) Other miscellaneous necessities that must be purchased frequently are kerosene for lamps; areca nuts, betel leaves, and lime for the betel chewing that is practiced by virtually all married women; tobacco and cigarettes for men; thread for mending and sewing; and school supplies for children.

(e) At least once or twice a year, every household gives at least a minimal contribution of some sort to the Buddhist temple and monks. In fact, the great majority of families may attend anywhere from three to twelve or more events at the two temples near Svay, at each of which some offering is made. These contributions may be relatively simple (e.g., some incense or a few riels) for lesser events. But on the major Buddhist holidays the customary offering is a special food dish (for which special ingredients may be purchased) and often some money or lesser gifts (candles, cigarettes, etc.) as well. While donations of actual cash are relatively limited, the total expenditures for contributions throughout the year can be considerable when one adds up the cost of other offerings, especially food.[75]

In addition to the preceding there are also other items or services that are purchased only infrequently or that only certain households will buy. Among these are the following: household items (e.g., bedding, furniture, kitchenware), agricultural and other work implements, animals, hired help for agricultural labor, transportation fares, entertainment, medicines or "medical" services (e.g., payments to midwives, medical practitioners), sponsoring of life-cycle or other ceremonies (also monetary gifts when guests at such events), and miscellaneous items and services (e.g., jewelry, cosmetics, photographs taken by professional photographers, musical instruments, songbooks).

---

[75] In Delvert's budgets (1961, 524–32), religious contributions accounted for 6 percent and 15 percent of the expenditures of two families of moderate means, and 6 percent for a wealthy family. One household (the only one with a deficit) reported no religious offerings.

West Svay's inhabitants do not yet have many of the material items that are not uncommon in other Southeast Asian villages (e.g., soap, condensed milk, sewing machines, radios [see, for example, Kaufman 1960, 55–59, 220–21, and Sharp et al. 1953, 208–9, 219–20 on Thai villages]). But the number of purchased items has undoubtedly multiplied through the years, and the Khmer villagers are increasingly exposed to a diversity of commodities that become desirable because they save the time and labor of making something at home, because they are obviously more efficient or efficacious than cheaper or homemade items (e.g., a pressure lamp contrasted to a wick in a tin can), or because they are symbols of prestige (e.g., wristwatches). The younger generation in particular is attracted to many of these material objects, and even many of their parents wish they could afford more conveniences and luxuries. The desire and need for cash thus also increases, though most of the money earned must still be spent on absolute necessities such as food and clothing. It is probable that this will continue to be the case, for the villagers must contend with a steadily rising cost of living that has risen from a base of 1 in 1939 to 85 in 1957 (Ministère du Plan 1958, 95) and that older people remarked upon frequently without the aid of statistical evidence.

CREDIT AND DEBT

The budgets of most families in West Svay have a precarious balance between income and expenditures that is easily upset by any emergencies or necessity for large cash outlays. The most common circumstances that disturb household finances are (1) a bad harvest, or landholdings too small to adequately support a family, such that rice for food or seed must be purchased or borrowed; (2) the need to sponsor a major life-cycle ceremony; (3) the need or desire to purchase cattle or some other expensive item; and (4) serious or prolonged illness of an adult member of the household that reduces a family's labor force (as well as necessitating the purchase of medical aids). (Cf. Delvert 1961, 517 who also cites the first three of these as the major reasons for borrowing among Cambodian peasantry; see also Firth 1964.) In such situations, if needed money cannot be earned by one means or another, the villager must borrow rice (if that is what he needs), borrow money, or sell some property.

Rice for food or seed may be borrowed outright, preferably from kinsmen or neighbors with sufficient resources, but often from rice brokers as well. Such loans are made usually on good faith against the promise of a forthcoming crop, with payment of the original debt and interest in kind. A common arrangement is five or six *tau* of rice in return for having borrowed four.[76] But since one's fellow villagers are apt to have little rice to spare, it is more common to borrow money to purchase rice.

Money for rice or other expenses may be borrowed from several sources by West Svay villagers: kinsmen or friends, rice brokers who advance money against the coming harvest, or other merchants or moneylenders (e.g., a jeweler in Kompong Tuol)

---

[76] This follows nineteenth-century law codes that specified repayment of one and a half for one for loans of rice or other provisions repaid at the end of the season (two for one if repaid the following year) (Aymonier 1900, 86). However, as Firth (1964, 30–31) points out, what appears to be interest may not in fact be so when one considers that rice has a higher value at the beginning of the cultivation season when a loan is made than it has at harvest time when it is repaid. But Delvert (1961, 517) notes that rice brokers take this fact into account when setting the terms of loans.

who will accept the pawn of some item of value (e.g., jewelry, a bicycle).[77] Loans
from kinsmen are considered preferable because usually (though not always) little or
no interest is exacted. Most of the persons who needed money to buy oxen or build
oxcarts for dirt hauling did ask relatives (often several) for loans (e.g., Rotha in House
4 borrowed 1,000 riels from his brother Sen in House 6 in return for his rice crop of
about thirty *tang*). But since one's kinsmen usually are not much better off then oneself, it is often necessary to borrow part or all of needed money from rice brokers or
moneylenders.

Loans from the latter do carry an often considerable interest rate. If the debt is
to be repaid in money, the creditor generally sets a certain interest rate per month.
For example, a loan of 100 riels from the jeweler in Kompong Tuol carries an interest
of 5 percent a month until the debt is paid (because the interest is computed against
the original amount of the loan without allowance for whatever portion of it may be
repaid from time to time, this adds up to a true interest rate of 120 percent a year
according to the traditional methods of calculating interest rates per annum [Marvin
Gelfand, economist, pers. comm.]). Such debts are usually allowed to stand for long
periods of time, so long as the interest charge is paid each month.[78] If a villager seeks
to borrow money from four to six months before harvest with repayment to be made
in rice from the forthcoming crop, the broker surveys the hopeful borrower's fields to
assess the potential yield and decide the terms of the loan. A loan may be refused if
the crop looks too meager. But should the loan be granted, the amount of rice to be
paid in return will depend upon the creditor's estimate of the probable price of the
rice at harvest time. In 1959 the terms were usually set at six *tau* of rice at harvest in
return for every 100 riels borrowed before harvest. Since, on the open market, four *tau*
of rice at harvest was evaluated at approximately 100 riels, the payment is actually 100
riels plus 50 riels interest (if, therefore, the loan were made for a five-month period,
the interest would be 10 percent a month).[79]

It is sometimes stated or implied that the Cambodian peasant is in a perpetual
state of debt to onerous Chinese moneylenders (see, e.g., Steinberg 1959, 205–6;
Morizon 1936, 186). It is impossible to give a precise calculation of the extent of debt
among the peasantry because people often do not like to admit indebtedness; but the

---

[77] There are also government credit facilities (see Steinberg 1959, 207–9; Delvert 1961, 518),
but none of these has been very successful in reaching a large number of peasants and reduc-
ing the role of Chinese and other private creditors. Certainly West Svay residents did not use
government credit arrangements. Steinberg (1959, 205–6) states that land can be used as collateral and that a moneylender may gain total usufruct of fields if a loan is not repaid (at present, a Chinese or other foreigner cannot hold actual title to land unless he is naturalized as a
Cambodian citizen or is married to a Khmer and registers the land in the spouse's name). But
this practice was not evident in Svay. Neither is it discussed by Delvert, so I do not know if such
land mortgage is common in Cambodia as a whole.

[78] But in nineteenth-century law, when the interest due became equal to the original amount
of the loan, the creditor could put the debtor up for sale unless the latter found a new creditor,
changed his debt into a contract of slavery (sometimes involving his family as well as himself),
or simply fled the country (Aymonier 1900, 98). Debt slavery is now abolished, but Delvert
(1961, 518–20) notes that a debt is sometimes repaid by the debtor or a member of his family
(often a daughter) going to work for the creditor.

[79] See also Delvert 1961, 516–17 for other details on terms of loans. He says that interest rates
usually average about 12 percent a month, and payments of six to ten *tau* of rice in return of
loans of 100 riels are common. (For interest rates and other conditions of loans in the nineteenth century, see Aymonier 1900, 86; Leclère 1898, 1:458–62, 466, 468).

Office du Crédit Populaire estimated that in 1952, three-quarters of 700,000 cultivators had debts averaging 1,000 riels (Delvert 1961, 519; see also 520–22). Delvert notes, however, that the number of debtors varies regionally, ranging from 10 percent of the population in some areas to 78 percent in others (1961, 419); and one of the striking facts to emerge from his research is the surprising absence of debts in the rice-cultivating region around Phnom Penh.

> The peasant within a radius of 30 kilometers from the city, especially to the south, has renounced buying on credit and borrowing. To get money, he goes to sell in the city, or to work in Phnom Penh (as coolie, cyclo, carpenters, masons), or expands his handicraft production (weaving) or fishing, or sells products of animal husbandry (eggs, ducks, pigs, oxen). Rural handicrafts, animal husbandry, work in the city, and movings about [déplacements] are very effective means of peasant liberation. This region is one of the most populous in the kingdom; and one of the poorest . . . [but] indebtedness is much more rare than elsewhere. (Delvert 1961, 522; my translation)

Delvert's conclusions are generally supported by the situation in West Svay. Despite the fact that most families have limited holdings and are by no means prosperous, indebtedness tends to be infrequent and/or relatively minor. Most villagers greatly dislike being in arrears to moneylenders or brokers; it makes them feel a "heaviness" pressing upon them (though indebtedness to kinsmen is considered in a different light as "sharing" among relatives). Accordingly, many people avoid borrowing if at all possible by tightening their belts when necessary, by seeking means of earning extra money, or by selling some valuable item of property such as oxen, jewelry, house materials or furnishings, trees, or even—in an extreme emergency— land. There are, of course, times when borrowing is unavoidable, or when a villager voluntarily enters debt to get something he desires. Even then, however, most of the borrowing is for short-term periods to tide one over an immediate exigency (see also Firth 1964, 29–30; Zadrozny 1955, 295) and for relatively small sums of money (usually under 2,000 riels). Moreover, once having incurred a debt, the villager in West Svay tries to rid himself of its burden as quickly as possible—again, by making do with the barest essentials, by searching more energetically for supplementary sources of income, or by selling some property. Often he is successful in clearing his debts within a year or so (though he might subsequently incur other debts).

During 1959 in West Svay there were more than the usual number of households in debt because of purchases of oxen or materials for oxcarts by families who wanted to engage in dirt hauling. Of eight families in debt, five had borrowed for precisely this purpose, while one household had gotten loans to buy an ox for the cultivation season and two households had needed money and rice for food during the preceding year. Six of these families cleared their debts (which ranged between 1,000 and 2,000 riels) completely by payments of rice from the 1959 harvest, money earned from dirt hauling and other activities, and/or sale of oxen that were no longer needed for hauling. (Two families continued to owe 500–1,000 riels to kinsmen, but loans from relatives can be paid in leisurely fashion.) The problem was, however, that in paying off the debts most of the households surrendered most or virtually all of their rice crop to brokers and kinsmen, and were thus faced with the prospect of having to buy or borrow rice for food in the coming year. Some of these families would be able to cope with the situation by extra effort, and it is likely that their budgets would be free of bad deficits within a year or so. For example, Kouch expected to buy rice for food and slowly repay his remaining debts to kinsmen by working more than usual as a cyclo driver in Phnom Penh, and by selling an ox should it become necessary.

There are, however, two or three families that are caught in a seemingly unbreakable cycle of annual debt because of grossly inadequate holdings. House 2 with its meager six ares of land for a family of seven must each year borrow money and rice for food (despite extra activities such as making palm sugar, raising pigs, driving a cyclo, dirt hauling, and odd jobs), give up its small harvest as payments for debts, and borrow again the next year.[80] Its situation is now somewhat ameliorated by the fact that the oldest son is of an age where he also can earn money by driving a cyclo; but it is likely that the family will be in tight straits until most or all of the children are grown. House 10 with four adults and three young children to support on thirty-four ares of land also has a difficult time, and in 1959 it also gave up virtually all of its harvest in payments for borrowed rice and money. Although Sophat, the resident son-in-law, is an energetic young man who sharecrops and plows for people without oxen, the family has no other sources of income (except that the father is occasionally hired to play music). It is probable that this household will also be in annual debt unless they undertake some supplementary occupations, or until the size of the household is decreased by the death of the elder couple.

Apart from debts, it is not uncommon to buy on short-term credit. Usually, either a token or a substantial part of the purchase price is given at the time of buying an item, with "a promise [to pay]" (*sŏng kee*) the rest at some date in the near future (generally within a month or so). Such arrangements may be made in transactions among villagers (e.g., in buying oxen), occasional purchases at the Chinese roadside stand (or in Kompong Tuol if the buyer is well known to the merchant), and purchases of items for weddings and funerals.

A word might be said here about the brokers and moneylenders with whom the villager deals, and who are not uncommonly stereotyped as heartless, mercenary Chinese preying on the peasants (see Monod 1931, 35–36, 42–45 for an extreme example). In point of fact, the rice brokers who come to West Svay are as likely to be fellow Khmer[81] or Sino-Cambodians (who are often culturally Khmer) as well as Chinese; and they are on very amiable and cordial terms with the villagers. Moneylenders or pawnbrokers in Kompong Tuol are Chinese, and they, too, treat their clients with courtesy and honesty.[82] Indeed, it is to the merchant's advantage to behave amicably and fairly with villagers since the latter can choose to go elsewhere; moreover, loans are often made on the basis of the merchant's prior knowledge, gained from a long-standing relationship, of the trustworthiness of a debtor. On the other side of the relation, the villager thinks debt is a burden and does not like to be in its thrall. But if he must become indebted, he accepts the conditions of the loan without complaint

---

[80] House 2 used to have twenty-five more ares of land that had to be sold to the normal school as a building site. Thus, they have had problems of sustenance primarily only within the past two years.

[81] Zadrozny 1955, 296 suggests that Khmer merchant-moneylenders may be a relatively recent development since World War II. Note, however, that one man in West Svay was a rice broker-moneylender more than thirty years ago, and that Svay villagers have long been accustomed to dealing with Khmer rice merchants.

[82] See Delvert 1961, 522–23 and Steinberg 1959, 42–44 for brief discussions of Chinese merchants in Cambodia.

because he knows of no other system or has no other recourse, and he does not feel that he is prey to a greedy ogre. The villager neither loves nor hates the merchants and lenders but looks upon them in a businesslike manner as convenient sources of sales and loans.

In the larger picture, such merchants serve an essential role in the economy at large. As in other peasant societies, these middlemen perform bulking, bulk breaking, storage, transport, and processing functions as well as providing credit and capital for the villagers (Mintz 1959, 23; Delvert 1961, 511–13). From one point of view, it seems onerous that interest rates are so high and that the merchant, not the villager, determines the price (usually low) at which the latter sells his rice. But from a different perspective, the merchant buying rice must deal with the fact that he is purchasing at a time when the national (and international) market is saturated with rice (which thus commands low prices); high interest rates and profits go to defray different aspects of the merchant's business overhead (for he, too, usually operates on credit with the next higher level of commerce such as wholesalers and export firms); and the merchant does provide the villager with a variety of services (see Delvert 1961, 511–13 for details).

## BUYING AND SELLING TRANSACTIONS

The official medium of exchange in Cambodia is, of course, the currency known as the riel, though (as noted earlier) bartering with rice is also common in some exchanges. Another sort of barter is simple swapping, such as trading one ox for another. In all transactions, bargaining is an essential and enjoyable concomitant. Fixed price is a rarity limited only to certain stores in Phnom Penh that cater mostly to foreigners.

The buying and selling of various items (and labor) take place within three main spheres: (a) intra- or inter-village exchange; (b) village and town (i.e., Kompong Tuol) exchange; and (c) village and city (i.e., Phnom Penh). The first two are of primary importance in providing Svay with its diverse material needs.

(a) Intra- or inter-village exchange. A number of things—for example, small surpluses of agricultural produce, craft items, chickens, cattle, snacks, and the services of specialists—are bought and sold within the village (even within the hamlet) itself by direct transactions between neighbors or acquaintances. Such purchases and sales are also common between the inhabitants of West Svay and people in either nearby or distant villages; either a purchaser seeks out a seller who is known or thought to have what one wants, or a seller may hawk his products from community to community (e.g., vendors of mats, sickles, etc., often come to West Svay).

(b) The market town. Kompong Tuol, several kilometers from Svay, is a relatively small but bustling market town located near the junction of two minor and one major highways. At the hub of the town are two large market pavilions crowded with stalls and counters of professional merchants selling meat, fish, cloth, spices, beverages, and a variety of fruits and vegetables (much of the fresh produce coming from within the surrounding area). Outside the pavilions are a profusion of other sellers: snack vendors, soft-drink carts, bread peddlers, and villagers with small amounts of fruits and vegetables spread out on mats. To either side of the marketplace, a succession of small, open-front shops stretch along the road; some are more or less specialized while others offer almost as wide a variety of goods as any American dime store. Among the items or services available here are cloth, sarongs, and other clothing for both sexes of all ages, shoes, household wares, tools and diverse "hardware" goods, gasoline and kerosene, medicine, toys, jewelry, stationery, tobacco and cigarettes, cosmetics, beauty parlors, a slaughter house, a brick yard, a lumber yard, photographers, tailors, jewelers, and renters of loudspeakers, phonographs and records, dishes, tables, and chairs for ceremonies.

In addition to the shops and stalls in town, there are also several traveling vendors who work out of Kompong Tuol and make frequent or occasional rounds of the villages in the area. One old man, who comes almost daily to Svay, carries a potpourri of goods in baskets hung from a shoulder pole: betel, areca, lime, candy, salt, dried fish, mirrors, thread, pins, toys, kerosene, etc., the exact inventory varying from day to day. Several times a week an old woman comes to vend cakes or other prepared food dishes, while a girl sells fruit or other produce. Several times a year, a dye-man may come with a pot of boiling, black dye perched on his bicycle. All of these peddlers are Chinese (as are the storekeepers in Kompong Tuol) and pursue their occupations full-time.

Kompong Tuol thus serves important economic functions for Svay and the other villages in this vicinity. First and most significant, it provides the villagers with a variety of foods and material objects gathered in from other communities both near and far, as well as manufactured or imported items channeled down from the city.[83] Second, the town furnishes an outlet for villagers to market produce or goods without the intervention of a middleman. Third, it is a minor source of employment for villagers as well.[84]

Somewhat intermediate between village–village and village–town exchange, but closer to the latter in its nature, is the small store located across the road from Middle Hamlet. Operated by two Chinese families (who are socially as well as geographically separate from the Khmer villagers), this shop carries a very limited supply of items: kerosene, cigarettes, candy, cakes, salt, sugar, and small or occasional amount of fish, fruits, and vegetables. Its essential function is not unlike that of the small, corner grocery store in relation to the supermarket of Kompong Tuol: villagers prefer not to buy at the shop because its prices are a few riels higher than in town, but they will do so when they run out of some essential and cannot get to town, when they are in a hurry, or when they wish to buy on short-term credit. The shopkeepers also serve as occasional buyers of palm sugar made by the villagers.

(c) The city. Phnom Penh has several large marketplaces for food and a myriad of shops and stores offering a vast array of both domestic and imported merchandise. Prices of items in Phnom Penh are usually cheaper than in Kompong Tuol, but since a trip to the former requires some time and bus fare, purchases in the city

[83] Cf. Mintz's (1959, 21 and passim) "horizontal" and "vertical" exchange. Horizontal exchange between "class equals" applies, strictly speaking, to the intra- or inter-village exchanges discussed previously, and to situations where villagers directly vend their wares in the marketplace. But there is a sort of horizontal (or, one might say, zig-zag) exchange when fruits and vegetables from nearby *chamkar* villages, or craft items made by village artisans in other areas, are sold through the mediation of Kompong Tuol's merchants to Svay villagers. Vertical exchange involves movements of goods "upward" to or (as is mainly the case here) "downward" from the city, where the producers and consumers of goods are of different classes.

[84] The latter two functions are relatively unimportant for West Svay. It is rare for West Svay residents to have an abundance of surplus goods to sell in Kompong Tuol, though this does occur on occasion. With respect to employment, four men had jobs in town: as gold artisan, metalworker (both for several years), worker in the lumber yard, and remorque driver.

are infrequent and usually limited to certain commodities that are not available in Kompong Tuol (e.g., better quality clothes, silk thread for weaving). Even rarer are direct sales of produce without the intervention of middlemen; as noted previously, West Svay sometimes sold their rice direct to merchants in Phnom Penh, but this practice has decreased since oxcarts were barred from entering the city (though villagers from other areas evidently bring their rice in by bus). Phnom Penh is, however, very important in offering temporary jobs for West Svay villagers, as well as other kinds of more permanent employment for those who emigrate from the countryside.

## PROPERTY AND INHERITANCE

A sense of property is highly developed in village life; virtually everything in and around the community—every tree, every length of rope, and even every fish that spawns in a bit of water—can be traced ultimately to some owner(s). The major types of property can be characterized as follows: (1) land: rice fields, house sites, and other land within the village proper, uncultivated land outside the village, and water holes; (2) trees; (3) houses and their furnishings; (4) various equipment, implements, and tools; (5) cattle and other domestic animals; (6) jewelry; and (7) personal possessions such as clothing. Such items may be acquired through inheritance, purchase, or gift. And once ownership is established, property rights, according to law (see Clairon n.d., 167–68), are absolute (with the exception of possible confiscation by the government in cases of public interest or emergency, such as happened when some West Svay villagers had to sell land for the building of the normal school) and perpetual. Further, property may be loaned, rented, sold, given away, or transmitted in inheritance, according to the owner's wishes.

Ownership of property is usually strongly individual in nature. Cases of joint ownership do occur and are usually instances where a husband and wife have purchased or otherwise acquired property through their mutual efforts or pooling of resources. Though it is legally possible for others, for example, siblings, to hold property in common, in practice such situations are quite rare because they lead usually to friction and eventual division. Even in marriage, property (apart from joint holdings) remains ultimately separate: each spouse retains title to whatever goods he or she brought to the union (or inherits during the marriage). It is true that for the duration of the marriage, husband and wife freely utilize one another's property, share the produce or proceeds therefrom, and ordinarily give little thought to what items belong to which spouse or bother to distinguish individual from common property. But one cannot dispose of a spouse's property without his/her consent. And in event of divorce, each spouse takes back whatever possessions he/she owned at the outset of, or acquired during, the marriage, while goods or money earned jointly during the marriage are divided equally between them (for other details on disposition of property in divorce, see chapter 6). In case of a spouse's death, the surviving widow(er) does not assume title to the deceased mate's property but has only rights of executor and usufructor unless there are no offspring or other close consanguineal kinsmen who qualify as heirs.[85] In village life, even minor children are recognized as having some rights of

---

[85] For a comparative study of legal codes regarding property in marriage, see Lingat 1955, especially vol. 2.

ownership, whether it be a possession that was received as a gift, purchased by the child's own earnings, or acquired in inheritance.[86]

Land is the most precious possession in village life and thus deserves some discussion; furthermore, certain points regarding ownership and use of land will apply to other items of property as well. In 1884 the French administration nullified the idea of royal domain over all lands and established the existence of private property holdings. There are still some areas of unused land that belong to the state or to temples. But individual property has increased in scope and importance.[87]

In and around Svay, which has been inhabited for generations and supports a dense population, every bit of land is owned by someone. There are no communal lands belonging to the village, nor lands held by a group of persons as a unit (apart from joint ownership by spouses). Title to land is acquired primarily through inheritance and sometimes through purchase.

Purchases and sales of land are relatively infrequent.[88] While land within the village may be sold without much hesitation to someone who desires a house site, sale of rice fields generally occurs only if the owner is in dire need, is emigrating from the village, has no offspring to inherit the property, or is forced to sell to the government. Correspondingly, purchases of land are not too common because most villagers lack the large amounts of money necessary to buy land. The price of land varies with its location or quality, as well as size of plot. Location is the important factor in sales of land for house sites: plots along or near the highway are favored (because of ease of access to and from routes of travel) and therefore more expensive, while sites further inland are correspondingly less desirable and cheaper. (Within West Svay, which is a few hundred meters from the highway, House 18 purchased a house site of about fifteen by thirty meters for several thousand riels [from House 27].) Quality of the soil is more important than location in determining the price of rice fields. A hectare of excellent paddy land can cost as much as 30,000–40,000 riels, while those of poor quality might sell for as low as one-tenth that price. Fields around Svay generally range from about 5,000 to 8,000 riels per hectare. (The government paid 5,000 riels a

---

[86] For example, when House 1 was in need of money and it was suggested that the parents pawn a bracelet belonging to their eighteen-year-old daughter, they refused to do so, saying that she had bought the jewelry with her own earnings and the bracelet was therefore not theirs to dispose of.

[87] In precolonial Cambodia, the king was said to be ultimate owner over everything—land, people, and waters—within his domain. However, individuals could live on, work, and transmit (in inheritance, sale, or rental) any plots of land that were not in royal domain, mortmain, or occupied by temples, officials, or royal serfs, by virtue of having cleared the land and/or three continuous years of usufruct, notification of the proper officials, and payment of taxes. Such rights were maintained so long as the land was used and lapsed only if the land were abandoned for three consecutive years (Aymonier 1900, 82–83). There has been considerable discussion by several authors as to whether individuals had mere usufruct of the land or whether true individual ownership did indeed exist among the ancient Khmer. For a review of differing viewpoints on this question, see Kleinpeter 1937; Morizon 1934; Delvert 1961; and Bruel 1924; also see Ricklefs 1967. All but Bruel argue that although the king was legally and theoretically the ultimate proprietor, individual ownership of land existed for all practical purposes. Kleinpeter (1937, passim) also offers an interesting discussion of various influences on and development of concepts of property through time in Cambodia.

[88] Of approximately 146 parcels of rice fields cultivated by West Svay inhabitants, only about twenty were acquired through purchase while the rest were inherited. Of thirty-two house sites, only two were purchased and the rest were inherited.

hectare for the land they expropriated in building the normal school, which price was considered niggardly by the villagers.)

Excluding sale of land to the government, land is almost always bought from or sold to someone within the community. Occasionally, fields may be purchased from someone in a neighboring community if a plot is located in the vicinity of Svay; or one might sell land to a former resident or to a kinsmen of a Svay resident who wished to move into the village. There is no obligation to restrict sales in such a manner (cf., e.g., the "closed communities" discussed by Wolf 1955, 1957), for legally anyone except a foreigner (e.g., a Chinese) could purchase land in Svay. In practice, however, peasant insularity and distrust of strangers makes it exceedingly unlikely that anyone would seek to buy land in and move into a community unless he were known in some manner to its residents.

Rights of usufruct are real and recognized in both civil law (see Clairon n.d., 189–93) and village life. In West Svay, the following kinds of usufruct arrangements are common. (1) Rights to usufruct may be tacit, and permission of the owner need not be asked. For example, members of a family or household generally freely utilize one another's property; during the dry season, oxen may pasture in anyone's rice fields; spaces of open land within the village proper are used constantly as thoroughfares, playgrounds, etc.; water holes are used to wash oxen or catch small quantities of fish. Note, however, that such free usufruct of someone else's property may be subject to sudden cancellation at critical moments when the owner wants to assert his exclusive rights. There are several examples of this (some of which have been mentioned previously). (a) For much of the year, cattle may graze or fodder may be obtained anywhere in the rice fields. But during certain months when food for cattle is difficult to obtain, grasses on the dikes of certain rice paddies are forbidden to anyone but the owners of the fields. (b) Similarly, villagers often fish in the several water holes by the hamlet. But after the end of the rainy season when fish are largest and most plentiful, one water hole is fenced off and no one but the owner's household may fish there. When the other water holes are drained, the fish within them are considered the rightful property of the holes' owners. (c) The uncultivated lands to the west of the hamlet ordinarily appear to be a no-man's-land where villagers are free to relieve themselves or gather wild plants. But when dirt-hauling operations were in progress, owners of these lands exacted fees from other villagers to dig dirt from, or even merely to drive across, their property.

(2) Rights to usufruct may be granted by the owner with no special arrangements or payment required; for example, dirt haulers from other villagers were allowed to set up temporary shelters on several persons' lands simply by requesting permission to do so, and no rental fees were charged. Things other than land are also frequently lent freely to kinsmen and neighbors: for example, Muoy (House 25) has free use of the house that belongs actually to her sister who has moved away; a bride often borrows jewelry and clothes from friends and kinsmen for the wedding ceremonies; House 27 purchased a brass gong specifically to lend to fellow villagers for life-cycle ceremonies; etc.

(3) Rights to usufruct may be granted by the owner on the condition of some payment for usage. Money rental of land does not occur in Svay, but sharecropping arrangements are common. Sugar palms, however, are often rented out for money; it is also possible to rent oxen if one has none.[89]

---

[89] It might be mentioned that the renting out of certain items may be undertaken as a commercial venture; e.g., a woman in a neighboring village rents out clothes and other finery for wedding costumes, and Chinese in Kompong Tuol rent out chairs, tables, dishes, loudspeakers, phonograph records, etc. to villagers for life-cycle ceremonies.

INHERITANCE

In discussing the Cambodian system of inheritance, there are two levels to consider: (1) the extensive and detailed legal statutes of the civil code (see Clairon n.d., 122–63; Lingat 1952–55, 2:130–35, 169–71),[90] and (2) the less formalized and simpler patterns of inheritance in village society that is our major concern. Both utilize the same fundamental principles (for the legal code is based to a great extent on traditional practices), but the operation of inheritance among villagers rarely becomes as complicated as some of the situations discussed in the civil code. Since, however, disputes over inheritance do occur in village life and must often be taken to officials or courts for adjudication, reference will be made to formal law codes for amplification of certain points.

The basic and ideal principles underlying inheritance in village life are the following. (1) Both males and females can transmit and inherit any kind of property; there are no rules that certain types of property must pass to a certain sex. (2) Inheritance is partible: the estate can be and usually is divided among a number of heirs. (3) Children are the first and foremost heirs. All legitimate or adopted offspring inherit equally, and sex and birth order are of no significance. (The surviving spouse acts as executor and usufructor of the deceased's estate on behalf of the children.) (4) If the deceased has no children, inheritance passes to the deceased's parents or, if the latter are already dead, to the deceased's siblings.[91]

Before discussing actual instances of inheritance, a word might be said first about the time and manner of transmission of property. Rice fields are almost always ceded to a child at the time he/she marries, rather than waiting until the parents' death. (Indeed, sometimes a child will have a certain paddy or paddies designated as his/her own upon reaching late adolescence.) Newlyweds often receive other property as well, such as land for a house site, trees, a parental home, jewelry, etc., because a young couple needs resources for the beginning of a new family.[92] Otherwise, wishes as to disposition of other property (e.g., to as yet unmarried children) are generally made known by parents before they die. Since 1920 the only legally valid will is a written

---

[90] For nineteenth-century and earlier legal codes on inheritance, see Leclère 1898, 1:340–43, 347–56, 361–72, 383, 467; 2:32, 38, 45, 480–82, 525, 550–51, 587–88; Aymonier 1900, 85.

[91] It was hard for informants to conceive of situations in which none of the preceding categories of heirs were present. In the legal codes, however, the following order of heirs is specified for cases in which the deceased has no offspring: (a) parents, (b) "ascendants," presumably grandparents, (c) siblings (step-siblings inherit only one-half as much as full siblings), (d) the surviving spouse, (e) aunts, uncles, or first cousins, (f) the state, if no heirs whatever can be found (Clairon n.d., 125–26). An additional complication is introduced by the legal principle of "representation" whereby the offspring of a possible heir who is already dead can claim the inheritance due his deceased parent, if that parent was a child or sibling of the legator: e.g., if X dies leaving a son and grandchildren born of a deceased daughter, the grandchildren can claim their dead mother's share of X's inheritance (Clairon n.d., 125–27). Non-relatives can also inherit property; but by law, only one-half of the deceased's goods can pass to non-kinsmen; the other half must be kept for the support of the surviving spouse and offspring unless they have been disinherited (Clairon n.d., 142–43; Lingat 1952–55, 2:171).

[92] Although land or a house may be verbally "given" to a child at the time he/she marries, in many cases land continues to be officially registered under a parent's name until the latter's death because of the bother involved in transferring title; the child, however, will have full usufruct of the land. Similarly, a house may continue to be occupied by parents (as well as the young couple) although it has been verbally passed on to a child.

one (either dictated to the sub-district chief in the presence of two witnesses who are not heirs, or written by the testamentary himself [Clairon n.d., 135–38]). The villagers themselves realize the value of written wills in averting possible quarrels among heirs, but verbal wills, spoken to family and trusted elders or friends, are still common.

There are, nonetheless, instances of deaths intestate with respect to certain property that may or may not be partible (e.g., a house or small paddy), or cases of disagreement among heirs as to the division of certain goods (especially with verbal wills). The heirs may be able to work out a satisfactory solution, such as selling the property and dividing the money equally among themselves, or otherwise agreeing on an equitable partition of the estate. If, however, the heirs do not reach an amicable settlement—and quarrels over inheritance are said to be common—the matter must be taken for adjudication first to the sub-district chief; if his judgment is not acceptable to the heirs, the district office is next consulted; or, as a final resort, the provincial court of appeals.[93]

It should be noted that the death of an individual does not mean the immediate dispersal of all of his/her property if there are a surviving spouse and children who must be supported. The widow(er) with children becomes administrator of and has rights of usufruct to the deceased spouse's property, which cannot be disposed of but must be maintained for the offspring. According to law, a widow also receives title to one-third the common property of the spouses (two-thirds if a widower) so long as she does not remarry, become a concubine, or lead an "unworthy" life. But if there are no children born of the marriage, a widow cannot become even executrix of her husband's estate and must give it up to other rightful heirs, though she may receive one-third the common property unless her husband had accused her of adultery while he was still alive. (See Clairon n.d., 128–30; Lingat 1952–55, 2:130–35, 169–70, for further details on the rights and obligations of the surviving spouse, especially a widow.)

To return now to the question of actual instances and patterns of inheritance in village life, in practice some of the ideal principles are followed while others are modified.

(1) Both males and females do indeed transmit and inherit all sorts of property. See, for example, the following cases of ownership and inheritance.

(a) Rice fields:

| | |
|---|---|
| owned by male, inherited from father | 4 cases |
| owned by male, inherited from mother | 4 cases |
| owned by male, inherited from "parents"[94] | 8 cases |
| owned by female, inherited from father | 6 cases |

---

[93] If the matter reaches court, the law provides for the establishment of as many shares of the estate as there are heirs (or branches of the family if the principle of representation is invoked), guided by local practices, the wishes of the majority of the heirs, and the nature of the estate. The heirs then draw lots for the different portions of the estate. If the estate cannot be divided without notably diminishing its value, it is given to one of the heirs on the condition that he will reimburse the others with the value of their rightful portions. If no agreement can be reached on the division of some goods, the property is sold and the proceeds divided among the heirs (Clairon n.d., 156).

[94] The term "parents" indicates that the informants were not certain whether a piece of property derived from the father or the mother, or that both parents were co-owners of some property.

|  |  |
|---|---|
| owned by female, inherited from mother | 10 cases |
| owned by female, inherited from "parents" | 5 cases |

   (b) Village land:

|  |  |
|---|---|
| owned by male, inherited from father | 2 cases |
| owned by male, inherited from mother | 6 cases |
| owned by male, inherited from "parents" | 4 cases |
| owned by female, inherited from father | 5 cases |
| owned by female, inherited from mother | 10 cases |
| owned by female, inherited from "parents" | 1 case |

   (c) Houses (and associated furnishings, etc.):

|  |  |
|---|---|
| owned by male, inherited from mother | 3 cases |
| owned by female, inherited from father | 2 cases |
| owned by female, inherited from mother | 10 cases |
| owned by female, inherited from "parents" | 1 case |

As is evident from the figures, there is a slight statistical tendency for women to out-number men as both transmitters and inheritors, especially with respect to houses. This fact is consistent with the tendency toward uxorilocal residence. Villagers noted that houses usually pass to daughters because they remain at home after marriage more frequently than do men, but this is by no means a definite rule. To a certain extent, some other goods tend to be sex-linked, for example, feminine jewelry and objects such as looms often go to daughters, or tools and cattle to sons; again, how-ever, this is not always the case.[95] (Some informants stated that jewelry is usually given to the favorite child or children, regardless of sex.)

(2) Inheritance is always partible, unless there is only one heir.

(3) Children are indeed the primary heirs to an estate, but the ideal of equal inheritance among offspring is often modified in practice. Many parents do attempt to follow the principle that inheritance should be equal in value, if not always in type of goods, for all children. For example, in the case of Vireak (House 1) and his two siblings, the rice fields were divided equally between Vireak and his brother, while the parental home (with all its furnishings, tools, etc.) and village land was given to his sister. But, villagers will admit, in practice there are numerous instances of unequal inheritance dictated by personal favoritism or individual circumstances, such that it is difficult to predict exactly how an estate will be divided among children. The primary considerations that may arise are the following.

(a) The child who has supported and cared for his/her aged parents until their death, either by staying on after marriage in the parental home or by taking the par-ents into his own home, will receive a larger share of the inheritance than those children who have had lighter responsibilities toward the parents. If the child has remained living with the parents, it is usual that he/she will get the family house and all that goes with it (in addition to land and/or other goods similar in amount to what his/her siblings have inherited).[96] For example, Kompha and Leak (House 20) have two sons, one of whom has emigrated to Phnom Penh and Rith who has remained

---

[95] Cf. the statement in Zadrozny 1955, 313 that "daughters tend to inherit more of such prop-erty as household belongings, money and jewels; sons generally receive a larger share of land."

[96] The house and all its furniture, utensils, tools, etc., as well as the house site and often cattle as well, often pass in one package to one heir, although that heir often distributes some items to siblings or other close kin.

with his parents and helps support them as well as his own family. Rith has already received about three-fifths of his parents' rice fields and will further inherit, upon his parents' death, the parental home and everything in it, the house site, and other land in the village, trees, cattle, all work implements, and jewelry. This is regarded as only fitting because, as his mother said, "His duties have been so heavy." (As noted in chapter 3, there is no clear-cut predictability as to which child, in terms of birth order[97] or sex, will remain at home to care for the parents though it is more likely to be a daughter than a son.)

(b) Any child who emigrates from the village upon marriage (e.g., to assume post-marital residence elsewhere) may not receive any rice fields, particularly when family holdings are small or there are a large number of children. To take one of numerous examples, Srey (House 1) was one of eight children. Four of her siblings who moved to other provinces upon marriage received no paddies (though they did get some portable property such as jewelry); rather, the rice fields and other land were divided equally among Srey and three other siblings who stayed in Svay.

There are, however, several qualifications to the preceding generalization. (i) A child who moves to a nearby village in marriage may well receive at least a small plot of land because he will reside close enough to work it. Thus a number of persons who came to West Svay in marriage own paddies near their natal villages, especially when they are from the neighboring communities of Ta Chas, Chouk, etc. (ii) If the parents' holdings are ample, even a child who emigrates to a distant community may receive and retain paddy land, letting relatives sharecrop it (e.g., Rith in House 20 sharecrops fields inherited by his brother who lives in Phnom Penh). (iii) Sometimes an emigrating child may inherit land within the village proper, if not rice fields. For example, Sen (House 6) did not get any paddies when he married because he went to reside in his wife's village, but he did receive some village land to which he eventually returned.[98]

(c) A child may receive a lesser share, or even no inheritance, if he/she marries someone who is relatively prosperous or, at least, owns enough rice fields to adequately support a family. This is particularly apt to be the case when the parental holdings are small relative to the number of children. As one example, Phana (House 3) is one of four siblings who remained in West Svay upon marriage (plus three more who moved elsewhere). He received no paddies because he married a woman from Middle Hamlet who inherited almost a hectare of rice fields; the other three siblings in West Svay each got a small portion of rice land.

(d) Another situation in which a child might receive a lesser inheritance is if the parents had financed a splendid wedding and/or new house for him/her before the former died. Upon the parents' demise, then, any still unmarried child or children might receive a larger amount of the estate because their marriages are yet to occur and their future in general must be provided for.[99]

---

[97] Cf. precolonial tradition in which, according to Aymonier (1900, 85), "The antique custom, sanctioned by law, gives a double share to the eldest [child] who had to support all his younger brothers, and to the youngest, the true pillar of support to his parents in their old age."

[98] Because of these three situations just described, there are a number of cases of individuals born in West Svay (or born of West Svay parents) who moved elsewhere upon marriage and then later returned to the hamlet to utilize land (paddies or house sites) that they had inherited in the community.

[99] One informant also stated that sometimes the first child to marry received somewhat more land than the other children would ultimately get, either because the parents were flushed with

(e) All of the preceding instances of unequal partition of inheritance are actually fair-minded attempts by the parents to equalize the situations of various children by taking various factors into account: those children who shoulder the heaviest burden for support of aged parents are compensated for their efforts by a larger share; those children who do not require land because of emigration or a prosperous marriage get little or no fields; etc. It is also possible, however, that parents may be quite arbitrary in their division of property and give a greater portion of inheritance to whatever child or children they happen to like most. Although ideally all children are loved equally well, villagers frankly state that it is not unusual for one or some offspring to be particular favorites. In most instances, the favored and most beloved child is the one who tends the parents in their old age, but this may not always be the case. (E.g., Pol's older brother resided with and cared for their parents in their old age, but Pol received a larger amount of rice fields than any of his siblings because his parents felt that he had been the most loving and thoughtful of all the children.) Conversely, there may also be situations in which little or nothing is given to a child who has quarreled with his parents, shown disrespect or ingratitude, failed to aid them when they were in need, or did not attend their funerals.[100]

(4) Finally, should an individual die without leaving any offspring, law and custom specify that his/her property should go first to the deceased's parents or if (as is likely) they are already dead, the inheritance passes to the deceased's siblings. However, village opinion decrees that the siblings should not retain such an inheritance but rather sell it to finance a splendid funeral for the departed. It is said that "persons of bad character" have been known to keep the property for themselves and their children, but such behavior is not condoned.

---

enthusiasm and generosity at the happy event, or because the parents might later give birth to more offspring and thereby upset what seemed to be an equal division of land at the time of the first marriage in the family.

[100] In fact, both the modern and ancient legal codes explicitly provide for the disinheritance of, or a reduction in inheritance for, an heir who was guilty of any offense toward the deceased, particularly neglecting to care for the deceased in his/her last illness and failing to attend the funeral (see Clairon n.d.,123–24; Leclère 1898, 1:348–51, 355).

# CHAPTER FIVE

# RELIGION

Theravada Buddhism is the official national religion of Cambodia that commands the sincere and devout allegiance of the Khmer peasantry. But the religious and ceremonial life of the village is better seen as a blend of elements not only from Buddhism but also from Hinduism and the traditional, indigenous folk religion as well. Hinduism, once dominant in some of the ancient kingdoms (but perhaps never fully understood and accepted by the masses), survives only as discrete elements of ceremonials, symbolism, and cosmology.[1] But the folk religion, which is the oldest religion of the Khmer, offers a variety of supernatural beings, as well as rituals and other practices, that are still firmly espoused in village life. It must be emphasized, however, that though it is possible (albeit sometimes difficult) for the observer to segregate various elements of village religious beliefs and practices as deriving from one religious tradition or another, the villager himself rarely conceives of observing separate religious traditions. Rather, for the ordinary Khmer, Buddha and ghosts, prayers at the temple and invocations to spirits, monks and mediums are all part of what is essentially a single religious system, different aspects of which are called into play at different, appropriate times.[2] However, for ease of presentation I shall discuss Buddhism and the animistic folk religion in separate sections.

## BUDDHISM (*PREA POT SASNA*)[3]

### THE TEMPLE AND ITS PERSONNEL

Buddhist temples and monks are ubiquitous parts of the Cambodian scene. (Various estimates of the number of monks in Cambodia in the 1950s range from approximately 37,000 to 68,000 while the number of temples is estimated to be between 2,500 and 2,800 [Martini 1955a, 409; Delvert 1961, 139].) Every village has either its own temple or one located nearby (see Delvert 1961, 219–20 on the distribution of temples). Svay villagers, in fact, attend two temples: Wat Svay, the village temple

---

Portions of this chapter have been published in Ebihara 1966.

[1] E.g., belief in certain minor deities (*tivoda*) derived from Hindu gods and goddesses, the use of white cotton thread in ceremonies, the *naga* (Khmer: *niĕk*) symbol, etc. See also Steinberg 1959, 73–74.

[2] Such blending of what Redfield called great and little religious traditions is common not only among other Theravada Buddhist cultures (see, e.g., Obeyesekere 1963 on the Sinhalese; Brohm 1963 and Nash 1963 on the Burmese; Kaufman 1960 on the Thai; various articles in Nash et al. 1966), but among peasants in general (see Redfield 1956; Wolf 1966). See also Gorer 1967.

[3] *Prea pot* = Holy Buddha, *sasna* = religion, from the Pali *Buddhasasana*. See Musgrave's glossary in Nash et al. 1966 (following p. 223) for the original Pali and Sanskrit words from which this and other Cambodian religious terms are derived.

situated at the eastern end of the community, and Wat Samnang located about two kilometers to the west on the road to Kompong Tuol.

Although the particular spatial arrangement and size of grounds may vary, temple grounds customarily have the following features. (1) A stone or cement wall (with several entrances) encloses the temple grounds and forms both an actual and symbolic boundary between the sacred and secular worlds. (2) The central temple proper (*vihiĕ*), built of painted stone or cement with an arching fluted roof and raised high upon a foundation with steps on all sides (though there is only one entrance to the temple that faces east), houses a resplendent altar with statues of Buddha and a colorful array of decorations. (3) The *salaa* (of which there may be more than one) is a roofed structure that is open on several or all sides and often contains a small altar. It is used for many purposes: for example, here the monks eat their meals and receive visitors; a large part of most ceremonies occurs in the *salaa* rather than in the temple proper; and the structure may serve also as a school classroom or shelter for overnight guests. (4) There may be one or more dormitories for the monks, built of cement or wood with various rooms for individual monks. The head monk often has a separate small residence. (5) There is usually a pond or water hole where the monks may bathe. In addition to the preceding, the temple grounds also often have a kitchen shed, a school building, small thatch shelters for persons who come to serve the monks or to meditate, monuments that hold the ashes of the dead or honor some important deceased personage, and some shrines for animistic folk spirits.[4] (See map 4 for layout of Wat Svay.) Various buildings are often in a state of partial construction because they are being newly erected or rebuilt, and work proceeds only as money is gradually accumulated through contributions. But the structures and grounds as a whole are well maintained and, because of the verdant growth of trees and other flora that is typical of temple grounds, the temple compound presents an aspect that is at once neat, colorful, and serene. Wat Samnang, with its spacious lands that have an almost forest-like tangle of growth (plus an active population of monkeys) attracts even visitors from Phnom Penh for picnic outings in its pleasant atmosphere.

Each *wat* or temple also has its own community that consists of the following individuals. (1) The monks (*look sŏng*, literally "master of the Sangha" or brotherhood of monks [Leclère 1899, 394]) themselves are differentiated on the basis of rank in the temple hierarchy. The head monk (*cau athikaa*, sometimes also called *mevat*), who is appointed by his superiors in the national hierarchy of monks,[5] has the main responsibility for supervision of personnel, property, and general maintenance of the temple according to both religious and secular law. He is assisted in this management and in the conducting of services by two assistant monks: the *kru sot* "of the right" and the *kru sot* "of the left." The remainder of the monks are divided into *pikuk*, fully ordained monks over twenty years of age, and *samne* or *niin* who are the novice monks under

[4] See Leclère 1899, 433–95 for a detailed discussion of temple grounds, architecture, interiors, statues of Buddha, altar decorations, religious paintings, etc.

[5] See Martini 1955b, 416–24, for discussion of the manner of appointment and the organization of the religious hierarchy above the temple level. This organization is autonomous in two senses. First, the Cambodian clergy has no structural ties to that of other Theravada Buddhist countries. Second, the two religious orders in Cambodia (see infra) each maintain separate though similar hierarchies with its own chiefs, various ranks, and regional councils that parallel the secular political division into provinces, districts, and finally the local unit. Also, see Martini 1955b and Leclère 1899, 393–94 for various terms for different kinds of monks.

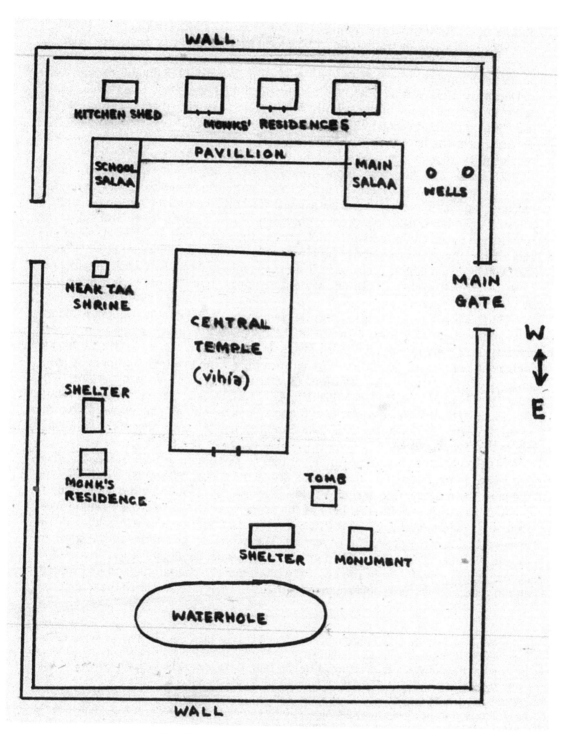

**Map 5** Schematic map of Wat Svay (not to scale)

twenty. (Both *pikuk* and *samne* tend to be ranked informally on the basis of the length of time they have been at the temple, but this is manifest only in the order in which they seat themselves or walk in line.) Because entrance into and departure from the monkhood are relatively simple and it is a common pattern for males to spend some period as a monk, the number of monks at any one temple will fluctuate through time. In December 1959 Wat Svay had ten monks (including novices) while Wat Samnang had twenty-three (many of the latter had entered the monkhood at other temples but had come to study at this temple). But the head monk and his two assistants are customarily men who have been monks for a good number of years and are committed to religious life (though they are technically free to leave it at any time).[6]

(2) *Konsüh look* (literally "monk's pupil") are young boys, ranging from about seven to twelve years of age, who are "given" by their families to serve the monks, receive religious instruction, and earn merit for both themselves and their parents. These temple boys, most of whom come from nearby villages, sleep and eat at the temple and assist the monks in various ways: they cook and serve food, wash and clean, carry things for the monks on journeys, etc. When not engaged in such tasks, the boys receive religious instruction from the monks and secular education at a public school. In December 1959 there were nine temple boys at Wat Samnang and ten at Wat Svay.

(3) Usually there are several adult laymen living at the temple. Generally elderly men and women, they come to reside at the temple for periods ranging from several days to several months to earn merit by performing various chores for the monks, as well as by prayer and meditation.[7] Sometimes they come for the latter alone, staying in isolated retreat for quiet devotion. (See also Martini 1955a, 414; Leclère 1899, 424–25.) These people live in small shelters on the temple grounds, though they must provide their own food (in contrast to the temple boys who eat the leftovers from the monks' meals). In December 1959 Wat Samnang had six such persons in residence, while Wat Svay had four.

(4) Finally, an important member of temple personnel, although one who does not reside there, is the *achaa*:[8] a layman who acts as liaison between the monks and the laity, the religious and secular worlds. The *achaa* is selected by the head monk in consultation with various members of the "congregation" as to what men are most liked and respected (the appointment must then be confirmed, as a formality, by the district chief and the provincial governor). The main responsibilities of the *achaa* are to lead the laity in prayers at ceremonies, to assist with the organization and conduct of temple festivals, to aid in the general management of the temple and its property, and in general to act as a spokesman for the laity in their relations with the temple and

---

[6] E.g., the head monk at Wat Samnang has been in the order for thirty-two years and is now a member of the district council of Mohanikay monks. The chief monk at Wat Svay has been a monk for forty-four years; he was ordained at Wat Svay, studied for some years at the Buddhist Institute in Phnom Penh, then returned to Wat Svay as its head. The assistant monks at both temples had been in the monkhood for eight to ten years.

[7] Cambodian Buddhism does not have nuns. But there are women called *don chi* who shave their heads, dress in white, lead a devout and ascetic life comparable to that of the monks, and render various services to the monks and the temple (Martini 1955a, 414).

[8] This term is also applied to men who are especially knowledgeable about religious-ceremonial matters and officiate at private rituals such as life-cycle ceremonies, but who are not attached to a temple. The term *achaa wat* ("temple *achaa*") is used to distinguish those who hold a formal position and responsibilities at a temple.

as a representative for the monks in their relations with the secular world. An *achaa*'s term of service varies according to his desires or abilities but is usually a number of years. Wat Samnang has two *achaa*; the one of second rank ("*achaa* of the right") assists the main *achaa* ("big *achaa*") in various duties and acts as a substitute when the latter is absent.

Life at Wats Samnang and Svay follows an orderly and disciplined routine that is dictated largely by the Vinaya (*viney*) code of conduct for monks and is similar to monastic life in other Theravada Buddhist countries (see, e.g., articles by Pfanner and Ingersoll in Nash et al. 1966; Kaufman 1960, 131–35; Nash 1965, 147–48 on Burmese and Thai monks). After waking at dawn the monks recite prayers before and after breakfast, which is served at about 7:00 a.m. During the morning they pursue whatever duties have been assigned to them by the head monk: some clean the temple grounds, while others study, speak with guests, teach in the school, or go to beg food in nearby communities. At 11:00 a.m. the second and final meal of the day is eaten, often in the company of laymen who have brought food or come to visit. (After noon, no solid foods can be eaten although beverages such as tea or water are permitted.) The monks spend the rest of the day performing more chores, punctuated by periods of leisure, until they recite brief prayers and retire to their spare cubicles at 10:00 or 11:00 p.m.[9] At Wat Samnang, noted for its educational facilities that draw monks from other temples, a good deal of time is spent in the teaching and learning of various religious and secular subjects (e.g., geography, history, religious doctrine, and Pali).

The usual daily routine of the monks varies with the occurrence of certain weekly, fortnightly, and annual or other observances: for example, the weekly Holy Day (see infra); the twice a month meeting of the monks for confessions of sins to one another (see Leclère 1899, 428–32; Martini 1955a, 415); the annual rainy season retreat during which monks are forbidden to leave the temple grounds; the observance of various annual Buddhist holidays; periodic invitations to the monks to participate in village ceremonies such as weddings and funerals; and special occasions such as visits by notable monks from other temples.

At all times a monk must observe ten major precepts: (1) do not kill any living beings (or even plants); (2) do not steal; (3) do not engage in any sexual activity; (4) do not lie; (5) do not drink any intoxicating beverages;[10] (6) do not eat after noon; (7) do not watch or participate in any sensual activity such as dance, song, the theater, etc.; (8) do not wear perfumes, cosmetics, or ornaments (9) do not sleep on a raised bed or sit on an elevated seat (except the prayer chair from which sermons are delivered);[11] (10) do not touch gold or money (see also Leclère 1899, 311–25; Martini 1955a, 411). In all there are 227 "sins," comprising the Patimok or code of errors in the Vinaya rules of conduct for monks, that must be avoided. These include not only the ten injunctions just listed but a variety of other rules such as not being alone in a room with a woman and never traveling alone. Punishment for infraction ranges from defrocking for the gravest sins (such as fornication), to various penances such as fasting for less grievous errors, to simple shame in the face of one's fellow monks for

---

[9] For further details of the monks' daily schedule, as well as their dress and possessions, see Leclère 1899, 413–17, 420–24; Steinberg 1959, 66; Martini 1955a, 413–15.

[10] Martini (1955a, 411) notes, however, that medicinal alcohol is permitted.

[11] I have, however, seen monks sitting on the slightly raised platforms that are common in village life for sitting while eating or talking.

the most minor offenses (such as impatience) (see Leclère 1899, 428–32 for details of punishments). In fact, apart from the ten precepts and the most serious sins listed by the Patimok, adherence to the entire 227 rules is not overly rigid, and the monks are not absolute paragons. Young monks have been known to break into giggles when they stumble over words in the midst of a chant; the head monk at one temple was interested in birth control in America, a topic that should be taboo for his ears; monks have obliquely or directly asked me for cigarettes or magazines, items that are not essential alms; monks are sometimes seen traveling alone; etc. Mohanikay monks in particular are often accused by Thommayut adherents as being lax in their observance of the monk's code of conduct.

Nonetheless, the monks do follow an ascetic and disciplined life that earns them supreme respect as living embodiments and spiritual generators of Buddhism. They are set apart from and above the secular world: they live in special quarters; they do not vote; they cannot be tried in ordinary law courts; they have distinctive dress; etc. There is also special etiquette governing interaction with monks: for example, laymen must speak to them or about them with special linguistic forms (that are used also by the monks in speaking among and about themselves); one must kneel, place one's hands in the greeting or prayer position, and bow to the ground three times when greeting or leaving a monk; one must hand them objects in the deferential manner of cupping an item in both hands; one must take care not to have one's head higher than that of a monk (which involves walking in a crouch when passing monks who are seated on the ground); one must step aside immediately and give a monk unimpeded passage on a path or stairway; etc.[12] This is not to imply that the villagers feel that all monks are aloof and remote creatures toward whom one must behave with complete reserve. One can chat and joke in ordinary conversation with them, or even indulge in horseplay in their presence (e.g., one day Rotha was poking the buttocks of Thol while the latter was serving food to monks at a festival). Respect mingled with affection, rather than fearfulness, is the common feeling toward many monks, especially those who reveal their humanity as well as spirituality. Many villagers had particularly deep affection and regard for the head monk at Wat Samnang, an exceptionally warm, lively, and intelligent man whose genuine love and concern for the villagers was expressed constantly in small acts such as giving fruit to a shy baby, asking someone the name of a visiting relative whose strange face he had spied at a temple festival, or quite simply, the smiles and general good humor that punctuated all of his conversations.

## Mohanikay and Thommayut

Before proceeding further, it should be noted that Cambodian Buddhism is divided into two orders: the Mohanikay ("the great congregation") and the Thommayut ("those who are attached to the doctrine"). The Mohanikay is the older and larger of the two, with over 90 percent of the total number of monks and 94 percent of all temples (Martini 1955b, 416–17). The Thommayut group originated in 1864 with a Cambodian monk who had studied at a Thommayut temple in Thailand, and considers itself more orthodox and strict than the Mohanikay. The number of Thommayut monks was estimated at less than 1,600 in 1955 (Martini 1955b, 417) and its

---

[12] Monks are also given favored seats on buses by even Chinese or Vietnamese drivers. In addition, the monks commonly receive free transportation on buses, trains, and cyclos because the drivers earn merit by giving them free rides.

temples are located primarily in Phnom Penh and the provincial capitals, but the order is important for having been adopted by the king and other high-ranking groups. Both orders share the same basic Theravada doctrine and texts but have separate and independent hierarchical organizations. There are also a few minor differences between the orders in the behavior of their monks (see infra) that arise from the Thommayut attempts to return to what they feel is a more pure and rigorous form of Theravada. (See also Leclère 1899, 402–3; Zadrozny 1955, 128; Martini 1955b, 416–18; Steinberg 1959, 70–72.)

It is interesting and perhaps somewhat unusual that both of these orders are represented in Svay.[13] Wat Samnang is Mohanikay, while Wat Svay changed from Mohanikay to Thommayut about seventy years ago. (The exact reasons for this shift are unclear; evidently the temple's head monk decided to leave the Mohanikay order and be ordained as a Thommayut monk. Some of the other monks followed his example, while the rest scattered to other Mohanikay temples.)

The villagers themselves feel that the distinctions between Mohanikay and Thommayut are minor. They say that Thommayut monks carry their alms bowls in their hands, recite Pali texts with non-Khmer pronunciation, will not accept objects directly from the hands of a woman, cannot go anywhere unaccompanied by another male, do not attend the movies or theater, and cannot carry money; while the Mohanikay monks carry their bowls suspended from the shoulder, recite Pali with Cambodian pronunciation, and have been known on occasion to perform the other acts just noted as being prohibited to Thommayut monks.[14] Thommayut adherents will often have a superior tone in their voices when discussing the allegedly less rigorous behavior of Mohanikay monks.) But, most villagers conclude, "They are really both the same," and they realize that the differences between the two orders are rather superficial ones.

In recognition of the fundamental similarities between the Mohanikay and Thommayut, fifteen households in West Svay either attend both temples equally often (saying, "Wherever there is a festival, we go"), or contain varying loyalties within the same family (the husband devoted to one temple and the wife to another). On the other hand, however, the remainder of the hamlet's households do feel strong loyalty to one order. There is an old tradition in West Svay that the houses in the eastern part of the hamlet are Thommayut, while those in the western section are Mohanikay. In fact, ten households, all of which are situated in the eastern part of the hamlet, are devoted to Thommayut Wat Svay.[15] This loyalty to a particular order is manifested

---

[13] Actually, within the radius of about five kilometers there are a number of other temples that represent both orders. So it is not unlikely that the dual or divided allegiance to the two orders that is found in Svay exists also in other villages in this area.

[14] Apart from the Thommayut attempt to return to a "greater piety and purity," the manner of carrying the alms bowl and pronunciation of Pali are the only major differences between the two orders that are noted by Martini (1955b, 417), while Leclère (1899, 403) cites only the method of carrying the bowl. The other differences mentioned by the villagers are thus evidently taken from their personal experiences of what they have seen or heard that monks do.

[15] An individual's or a household's allegiance to one or the other order was determined by questions as to which order the men of the family had been monks in, what temples one's parents attended, which temple was attended and/or preferred by present members of the household (if the response specified a particular temple, the person was asked if he ever went to the other temple), and by records of villagers ritual attendance at various events at both Wat Svay and Wat Samnang.

by attendance at one particular temple (some persons never go to the other temple, though others will go "if asked" or if a major festival is occurring) and by sending one's son, if he becomes a novice or monk, into the order to which one is devoted. Overtly, the choice between Mohanikay and Thommayut is dictated mainly by the fact that one's parents had attended, or men in the family had been monks in, one or the other order, or sometimes simply by a preference for one or the other temple and its monks as being "nicer," "more comfortable," etc. On a less obvious level, it might be noted that most of the Thommayut families are among the wealthier households in the village, and it may be that their criticisms of the Mohanikay on religious grounds are an expression of superiority that they may feel in other contexts but cannot ordinarily express in egalitarian village life.[16] The Mohanikay order does appear to be more populistic and is definitely the more popular order in West Svay.

Though the villagers ordinarily recognize this divided allegiance to the two orders, it is relatively insignificant and does not usually disrupt daily relationships. Thommayut adherents may make disparaging comments about Mohanikay monks, and those loyal to the Mohanikay order may criticize the monks at Wat Svay as being cold, aloof, and unsympathetic (making such remarks only to others of one's own order or to an impartial anthropologist). But the division is not so strong that, for example, parents who are devoted to one temple will not allow their children to attend an event at the other temple although they themselves would not go; or that husband and wife cannot have loyalties to different orders without creating family dissension; or that one would insist that one's children marry persons belonging to a particular order. It seems, however, that on rare occasions the different loyalties can become crystallized into opposing forces, as in the example (discussed in chapter 3) of West Svay's failure to hold a customary post-harvest festival in 1959 because resources were slim, and Thommayut villagers refused to contribute money if only Mohanikay monks were to be invited, while Mohanikay villagers were similarly adamant about declining support if only Thommayut monks were to be feasted.

## FUNCTIONS OF THE TEMPLE IN VILLAGE LIFE

"The temple is the center of rural life" (Delvert 1961, 220) in several respects. First and foremost, it is, of course, a moral center. The temple and its monks not only exemplify and disseminate the Buddhist teachings but also offer various opportunities for laymen to earn merit. Second, the temple is also a major social center. The various annual Buddhist festivals and other events are occasions for large festive gatherings and an important source of entertainment for the villagers; the Buddhist holidays, along with the stages of rice cultivation, are the main markers in the annual cycle of the village. Third, the temple retains importance as an educational institution. The temple schools or the period spent as a monk were once the only means of education for peasant children; in modern times, monk instructors and temple schools continue to operate as part of the public school system. Fourth, the temple provides a variety of other miscellaneous services.

---

[16] Recall that the royal family and upper classes in Phnom Penh are known to be Thommayut. In fact, Sihanouk himself once spent a very brief period as a monk at Wat Svay. [Actually it was an uncle of Sihanouk's who was ordained at Wat Svay, not Sihanouk himself.]

### (I) The Temple as Moral Center: Buddhist Beliefs and Practices

The intricacies of Theravada theology and doctrine are little known to the average villager (except perhaps those men who had been monks for a long period of time and have intellectual curiosity). But certain basic notions are known to all from sermons at the temple, recitations of the life of Buddha, chants or prayers committed to memory, or lessons at school. And the primary concepts of immediate significance to the villager are presented succinctly in a comment made by an eighteen-year-old girl: "I think I will go to three or four Katún festivals this year so that I will be reborn as a rich American." Several critical ideas underlie this remark: an individual goes through a cycle of reincarnations, and the average layman has little hope of achieving supreme Nirvana (*nipean*). But one's chances for a better existence in the next rebirth are determined by the number of good deeds accomplished in this lifetime. That is, by living according to the "law" (*cbap*), abstaining from sin (*bap*), and earning merit in numerous ways, an individual proceeds forward on the righteous path.[17]

There are godlike beings in village Buddhism. Buddha himself is considered by the common man to be a sort of god and is, in effect, supplicated for aid in times of crisis by ceremonies involving monks and offerings. There are also lesser deities or celestial beings, the *tivoda*,[18] or "beings who are very good" and live "up there."[19] But both Buddha and the *tivoda* serve primarily as examples of noble behavior to be emulated by ordinary people, rather than as controllers of man's fate. The individual himself determines what his future existence will be—whether as a human being of lower or higher standing, as an animal, or as a person consigned to a hell—by the tally of merits and sins he accrues in his present life.

There are a variety of ways to earn merit. (A) Becoming a monk (or novice) is the supreme means of earning merit for a male and is an act that radiates merit onto his parents as well.[20] Entrance into the monastic state (*bueh*) is an ideal of Cambodian culture that has been achieved by three-quarters of all males over seventeen years of age in West Svay. It is possible to become a monk for as short a period as a few months (often for just the duration of a *vossa*, the rainy season retreat of the monks), but for West Svay men the average length of stay in the monastery was two to three years, the shortest period being one year and the longest eight years.[21] (Twenty-four men had

[17] The term *cbap* is generally applied to secular rather than religious laws, but villagers may use it to refer also to moral (religious) as well as civil codes of conduct.

[18] Some of these *tivoda* are originally Hindu deities who were assimilated into the Buddhist pantheon. They include *prea ayso, prea norie, prea ùn, prea prum,* and *prea somanakoo.* The first four of these are equivalent to Siva, Vishnu, Indra, and Brahma respectively. Who *prea somanakoo* is, I do not know; it may refer to a Bodhisattva. Some villagers also spoke of ancestral spirits as being among the *tivoda,* and Steinberg (1959, 74) states that "for many rural Cambodians the tevoda [*sic*] merge into the world of *neak ta* [animistic spirits]."

[19] For discussion of Buddhist cosmology, see Monod 1931, 13–24; Porée and Maspero 1938, 189–93; Conze 1959, 49–51.

[20] According to Monod (1931, 61–62) and Porée-Maspero et al. (1958, 179) a male at the age of twelve should become a novice for a few months in honor of his mother and later be ordained as an adult monk, usually for a year, in honor of his father. This notion of two separate sojourns in the monastery is known in West Svay, but only Kompha (House 20) had actually done this, spending three years as a novice "for [my] mother" and two years as a monk "for [my] father."

[21] In the late nineteenth century, Leclère noted that it was rare for a man to spend less than a year as a monk and that shorter periods were disapproved of; he also stated that sojourns in the monastery had become less extended than in former times (1899, 401–2, 424).

entered the Mohanikay order, while six were ordained as Thommayut monks. A male from West Svay usually enters Wat Samnang or Wat Svay, but some had gone to other temples in the vicinity or in Phnom Penh.)

Becoming a monk is relatively simple. The basic requirements are that one desires to serve and can respond affirmatively to the various questions at the ordination. Prior to entering the monastery a young man or boy spends several months studying the Vinaya code of conduct for monks and various prayers under the guidance of a monk or temple *achaa*. Preceding the actual ordination at the temple, there are some ceremonies at the candidate's home during which his head and eyebrows are shaved, kinsmen and friends are feasted, monks are invited to pray, offerings are made to ancestral and other spirits, and other ritual acts may occur. On the day of ordination itself there is a symbolic reenactment of the young Lord Buddha's renunciation of his titled and wealthy secular life as the candidate, dressed in splendid clothes and sheltered by a parasol, rides a horse from his home to the temple amidst a colorful procession of kinsmen and friends carrying his monk's robes and equipment and offerings to the monks. In the temple, the chief monk asks the candidate the traditional questions posed in Theravada ordinations: are you twenty years of age; have you an alms bowl to beg food; are your monk's robes complete; do you have leprosy, sores, epilepsy, etc.; are you a slave; are you male; do you have the consent of your parents (or wife if married); do you have debts or owe any services to the king; are you a true human being and not a *yakh* (mythological ogre) or *nièk* (naga)? Other parts of the ordination ceremony include the donning of the monk's robes by the novitiate, the recitation of the 227 precepts for monks, and prayers. (Young boys who are becoming novices usually go through the same procedure except that the rituals are simpler and the ordination questions are not asked.) (For further details of these rituals and the ordination itself, see Leclère 1899, 405–12; Monod 1931, 63–65; Porée and Maspero 1938, 179–80; Porée-Maspero et al. 1950, 39–42; 1958, 45–48; Martini 1955a, 410–11.)

When a monk wants to return to secular life, he simply makes his wishes known to the head monk. After a brief, simple ceremony with prayers, the offering of food to the monks, and the ritual declaration that one wishes to "leave the monastic order" (*suk*), a man resumes lay status. (See Leclère 1899, 402 and Porée-Maspero et al. 1958, 48 for details.)

(B) Another crucial means by which laymen (especially women, who cannot become monks) can earn merit is to adhere to the various Buddhist precepts and other norms of conduct that are imparted to them in sermons, prayers, recitations of the life of Buddha, etc. While some villagers can more or less elucidate the famous Four Noble Truths and Eightfold Path[22] that are basic to Theravada doctrine, to most people they mean little more than a general injunction to practice proper conduct. Much more critical to the ordinary villager are the ten basic precepts that are the main guides for judging whether behavior is meritorious or sinful. These injunctions are identical to the ten major precepts observed by the monks, except that the layman need not be celibate but should abstain only from immoral sexual relations. For the

---

[22] The Four Truths are (1) existence is inevitably sorrowful because of the transiency of all things; (2) unhappiness is caused by desire for such things; (3) such sorrow can be avoided by the extinction of such desire; (4) desire can be stopped by following the eightfold path: right understanding, right purpose, right speech, right conduct, right vocation, right effort, right alertness, and right concentration. (See also Zadrozny 1955, 123–24; De Bary et al. 1958, 95–96.)

layman, however, only the first five precepts (*sùl pram*) that forbid killing, stealing, fornication, lying, and the consumption of alcoholic beverages, are to be observed constantly. The remainder are to apply only on Holy Days or only for the deeply devout.

The *sùl pram* do indeed exercise a powerful influence on village behavior, though often they are followed with varying degrees of fidelity. (1) The injunction against killing is the strongest precept. The murder of human beings is universally regarded as the greatest sin and horror. As noted in chapter 4, the slaughter of animals is also abhorred, and this task is delegated to Cham and Chinese butchers (although certain creatures such as frogs, crabs, snakes, insects, and fish are dispatched quite readily by most villagers, and chickens are a borderline case). Indeed, the especially devout, particularly old people, avoid keeping any domestic animals at all (except pets) because the latter will eventually be killed. (2) Theft is not a problem within the village itself, although the villagers are always fearful of being robbed by strangers. (3) The precept concerning immoral sexual relations is occasionally broken. Weddings of pregnant brides are not unknown (although they involve public shame and censorious gossip), and a double standard more or less sanctions adultery for males although it is actually rare among village men. There are also occasional stories of rape and illegitimacy. (4) Falsehoods, beyond white lies and evasion for one reason or another (e.g., not registering all of one's lands to avoid taxes) did not come to my attention. (5) The rule against consumption of alcoholic drinks is the precept upon which one's back is most easily turned, especially for men. It is not unusual for men to relax with a little beer or wine when money is available, and occasions such as weddings or New Year include liquor if it can be afforded. However, excessive drunkenness is definitely abhorred and is constantly cited as evidence of "bad character."

(C) Observance of the Holy Day and participation in the various annual Buddhist festivals or other temple events (e.g., sermons by important monks visiting from other temples) are a further means of acquiring merit.

On the eighth and fifteenth days of the waxing and waning moons falls *tngay sùl* (literally, "day of the precepts"), or what might be called the Holy Day. It is observed nationally by the prohibition of the sale of beef and alcoholic drinks and observed locally in various ways ranging from complete ignorance that it is Holy Day at all to the most rigorous observance by the devout. Ideally, one should go to the temple "to ask respectfully to receive the holy precepts" (*som sùl*) and perhaps remain the entire day to hear a sermon and recitation of scriptures by the monks (*look tIh*) (see also Leclère 1899, 382–83; Martini 1955a, 415). Or, like Grandfather Map, one can spend the day in quiet retreat at home, seclude oneself to avoid anger, upset, or the possibility of killing insects by walking outside, sip only liquids after midday, and meditate and pray.[23] But, in fact, usually only the elderly villagers go to the temple on Holy Day or make strict efforts to observe all of the ten basic precepts; most of the active adult population are generally too occupied with various chores to journey to the *wat* (though some of the more devout may drop in for an hour or two), while adolescents generally ignore this day altogether. Villagers make much more effort to attend the various temple festivals, but here again, attendance varies (see next section).

---

[23] It should be noted that virtually every house contains an altar to Buddha. Whether a small shelf or a large table, the altar is usually placed beneath a picture of Buddha and is decorated simply or elaborately with incense sticks, candles, and sometimes paper flowers and other ornaments. Here one may perform prayers or make offerings at home, and here attention is focused on occasions when monks are invited to one's house.

(D) The final major way to accumulate merit is through contributions of food, money, various objects, or labor to the temple and the monks. The situation that Ingersoll (1961) summarized succinctly for Thailand is also true for Cambodia: "The monk depends on the layman for goods; the layman depends on the monk for goodness." That is, through offerings of material support or services to religious personnel, activities, and structures, the laity receives spiritual support in return. Such contributions are made in different ways and on different occasions. (1) One may offer special services to the monks, such as is done by the temple boys and the elderly persons who reside temporarily at the *wat*. (2) One can answer a temple's request for aid in special tasks; for example, a *wat* about five kilometers away sent out a call for laborers to work on a new road leading to the temple, and Wat Samnang once asked villagers to bring food to feed a legion of monks who had come to take special examinations for passing to a higher rank in the religious hierarchy. In both instances, a number of West Svay villagers responded with their help. (3) Several times a week some monks come from West Svay to receive rice alms. Actually, however, only a few houses in the hamlet (families with old persons) give rice and sometimes a bit of other food. (4) Monks may be invited to one's own home or to the village on occasions such as weddings, funerals, housewarming rituals, ceremonies in honor of the dead,[24] ceremonies to cure illness, or the community post-harvest festival to recite prayers and give blessings. At such events the monks are often given an elaborate meal (*look chan*) in addition to other gifts such as money, cigarettes, incense, and candles. (5) Finally, every event or festival at a temple involves the contribution of some food, money, and/or services by the villagers. For Holy Days or other lesser events, some food or very small amounts of money (several riels) are given. For the important annual Buddhist festivals, the villagers typically contribute food in the form of special dishes and delicacies, some money, small offerings such as incense, and perhaps labor services (see also next section). (One also, of course, acquires additional merit from saying prayers, listening to sermons, etc.)

As part of this discussion of general religious beliefs and activities of the villagers, one should note that religious piety varies according to age and sex. Children become socialized into religion at an early age because youngsters accompany their mothers almost everywhere, including the temple, and parents attempt to teach even toddlers the proper etiquette and deference toward monks. It was both instructive and delightful to see children of three or four years of age "playing temple," sitting with their legs folded properly to one side, hands pressed together, chanting their own version of prayers, just as they sometimes played "house" or "store." Yet, while the more overt ritualistic forms are learned fairly quickly, the inculcation of Buddhist ideology is a slower process, and total adherence to the precepts is only gradually expected. The most illuminating example of this was noted previously in chapter 4: when a chicken needed to be killed, this task was often assigned to children on the assumption that the latter were still too young to be fully responsible for sins. Neither is the young child especially admonished to adhere to the Buddhist norms, for Cambodian parents

---

[24] Such ceremonies, called *san katièn*, involve the invitation of the monks to one's home to eat a fine meal and pray for the deceased members of one's family. Offerings are made to both the monks and the ancestral spirits. This ceremony not only gains merit for its sponsors but is thought to "help the dead in their progress toward Nirvana." (See also Leclère 1899, 384–85 on the concept of "intercession for the dead.")

are generally quite permissive. However, from the age of about eight or nine when the child does become more subject to discipline at home, is more able to comprehend sermons at the temple, and nowadays attends school where there is a course in "morals," gradual awareness and internalization of the Buddhist precepts begin. By the time of adolescence, some boys enter the monastery and girls aid in contribution of food and service to the temple. They have by now become religious "adults" in the sense that they are fully cognizant of earning merit and have begun in earnest to accumulate their own supply.

Religiosity reaches its peak in old age when individuals come to possess more physical and psychological leisure. The somewhat younger adult generations in full activity and vigor are usually observant enough, but the cares of the world often impinge upon them too heavily. A field must be transplanted whether it is Holy Day or not; a little surplus cash must be used for children's clothing rather than as a gift to the temple; a man is too exhausted from his labors to attend a temple ceremony. Although the desire for earning merit is present, practical realities and exigencies often override good intentions; although one's fate is determined by religiosity, one must survive within the present life of poverty and hard effort. However, when one's children are married and the labor and worries of subsistence are given over to them, their filial piety can now support the old people's religious piety, much as the layman supports the monk. Released from arduous labors and cares, and coming increasingly closer to the final tallying of merit, the old people have both the heightened motivation *and* the increased time for religious devotion. The woman past menopause cuts off her hair or shaves her head to signify renunciation of worldly vanities; both men and women become more observant of Holy Days and are seen at all religious festivals, large and small, staying through all the prayers and sermons about which the younger adults often do not bother or have no time to attend; some old people stay for extended periods of time at the temple to pray and meditate. Merit is accumulated in large quantities during these latter years of life, and the old people also earn a great deal of respect while they are still in this world.

Religiosity also varies somewhat with sex. Within Buddhism, women occupy a lower religious status than men; their sex presumably reflects a limited amount of merit in the previous incarnation. Moreover, women are barred from the monkhood, and various injunctions prevent them even from close contact with the monks. The woman begins with several strikes against her, and thus must work harder to compensate for them. This, plus the fact that food is perhaps the main contribution that villagers give to the temple, seems to account for the preponderance of women noted at various religious observances, some of the lesser ones being attended almost exclusively by females and a few old men. (See also Martini 1955a, 415.)

Men generally know more about Buddhism because of their experience in the monastery. But perhaps because they could obtain or had accumulated so much merit in this way, most active adult men and adolescent boys tend to participate in only the most important annual festivals, explaining non-attendance by comments such as "I'm too tired," "It's boring," "My wife is going for the family," etc. Men are also more likely to break certain precepts, for example, against alcohol, than do women who are characterized by more constant devotion and obedience to religion from an early age. Generally, men seem to "coast" until old age both releases and prods them into more active observance.

### (II) The Temple as Social Center

The various Buddhist festivals form a welcome punctuation of the usually drab and arduous cycle of village life (see appendix I on the annual cycle). The major annual ceremonies are eagerly anticipated for months in advance. Ostensibly, the main reason for participation in these festivals is to earn merit through one's attendance and contributions (villagers sometimes even journey to ceremonies at other temples in the area to gain extra merit). But an equally strong motive for going to these ceremonies, especially for the younger generation, is the chance to see people, to savor the color and excitement of the festivities, and to be entertained. The important holidays draw individuals from many different communities (including villages beyond the immediate vicinity and sometimes wealthy persons from Phnom Penh as well), such that villagers have an opportunity to visit and gossip with acquaintances not usually encountered in everyday life, or to meet new people. Of special interest is the chance for young men and women to see and be seen by one another, for the overtly casual and disdainful glances exchanged at temple festivals often lead to marriage proposals and village exogamy. At certain of the major festivals (especially New Year, Pchum, Katùn, and Bon Pkaa), the temple grounds assume a fair-like atmosphere with music; brightly colored decorations of bunting, banners, and flowers; and vendors selling soft drinks, confections, fruits, or even balloons and toys. Sometimes, too, the festivities may include an evening of sheer entertainment: music, an Indian movie, or a program of skits and songs.[25] The atmosphere of many festivals is far from the solemnity of church services in much of the Western world: children are free to run in and out of the *salaa* and about the temple grounds in noisy play, even during prayers; young men also roam about or stand outside the *salaa* to look at girls; gossip and conversation buzzes between prayers; even the monks smoke cigarettes and chat when they are not chanting. The Buddhist ceremonies are, therefore, not simply religious observances alone, but truly festive occasions.

The major annual temple festivals are briefly described below.[26]

(1) Col Cnam ("to enter the year"), the New Year, occurs around mid-April (month of Caet), its exact date determined by the royal astrologer. Considered the "biggest" and "happiest" holiday of the year, Col Cnam touches off a three-day round

---

[25] The monks themselves, however, are not permitted to watch such entertainment because of the precept prohibiting their participation in such activities. The monks (including those at Mohanikay Wat Samnang) always carefully retreat to their dormitories when such entertainment begins.

[26] I shall not attempt to offer a complete account of the rituals performed on these holidays. For details, see in particular Porée-Maspero et al. 1950 and Leclère 1899, 363–80; also Aymonier 1900, 45–46; Porée and Maspero 1938, 229–33; Zadrozny 1955, 336–43; Pym 1959, 141–47; 1960, 81–90, 159–67. It might be noted, however, that the descriptions given in Porée-Maspero et al. 1950 (which were taken from observations of ceremonies at the royal palace or temples in Phnom Penh, as well as from accounts written by various persons and submitted to the Commission des Moeurs et Coutumes du Cambodge) often report much more elaborate rituals than I observed at Wats Samnang and Svay (I attended part of all the annual festivals except Col Cnam, Col Vossa, and CEng Vossa). The differences between their data and mine may be due to several reasons. (a) Porée-Maspero et al. may be describing ideal traditional practices that have died out in various areas. (b) All Cambodian ceremonies seem to allow for a certain amount of variation in the inclusion, exclusion, or modification of various elements within certain broad outlines. Rural temples that are both geographically and socially removed from the great tradition may be particularly subject to deviation from ideal patterns.

of celebrations both at the temples and in the village itself. Each day the villagers take food and other offerings to the temple in the morning and hear sermons or recitations in the evening, while in the village there are music and dancing, games and general merrymaking. The temples draw large crowds because New Year is traditionally a time of reunion of families and friends when people return to their natal villages or visit kinsmen.

(2) Visak Bociė, the Anniversary of the Birth, Enlightenment, and Death of Buddha, comes on the full moon of Visak (May). In the morning the villagers take food and offerings to the temple and participate in brief prayers. In the evening there are more prayers, and various monks take turns reciting the life of Buddha throughout the entire night until daybreak. The most devout villagers remain at the temple all night, but most leave after a few hours.

(3) Col Vossa, the Entrance of the Monks into Rainy Season Retreat, is held on the full moon of Asat (July). Vossa is the three-month-long retreat of the monks during which they are confined to the temple grounds (except in event of emergency such as the illness of a parent). On the evening before Col Vossa there are prayers and sermons at the temple; the next morning the villagers take rice and other food and offerings to the temple and hear the monks recite the ten precepts and various prayers. The monks light a "*vossa* candle" that is kept burning for the duration of retreat.

(4) Pchum, the Festival to Honor the Dead, occurs sometime in late September or early October. The first day of the waning moon of Potrobot (September) initiates two weeks of ceremonies honoring the dead whose spirits are believed to return to earth at this time in search of their descendants and offerings. Almost every day of the two weeks preceding the main ceremony of Pchum, the monks are given offerings of food and other items, and there are prayers and sermons in the evenings. Particular hamlets or villages are asked to bring food on certain days, and the villagers usually respond conscientiously to this request. In fact, it is common on such occasions for even Thommayut adherents to make a rare trip to Mohanikay Wat Samnang (or for Mohanikay to go to Wat Svay) "because we have been asked to come." The day of the major Pchum ceremony itself is one of the most eagerly awaited events of the year. The temple grounds are gaily decorated and generally draw huge throngs. In addition to their usual contributions, villagers give the monks a special delicacy that is traditional on this holiday: *ansom*, a sort of cake made of glutinous rice mixed with meat or enclosing a banana, wrapped in a banana leaf boiled or steamed. Plain rice is also offered to the monks and to the spirits of the dead. After their midday meal, the monks offer special "prayers for the dead" (*bangskol*) and then chant their usual prayers with the laity. (In 1959, on the evening of the following day, Wat Samnang also presented a brief period of prayers and recitation from the life of Buddha, then showed an Indian movie as part of the festivities.)[27]

(5) CEng Vossa, the monks leaving retreat, takes place on the full moon of Asoit (October). The proceedings here are essentially the same as those for Col Vossa. In

---

[27] Porée-Maspero et al. 1950, 54–56 describe a number of rituals that occur at home or in the village during Pchum, but none of these are practiced at Svay. At one time, West Svay villagers used to kill chickens and look at their intestines for omens of the coming year; they also placed stakes with baskets of cakes, soup, rice, and chicken heads in the rice fields to obtain a good harvest. But these practices were given up about six or seven years ago because, according to one informant, "it is a sin to kill chickens." It is likely, too, that many families could not afford the expense of buying chickens.

addition, the monks confess their sins to one another and recite a special portion of the life of Buddha.

(6) Katùn, the festival to give gifts to the monks who have come out of retreat, may be held anytime between the first day of the waning moon of Asoit (October) and the full moon of Kadúk (November). Along with New Year and Pchum, Katùn is one of the most popular and festive events of the year. Its main object is to give new clothing to the monks, a practice that is said to have been initiated by the Buddha himself when his disciples had their robes soiled by the mud of the rainy season (Porée-Maspero et al. 1950, 59); but in fact it is customary to give an elaborate variety of gifts to the monks and the temple at this festival.

Great merit is earned by an individual or group who organizes a Katùn. This ceremony may be sponsored in any of several ways: (a) by one wealthy person or couple who underwrite the major expense of buying gifts for the monks, aided by contributions from relatives and friends; (b) by a group of individuals, such as a family, business company, or government office;[28] or (c) by the temple's entire congregation of villagers. In 1959, Wat Samnang's Katùn was sponsored by a wealthy man from Phnom Penh who had been a district chief in this area and was very fond of the temple; some of his close kinsmen and friends also contributed money and offerings. Wat Svay found no special sponsor for its Katùn, so villagers were asked to donate food and money, and eventually some wealthy people from Phnom Penh and several government officials in the area brought gifts that the villagers could not afford.

The gifts for the monks and temple are numerous and lavish, and go far beyond a simple offering of new robes. Each monk receives a package wrapped in bright yellow cellophane that contains not only garments but items such as incense, cigarettes, soap, sugar cubes, tea, and simple medicines, all placed on a metal tray (such a package costs about 400 riels). Special packages for head monks contain much the same items but are elaborately decorated with flowers or beads and cost 800–1,000 riels. The temple as a whole also receives a variety of items such as kerosene pressure lamps, mats, dishes, pots, stoves, pillows, umbrellas, urns, prayer chairs, etc. The cost of the material items presented to Wat Samnang in 1959 was probably about 30,000 riels, although Wat Svay was given much less. In addition there are donations of cash: Wat Samnang received 69,210 riels and Wat Svay 18,000 riels in their 1959 Katùn. (Such money is used for temple maintenance and building projects.) While villagers do give small amounts of money or little offerings, it is obvious that they can scarcely afford to buy such elaborate gifts for the monks or to amass such great sums of money from their meager resources. The villagers' main contribution consists rather of special food dishes and services as waiters and waitresses to feed the sponsors of the Katùn and numerous visitors from other communities or Phnom Penh who come to their temple.

Katùn is a very colorful affair, with music and the bustle of crowds filling the air. The gifts for the monks and the temple are arranged in a *salaa* and create an impressive and flamboyant display. Huge tent pavilions with tables and chairs are set up to feed guests in style and comfort, and after the midday meal a great procession is formed. Led by a band (composed of drums and either traditional or modern instruments), the sponsors and other persons carry the various gifts, offerings, and incense and flowers

---

[28] A common sight on the highways during *Katùn* season are buses decorated with religious banners and full of people on their way to a *Katùn* that they are helping to sponsor.

to the central temple. The cortege circles the temple three times before entering it to deposit the contributions, hear a brief speech by the sponsor(s), and participate in prayers. (The 1959 Katùn at Wat Svay also featured, on the night preceding Katùn, a sermon by the monks followed by a program of song, music, jokes, and comic acts performed by a group of government officials from a nearby town who had donated their services as amateur entertainers to help the temple's festivities.)

(7) Twèr Bon Phnom Srau, the Ceremony to Make a Mountain of Rice, is held shortly after the rice harvest (usually sometime in late January). This ceremony is not an integral part of the Buddhist calendar and is not held annually by all temples (e.g., in 1959 there was one at Wat Svay but not Wat Samnang). This simple ceremony consists of the villagers bringing small amounts of raw rice (ranging from a few handfuls to a basket or more) to make, literally, a small "mountain" of paddy in the *salaa* (this rice is later sold by the temple to obtain money for its building fund). There are also the usual prayers and a sermon.

(8) Mièk Bociè, the Anniversary of the Last Sermon of Buddha, occurs on the full moon of Mièk (February). This ceremony is virtually identical to that of Visak Bociè.

(9) Bon Pkaa (literally "ceremony of flowers") is a festival to raise money for the temple. A Bon Pkaa may be held at any time (except during Vossa) and even more than once a year if desired. Usually, however, a temple has only one such festival annually, during some period of leisure in the cultivation cycle. While villagers contribute whatever money they can afford (ranging generally from about 20 to 200 riels), their main role—as for Katùn—is to provide a meal and serve as waiters and waitresses for wealthy donors from Phnom Penh and visitors from other villages. Thanks mainly to numerous urbanites,[29] Wat Samnang garnered about 80,000 riels at their Bon Pkaa in 1959. (Wat Svay had no such festival during my residence.)

Counting the major holidays and various lesser events, there may be a dozen or more affairs at the temple(s) in the course of a year. But not all of them draw equally large crowds; attendance varies according to several factors: which holidays are considered most important or festive, which temple is holding the celebration, whether one can afford contributions, or simply whether one feels like going. Although a few households may have at least one of its members at every temple event, others attend only two or three. Most families probably participate in about half a dozen during the course of a year.[30]

New Year, Pchum, and Katùn are considered to be the major festivals of the year and draw enormous crowds of both sexes and all ages. But some of the other holidays that actually have great significance in Buddhist doctrine, such as the Anniversary of Buddha's Last Sermon or the monks' entry into retreat, attract relatively few people. Usually only the elderly of both sexes and adult women attend these latter ceremonies;

[29] Such urbanites who appear at the local temples may be persons who were born in the area, who once worked or held positions in the vicinity, who are familiar with the temple (e.g., Wat Samnang is a favorite picnic ground for people from Phnom Penh, while Wat Svay gains some recognition by having once had Sihanouk as a temporary monk), or who simply select any rural temple as the recipient of their generosity. Such persons also frequently bring their kinsmen and friends with them.

[30] E.g., records of attendance at five representative temple events (pre-Pchum ceremonies at both temples, Pchum at Wat Samnang, *Katùn* at Wat Svay or Samnang, a meal for a convocation of monks at Wat Samnang) showed that four households in West Svay attended one of these events, three households attended two events, eight households attended three events, nine households attended four events, and seven households attended all five (the average number of these events attended was three).

adolescents do not go because "it's no fun" and adult men are often "too busy." (E.g., the Visak Bociė at Wat Svay had an audience of about two hundred persons composed of about four times as many women as men; most of the females were matrons or elderly with a sprinkling of adolescent girls, while all of the men were middle-aged or old. Persons from about eight households in West Svay attended this event. By contrast, the Katùn at Wat Samnang attracted a throng of close to a thousand people of both sexes and all ages, including persons from twenty-nine households in West Svay.)

Wat Samnang generally draws larger crowds than does Wat Svay, for two reasons. First, the number of Mohanikay adherents in the area is greater than the number of Thommayut followers. Second, those families who have no firm commitment to either order will, if faced with a choice,[31] usually prefer to go to Wat Samnang because its celebrations are on a grander scale and its grounds are "more pleasant." (E.g., the Pchum at Wat Samnang drew individuals from twenty-one households in West Svay while the Pchum at Wat Svay, held on the same day, had persons from only six households in the hamlet. Two households sent representatives to both temples.)

Finally, apart from personal inclinations as to whether one wishes to go to a particular ceremony or not (cf. the previous discussion of age and sex differences with respect to religious piety), a family's attendance at various events may depend on its financial resources. A few households are rarely seen at either temple, and one suspects that this is due in most cases not to lack of religiosity but rather to lack of funds. Even though contributions can be as minimal as a few riels, some embarrassment is felt if one cannot take the usual offering of a special food dish (which may deplete the family's food supply or cost at least a fair sum of money) or give a gift that is more substantial than, for example, a few sticks of incense.

### (III) The Temple as Educational Center

The temple school or the instruction one received while a monk were once the major and sometimes the only means of education for villagers. Of thirty-five men in West Svay over eighteen years of age who are literate, all but four learned the rudiments of Khmer (and sometimes a smattering of other subjects) while they were monks.[32] Illiteracy among the adult men correlates directly with not having entered the monkhood; as one of them said, "I cannot read because I was not able to become a monk." Similarly, all females over eighteen years in West Svay are illiterate (with the exception of one girl raised in another province), partly because it was once thought that instruction in household matters was more important than formal education, and partly because neither the temple schools nor the monkhood were open to them.

While the school at Wat Samnang is now used only for the instruction of monks and novices because there is a public school in nearby Kompong Tuol, the school at Wat Svay has become part of the secular educational system. Its curriculum was

---

[31] Because there are two temples in the immediate vicinity, such choices must often be made if both *wats* are holding a ceremony on the same day, or if a family does not have the resources to make contributions to both temples if ceremonies are held on different days. In the event that a family's loyalties are divided or impartial, the problem of coping with two ceremonies on the same day may be solved by sending some members of the family to one temple and some to the other temple (if the household can afford offerings to both).

[32] The other four men who are literate attended public secular schools; one man who was a monk also received several years of public schooling.

expanded to include the range of subjects taught in grades one through three of public school, and its teaching staff now includes two laymen as well as one monk.[33] It is also open to both boys and girls. Indeed, over 80 percent of West Svay children of school age attend the school at Wat Svay because it is closer than the one in Kompong Tuol (though they must eventually go to the latter for higher grades). The temple has, therefore, now become a significant source of secular as well as religious instruction.

### (IV) Miscellaneous Functions of the Temple

In addition to the three main functions of the temple that have just been discussed, the *wat* and its monks also perform a variety of other services for the villagers. (1) The temple occasionally offers employment; in addition to using volunteer labor, it sometimes hires workers for its continual building projects. (2) The temple *salaa* has traditionally served as a safe hostel for travelers who need overnight lodgings when journeying in unknown regions. (3) The temple can be a source of information and news because its monks usually have access to radios, magazines, and other media, and in many cases possess more education than the ordinary villager.[34] (4) Certain monks have special skills or knowledge that villagers may call upon; for example, one monk at Wat Samnang is known as an expert repairer of various mechanical devices, while others have knowledge of curing techniques, astrological calculations, etc. (5) The temple may loan items such as dishes and tableware to villagers who need them for major life-cycle ceremonies and cannot afford to rent them. (6) Finally, it is often said that the temple acts as a poorhouse to feed and lodge monks and temple boys from destitute families. This may well be true in certain individual cases but is, in general, a moot point (see infra).

### BUDDHISM IN VILLAGE LIFE

A number of the various ways in which Buddhist precepts and doctrines influence or impinge upon village life have already been noted in preceding chapters and sections. It is beyond the scope of this chapter to explore all the interrelations between Buddhism and other sociocultural institutions, but I will examine in particular some of the connections between this religious system and economic organization, a topic that has been the object of some discussion (see, e.g., Pfanner and Ingersoll 1962; Nash 1965, 157–63; Spiro 1966; and other references cited below).

It is sometimes said or implied in the literature that Buddhism is a drain upon or hindrance to economic development because of the large numbers of men in the monasteries, because the doctrine of accepting one's fate is contrary to Protestant ethic drives for economic success, and because a high proportion of food and money are spent on religious contributions (see, e.g., Kleinpeter 1937, 76–78, 82–85; Gourou 1945, 381; Delvert 1961, 140–42). There is indeed some truth in these assertions, but

---

[33] On the former curriculum of and modernization of the temple schools, see Monod 1931, 133–34; Bilodeau, Pathammavong, and Hồng 1955; Zadrozny 1955, 133–40; Delvert 1961, 140.

[34] It might be mentioned that the monks at Wats Samnang and Svay played no role in political matters, other than occasionally acting as channels for dispersal of news about national events. However, in Phnom Penh, where political parties and conflicts occur among the intelligentsia and elite, monks have participated in political movements and debates. This tendency, however, has been discouraged and criticized by the king (Steinberg 1959, 301–2).

the generalizations should not be accepted without qualification because the reality at the village level is more complex than might be initially thought.

First, when one looks at a Buddhist nation as a whole, the large number of monks (an estimated one-tenth of the male population in Cambodia, according to Delvert 1961, 140) does appear to cut off a considerable supply of labor. But in West Svay, it is interesting to note who has not been a monk and why. Of the nine males over eighteen years of age who had never been monks, the following kinds of situations had been present. Apart from two who were quite simply more interested in secular concerns (e.g., one is a professional musician), these men had come from families that could not spare them because the father had died, because a brother or brothers were monks, or because the family was poor and needed all available manpower at work in other kinds of employment if not in the rice fields. In all of these cases, the men came from poor families to begin with, and most of them even now reside uxorilocally. Thus, while it can be true that the monastery can be a haven for the poor, it is also true that a monk cannot work the family's fields or remit regular income from other jobs. Thus, from the perspective of the family, a male usually will not become a monk unless he can be spared.[35]

Second, it is true that it is considered praiseworthy to use wealth for religious contributions, that religious efforts do absorb resources that might ordinarily be utilized for secular purposes, and that available margins of food or money, especially fortuitous surplus, are often (though not always) used for making merit.[36] (E.g., when House 11 won a lottery, the funds were used to finance a *san katièn* ceremony although the family could surely have used the money for other purposes because it is not at all wealthy.) But it is also true that families generally seem to give only what they can afford. Cash contributions are generally limited, from the equivalent of a few cents at lesser events to about a dollar at the larger festivals. More generally, since cash is scarce, contributions are made in the form of services and especially food. The latter raises a significant point: the food given is in the form of special dishes (chicken curry, beef, sweet delicacies, etc.) that the villager can afford to prepare only on very special occasions such as life-cycle or temple ceremonies. After the monks finish their meal, there is always considerable food remaining that the villagers themselves then reclaim and eat, gathering in small groups to pool various dishes brought by different families. The temple festivals are, therefore, one of the few occasions when the usual diet of rice and fish

---

[35] In all fairness it must also be stated that many men who were monks came from poor families, often with identical circumstances. But in these instances some arrangements were worked out whereby the men could be spared for a temporary period in the monastery (e.g., a brother-in-law supplied the necessary labor for the family in one case). Also, uxorilocality is a common residence pattern in general, but in the cases cited here it was due specifically to the male's lack of resources.

It should be noted, too, that sending a male into the monkhood may not be a hardship for a family if the individual is still a child or very young adolescent who contributes little or no labor power or income anyway, or if the period in the monastery is very brief. But neither of these patterns was common in West Svay. Of the men who had been monks, mid- or late adolescence was the usual age for entering the temple, and the time spent as a monk was at least a year and usually longer.

See also DeYoung 1955, 169 and Moerman 1966, 147 who make a similar point about families in Thailand not being able to spare men for monkhood.

[36] See section on "Finances" in chapter 4; also cf. Pfanner and Ingersoll 1962; Nash 1965, 160; Kaufman 1960, 221 for percentages of budgets spent on religious contributions in Burmese and Thai villages.

is supplemented by meat and other special foods through a small-scale redistributive system. Thus, while cash and service contributions bring important spiritual returns, the food donations generally bring returns to the stomach as well. To paraphrase an old Western proverb, in this instance the villagers have their merit and eat it, too.

Contributions for merit making are not necessarily a drain and bring other than purely spiritual rewards in two other ways. First, the temple has traditionally performed a variety of social services for the community, notably as an educational institution but also as a social center, hostel, etc. (see above). Religious offerings may thus substitute for money that might otherwise have been spent in taxes to support certain public services performed by government agencies. Second, in terms of the very long-range view of existence in the Buddhist doctrine, contributions for merit may also be considered as a sort of "investment" for future "profits" if they are thought to bring a better (and wealthier) life in the next reincarnation.[37]

Finally, it is said that the Buddhist doctrine of resigned acceptance of one's fate keeps the peasant from moving onward and upward to better and higher socioeconomic positions. Actually, for most peasants living several decades ago, I doubt whether mobility was probable or possible even with the greatest of ambition, and resignation was perhaps the only possible response. At the present time, however, an interesting development is taking place that highlights one of the major areas in which the secular sphere is having considerable impact upon the sacred. I was struck by the frequency of comments made by the villagers with the general tone: "We are so poor," "We must work so hard to earn so little," "Life is very difficult in the rice country." In part this can be seen simply as a realistic perception of one's fate. But this demanding and arduous fate is with one daily, and the statements contained a hint of sadness, sometimes even of bitterness or envy. The important fact is that mobility has become more possible in contemporary Cambodian society. A loosening of the traditional hierarchy has made high status more obtainable through achievement as well as ascription; and the expansion of public schooling makes education, the major means of mobility for the peasant, more accessible to all. It becomes increasingly clear that the doctrine of resignation does not in fact repress hopes of change, whether of geographical mobility to urban areas or of social mobility into the higher stratum, of the mechanic, the school teacher, the minor bureaucrat, etc. An interesting question is whether this desire for secular careers (and the training they require) will affect the number of males entering monasteries in future years. Although my sample is too small to be more than merely suggestive, one might note the following figures for West Svay:

| Age | Number of men who have been monks or novices | Number of men who have not been monks or novices |
| --- | --- | --- |
| 50 and older | 13 | 0 |
| 40–49 | 5 | 2 |
| 30–39 | 8 | 2 |
| 20–29 | 7 | 4 |
| 10–19 | one is now a novice | 12 |

[37] A similar point has recently been made by Spiro 1966.

Indeed, of the youngest group, none in the second column have any immediate plans for entering the monastery because of poverty, disinterest, or concern with obtaining a secular education. Moreover, consumer goods have become increasingly available and necessary, and their possession is now a symbol of success and prestige. Cash income, then, has assumed a much more significant role in contemporary life and may in future years seriously override the non-materialistic emphasis of traditional Buddhism.[38]

With respect to social structure, I will discuss the relation of Buddhism to individualism. It has been said in the literature that individualistic behavior is characteristic of a number of Southeast Asian societies and is encouraged, at least in part, by the Buddhist doctrine that each individual is responsible to and for himself. An individualistic and independent streak is undeniably present in the Khmer (see chapter 3). But again there is danger in too broad a generalization, for the data from West Svay suggest that Buddhism can encourage group action and integration as well as individualism.[39]

It is, of course, true that the accumulation of merit involves individual responsibility and rally. Yet merit making is frequently performed by some group, usually a family that has pooled its efforts and resources to provide a contribution from the unit as a whole, taken to the temple by one or two persons who are representatives for the entire family. The merit thus earned is, in effect, "divided" among the members, but nonetheless there is action as a unit. Similar group effort occurs, as mentioned, in the sponsorship of a Katùn festival. Moreover, the temple as a moral-religious center serves to integrate the villagers in its congregation into a religious community through shared norms and common participation in rituals. As a social center that offers opportunities for assemblages of people at ceremonies and other events, it also reinforces or creates social ties among individuals. (Sometimes, too, the larger religious order may crystallize relationships, as seen in the brief factionalism between Mohanikays and Thommayuts in West Svay discussed in chapter 3.)

Finally, no matter how much the Khmer villager may value independence and individualism, the social reality is that each individual is inextricably bound with others in his life. Buddhism recognizes this elemental sociological fact in its precepts which urge harmonious, courteous, and generous relationships with others. And although presumably only individual conscience and sensitivity to critical gossip dictate adherence to the religious norms, certain fundamental obligations and conformity are actually inescapable unless one becomes a criminal, an outcast, or a ne'er-do-well. For the persons who do voluntarily accept and wholeheartedly practice the Buddhist virtues and precepts, particularly those of generosity and kindness to those around them, there are the rewards of prestige, affection, and respect in this life, as well as excellent prospects for the next.

For, as De Bary has noted:

> The (Buddhist) ideal is a society in which each individual respects the other's personality, an intricate network of warm and happy human relations, mutual respect

---

[38] While I have just suggested that religious norms may not be as important in certain spheres of economic organization as is often thought, chapter 4 did point out other areas of subsistence activity that do evidence the influence of Buddhism, e.g., the firm adherence to injunctions not to kill certain animals and the equivocal attitudes toward raising pigs and chickens.

[39] Cf. Nash 1963, 291–92 on groupings in Burmese Buddhism, although he also emphasizes the individualism fostered by Buddhism (293–94; 1966, 161).

and affection between parent and child, teacher and student, husband and wife, master and servant, friend and friend, each helping the other upward in the scale of being. (De Bary et al. 1958, 116)

Buddhism thus can and does encourage integration in a society where the family, village, and nation are the only other institutions that can command much loyalty or influence behavior to a significant degree.[40]

## THE FOLK RELIGION

Buddhism has characteristically been tolerant toward other religious systems. In Cambodia (as also in Ceylon, Burma, Thailand, and Laos), it coexists with what might be called a folk religion that centers around belief in a variety of supernatural beings and essentially magical rituals and other practices. There is virtually no competition or conflict between the high religion and this folk religion.[41] Shrines for spirits are found on Buddhist temple grounds; magical practitioners are also devout Buddhists; life-cycle and other ceremonies combine offerings to both spirits and monks; appeals are made to Buddha and spirits in time of trouble; etc. Respect and/or fear for the folk religion's supernatural entities is almost universal among the villagers; even the few skeptics are more agnostic than atheistic in their doubts or may reject some aspects of the folk religion while clinging firmly to others.[42] Thus, while the Khmer are officially Buddhists, their Buddhism encompasses and is mingled with the indigenous, traditional folk beliefs.

The array of supernatural beings in the folk religion includes the following.[43]

(1) The *neak taa* are, in the most general sense, guardian spirits that maintain the welfare of the thing or area that they inhabit. But the designation *neak taa* is actually applied to a variety of different sorts of supernatural entities ranging from animistic spirits to celestial deities. The term itself can be literally translated as "ancestral person," and according to some sources (Leclère 1899, 151; Porée-Maspero et al. 1950, 27; Porée-Maspero 1962a, 6) certain *neak taa* can be traced to specific deceased

---

[40] See Leclère 1899, 496–530 for a discussion of various other ways in which he thinks that Buddhist ethics influence different aspects of Cambodian culture: law and government, slavery, the conduct of women, and some interesting views on the family. Also, cf. Pfanner and Ingersoll 1962; Nash 1963, 1965; Spiro 1966; and Moerman 1966, for comparative data on connections between Buddhism and economic and social organization in Burma and Thailand.

[41] The only instances of conflict between Buddhism and the folk religion that are known to me are that one folk ritual associated with Pchum was abandoned because it necessitated killing chickens; that some monks are said not to believe in various spirits of the folk religion; and that one kind of magical practitioner, the *tmòp* (see infra), is said to be forbidden to enter a Buddhist temple or worship Buddha because of his evil practices.

[42] E.g., the young man who was my interpreter was disdainful of "ignorant" people who believed in supplications to spirits to control crabs in the rice fields, while at the same time he showed profound deference to shrines of certain spirits and feared ghosts. Even the more well-educated or urban Khmer hold to traditional beliefs; e.g., the proprietress of an elegant store in Phnom Penh said that members of her family had seen ghosts, and it was rumored in 1959 that a royal entourage to Angkor Wat had been stopped because of bad omens encountered along the way.

[43] People's conceptions of these supernatural entities may vary somewhat according to region or to individual imagination and interest because several sources (to be cited infra) give slightly different or more detailed descriptions of various beings than do Svay villagers.

persons or are, in general, considered to be spirits of the dead. Often, however, a *neak taa* has no such specific origin and, as in Svay, are considered simply to be supernatural beings that have always existed (see also Porée-Maspero 1962a, 6). The *neak taa* are harmless if given proper deference but will bring illness upon men or animals, or other trouble such as drought, if ignored or treated disrespectfully. Sometimes they are also asked for aid in warding off or ameliorating difficulties such as sickness. Their tempers are appeased or their help is requested with supplications and offerings of fruit, foods, incense, etc.

While the exact nature of the various kinds of *neak taa* is not always clear, they may be tentatively classified as follows. (a) Some *neak taa* seem to be essentially animistic nature spirits that inhabit various parts of the natural environment such as trees, rice paddies, streams, forests, mountains, etc. They are thought to be especially populous in hilly or mountainous regions (which are, therefore, considered to be dangerous areas) but occur everywhere. In Svay itself there are said to be *neak taa* living in huge trees and in the rice fields. The latter are sometimes enjoined to prevent crabs from cutting the stalks of young rice seedlings; the former go largely unheeded except that when a large tree is cut down, a small offering must be made at its base to request the resident *neak taa* to move to another tree. These spirits are generally invisible, although they may appear as balls of fire flying from tree to tree, or assume human or animal form if they desire. (b) Other *neak taa* are associated with a particular territorial region, whether it be a province, district, village, or simply a certain area of land. Indeed, in some regions, these spirits are arranged in a regular hierarchy that duplicates secular sociopolitical organization, with a king or chief *neak taa*, lesser nobles, district *neak taa*, etc.[44] While the neighboring village of Ta Chas has a village *neak taa*, Svay does not. There is, however, a small stone shrine set in a deserted, uncleared area south of Middle Hamlet Svay that houses a small, fat smiling idol named Look Taa Tpól, his clay ox, and some stones that are further representations of this spirit.[45] This *neak taa* is supplicated by the villagers (with offerings of food and incense, and entreaties that must be presented with the greatest solemnity and deference) in event of trouble such as illness or drought. There are also shrines to *neak taa* at both Wats Svay and Samnang, the spirits being represented either by heaps of stone and rock (e.g., the "Grandmother" *neak taa* at Wat Svay) or by small statues of human form (e.g., the man and wife *neak taa* at Wat Samnang) that are the "form" or "body" (*rup*), the tangible manifestations of the *neak taa*. (c) Some *neak taa* also merge into, or are confused with, the *tivoda* or celestial beings of Hindu origin (see also Steinberg 1959, 304).

(2) *Kmauit* are ghosts of several kinds. (a) *Kmauit long* are comparable to ghosts in the Western sense, that is, spirits of dead persons (the term *kmauit* also means "corpse"), especially those who have committed suicide or been murdered. These ghosts wander about and may appear in human or animal form, although they usually vanish when approached too closely. (b) *Baysayt* are a type of *kmauit* that lives on dirt

---

[44] Porée-Maspero 1962a, 11–12, feels that these territorial spirits are the main type of *neak taa*. See also Porée-Maspero 1955a and Porée-Maspero et al. 1950, 27–31; Souyris-Rolland 1951.

[45] The origins of the idol and the shrine are unknown. (Note that CMCC 59.107 says that it is possible, in effect, to create a *neak taa* by erecting a shrine and making offerings, to which a spirit will then come.) The stone or rubble that is often seen as a representation of a *neak taa* may be ordinary rock or fragments of rubble from old statues of Hindu deities; sometimes, too, the *neak taa* is represented by a root or even an empty shrine (Porée-Maspero et al. 1950, 27; Porée-Maspero 1962a, 8; CMCC 59.107).

and excrement although they also eat rice and other foods that are sometimes placed in the fields for them. They, too, roam about and are capable of assuming animal or human appearance.[46] (c) *Priey* are another kind of *kmauit* that inhabit large trees and manifest themselves as balls of fire flying from tree to tree.[47]

The *kmauit* are a source of very real and constant fear to the villagers. Even husky, courageous men dread to walk alone at night because of the possibility of encountering a ghost; as one of them said, "I don't fear men, but I do fear *kmauit*." (Some people refuse even to talk about *kmauit* because it is such a frightening topic.) It is said that there are *kmauit long* who roam about the grounds of the normal school (the female students at the school will not open their dormitory windows at night for fear of both men and ghosts), as well as near Wat Samnang, and there is always the possibility that some will wander into Svay itself. There are also *priey* in some of the huge trees in the village, and some villagers claim to have seen the balls of fire (or at least know someone who did). One dreads encountering a *kmauit* because the terror would be so great that one would fall ill. The *kmauit* are also capable of causing illness through sheer malevolence or because an individual has offended them in some manner.

(3) *Arak* are similar to and are sometimes spoken of as *kmauit* in that they are spirits of dead persons.[48] They may appear as humans or animals but are notable primarily because they possess and speak through spirit mediums (the *rup arak*) in annual séances. While some speak of *arak* as mischievous spirits that can cause sickness, they may also be protective toward those who give them offerings. Sometimes small wooden shrines atop poles are erected to *arak*.

(4) *Bòngbèt* are similar to *arak* but possess individuals only occasionally and do not assume animal or human form or cause illness. The term also refers to the person who is possessed.[49]

(5) *Meba*, who are also sometimes referred to as *kmauit*, are ancestral spirits (not of specific ascendants but ancestors in general) who watch over the living members of the family. They are informed of important events in the family's life and receive offerings of food at life-cycle ceremonies, as well as on certain annual holidays such as New Year and Pchum. The *meba* do not appear in human or animal form but are capable of causing illness when someone in the family is guilty of sinful deeds or quarrels (the example most often cited is that of parents not allowing a child to marry someone whom he/she loves). Such sickness always strikes an innocent member of the family who must be treated with a ceremony in which the guilty person(s) ask forgiveness of and make offerings to the *meba*. (See also Leclère 1898, 1:156, 287–88.)

---

[46] CMCC 59.107 says that they have "hideous and frightening forms" but are "invisible except when they play tricks to frighten people." Porée and Maspero 1938, 223 state that they are "famished demons or wandering condemned souls" who are tall and thick with mouths no larger than the eye of a needle.

[47] CMCC 59.107 speaks of these as female spirits of light that haunt big trees and can cause illness by possessing people. Porée-Maspero 1962a, 4, says they are spirits of women who have died tragically (e.g., in childbirth or accidents). See also Porée and Maspero 1938, 223 for some other details concerning *priey*.

[48] Porée and Maspero 1938, 226 speak of *arak* as ancestral spirits, but Svay villagers gave the ancestral spirits another name. CMCC 59.107 speaks of *arak* as living in trees, forests, water, and sometimes haunting certain places or houses.

[49] Cf. CMCC 59.107, which says that "banbat" is the term used for the most powerful *neak taa* in a region, as well as for "one who has great influence over *neak taa*."

There are also the *cambuė cuė* (or *sambuė cuė*) who are similarly spoken of as ancestral spirits or ghosts of deceased members of the family.[50] They cause illness when ignored or angered at misdeeds of descendants.

(6) *Praet*, though not classified with *kmauit*, are said by some villagers to be spirits of dead persons who had committed some dreadful sin such as slaughter of animals. Others refer to them simply as malevolent spirits, rather like demons, that create trouble. They are capable of assuming human or animal form.

(7) *Cmnièng ptea* are house spirits that watch over a particular home's inhabitants "to see that the people are happy." They are the only spirits who are wholly benevolent and do not cause illness. Offerings of food are given to them occasionally, especially at weddings.

(8) *Mrin kònvIl* are the guardian spirits of various animals, both wild and domestic, such as oxen, buffalo, horses, elephants, etc. (but not pigs or chickens) who see that these beasts are treated with consideration.[51] Domestic animals must be fed properly and not beaten, allowed to be stolen, or otherwise mistreated lest the owner be struck down with illness. Offerings of food are occasionally set out for the *mrin kònvIl* within the house or underneath the dwelling where the cattle are stabled.

In sum, then, the world is thought to be populated with a host of supernatural beings, of which only the house spirits (*cmnièng ptea*) are completely altruistic and never create trouble. The *neak taa*, ancestral spirits (*meba*), and guardian spirits of animals are harmless if proper conduct is followed; some may even be beneficial if aid is requested of them. But an individual who displeases them will be struck down with illness. The rest of the supernatural entities are testy or malevolent creatures whose ill nature characteristically manifests itself by causing persons to become sick. In order to keep the spirits in good humor, atone for misdeeds, banish misfortunes, ward off potential disasters, or obtain special powers, the villagers have recourse to offerings, supplications, rituals, charms, potions, etc. Certain persons acquire distinct competence in mediating with spirits; these specialists are of the following kinds.

(1) The *kru*[52] is a practitioner of magic who may possess any of a variety of talents or techniques such as curing, finding lost objects, making charms or potions to obtain love or invulnerability or to ward off misfortune, exorcism of spirits, etc. *Kru* are almost always males, and knowledge often passes from father to son if the latter has an inclination to learn to be a *kru*, possesses a favorable horoscope, and has the discipline to conduct himself properly.

Kosal (House 8) is both respected and somewhat feared as a *kru*. He had learned the various procedures of the profession from an old *kru* in a distant village with whom he had studied for three years because his own father, who was also a *kru*, became senile before transmitting his knowledge to his son. As is true of most *kru* in the area, Kosal's major skill is curing illness. Certain minor ailments, such as strained

---

[50] Cf. CMCC 59.107 who says the "cuor cambuor" are "araks that are respected from generation to generation" that must be propitiated by "all the descendants of a same line."

[51] According to Porée-Maspero 1962a,15, these spirits are the servants of or actually are *neak taa*, who look like "children of seven to ten years of age with dark skin," live in trees, and are invoked to keep animals from ravaging the fields. CMCC 59.107 notes that hunters make offerings to these spirits so that animals will be directed to come to them.

[52] The term *kru*, from the Sanskrit and Pali *guru* or "master" is applied actually to any specialist in a particular realm of knowledge, e.g. schoolteacher = *kru bòng rièn*, medical doctor = *kru pEt*, etc.

muscles or a temporary stomachache, are treated simply with one or another concoction of plants and herbs, or by "blowing" (*plom*) on the affected part of the body.[53] But more complex, severe, or long-lasting illnesses must be diagnosed by an examination of the patient's horoscope (i.e., the year, month, and day of birth),[54] which will yield clues as to the cause of the sickness: perhaps a *kmauit* has fallen in love with the patient and is making him ill by attempting to possess his body; or perhaps the individual or someone in his family has offended a spirit in some manner. Kosal then proceeds to the cure, which is likely to involve a combination of herbal medicines, "blowing," incantations, offerings of food or various ritual objects, and other procedures (e.g., making a love charm that will entice the ghost to leave the patient's body) that will exorcise the spirit or appease its temper. Kosal can also help an individual ward off illness or other misfortune by preparing special amulets or charms; he can occasionally find lost objects if the individual's horoscope is favorable; and he knows how to make some love charms (although he says there is no call for them because another *kru* in a nearby village specializes in *snay*, or techniques of making someone fall in love). He is paid for his services usually in kind, that is, fruit, cakes, cigarettes, etc., and occasionally by sums of money.

Though I never saw Kosal conduct a curing ritual (except for "blowing"), House 26 once called in a *kru* from another village to cure a visiting grandchild. A variety of ritual objects were constructed and set out with dishes of meat, rice, and vegetables for the *kmauit* that was causing the illness. The *kru* chanted an invitation to the *kmauit* to recognize and receive the offerings. The ritual objects were then taken out to a deserted field near the village; the people who carry out these objects must not look back, once they have deposited the things, for fear that they might see the *kmauit* come and take the offerings. (For details of the various ritual objects and offerings used in curing and other ceremonies, see Porée-Maspero et al. 1950, 11–14; 1958, 19–25; Porée-Maspero 1954.)

(2) The *tmòp* is a special kind of *kru*, always male, who specializes in a unique form of malevolent, magical murder: the *tmòp* can cause a knife, piece of sharp bamboo, scissor, razor, or similar sharp object to enter and swell up inside a victim's body.[55] Intense pain, vomiting, spitting of blood, and eventual death results unless another

---

[53] Kosal is well aware of the efficacy of "secular" or "scientific" medicine, as well as what might be called "ritual" medicine or treatment. He sometimes came to me for ointment or pills for his own ailments, and he was not upset when his patients had recourse to medicines such as penicillin or consulted trained medical personnel.

[54] I cannot explain exactly how one diagnoses illness on the basis of an individual's horoscope, but it involves a complex system of astrology that is of great importance in other spheres as well, such as deciding whether potential marriage partners will be compatible. The astrological calculations are based (as in China) on a twelve-year cycle with each year bearing the name of a particular animal. For details, see Porée-Maspero et al. 1950, 17, 85; 1958, 11–17; and especially Porée-Maspero 1962b.

[55] CMCC 55.002 and Porée and Maspero 1938, 225–26 say that buffalo hide, a piece of cooked meat, and cattle horns may also be sent to expand within a victim; Porée and Maspero also give further techniques that the *tmòp* uses for murder. CMCC 51.005 and 51.006 note several interesting points: that one cannot learn to be a *tmòp* from one's father because one will not be powerful and will die young; and that one who wishes to be a *tmòp* must not enter a Buddhist temple, pass in front of or salute a statue of Buddha, or bathe during one's entire lifetime. The first two prohibitions are significant in their recognition that the *tmòp*'s calling violates the cardinal Buddhist precept against the taking of life. Also, Leclère 1898, 1:133, cites an ancient law code stating that accused *tmòps* would have their property confiscated and be decapitated.

*kru* is called to exorcise the object. There are no *tmóp* in the vicinity of Svay, though their existence is known of and feared.[56]

(3) The *rup arak* is a spirit medium whose body is entered by *arak* in a possession ceremony (*cuèn arak*) that occurs once a year during the month of Mièk (February).[57] *Rup arak* are usually women who are not trained in their calling, as are *kru*, but simply find themselves able to receive spirits into their bodies. There are no *rup arak* in Svay, but I witnessed a *cuèn arak* ceremony in another village. The medium, named Yuan, was a women in her midforties who had experienced possession since she was an adolescent. In a cloth pavilion outside her home, Yuan sat before a number of ritual objects and food offerings while hired musicians sang invitations to the spirits.[58] When she became possessed by an *arak*, Yuan would begin to quiver; her trembling and shaking would become more and more violent (while the onlookers clapped and shouted encouragement) until she would begin to weave back and forth in a sort of seated dance in time to the music that reached a crescendo. In the midst of a possession, she would variously shout out, weep, put powder and oil on herself or on spectators, utter angry words, joke, make charms, or perform various other actions according to the inclination of the spirit within her. When an *arak* left her body, she returned to a normal state and rested until the next possession. In all, Yuan was entered by some ten *arak* (she usually contacts twelve, but two did not appear this year), as well as two *priey*. The *arak*, who have names and are either male or female spirits of persons long dead, may simply express their personalities when they possess the medium (e.g., a young bachelor spirit made Yuan act gay and flirtatious, saying that "he" wanted a nice young woman and would make a good husband), or speak to their descendants (e.g., one spirit was angry because kinsmen were quarreling), or simply pass out "good luck" (e.g., during possession the medium may blow on, wipe powder or oil on, or give pieces of string or charms to spectators). After the séance had ended, the ritual objects were taken out to a deserted field and left for the spirits. It is interesting that some of the audience, especially the young men, laughed at and made derisive comments about the possessions. Most of the onlookers, however, were convinced and impressed by the ceremony (to which they contributed items such as fruit, betel, and small sums of money), and it is said that Yuan is much respected and feared, even by the spirits themselves, for her powers.

(4) The *bóngbèt*, according to villagers, is similar to a *rup arak* in being capable of possession by spirits. But rather than being possessed annually, the *bóngbèt* is entered by spirits only occasionally and is characterized as being a person (either male or female) of exceptionally good character.[59]

---

[56] According to village gossip, a Svay woman once attempted to disguise a presumed abortion or infanticide by crying out that a *tmóp* had put a knife in her stomach.

[57] Cf. Porée and Maspero 1938, 226 who state that every family has a *rup arak* and that possession may occur anytime a family member falls ill. This was not true in the Svay area. But see Porée and Maspero 1938, 226–27, and CMCC 59.107 for other descriptions of a possession ceremony.

[58] The spirits are said to be especially fond of music, which constitutes an offering in itself. Music is also "offered" to Buddha in curing rituals that involve monks rather than magical practitioners.

[59] Cf. Porée and Maspero 1938, 224 who describe a "bangbot" as similar to but less powerful than a *kru*, who may have various skills such as reading omens, making amulets, warding off evil, and causing thieves to be covered with burns unless they return stolen goods.

(5) Finally, there is the *achaa*; not the temple *achaa* discussed in a previous section, but an *achaa* who officiates at various familial ceremonies such as life-cycle rituals. (Such *achaa* are usually differentiated into *achaa kaa*, who specialize in weddings, and *achaa yoki* who specialize in funerals, although in fact either one may officiate at other kinds of ceremonies as well.) The *achaa* is not, strictly speaking, a magical practitioner or spirit specialist in the manner of the *kru*, *rup arak*, etc. His main function is, rather, to be the "master of ceremonies" in the literal sense: to preside over rituals, guide the participants through their ceremonial roles, and see that the ceremony is properly conducted. In the practice of his profession, the *achaa* must know not only the component parts of various rituals, but such things as how to fashion ritual objects, what invocations and offerings must be made to particular spirits on certain occasions, and how to make astrological calculations to determine, for example, auspicious days for holding ceremonies or whether potential marriage partners will be compatible. In addition, an *achaa* may possess certain skills such as curing or making charms against misfortune. An *achaa* is paid in money and/or kind, the amounts varying according to the services rendered.[60]

There are two *achaa* in West Svay: Kompha (House 20) and Samnang (House 22), both of whom are primarily "wedding *achaa*" although they occasionally preside at other kinds of ceremonies as well. Kompha learned the fundamentals of his profession from monks at a temple near Phnom Penh (after he himself had left the monastic order), while Samnang was instructed by Kompha and another *achaa* in the neighborhood. Both are frequently called upon to supervise the life-cycle ceremonies in Svay and sometimes neighboring villages as well; Kompha also knows how to cure by "blowing" and is consulted for minor ailments.

There is occasional skepticism about some of the skills of these various specialists, for example, the *kru*'s ability to find lost objects, or whether a *rup arak* is truly possessed or only pretending to be. In general, however, the average villager believes as firmly in these specialists and their efforts to control supernatural elements as they do in various spirits. For example, charms to ward off sickness or misfortune are worn by numerous villagers;[61] and severe or extended illness always initiates consultation with a *kru* or *achaa* and some sort of curing ritual that involves offerings to spirits (sometimes there is an additional ceremony with offerings to Buddha and the monks as well). As one man said, "Illness cannot be cured with medicine alone."

Perhaps the major significance of the folk religion is its supplementation of Buddhism. Buddhism can explain transcendental questions such as one's general existence in this life and the next. But the folk religion can give reasons for and means of coping with the more immediate and incidental, yet nonetheless pressing, problems and fortunes of one's present existence. The accumulation of Buddhist merit may enable a better rebirth in the next life, but in the meantime there may be problems

---

[60] E.g., for officiating at a wedding, Kompha is customarily paid 50–100 riels, two bunches of bananas, sixteen *ansom* cakes, two coconuts, and five kilograms of candles. For "blowing" on a minor ailment, he takes whatever fruit or other kind the patient offers.

[61] These may be knotted or braided string, old coins, *kataa* or metal cylinders enclosing Pali incantations written on paper or thin metal, magical symbols drawn on paper or cloth, etc. Sometimes these charms are blessed by monks as well as being chanted over by *kru* to yield a double efficacy. One man in West Svay also has special tattoos that presumably make him invulnerable to bodily harm. See also Steinberg 1959, 76; Porée and Maspero 1938, 221–23 on charms and amulets.

such as drought, illness, or unrequited love in this life that need attention, and worry can be relieved by recourse to the folk religion.[62]

Moreover, it is important to note that the folk religion also provides certain norms for behavior with sanctions that are more instantaneous in their punishment for misconduct than in Buddhism. For example, Buddhism certainly urges harmonious relations among kinsmen (see, e.g., the Sigalovada Sutta in Burtt 1955, 109–10), but the consequences of antagonistic behavior toward relatives are remote at best in its doctrine. In the folk religion, on the other hand, quarrels or dissension within the family or among kinsmen immediately invoke the wrath of the ancestral spirits who will strike down an innocent member of the group. The fear of arousing the anger of these spirits is a very real one, and although it does not succeed in suppressing all discord, it has certainly conciliated more than one family squabble. In much the same manner, the belief concerning the guardian spirit of animals specifies that these creatures, which Buddha says should not be killed, must also be cared for properly lest the owner be punished with a sickness. Thus, animals as well as kin relations receive a double-barreled religious protection. A further interesting and important point is that illness is the characteristic form of retribution for offense to the spirits. Surely various forms of physical ailments are endemic in a peasant population, and the folk religion thus offers a variety of explanations and cures for ill health.

---

[62] Other writers have made this same point with respect to the coexistence of both a great and little religious tradition; see e.g., Mandelbaum 1966; Nash 1965, 166; Steinberg 1959, 75; Wolf 1966, 101–2.

# CHAPTER SIX

# THE LIFE CYCLE

The different stages in an individual's life are distinguished by various terms denoting broad age groups or statuses, as well as by particular activities, dress, and sometimes ceremonial observances, that are described below.

## PREGNANCY AND BIRTH

Villagers sometimes comment that their meager resources make it difficult to support children as well as one would like. But the birth of children, either male or female, is always welcomed with pleasure even in already large families. While there is no special value attached to producing a great number of offspring, the other extreme of barrenness is regarded as highly unfortunate and undesirable. Indeed, a sterile couple will commonly ask a close kinsmen to let one of the latter's children come to live with them. Similarly, old couples whose own children are already married or moved away will have grandchildren come to enliven their homes for weeks or months at a time.

The villagers realize that sexual intercourse causes pregnancy, but there is no clear idea as to exactly how conception occurs, although women will speculate that it involves the union of the man's "fluid" with something in the female. They do know that contraception is possible; it is said that prostitutes and people in Phnom Penh have "medicines" that prevent or abort pregnancy.[1] But, as Srey said: "We [villagers] do not know how to use such things—those women in Phnom Penh are lazy about having children." Furthermore, of course, the Buddhist prescription against the taking of life is a powerful deterrent against abortion or infanticide.[2]

Once pregnancy has occurred (evidenced by cessation of menstruation, periodic malaise, and swelling abdomen), the woman continues her various chores, even arduous work such as transplanting, for as long as possible. She has no special dietary restrictions, except for purely individual feelings about not eating certain foods, but women generally agree that having hot spices is not advisable.

At birth (clóng tonle or "crossing the river") the woman is assisted by several of her female relatives and friends in addition to a midwife (cmòóp, smòóp). West Svay women customarily call in a midwife from the neighboring village of Sandan, an old lady who learned her profession simply by attendance at numerous births. (There is also a midwife in Kompong Tuol who was trained at the midwifery school in Phnom Penh established by the World Health Organization; but she is sent for only in cases

---

[1] Villagers also know of the existence of condoms, but these are considered to be devices to prevent men from contracting venereal disease rather than contraceptives. On the question of whether contraception is contrary to Buddhist doctrine, see Lorimer 1954, 187–88, which discusses Bruce Ryan's survey of opinions among Sinhalese Buddhist monks.

[2] There was, however, one instance of suspected abortion or infanticide in West Svay; see infra. See also Leclère 1894, 352–53 on law codes regarding infanticide and abortion.

of complicated births that cannot be handled by the village midwife and *kru*.) Men, unmarried females, and children are not allowed to witness births, although the husband and other assorted bystanders gather to wait, listen, and talk outside the house. I was not allowed to observe a birth because of my unmarried status, but it is said that the woman reclines and her labors are assisted by massage and gentle pushing on the abdomen. Once the infant has been expelled, the midwife cuts and ties the umbilical cord and washes the child. The umbilical cord and the afterbirth are later buried by the midwife in some deserted spot.[3]

After the birth, the mother customarily lies for three days upon a raised bed of bamboo slats under which small fires burn continuously in clay pots.[4] This procedure, called *ang pløøng* or *cau pløøng*, is considered necessary to the mother's health because "coldness leads to illness" while heat is therapeutic and healing.

On the third day after birth there is a ceremony (*bon prokak cmòóp*) to honor both the midwife and new child. The mother "asks forgiveness of the midwife" (*som too cmòóp*) for having subjected her to trouble and presents her with gifts of betel, candles, incense, rice, and perhaps fruit or a bit of meat, and whatever sum of money the family can afford (usually fifty riels). In turn, the midwife ties white string upon the infant's wrists for good luck (and may also pierce the ears of a female child). The parents give offerings to ancestral spirits and provide a meal for the midwife and a few close kinsmen and friends (although the latter do not reciprocate with gifts for the child). Although not necessary parts of the ceremony, the child is often named at this time and also receives a small daub of rice flour (the *bòng haoy*) upon the fontanel to "make the skull close up" (this daub will be worn for several months).

The mother customarily remains in the house for a week or longer after birth, resting until she feels able to resume her normal tasks and receiving visitors who come to see the new child. Apart from a certain type of fish and pigs' heads, there are no special food restrictions after birth. Sexual intercourse is usually suspended for about a month (as it was prior to the birth as well), but there are no set rules concerning this matter.

## INFANCY AND CHILDHOOD[5]

Breastfeeding (*bau doh*) provides the main nourishment for babies.[6] The child is granted the breast whenever it seems hungry or cranky, even if feeding interrupts the mother at some task. Such nursing may continue up to the age of three or four

[3] Cf. Porée-Maspero 1958, 33, which states that in some families the father disposes of the placenta by various means; this source also says that "in the countryside" delivery occurs in a small shed that is especially constructed apart from the house proper. This was not, however, true in West Svay where births took place in the house itself.

[4] This custom is widespread throughout Southeast Asia and occurs among the Burmese, Thai, Laotians, Malays, Vietnamese, and even some Philippine groups (see Hart, Rajadhon, and Coughlin 1965; Nash 1965, 258; Kaufman 1960, 142–43; 1961, 42–43; Fraser 1960, 195). For further details of "roasting" the mother and other observances connected with birth among the Khmer, see Porée-Maspero 1958, 31–34; Porée and Maspero 1938, 204–6; CMCC 31.005, 31.006, 42.024, 42.003.

[5] Infants are termed *kon ngait, kon ngaa*, or *kon kchay*. Children up to the age of adolescence are variously referred to as *kon* (child), *kmeng* (young), or *kon kmeng*.

[6] Canned milk, known as "cow's milk," is used only by urban families or for a village baby whose mother has died. It is interesting that mothers say that when an infant is fed on canned milk, it is fed on a schedule and not on demand.

depending on whether another infant is born in the meantime or on the permissiveness of the mother. Some women prefer to wean a child at one and a half or two years of age; others allow their children to nurse for several years. When weaning is necessary, the mother tries to increase the amount of solid foods given to the child and usually has to resort as well to applying pepper or quinine to the nipples. Apart from milk, babies are fed thin rice gruel from about the fifth or sixth month, sometimes earlier. Ordinary rice, fish, meat, and fruit are not part of a child's diet until it has a good set of teeth at a year or more of age. They are fed most of their meals by an older person up to the age of three or four when they can manage to eat with their own fingers or using silverware.

The development of various motor skills appears to follow the pattern common to children in the Western world. From observations and mothers' reports, babies can usually sit alone at about half a year, crawl and stand with aid at about ten months to a year, and walk at about a year or more of age. Certainly the baby becomes accustomed to being in an upright position from an early age because it is inevitably held on someone's lap whenever it is awake; and crawling and walking can be practiced without the hindrance of much clothing but with the aid of many encouraging comments and helping hands. Frequently, however, even after such motor abilities are well developed, the child continues to be carried (straddling someone's hip) for a good deal of the time.

Infants are usually naked except for a string necklace, ankle bracelet, or some other ornament. From the age of a year or so, female children may be clothed in a small sarong or pants, but boys often continue to run naked up to the age of seven or eight except on special occasions.

The child in the first few years of life, if no younger sibling is born in the meantime, is the recipient of a great deal of affection from family, kinsmen, and neighbors. Its most intimate association is, of course, with the mother; the child is continually in the mother's presence, whether about the house, in the fields, at a temple ceremony, or asleep at night next to her, and always able to receive the breast, a soft lap, and soothing words whenever it desires. An infant receives a good deal of attention from others as well. Babies are cuddled and adored by everyone, passed from one person to another to be admired, always capable of finding someone to provide warm arms, smiles, gentle words, and sniffing kisses. Even adolescent boys will cradle and chuckle at a baby, and fathers, who will later come to assume more and more of an authoritarian pose as the child grows older, are unashamedly affectionate to an infant child. Because of this constant attention and love, immediate fulfillment of demands, and permissiveness, the child in the first year or so of life probably views the world as being warm and receptive.

But the child is eventually propelled from the Eden of its infancy into a harsher environment, either because a younger sibling is born or because the child attains an age (usually three or four) when he is expected to begin accepting some discipline. In either case, he must stop breastfeeding, become less dependent on his mother, resign himself to receiving less attention and the immediate gratification of his wishes, begin learning to feed and bathe himself and to control elimination, and start to assume some minimal responsibility for small chores as well as his behavior in general.

For a young child less than five or six years of age, the birth of a new sibling means above all the sudden withdrawal of all the attention and spoiling he has received as the youngest of the family. He (or she) is likely to become petulant, sullen, or mischievous, often tugging at his mother's skirts, trying to cuddle in her lap at every opportunity, and teasing the younger child. As the child grows older, the hostility toward the younger sibling (or siblings) will be displaced to a large extent as the former's role changes from competitor to surrogate parent. This is especially true for girls who, from a very young age, are given the responsibility of caring for younger children and who usually assume this task with as much pleasure as the Western child playing with dolls. There are inevitably quarrels among siblings, sometimes quite violent ones in which older children will scream at, tease, or hit the younger ones in a manner much harsher than parents treat offspring. But, in general, affection and a sense of responsibility for younger siblings usually increase with age.

Another problem that arises, with or without the birth of another child in the family, is the fact that there is some inconsistency in the affection and discipline given a child past the age of three or four. Sometimes his tears are soothed at once; at other times his cries are ignored or even laughed at. Sometimes his mischief is tolerated with amusement; on other occasions it will bring disapproval. While the parents, especially the mother, continue to be generally affectionate and permissive, the child learns that the world is no longer all warmth and smoothness. He also becomes subject to correction and punishment by parents, older siblings, and other adults. Actually such chastisement is not severe and limited usually to yelled threats of "Don't play around," "I'll break your head," or "I'll hit you this instant," although in fact physical punishment is resorted to only in the extreme. Even then it never goes beyond a slap on the arms or legs, or a quick rap of knuckles on the head, because parents feel that too much physical castigation makes a child "rotten" (*koit*). In addition, children become subject to teasing from their peers, older children and adolescents, and sometimes adults; someone will make a scary face at the child, make a frightening feint of hitting, or tease a small girl that so-and-so is her fiancé until she bursts into tears. Some children respond to chastisement or teasing with nonchalance. But most will break into whimpers or cries, give a gesture of defiance by making a face or turning one's buttocks toward the offender, or react with fiery anger by screaming curses and striking out with wild blows (sometimes even at parents). Temper tantrums with prolonged shrieks and tears or wrath are less common than one might expect. But children between the ages of about four and ten often exhibit behavior that seems to manifest a certain frustration, defiance, and willfulness.

The first things that are deliberately taught to a child are simple tricks that amuse adults, such as Mias learning to tap her feet and wave her hand when one says "Dance," or Paa groaning and rubbing his stomach when one says "Bellyache." The child also learns the appropriate replies to questions such as "What year were you born in?" "Whose child are you?" "Where did mother go?"; or to put his hand on different portions of the anatomy as a list of body parts is recited. Different persons and kinship or relative age distinctions are distinguished as the child hears "Give it to Aunt Sau" or "Come to older sibling." Etiquette is taught when an adult places a child's hands together in the appropriate gesture of salutation, or admonishes a child to sit properly with legs folded to one side in front of a monk, or tells a little girl not to expose her sexual organs. Other things are taught in a more laissez-faire manner as youngsters (even two- or three-year-olds) are permitted to handle a machete or play with a lighted cigarette to learn for themselves what the dangers may be. The child also learns gradually to feed and bathe himself and to eliminate properly. Urination is treated lightly up to the age of about three; children are allowed to urinate at will through the floorboards of the house, on the ground, or in their clothes, with little or no effort to clean either the child or the soiled area afterwards. But some effort is made to control defecation from about the age of one and a half or two. Soiling one's clothes or trafficked areas is met with disapproval, and the child is told to defecate only in the bushy, uncleared areas around the hamlet where adults customarily evacuate.[7]

From the age of about five, the child gradually relaxes his dependence on the mother and moves into more frequent association with other children. Though the youngster still frequently tags after his mother, he is now seen equally or more often engaged in play and games with age mates or in carrying out small chores. Toys are scarce in the village and usually limited to simple objects that can be fabricated from readily available materials: a slingshot of wood and a rubber band, a bamboo pinwheel, a crude hobby horse of palm stalks, a paper kite, etc. There are also a number of games with formal rules that may involve several or a crowd of children: a form of hopscotch, a sort of bowling game with palm seeds used as balls and pins, a game analogous to marbles but using small seeds, etc. Something that strikes the observer is the absence of games involving competing teams, or in which one person is "it" and pitted against all the others, such as is common in Western games. There is certainly some competition in several games in that skills are matched against one another, but the stress seems to be more on the playing than on winning.[8]

A good deal of play, however, involves neither toys nor formalized games: climbing trees, splashing and throwing mud in the rice paddies, fishing and catching crabs, singing, and simple exuberant running about the village. More elaborate play involves imaginative imitation of adult life: playing "house" in a small shelter of cloth draped over some convenient poles; playing "plowing" with two younger siblings or friends as oxen; playing "restaurant" selling meals of chopped leaves on pieces of broken pottery in return for "money" of torn bits of paper; playing "temple" by kneeling and chanting replicas of Buddhist prayers; and, a special favorite of young girls, dressing up in scarves and borrowed jewelry to dance gracefully to music sung and drummed by obliging adolescents or adults. In such play activities children associate most with those of the same sex, but it is not unusual to see groups of both boys and girls. It is also common for children of different ages to play together. Although the closest friendships evolve between those of approximately the same age, games and play may involve youngsters who are five or more years apart in age and even, on occasion, adolescent girls of eighteen or nineteen who still find delight in games.[9]

The child's life, however, is not spent exclusively in frolic and sport, for he also acquires small duties from the age of about six or seven. The first chore usually given to children of both sexes is the collection of kindling for fires, an essential daily chore of village life. Small girls take care of younger siblings and are generally quite competent babysitters (although sometimes they can barely lift their charges onto their

---

[7] For other comments on child-rearing practices in Cambodia, see Zadrozny 1955, 326–27; Steinberg 1959, 79–81; Porée and Maspero 1938, 194; CMCC 42.024, 42.003.

[8] This is also seen in one form of adult "play," the *ay yay* song form, in which a man and woman trade remarks in song (according to a particular pattern of melody and stanza); essentially one is trying to get the better of the other, but the listener's delight comes from the wit and skill of the exchange itself, rather than seeing which singer wins the verbal contest. This may be a reflection of the general absence of competitiveness in Khmer society and is also perhaps consistent with the Buddhist ethic that an individual should strive for individual excellence (in meritorious behavior) but not at the expense of depriving others.

[9] This aspect of play also struck me as unusual, but is understandable when one realizes that the rough age grading imposed by schools is not as strong as in our own culture.

small hips). By about the age of ten, a girl has learned how to do some simple cooking and may be given the responsibility of preparing rice for a meal, while boys are often sent to watch cattle at pasture and help tend them in other ways.

Nowadays children of both sexes, from the age of six or seven, are also sent to receive formal education in the public schools for six hours a day, five days a week, nine months a year. The first three years of school concentrate upon the Khmer language (grammar, vocabulary, writing), along with elementary instruction in subjects such as hygiene, mathematics, geography, civics, "morals," and physical education. If one passes the state examinations at the end of the three years and is granted a "certificat" for satisfactory completion of the "études élémentaires," the child advances to another three-year cycle, grades four to six, which add the French language to further study of the Khmer language and other topics. Apart from a few children who dislike school and whose tolerant parents permit them to stay home for days or even years at a time, absenteeism from school is quite rare because most of the youngsters and their parents realize the value of education.

## ADOLESCENCE

In the earlier part of this century the villagers observed several rituals that marked the transition from childhood to a more mature stage. These ceremonies were the following. (a) An old custom in Cambodia was keeping a child's head completely shaven except for a tuft of hair at the top of the crown. At the age of about thirteen[10] a ceremony was held in which the topknot was ritually cut off by an *achaa*, kinsmen and friends were feasted, and monks were invited to recite prayers. Wealthier persons even hired an orchestra and professional entertainers to make a grand display. But this ritual has not been practiced in the village for some fifteen or twenty years. At present, only one child in West Svay has a shaved head with a true topknot, although many female children observe a remnant of this tradition by tying up a lock of hair on top of the head. (b) A special ritual for girls, which has not been practiced in Svay for some forty years, was the "entrance into the shade" (*col mlop*) at the appearance of the first menses (which is said to occur anytime between the ages of thirteen and seventeen).[11] The girl was secluded in a special, curtained section of the house, allowed to see no men (not even her father and brothers), forbidden to go outdoors except in the dark of night when the males of the village would be asleep, and prohibited from eating fish or meat. This seclusion lasted anywhere from several months to as long as a year, during which time the girl passed her days by learning skills such as sewing or basketry. The "coming out of the shade" (*cEng mlop*) was celebrated with feasting of kinsmen and friends, offerings to ancestors and spirits, and various rituals performed by an

---

[10] Cf. Porée-Maspero 1958, 35 who say that the topknot was cut between the ages of seven and twelve. See Porée-Maspero 1958, 35–37; Porée and Maspero 1938, 136–44; and Monod 1931, 50–52 for details of the ceremony. The Thai and Laotians also observe this practice (see Kaufman 1960, 147; 1961, 45).

[11] There was/is no comparable *rite de passage* for boys. However, a number of males become novice monks during early adolescence. The ceremony that accompanies entrance into the monastery (see chapter 5) is meant to mark a transition from secular to sacred status rather than from one stage of life to another. But in another sense, entry into monkhood could be considered as recognition that the boy had reached a point in life when he was sufficiently mature to accept monastic discipline and profit from an education.

*achaa* that are identical to those observed at weddings, as if to signify that the girl was now physically ready for marriage. (See Porée-Maspero et al. 1958, 39–44; Porée and Maspero 1938, 207–9; Monod 1931, 69–70 for details of the ceremony.) The girl's first menstruation is now observed with secrecy rather than celebration.[12] (But there is a sort of survival of the concept of "the shade" in the feeling among women that menstruation should be concealed from and never mentioned in the presence of men.)

Now that the rituals of cutting the topknot and menstrual retreat are no longer observed, there is no clear-cut demarcation between childhood and adolescence. Through the early teens, village youngsters remain much like children in their physical development and activities. The young adolescents have few household chores and are still free to play a good deal of the time. They do, however, become increasingly decorous in behavior and begin to show concern for their personal appearance. The girls in particular become very modest even about their still childlike figures and usually get their first beauty salon permanent at the age of about thirteen.

At the age of about sixteen, however, when both sexes begin to show definite signs of physical maturation, adolescents are recognized as being at the threshold of adulthood. They are no longer referred to as "children" but as *kromom*, "unmarried female," and *krolaa*, "unmarried male,"[13] with the implication that they are now eligible for marriage, which will mark their passage into true adulthood.[14] With this end in view, both sexes now take an increasingly active role in household and subsistence tasks. Boys learn the techniques of rice cultivation, driving oxcarts, repairing tools, elementary carpentry, etc. Girls transplant and harvest alongside their mothers, learn how to cook various dishes, sew, and act as real surrogate mothers for younger siblings. Adolescents of both sexes sometimes take extra employment to earn money for both themselves and their families. They also become active participants rather than mere onlookers in ceremonial activity, whether as wedding attendants or waiters and waitresses at temple festivals. They become quite conscious, too, that they are now responsible for their actions and will express concern for earning merit, as well as fear of incurring the retribution of "spirits" (*kmauit*) for bad behavior. They also become noticeably more obedient and respectful toward parents, accepting the latter's decisions without the sulking or defiance with which young children often respond to parental orders.

But despite this increasing seriousness, there is still a good deal of carefree frivolity in adolescent life. Various chores notwithstanding, there is considerable free time for young men to sit in small groups talking and joking and, especially in the evenings, playing music in impromptu jam sessions. Girls are similarly seen gossiping, discussing clothes and men, singing popular songs, and sometimes even playing games with little girls. The closest friendships are formed between individuals of the same sex and

---

[12] Porée-Maspero 1958, 35, 39 also state that both the cutting of the topknot and menstrual seclusion are becoming increasingly rare practices in modern Cambodia.

[13] The term *cumtung* or, more rarely, *pum cre* may be used for preadolescents and adolescents of approximately ten to eighteen years of age, but these words are actually little heard. Spinsters of about thirty to forty years of age are called *kromom sau kay*, while those older than forty are termed *cah kromom*. Similarly, old bachelors are called *cah krolaa*.

[14] The minimum legal age for marriage is fourteen for females and seventeen for males, though it is possible to obtain dispensation for a girl to marry as early as twelve and a boy at fifteen (Clairon n.d., 56). In village life, however, girls are usually not considered marriageable until the age of about sixteen and boys at about nineteen.

approximate age, but groups of mixed sex often gather at someone's house to banter and joke in easy camaraderie born of long years of association.

The gaiety of this age period is also reflected in the clothing of adolescents and young unmarried adults, which is more varied and stylish than that of any other age group. The adolescent girl must have her hair long and artificially curled and dresses ordinarily in bright flowered sarongs and cotton blouses (with a camisole or brassiere, for breasts are an object of extreme modesty at this age). On special occasions, such as temple ceremonies, the village girls are particularly striking creatures with special silk sarongs in rich hues, brightly colored sheer blouses, Western-style sandals or mules, family jewelry, and powder and lipstick as well.[15] The young men are also dandies in their own manner. While shorts or plaid sarongs are usual for ordinary wear, special occasions find the young man handsomely turned out with pomaded hair, Western-style shirts, Western or traditional silk trousers, shoes or rubber sandals, and perhaps even sunglasses or a wristwatch if he is wealthy.

This attention to personal appearance is geared, of course, to one of the primary concerns of this age: attraction of the opposite sex. Some of the adolescent girls occasionally express apprehension about the work and pain of marriage and childbearing and laughingly assert that they intend to be spinsters who will live with a married sibling. But even they, as do the other young unmarried people, have a constant interest in the other sex. There are continual discussions of who are the most attractive *kro-mom* and *krolaa* in the village, excited anticipation of and meticulous primping before temple festivals or any other events that draw crowds and are thus good hunting grounds for potential spouses, and constant teasing about so-and-so being someone's fiancé(e).

Despite this preoccupation with the opposite sex, there is relatively little premarital sex in village life. Adolescents are certainly not totally ignorant about sexual practices and organs when, for example, children often go naked (and little boys in particular are often teased about their penises), one often sees dogs or cats copulating, ribald stories are related in the presence of children or adolescents, and the most common expression used in anger, surprise, or mere exclamation can be translated as "have intercourse with a widow" (*coy kaduy memay*). But for all this, adolescent girls at least are often uncertain about the exact nature of intercourse and childbirth. Young women are, moreover, rather strictly chaperoned in that they are never permitted to go out alone at night, or even out to deserted rice fields in the daytime by themselves. They are also strongly imbued with fears of possible rape or abduction by strange men,[16] and the fact that both Buddhist precepts and ancestral spirits frown upon fornication. Villagers say that premarital sex is common in Phnom Penh where there are looser morals and prostitutes, but that there would be "great shame" and "bad-smelling talk" should any of their young people be guilty of this sin.

---

[15] Western-style dresses are considered "embarrassing," although schoolgirls and little girls will wear short skirts. The males are much more receptive to Western dress.

[16] See chapter 7 for the story of two girls from a nearby village who were abducted by some men, and other incidents that reinforce such fears. Aymonier 1900, 33 states that there is an old tradition that girls and women could be raped if they were indecent enough to venture out alone at dawn, noon, or twilight. But there were also numerous legal statutes in the nineteenth century and earlier that punished seduction, rape, fornication, and even mere propositions to women (see Leclère 1894, 374–82, 411–20, 423–25).

But in fact premarital sex does occur on occasion. A young woman in East Hamlet was four months pregnant at her marriage, and villagers acknowledge that similar situations do happen "once in a while." These pregnant brides do, however, bring censorious gossip upon themselves and their families (though the fact tends to be forgiven and largely ignored after several years of marriage). More striking and decidedly unusual is the case of the girl in West Svay who appears to be the mistress of an "official" from Phnom Penh. She, too, is the object of considerable disapproval, as are her parents for permitting such behavior.[17] Another exceptional case in West Svay that occurred several decades ago was that of a young unmarried woman who was said to have had affairs with and borne the children of two men (and may even have aborted or practiced infanticide on another child).[18] In general, though, cases such as the latter two are rare. While young men sometimes say wistfully or jokingly that they wish the situation were freer, the young unmarried women are generally fearful of premarital relations, and public opinion and the closeness of village life are strong deterrents to fornication.

## BETROTHALS

According to ideal custom, a young man makes his own choice as to whom he wishes to marry and, once having decided, asks his parents to begin negotiations with the girl's family. When the latter receives a marriage proposal, the young women herself is consulted and, again according to tradition, is free to accept or reject the offer. Theoretically, the parents cannot force a child into a marriage that the latter does not want, or prevent him (her) from wedding the person of his (her) choice without incurring the wrath of ancestral spirits. Villagers deny that parents ever arrange marriages; "boys and girls do as they wish." This ideal is actually followed to a great extent: the male does indeed initiate marriage negotiations; individuals do often make their own choices; and parents generally do not explicitly force a child into or away from a union that they themselves may favor or disapprove of. But in fact, parents often exert more oblique and subtle influence over whom their child marries: by suggesting possible spouses, by extolling the virtues of one suitor over another, by discouraging a child from making or accepting a proposal on the grounds that he (she) is not yet ready for marriage, etc. (see also Zadrozny 1955, 315). If a child is absolutely adamant, the parents will generally suspend whatever reservations or objections they may have. But in many instances, a girl or boy is willing to defer to the presumably greater wisdom of the parents and accept without demur what the latter thinks is best. Oftentimes, then, it is actually the parents who make the major decision about the marriage partner, and the child acquiesces because of a sense of obedience or because she/he has no strong feelings about marrying a particular person. For example, San, who became engaged to and married a mechanic from Phnom Penh during my stay, was gloomy and negative throughout her betrothal and kept postponing the wedding date on one pretext or another. She honestly did not want to get married but did so in the end because

---

[17] Cf., however, LeGallen 1929, 220 who notes that some parents may, because of "vanity or cupidity," allow their daughters to become second-rank wives or concubines of men of high standing in order to "get honor or wealth."

[18] Illegitimate children are called *kon prey*, "children of the wilderness," because lovers usually seek deserted areas to have sexual relations; there is also an expression *paèm prey*, "to become pregnant in the wilderness."

she knew that her divorced mother could barely support the family and wanted desperately for San to marry this young men who gave evidence of being a decent person and a good provider. Or, to take another case, the various proposals received by Neary have been rejected really by her parents who feel that she is still too young to marry, and Neary accepted her parents' feelings because she felt no special attraction for any of her suitors.

A man may find a potential fiancée in various ways: she may be someone in his own or a nearby village whom he has known (well or slightly) for years, or someone whom he has only seen or met fleetingly at a temple festival or on a visit to another community, or someone who has been recommended by kinsmen or friends as a good spouse. The physical attractiveness of an individual, especially a girl, is an important attribute when young people discuss marriage partners, and it is obviously a powerful magnet in attracting attention and consideration as a possible mate.[19] (E.g., Neary, who is regarded as one of the prettiest girls in West Svay, has already received four or five proposals by the age of eighteen, while Phany, a homely young woman, has just received her first offer at the age of twenty-five, and that one probably because she stands to receive a good inheritance.) But in the final decision, other qualities may assume greater significance. First, one of the most important attributes stressed by villagers is "good character": a young woman should be modest, have an untarnished reputation, and not be lazy or flighty; a young man should not drink, be industrious and capable of supporting a family adequately, and be generally well mannered and respectful in demeanor. A second consideration, although it is not explicitly stated, may be the economic status of a possible marriage partner. For example, someone in a poor family with little land may be encouraged to marry an individual who will inherit enough property to support a family; and a number of parents would prefer their daughters to marry men who have non-agricultural occupations or professions (teachers, government clerks, etc.) rather than rice cultivators. Third, there may be other factors to consider; for example, a man or woman will think twice about marrying a widow or widower (or divorcé[e]) with children unless he or she has no other prospects; and a man normally seeks someone of his own age or younger, although in some marriages the woman is several years older than the husband. Fourth, one final matter is of critical importance; after everything is taken into consideration and a man and woman have expressed interest in one another as potential spouses, the horoscopes of both persons must be examined by an *achaa* to make certain that they will be compatible. Each individual is born in the year of a particular animal and, according to astrological calculations, unions between persons born in certain years are favorable for marriage, while combinations of other years would be either risky or disastrous (for charts of favorable and unfavorable combinations, see especially Porée-Maspero 1962b).

The formal procedures and ceremonies of betrothal may vary somewhat according to region and the extent to which traditional customs are maintained, but the basic elements are usually the following.[20] (1) The man tells his parents of the woman he

---

[19] Some of the qualities of beauty or handsomeness are medium height and build, olive skin that is neither too white nor dark, medium-sized eyes that are neither too owlish nor small, and regularity of features. Cf. Steinberg 1959, 38 who gives different standards of attractiveness.

[20] I shall not attempt to give the full ceremonial details of betrothal proceedings. For accounts thereof, see Leclère 1916, 535–39; Porée-Maspero et al 1958, 49–53; Monod 1931, 71–73; Steinberg 1959, 84.

has selected and asks their approval. If this is granted, the traditional practice is for the parents to select an older woman who has reputable character and is knowledgeable about etiquette to act as a go-between (*neak plau* or "person of the road") in handling negotiations with the girl's parents. In some cases, however, the suitor's parents may go directly to the girl's family, an orphan may ask a friend to act as a substitute parent and intermediary, or a young man away from home may himself go directly to the girl's parents.

(2) Ideally, the intermediary (or whoever speaks for the man) pays three visits to the girl's parents or the latter's representative (the *meba*), taking small gifts (cakes, fruits, betel, etc.) and gradually, obliquely tendering a marriage offer. The girl's parents give encouragement or discouragement in return, depending on their daughter's wishes. In practice, the number of visits may be less, the proposal made quite directly, and (as noted previously) the parents themselves may make the final decision.

One important point in these negotiations, apart from the various considerations cited above, is the amount of the monetary gift (called either *cumnuèn*, "gift," or *tlay ptea*, "the worth of a house") that is customarily given by the male's family to the girl's parents.[21] The sum is decided upon by bargaining between the two sides. In village marriages the amount usually ranges from 2,000 to 5,000 riels (though it may go as high as 10,000 riels), depending upon the financial resources of the man's family and the desirability of the young woman (e.g., a homely girl, widow, or divorcée commands less money). This gift is used by the girl's family to buy her clothing and jewelry and to help defray other wedding expenses.

(3) If the negotiations proceed smoothly, the final betrothal ceremonies occur on the third and last visit. Ideally this involves a gathering at the girl's home of the intermediaries, both sets of parents, and some kinsmen and close friends. The male's family offers more gifts to the girl's parents; the ancestral spirits are notified of the event and given offerings; a small feast is prepared by the girl's family; and sometimes monks are invited to recite prayers and give blessings. This constitutes "the fixing of the word" (*pcuóp pièk*), and the man's parents now "ask for the date of the wedding" (*som cuun piliè*) to be set by an *achaa*. The couple are now formally fiancés (*sòng saa*).[22] Should an engagement be broken after this point, the girl's parents must return to the rejected fiancé's family a sum of money equal in value to all the gifts they have received from the latter.

After a betrothal was formalized, it was once customary for the fiancé "to serve" (*twèr bumraè*) his future parents-in-law until the wedding. The young man worked in his prospective in-laws' fields, did chores about the house, and sometimes actually lived with his fiancée's family, while his industriousness and good character were closely scrutinized and assessed (see also Leclère 1916, 539; Porée-Maspero et al. 1958, 52; Monod 1931, 74). This tradition was practiced in West Svay as recently as fifteen years ago when the fiancé lived in the same or a neighboring village. But nowadays it is rarely followed except that the young man may proffer some aid during

---

[21] Leclère 1916, 538; Porée-Maspero 1958, 55; Steinberg 1959, 85 refer to this monetary gift as "the price of the mother's milk," but West Svay villagers had never heard of this term. (The notion of payment for the "mother's milk" is, however, found among the Sedang, a Mon-Khmer tribal people in Vietnam [LeBar, Hickey, and Musgrave 1964, 17] and among the Thai [Blanchard et al. 1958, 434]).

[22] The term *sòng saa* may also be used as a euphemism for lovers engaging in premarital sex who are not actually affianced.

the busiest periods of cultivation if he resides nearby. Villagers attribute the decline of this custom not only to weakening tradition but to the fact that a number of village girls now marry young men with non-agricultural occupations that do not permit time off for bride service.

Another custom that is now rarely observed is the obligation of the fiancé to build a new house for himself and his bride-to-be (see chapter 3). The reasons for the passing of this practice are, according to villagers, the great expense of building houses and "the laziness of young men nowadays." But this tradition is recalled in the monetary gift given by the male's family to the bride's parents, which is called "the worth of a house," if a house is not actually built.

## WEDDINGS

Weddings (*rièp kaa, kaa,* or *apièpipiè*) are the most joyous, delightful, and (along with funerals) the most extravagant and elaborate of all life-cycle ceremonies. Until about twenty years ago, the festivities lasted for three days; at present the actual ceremonies have been cut to one and a half days to reduce both expenses and fatigue. But various preparations begin long beforehand, and the occurrence of a wedding involves considerable effort and expenditures.

The date of the marriage is set by an *achaa*. Weddings may take place only during certain months,[23] and the exact day is determined by the horoscopes of the bridal couple that will dictate propitious or dangerous dates for marriage. For weeks prior to this time excitement mounts among the two families, their kinsmen, and friends; and the villagers in general look forward to a bright moment of gaiety and entertainment to enliven their days. Because the wedding is held at the girl's house, her family is busiest with arrangements: renting a loudspeaker and phonograph records because no wedding is complete without continuous music; hiring, in addition, live musicians to play traditional melodies for ceremonies and dancing; borrowing or renting cooking implements, dishes, tables, and chairs (and sometimes hiring a special cook) for the several meals that will be offered to guests; buying decorations for the house, offerings for the monks, and traditional gifts for the groom's family; selecting an *achaa* and various wedding attendants; making scores of *ansom* cakes that are a traditional delicacy at weddings; sending messengers to notify kinsmen in distant communities of the wedding date; and the bride must get a new permanent and either buy elegant wedding clothes or rent a wedding costume from an old lady in a nearby village.

Although news of a prospective wedding spreads rapidly throughout and beyond the village by word of mouth, formal invitations to the ceremony are extended in the form of areca nuts and betel leaves (or banana leaves) that are distributed to invited guests a few days prior to the nuptials by a family member, kinsman, or friend. Whether or not such an invited guest (and his family), who is not a close relative or friend of the bridal couple, will actually attend the ceremony depends partly on whether he has time to spare but mostly upon whether he has money to spare as a wedding gift (*còng day*).[24] This contribution ranges from about 20 to 200 riels, depending

---

[23] These months are Boh, Palkun, Visak, Asat, and Kadŭk, which coincide roughly with January, March, May, the first part of July, and November.

[24] The term *còng day*, literally "joining of hands," refers also to the ritual of tying strings on somebody's wrists for good luck (see infra).

on the closeness of kinship or friendship, and without such a gift one would feel ashamed to attend and eat at the wedding feast. A wedding will also draw numerous spectators (even from other villages) who were not specifically invited but who will come by in the evening (after the meals are finished) to watch the festivities and give regards to the couple.

On the wedding day itself there is a flurry of commotion in and around the bride's house as kinsmen and neighbors help to prepare food; make frantic last-minute shopping trips; put up decorations and tables, chairs, etc.; borrow brass bowls, a gong, and other ceremonial objects; go to remind the monks that they are due at a certain hour; etc. Cloth hangings partition off a small corner of the house as the bride's chamber; and here she sits nervously (except when called forth for certain rituals), surrounded by female relatives and friends who will help her change clothes, fan her in the stifling heat of the small room, and keep up a steady flow of chatter and laughter. The groom similarly sits with his attendants, kinsmen, and friends in a small bamboo and thatch shelter that has been specially built for him near the bride's house. Music begins early in the day and continues almost non-stop through the entire event, broadcasting gaiety through the loudspeaker for kilometers around. Guests arrive in sequence to sit and talk in and around the house, eating and chewing betel.

The ritual procedures and paraphernalia (as well as their symbolism and mythology) of a wedding are too detailed to be described minutely, although a brief account of the major parts of the ceremony will be given (cf. the descriptions presented in Aymonier 1900, 33–34; Leclère 1916, 54–62; Monod 1931, 74–77; Porée and Maspero 1938, 209–14; Porée-Maspero et al. 1958, 54–62).[25] It might be noted that weddings vary somewhat on several counts: (1) certain rituals may be included, omitted, or carried out somewhat differently according to the dictates of the *achaa* in charge; (2) simple weddings, called *vee*, omit certain customary accouterments such as a live orchestra because the family is poor and cannot afford the expense; and (3) weddings are supposed to be less elaborate for the remarriage of a widow or divorcée, although in fact they are often as extravagant as those of first marriages if the family has the resources.

Apart from the bride and groom themselves, the main actors in the wedding ritual are the following. (1) The *achaa* presides over all ceremonies, supervises the making of ritual objects, and directs the participants to follow the proper procedures. (2) The *neak moha*, representing the groom's family, and the *meba*, representing the bride's side, assist the *achaa* in seeing that the rituals are conducted correctly, help to prepare ritual objects, and act as ceremonial representatives of the two sides. Theoretically, the *neak moha* and the *meba* are the intermediaries used in betrothal negotiations who now appear under new titles, but in practice they are often individuals who have been especially selected for the wedding because of their knowledgeability in the conduct of wedding ceremonies. They should also be persons who are old, of good character, and never widowed or divorced; they are often kinsmen but need not necessarily be so and are equally often persons who customarily preside in these capacities (e.g., Grandmother Leak [House 20] is frequently called upon to act as a *neak moha* or *meba* for weddings in the village). On occasion, too, one or another of these positions may be dispensed with or combined into one person; indeed, at one wedding, Kompha was *achaa*, *neak moha*, and *meba* all rolled into one. (3) Finally, the bride and groom each have two (possibly three or four) attendants (*kômdòò*) who stand by during

---

[25] I observed parts or all of seven weddings in Svay and a neighboring village.

various rituals. These bridesmaids and groomsmen, chosen by the couple's parents, are usually siblings or first cousins, although close friends may also be selected. The important point is that an attendant should have both parents alive and harmoniously married, for one with but a single parent would augur widowing or divorce for the bridal couple.

The actual wedding rituals, taken in sequence, are the following. On the night before the wedding there is a short ceremony "to enter the groom's shelter" (*col rung*). The *achaa* leads a procession composed of the groom, his attendants, relatives, friends, who carry his clothes, betel boxes, and a gong into the shelter. Here the *achaa* recites invocations; the *neak moha* and *meba* give best wishes for the marriage; offerings are made to ancestral spirits; and the *achaa* ties strings upon the groom's wrists for good luck.[26] The ritual ends with the pounding of a brass gong and cheers from the spectators.

The first day of the wedding encompasses a whole series of separate rituals. (1) In the morning, gifts of betel and areca, fruits, *ansom* cakes, and other delicacies are carried from the groom's shelter to the bride's home. (Part of these are kept for the girl's family while the rest are distributed among the guests.) In return, the girl's family presents certain traditional gifts (such as heavy silk sarongs and a scarf) to the groom. The ancestral spirits are informed of and invited to participate in the wedding and give their blessings to the couple, as well as given small offerings of food and ritual objects. (2) After guests are given a simple midday meal, the "hair-cutting" ceremony takes place in the early afternoon. First the *achaa* ritually snips a lock of hair from both the bride and groom, then the couple is given a general hair trimming by some relatives or friends who must either have both parents alive or are themselves happily married.[27] (3) In the late afternoon monks from one of the local temples are invited to recite prayers (along with the guests), and the head monk sprinkles holy water onto the couple who bow low before him. In return for their services, the monks are given liquid refreshment, cigarettes, and a contribution of money. (4) After a splendid evening meal of special dishes, delicacies, and assorted refreshments have been given to the guests, there may be a brief ceremony (called *krong pêli*) in the groom's shelter to present food and ritual objects to various spirits (cf. Porée-Maspero 1958, 24–25; Leclère 1916, 543). (5) The most important rite of the evening is the *còng day* or tying of threads upon the couple's wrists for good fortune. First the bride in her home, then the groom in his shelter, lies semirecumbent holding a betel nut crusher, lime container, and betel leaves[28] in cupped hands, while the *achaa* and various kinsmen and friends tie threads upon his/her wrists and offer best wishes. (6) There are sometimes two other rituals in the evening. First, there may be the ceremony of "drinking coconut juice" (*pùk tùk dong*) in which the *achaa* feeds three spoonfuls of coconut juice to both the bride and groom. This is considered to be a substitute for the ceremony of "doing the teeth" (*twùr tmeng*), that is, wiping the teeth or, in former times, of

---

[26] See Porée-Maspero 1958, 20 on the significance of cotton thread in rituals.

[27] For West Svay villagers, the ritual cutting of hair (which occurs in other ceremonies such as the cutting of the topknot, shaving of head when death occurs in the family, etc. [see Porée-Maspero 1958, 231]) has no rationale other than tradition. According to Porée-Maspero 1958, 23, it is meant to ward off misfortune. It is possible that the alteration of a physical feature (i.e., hair), may also symbolize the acquisition of a new social status.

[28] According to Porée-Maspero 1958, 58, these objects symbolize union.

lacquering the teeth black.[29] Second, and more rarely, there may be a ritual discussion of the payment to be given by the groom's family to the bride's side, after which the bride expresses gratitude and gives small gifts to her parents for having raised her.

After these ceremonies are completed, the wedding bursts into merrymaking with music, dancing,[30] and often singing by the bridal attendants and younger guests (although the bride and groom themselves must maintain a solemn demeanor and can only watch the fun). The young women delight in showing off their grace, and they are sometimes jokingly imitated and impersonated by a few young men who don garish female costumes. The older guests enjoy this entertainment while chatting with one another; and if liquor is served, some of the men will become pleasantly high. This is the part of the wedding that draws the most uninvited spectators, and the revelry may continue well into the early morning hours until people finally return to their homes or simply lie down to sleep on any available space, even a tabletop.

The second and final day of the wedding begins extremely early for the major participants, and official ceremonies will culminate by midmorning. Before daybreak, the *yop piliĕ* ceremony to greet the dawn is held outside the house with the *achaa*, the groom and often the bride, and the *neak moha* and *meba*. This is a short ritual with prayers of blessing by the *achaa* while the participants await the auspicious moment (the *piliĕ*) when the darkness yields to a certain amount of light, and one bows to the rising sun. After the bride slips back into the house, the *achaa* leads a procession of the groom and his attendants, relatives, and friends to the girl's home. There the young man is greeted by his bride who ritually washes his feet and gives him a betel quid in return for a small sum of money before she retires to her chamber.

Finally, the last major ritual, the *kan slaa*, occurs. First the groom, then the bride (escorted by her attendants and sometimes preceded by a musician with a sword who sings and dances to traditional airs during the ceremony), comes forth to sit in front of the *achaa* and make obeisance to each of three stalks of coconut flowers lying on a pillow. Both bride and groom then lie semi-recumbent, holding betel leaves and the implements of betel chewing in their hands. A group of attendants, kinsmen, and friends (ideally four men and four women but often more than this) form a circle around the couple and pass a *popll*[31] (a small, metal, leaf-shaped object) from hand to hand around the circle to wish the couple good fortune. Ritual objects called *pkaa slaa* ("areca flower"), formed of stalks of coconut flowers, are then given to the spectators who break off the seeds and throw them on the couple, much as rice is thrown in Western weddings.[32]

---

[29] This tradition is explained by a myth in Porée-Maspero 1958, 23–24, but the villagers know nothing of this story. "Doing the teeth" occurs also when a girl comes out of menstrual retreat and when a man enters the monastery. Again, this might be seen as another physical representation of a change in social status.

[30] The popular form of dancing, called the *lamton*, is said by villagers to have come from Thailand. Groups of men and women dance in a circle (one following behind another) and step in time to the music while performing sinuous, delicate movements with their arms and hands that are much simpler than, but reminiscent of, the postures of the classical dance as performed in theater and by the "royal ballet" group. For details of the classical dance and orchestra, see Thiounn 1956.

[31] See Porée-Maspero 1958, 20–21 on the symbolism of the *popll*.

[32] There are three *pkaa slaa* that, according to Porée-Maspero (1958, 56, 61), represent the father, mother, and elder sister who are important in raising children. One *pkaa slaa* is kept intact and taken to the temple after the wedding so that a monk can throw the seeds on the couple.

The *achaa* then ties cotton thread upon the groom's and bride's wrists for good luck, as do various other spectators. The music, which has played continuously, becomes increasingly louder and faster through the final phases of the ritual, then suddenly stops as the *achaa* recites a last invocation and blessing. The ceremony ends (as had several other rites of the preceding day) with the banging of the gong and the final statements of the *achaa* that are echoed or answered by the crowd: "Victory!"; "Victory!"; "Happiness!"; "Happiness!"; "Health!"; "Health!"; "This is a good day, is it not?"; "It is!"; "What do you accept?"; "[We] accept this fine couple." To the sound of cheers and claps, the bride rises and rushes to her chamber, followed quickly by her groom who must catch the end of her scarf as she goes (an attempt that often brings laughter from the crowd).[33] A few moments later the couple emerges again to receive from the *achaa* the mat that they had sat on during the various rituals (an act that brings jokes from the spectators because this will be the mat the couple sleeps upon) and to hear a brief lecture on marital and filial duties.

A midmorning meal concludes the wedding so far as the guests are concerned, and the village returns to a state of tranquility. In the coming night the bridal couple will be allowed to sleep together for the first time (usually in the bride's house). It is traditional for the *achaa* and a couple of old women (kinsmen or neighbors) to perform a small ceremony and to inform the bride about sexual matters before the consummation, but this custom is rarely practiced nowadays.

As mentioned previously, a wedding is not only the most joyous but also one of the most expensive life-cycle ceremonies. The possible expenditures (in approximate figures) are as follows:

| | |
|---|---|
| Food (rice, meat, vegetables, beverages, etc.) and other necessary items such as candles, incense, betel, cigarettes, decorations, etc. | 1,000–6,000 riels |
| New clothes for the bride | [amount varies] |
| or rental of bridal costume | 100 riels |
| Gifts given by bride to groom | ca. 500 riels |
| Payments to achaa, meba, neak moha for their services, usually 30–50 riels each plus gifts of food, candles, etc. | 90–150 riels |
| Contribution to monks | 100–200 riels |
| Rental of loudspeaker and phonograph records | 300–400 riels |
| Hiring musicians (usually four or five at 200 riels each) | 800–1000 riels |
| Rental of dishes, tables, chairs, etc. | 300–400 riels |

The bride's family can, therefore, spend anywhere from about 3,000 to 8,000 riels on a wedding, a great sum for an ordinary household's budget. A good part of the expenses are defrayed, first, by the monetary gift from the groom's family, which is usually from 2,000 to 5,000 riels, and second, by the monetary contributions of

---

[33] See Porée-Maspero 1958, 60–62 for the myth that explains this custom. It was rumored in 1959 that when one of the royal princesses was forced into a marriage with a man she did not like, she refused to let him catch the end of her scarf and locked him out of her chamber.

guests, which may total anywhere from about 1,000 to 6,000 riels depending on the number of guests and their generosity.[34] If there is any money left after the wedding is paid for, it is given to the couple. As likely as not, however, a family will only break even, or may be temporarily in debt for a greater or lesser sum of money. Actually, much of the wedding is financed on short-term credit or loans because, although the groom's gift is usually paid before or at the time of the wedding, the money from guests is not received until the ceremony takes place. But large-scale indebtedness for weddings is not common because a family will try to fashion the ceremony to fit their financial resources, dispensing with certain items if necessary (e.g., not hiring musicians) or cutting back on others (e.g., serving simple meals).

In addition to the ceremonial sanctification of a marriage, for the past thirty years or so it has become common to officially register one's marriage at the sub-district chief's office. This registration is called, using French terminology, *état civil*. A marriage that is not so registered would still be considered valid in the eyes of the villagers if the traditional ceremonies had been observed, and there would be no government action against a couple who were not *état civil*. But a couple who had not registered themselves would have subsequent difficulties if there should ever be divorce proceedings, inheritance disputes, etc. Thus, all the village couples that have married within the past few decades have observed the *état civil*.

## MARRIAGE

A bride and groom may be relatively young: most village girls marry in their late teens and early twenties, while young men usually wed in their early to mid-twenties.[35] And in cases where the couple go to reside in the household of one or the other spouse, the elder parents will still wield considerable authority over their married child and son- or daughter-in-law. Nonetheless, marriage marks the young man's or woman's attainment of adult status: legally, one attains majority either at the age of twenty-one or upon marriage (Clairon n.d., 104); and socially, an individual now forms part of a new social unit, has responsibility for the support of oneself and others, becomes a full-fledged property owner, etc. Associated with the change in status is an alteration in behavior that can be broadly characterized as a change from relative frivolity to seriousness, from spending a good deal of time in lighthearted concerns to assuming all the chores and worries of maintaining a household. Even clothing and personal appearance, especially among women, reflects this modification. In contrast to the bright plumage and preening of unmarried youth, married women put cosmetics and jewelry into storage, cut their hair short and forsake permanents, and wear sober (usually black) shirts and simple, high-necked blouses.[36] Married men are

---

[34] For example, San's (House 25) wedding cost about 5,000 riels. But her mother received 3,000 riels from the groom and contributions of 2,650 riels from guests.

[35] Of the married couples in West Svay, the average age at which an individual married for the first time was twenty years of age for women and twenty-four for men. But some women were married as early as fifteen years of age or as late as thirty-seven, while men married as early as seventeen and as late as thirty. Marriage in the teens seems to have been more common in the earlier part of the century.

[36] Married women also become avid betel chewers. Adolescent girls occasionally chew betel but only as a sort of treat; it does not become a habit until after marriage. Men chew betel only infrequently.

usually seen in black shorts for work (a sarong for leisure hours), perhaps an old shirt or undershirt, and often a battered hat.

A village family's daily round of activities varies from season to season according to the stages of rice cultivation, the ceremonial calendar, etc. Generally, however, the woman of the household is the first one up at daybreak (5:30 or 6:00 a.m.) to start a fire and prepare the simple morning meal of rice gruel and fish. If school is in session, older children are off to classes by about 7:00 a.m. while the adults begin various chores: cleaning house, washing clothes, repairing implements, making mats or other items, going to market, taking cattle to pasture, working in the fields, etc. The morning is the best time to work, especially on any arduous tasks, because the air is still relatively cool and fresh. At about 10:00 a.m., women must start cooking the midday meal; children will return from school at about 11:30 for lunch and play until classes again resume at 2:30. Unless it is a particularly busy season in the cultivation cycle, the oppressive sun imposes a somnolence upon the village during the early afternoon that is spent in napping, in quiet tasks, or in one of the favorite pastimes of village life: sitting and chatting with friends. Respite from the heat begins in the late afternoon, and the village again becomes lively as older children return from school and erupt into play, women begin preparing the evening meal, people sluice themselves off at the family water jar or one of the village wells, cattle are brought back from afternoon pasture, and families gather for supper.[37] After sundown the village again becomes quiet. Some visiting may continue into the night, but unless there is a temple ceremony or other event, most families retire into their houses when it becomes dark. Some activity may continue to the light of tiny kerosene lamps until the sleeping mats, pillows, and mosquito nets are laid out. Many nights the villagers fall asleep to the pleasant sound of music played by a group of young men who often gather for impromptu musical sessions. But by 11:00 p.m. or midnight, the village is dark and still except for a few men quietly patrolling on guard duty.[38]

Although the adolescent girl usually views sexual intercourse with trepidation or fright, the married woman comes to accept it with at least resignation or equanimity, sometimes with pleasure, and often a wry humor. Actual intercourse is evidently executed very quickly and quietly with little or no foreplay and rapid male orgasm[39] because a couple usually sleeps in the same room as the other members of the household, or even with a small child under the same mosquito net. Intercourse is suspended during the woman's menstrual period and for a month or so before and after birth.

---

[37] In addition to steamed or boiled rice, the midday and evening meals include various side dishes that are usually simple and limited in quantity. The most common accompaniments are fish in various forms; soups made from fish, crabs, vegetables, etc.; or some mixture of cooked fruit and/or vegetables. Meat is rarely a part of ordinary daily fare (see Delvert 1961, 154–55), although it is an ingredient of dishes for special occasions. Villagers also have numerous snacks during the day: fruits, dried crusts of rice, cakes and other sweets (of which there are a great variety), sometimes dried insects of a particular sort, etc. The common beverage is plain water, although wealthier families may have tea with their meals. For some other details of Cambodian cuisine, see Saris-Yann 1955; Martini 1955d.

[38] Although villagers can in fact determine the exact hour of the day with considerable accuracy by noting the position of the sun, they reckon time more generally in terms of the periods of the day: *prŭk* from daybreak to noon, *rosièl* from midday to about 2:00 or 3:00 p.m., *lŭngiet* from midafternoon until darkness falls, and *yop* or nighttime. These periods correspond with the rhythm of daily activities described above.

[39] Intercourse is usually performed with the male assuming the superior position; occasionally the man may lie beneath the woman. Other positions are unreported.

There is a legal double standard in that a man can divorce his wife if she commits adultery, but he himself can be adulterous without invoking any legal sanctions and can, moreover, be polygynous as well. Actually, both adultery and polygyny are relatively rare in village life. The former is deterred by Buddhist injunctions against immoral sexual relations, lack of money and time to frequent prostitutes in Phnom Penh,[40] and the general inaccessibility of village women who are usually staunchly moral. And polygamy, while legally permitted,[41] has long been limited mainly to the upper social strata and is rare among the populace at large (see Thierry 1955, 121–22, 157 for figures; also Aymonier 1900, 83; Condominas 1953, 600; Zadrozny 1955, 318; Steinberg 1959, 77; Clairon n.d., 51). It is especially uncommon among villagers because most men lack resources to support more than one wife and set of offspring. A final strong obstacle to both adultery and polygyny is the fact that although men may find such relationships to be attractive, village women commonly react to a husband's philandering with at least irritation or dejection, and more usually with fierce wrath, recriminations, tears, and threats (see also LeGallen 1929, 221). Despite the legal primacy and privileges held by the first wife, the village woman feels that polygyny is contrary to her own and her children's best interests because they would have to share not only the husband and father's affections but his income and property as well.

It is not unlikely that men who leave home for temporary employment may have occasional affairs or recourse to prostitutes. For example, a man in West Svay admitted to having once lived with a woman for several months while working as a cyclo driver in Phnom Penh. But he was greatly chastened by his wife's anger when he confessed his escapade to her and by the fear that he may have contracted a venereal disease from his mistress, and he never again attempted adultery. Sometimes, too, acquiescent women might be found even in the villages; for example, it is said that the father of at least one of the illegitimate children borne by the woman discussed in a previous section was a married man living in West Svay. But from all available evidence, adultery is relatively infrequent among village men and non-existent among married village women.

Two village men attempted polygamy during my stay, one in West Svay itself and one in the neighboring community of Ta Chas. In both cases the men have non-agricultural occupations (one operates a roadside restaurant and the other is a chauffeur at the school) and are thus more affluent than ordinary villagers. Both men had met other women while traveling or visiting elsewhere and wanted to take them as second wives or concubines. And in both instances, the wives reacted immediately and vigorously with such tremendous furor that, after brief attempts to assert male authority, both men capitulated and renounced their polygamous aspirations. Neither in Svay nor the neighboring villages are there any cases of polygynous marriages.

[40] It might be mentioned that there are male as well as female prostitutes in the city, but male homosexuality is not practiced by villagers. In East Hamlet there are two spinsters in their forties who live "as man and wife and do not like men, only each other." It is unclear, however, whether this is an instance of true lesbianism. (Leclère 1898, 1:185 cites the old legal codes that forbid homosexual relations among palace women.)

[41] Not only may a man take second- and third-rank wives (with the consent of the first wife), but additional concubines as well. For various legal statutes concerning the privileges and restrictions of different rank wives with respect to marriage ceremonies, inheritance, status of offspring, divorce settlements, etc., see Leclère 1890, 90–118; Aymonier 1900, 33; Daguin n.d.:passim but especially 64–66, 73; Lingat 1952–55, 2:144, 168–71; Thierry 1955, passim; Steinberg 1959, 79; and especially Clairon n.d., 51–55, 57, 64–65, 68, 73–74, 121, 127, 129–33, 162–63, and passim.

## DIVORCE

Divorce (*leng knia*) is sanctioned in the civil code on the following grounds: (1) adultery on the part of the wife, (2) prolonged absence of a spouse without acceptable excuse, (3) failure to provide adequately for the support of the family, (4) repeated or serious physical attacks upon the spouse (or his/her parents or other kinsmen on the first ascending generation), (5) commission of a criminal offense and conviction to death or forced labor, (6) immoral conduct such as gambling, alcoholism, drug addiction, etc., (7) withholding of sexual privileges for over a year (Clairon n.d., 69–70). The villagers themselves cite the first, second, third, and sixth points as causes for divorce, along with "failure to respect the parents-in-law" and simple incompatibility that expresses itself in constant quarrels. Divorce is not unknown (although not frequent) in village life. Within the past twenty years there have been four cases of divorce among West Svay inhabitants for the following reasons: an irresponsible husband who was given to gambling and drunkenness, a husband who was guilty of theft and murder while an Issarak, and two cases of incompatible temperaments.

Either the husband or the wife may initiate divorce proceedings by presenting a written request to the sub-district chief that is then sent to the district office and finally to a court in Phnom Penh. If one spouse contests the divorce or there is disagreement about custody of the children or division of property, the case may have to undergo several hearings. But otherwise the final decree for divorce by mutual consent is usually obtained within a few months.

Upon divorce, each spouse takes back whatever property he/she brought to the marriage. The common property was formerly divided into three parts with two-thirds going to the man and one-third to the woman, but at the present time it is split equally between the two. In many instances, objects of common property (especially non-partible items such as a house, a rice paddy, an ox) are sold and the money divided equally between the man and woman, or one spouse will keep a piece of property and reimburse the other for one-half its value. In two instances, however, all of the common property may go to one spouse: to the wife if she has been abandoned by her husband, or to the husband if the wife has been guilty of adultery.

Custody of offspring is decided mainly on the basis of the children's ages or their own inclinations. Villagers say that children under ten or so years of age almost always remain with the mother, while those old enough to express a definite preference may go with the parent of their choice (sometimes the father will take the older ones if the latter do not object).[42] Villagers stress that the personal preferences of the youngsters themselves are always respected, and that usually *all* children will elect to stay with the mother. This was true in all the cases of divorce in West Hamlet.

The husband is legally bound to pay some sort of maintenance alimony to his ex-wife if she has not remarried and does not have adequate resources to support herself and the offspring.[43] In village life, however, such alimony is extremely rare because the

---

[42] Cf. the civil code that states (1) that children over sixteen years of age may make their own decision, and (2) that for children over five years of age, the mother should have custody of daughters and fathers of sons (Clairon n.d., 74).

[43] For details of this and other statutes in the civil code concerning divorce, see Clairon n.d., 68–74; Lingat 1952–55, 2:168–69; Daguin n.d., 67–77. For earlier law codes, see Leclère 1890, 140–52; 1898, 1:258–59.

man disappears (if he has not already abandoned the family), because the ex-husband is often improvident or has little money himself, and because the divorced woman is often supported by her family of orientation or remarries within a few years.

A divorcée (*memay*) almost always returns to the household of her parents (if they are still alive) and resumes her former role as daughter. And if she is relatively young, it is highly likely that she will find another husband within a short while.[44] But the older divorcée without a family to fall back upon and little prospect of remarriage often finds herself in a difficult situation unless she has sufficient land to support herself and the offspring. For example, Muoy (House 25), who was divorced in her late thirties and had inherited no land in West Svay because she had moved to another province after her marriage, now barely manages to subsist on a small plot of purchased land, has shelter thanks only to a sibling who moved away and left a vacant house, and must send two of her children to live for part of the year with a married daughter. The divorced man (*puėmay*) may also, if he is young, return to his family of orientation. But he is more likely to maintain an independent status and will either quickly find another wife or, like my landlord, lead a carefree life of bachelorhood regained.

## WIDOWHOOD

The marriage bond is cut by widowing much more frequently than it is by divorce. The fact that widowhood is a common occurrence in village life is illustrated in a game that children and adolescents play to the cries of the gecko lizard. Similar to our playing "she loves me—she loves me not" with daisy petals, one recites "*kromom* (unmarried woman)—*memay* (widow)" to successive croaks of the gecko; and whichever of the two coincides with the last croak will indicate what sort of woman one will be or marry. This game also suggests that remarriage of widow(er)s is common, which is indeed the case when the widowed person is still in his/her forties or younger. The young widow(er) can and often does return to his/her natal family for support. But those of older age often do not have such a refuge because the parents have already died or are too elderly to be of much aid; and a widower is likely to be left with relatively young children who need a woman's care, while a widow finds herself in need of male labor power to work the fields. Thus, there is considerable incentive to remarry. Although a widower with children is no bargain for a young girl, there are other women—usually divorcées or spinsters in their late twenties and thirties—who are willing to undertake such marriages. Similarly, a widow with children would seem to be an unappealing match, but the fact that she may own property and/or is usufructor of her late husband's estate can be a strong attraction for a man with little or no resources of his own.[45]

Upon remarriage the new spouse seems to replace the deceased mate or parent with relative ease. Although the children may be initially bewildered or wary, there

---

[44] Of the three women in West Svay who have been divorced, two remarried. In the other hamlets, however, there are several instances of divorced women living with their families of orientation.

[45] Of the widowers in West Svay who remarried, one married a divorcée, while four others married women in their late twenties and thirties who were on their way to spinsterhood; only one man (without children) married a girl in her early twenties. All of the widows in West Svay who remarried were wed to poor men who brought no property of their own to the match. Remarriage may, according to villagers, take place at any time after the death of the first spouse, but it is customary to wait for about a year after one's mate has died.

is no tradition of the evil stepparent, and from all evidence a new parent comes to be accepted with at least a tolerant respect and often genuine affection.

Persons who are widowed in their late forties and fifties usually forego remarriage because their remaining years of hardiness and fertility are numbered and because they generally have children who are old enough to provide supplementary labor power. It is common for one of the offspring to continue to reside at home after marriage and to assume (along with his/her spouse) the main burden of maintaining the household.

## OLD AGE[46]

From the age of about fifty or sixty, the individual enters a period where he or she enjoys relative leisure, devotes him/herself increasingly to religious activities, and earns respectful deference from others. As physical power wanes and bouts of illness become an increasing problem, most of the work is passed onto the more vigorous younger generations. The old people are by no means idle or incapable: women of sixty can still transplant rice and outstrip hardy adolescent girls in speed and skill; Grandfather Kompha at age sixty-six can still chop down a tree; and Grandfather Map at age eighty still has hands that are nimble enough to sew thatch. But arduous labor is no longer a necessity for the elderly who can be left to pursue less demanding tasks such as twining rope, making baskets or mats, repairing equipment, cooking, and tending grandchildren; and to enjoy extended periods of leisure that are spent in chatting with neighbors, extended visits to see married children and grandchildren in other communities, and especially, acts of religious devotion. It is interesting, too, that women at about the time of menopause customarily shave their heads or crop their hair an inch or so from the scalp, a practice that seems to symbolize their renunciation of worldly concerns (just as monks shave their heads), and that also neutralizes their sex (it is often impossible for an uninformed observer to distinguish between elderly males and females).

Because of traditional respect for old age and because of the usually exemplary behavior of the elderly, the latter are given deference by the younger generations. The old people are the ones who tend to have the most informal authority in village affairs, who are asked to take important roles in life-cycle ceremonies, and whose fund of experience is tapped for opinions and advice. But it must be noted that respect for elders does not necessarily mean that they must be treated with complete sobriety and distance. Old people, especially women, are often exceptionally demonstrative in giving and accepting affection, and they are not above indulging in or being the objects of good-natured teasing and joking in their relations with younger people.

## FUNERALS

When death is imminent, monks and/or an *achaa* are called to the house to recite Buddhist prayers and texts, and certain ritual objects are prepared by the *achaa* and kinsmen or friends of the dying person.[47] After death the corpse is bathed (with water

---

[46] Middle-aged and old people are referred to as *cah cah* ("old ones"); the elderly are also called *sòk skøu* ("silver haired").

[47] The following account of funerals (which does not include all possible ceremonial details) is based upon observation of the only funeral that took place in Svay during my residence and upon information from informants. Cf. the descriptions of funerals in Porée-Maspero 1958,

blessed by monks) by the *achaa* and the deceased's children, and then dressed in white clothing with a scarf worn over one shoulder (as is customary when one attends the temple). An old coin is placed in the corpse's mouth; a folded banana leaf containing areca, betel leaves, and incense is put between its hands that are folded as if in prayer; a cloth is laid over the face; and thread is bound around the neck, waist, and legs. The monks recite prayers for the dead and continue to chant throughout the night following the death.

In the meanwhile there is bustle and noise outside the house. A funeral is, next to weddings, the most elaborate of all life-cycle ceremonies, and because it cannot be planned and organized well in advance as for a wedding, the necessary preparations must be compressed into a day or two of hurried activity. News of a death spreads rapidly throughout and beyond the village, bringing kinsmen and friends hurrying to the scene to pay their respects and aid in the various preparations.[48] Messengers are immediately dispatched to fetch close kinsmen who live in other communities; a coffin is purchased in Kompong Tuol and is assembled and decorated with colored paper; an elaborate funeral pyre is constructed of bamboo and banana stalks that are carved with delicate designs; a loudspeaker and phonograph records are rented or borrowed; and quantities of food are bought and prepared to feed the monks, numerous guests, and helpers.

Cremation is the usual means of disposing of the dead (except for those who commit suicide who are buried). Among the upper social strata the corpse may be kept several months or even years before cremation, but in the village the body is usually cremated a day or two after the death in some open area near the deceased's home. (In other communities, the local temple may have a crematorium.) The coffin is borne from the house to the pyre in a procession led by the *achaa*. After him come musicians with muffled drums, a gong, and perhaps other traditional instruments; a kinswoman who scatters rice upon the ground from a basket of rice that had been placed at the feet of the deceased while he was dying;[49] the coffin carried by four to eight sturdy men; a monk; members of the immediate family who have shaved their heads and donned white mourning clothes; and assorted relatives and friends who wish to join the cortege. After the group circumambulates the pyre three times,[50] the coffin is placed on the pyre. Various kinsmen and friends come forward to stick incense on the pyre, then join the *achaa* and monks in reciting prayers.[51] The *achaa* and several men who will

---

73–81 (which gives the best account of the rituals and their meaning); Aymonier 1900, 47–48; LeGallen 1929, 222; Monod 1931, 77–80; Porée and Maspero 1938, 215–21; Vanell 1956. For funerals of royalty, see Porée and Maspero 1938, 334–36, Zadrozny 1955, 334–36; Marchal 1956.

[48] Note that much of the preparation and even important parts of the ritual are performed by persons who are but distant kinsmen or simply friends of the deceased.

[49] This basket of rice (*srau ponle* or *srau nciĕng tbong*) is also used in birth ritual; according to Porée-Maspero 1958, 75, 22, it symbolizes the continuing rebirth of life just as seed produces seed, although villagers view it simply as "custom."

[50] The circling of the funeral pyre is similar to the circumambulation of the temple that is performed in many Buddhist festivals, except that in a funeral the procession proceeds counterclockwise with the left side of the body toward the pyre, rather than clockwise with the right shoulder toward the temple as in Buddhist festivals.

[51] In contrast to other familial rituals in which perhaps half a dozen monks are invited for a brief recitation of prayers and blessings, a number of monks are in almost constant attendance at funerals. Four to six monks are present shortly before and after death, and throughout the

start the cremation fire, carrying incense and the candle that was lit at the moment of death, again circle the pyre. The *achaa* then removes the coffin lid, opens the mat and shroud encircling the corpse, cuts the threads binding the body, and ignites the coffin.

The body is slowly consumed over several hours as both traditional and popular music is heard over the loudspeaker. While the incineration proceeds, the guests are served food, liquor, and betel. There is no air of mandatory gloom and solemnity throughout the funeral observances. The immediate family and close kin of the deceased do feel a grief that is manifested by periodic tears and sad reminiscences about the deceased.[52] But the sorrow of death is, of course, tempered by the thought that the deceased will pass into another, and hopefully better, reincarnation. So members of the mourning family and the guests chat and joke amiably with one another (even indulging in occasional horseplay); children run about as usual; and men may get a bit drunk.

After three or four hours the corpse is virtually reduced to ashes and the fire is extinguished with water. Relatives and friends look through the ashes for remnants of bone and teeth that are collected and washed with coconut milk and perfume. These fragments will eventually be placed in an urn that is kept either at home or placed in a *cheday* monument at a temple.[53] Monks recite more prayers (as they will again that evening) and a final meal is served to all.[54] There are no strict mourning injunctions, and members of the family resume their usual routine after the funeral.

The expense of a funeral can be considerable, ranging from about 3,000 to 10,000 riels for various items such as the coffin, decorations for the coffin and pyre, rental of a loudspeaker, food and beverages for monks and guests, payment for the services of an *achaa* and monks, and miscellaneous purchases such as candles, incense, betel, and cigarettes. The immediate family of the deceased (i.e., the family of procreation if the deceased is a married adult, the family of orientation if the deceased has no offspring or is still unmarried) bears the major expense of the ceremony, aided by contributions of money and services from kinsmen and friends. Guests bring small monetary gifts (as they do for weddings), and frequently musicians will play without recompense or a temple may lend a loudspeaker free of charge for funerals.

(It should be noted here that children do not receive the full pomp of adult funerals. Monks are invited to pray at the house of a deceased infant or child, and after

---

night following the death; while a great crowd of monks are invited for the cremation (e.g., more than thirty monks from both local temples attended the funeral I observed in East Svay). The importance of monks in funeral rituals is, of course, understandable because death is the time of passage to a new reincarnation and should be attended by numerous prayers that may ameliorate the lot of the deceased.

[52] Cf. an old legal code that states that the deceased's parents, siblings, and children must lie weeping upon the ground (Leclère 1898, 1:234).

[53] Wealthy persons may have a special tomb or *cheday* constructed for the remains of one or several members of the family, but ordinary villagers usually deposit the ashes of family members in a *cheday* at the local temple that receives the remains of many persons in the area.

[54] The different parts of the funeral ritual may occur at different hours and on different days depending on the time of death, the rapidity with which various preparations can be carried out, and auspicious days for cremation. E.g., Peou in East Svay died on a Monday morning; she could not be cremated on Tuesday, which is an inauspicious day for funerals, so her coffin was simply taken to the pyre on Tuesday afternoon, and the incineration was held on Wednesday morning. In other funerals, however, the cremation might take place on the very next day or even on the same day as death.

another simple ceremony of prayers at the temple, the child is cremated. The death of a baby or youngster creates hardly a ripple in village routine and passes almost totally unremarked except among the immediate family and close kin, for the child has had little time to create a definite place for himself within society and hence does not cause a noticeable sense of loss when he dies. The death of an adolescent, however, may well occasion a funeral similar to that for an adult although it may not be as elaborate.)

Ceremonies in honor of the dead are held on the seventh and one hundredth days after death, and ideally upon the yearly anniversary of the death. For the villagers, these observances consist mainly of inviting some monks to recite sacred texts and chant prayers in the evening, and offering them a midday meal on the following day.[55]

---

[55] When the director of the primary school in Kompong Tuol observed the one hundredth–day anniversary of his father's death, over a hundred monks from six or seven temples were invited to receive food and other offerings. Villagers, however, usually invite just a few monks from one of the local temples.

# CHAPTER SEVEN

# POLITICAL ORGANIZATION

Although village chiefs are probably an ancient and indigenous element in Khmer society, the nature of formal village political organization in modern Cambodia is determined primarily by the structure and constitution of the national government as a whole, which was greatly influenced by French administrative practices. Beneath the king, prime minister, councils, the legislature, and the various ministries in Phnom Penh, regional government is organized in several descending levels.

(1) The administrative region, or groupings of provinces, is of minor importance. Its main function is the election of a representative to the upper house of the legislature. (2) The province (*khayt*) is the first and major link between national and local government, with a full complement of officials including the provincial governor (*covaykhayt*) and deputies of various national ministries and departments. (3) The district (*srok*) is perhaps comparable to an American county. It is the lowest rung of regional administration that is staffed by professional civil servants appointed by the central government. The district administration includes a district chief (*covaysrok*) and representatives of some government bureaus.[1] (4) The sub-district (*khum*), a grouping of several villages and towns into one administrative unit, was created by a royal ordinance in 1908 and further defined in 1919 (see Bruel 1924, 19–22; Delvert 1961, 199–200). The *khum* is an "artificial creation . . . not a historic or geographic reality" (Delvert 1961, 199) whose territorial limits were arbitrarily defined by the government. But its chief (*mekhum*)[2] may be of considerable importance to contemporary villagers (see infra). (6) Finally, the *phum*, the village or hamlet, is the smallest unit and lowest level of government with a village chief (and some minor officials) of limited importance. According to Delvert (1961, 201–4), the administrative units known as *phum* have sometimes been arbitrarily delimited by the government without regard for the various kinds of natural local groupings and settlement patterns that exist. (But this does not seem to be true for Svay, although it has three hamlets that could conceivably exist as separate villages.)

In sum, then, *phum* Svay is part of *khum* or sub-district Treang (that contains six other villages), *srok* or district of Koh Thom (along with twenty-five other *khums*), and

---

[1] Aymonier (1900, 70) notes that a territorial-administrative unit known as the *srok* (which also means "country" in the senses of both "countryside" and "nation"), as well as an official called the *covaysrok*, existed in precolonial times. These *srok* were then modified into provinces, of which there were fifty-seven in the late nineteenth century (see Aymonier 1900, 70–72 for details of nineteenth-century regional administration and officials). At the present time there are seventeen provinces (three of very recent creation) and an unknown number of *srok*.

[2] Both Zadrozny 1955, 164 and Steinberg 1959, 133–39 are erroneous in their description of *mekhum*. The former refers to it as a "group of notables," while the latter calls it a city or village mayor.

*khayt* or province of Kandal.[3] The first three levels are the ones of primary significance for the villager.

## FORMAL ADMINISTRATIVE STRUCTURE

### THE DISTRICT LEVEL

The district office (*salaa srok*), located in a small wooden building on the outskirts of Kompong Tuol, is usually the highest level of government with which villagers have face-to-face contact. The district chief is a civil servant within the Ministry of the Interior who is appointed to his post by his superiors for an indefinite term of duty. His primary duties, in the broadest sense, are to act as an intermediary between the national and provincial government and the lower levels, to oversee various administrative matters pertaining to his district (including the duties of the various sub-district chiefs), and to supervise the operation of several departments in his office. His administrative staff includes an assistant chief, a police chief, an official in charge of land registration (Division Cadastrage), and several "secretaries," all of whom are similarly professional bureaucrats.[4]

It is sometimes necessary for the villager to visit the district office about matters that the sub-district chief must refer to a higher authority. Such contacts between the villager and the district officials are very formal and impersonal. The district chief, well educated with urbane manners and outlook, is considered by the villagers as a "big person" (*neak tom*) demanding of respect and distance: "When the district chief sees you, sometimes he will speak to you and often he won't." When he appears, for example at a temple festival on one of his innumerable and indefatigable tours about the district, the villagers immediately speak quietly only when spoken to and make the deferential gestures that one assumes in the presence of an individual of clearly superior rank. The other members of the district staff are, to a somewhat lesser extent, similarly treated. Because all of these administrators are likely not to be natives of the area (in contrast to the sub-district and village officials), they are known only in their official capacities, as professional civil servants representing the central government, which makes them figures of respect and authority.

### THE SUB-DISTRICT LEVEL

The official with whom Svay villagers have the most frequent contact is the sub-district chief or *mekhum* (also occasionally referred to by an older term, *mesrok*).[5] The relationship between villagers and the sub-district office is much more informal and

---

[3] At one time there was a further territorial division called the *khand* that was intermediate between the district and sub-district (see Bruel 1924, 19; Office of Strategic Services 1944, 29). But evidently this was abolished at an unknown date. [The Khand is division within the city, a neighborhood that has local political representation.]

[4] Apart from the district office itself, Kompong Tuol also has a post and telegraphic office, a midwife trained under government auspices, and a bulletin board in the central marketplace that posts news, proclamations, etc., issued by the government.

[5] In the nineteenth century, the title *mesrok*, "chief of the country," referred to the head of a "small canton or large township" who was appointed by the provincial governor and aided by "hamlet chiefs" (Aymonier 1900, 72).

friendly. For while the *mekhum* deserves and receives respect for his official p
he and his staff are residents of the area, basically peasants like everyone else wnu
are also known as kinsmen, neighbors, or acquaintances, and hence easy to approach.

Moreover, the *mekhum* is selected by the villagers themselves in a popular election
held every four years. Any aspirant to the position may submit an application for candidacy to the district chief and take a literacy examination; the *covaysrok* then selects
two to four candidates from among the applicants. Officially, the main qualifications
for the post are literacy and evidence of competence and good character. Unofficially,
the *mekhum* is also apt to be a person of at least moderate wealth (since his duties are
time consuming and the salary is limited);[6] and, according to Smith (1964, 654), he
must also be found by provincial authorities "to be loyal to the regime."

In an election that occurred during my stay, the incumbent *mekhum*, Deth, was
running against one other candidate. On election day, from 6:00 a.m. to 5:00 p.m.
when the polls were open, a stream of people walked or rode on bicycles or in free
remorques to the temple school in Stoung (the village neighboring Svay to the east)
where voting was conducted. Upon presenting a slip of paper with one's name and
an official stamp that designated a qualified voter (anyone over twenty years of age
who is not a monk, criminal, or in military service) and having one's name checked
in a register of voters, the villager received two ballots, each one bearing a picture of
a candidate. After considering the ballots in the privacy of a curtained room, the voter
folded them and emerged to drop the ballot for the candidate of his choice into a ballot
box and discard the other in a jar. The votes were later tallied by several "secretaries"
(local villagers recruited by the *mekhum*) who were searched for hidden ballots and
then locked in a room by the district police chief (according to one of the secretaries,
the counting was conducted with strict honesty). The people of West Svay were interested and conscientious voters, with every house in the hamlet sending one or more
qualified voters. The women, who had been granted the vote in 1956, were especially
enthusiastic constituents. People from other villages in the sub-district evidently felt
similarly, for well over 1,000 votes (about half of which were submitted by women)
were cast out of a total number of 1,693 possible voters. The incumbent was reelected
by a margin of about fifty votes. (There is a clear tendency for a man, once elected, to
remain in office for long periods of time: the incumbent had been *mekhum* for thirteen
years, his predecessor held the post for about twelve years, while Map [House 27] had
been *mekhum* for twenty-four years until he voluntarily resigned the post.)[7]

The "office" for sub-district Treang is located wherever the *mekhum* resides, in this
instance in a one-room structure near Deth's house in Stoung (about one and a half
kilometers from West Svay). The *mekhum*'s duties are numerous and varied; among
them are (1) supervising the collection of taxes; (2) adjudicating any disputes that
are brought to him for settlement; (3) registering all births, marriages, and deaths
(which must be reported to his office within three days after the event); (4) handling
the initiation of proceedings for divorce or annulment of marriage; (5) keeping lists
of all qualified voters and taxpayers; (6) issuing identity cards that must be carried

---

[6] According to Map (House 27) who was a *mekhum* from about 1910 to 1934, in the earlier part
of the century a candidate for office *had* to give evidence of wealth as well as literacy and good
character. The present *mekhum* has about three hectares of rice fields (though some have been
passed on to children) and may thus be considered to be better off than the average villager.

[7] There is, however, no evidence that the post tends to be passed on within a particular family,
or that a retiring *mekhum* designates his successor in any way.

by all males over eighteen years of age when traveling any distance from home; (7) writing bills of sale for transfers of land, cattle, and houses; (8) assessing the character of anyone from another region who wishes to live in the sub-district and granting permission to do so if the person is reputable; (9) supervising the organization and execution of any public works; (10) conscripting men for work on government projects; (11) organizing communal effort and relief activity in case of any emergencies or calamities such as epidemics or fire; (12) supervising the election and conduct of village chiefs; (13) acting as a representative of the police in apprehending any criminals, reporting accidents and assessing fines and damages, supervising the *civapol* or village guards, and in general maintaining the safety of the villagers; and (14) passing down any proclamations, ordinances, propaganda, etc. from the central government to the village level (see also Bruel 1924, 19–22 for duties of the *mekhum* as defined by the royal ordinance of 1919). In general, then, the *mekhum* is responsible for general welfare and order within his territory, acts as a representative of both his constituents and the central government vis-à-vis one another as the situation demands, and operates as a critical link in the chain from the national government to the village. (*Mekhum* Deth, when not busy at his office, visiting a village for one reason or another, or attending some meeting, is most often seen on his bicycle peddling hurriedly to or from the district chief's office.)

For the performance of these duties, the *mekhum* receives a salary of 700, 750, or 800 riels per month, depending on whether his *khum* is of third, second, or first rank according to size of population (*khum* Treang is of second rank, so Deth gets 750 riels).[8] In addition, a fee of twenty riels is charged for issuing bills of sale, half of which is kept by the *mekhum* while the remainder goes to the district office. It is not unlikely that the *mekhum* (and higher officials as well) also occasionally receives small, informal "gifts" for expediting various matters.

The *mekhum* is aided in his responsibilities by a small staff of minor officials who, like him, are local inhabitants. These are (1) a "secretary" (*smiln*), appointed by the provincial governor from among candidates recommended by the *mekhum*, who keeps all registers and records for a salary of 700 riels a month; and (2) three tax collectors (*cumtuk*) who are selected by the district office and receive 350 or 250 riels a month. (Taxes are paid once a year but at no specific time. These collectors tour each village twice a month, beginning in January of each year, to receive payments from families whenever the latter have managed to accumulate the required amount.)[9] In addition to the officials just mentioned, there is also a position called the *protièn khum* whose duties are presumably to aid the *mekhum* and to see that the latter is competent and honest; in practice, however, the *protièn khum* evidently does little because there is no salary for the post and its holder is usually fully occupied with earning a living.[10]

It might be noted here that litigation rarely goes beyond the district or sub-district levels. Disputes that are not settled by the parties themselves (which usually

---

[8] During Map's term of office (1910–34), the *mekhum* received no set salary but kept 3 percent of the taxes collected from residents of the *khum*.

[9] According to Steinberg 1959, 185, the post-colonial government has had difficulty in collecting taxes because of reluctant villagers, lack of well-trained and honest tax collectors, and the general problems of establishing an independent government.

[10] I believe that the post of *protièn khum* is filled by whoever receives the second largest number of votes in the election of *mekhum*. Beginning in 1960, the sub-district was also to have a council as well as a *mekhum*, elected at the same time as the latter (Smith 1964, 653–54).

arise from disagreements over property lines, quarrels over inheritance, fights over water in the rice fields, and personal altercations that involved fisticuffs) are taken for adjudication usually to the sub-district chief. According to the nature of the case, the latter may try simply to mollify and reconcile the disputants, order damages to be paid by one party to another, or dictate some other sort of settlement. If the *mekhum's* judgment is not accepted by the litigants, the case is taken next to the district chief (in some areas there is a regional justice of the peace). Villagers usually do not carry proceedings further because of timidity, lack of money to finance court costs, and ignorance about litigation procedures. They do, however, know of the existence of the *sala dambong* or provincial tribunal that accepts appeals from lower levels, and the *sala otoo* or higher court of appeals in Phnom Penh (for further details of the court system, see Zadrozny 1955, 165–72; Steinberg 1959, 130–32; Smith 1964, 652–53). The legal code used by the courts is modeled strongly on French law although it continues to recognize certain indigenous traditions (see Clairon n.d., 10–11; Thierry 1955, 74–76; Lingat 1952–55, 1:149–50).

THE VILLAGE LEVEL

At this lowest level of local government, there is a village chief, officially designated since 1955 as the *protièn phum* but still commonly referred to as the *mephum*. Candidates for this position are nominated by the villagers themselves who are polled by and make their wishes known to the *mekhum*. An election (similar in procedure to that for the sub-district chief) is then held at the village temple.[11] Elections are not, however, conducted regularly; the *mephum* remains in office until he voluntarily resigns, dies, or loses favor with his constituents because of clear incompetence or corruption (in this latter case, the villagers can ask the *mekhum* to remove the village chief from office). Good character, literacy, and a certain competence are cited as the major qualifications for office; wealth is not considered to be of particular importance (although evidently it was of significance in earlier times).

Aiding the *mephum* are an assistant chief (*anup protièn phum*) and two other officials (known as *samacek*) who are, respectively, those candidates who received the second, third, and fourth highest number of votes in the election for village chief. These three persons and the *mephum* himself form a sort of village council called the *kanak kamakaa*. None of these officials receives any salary although they are charged with several minor responsibilities. Their formal duties are (1) transmission of any policies, orders, etc. from the central government (via the sub-district office) to the community; (2) maintenance of law and order, for example, the apprehension of petty criminals and supervision of the village guards; (3) assessment of the character of any person who wishes to stay overnight or reside in the village; and (4) adjudication of any disputes brought to them for settlement.[12]

---

[11] According to the villagers, in former times (I think prior to 1955) the village chief was appointed by the sub-district chief after polling the opinions of all males over twenty years of age in the community as to what man was most favored for the position. Cf., however, a description in Zadrozny 1955, 310–11, given by an informant from a village in Battambang province on the procedure for selecting a village chief.

[12] Contrary to Zadrozny 1955, 311, the village chief, at least in Svay, does not collect taxes. Cf. also the extensive list of the village chief's duties that are listed in Cady 1964, 557 (taken from

To the residents of West Svay, and evidently of the other hamlets as well, the village chief is a non-entity; some villagers do not even know the chief's name (Mau) or where he lives (Middle Hamlet). Instead, the sub-district chief is the main figure of official authority who is appealed to directly for any legal or governmental matters. This situation is probably not typical of Khmer villages in general, and the weakness of the village chief in Svay is perhaps due to several factors. First, because the functions of the village chief are but lower-level duplications of some of the *mekhum*'s duties, and because the latter lives only a kilometer or so away, the villagers feel that it is sensible to go immediately to the figure of higher authority. Second, the *mekhum*, on his part, does not discourage such bypassing of the village chief. Indeed, perhaps because Svay is so nearby, he superintends its affairs more than he has to, and often takes action himself when he could very well delegate jobs to village officials.[13] Third, Svay as a whole is relatively large, both in population and area, as well as split into hamlets that are socially self-sufficient to a good degree. This makes it somewhat difficult for everyone to know the village chief well if, like Mau, he makes no effort to acquaint himself with all the inhabitants or to assert what small authority he has. It is likely that in smaller, more centralized villages that are located a greater distance from the sub-district office, the village chief has much greater prestige and authority than he does in Svay.

### The *Civapol*

Another aspect of local government must be mentioned: the *civapol* or village guards. The *civapol* system was initiated by Sihanouk in the mid-1950s to provide an adjunct to the police and provincial guards (self-defense units organized in various larger villages) in protecting the countryside against bandits and especially subversive groups that have been a major concern of the government in recent years (see Steinberg 1959, 98, 135–37 for details). West Svay has its own *civapol* unit, composed of all able-bodied males from twenty to fifty years of age, whose main duty is to "protect the hamlet from thieves and people sneaking in from Thailand and Vietnam [i.e., subversives]."[14] Working in teams of several persons (equipped with two ancient rifles), each man takes a turn about once a week in patrolling the hamlet and guarding its entrances from sundown to daybreak. In addition, about once a year the *civapol* are called into Phnom Penh for a day of maneuvers, drill, and lectures (which duty is considered a trial by many men because they must purchase special clothing for the

---

Bell 1926). The latter, however, deals with the Cambodia of several decades past, and it would seem that the village chief's authority and responsibilities have been diminished in recent years.

[13] In addition, the district chief seems to accord responsibilities to the *mekhum* that could just as well be given to village chiefs. For example, when I was making arrangements to reside in Svay, it was presumably the village chief's responsibility to assess my character. In fact, I was never referred to him and never saw him. Rather, the *mekhum* was the first on the scene (having been sent by the district chief) and the one who assumed the major responsibility for my welfare.

[14] Relations between Cambodia and these two countries have always been tumultuous (see Smith 1965, chap. 5). And in the late 1940s and early 1950s there were real problems with Vietminh infiltration from Vietnam, as well as, in the late 1950s, presumed rebel plots to overthrow Sihanouk that were supposedly directed by former Khmer officials who had fled to Vietnam and Thailand (see Steinberg 1959, 96; Smith 1965, 164–65). In 1959, government propaganda had made the villagers aware and fearful of the latter.

turnout). They may also be ordered to participate in reception ceremonies for visiting dignitaries.[15]

Of some significance in formal political structure, at least in West Svay, are the village leaders of the *civapol*, one of whom is Phana (House 3) (the other resides in Middle Hamlet). Selected by the sub-district chief, these *civapol* leaders have only minimal official responsibilities: supervision of the village *civapol* (e.g., seeing that schedules of guard duty are made up), attendance at any meetings in Phnom Penh that concern the *civapol*, checking on any suspicious strangers that pass through or wish to stay in the village, and apprehending criminals. But they may also be asked by the *mekhum* to aid in other endeavors; for example, when the government provided some funds toward the construction of a new well in West Svay, Phana was in charge of collecting money from each household to pay for the remainder of construction costs (plus food for the workers) and of organizing the materials and labor to build the well. So far as West Svay is concerned, Phana is the most immediate representative of the government. Though his position and duties are actually quite limited, he is sometimes referred to as "the village chief's assistant" or as "the *mekhum*'s helper"; and he may be called upon as a representative of official authority, especially when there is no time to get to a higher official.

In sum, the interaction between the central government and the village, as mediated through the various regional officials, is primarily a one-way road. The government sends down policies, programs, propaganda, and laws, while little more than taxes and vital statistics pass upward. The situation described for a village in Thailand is equally apt for villages in Cambodia: local officials, "instead of being supported from below by their constituencies, are suspended from the governmental pyramid above, being responsible to, dependent on, and largely controlled by district officials representing central government"; while the lowest chiefs have some authority, they are mainly passive agents of government bureaucracy who help maintain law and order and provide a channel for passing policy down, but who have little real authority to push things through from below (Sharp et al. 1953, 45–46).[16]

---

[15] It should be noted that village men are also called to work on government projects. Corvée labor was common in precolonial Cambodia when every able-bodied male between the ages of twenty-one and fifty owed the government up to ninety days of labor of year (Aymonier 1900, 73). In 1958, after a visit to Peking, Sihanouk revived a sort of corvée by decreeing that all government officials and civil servants should spend two weeks a year in "*travail manuel*" to give new dignity to manual labor (see the famous picture of Sihanouk, clad in shorts and wielding a hoe, in *Time Magazine*, August 18, 1958, p. 21). All able-bodied village men from twenty to fifty years of age were also conscripted in 1959, the men of West Svay spending five days working on river dikes several kilometers from the village. In theory, participation in this program was not compulsory. But no villager dared to refuse to cooperate for fear of being branded a subversive "follower of Sam Sary" (a former high government official who in 1959 was accused of plots to overthrow Sihanouk), and there was actually no overt grumbling about being called to work. (Neither, to my knowledge, did any of the urban officials and civil servants refuse to participate, though some of the latter of my acquaintance approached the prospect of two weeks at hard labor with more than a little trepidation.) In fact, they labored only four hours a day and were regaled the rest of the time with free food, wine, and radio entertainment.

[16] Further, Steinberg (1959, 275) suggests that the principal role of any leader in Cambodian society is to explain political situations to the people, rather than seeking support for one's policies or person, and to establish lines of authority and responsibility between the government and the governed so that people will cooperate instead of withdrawing from or ignoring what the leader wants them to accept. The implication is that the people are primarily in the position

## GOVERNMENT, POLITICS, AND THE VILLAGE

### GOVERNMENT PROGRAMS AND THE VILLAGE

Despite the essential passivity of local officials and the populace, it must be said in all fairness that the post-colonial government has become more aware of the needs of the peasantry and has adopted a more benevolent and sympathetic attitude toward them than was formerly the case.[17] This is due in large measure to the humanitarian outlook of Sihanouk whose administration has received substantial financial and advisory assistance from a number of European, American, and Asian private and governmental organizations.[18] Some developments were begun under the French, but after Cambodia gained independence, the government has expanded or initiated practices or services that directly or indirectly affect the villagers with varying degrees of success. A few examples follow.

(1) One of the most dramatic developments of the post-war era is the greatly increased opportunity for education. The government realizes the need for more trained personnel to fill administrative, commercial, and professional roles (most of which are presently held by non-Khmer), and funds for education are the highest of all allotments in the national budget (Steinberg 1959, 186, 252). With the incorporation of the temple schools into the public educational system (which policy was begun by the French) and increased construction of new schools, the number of primary schools and enrollment virtually tripled between 1951 and 1957 (Steinberg 1959, 252–53). There are still problems such as an insufficient number of adequately trained teachers and the lack of funds that hinder most village children from obtaining secondary schooling. But desire for education has certainly penetrated peasant values, and there should be substantial increase in literacy (especially for females) in the future. (For details of the educational system, see Bilodeau, Pathammavong, and Hòng 1955; Zadrozny 1955, 131–47; Steinberg 1959, 251–53; Smith 1964, 655–59.)

This expansion of education is quite obvious in West Svay. As noted in a preceding chapter, in former times the primary means of education were temple schools or instruction received while a monk; while a small school with three grades was available in Kompong Tuol since 1911, it was evidently little attended. Three-quarters of all males over thirteen years of age in West Svay have at least minimal literacy in the Khmer language, all but four of whom had received their education while monks, while all females in the hamlet over eighteen years of age are illiterate, with the exception of one girl raised in another province. At present, there are two primary schools in the area: the public school in Kompong Tuol has expanded to six grades with sixteen teachers and an enrollment of about 745 pupils (of which about one-third are

---

of listening and questioning only to clarify matters, rather than actively contesting or opposing what is presented to them.

[17] According to inscriptions, some of the ancient kings also had a humanitarian concern for the masses and built them hospitals, gave rice to the needy and sick, etc. (Steinberg 1959, 240–41). But most of them, except in theory, seemed largely to ignore the condition of the populace.

[18] These include various agencies of the United Nations (WHO, FAO, UNESCO, etc.); the United States Overseas Mission (with its various departments of agriculture, education, health, etc.); aid from the French, Russian, Chinese Communist, Japanese, and other governments; and some private organizations such as Medico, the Asia Foundation, and the Unitarian Service Committee (the latter in a non-religious capacity). For a discussion of foreign aid to Cambodia, see Steinberg 1959, 233–37 and passim; Smith 1964, 661–62, 663–71; 1965, 113, 122–27.

girls), while the temple school at Wat Svay is now under public school administration and has four grades, about one hundred pupils, and two regular teachers plus one monk instructor.[19] With only a few exceptions (and occasional hooky playing), all the children of West Svay, up to the age of about sixteen, attend one of these schools and receive instruction in various subjects.[20] Relatively few go on to the secondary schools (*lycées* or *collèges*) that are located in Phnom Penh because of lack of motivation, inadequate funds, or because their labor is needed at home; only one girl in West Svay is now attending a secondary school in the city (her father earns a regular salary working at the normal school).[21] However, the value of education, for females as well as males, is now clearly recognized by most parents and children who see it as the major means of escape from the difficult life of the rice cultivator. This attitude has probably been reinforced by the proximity of the normal school where villagers see and meet many young people, born of peasant parents, who are on their way to a white-collar profession. Thus, several West Svay children now dream of secondary education and the possibility of becoming teachers or civil servants, though it is uncertain how many of these aspirations will actually be fulfilled unless the government can expand scholarship programs.[22]

(2) In the realm of health, the government has been aided by the World Health Organization, a program of Fundamental Education (Éducation du Base) staffed mainly by United Nations personnel, Medico, and aid missions from various countries. Many activities are directed toward the improvement of village conditions and health, for example, the digging of wells and privies, spraying of malarial regions, training of midwives, building of hospitals outside Phnom Penh, attempts to give instruction in Western concepts of hygiene, etc. (see Steinberg 1959, 238–49 on health and welfare programs). But it is questionable as to whether a large proportion of the peasantry has been affected by such efforts. Probably the greatest boon to health in this century is the practice of inoculations against the great epidemic diseases that was begun under the French. Old villagers noted that smallpox, cholera, and plague were greatly feared in the earlier part of this century; but now, smallpox

[19] Technically, grades one to three are called *école élémentaire*, while grades four to six are known as *école complémentaire*. Education is theoretically compulsory through all six grades, though in practice it is said that a number of children do not go beyond the first three years.

[20] In 1959, thirty-eight children from West Svay were attending primary school; these included eighteen boys and twenty girls, ranging in age from five to fifteen. Thirty children were in the first three grades, the rest in grades four to six.

[21] In the entire village of Svay, there are only a handful of individuals who had received partial secondary education or training, and only one young man who spoke enough French to act as an interpreter. (Although, of course, those who had gotten considerable education would not be likely to remain in the village.) Evidently the secondary schools still graduate very few students, especially from the complete six-year program that leads to a *Baccalauréat* (Steinberg 1959, 254).

[22] It is indeed possible for very ambitious and intelligent village children to obtain quite high positions. One young man of my acquaintance, born of peasant parents in Battambang province, eventually won scholarships to American universities and returned to a high position in the Cambodian government when he was only in his mid-twenties. On a more modest level, the director of the primary school in Kompong Tuol was similarly born into a rice-cultivating family in the area. The normal schools now recruit able students by providing education and room and board in return for the promise of ten years of teaching service once training is completed. It is also possible to obtain government or other scholarships for secondary school and college-level training, as well as graduate study abroad, through competitive examinations.

vaccinations are ubiquitous in West Svay, and the other diseases have been greatly suppressed. West Svay has also benefited from a government-financed well and the presence of a trained midwife in nearby Kompong Tuol (although women continue to rely primarily upon an old peasant midwife). The villager has also become aware of the efficacy of modern medical techniques to the extent that medicines such as penicillin are purchased by those few who can afford them, and the professional midwife from Kompong Tuol is sent for in cases of difficult births. But there are no hospitals or medical centers in the area (in one emergency when Ny of House 12 fell unconscious after a trying birth, the midwife had to telephone from Kompong Tuol for an ambulance to take her to a hospital in Phnom Penh), and very few villagers can afford to consult private physicians in the city. Various ailments such as trachoma and dysentery are still endemic in West Svay, and there is still heavy reliance on native remedies (though some prove to be quite efficacious) and traditional curing practices.

(3) It is obviously to the government's advantage to make agriculture more efficient and productive, and both the colonial and present administrations have supported experimental agricultural stations and an agricultural school to train farm agents, instituted water control and irrigation programs, experimented with mechanized farming, made limited efforts to distribute better quality seed, and give instruction in means of improving production (see Zadrozny 1955, 294–300; Steinberg 1959, 195–96, 202; Delvert 1961, 653–55; Smith 1964, 659–60). But evidently such efforts have had little effect on rice cultivators in general and West Svay villagers in particular. The latter have experienced only one government-sponsored attempt to improve agricultural methods. This was a meeting in 1959 at a nearby temple, organized by the Fundamental Education program and attended by regional officials and representatives (chosen by the sub-district chiefs) from various villages (including two men from West Svay), at which methods of obtaining better yield from rice and sugar palm production were discussed. It was hoped that the village delegates would then disseminate this knowledge to their neighbors. The men from West Svay did indeed pass on some of the information to anyone who was interested, but it is doubtful that any villager was impressed enough to depart from tried and presumably true traditional methods.[23]

(4) With respect to agriculture, a more urgent concern of the government has been the problem of peasant finances and, in particular, debt. The system of agricultural credit and cooperatives (begun under the French) has been reorganized and expanded (see Steinberg 1959, 191–93, 207–9, 222–24; Delvert 1961, 654–55), and evidently an increasing number of peasants are taking advantage of government loans

---

[23] A further point is that none of the delegates from Svay with whom I was acquainted were actually practicing farmers or palm tappers. Daen (House 28) is basically a carpenter whose fields are worked by his brother-in-law or hired labor; Rina (House 4) is also a carpenter who is now supported by his son-in-law, and Chhean (a delegate from East Hamlet) is an educated young man who worked as my interpreter, rarely labors in the fields, and wishes to escape the countryside. The sub-district chief probably chose these men because they were intelligent persons who could accurately understand and report what was presented to them in the meeting, but they were certainly not villagers who might actually try some of the new methods themselves. See Nash 1965, 237–39 for a similar occurrence in a Burmese village that further points out some of the unforeseen difficulties in such government programs.

with lower interest rates and the greater security of selling or purchasing through a cooperative. But cooperatives will have to become more widely dispersed through the countryside (there were only nine in 1955), and villagers must be encouraged to greater patronization of government credit facilities. As noted in chapter 4, villagers in West Svay (and probably most other communities as well) still rely on private moneylenders and sell their rice at relatively low market prices. It was also mentioned, however, that a cooperative for marketing rice was being built near Svay in early 1960, and that the government was considering the possibility of purchasing palm sugar.

(5) The French instituted an extensive program of road building that has been continued, to a lesser degree, by the present government (see Zadrozny 1955, 32–35; Steinberg 1959, 27–28, 224–45). These routes, coupled especially with the expansion of privately owned bus systems, have greatly increased the ease and possibility of travel for villagers and enabled diverse activities such as marketing rice in Phnom Penh, obtaining temporary urban employment, seeing kinsmen in other communities more frequently, etc. In general, the growth of transportation and communication systems has reduced the traditional insularity of village life.

(6) Finally, two measures have attempted to increase the peasant's voice in government: the expansion of voting rights and the creation of the National Congress. With respect to the former, women were granted the franchise in 1955, and villagers now have the right to elect village chiefs, sub-district chiefs, and delegates to the National Assembly (the central legislature). In one sense, much of this means relatively little; for example, in West Svay the village chief, though elected, is a non-entity; and the regional delegate to the National Assembly is a vague and remote figure who is supported because he has Sihanouk's endorsement.[24] Many villagers participate in elections mainly because of the simple novelty and pleasure of going through the motions of voting. In another sense, however, voting can be a genuine expression of preferences when the candidates are well known. Moreover, even in national elections and referenda, the villager is made to think that his vote is meaningful (though in fact all he usually does is to rubber stamp what Sihanouk advocates) and thus comes to feel that he has at least a minimal voice in government. Sihanouk has attempted to increase this feeling further by the innovation in 1955 of the National Congress: a biannual meeting in Phnom Penh of Sihanouk, delegates from his party, ministers or other officials called upon to give reports or answer questions, and, theoretically, masses of common people. Various domestic and foreign policies are discussed at the Congress, and anyone may ask questions of or present grievances against the government.[25] The Congress has two ostensible functions: first, to permit and encourage

---

[24] The National Assembly initially had one delegate for every ten thousand voters, but when the granting of the franchise to women greatly enlarged the electorate, the representation was lowered to one for every thirty thousand voters (Smith 1964, 624). Smith also notes that "members of the National Assembly have been only nominal representatives of the people. Except when campaigning for votes, they have tended to concentrate themselves in Phnom Penh, have been indifferent to the needs and desires of their constituents, and have not tried to cultivate a following among them" (1964, 650–51).

[25] Actually this is an old tradition in modern guise because Khmer kings from the time of Angkor are supposed to have held daily audiences at which presumably even the humblest commoner could present his grievances and petition the monarch for redress or advice.

the common man to voice his opinions and problems without intermediaries; and second, to pass resolutions that will then be enacted by the legislature and other governmental bodies (Smith 1964, 623). These meetings evidently do draw large crowds of peasantry and other common folk (though no one from West Svay has ever been to or expressed any interest in attending the Congress), and its conception is admirable in theory. In practice, however, the Congress's agenda is prearranged by the dominant Sangkum party; the audience is usually passive and quiet; and Sihanouk (or whoever is prime minister) presides over the meetings and is able to influence the course of discussions and control what resolutions are passed (Smith 1964, 647). The Congress has, however, stimulated some significant legislation, such as the granting of the vote to women.

From the preceding, it is evident that the peasant is coming to gain increasing recognition and benefits from the central government. However, more government personnel and facilities are needed in numerous areas to effect widespread amelioration among a substantial number of the rural population. There is, in addition, the perplexing problem of how to convince the villagers of the need to alter permanently certain basic patterns of daily and annual life, whether it be techniques of cultivation or remembering to wash one's hands before cooking meals. And, in sum, the peasant remains a passive recipient of, rather than an active agitator for, any improvements in his life.

## POLITICS AND THE VILLAGERS

There is only one instance, temporary but turbulent, in which national political factionalism manifested itself in Svay: the period of the Khmer Issarak agitation after World War II and prior to Cambodia's gaining of independence. The Khmer Issarak (Free Khmer) movement, in its initial or pure form, was a militantly nationalistic group that opposed Sihanouk (who was then king) and the central government for being too slow and pliant in negotiations with the French for independence. In time, however, the situation became confused and complicated by a variety of factors (e.g., Issarak relations with Vietminh), and the rebels were splintered into virtually autonomous groups with different leaders and varied activities: "this name Issarak has served as a cover denoting Cambodian nationalists and communists, ranging from semi-bandit bands to disciplined political organization" (Zadrozny 1955, 174; for other details on the Issarak, see Zadrozny 1955, 174–209, Steinberg 1959, 101–6; Smith 1964, 608–9, 1965, 31–33, 37–38, 40–43). Issarak groups were spread throughout the country, and the area southwest of Phnom Penh, which fell under the provenance of a particular leader, was frequently the scene of considerable rebel activity (see Zadrozny 1955, 174ff. for details).

The Issarak movement managed to recruit a fair number of adherents from Svay itself. It is difficult to estimate how many men actually became active rebels, but a number of former Issarak still reside in Svay, including two men in West Hamlet. Some had joined the Issarak because they believed sincerely in the quest for autonomy from the French. But knowing the general unconcern for political affairs that usually exists among the villagers, it is likely that most men were lured more by the prospect of adventure, fighting, and wielding some sort of power, than by the ideology of nationalism. The villagers say that the majority of Svay's residents remained neutral or even hostile to the Issarak.

Some people look back on this period[26] with the nostalgia of old generals recalling great battles; others discuss it dispassionately; and not a few villagers recall bitterly the dissension and turmoil that disrupted their lives.

> The Issarak were their own law. They killed anyone they wanted to kill. . . . Sometimes siblings could not speak to one another because one was an Issarak and the other worked for the government in Phnom Penh. They never saw each other's faces. . . . The Issaraks were very bad people. My wife's own brother-in-law was an Issarak, and once he took a knife and threatened to kill me. My wife cried and cried, and I had to tell her to go in the house while I persuaded him not to murder me. But then he stole many necklaces and bracelets from my wife, and also several thousand riels.

A number of families emigrated temporarily to Phnom Penh for safety's sake[27] because the Issarak not only stole but were known also to commit murders. (Presumably they killed "enemies of Cambodia," but the identification of these was evidently sometimes quite arbitrary.) At times, too, they might force a non-Issarak villager to aid them in their activities on pain of harm to him or his family.

Because of such excesses, one Issarak adherent was ostracized permanently from West Svay for unforgivable aggression and sins against his neighbors. Others, however, were only temporarily ostracized (actually or literally); and in time, they were reaccepted on friendly terms by their neighbors and are now ordinary, indeed sometimes upright, members of the community. In retrospect, most villagers feel that much of the activity of the Issarak was undeniably "bad," but that some of their behavior is at least partially excusable as having been "against the French, not Cambodia itself."

Once the Issarak movement died down, West Svay returned to its normal placidity and passivity concerning political affairs. Political conflicts and parties do exist in Cambodia, but they are usually almost exclusively a phenomenon of the urban elite and intelligentsia, and Svay's inhabitants know nothing of them.[28] So far as the villagers are concerned, there is only Norodom Sihanouk, the nation's leader, and the monarchy with which he is identified. Once the nation's king (from 1941 to 1955), Sihanouk abdicated from the crown to assume the post of prime minister[29] (although

---

[26] Issarak activity in Svay was strongest from approximately 1951 to 1953.

[27] According to Delvert 1961, 435, movement to Phnom Penh because of insecurity in the countryside during the post-war years was common throughout the district of Koh Thom and the neighboring district of Bati.

[28] For discussions of political parties in the post-war era, see Steinberg 1959, 95–114; Smith 1964, 619–51. In 1959, Sihanouk's Sangkum Reastr Niym (People's Socialist Community) party was overwhelmingly dominant, while the Communist Pracheachon (People's) party and the Pracheathipatey (Democratic) party had minimal followings. Opposition to Sihanouk's policies has come primarily from those who hold (or held) high government positions and discontented "jeunes intellectuels" (Smith 1964, 627–31, 638–41). Smith notes that "when political parties existed, they were not national organizations with which the people could identify themselves" (1964, 651).

[29] In 1959, Sihanouk's official title was prime minister, and his parents were king and queen. After his father, King Suramarit, died in April 1960 and no successor was agreed upon, Sihanouk assumed the title of chief of state with monarchic powers. But this is evidently a temporary solution to the problem of succession to the throne, and the monarchy has not been abolished (see Smith 1964, 626, 643).

villagers still frequently refer to him as "king") because, as he said, "As a king it was difficult to keep informed. . . . The true face of the people was hidden from me" (see his speech quoted in Steinberg 1959, 99). In both domestic and foreign affairs, Sihanouk has proven himself to be an intelligent and skilled administrator and politician who has a deep and sincere concern for his nation and his people.[30] With respect to the latter, "more than any other ruler in Cambodia, Sihanouk has fostered intimacy with the peasantry" (Smith 1964, 645) and has changed the old "image of remote power indifferent to the needs of the people" to "one of benevolent paternalistic authority" (643). His legislation attempting to ameliorate the lot of the peasants, his trips through the countryside to visit villages, his ebullient nature and lack of hauteur, his dedication to Buddhism, and his attempts to make the people feel that their opinions and grievances matter to him have won Sihanouk a tremendous popularity. While West Svay villagers sometimes grumble about the government, such as arrogant or dishonest officials whom they may have encountered, Sihanouk himself is spoken of with only the greatest of loyalty, affection, and respect. Whatever or whomever he espouses is therefore accepted.

News of national and international politics does reach the village in several ways, although Svay residents have relatively little access to most media and are often uninterested in political affairs. There are only two radios in the entire village (both located in the other hamlets), although I brought one into West Svay and there are others at the local temples and in Kompong Tuol. The Khmer Broadcasting System (Radio Diffusion Khèmre), operated by the government, offers music, drama, news, and speeches on its one station.[31] As a source of news the radio is of limited utility to villagers because the news broadcasts are either in French or in the formal Khmer speech used by educated people that is barely intelligible to most peasants. Whenever Sihanouk is on the radio, he arouses great interest and attention (and it is a credit to Sihanouk's cleverness that, in such speeches to the populace, he always uses "colloquial" language in at least part of his talk so that ordinary people can understand him). Otherwise, however, West Svay villagers are much more interested in listening to music and especially dramas (which always drew great crowds around the radio). Similarly, although there are a variety of newspapers and magazines published in Phnom Penh, these rarely reach the village except as wrappings for food purchased at the market. Very occasionally a paper or periodical may be brought from the city or perhaps borrowed from someone. Newspapers seem to excite less interest than do magazines whose pictures are meaningful and entertaining to even the illiterate; but ultimately, both are valued perhaps as much for their utility as wallpaper as for the information they impart.

There are two more important sources of news. First, a bulletin board maintained by the district office in the central marketplace of Kompong Tuol, and one at the sub-district office as well, post various government news releases, posters, and other official communications. These are usually given at least a cursory perusal by literate villagers. Second, word-of-mouth transmission of news is still a significant means of information dispersal. There are numerous persons who act as carriers of news: for example, local officials such as the sub-district and village chiefs who pass on

[30] For a cogent and succinct analysis of Sihanouk as a political figure, see Smith 1964.

[31] For a more detailed discussion of radio and other media in Cambodia, see Steinberg 1959, chap. 10.

information either as part of their duties or because they have more access to news of government affairs; individuals who have returned from Phnom Penh, especially the men who have temporary employment as cyclo drivers and have occasion to see and hear a great deal on their rides about the city; urbanites visiting rural kinsmen; persons such as merchants or bus drivers who make frequent journeys between the countryside and city; and more well-educated and affluent persons such as schoolteachers or monks[32] who have greater access to media such as radios and newspapers, and are likelier to take more interest in public affairs. Such word-of-mouth communication is often surprisingly efficient and rapid in its disseminations of news (including some items that do not appear in official press releases).[33]

Because the government exercises considerable control over the various communication media through its Ministry of Information, Smith points out that

> dissident views are not transmitted to the populace through three channels, and thus they [the people] possess an uncomplicated view of power politics in the capital. Thus political views are a simplified version of the prince's [Sihanouk's] public statements, and they adopt them unquestioningly because they believe that there is no wisdom greater than that of the prince. (1964, 641)

This situation is clearly evident in West Svay. The villagers generally know little about national or international issues, both in depth and scope, and whatever opinions and information they do have are clear reflections of government views. As example, some of the major "political" attitudes and notions of the villagers are given below.

(1) Smith (1964, 643) notes that Sihanouk has deliberately used the concept of "nation" as part of his effort to instill an esprit de corps among the people. West Svay villagers are very much conscious of "we Khmer" as a distinct nation and culture,[34] and feel moreover that it is an important one. (When confronted with a map of Southeast Asia, villagers were always shocked that Cambodia is small because they thought that its size would be commensurate with its presumed importance.) They believe, moreover, that Sihanouk makes great efforts on behalf of his country: that in the domestic sphere he has the best interests of the people at heart, and that in foreign policy he maintains Cambodia's treasured independence while simultaneously obtaining foreign aid (from countries such as Russia, Japan, and the United States) that benefits the nation in various ways. (2) In response to my queries about communism,

---

[32] Steinberg (1959, 142) emphasizes the temple as "a key point in the relay of information and in opinion formation." This may well be true in some regions and for isolated villages, but (as mentioned in chapter 5) this was not the case in Svay. While several monks at the local temples are impressively intelligent and well informed, they do not appear to be significant sources of secular news and information for the community. Neither do the Svay villagers make a point of congregating at the temples to read books and papers or listen to the radio as Steinberg suggests.

[33] For example, once I returned to Svay after a day in Phnom Penh where I had heard (from American friends) of a minor scandal involving a royal princess. I did not mention this to the villagers, but a day or so later, the same news was brought to the village by a man who was working as a cyclo driver in the city.

[34] Cf. Smith (1964, 643) who goes on to say that the peasants have difficulty understanding the concept of "nation" because they have long been accustomed to village life. West Svay villagers, however, frequently use the phrases "we Khmer" (*khmay yoeung*), or *srok khmay* (Cambodia) to speak of Cambodia as a territorial nation and Cambodians as an ethnic group.

a number of villagers knew of its existence and the fact that China is communist (viz. Sihanouk's various visits to Peking). Rith (House 20) succinctly explained the doctrine of the "komunii" as "Poor people like communism because they [the communists] want to share everything and no one would be rich or poor; but rich people don't like this idea." It was said further that some of the poor Chinese in Kompong Tuol are communists, but that Svay villagers were not interested in and even negative toward communism. One might expect that communism, especially in its simplified form as presented by Rith, would be attractive to poor peasants. But the villagers' rejection thereof is understandable if one realizes that in 1959, Sihanouk was attempting to suppress subversive communist activity within the country itself and was also striving to maintain his neutralist stance by alternating between favorable and unfavorable comments about the major foreign powers, that is, the United States and the Communist Russian–Chinese bloc (for details, see Smith 1965, chap. 4; Steinberg 1959, 106–16). (3) The centuries-old enmity between Cambodia and its neighbors Thailand and Vietnam continues to the present day (see Smith 1965, chap. 5; Steinberg 1959, 4, 103, 114, 152–53, 206, and passim). Svay villagers view these countries with suspicion and hostility as harbingers of subversion and aggressive encroachers on Khmer territory, the two issues that have most aggravated the Cambodian government in recent years. (4) The villagers fear subversive activity (viz. the *civapol* guards) and scorn anyone who is publicized as a traitor to the country. In 1959 the government directed particular attention toward Sam Sary, a one-time high official who was accused of conspiracy to overthrow Sihanouk (for details, see Steinberg 1959, 96; Smith 1965, 164–65, 114). Villagers came to use the name of Sam Sary as a synonym for traitor and feared that any expression of disloyalty toward the government would brand them as "a follower of Sam Sary."

From the preceding, then, it is evident that village political opinion mirrors national government (i.e., Sihanouk's) policies. The example of the Issarak movement in Svay shows that it is possible, on occasion, for villagers to hold opposing political views, but this situation occurred during a time of national unrest when central leadership was relatively weak. Now that Cambodia has become stabilized under the firm control of Sihanouk, it is not likely that diverse political attitudes and loyalties will appear among the general populace unless his power wanes, and other leaders and parties can gain real strength.

# CHAPTER EIGHT

# RELATIONS OF THE VILLAGE WITH THE SURROUNDING WORLD

Svay is a rather self-centered and self-sufficient community in some respects: its inhabitants spend most of their lives and satisfy many of their social and material needs within its confines, and their outlook on the surrounding world is basically provincial and insular. But it is by now a truism that any community, especially a peasant village in a modern complex nation, cannot be studied in isolation from the larger society that encompasses it,[1] and Svay is no exception. Some of the varied kinds of relations between West Svay and other villages, the town, and the city have already been mentioned in the preceding discussions of economic, social, and political organization.

In this chapter, special attention will be focused upon the kinds and frequency of direct contacts that West Svay villagers have with other communities or regions[2] and upon their conceptions of and attitudes toward other ethnic groups and nations.

## MEANS OF TRANSPORTATION AND COMMUNICATION

Thanks primarily to the efforts of the French colonial administration, an extensive network of roads and highways interlaces Cambodia. Svay is located on a minor highway that connects it with several neighboring villages and the market town, and that intersects a major highway leading to Phnom Penh. But up until the past decade, villagers did relatively little traveling outside the immediate area because means of transportation were limited mainly to walking and to oxcarts. A trip to Phnom Penh or other distant points thus meant long, arduous journeys (e.g., even the nearest bus connection to the city was twenty kilometers away) that were not easily undertaken. At the present time, however, the mobility of the villagers has been greatly facilitated by the increased number and range of buses that have become the main means of long-distance travel. After World War II, various bus systems (operated mainly

---

[1] I shall not attempt to review here the numerous models (e.g., the folk–urban continuum, levels of integration, great and little traditions, fields of interaction, social network maps, etc.) that have dealt with this problem; see, among others, Redfield 1955, 1956; Steward 1950; Barnes 1954; Marriott 1955; Stewart 1958.

[2] Following a suggestion by Professor Michael Mahar (Department of Oriental Studies, University of Arizona, pers. comm.), I was particularly interested in keeping an actual count of the number (and purposes) of trips made by villagers to other points, in an effort to specify more precisely the exact nature and frequency of villagers' interaction with other communities. To my knowledge, this sort of data has been collected by few investigators (Redfield and Rojas 1962, 8, and the "Diary of Events in Alitoa" in Mead 1947, are exceptions; see also Opler 1956).

by Chinese) expanded rapidly and now traverse almost all roads. Now, at Kompong Tuol, a villager may catch either of two buses that leave for Phnom Penh (by different routes) every hour throughout the day, and buses for other points may be caught in the city or at various crossroads.[3] Most of these vehicles are rather decrepit and shaky conveyances, but they manage nonetheless to carry a great number of passengers, as well as an awesome load of goods on top of the bus.

There are, in addition, other means of transportation within the area. The oxcart is still used occasionally when loads must be transported (e.g., traveling to and from marshlands to get food for cattle), although the small, light cart that was used for "visiting and going to the temple" has disappeared in favor of other conveyances.[4] Primary among the latter for short-distance travel is the remorque or rural pedicab that can carry four (or, if necessary, more) people or sizeable loads, and whose fares are relatively cheap. Bicycles are rare in Svay because even a secondhand model may cost as much as 1,000 riels; there are only three in the hamlet, although they are freely lent to kinsmen and friends who use them for journeying within the region and sometimes even as far as Phnom Penh. Finally, walking is still common for distances up to several kilometers, either because some communities can be reached only on foot or because one wishes to save money. In fact, it is not unknown for hardy men to walk sixty kilometers to and from Phnom Penh for lack of bus fare, and one man walked a total of about one hundred kilometers in five days while seeking to purchase an ox.

Communication between villagers in different communities is limited almost entirely to face-to-face transmission of messages and news. Although there is a post office and telegraph station in Kompong Tuol, telegrams are never sent and letters are written only rarely because of lack of money and the difficulty of addressing messages to individuals in other villages. Rather, when relatives and friends in another community must be notified of some critical event, such as the illness of a parent or the occurrence of a life-cycle ceremony, someone is sent to carry the news even if it means a long or difficult trip. (Thus, when Cheang's mother was dying while he was working in Phnom Penh, a villager was dispatched in the dead of night to ride a bicycle to the city and bring Cheang back to Svay; similarly, Muoy traveled some two hundred kilometers to Battambang to notify her married children that their sister was to be married.) Apart from such personal communications, news of local events in general—accidents, deaths, marriages, unusual occurrences, etc.—are also relayed by word of mouth and can travel surprisingly quickly from community to community. (For example, one day in Svay we heard of a terrible bus crash on the highway about twenty kilometers distant within a few hours of the event.) It is, therefore, common for West Svay's inhabitants to be abreast of any major happenings in the surrounding area.

---

[3] Two other means of long-distance travel for villagers (although rarely used by West Svay's residents) are boats and the railroad. The former is especially important for riverbank villagers. The latter runs only in a northwesterly direction from Phnom Penh to the Thai border.

[4] There are three main types of oxcarts: (1) the *rotEh kayt*, a medium-sized cart capable of tipping on its axis to dump loads; (2) the *rotEh pret*, a larger cart also used for carrying loads that does not tip; and (3) the *rotEh sale*, a small cart used for transporting people. See also Delvert 1961, 229–31 on oxcarts.

## KINDS OF CONTACTS WITH OTHER COMMUNITIES

When villagers make trips to other communities (or, conversely, when visitors come to West Svay), they do so for a variety of purposes of which the following are primary.

(1) Visits to kinsmen. As discussed in chapter 3, a high proportion of West Svay marriages are exogamous to the village. Thus, virtually everyone in the hamlet has kinsmen in other communities, whether they be parents, siblings, and other relatives left behind in one's natal village; siblings, married children, or other kin who have moved away in post-marital residence or assumed employment elsewhere; cousins, nephews and nieces, and grandchildren who were born and reside in other areas; etc. This kinship web spreads out from Svay mainly to other villages within a ten-kilometer radius, but it is not uncommon for individuals to have ties with persons in Phnom Penh or distant localities.[5] Such kinsmen (especially siblings, parents and children, grandparents and grandchildren) commonly maintain contact through mutual visiting, whether it be frequent or occasional contacts of short or long duration (see chapter 3).

It should be noted that one may make special trips to see non-kin friends in other communities as well, but usually only when such friends live relatively nearby. The exception is when non-kinsmen assume a *towaa* or fictive kin relationship, in which case individuals may travel great distances to visit *towaa* relatives.

(2) Attendance at ceremonial events. Individuals may travel to other communities (or come to Svay) to attend major life-cycle rituals, temple ceremonies, or annual celebrations. People will journey far distances to participate in the weddings and funerals of close kinsmen, and these events also draw a variety of other relatives, friends, and even (in the case of weddings) mere nodding acquaintances from other villages who come to watch the festivities. Villagers may also attend festivals or other events at various temples within the region (or sometimes in Phnom Penh) to earn merit, to see new people and places, or to return to one's natal region to visit with kinsmen and old friends. Other affairs, such as a spirit-possession ceremony or a post-harvest festival in another community, or the annual Water Festival or other events in Phnom Penh, can also occasion trips outside Svay.

(3) Exchanges of goods and services. As noted in chapter 4, West Svay has contacts with other villages, the town, and the city in the exchange of goods and services. The hamlet's residents may find employment elsewhere, whether as musicians at a wedding in another village or as cyclo drivers in Phnom Penh, just as a midwife, a *kru*, hired agricultural workers, etc. may come to West Svay from other communities. The purchase of oxen and items not available locally may also necessitate trips to the city or other localities, and vendors of various goods often come through Svay to hawk their wares.

(4) Miscellaneous. Svay residents may make other trips for various purposes: to the sub-district or district offices (or even to the city) for legal-governmental matters; to uninhabited areas to gather food for cattle or bamboo shoots; to tend one's fields

---

[5] To take but one example, Chea (House 18) has a brother and his family in a village about twenty kilometers away; aunts, uncles, or cousins in Ta Chas, Chouk, two other communities about twelve kilometers distant, Pochentong (a settlement next to Phnom Penh), and Phnom Penh; and various in-laws in Sandan, Phnom Penh, and Battambang province.

in other villages; or to visit certain places for sheer pleasure and adventure (this latter is, however, quite rare because of lack of money).

### FREQUENCY OF CONTACTS WITH OTHER COMMUNITIES

(1) Svay and other villages. Not surprisingly, the hamlet's residents have the most frequent contacts with the immediately neighboring villages: Ta Chas (about half a kilometer to the west), Sandan (one kilometer to the east), and Chey and Chouk (two to three kilometers to the south). These villages are linked not simply by geographical proximity but by numerous bonds of kinship and friendship. More than 40 percent of all village exogamous marriages in West Svay were made with individuals from these four communities (with post-marital residence in either Svay or the natal village of the other spouse) such that a number of the hamlet's inhabitants have close relatives and friends in these other settlements. Such kinsmen (or friends) exchange periodic visits and participate in one another's life-cycle rituals. Villagers from within this region may also attend other ceremonial events in the different communities or temples in the area, exchange goods and services, go to tend rice fields near other villages, or journey to the sub-district chief's office in Sandan.

A number of West Svay villagers also have relatives or friends in other communities within a ten- or fifteen-kilometer radius, whom they will see periodically. They might also travel to other communities within this region to purchase cattle or other items or to attend festivals at other temples. Similarly, individuals from other communities come to sell things in Svay or to celebrate holidays at Wats Svay or Samnang.

There is, however, a general distaste for journeying to villages outside the immediate area of a few kilometers. The villagers claim that they enjoy seeing different places and meeting new people, and certainly visitors to their own community are generally treated with great hospitality and courtesy. Yet there is a basic insularity and parochialism in the villagers' attitudes that brand the inhabitants of most other communities (even neighboring Sandan) as robbers, rapists, murderers, and generally "people of bad character." To take one of numerous examples of this outlook, a kindly old lady, who had come to a wedding in Middle Hamlet Svay, invited me to visit her village about twenty kilometers distant. Despite the fact that this village was well known by name and had been visited by several of West Svay's inhabitants, my closest friends in the hamlet adamantly refused to let me accept the lady's invitation on the grounds that they feared for my safety there. The amusing thing was that the old lady and her friends were equally frightened of being in Svay and did not dare to venture out of their hosts' home at night. Similarly, during the dirt-hauling project when Svay was crowded with strangers from other communities who camped in the area for some time, the hamlet's residents were very uneasy and fearful for the safety of their goods and persons, and no doubt the immigrant dirt-haulers felt the same way. In point of fact, stories do arise from time to time that confirm and reinforce these suspicions and apprehensions of unknown persons and places. Not only does government propaganda nurture distrust of strangers as possible subversives and bandits, but villagers themselves experience or hear of unpleasant occurrences. Sometimes they are minor incidents, such as Kosal returning angrily from a Buddhist festival held about fifteen kilometers away, muttering how his new shoes had been stolen when he left them outside the central temple to enter and give offerings to the monks. It is also not uncommon for insulting or lewd remarks to be made to West Svay youths, especially the girls, by strangers encountered at temple festivals or on travels abroad.[6] On a more serious level, there is the unusual account of how two young women from Chouk, who had been hired along with several other girls to dance at a festival in another community, were abducted and "made to be like wives" by several men. (One of the girls did not reappear for two weeks, while the other was still missing after a month's time when I left the area.) It is, therefore, not surprising that villagers do not venture outside their region with confidence; men carry knives and proceed with constant caution when they must travel to unknown places, and people feel uneasy even when visiting kinsmen in strange communities.[7]

In sum, West Svay has frequent and relaxed social intercourse with certain familiar communities within a few kilometers radius. I gave up attempting to keep an exact tally of visits to or from these villages because they were so frequent. I would estimate, however, that someone from West Svay went to, or an individual came from, Ta Chas at least several times a week, to or from Sandan on the average of once a week, and to or from Chey and Chouk (both of which are accessible only by footpaths through the rice fields) on the average of about once a month. The majority of such interaction is visiting between kinsmen and friends. But trips further afield are less common. During a nine-month period, there were about twenty trips (involving individuals from eleven households) to other communities within a twenty-kilometer radius. (One of these journeys was to visit kinsmen, but all the rest were for other purposes: to tend fields elsewhere, to purchase something, to attend a temple festival, to see a spirit-possession ceremony, or to participate in a wedding. Conversely, West Svay inhabitants received five visits from persons within this larger region, all of whom came to see kinsmen in the hamlet.)

There is even less travel beyond a twenty-kilometer radius (except to Phnom Penh). For although villagers have heard of and are curious about other regions of the country (such as the seacoast or Angkor Wat), their lack of money and fear of unknown places prevents extensive journeys. During a nine-month period there were only eight trips (involving individuals from six households) to distant provinces such as Kampot, Kompong Cham, Kompong Chhnang, Kompong Thom, and Battambang. (Six of these journeys were for the purpose of seeing kinsmen;[8] one trip was made to find employment; and one was a simple pleasure trip.) Some West Svay men have in the past held occupations or taken journeys that carried them as far as the wilds of eastern Cambodia or the extreme northwest of the country. But in all, only eleven residents of the hamlet have traveled to regions more than one hundred kilometers away. Similarly, inhabitants of distant areas rarely come to West Svay; in nine months there were only three visits to the hamlet by persons who resided further away than

---

[6] For example, at one temple festival several young women from West Svay became embroiled in a heated verbal exchange with girls from another village who made insulting comments about the formers' dress. And on one grass-cutting expedition to the marshlands, West Svay girls were frightened by some strange men who called out suggestively: "Hey, girls, come help me cut this grass—it is so high." (To which a West Svay man angrily retorted: "Cut it yourself!")

[7] Another indication of the apprehension that villagers feel about unfamiliar regions is the custom of the *towaa* or fictive kin relationship. As noted in chapter 3, such relations are often established when one is traveling or residing in a strange area in order to assure (among other things) that one will have safe refuge in at least one home.

[8] Sometimes such journeys to kinsmen's homes are not simply social visits; e.g., a villager may go to fetch an aged parent or young child who has been staying temporarily with some relatives; or one may combine a visit to kinsmen with a detour to some famous spot such as the seashore.

twenty kilometers (exclusive of Phnom Penh), all of whom came to see relatives (or, in one instance, a fictive kin *towaa* parent).

(2) Svay and the town. Kompong Tuol, about two and a half kilometers distant and easily accessible by foot or remorque (for a fare of about three riels one way), serves the surrounding communities as an economy, political, and educational center. It also offers bus connections to the city and other points, and occasional commercial entertainment.

Schoolchildren in the upper grades, of course, go to Kompong Tuol five days a week for classes. Adult villagers from almost every household in West Svay travel there on the average of three to four times a month. They go primarily to purchase food and other essentials, secondarily to buy other items or services, and occasionally to visit the district chief's office. Several times a year there is also some sort of enter-tainment available in town: traveling theater groups[9] or carnival rides. Both attract fairly large crowds, especially of the young, although relatively few persons from West Svay actually see the theatrical performances or go on the rides because of lack of money. It is significant that West Svay residents do *not* go to Kompong Tuol to visit kinsmen or friends because the town's population is composed mainly of Chinese or Sino-Cambodians with whom villagers have commercial but not social relationships.[10] Neither are the villagers on visiting terms with the Khmer residents of Kompong Tuol who are mainly schoolteachers, government officials, and others of higher socioeco-nomic status. In brief, then, the people of West Svay have frequent occasion to go to the town, but the ties between the townsmen and villagers are *gesellschaft* rather than *gemeinschaft* in nature.

(3) Svay and the city. Phnom Penh is the nation's administrative, commercial, religious, and educational center. It is also the only truly urban and relatively sophis-ticated, cosmopolitan settlement in the country, with its large and diverse population of Khmer, Chinese, Vietnamese, Indians, French, and other Europeans and Asians.[11] Situated at the confluence of four rivers, Phnom Penh is a graceful city that shows French influence in its broad tree-lined boulevards and numerous buildings of Euro-pean style. But indigenous and oriental elements are also evident in the wooden or thatch dwellings of the ordinary populace who cluster in different parts of the city, the bustling marketplaces, and the crowded Chinese quarter. Here also are the Royal Palace, various government buildings, foreign embassies, a museum, temples, banks, movie theaters, hotels, restaurants of various ethnic tastes, numerous shops, etc. On the streets are a confusion of cyclos, bicycles, motor scooters, and cars, and on the

---

[9] These theatrical troupes perform plays (evidently based on original scripts) that are mixtures of comedy, tragedy, adventure, and romance, involving much broad drama, slapstick, sword-play, dance, and song. Even the costumes are a mélange of Indian, Khmer, and Western dress (including one character dressed like Tarzan in a play that I saw). The plays are often given on a cliffhanger basis, continued serially over a period of several nights.

[10] The only time that I saw Chinese from Kompong Tuol in West Svay, other than the traveling vendors, was when some village men were gambling on fighting fish. The Chinese had been invited to participate in the gambling not for the sake of friendliness but in order to stimulate betting. It might also be mentioned that a few Chinese from town occasionally come to Thera-vada festivals at Wat Samnang; but Khmer villagers make no effort to attend or observe Chinese festivals in Kompong Tuol.

[11] The population of Phnom Penh in 1956 was 592,000 (Ministère du Plan 1958, 11). In 1950, about 41 percent of the residents were Khmer, 29 percent Chinese, 29 percent Vietnamese, and 1 percent "Europeans" (11).

sidewalks a variety of people ranging from French teenagers to Vietnamese "taxi girls" to Chinese merchants to Cambodian monks.

To some villagers, especially the older ones who enjoy the calm security of home and countryside, Phnom Penh seems to be a welter of noise, confusion, crowding, unsavory characters, immorality, danger, and expense, to be endured only when absolutely necessary. Some people who have been there, especially the men who work as cyclo drivers, bring back stories of immodest women, attempted or accomplished thievery, physical violence, and other lurid accounts or varied complaints.[12] But for other villagers, especially the younger generation, Phnom Penh is the epitome of excitement, sophistication, and glamour, the symbol of wealth and escape from peasant life. They visit the city eagerly and describe its sights with glowing eyes.

At the present time, with bus transportation readily available, trips from Svay to Phnom Penh are fairly common although still limited by the fact that many villagers lack money for bus fare (eight to ten riels one way) and for expenses during one's stay. (Even though one always lodges with relatives or friends while in the city, one must still spend money on cyclo fares and snacks or meals, such that a day's stay in Phnom Penh may cost anywhere from about 30–100 riels per person.) During a nine-month period, West Svay inhabitants made approximately forty trips to the city.[13] This number can be deceptive because some persons went more than once while others went not at all. The figure should thus be qualified by stating that these trips involved twenty-three persons (over fifteen years of age)[14] from seventeen households. These journeys were made for the following purposes.

(a) Visits to kinsmen (or, in one instance, to attend a kinsman's funeral) accounted for 36 percent of the trips to the city (fourteen journeys involving one or more persons from nine households). A number of former West Svay residents have emigrated to Phnom Penh, either through marriage to a city dweller or to hold permanent occupations in the city, such that there are bonds of friendship and kinship linking villagers and urbanites. And regardless of possible status differences between the two,[15] frequent contacts are maintained between close kinsmen (especially parents and married children, and siblings). (b) About one-quarter of the trips (eleven journeys made by six men) were for the purpose of obtaining some temporary employment in the city. The men usually become cyclo drivers and stay in Phnom Penh for periods of time ranging from several weeks to several months (although some have held other

[12] As a further comment on Phnom Penh and its way of life: a Khmer urbanite of my acquaintance, a young man who was born and raised in a rural village but became a high government official, invited his mother to come visit him in his handsome Western-style apartment in the city. When the old peasant lady was asked what she thought of her son's apartment, her only reply was that she felt as if she were suffocating within the stucco building.

[13] Actually, more trips were made if one takes account of the fact that men working as cyclo drivers in Phnom Penh return home periodically to bring money to their families. But I counted only a man's initial journey to the city to obtain the job, not any subsequent trips he made back and forth between Svay and Phnom Penh during the course of employment.

[14] This age limit excludes young children who accompany their parents on trips, but does include adolescents who might go by themselves.

[15] Actually, in recent years only two former residents of West Svay have attained markedly superior socioeconomic status: House 20 has a son who is a protocol official at the Royal Palace, and House 27 has a son who is a medical technician. Others from the hamlet hold (or are married to men who have) occupations, such as busboy at a hotel, soldier, or mechanic, that are less elevated.

occupations for as long as a year or more).[16] Such urban employment has significance beyond the earning of income, for the men have diverse experiences in Phnom Penh (such as contact with other ethnic groups, freedom to do things that they might not or could not do in the village, exposure to both the hazards and pleasures of urban living) that broaden their horizons regardless of whether they like or dislike the city in the final analysis. These men can also be sources of information for other villagers, whether it be specific news of political or other activity, or simply reports of urban life, that are brought back to the countryside. (c) The remainder (approximately one-third) of the trips to Phnom Penh were made for diverse reasons. (i) Five journeys were shopping expeditions because the city carries a greater variety of items for cheaper prices than in Kompong Tuol, as well as stocking certain goods that are not locally available. (ii) Six households attended the Water Festival (*Omtuk*), an annual event in which hundreds of colorful boats engage in numerous races on the Tonle Sap River (for details, see Porée-Maspero et al. 1950, 62–64; Steinberg 1959, 26, 283). This festival falls sometime in November during a lull before the rice harvest and thus presents an opportunity for villagers to visit the city and have fun. But most West Svay families are prevented from attending because of lack of money. (iii) Elders from two households attended a sermon given by the highest ranking monk in the Mohanikay order at one of the major temples in the city. (iv) Finally, one household sent two children to receive schooling in Phnom Penh.[17]

Villagers not only go to the city but are visited by urbanites who, in virtually all instances, are close kinsmen (and sometimes friends of the latter who come along for an excursion to the countryside). During a nine-month period, individuals from Phnom Penh paid approximately twenty visits to seven households in the hamlet.[18] Most of these visits are made for sheer pleasure and conviviality (former residents come to see parents and siblings, or their urban-born children come for extended stays with grandparents or aunts and uncles). City dwellers may also come to celebrate Buddhist holidays at the local temples (especially New Year and *Pchum*, which are traditional times for family reunions), to attend life-cycle ceremonies, to recuperate from illness in the quiet countryside, or sometimes to lend a hand for transplanting and harvest.[19] (Occasionally, too, traveling merchants [e.g., the pig dealers] may come from Phnom Penh.)

A question raised and briefly considered in chapter 1 was whether the proximity of Phnom Penh has made Svay more "urbanized" than most Khmer villages. Although definite answers cannot be given because of lack of necessary data on other communities, the question of "urbanization" (used here in the broad sense of the city's impact on the countryside) will be discussed at further length here.

If urbanization means migration from rural areas to urban centers, this has been and is occurring within the country as a whole; the population of Phnom Penh has

---

[16] As noted in chapter 4, some West Svay men have had extended employment in the city as a gold artisan, clerk in the railroad station, printer, worker on an experimental farm station, hospital attendant, and ice vendor.

[17] Occasionally, it may also be necessary for a villager to travel to the city because of a legal or administrative matter that has been referred to ministries or courts in Phnom Penh.

[18] In many instances, the same relative(s) paid several visits to one household, but some families in West Svay were hosts to different kinsmen at various times.

[19] Friedl (1959) describes similar visits between urban and rural kinsmen in Greece.

expanded considerably in recent years.[20] West Svay, however, has contributed little to the city's growth. Within the past thirty years, only seven persons born in West Svay have emigrated permanently to Phnom Penh (others leaving the hamlet have moved to other villages). However, as noted in previous sections, a number of villagers have lived and worked in Phnom Penh for varying lengths of time, and the advent of the bus connections between Kompong Tuol and the city has enabled more villagers to make more frequent brief visits to Phnom Penh.

As a corollary to the above, urbanization may imply the abandonment of agricultural for other occupations. Thus far, of course, cultivation remains the basic subsistence activity of most West Svay villagers, and three-quarters of the emigrants from the hamlet within the past few decades have continued to be farmers in other villages. However, it is significant that temporary urban employment has become a major means of earning extra income (supplanting traditional rural pursuits such as making palm sugar), and that many of the younger generation aspire to attain (or marry someone who holds) an urban occupation. Probably most of these young people will continue to be rural peasants, but the expansion of education and heightened motivations may, in the future, enable an increasing number of village children to obtain blue-collar or white-collar positions. Even among the older generation, one-quarter of the emigrants from West Svay were able to assume (or marry someone who had) one of a variety of non-agricultural occupations such as coolie, soldier, mechanic, tractor driver, busboy, merchant, bus driver, medical technician, and minor government official.

If urbanization involves use of goods that are manufactured or imported rather than made at the local level, the material culture inventory of the villager is coming to include more and more of the former. Certainly these products are desired by most villagers. But the fundamental poverty of most West Svay residents limits purchases to essential necessities, and many items of daily use are still fabricated at home.

Urbanization may mean the acceptance of the ideology and attitudes of the urban elite and intelligentsia. Actually, of course, the latter have affected the village since the time of the ancient kingdoms, especially with regard to the interaction of great and little religious traditions. At the present time, the outlook and values of urbanites penetrate the village in two major respects (both of which have been discussed in previous sections or chapters). First, the central government firmly molds the peasants' understanding of and attitudes toward political affairs. Second, many villagers (especially the young) have come increasingly to feel that non-agricultural occupations and urban styles of living are more desirable than the life of the rural cultivator. With regard to the latter, however, it must be strongly emphasized that there are still many other villagers who maintain a profound attachment to the land and countryside, negative attitudes toward the city and its way of life, and a basic provincialism. (Indeed, even those with strong desires to escape the village are often ambivalent about rejecting rural life altogether.)

---

[20] Phnom Penh's population increased more than fivefold from 1948 to 1956 (see Ministère du Plan 1958, 9), due partly to natural expansion of population and partly to immigrants from both rural areas and other countries. Apart from the growth of Phnom Penh itself, however, Cambodia has not experienced urbanization in the sense of the development of other comparable urban centers. The provincial capitals continue to be more like large towns rather than real cities.

In general, I would guess that Svay is not markedly less "rural" than many other Khmer villages. While its residents have more opportunity for direct contacts with the city than do people in more remote regions, they cannot or will not completely adopt urban styles of life and attitudes because of lack of money and certain deeply rooted peasant values. And if the city has had certain kinds of impact on Svay (as discussed above), I suspect that it has the same influence on numerous other villages throughout Cambodia.

## KNOWLEDGE OF THE LARGER WORLD AND
## ATTITUDES TOWARD OTHER GROUPS

While the various provinces and major cities or towns in Cambodia are well known to the villager (by name if not direct experience), the world beyond Cambodia's borders is largely terra incognita. The country's immediate neighbors—Thailand (*srok siùm*), Laos (*srok liu*), and Vietnam (*srok yuên*)—are the only nations whose exact locations are known and whose names are recognized in some meaningful fashion. (Sometimes villagers even have acquaintances who have actually been to Bangkok [*bùngkòk*] or Saigon [*prengko*].) But mention of other Southeast Asian nations, such as Malaya (*srok malayu*), Burma (*srok pomiê*), and Indonesia (*srok Endonesi*), is likely to provoke a mystified look from all but the more well-educated persons. The rest of the world floats in a nebulous haze somewhere "out there." Villagers realize that certain countries exist because they have heard of them for one reason or another, or perhaps even come into contact with persons of these nationalities. For example, France (*srok peang*) is obviously recognized because of its former colonial rule; China (*srok chEn*) is known as the homeland of resident Chinese (and because of Sihanouk's political relations with Communist China); Japan (*srok cipun*) is recognized because of the Japanese occupation of Cambodia during World War II; India (*srok klùng*) is known because of the popularity of Indian movies; and America (*srok amêrik*) became familiar thanks to my presence. But most people are almost totally ignorant of the locations of these nations and the nature of their cultures. This is not to say, however, that the villagers are uninterested in the rest of the world. On the contrary, there is tremendous curiosity about other people and places: a map on my wall provoked constant attention and perusal, and at least once a week I was asked in what direction a particular country lay,[21] how long it took to get there, and whether or not rice was grown there.

---

[21] In traditional Hindu cosmology that influenced early Khmer culture, the world is considered to be flat (see Heine-Geldern 1956). I am not certain whether the villagers, especially the older ones, fully believed that the world is round. One of the most frequent questions asked of me was: "In what direction do you go to get to America?" (Cambodians orient themselves spatially mainly by the four cardinal directions.) This query always perplexed me because one can go either east or west from Cambodia to reach America, which reply always invoked a polite but mystified sound from the questioner. I would then take an orange or some other sphere to demonstrate my answer, but I am not certain that the villagers were convinced by my explanations. Villagers were also greatly surprised at the size of the world when told how long it would take to fly to various countries. It should be noted, however, that there were two highly intelligent and well-informed monks at Wat Samnang who had extensive knowledge of geography (one even knew the names of major American cities); and a number of Khmer officials and intelligentsia in Phnom Penh have actually lived in France, the United States, or other Western countries while obtaining higher education. Furthermore, the present school-age generation of villagers does receive instruction in geography at school.

Since villagers are generally suspicious of strangers of even their own ethnic group (although at the same time they feel loyalty and patriotism toward their nation as a whole), it is not surprising that their attitudes toward individuals of other ethnic groups are usually negative or ambivalent.

West Svay residents have frequent contacts with the Chinese in Kompong Tuol and, by and large, view them with neither special affection nor extreme distaste. The nature of actual interaction between the two depends to some extent on individual cases: for example, many of the Chinese merchants both treat and are treated by the villagers with cordiality and courtesy; some of the Chinese vendors are often teased or spoken to peremptorily; and the Chinese who operate the small shop across the road are viewed slightly negatively as a convenient source of goods but one that the villagers would just as soon not patronize. In general the Khmer and the Chinese deal with one another in a rather formal manner, and social distance is maintained between the two groups. There are, however, two persons in the hamlet (and others in the rest of Svay or in neighboring communities) who are perhaps one-eighth or one-sixteenth Chinese. Villagers would rarely marry or accept a full-blooded Chinese into their midst because of the strong cultural differences, but such Sino-Cambodians are not regarded askance because they are thoroughly Khmer in culture and usually appearance as well.[22]

By contrast, the Vietnamese (*yuên*) are categorically, unconditionally, and actively detested.[23] They are considered to be mean, depraved, violent, and altogether disreputable, and several villagers will tell stories of unfortunate encounters with Vietnamese thieves, attackers, and immoral women in the city. This unfavorable attitude is encouraged and reinforced by the national government, which speaks of the Vietnamese as encroachers on Khmer territory and conspirators against the kingdom.

The Cham-Malay minority (*cham, cham arab*) are represented in the Svay area by two cattle butchers (one in Kompong Tuol and another in a town several kilometers away). The villagers are conscious of the physical similarity but cultural differences between Khmer and Cham in dress, religion, and other customs. And while Chams are treated amiably enough in face-to-face encounters, the Khmer villager feels a deep-seated repugnance toward persons who slaughter animals as an occupation.

---

[22] Cf. Steinberg 1959, 44–47 who states that "Chinese are eagerly sought as marriage partners" because of their "reputation for industry and financial shrewdness," the Khmer "preference for light skin," and "the belief that such inter-marriage strengthens the Cambodian ethnic stock." Such atti-tudes were not evident in Svay. But in the country as a whole there has been a good deal of Chinese–Cambodian intermarriage for many centuries, especially in the cities and among Khmer in government or business (although Steinberg also notes that marriages between full-blooded Chinese and full-blooded Khmer are evidently decreasing in recent years) (see also Delvert 1961, 25). As noted in chapter 2, Sino-Cambodians assume either Chinese or Khmer cultural identities and are not a group set apart (such as Eurasians tend to be). Cf. also an interesting legal statute dated 1875 that states that it is a "crime against religion" to offer one's daughter in marriage to a wealthy foreigner for mercenary reasons, and "penalties are made to prevent people from abandoning their religion to follow another" (Leclère 1898 2:265).

[23] It is interesting that Khmer refer or speak to Chinese using any of several terms of neu-tral emotional content. But Vietnamese are frequently referred to by insulting designations (e.g., *asükøy*, which can be roughly translated as "one with gills"), and Khmer try to avoid any terms of address in speaking directly to them (Dale Purtle, linguist at the American Embassy in Phnom Penh, pers. comm.).

The French (*barang, peang*), and by extension all Caucasian Westerners who are usually lumped with them, are viewed with both respect and wariness. Villagers do not often come into direct contact with such Europeans or Americans, but if such an encounter should occur, the villager generally assumes a subservient posture while feeling, at the same time, curiosity, wariness, and great reserve.[24] There are, too, negative or derisive accounts of Westerners: for example, the story of a Frenchman who deserted a Khmer woman and two of his children in the neighboring village of Ta Chas; or an amusing tale told by a prostitute visiting from Kompong Tuol of the unusual size and color of an American client's sex organ.

Several villagers came into contact with Japanese (*cipun*) during World War II and regarded them in a favorable or neutral light. The Japanese occupation barely affected the countryside, and no ill feelings were generated toward the Japanese.

Thai and Laotians are thought to be "of the same flesh" (i.e., physically similar to) the Khmer. But Thailand is considered to be a traditional and noxious enemy of Cambodia, and Sok (House 26), who once worked with some Thais, relates several stories about the latter's brutishness and lack of propriety. (There are no special feelings about Laos and Laotians.)

Indians (*klŭng*) are not known to villagers personally but only from movies and occasional glimpses of Indian residents of Phnom Penh. Thanks to the cinema in which India appears to be an exotic land of adventure and romance, Indians are greatly admired.[25] (Adolescent village girls in particular are completely enamored of them and attempt to imitate Indian dress when posing for portraits at the photographers' studios in Kompong Tuol.)

Only one man in West Svay has actually seen any tribal people, who are known collectively as *phnong*. The rest of the villagers know of the latter only by hearsay and consider the tribal groups to be uncivilized people with strange customs who live in the wilds of eastern Cambodia.

In conclusion, then, West Svay villagers have relatively frequent contacts with various communities outside their own village, some interaction with other ethnic groups, and at least minimal awareness of the world beyond their own nation. But although the village is not socially, politically, or economically isolated, the outlook of its inhabitants is fundamentally insular and parochial.[26] The villagers feel most secure with their own community, and when they venture beyond its boundaries the majority of their trips are visits to kinsmen, while most of their other journeys are impelled by some necessity such as seeking temporary employment. And their attitude toward persons who are not kinsmen or acquaintances—even though the latter are fellow Khmer (and even fellow peasants)—is generally one of wariness, distrust, or downright dislike. On a larger scale, such feelings are also manifest toward other ethnic

---

[24] The respectful demeanor that Khmer often assume in the presence of Westerners probably accounts for the impressions of many French writers that Khmer are docile, quiet, and shy. They can indeed be so, but there is also a good deal of exuberant, noisy, aggressive behavior when villagers interact with one another.

[25] For another discussion of general Khmer attitudes toward India and other countries, see Steinberg 1959, 286–88. Contrary to Steinberg, however, Svay villagers are not cognizant of Hindu influence on Khmer culture; nor do they feel that China is "part of the family." (See also Smith 1965 for the government's political attitudes toward various nations.)

[26] Such an outlook is typical, of course, not only of peasants in general (Wolf 1966, 47), but of tribal and other cultures.

groups and nations. Other Khmer may be viewed with apprehension in some respects, but the character and behavior of Khmer in general are considered to be unquestionably better than that of most other ethnic groups. Moreover, the villagers feel patriotism and loyalty toward the nation as a whole, reinforced by the government's presentation of Cambodia as a country attempting to maintain its territorial integrity, political independence, and cultural identity in the face of other political powers.

# CHAPTER NINE

# CONCLUSION

Having presented a general overview of life in a Khmer village, in this final chapter we go beyond its boundaries to two larger concerns. The first problem is the nature of Southeast Asian cultures and a comparison of the Khmer with other groups in this region (particularly the mainland). The second is a consideration of Khmer village life as an example of a social type that has become commonly known as peasantry.

## SOUTHEAST ASIAN CULTURES

There have been some attempts to delineate those qualities that are particularly distinctive of Southeast Asian cultures and distinguish this area from other parts of the world. One of the earliest characterizations was proposed by Elizabeth Bacon (1946) in her courageous effort to formulate culture areas for Asia. In the region with which we are concerned, she differentiated the "Southeast Asian primitive nomadic" hunting and gathering groups from the "Southeast Asian-Indonesian" culture area, which included mainland Southeast Asia, Indonesia, and the Philippines. For the latter, the following basic features were abstracted from what she realizes to be a quilt of various cultures whose diversity was encouraged by broken topography, ecological adjustments to differing environments, etc. (1) Subsistence is based upon agriculture: wet-rice cultivation wherever irrigation is possible, and shifting agriculture in the highlands. Rice is the main crop, though in some regions it is being displaced by maize. (2) Pigs and chickens are the main food animals (except among Islamic groups that prohibit pork), and fish provides a staple part of the diet. Water buffalo are major draft animals, though milk products are never used. (3) Houses are constructed of mud or stone with thatch roofing in the highlands, and of bamboo and thatch, often set on piles, in the rest of the area. The balance pole is a common means of transporting goods. Coastal people have also developed skilled techniques of navigation. (4) Politically, the forms of central government show the influence of concepts from other high civilizations, for example, the notion of kingship that was brought from India or that of bureaucracy from China. But the village remains the basic sociopolitical unit, and among the peasantry is found a "democratic communalism" with village chiefs whose position is often inherited but must be confirmed by vote and whose authority is checked by a council of elders. (5) The traditional, indigenous religious system is strongly animistic and has an ancestor cult, as well as "marked preoccupation" with the dead (propitiation of spirits, care of the dead, etc.). Shamanism is frequent. In many areas, however, this folk religion was subject to impact from and merging with several high religions: Hinduism, Buddhism, and Islam.[1]

---

[1] See also Burling (1965a, 2–4) who suggests these common features for Southeast Asia: (1) women hold positions of respect and freedom; (2) families are small and relatively autonomous, and large kin groups are not very common; (3) belief in a variety of malignant spirits;

Bacon's formulation is problematical in several respects, as was pointed out by Kroeber (1947) among others. Among the various criticisms of her scheme, one point is particularly important. What Bacon did in part of her analysis, namely the segregation of the "primitive nomadic" cultures from the agricultural groups, was actually to delineate culture types within a geographic area.[2] To be wholly consistent with this line of thought, she could or should have separated the tribal groups and the state-organized sedentary agriculturalists that she put together in one "culture area." Bacon does, in fact, implicitly recognize the distinction between the two when she notes that the "uplands" and lowlands sometimes have different features, and that influences from the civilizations of India and China affected some groups.

On the one hand, there is justification in asking what both the tribal peoples and lowlanders of Southeast Asia have in common.[3] For the tribal groups can be said to offer clues to, if not an exact representation of, the pre-Indianized-Sinicized culture[4] that has shown sturdy viability in many of its features despite the formidable impact of and modifications wrought by contacts with India and China. While the importance of these influences cannot be underestimated (see below), it must also be recalled, first, that the Southeast Asian cultures were selective in what they adopted from the high civilizations and, second, that the populace at large was less profoundly affected than the ruling stratum. Thus, the lowland groups continue to share a number of features with the tribal uplanders: for example, reliance on agriculture with rice as a major crop; buffalo, pigs, and chickens as domestic animals; similarity of house types and other items of material culture; animistic beliefs; etc.

On the other hand, however, it is also meaningful to distinguish between the tribal groups of the highlands and the dominant cultures of the lowlands as two different culture types. For the two do have distinctive characteristics, not only in terms of Steward's criteria for delimiting culture types—differing "cultural-ecological adaptations" and "levels of socio-cultural integration" (1955, 89)—but in sociopolitical organization as well.[5] The tribal peoples of Southeast Asia—though they show diversity among themselves with regard to details of economy organization, kinship systems, religious

---

(4) rice as a staple food; (5) rectangular houses of bamboo or thatch, usually on piles; (6) iron tools and frequent use of bamboo for items of material culture; (7) the widespread custom of "roasting" the mother after childbirth. See also Fisher 1964, 69–78 and Embree 1950, 182 who cite some of the same features given by Bacon or Burling.

[2] For a discussion of culture types as contrasted to culture areas, see Steward 1955, chap. 5. As he notes, a culture area is "essentially a geographical delimitation of peoples sharing certain features," while a culture type abstracts features that "first, are determined by cross-cultural regularities of cultural ecological adaptation and second represent a similar level of socio-cultural integration" (82,89). Kroeber (1947, 329) also notes that "'culture areas' are of course not areas at all but kinds of cultures which are areally limited."

[3] Kroeber in his critique of Bacon says, "actually there is enough solid and clear-cut basis for a farther India-East India culture area," with the diversity due not so much to "intrinsic variation but . . . to survival of the old general culture only in spots between the invasion and spread of literate cultures" (1947, 323).

[4] For reconstructions of this culture, see Linton 1955, 174 and Coedès 1953, 370–71; a summary is also given in chapter 2 of this dissertation.

[5] On different kinds of sociopolitical organization, see, e.g., Linton 1936, 231–52; Lowie 1948, chap. 14; Service 1962, chaps. 4, 5. These different authors have somewhat varying classifications of types of sociopolitical organization, but the general outline of their schemes are in basic agreement.

beliefs, degree of acculturation to the larger society, etc.—usually rely on shifting cultivation, reside in relatively autonomous villages that are the primary sociopolitical units, possess unilineal kinship systems with important kin groupings beyond the family, have egalitarian social structures with only limited specialization and hierarchical ranking, and have limited or no political organization beyond the community.[6] This last feature implies a further critical difference from the peoples of the lowlands: although the tribal groups came under the nominal suzerainty of some kingdom or empire, most of them were never wholly integrated into a state organization. Though they often had (or have) various kinds of relations with the lowlanders (trade, labor, even intermarriage), the tribal peoples remained relatively isolated from the central government and the Indian- or Chinese-influenced civilizations that developed in the plains and on the coasts. In these latter regions, by contrast, the lowland peoples were brought to a new level of sociocultural integration. The Burmese, Thai, Lao, Khmer, Vietnamese, Malays, and various Indonesian groups evolved state forms of political organization with centralized, monarchical governments that often ruled extensive territories and populations. Corollary development of other features included clear-cut social stratification, specialization of occupations or professions, wet-rice cultivation enabling increased production and surplus, the religious-philosophical-social systems of Hinduism, Buddhism, and Islam, codification of law, etc. (see chapter 2).[7]

Because of these significant contrasts between the tribal groups and the cultures of the lowlands, it seems appropriate to compare the Khmer to those who represent the same level of sociocultural integration. At the present time, the dominant ethnic groups of Cambodia, Burma, Thailand, Laos, Vietnam, Malaysia, parts of Indonesia (especially Java), and the Philippines bear many resemblances to one another. In gross terms, the Khmer are most similar to the Burmese, Laotians, and particularly the Thai, all of whom share the same Indian tradition, Buddhism, and numerous other traits. The Malays and certain Indonesians, although they too were "Hinduized," diverge somewhat because of their eventual adoption of Islam. The Vietnamese, however, stand apart because of their Chinese heritage (as do the Filipinos who were rather isolated from both Indian and Chinese influences and underwent a seemingly more profound Westernization than did the other countries).[8]

In brief summary, the Khmer peasantry share the following features with the aforementioned Southeast Asian groups.[9] Significant exceptions to the general patterns will be noted.

---

[6] There are exceptions to the preceding characterization. Some tribal peoples are bilateral. Further, a number of groups (such as the Kachin, Chin, Karen, Meo, Palaung) may practice wet-rice cultivation when possible; have supra-village political organization that might, in some instances, be called semi-feudal petty states; and may have distinctions between nobles, commoners, and slaves (see, e.g., LeBar, Hickey, Musgrave 1964, 52, 62, 64, 74, 110, 125, 188; Leach 1954). In Service's terms (1962, chap. 5) such societies are a type designated as "chiefdoms" intermediate between tribe and state forms of sociopolitical organization.

[7] Such developments are, of course, similar to those that occurred in the rise of other early civilizations; see, for example, Steward 1955, chap. 11; Service 1962, 171–77.

[8] Many discussions of Southeast Asia include also Borneo and the Philippines that I shall omit purely for reasons of limited energy. It is important to note, however, that various of the Bornean groups (e.g., the Dayak) and both lowland and upland Philippine groups have some marked resemblances to other Southeast Asian cultures.

[9] The following sources were consulted for comparative data. General works on Southeast Asia: LeBar, Hickey, Musgrave 1964; Condominas 1953; Burling 1965a; Murdock 1960b; Ward

(1) Settlement patterns. Urbanization in Southeast Asia is still limited. Any one country usually has only one or two large, relatively cosmopolitan centers although there are often a number of provincial or market towns. The bulk of the population lives in villages that may be of linear, nucleated, or sometimes dispersed habitation. The size of these communities varies from less than a hundred inhabitants (e.g., in Laos) to many thousands (e.g., in Vietnam), depending on regional distribution of population densities according to ecological resources. The norm probably ranges from about four hundred to eight hundred residents per village. In larger communities, division into hamlets is common. Interspersed with gardens and trees are houses of rectangular form, constructed commonly of wood, bamboo, and/or thatch, and raised on piles (except Vietnam and parts of Java). The village frequently has some sort of religious center, whether it be a Buddhist *wat*, Islamic mosque, Vietnamese *dinh* temple, or Christian church.

(2) Economic organization. The economies of Southeast Asian nations as a whole are examples of what are often called "dual" economies, divided between an agricultural sector and a usually weakly developed entrepreneurial and industrial sector (with the latter usually operated mainly by non-indigenes such as Chinese and Indians). Agriculture is by far the dominant occupation for most of the population of Southeast Asia, with the bulk of the land given over to cultivation of wet rice (although dry rice is grown in some regions of all the countries). The techniques of rice agriculture are basically the same everywhere (initial plowing, seeding of nursery beds, transplanting, etc.), although certain details may vary (e.g., type of plow, varieties of rice sown, amount and kind of fertilization, reliance on rainfall or irrigation systems, flat paddies or terraces, etc.). Labor is supplied primarily by the family or household group, with either cooperative exchange or hired labor during the busy seasons. There is variation as to whether one or more crops are produced annually, and whether the rice is mainly for consumption or for the market. It seems that, in general, the majority of villagers in every country grow rice primarily for household consumption, with significant surpluses for the market produced only in certain regions (e.g., lower Burma, the Thai delta, some provinces in Cambodia) (see Dobby 1960, 349–50 and passim). In addition to rice (and kitchen gardens and fruit trees that provide supplements to the family diet), maize may be grown as a secondary crop to augment food resources; in some regions the latter may become a major crop. Some regions may concentrate on fruit and vegetable cultivation (e.g., the dry zone of upper Burma, the riverbanks of Cambodia) and/or cash crops of various sorts (e.g., tobacco, cotton, rubber), either as the main means of livelihood or as a secondary activity.

Fish in various forms is a staple of Southeast Asian diets, and fishing may, in fact, become the dominant occupation of riverine or coastal villages. More usually, however, villagers everywhere use a wide variety of techniques to catch fish from any available water source for family consumption.

---

1963; Hart, Rajadhon, and Coughlin 1965; Dobby 1960. Specific works on particular cultures: Burma—Brant 1954; Shway Yoe 1963; Khiang 1963; Nash 1965; Thailand—Sharp et al. 1953; DeYoung 1955; Kaufman 1960; Rajadhon 1961; R. Benedict 1952; Laos—Kaufman 1961; Ayabe 1961; LeBar and Suddard 1960; Halpern 1964a, 1964b; Vietnam—Gourou 1955; Condominas 1956; Hickey 1964; Malaya—Firth 1946; Ginsburg and Roberts 1957; Djamour 1959; Fraser 1960; Swift 1965; Indonesia—Kattenburg 1952; Koentjaraningrat 1957; Skinner 1959; H. Geertz 1961, 1963; C. Geertz 1963a, 1963b.

Ubiquitous domestic animals in Southeast Asia are the water buffalo or oxen (used for draft labor), chickens and/or ducks, and pigs (except among Islamic groups that often keep sheep or goats instead).

Crafts of various kinds—basketry, matting, pottery, metal work, weaving, etc.—are still widespread despite increasing reliance on manufactured goods. These crafts are pursued often on a part-time basis by cultivators or by a few full-time specialists within a village. Sometimes, however, whole villages may specialize in a particular craft.

Apart from traditional economic pursuits, those with limited resources may seek temporary employment as wage laborers: for example, hired agricultural workers for other peasants, menial laborers in cities, towns, or on plantations. In addition, some may turn to other income-producing activities such as selling cooked foods, renting out equipment, etc.

The Southeast Asian peasant is often involved in credit and debt arrangements because of the generally small landholdings, the often unpredictable and limited yields from cultivation, and the necessity for cash outlays, whether small (for food and other necessities) or large (e.g., for life-cycle ceremonies). The creditors are commonly Chinese, who are ubiquitous shopkeepers, brokers, and merchants throughout Southeast Asia, but fellow countrymen (e.g., wealthy kinsmen, landlords, or native merchants) may also be sources of credit or loans. Also, in some regions (e.g., Vietnam), mutual aid and loan societies are found among villagers. The extent of peasant debt can vary, however, from region to region (or even from household to household) within the same country.

With respect to property, individual ownership of land and other items by both men and women is usual in Southeast Asia (with some exceptions noted below), though a married couple (or sometimes siblings) may sometimes jointly hold property. Among groups where such individual ownership obtains, inheritance is usually, in theory, divided equally among the children.[10] But in practice, it often happens that a certain child (or children) may be favored according to particular circumstances; for example, a child who remains at home after marriage to care for aged parents will receive the most. This notion of equal inheritance has led to extreme parcelization of land in many areas. But a problem of another sort, common in the southern parts of Burma, Thailand, and Vietnam, is that certain individuals have amassed large tracts of land, and much of the population is reduced to tenant farming for either resident or absentee landlords.

Exceptions to individual ownership and equal inheritance are found in Vietnam, Java, and Negri Sembilan-Minangkabau. (a) In Vietnamese villages there are communal lands, cult lands, and lands collectively held by a patrilineage (or segment thereof), as well as individually owned lands. Patrilineal inheritance (with either ultimo- or primogeniture) is traditional, but women also inherit in South Vietnam.[11] (b) Among the matrilineal Malays of Negri Sembilan and the Minangkabau, title to rice land and houses is normally vested in women and inheritance passes to daughters. Rubber

---

[10] In cases where there are no children, the order of inheritance by other lineal or collateral relatives varies in different cultures. Also, the surviving spouse may or may not have rights of inheritance from the deceased.

[11] The Vietnamese patterns of land tenure and inheritance are complicated by both land-reform schemes and changing systems in both North and South Vietnam. For details, see Hickey 1964, 42–44, 132–33; LeBar, Hickey, Musgrave 1964, 165.

land, however, is held by males. (c) Java and Bali also have some communal village land that is parceled out to individuals for usufruct, in addition to private property holdings that are divided among offspring.

(3) Kinship and social organization. Except for some unilineal groups that will be discussed below, bilateral kinship systems are usual in Southeast Asia. Marriage is based either on free choice or parental selection; rules or preferences for community exogamy or endogamy vary in different groups. Polygyny is legal in all the societies, but monogamy prevails among most of the population. (Divorce is relatively easy to obtain and is very common in some groups.) After marriage, neolocality is often the preferred pattern or ideal, but this frequently occurs after an initial period of either uxorilocal or, less commonly, virilocal residence. Permanent uxorilocality or virilocality is also found, particularly because of the widespread pattern of one child (usually the youngest and often a daughter) remaining home after marriage to care for the parents. Associated with such residence patterns, the nuclear family is generally both an ideal and a statistical norm. But it is also exceedingly common to find stem families and households composed of a nuclear family plus some other relative(s), such as a spouse's sibling, grandparents, etc. Beyond the family there are no larger kin groups except what might be termed a personal kindred that is loosely defined and segments of which assemble on an ad hoc basis for life-cycle ceremonies, cooperative labor, etc. There are usually no firm prescriptions governing interaction with kinsmen, and the individual has considerable latitude to decide how intimate he will be with particular relatives on the basis of his personal feelings or motives. The kin terminological systems show some variation in details, but some common points are present in all: first ascending generation either lineal or bifurcate collateral; cousin terminology either Eskimo or Hawaiian; and distinctions of relative age not only for siblings, but often parents' siblings and cousins as well.

Unilineality is found among the patrilineal Vietnamese, matrilineal Negri Sembilan of Malaya and Minangkabau, and some Indonesian groups (e.g., the patrilineal Toba Bataks). Even in South Vietnam and Negri Sembilan, nuclear families are a common residence unit despite traditions of virilocality or uxorilocality. But the larger kin grouping, whether lineage or clan, may have important functions in owning property, governing the actions of its members, holding ceremonies, etc. The unilineal principle may also be important for inheritance of property.

The more general social organization of the Southeast Asian village is, by and large, egalitarian in nature. Although variations in wealth may be recognized and manifest in style of living, there are generally no clearly defined social classes within the village itself. In some areas (e.g., Vietnam) a wealthy individual may have easier access to formal or informal authority, but other features such as age or religiosity are usually equally or more important in gaining respect and prestige. Egalitarianism is manifest also in the position of women; though subordinate to the male in civil law and religious ideologies, the female is generally granted considerable freedom, responsibility, and voice both within and outside the home.

Non-kin neighbors and friends are likely to be as important as relatives in the formation of friendship cliques, providing aid for family ceremonies, cooperative labor exchanges, etc. But indigenous non-kinship associations tend to be relatively rare in Southeast Asian villages, except in recent years in some areas where the government, political parties, or religion may have organized various clubs and other groups.

All villagers feel a certain identification with and loyalty to their community as one sort of in-group and have strong bonds of kinship or friendship with fellow residents, as well as attachment to the land when they own their own fields. But the degree and nature of village solidarity, as well as the extent of communal activities, seems to vary.[12] On the one hand there are, for example, Javanese villages that Wolf (1957) characterizes as "closed" communities with strong group feeling, resistance to both outsiders and outside influences, community jurisdiction over free disposal of land, relative self-sufficiency, etc. Villages in other regions that have communal land (e.g., Vietnam) or, for example, irrigation systems that demand maintenance by the entire village also show a strong sense of community. But in Cambodia, and probably in Burma, Thailand, and Laos as well, there are no firm rules that dictate or clearly define village solidarity. The village as a whole may cooperate in certain endeavors (e.g., public works, sponsoring community festivals, etc.), but these may be relatively infrequent or minor activities.

Within the larger social structure of the nation as a whole, the rural population constitutes a strata subordinate to the upper levels of aristocracy or high government officials, businessmen and merchants, white-collar workers, etc. The exact nature of the overall system of stratification, and its relative rigidity or looseness, varies in different countries (e.g., Burma is said to have a flexible national social structure, while the Javanese and Balinese appear to have a relatively rigid one). But the possibility of upward mobility within the larger society seems to be present in all nations. The expansion of public education throughout Southeast Asia undoubtedly gives the villager a greater chance to attain non-agricultural occupations or professions than in the past, but it is still probable that only a small proportion of the peasantry are actually able to rise to higher socioeconomic statuses.

(4) Religion. All of the lowland cultures of Southeast Asia espouse a high religion that was imported from without: Theravada Buddhism among the Burmese, Thai, Khmer, and Laotians; Islam among the Malays and most Indonesians; a combination of Mahayana Buddhism, Confucianism, and Taoism among most Vietnamese; and some form of Christianity among some Vietnamese, Filipinos, and a few Indonesian groups such as the Toba Batak.[13] All of these religions, of course, involve a complex system of ideology, prescribed behavior, holidays and other rituals, priests or officiants, religious buildings, etc. Villagers are generally ardent believers and participants in their respective religions that may permeate other cultural institutions in various ways.

But in addition to the high religions, villagers (and often urbanites as well) maintain beliefs and practices of indigenous, traditional religious systems. These usually center around animistic spirits (e.g., the *nats* of Burma, the *phi* of Thailand and Laos, the *neak taa* of Cambodia, the *hantu* of Malaya) and a variety of other supernatural creatures such as ancestral spirits, ghosts, demons, etc. To deal with such beings, who are frequently conceived of as malicious and harmful if not properly propitiated and respected, there are various sorts of specialists (curers, exorcists, mediums, etc.), ceremonies, offerings, charms, formulae, etc. Whether or not such folk religions are condoned by the priests or officiants of the high religions, the villager has a firm belief in the existence of the various supernatural beings and the efficacy of essentially magical practices.

---

[12] It is not always easy to abstract this dimension of village life from available monographs.

[13] Vietnam also has other religious systems of indigenous origin in the Cao Dai and Hoa Hao sects. Both are considered to be reform Buddhist movements, but the Cao Dai has syncretistic elements from a variety of other religions as well (see Hickey 1964, 55, 290–94).

(5) Political organization. The formal political organization of the Southeast Asian village is everywhere incorporated into the hierarchy of the national government (which may take the form of a constitutional monarchy or a republic). The village chief is usually elected (although in some instances this may be only a nominal ratification of what is actually appointment by a higher official or the previous holder of the office, or hereditary succession). He is assigned certain duties of greater or less significance and has at least a modicum of official power, but in practice his effective authority may or may not be great depending, it would seem, on the qualities of the man himself. The chief is usually assisted by some lesser officials or a council of some sort (e.g., household heads, hamlet chiefs, elders, etc.).

The national government impinges on the villagers in different ways in different countries. Everywhere, of course, the villager must pay taxes and accept statutes imposed from above. In turn, he may also have received some real benefits such as expanded education, medical facilities, agricultural improvement programs, etc.; he may also be able to express some minimal voice in government by voting for national offices or joining a political party. (With respect to the latter, however, political parties and interest in national politics are evident at the local level in some areas [e.g., Burma and Java], but villagers in other regions [e.g., Thailand and Cambodia) are generally ignorant of or uninterested in the national political scene.) In general, the villager is essentially a passive agent who is acted on from above rather than agitating from below; moreover, although overt deference is usually given to the government officials who occupy superior social positions, the central government as an institution is often viewed with resignation, indifference, or even hostility.[14]

In addition to formal political organization, villages have informal means of social control and often unofficial leaders as well. Traditional methods of control such as gossip, shaming, and ostracism can effectively maintain proper conduct, although the loose structure of many Southeast Asian cultures permits considerable variation in behavior short of infringement of serious norms. (Where unilineal kin groups exist, these may also exert special control over their members.) Informal leaders are also frequently found where official chiefs are weak. Such a leader may acquire authority through age, wealth, strong personality, or other qualities, and can exercise significant control over both communal and individual affairs. Sometimes, too, religious personnel, such as Buddhist monks or the Muslim imam, may become figures of authority and advice in secular matters.

(6) Life cycle. In Southeast Asia, as in all societies, major events in the life cycle are marked by ritual observances of greater or lesser magnitude. For this region, the main *rites de passage* are the following. (a) After the birth of a child, a virtually universal custom Southeast Asians practice is that of "roasting" or keeping the mother near or over a source of heat for a period of time. Some sort of ceremony for the newborn is also held. (b) During childhood or adolescence, different groups have diverse ceremonies at various times of life. The Thai, Laotians, and Khmer have a tradition of shaving a child's head or cutting off a topknot in infancy (Thailand) or in late childhood or early adolescence (Laos and Cambodia), though this custom is now waning. The Burmese have an ear-piercing ceremony for girls that is an important ritual, while in Laos and Cambodia a girl is secluded at her first menses. In Islamic

---

[14] On occasion, however, certain leaders may achieve great popularity with the populace, e.g., Sihanouk in Cambodia, and probably U Nu and Sukarno in their better days. Also, in Thailand and Cambodia the institution of monarchy and the king are accorded great respect.

cultures, the circumcision ceremony for pubescent boys is a major event. There is no comparable puberty ritual for boys in the Theravada Buddhist countries. However, ordination as a novice monk, which is preceded by elaborate ceremony, often occurs during early adolescence. (c) Details of betrothal and wedding procedures vary from group to group, but marriage is an important event whether the ceremony is relatively simple (e.g., in Burma) or accompanied by extravagant festivities (e.g., in Thailand and Cambodia). The Khmer and Vietnamese have a tradition of bride service whereby a fiancé labors for his prospective in-laws to prove his worth. (d) Funerals also may be either simple (e.g., among Malays) or elaborate (e.g., in the Buddhist countries), with exact ceremonial procedures differing in the various cultures. Final disposal of the body is either by burial or cremation. (In a number of the groups, a distinction is made between death by natural and unnatural causes, e.g., accidents, childbirth, etc., and the latter may be treated differently or more hastily.)

With respect to other significant aspects of the life cycle, the socialization of children is almost everywhere indulgent and permissive in nature. Marriage usually occurs in late adolescence or in the early twenties and implicitly or explicitly marks the attainment of adulthood. Elderly persons are accorded special deference because of respect for age (there is also a concern with relative age in general whereby anyone older than oneself should be greeted with some respect).

In final summary, while I do not claim to have conducted an exhaustive review or definite analysis of the literature, the geographical region of Southeast Asia can be viewed as composed of the following (provisional) culture types and sub-types.

| Tribal Cultures | | | State-organized Cultures with Peasantry | | | |
|---|---|---|---|---|---|---|
| Hunting and gathering groups | Agricultural Groups | | "Hinduized" Cultures | | | "Sinicized" |
| | Shifting cultivators; | "Chiefdoms"; | Theravada Buddhist | Islamic | | Vietnamese |
| | relatively autonomous villages | sometimes sedentary cultivators | (Khmer, Thai, Laotians) | Bilateral (e.g., Malay, Javanese) | Unilateral (e.g., Negri Sembilan) | |

Within this framework, then, the Khmer can be considered to be part of a general Southeast Asian culture type (or area).[15] But, more specifically, they share various features with the other state-organized groups and show the most marked resemblances to the "Hinduized" cultures. Even more particularly, the Khmer have striking similarities in virtually all aspects of culture to the other Theravada Buddhist cultures of the Thai, Laotians, and Burmese. The Khmer, Thai, and Laotians are especially alike because of the cultural-linguistic relation between the latter two, and the considerable

---

[15] I realize that I have used varying criteria for delineating the sub-types; e.g., I took economic and sociopolitical features in differentiating between tribal groups, while broad cultural influences and religion were utilized in distinguishing different kinds of state-organized cultures. While such variation of criteria can be criticized, I feel that the distinctions I have made are critical ones for classifying whole cultures in Southeast Asia. But there can be, of course, other typologies based on different criteria.

cultural interchange between the former two that has occurred through the centuries despite periodic political enmity.[16]

## THE CONCEPT OF PEASANTRY

In the intellectual history of the social sciences there have been various attempts to categorize types of societies. The earlier classifications were made primarily in terms of a broad dichotomy or polarity between "more primitive" and "more civilized "societies (or features thereof), as in the distinctions between Maine's status and contract or kin and territory (*Ancient Law*, 1861), Spencer's militant and industrial (*Principles of Sociology*, 1874), Tönnies's *gemeinschaft* and *gesellschaft* (1887), Durkheim's mechanical solidarity and organic solidarity (*The Division of Labor in Society*, 1893), Redfield's folk and urban (*Folk Cultures of Yucatan*, 1941), etc. (see also Boskoff 1957 and C. Geertz 1962). In recent years, as more and more ethnological research takes place among communities in modern nation-states, anthropology has become concerned with a social type that seems to stand intermediate in the continuum between "primitive" and "civilized," and partakes of aspects of both: namely peasantry.[17] Peasantry has been accorded its own status distinct from "tribal" and "urban" societies, and attention is now focused on attempting to define its characteristic features.[18]

With respect to this latter endeavor, several names are outstanding: Kroeber (1948), Redfield (1955, 1956), Steward (1950, 1955), and Wolf (1955, 1966). There is basic agreement that the peasantry are, in Kroeber's phrase, "part-societies with

[16] The early Thai kingdoms (e.g., Sukothai, Ayutthaya) adopted a number of traits from the ancient Khmer, e.g., an alphabet, the concept of divine kingship and various administrative practices, juridical code, elements of material culture, etc. (Blanchard et al. 1958, 26–27, 76–77). In fact, political conflicts aided cultural interchange because the Thai periodically captured parts of Khmer territory and carried off Khmer officials, intelligentsia, artisans, etc., who acted as cultural instructors to their captors, while the Khmer did the same to the Thai. Culture elements diffuse between the different countries even at the present time; e.g., a popular dance form in contemporary Cambodia comes from Thailand. Similar interchange occurs between other Southeast Asian cultures as well; witness the Vietnamese adoption of a Khmer type of plow (Hickey 1964, 136).

[17] Actually, groups that we now call peasantry had, in fact, been discussed by several of the writers just mentioned (e.g., Tönnies, Maine) but were not distinguished as a separate type (see also C. Geertz 1962, 1). Peasants have also been studied by scholars in other disciplines, such as historians (e.g., Marc Bloch, *Feudal Society*, University of Chicago Press, 1961; Jerome Blum, *Lord and Peasant in Russia*, Princeton, 1961), economists (particularly economic historians, agricultural economists, and economists specializing in development: e.g., B. H. S. van Bath, *The Agrarian History of Western Europe*, St. Martins Press, 1963; Theodore Schultz, *Transforming Traditional Agriculture*, Yale, 1964); political scientists (e.g., Daniel Lerner, *The Passing of Traditional Society*, Free Press Macmillan, 1958), and sociologists (e.g., Max Weber; W. I. Thomas and F. Znaniecki, *The Polish Peasant in Europe and America*, Knopf, 1927; Barrington Moore, *Social Origins of Dictatorship and Democracy: Lord and Peasant in the Making of the Modern World*, Beacon, 1967). (See also the bibliographies in Chiva 1958; C. Geertz 1962; and Wolf 1966, as well as journals such as *Études Rurales* and *Economic Development and Culture Change*.) Works in other fields, however, have focused mainly on European cultures (with some important exceptions such as the historian Daniel Thorner's *Land and Labour in India*, Taplinger, 1966) and have not been concerned with defining peasantry as a social type.

[18] In addition, there has been discussion of methods for studying peasant and other kinds of communities within larger wholes; see C. Geertz 1962, 7–34 and, among others, Redfield 1955; Steward 1950, 1955, chaps. 3, 4; Arensberg 1954, 1957, 1961; Manners 1957. This problem is, however, not the immediate concern of this chapter.

part-cultures" (1948, 284), but different writers stress different aspects of the relations between the part and the incorporating whole. Redfield discusses peasantry primarily in terms of its values, worldview, and style of life as contrasted to the gentry; while Steward is more concerned with economic organization and the way in which peasantry is articulated within a nation-state (Geertz 1961, 3–4). And Wolf, in his most recent work (1966) seems to be influenced by both Steward and Wittfogel in emphasizing the economic and political status of peasantry within the larger society. In addition, in an effort to delineate more precisely the diverse aspects of the relationship between the peasantry and the wider society, as well as features specific to itself, a number of other anthropologists and works have discussed topics such as peasant social structure, patterns of interaction within the community, peasant economic organization and market systems, power relations, "cultural brokers" who mediate between the part and the whole, interchange between the great and little traditions, etc. (see, for example, Firth 1951, chap. 3; 1964; Fallers 1961; Fitchen 1961; Foster 1961a, 1965; Lewis 1955, 1961; Firth and Yamey 1964; Mintz 1959; Wittfogel 1957; Wolf 1956; Marriott 1955; Potter, Diaz, and Foster 1967; among others).[19]

A provisional model of peasantry as a social type can be constructed by combining the features of peasant society as discussed in various works.

(1) Economic organization. (a) Peasants are an agricultural, rural population for whom cultivation is at once both "a livelihood and a way of life" (Redfield 1956, 27), and holdings both "an economic unit and a home" (Wolf 1966, 13).[20] (b) As agriculturalists, peasants generally have a profound attachment to land that is not only pragmatic but can be reverential as well (coupled sometimes with denigration of the non-agricultural work and values of the townsmen) (Redfield 1956, 112, 123, 140; Firth 1951, 87; Kroeber 1948, 284; Wolf 1955, 459). Wolf feels that one of the defining characteristics of peasantry is "effective control" over this land through individual ownership, undisputed squatter's rights, or rental, and excludes "tenants whose control of the land is subject to outside authority" (1955, 453). Redfield (1956, 28) and Firth (1964, 17), however, feel that particular forms of tenure are not so important as actual usufruct of and attachment to the land; Steward (cited in Padilla 1957, 25)[21] also speaks in broad terms of "individual ownership or individual rights over the productive unit." (c) In most parts of the world this land is worked by relatively simple technology, utilizing what Wolf (1966, 19–21) calls a "paleotechnic ecotype" of human and animal labor power plus, perhaps, simple machines (see also Firth 1951, 87; 1964, 17; Steward in Padilla 1957, 25). The family or household group (whatever form it may take) provides the basic labor force on the land under its use or control, aided by cooperative or hired labor when necessary (Firth 1951, 88; Fitchen 1961; Steward in Padilla 1957). (d) Peasants may cultivate subsistence crops and/or cash crops; if both, the relative proportions of the two

---

[19] See also Casagrande 1959 on the concept of the "intermediate society" that subsumes peasantry, as well as other papers in Ray 1959. In addition, Chiva 1958, C. Geertz 1962, and Friedl 1963 offer general surveys of recent literature on peasantry and related topics.

[20] Cf., however, Firth (1951, 87; 1964, 18) who would include rural craftsmen, fishermen, and even marketers in the category of peasantry "if they are part of the same system" as agriculturalists. Wolf (1955, 453) specifically excludes fishermen, as well as livestock breeders, strip miners, rubber gatherers, etc. Lewis (1961) also excludes craftsmen and other non-agriculturalists.

[21] The article by Steward cited in Padilla is titled "The Family-Cultivated Farm as a Cross-Cultural Type," 1956, mimeo.

will vary in different groups. In any event, the main aim of the peasant is production for subsistence, rather than reinvestment of income to expand productivity as does the farmer (Wolf 1955, 454; Redfield 1956, 27; Steward in Padilla 1957, 26; cf. Firth 1964, 17). Surplus produce or income from crops is used primarily for the needs of the peasant himself (to feed animals, to replace or repair necessary work equipment or household items, to sponsor socially sanctioned ceremonies, etc.) or to pay "funds of rent," such as taxes, to persons in power who have liens on peasant produce (Wolf 1955, 454; 1966, 5–13). Note also that the peasant often turns to part-time craft specializations or the selling of his labor power to augment his resources (Wolf 1966, 445). (e) Despite this focus on subsistence, the peasant household or community is by no means an autonomous economic unit. For both the sale of produce and purchase of needed items, the peasant is tied (in a greater or lesser degree) to markets[22] that involve regional and often international trade and thus constitute one of the major links between peasantry and the larger whole (Wolf 1966, 40–48; Firth 1964, 17; Redfield 1956, 49; Mintz 1959). Peasant marketing differs from the commercial marketing of industrial societies because of the peasant's limited production, limited purchasing power, and limited withholding power (Wolf 1966, 48). But the market may have at least a minimal and often a considerable effect on the organization of not only the peasant's economy but other spheres of his life as well (see also Firth 1951, 90–100). (f) In addition to involvement with a market system, the peasant is also frequently bound in credit and debt relationships with merchants and moneylenders (as well as with fellow villagers, kinsmen, etc.) because of meager savings, shortages before harvest, crop failures, special ceremonial expenditures, etc. (Firth 1964, 29–33).

(2) Social organization. Fitchen (1961), using data drawn primarily from European and Latin American peasantry, has proposed several features characteristic of peasant social structure, some of which have also been suggested by other writers. (a) In contrast to tribal societies in which kinship plays a basic role in structuring interpersonal relations, peasant society gives predominance to non-kin, volitional relationships among individuals that are often contractual and temporary in nature (Fitchen 1961, 114–15). Wolf (1966, 78–91) also implies the same notion in his discussion of "coalitions": peasants become involved in different alliances with other persons and households for various reasons, but characteristically on a temporary basis for short-range ends so as to avoid overcommitment.[23] (b) Despite the fact that kin relations in general are relatively insignificant in ordering social organization, there is one kin grouping that assumes great importance in peasant life: namely, the family or

---

[22] See Wolf 1966, 40–48 for two major kinds of market systems with which peasants deal.

[23] In an extension of this idea, but emphasizing the quality of interpersonal relations, Foster (1961a) has proposed that peasant societies are characterized by conflict, enmity, distrust, back-biting, etc., because economic (and other) resources are conceived to be in limited quantity, such that one person's gain must be another's loss (this notion is further elaborated in Foster 1965; see also Wolf 1955 on "institutionalized envy" in the "closed" peasant community). There are, however, challenges (on both substantive and methodological grounds) to Foster's characterization of interpersonal relations (see Redfield 1956, 140; Lewis 1961; Pitt-Rivers 1961) and his concept of "limited good" (see, for example, Piker 1966; Kennedy 1966). Furthermore, Foster (1961a, 175) himself notes that his generalizations may not apply to Southeast Asian peasantry; see also Piker 1966 whose comments on Thai society generally hold true for Khmer as well.

household. Whether this domestic group is a nuclear or some form of larger family,[24] it forms a relatively autonomous and self-sufficient group (i.e., it is not necessarily bound to a larger kin group in bilateral societies, nor compelled to permanent alliances with other households). It constitutes the primary economic unit of consumption and production with its shared property and cooperative labor and is also a focus of social and religious activity (Fitchen 1961, 115–16; Wolf 1955, 459, 464; 1966, 38, 45, 62–72, 91). (c) The local community may be a unit of importance second to none but the household, by virtue of common economic activities, strong in-group feeling, and sometimes the holding of communal property or high incidence of endogamy (Fitchen 1961, 116; see also Wolf 1955 and 1957 on the "closed" community). However, the economic and/or social autonomy of the community may vary; see, for example, the exogamous villages of North India (Lewis 1955) or Wolf's "open" community (1955). (d) Fitchen proposes further that there are no sharp or immutable "vertical divisions" (such as lineages) or "clearly defined horizontal strata" among the peasantry, such that there is "mutability of social units within the same level of integration" (1961, 116–17, 118). She notes that this does not apply to all peasant societies, notably India; neither would the generalization hold for Southeast Asian peasants with unilineal kinship. But her point is generally well taken that, although there may be "neighborhood schisms, economic and political factionalism," and various status distinctions, most peasant communities have "only minimal and non-rigid internal segmentation" (116, 117). Wolf (1955, 1957) also notes that in his "closed community" peasant type, status differences are firmly leveled by a "cult of poverty" and "institutionalized envy" (see also Foster 1965), although there is great concern with status positions in the "open" community. (e) While there are no clear-cut strata within the peasantry itself, in relation to the larger society they do form a class segment that is subordinate to dominant groups of aristocracy, officials, landlords, merchants, etc. (Kroeber 1948; Redfield 1956; Fitchen 1961; Wolf 1966). The peasant is conscious of social distance between the classes and usually views townsmen and urbanites with some ambivalence (Redfield 1956, 140; Wolf 1966, 46–47). On the one hand, the latter may be admired, envied, and granted at least overt respect and deference; on the other hand, they may also be viewed with suspicion, distaste, and feelings that urbanites are immoral, lazy, etc. Bridging the gap between the different socioeconomic strata (and helping to relate the peasants to the larger whole) are various mediators or "cultural brokers" (Wolf 1956) such as local officials, schoolteachers, doctors, etc. (see also Redfield 1956, 60). The possibility of mobility from the peasant strata into upper levels varies from society to society but is in general hindered by not only poverty but a general conservatism and commitment to tradition.[25]

(3) Political organization. According to Wolf, one of the defining features of peasantry is its integration within a state (not simply interaction with a city) (1966, 11). While the local community has some sort of political organization of its own (that may possess considerable authority and significance in the lives of the peasants), it lacks political autonomy (Kroeber 1948, 284) and is ultimately under the control

---

[24] See Wolf 1966, 65–76 for a discussion of conditions favoring the existence of either the nuclear or an extended form of the family, as well as factors involved in partible or impartible inheritance within the family.

[25] This conservatism and traditionalism, a feature of peasantry that has been noted by others (e.g., Redfield 1956, 137) is seen by Wolf (1966, 16–17) as an advantage in helping the peasant maintain a certain autonomy and ability to survive within the larger system.

of higher authority. Corollary with the elite's political authority over the peasant is economic power to command part of the peasant's produce or labor in the form of tribute, taxes, rents, or corvée (see Wolf 1966, 10 and 50–57 on types of domain). The peasant attempts, however, to maintain a balance between his own needs and the demands of outsiders (Wolf 1966, 13).

(4) Religion and ideology. The religious, intellectual, and ideological sphere of peasant culture has been discussed by Redfield (1956, chap. 3) and others (e.g., Marriott 1955) in terms of great and little traditions. In Redfield's conceptualization, the "great tradition of the reflective few" is cultivated and carried by various members of the upper strata such as the intelligentsia and aristocracy who have both "secular and sacred power," while the "little tradition of the largely unreflective many" is nurtured among the peasantry (1956, 70). But the two traditions are conceived to be in continuous interaction and communication: aspects of the little tradition disseminate above and beyond the village level, while elements of the great tradition come down to the peasantry through natural filtering or imposition (viz. Marriott's "universalization" and "parochialization" [1955]). Thus, peasant ceremonio-religious systems and cosmologies are commonly a blend of the two traditions, combining, for example, adherence to a high religion and belief in traditional spirits (see, e.g., Redfield 1956, 71ff.; Marriott 1955; Obeyesekere 1963; Brohm 1963; Wolf 1966, 102–3). Wolf further characterizes peasant religion in the following terms: "Peasant ceremonial focuses on action, not on belief. It emphasizes the regulative character of norms . . . social order is the objective. Peasant religion is both utilitarian and moralistic, but it is not ethical and questioning" (1966, 99).

The culture and society of the Khmer rice cultivator, as presented in the preceding chapters, shows a close fit with the model of peasantry that has just been presented. Without troubling to recapitulate the Khmer data point by point, it can be said that, in general, Khmer village life validates virtually all of the various features that different anthropologists have proposed as characteristic of peasantry in other ages and/or other regions of the world. The few points of question that I would raise, on the basis of the Khmer material, are the following. (1) There are individuals in Svay who have no land whatsoever or who subsist largely by non-agricultural pursuits; yet in every other respect they are like their fellow villagers.[26] Whether these persons should be categorized differently than their neighbors, that is, as non-peasants, is a moot point. But I would tend to agree with Firth in allowing for a looser definition of peasantry to include, for example, rural craftsmen who are, in his terms, "part of the same social system" as agriculturalists (1964, 18). (2) Fitchen's point that kinship relations are relatively less important in peasant societies as contrasted to tribal societies is, in general, well made. But this should not obscure the fact that, among the Khmer at least, ties of kinship are important in many areas even though one has the option of choosing among or even ignoring relatives. (3) Fitchen also suggests that the community as a whole may be second in importance to the household. It was seen that for Svay villagers the community is the object of loyalty and identification, but there are

---

[26] It was seen, moreover, that even many of the landowning cultivators in Svay had to resort to diverse non-agricultural pursuits to meet their needs, a practice that Wolf notes (1966, 45) is common among peasantry in general. Such situations raise this question: Does, then, the classification of an individual or household as peasant in the strict sense (i.e., as a cultivator) depend on the relative proportion of agricultural and non-agricultural activities, on the villager(s)' subjective evaluation of which is the most important, or on some other criteria?

relatively few communal activities and no firm sanctions dictating village solidarity. Though the data is not always explicit on this point, the same appears to be true for a number of other Southeast Asian communities (see previous section in this chapter). Fitchen is wise, then, in specifying that this feature of peasantry is not a universal one.

We pass now from a consideration of peasantry in general to the problem of kinds of peasantry. Of special significance in this respect is Wolf's provisional delineation of types of peasantry in Latin America (1955), and particularly the distinction between the "open" and "closed" communities. His characterization of at least one Southeast Asian society, the central Javanese, as an example of the "closed" community (Wolf 1957) raises the question of the wider applicability of his types. The following discussion will be concerned with whether Khmer peasantry fits either of Wolf's models.

Wolf's typology is based on certain kinds of structural relationships between particular sorts of communities and the larger sociocultural whole, with special emphasis on economic and sociopolitical features that rise in response to certain historical conditions (1955, 454–55). He begins by limiting use of the term "peasant" to "an agricultural producer in effective control of the land who carries on agriculture as a means of livelihood, not as a business for profit" (Wolf 1957, 1). Two features shared by both the open and closed types are traditional technology in cultivation and the family as ultimate unit of production and consumption. Otherwise, however, the two are contrasted in a number of respects. In brief summary, the salient features of the types are as follows.

The "closed corporate community" is a "bounded social system with clear-cut limits in relations to both outsiders and insiders" (Wolf 1955, 456);

> they are corporate organizations, maintaining a perpetuity of rights and membership; and they are closed corporations, because they limit these privileges to insiders, and discourage close participation of members in the social relations of the larger society. (Wolf 1957, 2)

Resistance to both outside influences and immigrant strangers is aided by community jurisdiction over free disposal of land (some of which may be communally owned, but even privately held lands are subject to sanctions prohibiting sale to outsiders). Given the nature of the land and technology, productivity is low and the peasants are poor, thus furthering the isolation of the closed community. Though linked to certain kinds of markets, both sales and purchases tend to be limited and there is minimal influx of material goods from the outside. Within the community itself there is a distinct tendency to level status differences by a "cult of poverty" extolling hard work, asceticism, and adherence to certain standards of consumption; by "institutionalized envy" (gossip, witchcraft, etc.) that discourages individual mobility and accumulation of wealth; and by community pressures to redistribute or destroy surpluses in, for example, the financing of religious ceremonies. (For further details, see Wolf 1955, 456–59; 1957.)

By contrast, the "open" community is linked to the larger society in a number of ways. Membership in the community is unrestricted, and privately held lands may be disposed of according to the owner's wishes. Apart from a subsistence crop, some sort of cash crop is regularly sold (though the income therefrom may be small) in speculative markets tied to national and international trade; in the production of such cash crops, outside capitalization (though generally small-scale and intermittent) from urban patrons may be involved, and the peasant can respond to the market by shifts in production when necessary. The community is also open and receptive to the influx of both outside ideas and goods. Within the community, status differences are permitted and, indeed, expected; there are no sanctions against accumulation of wealth and conspicuous display thereof, and readjustments in and redefinitions of status (both upward and downward) are constant. (For further details, see Wolf 1955, 461–66.)

Khmer rice cultivators, as known to us from Village Svay and from other data, manifest features representative of both the open and closed communities. The Khmer community is open in that there is no communal land and no explicit communal sanctions against the free disposal of privately owned lands as one wishes (e.g., emigrants from the community can keep land inherited in the village; land can be rented or sold to outsiders; cf. Java [see Wolf 1957, 2]). Neither are there any restrictions of immigrants into the village (except that they must be checked by a local official for "good character"). There is also a high degree of village exogamy and consequent bonds of kinship and friendship with neighboring communities. On the other hand, however, there are also deep-rooted parochial and insular attitudes that lead to distrust and fear of outsiders from or in strange communities. Thus, despite the lack of definite prohibitions against immigration or sale of land to outsiders, the Khmer community is closed in that it is highly unlikely that an individual would dare to buy land and settle in a village unless he were originally native to the community, were marrying into the village, or had kinsmen there. Thus, it is not so much explicit community sanctions but rather deep-seated village parochialism that inhibits the influx of outsiders into the community.

Because of the traditional technology, mediocre soils, and relatively small landholdings (due to population pressure and parcelization through generations of inheritance), Svay and many other villages cultivate rice mainly for subsistence. Sale of surplus tends to be limited and/or occasional (except in certain regions that produce mainly for the market). Thus, the Khmer community tends to be relatively poor and must often turn to supplementary activities to meet various needs. Furthermore, poverty limits the influx of material goods from the outside mainly to functional items, and the villagers continue to fabricate a number of necessities themselves. All of the preceding features are characteristic of the closed community, but the Khmer community is also open in that there are definite ties to complex markets involving national and international trade, and the villagers are not only receptive to outside goods but show increasing dependence on and desire for them. (The openness of the community is undoubtedly heightened in the case of the *chamkar* cultivators who grow vegetables, fruits, and various cash crops; dispose of most of their produce on the market; and have much higher incomes than do rice cultivators.)

With respect to patterns of consumption and wealth accumulation, the Khmer do not exhibit the "institutionalized envy" or other firm sanctions against the amassing of fortunes that Wolf describes for closed communities. Neither is there a real "cult of poverty" (although villagers do often refer to themselves as "we poor peasants who must work so hard" and will pull in their belts when necessary). Indeed, the accumulation of wealth and achievement of social mobility are admired, vaguely envied, and even desired (although fervent pursuit thereof is relatively rare). Nonetheless, however, accumulation of wealth does not occur easily or frequently because of meager resources, and fortunes are made primarily by emigration from the village and pursuit of non-agricultural occupations. Moreover, although there are no explicit sanctions against rising above certain patterns of consumption (indeed, one expects that wealthier people will exhibit a higher standard of living), the richer folk in Svay are modestly unassuming. They have nicer homes, better and more furnishings, clothing, food, etc., but their general appearance and demeanor is little different from that of poorer fellows, and they do not indulge in conspicuous displays of wealth. This is not because they fear gossip, jealousy, or witchcraft from their neighbors; their modesty seems due rather to the fact that these wealthy villagers are also devout Buddhists who believe in the Buddhist ideal that spiritual achievement is more important than material wealth or display. The Khmer village has an egalitarian tenor in general that probably stems mainly from this religious ideal, and there is none of the great concern with redefinitions and realignments of status that Wolf cites as typical of the open community.[27] A further point with respect to religion is that, as in the closed community, a good deal of Khmer villagers' surplus can be drained off for religious purposes (i.e., contributions to the Buddhist temple). But where this occurs in Wolf's examples of closed communities because of communal pressure to participate in village rituals, it happens in Khmer villages because of individual desire to earn religious merit.[28] (The acquisition of such merit can also bring one prestige within the community, but the political and religious systems of the Khmer village are not meshed in the way that Wolf describes for Meso-America.) The celebration of life-cycle ceremonies, annual holidays, curing rituals, etc., can further diminish surplus (and, it should also be noted, throw many families into debt as well).

Finally, the Khmer peasant community may be considered closed in the sense that there is social distance between the rural villagers and the upper strata or urban segments of the larger society; villagers maintain certain conservative and traditional attitudes and mores; and the bulk of daily interaction and an individual's life cycle occur within the confines of the community. But, simultaneously, it is also open in that the Khmer community is not as tightly knit and cohesive as those that Wolf describes (e.g., there are few real communal rituals; formal village political organization is weak [at least in Svay]); the village maintains important ties to other communities including the town and city; and many villagers (especially the younger generation) are curious about and receptive to many (if not all) goods and ideas from the outside.

Wolf emphasizes that the different types of communities rise in response to certain factors in the larger society. He discusses the historical conditions that led to the renaissance of closed communities in Meso-America and Java: (1) conquest and colonialism dualized the economy into a dominant entrepreneurial sector and a subordinate peasantry, and land restrictions were decreed to force the cultivators to become part-time laborers for entrepreneurial activities; (2) simultaneously, there was dualization in the political sphere between the colonial and the native administration, and the village communities became relatively autonomous political entities under the jurisdiction of the latter. (Wolf's entire argument cannot be presented here; for details, see 1957, 7–12.) The open community in Latin America developed "in response to the rising demand for cash crops which accompanied the development of

---

[27] It may seem contradictory to say that the Khmer allow or even desire accumulation of wealth at the same time that they hold to an ideal of egalitarianism. That the two can coexist might be explained by the following. First, the achievement of material success can be considered as an indication of religious merit accumulated in previous existence; second, the increasing desire for material wealth and upward mobility (especially on the part of the young) shows a relative weakening of Buddhist norms (see chapter 5).

[28] Such desire to earn merit can be said to be communally sanctioned in that it is a cultural norm. But there is no community condemnation of those who have but minimal participation in temple activities or donate little to the monks.

capitalism in Europe"; thus, it "emphasizes continuous interaction with the outside world and ties its fortunes to outside demands" (Wolf 1955, 462). This type of community also manifests patterns of hierarchical relations and consumption of prestige goods (that can be acquired only in the market and only with money) that were originally transplanted from the old world (462).

Cambodia also experienced colonialism and a dualization of the economy, but that entirely closed communities (in the form described by Wolf) did not develop may be due to several factors.

(1) Unlike the Spanish in Meso-America and the Dutch in Java, the French in Cambodia did not restrict the lands available to the peasantry in order to create a labor force. Rather, the French maintained and encouraged the agricultural resources of Cambodia, notably the extension of cash-cropping on the river banks, but even rice cultivators now had an opportunity to become involved with complex markets as rice became a major export. Labor needed for other enterprises stimulated by the French, for example, rubber plantations, was provided by immigrants such as Chinese and Vietnamese rather than the native Khmer, the overwhelming majority of whom remained more or less full-time cultivators on their own lands. If communities in various regions of Cambodia are faced with a limited amount of land, this is due not to government fiat but rather to natural increase of population density in areas where expansion onto new lands is impossible.

(2) There was no tradition of a communal land system in Cambodia. As a means of increasing revenue for those in power, land has long been held in virtual or actual private ownership by individuals who had free right of disposal thereof. Thus, there is no tradition of communal jurisdiction over land, nor one of rigid restriction of membership in the community.[29]

(3) As in Meso-America and Java, the European officials in Cambodia maintained the outlines of native administration, and there was little contact between the colonials and the indigenous peasantry. But, although local political organization was encouraged (e.g., granting villagers the right to elect village and sub-district chiefs), the Khmer community does not seem to have had (or have) the political autonomy of the Meso-American or Javanese community. Although local chiefs had various responsibilities and some authority, it appears that attempts were made to integrate villages more tightly into a national administrative hierarchy (e.g., all taxes now went to the central government and local officials no longer kept a percentage thereof) in order to replace the precolonial system of patron–client relationships.

But if completely closed communities did not develop in Cambodia, neither did completely open ones such as Wolf describes for Latin America. This seems due to several factors that have already been noted in the preceding discussion. I recapitulate some of these. (1) In contrast to the cash cropping of open Latin American communities, meager holdings and the nature of the crop in Khmer villages such as Svay mean

---

[29] Apart from the lack of communal lands, it is not entirely clear why the Khmer village is relatively open to outsiders. It may be because, when the Khmer were in the process of expanding onto new lands during ancient and even relatively modern times, the typical settlement pattern was probably that of small communities of kinsmen (see also Delvert 1961, 206–7). Such communities may well have had to practice exogamy to find suitable marriage partners, such that acceptance of outsiders—at least through marriage—became common. Delvert also feels that contemporary Khmer change habitation easily (for "economic, familial, and religious reasons") (1961, 198), though I do not entirely agree with him.

that cultivation is primarily for subsistence. Thus, ties to the market are limited at the same time that the peasant has become inextricably bound to the market by dependence on outside produce and goods. (2) While accumulation of wealth is permitted, elaborate concern with status and display within the community is mitigated by the difficulty of amassing riches and by Buddhist ideology. (3) Peasant parochialism, insularity, and conservatism prevent complete openness to outside immigrants and ideas.

In sum, the Khmer do not fully approximate the models of either the open or the closed community but show features of both. This does not invalidate Wolf's typology, for he not only presented it as a provisional statement but explicitly recognizes the existence of other possible types (1955, 467–69; 1957, 6–7). Though Wolf found closed communities in Java, the example of the Khmer indicates that further refinement of types of peasantry is needed for Southeast Asia (and probably even for different kinds of cultivators within this region).[30] It is beyond the scope of this work to delineate such a typology here, but obviously this is an important area for further research and analysis.

---

[30] Note also that in certain instances where the Khmer do resemble Latin American or Javanese communities, the similar features have different historical or functional determinants that must also be taken into account.

# APPENDIX A

# ETHNOLOGICAL LITERATURE ON THE KHMER

A totally comprehensive account of the literature on Khmer culture would have to be an extensive annotated bibliography, a project that is beyond the limited time and space available for this dissertation. My immediate purpose here is to offer a brief assessment of the major sources on Khmer society and culture.

For information on late nineteenth-century (or earlier) Cambodia, two names are outstanding. The first is Adhémard Leclère who simultaneously pursued his duties as a French colonial administrator and produced an impressive array of scholarly works. Much of it (Leclère 1890, 1894, 1898) deals with nineteenth-century and earlier legal codes. A variety of valuable information on topics ranging from kinship to fornication can be gleaned from these statutes, but one must recall that the data is often mainly of historical interest rather than applicable to the contemporary scene, and that legal rules do not always reveal actual practice at the local level. Leclère also wrote some significant accounts of religious-ceremonial life (Leclère 1899, 1916). Second, Etienne Aymonier was an epigrapher whose main interest lay in the ancient Khmer. But his *Le Royaume actuel* (1900) presents numerous facets of nineteenth-century Cambodian society and culture (particularly the overall social structure) in valuable detail.

For data on the contemporary Khmer, again, two names are predominant. First, Éveline Porée-Maspero, continuing in the tradition of her father (Georges Maspero, a scholar of Khmer history and archeology), has given us numerous works on ceremonio-religious life. Although she is not a professional ethnographer and her accounts do not always distinguish between the ideal form of ceremonial procedures and their actual practice (though she has stated that she realizes the difference between the two), she has performed a valuable service in presenting information from the files of the Commission des Moeurs et Coutumes du Cambodge and from her own experience in Cambodia. Second, the recent publication of Jean Delvert's *La Paysan cambodgien* (1961) is a signal contribution to our knowledge of Khmer peasantry. Delvert is the first scholar to focus exclusively upon the peasants, a crucial segment of Cambodian society that was heretofore either neglected or mentioned only in passing. As an economic geographer, he naturally concentrates on peasant economic organization and activities, but he also throws valuable light on topics such as settlement pattern and diet, and discusses everything in excellent detail and breadth (see also Ebihara 1963).

In addition to the above, some other French works that are of utility are the following: the special edition of *France-Asie* (1955) for a collection of articles dealing with varied aspects of Khmer culture; Monod (1931) for a romanticized but interesting account of a fictional village family; Thierry (1955) for a discussion of the status of Khmer women through the ages; and Daguin (n.d.) and Lingat (1952) for consideration of marital practices and laws.

The only extensive information in English to be found on the Khmer are several volumes produced under the auspices of the Human Relations Area Files that offer general surveys of Cambodian culture and society.[1] The first of these (Zadrozny 1955) is by far the best. Although it does little more than to translate and summarize data from other works (primarily French sources), it draws together diverse materials and cites the sources from which information was derived. The other work (Steinberg 1959, which is a revised edition of an earlier book issued in 1957) repeats (in condensed form) the material in Zadrozny and adds some new information; but there are no source citations, and one cannot be certain where and how the data were gotten, nor how accurate they may be (see also Groslier 1957). It is, however, quite useful for its discussion of topics such as the organization of the central government.

---

[1] Brief articles on the Khmer have been written by Ebihara (1964, 1966). In political science, some excellent work has been done by Roger Smith (1964, 1965), who did actual field research in Cambodia. William Wilmott has done research on the Chinese minority, but I have not seen his published work (*The Chinese in Cambodia*, Vancouver, University of British Columbia, 1967).

# APPENDIX B

# CIRCUMSTANCES OF THE RESEARCH

My fieldwork was sponsored by the Ford Foundation Foreign Area Training Fellowship Program that awarded me a grant in 1958. After spending the summer of 1958 reading some of the available literature on the Khmer, studying phonetics and phonemics, and searching fruitlessly for a tutor in the Khmer language, I left the United States in November 1958. En route to the field, I spent two weeks in Paris to visit museums, libraries, and especially to meet French scholars (G. Coedès, É. Porée-Maspero, F. Martini, C. Archaimbault, and G. Condominas) who are specialists in Southeast Asian studies.

I arrived in Cambodia in January 1959 to begin my fourteen-month stay in the country. For the first three and a half months I pursued three basic tasks: speaking to various individuals who knew the country well, touring the countryside to survey various villages, and learning the rudiments of the Khmer language.

Having decided upon a particular community and having received government permission to reside there, I moved into West Hamlet Svay in April 1959. I obtained a small house (willingly vacated by a divorced man in return for rent) that was well situated within the hamlet (see map 3). In response to my request for a housekeeper, the villagers brought forth two young women on the grounds that both needed money and would share the work. Neary and San were not only dutiful housekeepers but delightful companions who provided valuable bonds to village families. In the same manner, a young man from East Hamlet, Chhean, was presented to me as the only person in Svay who could speak French. His command of French was actually rather meager, but he was a willing and able interpreter if not a perfect one.

During the first few months Chhean interpreted for me for several hours a day; subsequently I used him periodically as a guide on excursions and as reference for difficult interviews. My command of Khmer, after the first months during which I had to adapt from the more "formal" language learned in Phnom Penh to the more colloquial speech of the villagers, became sufficient to understand most or all of my conversation or interview. In honesty, however, I am not completely fluent in Khmer, nor do I know how to read the language.

My initial reception into the village seemed to me, at the time, to be completely free of difficulty. From the beginning I felt a genuine hospitality and warmth from the villagers, especially the older ones. I was quite surprised when one of my best friends told me, just before I left Svay, that many villagers had actually been very suspicious of and upset by my entrance into their community, and that I had been saved from expulsion only by the efforts of some tolerant persons (one of whom was Kompha, the informal leader of West Svay) who admonished the people to "wait and see." But after a month or so, as the villagers observed my activities, they came fully to believe and understand my stated intention: that I came as a student to study Khmer customs. My presence then became a source of pride or flattery to them, and my neighbors would explain to strangers: "She has come to see Cambodian customs; she asks and watches; and when she is done, she will go home in an airplane and write a book about us." My house became a place to visit for company or curiosity, to listen to the radio, and to receive simple medications. Conversely, their homes became sources of companionship and advice, as well as information, for me. I developed very close bonds of affection and fictive kinship with certain individuals and families (especially Houses 1 and 20 who watched over me as if they were my real parents and grandparents). I believe that the villagers gave me honest and accurate information, with vagueness or hesitation only when they themselves were not certain of something. For although they knew that I would write "a book," their notion of publicity was not clear enough to make them lie or hide illegal or immoral activities, especially in the course of informal conversations.

Within Svay I collected data by the traditional ethnographic techniques of casual conversations, formal interviews, censuses or questionnaires on certain topics, participant observation, and still photography. In addition, material on Khmer culture outside Svay was gathered from talks with urban Khmer, Frenchmen who were long-time residents of the country, Americans with the United States Foreign Service or Overseas Mission (USOM), Europeans with United Nations organizations such as UNESCO or WHO, and especially research in the files of the Commission des Moeurs et Coutumes du Cambodge in Phnom Penh. The latter is a collection of documents written by Khmer (from various provinces and walks of life, e.g., students, local officials, lay priests) on numerous aspects of Khmer culture ranging from "Domestic Animals" to "Spirits." It was not possible to cover the files completely (they contain one hundred categories, each filled with a greater or lesser amount of documents), but I did carefully investigate those topics that most interested me for comparative data on practices in other parts of Cambodia. Also, after my return to the United States in 1960 I read more of the existing literature on the Khmer, as well as rereading works I had examined before I went to Cambodia, and found the written sources much more meaningful than they had been prior to my fieldwork. Before I went to Cambodia I had had no way to assess the quality or validity of the extant ethnographic data. But after I had been in the field, I could see that some of the information in the literature was erroneous, or that certain traditions had fallen into disuse or were practiced only in certain areas, or that other customs did seem to be widespread throughout the country.

Having described some of the actual circumstances of my research, I will state some ways in which my data may be limited or biased. First, my status was defined by the villagers as that of a foreign,[1] young, unmarried woman. As a foreigner I could do and say much that is not ordinarily allowed to Khmer females, and my advanced academic status allowed me to interact with even the oldest people on a relatively equal basis. But as a young, unmarried female I was restricted from certain activities such as witnessing the birth of a child, traveling alone at night or to distant regions, being alone with monks, or participating in male friendship cliques, lest I be considered

---

[1] My ethnic identity was confusing to the villagers because my ancestry is Japanese but my citizenship is American. This duality was never fully understood, and the villagers usually called me a "Eurasian" from America. (I might also note that my mongoloid physical type was advantageous in allowing me to blend fairly inconspicuously into the population.)

quite indecorous. My knowledge of men's intimate thoughts, attitudes, and behavior is therefore limited as compared to the information I have on women.

Second, I was extremely enervated by the Cambodian climate. While I never fell seriously ill, I found that fatigue and lack of stamina prevented me from activities such as accompanying the villagers on their journeys to distant marshlands to get food for cattle, or visiting certain neighboring villages that were accessible only by walking several kilometers across the paddies.

Finally, the depth and extent of my material varies according to my research interests. My field investigations concentrated on the two least known aspects of Khmer village life. The first and greatest gap in our knowledge (and the one in which I was most interested) was social organization in general and kinship organization in particular (especially residence patterns and the nature of the "kindred," both of which had been raised as problems in the anthropological literature of the late 1950s and that were discussed in a seminar on social organization with Dr. Morton Fried in 1957. The second focus was economic organization, particularly the nature of rice cultivation because Dr. Harold Conklin was one of my original advisors (and, at that time, the work of Delvert had not yet appeared). I was also personally interested in the relations between the village and other communities. I was not overly concerned with ceremonio-religious life and political organization, partly because of personal lack of interest in these subjects and partly because the former at least is already treated extensively in the French literature on Cambodia. I did collect some data on these latter topics (as on the life cycle), but with less enthusiasm and detail.

# Appendix C

# Demographic Analysis of West Svay's Population

The age and sex composition of the hamlet's inhabitants is presented below.

| Ages | Male | Female | Total |
|------|------|--------|-------|
| 0–9 years | 21 | 21 | 42 |
| 10–19 | 13 | 17 | 30[a] |
| 20–29 | 12 | 11 | 23 |
| 30–39 | 11 | 11 | 22 |
| 40–49 | 8 | 11 | 19 |
| 50–59 | 7 | 5 | 12[b] |
| 60–69 | 4 | 5 | 9 |
| 70–79 | 1 | 1 | 2 |
| 80–89 | 1 | 0 | 1[c] |
| Totals | 78 | 82 | 160 |

[a] 45% under 20 years
[b] 47.5% ages 20–60
[c] 7.5% over 60 years

The proportion of broad age groups is roughly similar to that for the village as a whole, which has 44 percent of its total population under twenty years of age, 46 percent within the ages of twenty and sixty, and 9 percent over sixty years of age. But it varies from one estimate of the national rural average in having a lower proportion of young people under twenty years of age and a correspondingly higher ratio of adults and especially old people over sixty.[1]

An estimation of the crude annual birth rate in West Hamlet is, in traditional demographic terms, 21.25 births per thousand persons; or, to transpose this to a smaller scale, an average of about three to four births per year for a group of 160

---

[1] The rural population of Cambodia as a whole is estimated to have 54 percent ages zero to nineteen, 42 percent ages twenty to sixty, and 4 percent over sixty (Delvert 1961, 317). Delvert does note, however, that in Kandal province the proportion of those under twenty years of age is 45 percent (1961, 316), so that Svay does not vary significantly from the provincial average.

persons.[2] In fact, for the past two years there have been about four births per annum in the hamlet. This rate is much lower than one rough estimate that in Cambodia as a whole the number of annual births is about forty-five per thousand (Steinberg 1959, 31; Delvert 1961, 317–19). Female fertility in West Svay also seems to be lower than the national average; one estimate cites 117 children less than five years of age for one hundred women between the ages of twenty and forty-four in Cambodia (Steinberg 1959, 31; Delvert 1961, 319), while in West Svay there are seventeen children under five years of age for thirty women within this age range (or 56.6 per 100). The average number of children born per couple in West Svay is 3.6, the range being from one to eight children.[3] This figure seems consistent with one rural survey that gave an average of five persons per household (if we assume that one or two of a house's inhabitants are parents), although it is less than Delvert's estimate that a Cambodian family averages five living children (see Delvert 1961, 319, for discussions of both estimates). The reasons for this relatively low birth rate in West Svay are unclear. Apart from abstinence, there are no means of limiting conception (see chapter 6). The long period of suckling children may be a factor in limiting births, although lactation is evidently no guarantee against pregnancy (see Kehoe 1960). It is usual to breastfeed children until the age of two or even later, and one notes that the majority of children in West Svay families are spaced at least two or three years apart. It is not unusual, however, for siblings to be five or more years apart, or for a number of years to elapse before a newly married couple has their first child, so there must be some other factors inhibiting fertility.[4] (There is one instance of outright sterility in West Hamlet, and the villagers have known of other cases.)

It is difficult to calculate exactly the mortality rate for West Svay because my records of deaths is less complete than that for births.[5] I do know of seventeen deaths

---

[2] The birth rate is calculated by the formula (from Goode and Hatt 1952, 297–98): 1/5 (number of children ages 0–4 years/total population) x 1000. By comparison, this is roughly similar to the crude annual birth rate for Bang Chan, Thailand, of 20.3 (Sharp et al. 1953, 25), but lower than the rates for Burma, Thailand as a whole, and Java (see United Nations 1951, 161).

[3] In the genealogies of residents, the largest number of children born to any known couple was ten.

[4] Nash and Nash (1963) have suggested several factors that inhibit population growth in two villages of upper Burma: late marriage age, a high percentage of bachelors and spinsters, and infrequency of remarriage, all of which will delay or withdraw women from the breeding population. In testing the applicability of these factors to West Svay, it was found that only the first was of some significance. As in Mandalay, females in West Svay usually marry in their late teens and early twenties, men in the early to midtwenties, such that some of the fertile years for female procreation are lost. But the proportion of bachelors and spinsters in Svay is not as marked as in the Nashes' communities. Further, while at first glance there is a relatively high percentage of widowed or divorced persons in Svay who have not remarried (especially women), deeper investigation shows that most of them were past the age of reproduction (or close to it) at the time they were widowed. Indeed, it is usual for widow(er)s and divorcé(e)s to remarry if they are under forty years of age. (Calculations were made to support these statements, but I shall not present the figures here.)

[5] I did not always check the date of death of siblings of West Svay adults. Moreover, the death of young children, especially babies, passes with very little community comment or notice. Thus, it is possible that the villagers did not mention some of the deaths of children in the past, although I tried to get complete information on infant and child mortality in past and recent years. In any event, a formula calculation of mortality rates must be subject to further analysis in terms of the age composition of the total population and the age of death to be fully meaningful (see United Nations 1951, 9–15).

in West Hamlet within the past fifteen years (eleven adults and six children under five years of age). This yields an average of about one death per year in the hamlet, but this figure may be too low because it is possible that not all deaths in the recent past were brought to my attention. For in one actual year (March 1959 to March 1960) there were three deaths in West Svay, though in the previous year there had been only one death (and that one accidental).[6] For purposes of comparison, Delvert (1961, 319) estimates that in the regions of Cambodia he studied, annual mortality is 2 percent or less of the population (in 1959–60 for West Svay, the deaths were 1.25 percent of the population).[7]

From limited figures, Delvert (1961, 320–21) also suggests that (a) infant mortality before one year of age is not extremely high in Cambodia, amounting to perhaps 12 percent of all births; (b) childbirth traumas, however, cause a relatively high rate of death for women between the ages of fifteen and forty-four; and (c) the greatest number of deaths come after the age of fifty-five, due to enfeeblement caused primarily by intestinal parasites and, perhaps, deficient diet. Except for mortality of women from childbirth,[8] the first and last of these points are applicable to Svay. The deaths in West Hamlet in 1959–60 were, specifically, one infant several months old, one child of three who died from unknown illnesses, and one old woman of sixty-seven who finally expired after a year of lingering ailments aggravated by age. In general, various illnesses seem to be the main cause of mortality in Svay. Villagers are often debilitated or incapacitated with various ills that are difficult for laymen to diagnose accurately but seem to indicate bronchial and/or intestinal problems as being primary. It is probable that tuberculosis, pneumonia and bronchitis, parasitic infections, and especially prolonged amoebic dysentery are common causes of occasional or chronic sickness (see also Delvert 1961, 321; United Nations 1951, 15–16).[9] In the absence of effective medical treatment (usually only traditional folk cures are utilized) such conditions may eventually prove to be fatal, particularly for the very young and the old (although, with respect to the latter, the age composition of Svay's population does not show a sharp decline until the age of seventy). Deaths from accidents seem to be relatively rare, although in 1958 a West Svay man was killed when he fell from the top of a sugar palm while collecting its sap.

---

[6] During this same period of 1959–60 there was only one adult death in the other hamlets of Svay, though it is not unlikely that there were cases of infant or child mortality not brought to my notice.

[7] Cf., for example, mortality rates per thousand of 10.6 in Thailand (1949), 16.6 in the Philippines (1940), and 20.3 in Java and Madura (1940) (United Nations 1951, 203).

[8] Of adult deaths from non-accidental causes in the past fifteen years, six were men and four were women. None of the latter died in or immediately after childbirth, although two of the women died a year or two after giving birth and may have been weakened by that experience.

[9] There also exist in Svay a number of other endemic ailments such as trachoma, ulcerous sores and other eruptions (due to yaws or dietary deficiencies?), headaches, etc. Malaria is not endemic to the Svay area, although individuals might contract it while traveling elsewhere. In the past, epidemic diseases such as smallpox and cholera were evidently of considerable danger to the villagers, but these are now largely controlled. Virtually every West Svay resident has a smallpox vaccination, and cholera and typhoid have been suppressed within the country as a whole.

# CENSUS OF HOUSEHOLDS
# IN WEST SVAY

In the parentheses following names, M = male, F = female, kinship relations to household heads are stated when necessary, and numbers indicate age. Plus sign (+) means a marriage bond, and unmarried children are listed immediately beneath the names of their parents (or parent). Household composition is as of December 1959.

| | |
|---|---|
| House 1 | Vireak (M, 42) + Srey (F, 40)<br>7 children (ages 3–18) |
| House 2 | Say (M, 50) + Pheap (F, 43)<br>5 children (ages 1–20) |
| House 3 | Phana (M, 30) + Bopha (F, 43)<br>1 child (5) |
| House 4 | Rina (M, 52, widower)<br>2 children (10, 15)<br>Rotha (Son-in-l., 39) + Setha (Rina's Da, 20) |
| House 5 | Vannary (F, 54, widow)<br>1 child (25) |
| House 6 | Sen (M, 52) + Heat (F, 44)<br>6 children (ages 5–20)<br>Pisith (Heat's Br, 40) |
| House 7 | Ang (F, 50, widow)<br>2 children (20, 23)<br>Mom (Son-i-l., 48) + Narom (Ang's Da, 29) 1 child (2) |
| House 8 | Kosal (M, 54) + Ra (F, 48)<br>5 children (ages 10–21) |
| House 9 | Pol (M, 54) + Rouen (F, 48)<br>3 children (ages 7–21) |
| House 10 | Many (M, 64) + Seng (F, 67)<br>Sophat (Son-i-l., 27) + Touch (Da, 27)<br>3 children (ages 3–7) |
| House 11 | Kouch (M, 45) + Thida (F, 37)<br>5 children (ages 1–19)<br>Ken (Thida's Si, 26) + Peou (M, 30) |
| House 12 | Van (M, 71) + Many (F, 67)<br>Kouch (Son-i-l., 21) + Ny (Da, 30)<br>1 child (newborn) |

*(Continued)*

| | |
|---|---|
| House 13 | Vanna (F, 51, spinster)<br>Neang (Vanna's niece, 33) + Yat (M, 31)<br>2 children (6, 12) |
| House 14 | Ran (M, 39) + Ry (F, 34)<br>3 children (ages 4–12) |
| House 15 | Rattana (M, 39) + Seila (F, 38)<br>3 children (ages 7–15) |
| House 16 | Temporarily vacant.<br>Occupants gone to Phnom Penh. |
| House 17 | Sithouk (F, 56, widow)<br>1 child (20)<br>Phal (Son, 24) + Pich (F, 26)<br>1 child (1)<br>Vichet (Sithouk's *towaa* son, 20) |
| House 18 | Chea (M, 35) + Mean (F, 26)<br>3 children (ages 1–7) |
| House 19 | Sam (M, 35) + Phalla (F, 34)<br>2 children (4, 8) |
| House 20 | Kompha (M, 66) + Leak (F, 60)<br>Rith (Son, 42) + Nara (F, 35)<br>4 children (ages 4–15) |
| House 21 | Heng (M, 69) + Seang (F, 61)<br>2 children (20, 26) |
| House 22 | Samnang (M, 60) + Phoan (F, 58)<br>1 child (14) |
| House 23 | Nen (M, 33) + Sophal (F, 32)<br>3 children (ages 1–7) |
| House 24 | Sein (M, 48) + Dany (F, 31)<br>1 child (10) |
| House 25 | Muoy (divorcée, 45)<br>1 child (20)<br>Kanga (Muoy's niece, 30) + Hak (M, 36)<br>2 children (1/2, 5)<br>Poas (Muoy's nephew, Kanga's brother) |
| House 26 | Rom (widow, 68)<br>Sok (Son-i-l., 47) + Sreypich (Rom's's Da, 35)<br>1 child (8) |
| House 27 | Map (M, 80) + Sethol (F, 71) |
| House 28 | Daen (M, 51) + Oeurn (F, 46) |
| House 29 | Bun (M, 45) + Nary (F, 42)<br>4 children (ages 7–19) |
| House 30 | Peng (M, 53) + Aun (F, 40)<br>4 children (ages 6–22) |
| House 31 | Sareth (divorcé, 25) |
| House 32 | Bros (M, 34) + Noch (F, 41)<br>2 children (9, 18) |

# KINSHIP TERMINOLOGY

Two aspects of Khmer kinship terminology will be discussed: formal terms of reference and common terms of address. There is also a system of what might be called informal terms of reference that largely parallels the system of address. The description will be based primarily upon data given by Svay villagers, with some reference to the minimal information on kin terminology in some of the literature on Cambodia.

## FORMAL TERMS OF REFERENCE

By formal terms of reference I mean the most complete designation of a particular category of kin. Tables A and B list the primary terms and their denotata for consanguineal and affinal relatives and a schematic diagram of the terminology for consanguineals is presented in diagram 1. An examination of this list will reveal that the following principles (see Kroeber 1909) underlie the system.

(1) Generation. Each generation has distinct terms (even the modifiers that designate an affinal relation are strongly generational). In common usage, recognition of kin extends to five generations, above and below Ego, although Guesdon's (1930) dictionary and Leclère (1898) cite terms that would encompass seven generations in each direction. In actual practice, the effective range of kin is further compressed to two generations above and below Ego.

(2) Lineality and collaterality. In the system of formal terms of reference, the nuclear family and its direct lineal ascendents and descendants are terminologically demarcated from collateral relatives such as cousins, uncles, nephews, etc. (In terms of address and informal terms of reference, however, the line between lineals and collaterals becomes blurred or almost non-existent on Ego's and descending generations; see below.)

An examination of diagram 1 shows that terminology for collaterals has uneven range on different generations. The furthest lateral extension is on Ego's generation where a term exists for fourth cousin. But in practice, as noted in chapter 3, villagers rarely have a clear idea of connections beyond first and second cousins. Despite the fact that cousin terms explicitly refer back to common progenitors, villagers often have hazy recall of even grandparents and are not accustomed to tracing the rather complicated upward and downward lineal and collateral links that relate remote cousins.[1]

On ascending and descending generations there are distinct terms for only one outward degree of collaterality: parents' siblings and siblings' children. In village life there are no distinct terms for other collateral kinsmen such as grandparents' siblings, children of first cousins, etc. If necessary, such relatives can be designated by descriptions of the relationship that use existing terms (e.g., children of first cousins = *kmuy cidon muy* or *kon cidon muy*, where *cidon muy* = first cousin; *kon* = child; *kmuy* = in the narrow sense, niece/nephew and in the broad sense, collateral relative of the first descending

---

[1] Burling (1965b, 116) makes a similar point for kin reckoning among the Burmese.

generation). But there is sometimes considerable uncertainty as to the proper designation for some categories of kinsmen. When asked, for example, as to the term(s) for grandparents' siblings, villagers gave a variety of responses ranging from comments such as "They are dead; there are no words for them," to suggestions of possible terms such as "grandparents' siblings" (*bòng p?on cidon citaa*), "grandmother aunt" (*cidon ming*), or "grandfather uncle" (*citaa miê*). (Similar confusion is evident in Guesdon's dictionary, which gives a variety of terms for great-aunt and grand-uncle [see 1930 1:521, 805; 2:1345, 1359, 1381.) In any event, this lack of universal agreement (or sometimes even any notion whatsoever) as to terms for such collaterals is consistent with the fact that villagers do not readily remember or trace extended genealogical connections.

(3) Sex of relative. Inherent sex distinctions are present only in the ascending generations where there are distinct terms for grandmother, grandfather, aunt, uncle, mother, and father. In Ego's and descending generations, there are simply blanket terms for "child," "sibling's child," and "grandchild" that apply to both sexes. Sex differentiation can be made, if desired, by appending the words for "male" (*proh*) or "female" (*srêy*) onto a kin term (e.g., *kon proh* = son, *kon srêy* = daughter), but consideration of sex is by no means a primary one.[2] If a villager says, "My child . . ." and one inquires, "Which child?" one is just as likely to be answered with "My eldest child," "My child in Phnom Penh," or some other distinguishing characteristic as that of sex, unless the sex of the child is specifically questioned or unless sex is an important distinguishing feature.

(4) Relative age. The terms for "older" (*bòng*) and "younger" (*p?on*) are among the most ubiquitous words in Khmer, and the principle of relative age is important in both Ego's and the first ascending generation. On Ego's generation, siblings and cousins are distinguished on the basis of their chronological age relative to Ego's age. Aunts and uncles, however, are differentiated on the basis of their chronological age relative to the age of the connecting parent (i.e., the parent's older brother and sister are distinct from the parent's younger brother and sister).

Moreover, the general principle of calculating another person's age relatively to one's own becomes critical in determining what kin term will be used to address others; indeed, this principle can override the fact of actual genealogical relationship in choosing terms of address (see below).

(5) Consanguineals vs. affinals. There are no special terms used only for affinals, except the terms for husband, wife, and one's child's parents-in-law. But consanguineal relatives may be distinguished from affinal kinsmen by the use of modifiers placed after the basic kin terms. For example: *bòngkaüt* = consanguineal, full, or close kin; *kmek* = affinal of the first ascending generation. In practice, the distinction between the relatives by blood and those by marriage is often not specified unless specifically questioned. But the term *bòngkaüt* is of great importance to the ethnologist for distinguishing consanguineal relatives when reference terms are often used in an ambiguous manner, assigned on the basis of relative age, or extended to non-kin. Thus, when a villager says "This is my *bòng*," one can ask: Is that your *bòng bòngkaüt* (actual sibling), or *bòng cidon muy* (cousin) or *bòng tlay* (spouse's sibling or sibling's spouse), or what?

---

[2] Some authors (e.g. Guesdon 1930) cite separate terms for son, daughter, nephew, niece, etc., by appending the words for male or female as noted. But this is an ethnocentric imposition of European kinship terminology. On the other hand, other writers translate a term such as "bong" as "older brother" when actually it applies to elder siblings of both sexes. Zadrozny 1955, 314 also errs in saying that sex distinctions are made throughout the system.

(6) Sex of speaker. The sex of the speaker makes no difference, except that there are different terms for "husband" and "wife."

Before concluding this section on reference terminology, it should be remarked that apart from what I have called the formal terms of reference, there is also what might be considered a system of more common or informal terms of reference. That is, when villagers identify another person as a relative, even to me who was a relative stranger in many respects, the terms they used were rarely as complete as the full, formal terms presented in table A.[3]

Many "informal" reference terms are either abbreviated or extended to cover various other kin (see the example of "*bòng*" above) such that the exact relationship is often unclear and further probing is needed to uncover the exact genealogical tie. Villagers realize, however, that the terms apply in a strict sense to particular categories of relatives, or to near rather than more remote kin (see also Burling 1965b, 114, 116 for a similar situation in Burmese terminology). See table B for the most commonly used terms of reference and their designata.

TERMS OF ADDRESS

Kinsmen are directly addressed in a variety of ways that can be summarized as follows: (1) formal kin terms, (2) contractions or variations upon the formal kin terms, (3) formal names or nicknames (either common nicknames or such personal nicknames as "Shorty"), (4) kin term plus personal name, (5) term applied to an individual of a certain age group or sex, (6) second person personal pronoun, or (7) teknonymy between husband and wife. The various modes of address presented in table C need no special explanation for the most part, but a few points warrant some comment.

(1) A comparison of the system of address and the formal terms of reference reveals some interesting differences. Generationality is still strongly evident, as is relative age. But the latter, in the sense of age relative to Ego, takes on a much more significant role (see below). The distinction between lineals and collaterals is still present on the first ascending and descending generations, but cousin terminology changes from Eskimo to Hawaiian (cf. a similar situation among the Subanum as noted by Frake 1960, 59). (Moreover, the terms *bòng* and *p?on* are used not only by siblings and cousins, but by husband and wife to one another.) Furthermore, there is great extension of terms for collaterals to other or more remote kin of the appropriate age. Sex distinction remains in terms for grandparents, parents, and parents' younger siblings but is lost for parents' older siblings. The distinction between consanguineals and affinals is lost altogether. (Except that the second person personal pronoun, *neak*, seems to be used only for affinals, the latter are addressed by the same terms of address used for consanguineals.)

(2) Individuals may address a relative by a kin term that is determined on the basis of relative age rather than actual genealogical link. Theoretically the genealogical tie should govern the choice of terms; for example, a nephew who happens to have an uncle younger than himself should still address him as "uncle." In practice, however, age differences play an important role, and a common situation is, for example, a child of ten addressing a female cousin of thirty as "aunt" rather than "cousin." This may

---

[3] This seems to be similar to what Frake (1960, 59) describes for the Subanum of the Philippines in saying: "[An individual] chooses among alternative designative terms according to the degree of specification required in a particular cultural context."

even carry over into reference terminology where such a cousin might be designated as "aunt-cousin" (*ming cidon muy*), connoting that this is a cousin whose age (relative to the speaker) is equivalent to that of an aunt. In fact, the primacy of the relative age criterion over that of actual genealogical connection is very useful in a society where careful accounting of extensive genealogical linkages is rare. Thus, when one knows that so-and-so is a relative but is not certain exactly what sort of kin he is, a kin term can be properly assigned on the basis of relative age differences and the feeling of kinship can be maintained.

(3) Whether one uses a kin term or an individual's personal name in addressing someone has significance of several sorts. (a) Use of the kin terms (or a variation thereof) can imply respect toward elders who should be treated with deference.[4] Grandparents and parents are never called by personal names; parents' siblings are usually addressed by kin terms; and older siblings and cousins ideally should be called *bòng* (older person) rather than by name. (b) When personal names are used in free variation with or in place of kin term, it generally indicates a relation of affection and familiarity. Aunt or uncle might be addressed by personal names when they have very warm and informal relations with nephew/niece. Similarly, individuals of one's own or descending generations are addressed by name with as great or greater frequency than kin terms because relations with one's peers usually involve familiarity and informality, while interaction with younger people need not involve punctilio. (Note also that the use of personal names also has a certain convenience when kin terms can and often are extended to numerous individuals, e.g., in catching someone's attention in a group where a number of people could respond to the same kin term.) (c) But if a kin term is used exclusively in addressing someone on one's own or descending generation, this usually indicates a certain politesse toward a kinsman with whom one is not especially intimate (though not necessarily unfriendly).

(4) Two non-kin terms of address are frequently used. (a) *Niêng*, in the narrowest sense, can be translated as "woman" or "you (female)" (see also Guesdon 1930 2:884). It is also, however, frequently used to address young males (up to the time they become monks), as well as females (up to about the age of forty). The prefix *m* is usually added in addressing females (*m'niêng*) and *a* for males (*aniêng*). (b) *Neak* is the second person personal pronoun (it also means "people" or "person"). Interestingly, it seems to be used only in addressing affinals (e.g., cousin's spouse, brother-in-law, etc.), although it is not the only form by which affinals are addressed. (It is unclear whether *neak* may imply a certain formality toward affinals.)

(5) The greatest number of alternative forms of address exists between husband and wife. During the period of betrothal and the outset of marriage, the male is traditionally addressed by the fiancée/bride as "elder person" (*bòng*), while he calls her "younger one" (*p?on*). (This might be viewed as serving to put the affianced or new spouses, who are sometimes virtually unknown to one another, in a sort of "kinship situation," with the male assuming the position of authority, strength, and protectiveness.) With the birth of children, teknonymy is a common practice (usually using the

---

[4] One can indicate special deference by preceding a kin term with *look*, which, in this instance, is comparable to "sir" or "madame," e.g., *look taa* = sir grandfather, *look ming* = madame aunt. In such cases the person addressed is usually someone with whom one is not very familiar. Zadrozny 1955, 319 states that "Sanskrit kin terms are used in situations where extreme deference is called for." This may be true among more educated urbanites but was not evident in village life.

name of the eldest child if there are more than one offspring). Other variations also occur: *neak* to address the husband, *niêng* to address the wife, and sometimes humorous or private nicknames such as "ancient one" or "Old Lady Diamond." In later life, a couple may address one another by grandparent terms, teknonymy using the name of a grandchild, or personal names. And some couples prefer not to use any terms or names whatsoever in speaking to one another (the structure of the Khmer language being such that the second person personal pronoun or equivalent can easily be omitted).

(6) When one can trace a kin relationship to another person through both oneself and one's spouse, one may elect to address that relative by either one of the terms designating the genealogical connection. For example, Chhean is both Pol's first cousin and Pol's wife's aunt; and Pol chooses to address her as "aunt" "as my wife does."

## EXTENSION OF KIN TERMS TO NON-KIN

An important and common practice in both rural and urban life is the use of kin terms to address (or sometimes refer to) individuals who are not really genealogical kinsmen (see also Bitard 1955). Neighbors, friends, and even absolute strangers with whom one comes in fleeting contact may be addressed by a kin term, with the important proviso that the individual so addressed is of an equal or lower social status. (A strong feeling for proper punctilio and respect for superiors, such as government officials, dictates that impersonal, formal, non-kin terms be used in speaking to those of higher status.)[5]

The use of a kin term in speaking to a non-kinsman has different implications depending on the situation. (1) A kin term may be used in reference to (or in addressing) a person who is considered to be a very close friend, as an expression of affection and intimacy. Only in this case of close friendship will a kin term be used in reference to a non-kin (in actual address, personal names are more likely to be used unless it is a *towaa* fictive kin relationship). (2) A kin term may be used in speaking to acquaintances or even strangers (e.g., people from another village whom one hardly knows or has just encountered) as a mark of cordiality, respect (especially toward older people), and a tacit acknowledgement of being on the same social level (one does not place oneself in an inferior social position by using terms commonly employed for individuals of higher standing, nor can one be accused of putting on airs if common kin terms are used). (3) A kin term may be used in an impersonal manner to strangers with whom one comes in transitory contact, such as pedicab drivers or market vendors, because they are convenient forms of address. In such situations the other party (who is usually in a position of offering some service) may respond with "sir" or "madame" rather than a reciprocal kin term if he feels that the speaker should be accorded some deference.

One chooses a particular kin term to address a non-kin depending on the latter's age relative to oneself. An individual who is considerably older than oneself will be called "grandfather" (*taa*) if male, "grandmother" (*yeey*) if female, or perhaps "parent's older sibling" (*tom*) for either sex (see also Maspero 1915, 268). A person who is perhaps fifteen years or more older than oneself will be addressed as "parent's younger sister or brother" (*ming* or *puu*) depending on sex. Someone who is slightly older than oneself will be called "older sibling or cousin" (*bŏng*), while a slightly younger person will be addressed as *p?on*. Those of a younger generation will usually be called

---

[5] Such terms are *look* for males, *look srêy* for married or older women, and *neak srêy* for young women.

"sibling's child" (*kmuy*) or sometimes "child" (*kon*). Much younger individuals are addressed as "grandchild" (*cau*). Thus, a man who is thirty years of age may be called "grandfather" by a child of two, "uncle" by an adolescent, "older brother" by a person of twenty, "sibling's child" by an individual of forty-five, and perhaps "grandchild" by someone who is seventy. He in turn will usually use the appropriate reciprocal kin term in reply, unless some other non-kin form of address is in order.

TABLE A
FORMAL TERMS OF REFERENCE

Note: in addition to the standard abbreviations for designating kin, the following will also be used.

Sib = sibling        Ol = older
Pa = parent         Yo = younger
Gr = great or grand   Ch = child or children

GENERAL TERMS

*bong-p?on* = relatives in general (literally: older-younger)
*cidon-citaa* = ancestors, or general lineal ascendants (literally: grandmother-grandfather)
*kon-cau* = descendants in general (literally: children-grandchildren)
*may-au* = parents (literally: mother-father)

BASIC SPECIFIC TERMS

| | | |
|---|---|---|
| *cóng kêl* | ជុងកុល or ជុងគល់ | "Head of the line" (Guesdon 1930 1:521). By implication the 7th ascending generation progenitor. This term is not used by villages, although it may be utilized in some strata of the society (e.g., royalty) where genealogical connections can be of importance. Cf. also Leclère 1898 2:480. |
| *cipa* or *tum kêl* | ជីប៉ា | Sixth ascending generation lineal ascendant. The first term is given by Guesdon 1930 1:521 but is not used by villages. The latter have heard of the second term (cited also in CMCC 42.004) but, again, it is not in common usage. |
| *cidon liê* | ជីដូនលា | GrGrGrGrMo<br>These ancestors of the fifth ascending generation are the limit of kin terminology among the villages. |
| *citaa liê* | ជីតាលា | GrGrGrGrFa |
| *cidon luêt* | ជីដូនល្អុត | GrGrGrMo |
| *citaa luêt* | ជីតាល្អុត | GrGrGrFa |
| *cidon tuêt* | ជីដូនទ្អុត | GrGrMo |
| *citaa tuêt* | ជីតាទុត | GrGrFa |

| | | |
|---|---|---|
| *cidon* | ជីដូន | GrMo (i.e., MoMo, FaMo) |
| *citaa* | ជីតា | GrFa (i.e., MoFa, FaFa) |
| *aupok* | ឪពុក | Fa |
| *aupok cong* | ឪពុកចុង | step-Fa |
| *aupok som* or *reaksa* | ឪពុកសុំ or រក្សា | adoptive Fa |
| *num proh* | ញោមប្រុស | term for Fa used by a son while the latter is a monk |
| *mday* | ម្ដាយ | Mo |
| *mday cong* | ម្ដាយចុង | step-Mo |
| *mday som* | ម្ដាយសុំ | adoptive Mo |
| *num srey* | ញោមស្រី | term for Mo used by a son while the latter is a monk |
| *aupok tom* | ឪពុកធំ | FaOlBr; MoOlBr; FaOlSiHu, MoOlSiHu (note: *tom* = big) |
| *mday tom* | ម្ដាយធំ | FaOlSi, MoOlSi, FaOlBrWi, MoOlBrWi |
| *miê* or *puu* | មា or ពូ | FaYoBr, MoYoBr; FaYoSiHu, MoYoSiHu (note: *miê* seems to be used only for reference and never address, while *puu* is used often in address and only occasionally for reference)[a] |
| *ming* or *mday mingm* | មីង or ម្ដាយមីង | MoYoSi, FaYoSi, FaYoBrWi, MoYoBrWi |
| *bòng*[b] | បង | OlSib |
| *p?on* | ប្អូន | YoSib |
| *bòng-p?on cidon muy* | បងប្អូនជីដូនមួយ | First cousin (note: *cidon muy* = one grandmother) |
| *bòng cidon muy* | បងជីដូនមួយ | first cousin older than Ego |
| *p?on cidon muy* | ប្អូនជីដូនមួយ | first cousin younger than Ego |
| *bòng-p?on cituêt muy* | បងប្អូនជីទួតមួយ | Second cousin (note: *cituêt muy* = one GrGrPa) |
| *bòng cituêt muy* | បងជីទួតមួយ | second cousin older than Ego |
| *p?on cituêt muy* | ប្អូនជីទួតមួយ | second cousin younger than Ego |
| *bòng-p?on ciluêt muy* | បងប្អូនជីល្អួតមួយ | Third cousin (note: *ciluêt muy* = one GrGrGrPa) (same distinction between older and younger as above) |
| *bòng-p?on ciliê muy*[c] | បងប្អូនជីលាមួយ | Fourth cousin (note: *ciliê muy* = one GrGrGrPa) (same distinction between older and younger as above) |
| *Kon* | កូន | child or children |
| *kom som, kon cùm* | កូនសុំ, កូនចិញ្ចឹម | adopted Ch |
| *look kon, look kru* | លោកកូន, លោកគ្រូ | terms by which parents refer to and address a son while the latter is a monk, and ideally even afterwards as well |

*(Continued)*

**(Continued)**

| | | |
|---|---|---|
| *kmuy* | ក្មួយ | in the strict sense: Si's Ch<br>in the broadest sense: the child of a collateral relative (e.g., the term *kmuy cidon muy* is sometimes used to designate children of first cousins)[d] |
| *cau* | ចៅ | in the strict sense: GrCh<br>in the broadest sense: GrCh of collaterals and descendants in general |
| *cau tuêt* | ចៅទួត | GrGrCh |
| *cau luêt* | ចៅលួត | GrGrGrCh |
| *cau liê* | ចៅលា | GrGrGrGrCh |

[a] Leclère 1898, 2:169–70, says that *aupok tom* and *mday tom* are paternal uncle and aunt, while *miê* and *ming* are maternal uncle and aunt. On the other hand, Guesdon 1930, 2:1236, states that *puu* is paternal uncle. Both seem in error. CMCC 42.004 says that in some regions, *puu* is FaYoBr and *miê* is MoYoBr; I do not know if this is true.

[b] *Bòng* can also be used as a verb to mean "to be older than," e.g., Vireak bòng Srey = Vireak is older than Srey.

[c] Leclère 1898, 2:525, gives the term *ci sandan* for fifth cousin, but this is not common usage.

[d] *Kmuy* also means "clients, servants, attendants," according to Guesdon 1930, 1:190.

## Modifying Terms

The following terms may be appended after a basic kin term to specify consanguinity or affinity (an affinal relative may be either a consanguineal kinsman of one's spouse, or the spouse of a consanguineal relative).

| | | |
|---|---|---|
| *bòngkaùt* | បង្កើត | literally: "to beget, create" (Guesdon 1930 2:919). When added to a kin term (e.g., *bòng bòngkaùt*), it means that the kinsman is a true, full consanguineal relative (as opposed to a fictive, step-, half, or affinal kin). |
| *tlay* | ថ្លៃ | an affinal of one's own generation |
| | បងថ្លៃ | e.g. *bòng tlay* = sibling's spouse, spouse's sibling |
| | ជីដូនមួយថ្លៃ | *cidon muy tlay* = cousin's spouse, spouse's cousin |
| *kmek* | ក្មេក | affinal of an ascending generation who is a consanguineal relative of one's spouse |
| | ឪពុកក្មេក | e.g. *aupok kmek* = Fa-in-law |
| | ម្ដាយក្មេក | *mday kmek* = Mo-in-law |
| | ជីតាក្មេក | *citaa kmek* = spouse's GrFa |
| *pròsaa* | ប្រសា | affinal of a descending generation who is married to a consanguineal relative |
| | កូនប្រសា | e.g. *kon pròsaa* = Son-in-law or Da-in-law |
| | ក្មួយប្រសា | *kmuy pròsaa* = spouse of niece or nephew |
| | ចៅប្រសា | *cau pròsaa* = spouse of GrCh |

OTHER TERMS FOR AFFINALS

| | | |
|---|---|---|
| *pday* | ប្ដី | Hu |
| *prapun* | ប្រពន្ធ | Wi |
| *tlong* | ដង្កង | the parents of one's child's spouse |

MISCELLANEOUS

If necessary, the distinction between paternal and maternal relatives may be designated by the use of the terms:

| | | |
|---|---|---|
| *khang aupok* | ខាងឪពុក | on the Fa's side |
| *khang mday* | ខាងម្ដាយ | on the Mo's side |

Kinsmen can also be distinguished as:

| | | |
|---|---|---|
| *khang pday* | ខាងប្ដី | on the Hu's side |
| *khang prapun* | ខាងប្រពន្ធ | on the Wi's side |

(Some data on Khmer kinship terminology, generally fragmentary, may be found in the following sources: Guesdon 1930, passim; Leclère 1898 1:223; 2:169–70, 480, 525; Maspero 1915, 264, 267–68; Bitard 1955, 475–76; Zadrozny 1955, 314, 319; Murdock 1957, 680; CMCC 42.003.)

TABLE B
COMMON TERMS OF REFERENCE

The most commonly used terms of reference and their designata are as follows:

| | | |
|---|---|---|
| *cidon* | ជីដូន | GrMo |
| *citaa* | ជីតា | GrFa |
| *mday* or *may* | ម្ដាយ or ម៉ែ | Mo, StepMo, adopted Mo |
| *aupok* | ឪពុក | Fa, StepFa, adopted Fa |
| *mday tom* or *tom* | ម្ដាយធំ or ធំ | PaOlSi, PaOlBrWi |
| *ming* | មីង | PaYoSi, PaYoBrWi, or collateral kinswoman on first ascending generation |
| *miê* | មា | PaYoBr, PaYoSiHu, or collateral male kinsman on first ascending generation |
| *bòng* | បង | OlSib, Ol cousin, or relative in general on Ego's generation |
| *p?on* | ប្អូន | YoSib, Yo cousin, or relative in general on Ego's generation |
| *cidon muy* | ជីដូនមួយ | cousin |
| *kon* | កូន | Ch, stepCh, adopted Ch, Ch-in-law |
| *kmuy* | ក្មួយ | Si's Ch, Ch of first cousin or other collateral relative on Ego's generation, i.e., a collateral on the first descending generation |
| *cau* | ចៅ | GrCh of oneself or any collateral relative |

Note that affinals (whether the spouses of consanguineal relatives or the consanguineal kin of one's own spouse) are also frequently referred to by the preceding
terms, as well as by a term plus the appropriate modifier for affinals, or by the modifier alone (e.g., "She is a *tlay*").

TABLE C
COMMON TERMS OF ADDRESS

| Kinsman | Formal Reference Term | Forms of address |
|---|---|---|
| GrGrFa | *citaa tuet* (ជីតាទួត) | *taa, tuet* (តា, ទួត) |
| GrGrMo | *cidon tuet* (ជីដូនទួត) | *yeey, tuet* (យាយ, ទួត) |
| GrFa | *citaa* (ជីតា) | *taa* (តា) |
| GrMo | *cidon* (ជីដូន) | *yeey* (យាយ) |
| GrPaSi | | *yeey ming* (យាយមីង) |
| GrPaBr | | *taa puu, taa mie* (តាពូ, តាម) |
| Fa | *aupok* (ឪពុក) | *au, pok, paa,*[a] *aupok* (ឪ, ពុក, ប៉ា, ឪពុក) |
| Mo | *mday* (ម្ដាយ) | *may* (ម៉ែ) |
| PaOlBr, PaOlSiHu | *aupok tom* (ឪពុកធំ) | *may* (ម៉ែ) |
| PaOlSi, PaOlBrWi | *aupok tom* (ឪពុកធំ) | *tom, om* (ធំ, អុំ) |
| PaYoBr, PaYoSiHu | *mie, puu* (ម, ពូ) | *puu* (ពូ), sometimes name |
| PaYoSi, PaYoBrWi | *ming* (មីង) | *ming*, sometimes name |
| OlSib | *Bong* (បង) | *bong* (ideally), name |
| YoSib | *p?on* (ប្អូន) | *p?on, oon*, name, nickname |
| Ol cousin | *bong cidon muy* (បងជីដូនមួយ) | *bong, name, niêng, ming, puu* |
| Yo cousin | *p?on cidon muy* (ប្អូនជីដូនមួយ) | *p?on, oon, name, niêng* |
| Hu | *Pday* (ប្ដី) name or nickname, nothing | *bong* (បង), teknonymy, *neak* (អ្នក) |
| Wi | *prapun* (ប្រពន្ធ) name or nickname, nothing | *p?on* (ប្អូន), teknonymy, *niêng* (នាង) |
| Affinals of the first ascending generation, consanguineals of one's spouse | *kmek* (ក្មេក) | addressed as consanguineals, or as spouse addresses them e.g. Fa-in-law addressed as Fa |
| Affinals of first descending generation, spouses of consanguineal kin | *prosaa* (ប្រសា) | addressed as consanguineals |
| Pa of Ch's spouse | *tlong* (ថ្លង) | *neak* (អ្នក) |

[a] Some villagers suggested that paa was derived from French.

## TABLE D
## COMMON KIN TERMS OF ADDRESS AND THEIR DESIGNATA

| | | |
|---|---|---|
| *taa* | តា | GrFa, or any male kin of grandparental age relative to Ego |
| *Yeey* | យាយ | GrMo, or any female kin of grandparental age relative to Ego |
| *May* | ម៉ែ | Mo, step-Mo, adopted Mo, Mo-in-law |
| *au, pok, aupok, paa* | ឪ, ពុក, ឪពុក, ប៉ា | Fa, step-Fa, adopted Fa, Fa-in-law |
| *tom, om* | អុំ | PaOlSib, PaOlSibSpouse, or any male or female kin of the appropriate age relative to Ego |
| *Puu* | ពូ | PaYoBr, PaYoSiHu, or any male kin of the appropriate age |
| *Ming* | មីង | PaYoSi, PaYoBrWi, or any female kin of the appropriate age |
| *Bong* | បង | OlSib, Ol cousin, or any male or female kin slightly older than Ego; also Hu (woman speaking) |
| *p?on* | ប្អូន | YoSib, Yo cousin, or any male or female kin slightly younger than Ego; also Wi (man speaking) |
| *kon* | កូន | Ch, Ch's spouse (the word may also be used to mean "child" or "children" in the non-kin sense) |
| *kmuy* | ក្មួយ | SibCh, SibChSp, children of any collateral relative on Ego's generation (and their spouses), or any male or female kin of the appropriate age relative to Ego |
| *Cau* | ចៅ | GrCh, GrChSpouse, GrCh of collaterals, any male or female kin of the appropriate age relative to Ego |

| | | | | | | |
|---|---|---|---|---|---|---|
| +5 | GrGrGrGrFa citaa lié | GrGrGrGrMo cidon lié | | ‖ Lineal cf. collateral | | |
| +4 | GrGrGrFa citaa luét | GrGrGrMo cidon luét | | —— Generation | | |
| +3 | GrGrFa citaa tuét | GrGrMo cidon tuét | | ----- Relative age | | |
| +2 | GrFa citaa | GrMo cidon | | ⋮ Sex distinction | | |
| +1 | Fa aupok | Mo mday | PaOlBr ┊ PaOlSi<br>PaYoBr ┊ PaYoSi | | | |
| EGO | Ol sibling bòng<br>Yo sibling p?òn | | Ol 1st Cousin<br>Yo cidon muy | Ol 2nd Co.<br>Yo cituét muy | Ol 3rd Co.<br>Yo ciluét muy | Ol 4th Co.<br>Yo cilié muy |
| –1 | Child kon | | SibCh kmuy | | | |
| –2 | GrCh cau | | | | | |
| –3 | GrGrCh cau tuét | | | | | |
| –4 | GrGrGrCh cau luét | | | | | |
| –5 | GrGrGrGrCh cau lié | | | | | |

**Schematic diagram 1** Terms of reference

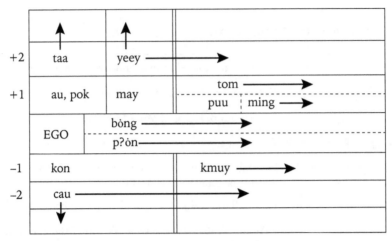

**Schematic diagram 2** Terms of address

# APPENDIX F

# CULTIVATED FLORA
# IN WEST SVAY

N.B. For the scientific identifications, I am indebted to M. Ho Tong Lyp (designated as HTL), botanist with the Agronomy Division of the Khmer government. See also Vialard-Goudou 1959 (abbreviated as VG).

| Western name | Cambodian Name | | Scientific name |
|---|---|---|---|
| lemon grass | *sluk kree* | ស្លឹកគ្រៃ | *Cymbopogon citratus* (HTL) |
| red pepper | *mtIh plaot* | ម្ទេសផ្លោក | *Capsicum annum Linn.* (HTL, VG:83, 86) |
| another pepper | *mtIh kmang* | ម្ទេសខ្មាំង | *Capsicum* (HTL) |
| turmeric | *romiet* | រមៀត | *Curcuma longa* (HTL) |
| basil | *cii* | ជី | *Ocimum basilicum Linn.* (HTL, VG:83, 86) |
| mint | *cii po hue* | ជីប្រហើរ | *Mentha Linn.* (HTL, VG:82, 86) |
| galanga | *medeng* | ម្ទេង | *Alpinia conchigera* (HTL) |
| loufa gourd | *ronung*[a] | ននោង | *Luffa cylindrica/acutangula* (HTL) |
| type of gourd | *trolayt* | ត្រឡាច | *Cucurtftacerifera* (HTL) |
| type of gourd | *peneu* | ផ្នៅ | *Aegle marmelos* (HTL) |
| sweet potato (vine) | *damlong cvie* | ដំឡូងផ្លា | *Ipomoea batatas* (HTL) cf. *Dioscorea alata or Linn.* (VG: 46, 53) |
| yam | *damlong dong* | ដំឡូងដួង | *Dioscorea* (HTL) |
| white potato | *damlong barang* | ដំឡូងបារាំង | *Solanum tuberosum Linn.* (HTL, VG:88, 91) |
| cucumber | *trosaak* | ត្រសក់ | *Cucumis sativa Linn.* (HTL, VG:88, 91) |
| (summer squash?) | *ropou* | ល្ពៅ | *Cucurbita pepo DeCand.* (HTL, VG:88, 91) |
| beans | *sendayk*[c] | សណ្ដែក | *Phaseolus sp.* (HTL) |
| eggplant | *trop veng* | ត្រប់ វែង | *Solanum melongena Linn.* (HTL, VG:85, 86) |
| celery | *vansoy* | វ៉ាន់ស៊ុយ | *Apium graveolens Linn.* (HTL, VG:84, 86) |
| tomato | *pEng poo* | ប៉េងប៉ោះ | *Lycopersicum esculentum Mill.* (HTL, VG:42, 45) |
| sugar palm or lontar | *dam tnaot* | ដើមត្នោត | *Borassus flabillefera* Linn. (HTL, VG:42, 45) |
| coconut | *dam dong*[d] | ដើមដូង | *Cocos nucifera Linn.* (HTL, VG:43, 45) |

*(Continued)*

(Continued)

| Western name | Cambodian Name | | Scientific name |
|---|---|---|---|
| banana | ceek[e] | របក | *Musa paradiseaca Linn.* (HTL, VG:47, 53) |
| papaya | lehong | ល្ហុង | *Carica papaya Linn.* (HTL, VG:75, 79) |
| guava | trobayt | ត្រប៉ែក | *Psidium goyava Linn.* (HTL, VG:76, 79) |
| orange, tangerine | kroit[f] | ក្រូច | *Citrus sp.* (HTL) |
| grapefruit | kroit tlong | ក្រូចថ្លុង | *Citrus grandis* |
| sweet sop | tiep | ទៀប | *Annona squamosa Linn.* (HTL, VG:51, 53) |
| mango | svay | ស្វាយ | *Mangifera indica Linn.* (HTL, VG:69, 70) |
| sapodilla | lemut | ល្មុត | *Sapotaceae family* (HTL, VG:80, 86) |
| ebony | can | ចន្ទ | *Diospyros dodecandra Lou.* (HTL, VG:56, 61) |
| tamarind | ampll | អំពិល | *Tamarindus indica Linn.* (HTL, VG:56, 61) |
| jackfruit | keneu | ខ្នុរ | *Artocarpus heterophylla Lam.* (HTL, VG:49, 53) |
| gooseberry | kantuet | កន្ទួត | *Averrhoa acida* (HTL) |
| egg fruit | seetdaa | សេដា | *Sapotaceae family* (HTL) |
| betel | mluu | ម្លូ | *Piper betel* (HTL) |
| areca | slaa | ស្លា | *Areca catechu Linn.* (HTL, VG:42, 45) |
| black dye-producing tree | makloe | មករ្លើ | *Diospyros mollis* (HTL) |
| kapok | koo | គរ | *Cerba pentandra* (HTL) |
| bamboo | rosey | ឫស្សី | *Bambusa Schreber* (HTL, VG:40, 45) |

[a] Several types of *ronung* are recognized in West Svay, including *ronung crang* (*Luffa acutangula* Roxb., VG:87, 91), *ronung sayn* (*Hibiscus esculentus Linn.*, VG:73, 79), and *ronung prahêu* (*Luffa cyclindrica Linn.*, VG:87, 91).

[b] Another plant categorized by the villagers as a type of *damlong*, but not cultivated, is *damlong coo* or cassava (*Manihot utilissima*, HTL) which grows in the uncleared area west of the hamlet.

[c] Various sorts of *sendayk* are differentiated by the villagers, including *sendayk kcisey* or green bean (*Phaseolus vulgaris Linn.*, VG:59, 61) and *sendayk bay* (*Phaseolus aureau Roxb.*, VG:59, 61), both of which are cultivated in the hamlet. Also classified as *sendayk*, but not grown in Svay, are peanuts and soybeans.

[d] Villagers distinguish three sorts of coconuts.

[e] There are a great variety of bananas in Cambodia, long and short, green and yellow, with different names. Popular in West Svay are a short, fat, yellow variety (*ceek pong mwan*) and a long, green-skinned variety.

[f] The category of citrus fruits, termed *kroit* by the villagers, includes various kinds of fruits of the orange and tangerine family whose scientific designations are not altogether clear. See VG:65, 66, 67, 70 for his identifications of some Khmer terms for types of oranges or tangerines. (Note also that villagers classify lemons and limes as part of the *kroit* category, although these are not grown in Svay.)

# OWNERSHIP OF PROPERTY AND ADDITIONAL SOURCES OF INCOME

| House | Rice fields owned | Sugar palms owned | Oxen owned | Other activities providing income* |
|---|---|---|---|---|
| 1 | 1 ha. | 20 | 1–2 | makes palm sugar, drives pedicab |
| 2 | 6 a. | 0 | 1 | raises pigs, makes palm sugar, drives pedicab, works as wood cutter |
| 3 | >1 ha. | 5 | 2 | raises pigs and chickens, drives pedicab |
| 4a† | 0 | 0 | 0 | carpenter |
| 4b | 1 ha. | 8 | 3 | raises chickens, makes palm sugar, sells sugar palm fruit |
| 5 | 1 ha. | 20 | 0 | occasional work as coolie |
| 6 | 0 | 0 | 0 | works at normal school, raises pigs and chickens, sells snacks, sometimes is a gold artisan |
| 7 | 1+ ha. | 20 | 2 | occasional work as coolie |
| 8 | 1+ ha. | 9 | 4–5 | raises chickens, magic practitioner |
| 9 | 2 ha. | 30 | 2 | made palm sugar in the past |
| 10 | 34 a. | 1 | 1 | musician, makes palm sugar, hires out as agricultural help for others |
| 11 | 60 a. | 10 | 0 | drives pedicab, coolie labor, metal worker, sells snacks |
| 12 | 80 a. | 5 | 3 | made palm sugar in the past |
| 13 | 60 a. | 0 | 2 | made palm sugar in the past |
| 14 | 60 a. | 0 | 2 | raises chickens, coolie labor, made palm sugar in the past |
| 15 | 50 a. | 3 | 1 | raises pigs, drives pedicab, coolie labor, made palm sugar in the past |
| 17 | 1 ha. | 0 | 2 | coolie labor, made palm sugar in the past |
| 18 | 53 a. | 0 | 3 | raises pigs, drives pedicab, made palm sugar in the past |

*(Continued)*

| | | | | |
|---|---|---|---|---|
| 19 | 0 | 0 | 0 | works as coolie at normal school, raises chickens, made palm sugar in the past |
| 20 | 2 ha. | 20 | 2 | lay priest (achaa), weaving, sells snacks, made palm sugar in the past |
| 21 | 1 ha. | 7 | 0 | coolie labor, made palm sugar in the past |
| 22 | 50 a. | 10 | 2 | lay priest, made palm sugar in the past |
| 23 | 20 a. | 0 | 1 | gold artisan |
| 24 | (works with house 21) | 0 | 3 | makes palm sugar, drives remorque cab |
| 25a | 0‡ | 0 | 0 | sells fruits and vegetables |
| 25b | 0 | 0 | 0 | musician, barber |
| 26 | 1 ha. | 5 | 0 | chauffeur at normal school |
| 27 | 4 ha. | 100 | 0 | 0 |
| 28 | 2 ha. | 93 | 0 | carpenter |
| 29 | 1 ha. | 13 | 2 | raises pigs |
| 30 | 2 ha. | 0 | 4 | raises pigs and chickens |
| 31 | 30 a. | 10 | 0 | drives pedicab, sells surplus fruit |
| 32 | 50 a. | 0 | 2 | operates roadside restaurant |

* Such activities may be pursued by different members of the family, or more than one individual may engage in a particular pursuit (e.g., both a father and son may work as pedicab drivers).

† The letters a and b designate different nuclear units within the same household when it is appropriate to consider them separately.

‡ This woman owned no rice fields but had purchased twelve a. of chamkar fields in another village that were worked on a share-crop basis by another family; she then sold her share of the produce.

APPENDIX H

# THE DIVISION OF LABOR IN COMMON ACTIVITIES

| Activity | Males | Females |
|---|---|---|
| Preparing rice fields for planting | x | x |
| Plowing and harrowing fields | xx | very rare |
| Pulling seedlings | o | x |
| Transplanting | occasional | xx |
| Harvesting rice | x | x |
| Threshing rice | xx | x |
| Winnowing rice | x (by machine) | xx (by hand) |
| Fishing | x | x |
| Gardening | x | x |
| Caring for cattle | xx | x |
| Caring for pigs and chickens | o | x |
| Driving oxcarts | xx | possible but rare |
| Cooking | only if necessary | xx |
| Cleaning house | o | x |
| Caring for children | x | xx |
| Sewing and mending | possible but rare | xx |
| Washing clothes | possible but rare | xx |
| Gathering firewood and carrying water | x | x |
| House construction and carpentry | x | o |
| Weaving | o | x |
| Making thatch | x | x |
| Making wicker baskets | x | o |
| Making palm leaf bins, mats, etc. | o | x |
| Ordinary marketing | x | xx |
| Buying or selling of rice, pigs, and food | o | x |

*(Continued)*

(Continued)

| Activity | Males | Females |
|---|---|---|
| Buying or selling of cows and chickens | x | o |
| Buying or selling of land | xx | x |

*Note:*

xx = activity performed primarily by one sex

x = activity performed

o = activity not performed

# THE ANNUAL CYCLE

| Months | Rice cultivation | Other activities | Ceremonies |
|---|---|---|---|
| *Caet* April | | Making of palm sugar; thatch work; weaving | New Year |
| *Visak* May | Clear & prepare fields; plow & harrow seedbeds; sow seedbeds | Palm sugar season ends | *Visak Bociê* Weddings |
| *Ceh* June | Plow other fields; pull seedlings; transplanting | | |
| *Asat* July | | | Weddings (first half of the month) Monks enter *vossa* |
| *Srap* August | [Rice left to grow] Weed; catch crabs | Cut grass for cattle Other employment Visit relatives | |
| *Potrobot* September | | Fishing | Prachum |
| *Asoit* October | | Palm sugar season begins | Monks leave *vossa* *Katûn* |
| *Kadûk* November | Harvesting; threshing; winnowing | | Weddings (Water festival in Phnom Penh) |
| *Mukase* December | [Peak period of harvest] | | |
| *Boh* January | | Weaving; repair houses, etc.; make palm sugar | Weddings "Mountain of Rice" |
| *Miêk* February | | Other employment; visit relatives | *Miêk Bociê* Spirit possessions; community festival |
| *Palkun* March | | | Weddings |

# REFERENCES

Adam, Leonhard. 1948. "'Virilocal' and 'Uxorilocal.'" *Man* 48:12.

Appell, G. N. 1967. "Observational Procedures for Identifying Kindreds: Social Isolates among the Rungus of Borneo." *Southwestern Journal of Anthropology* 23:192–207.

Arensberg, Conrad. 1954. "The Community Study Method." *American Journal of Sociology* 60:109–24.

———. 1955. "American Communities." *American Anthropologist* 57:1143–62.

———. 1957. "Discussion of Robert Manners' 'Methods of Community Analysis in the Caribbean.'" In *Caribbean Studies: A Symposium*, edited by V. Rubin. Kingston: B. W. I. Printers.

———. 1961. "The Community as Object and Sample." *American Anthropologist* 63:241–64.

Ayabe, Tsuneo. 1961. *The Village of Ba Pha Kao, Vientiane Province, a Preliminary Report.* Laos Project Paper No. 14, ed. J. Halpern. Los Angeles: University of California (mimeographed).

Aymonier, Etienne. 1900. *Le Royaume actuel.* Paris: E Leroux.

Ayoub, Millicent, and Samuel Lieberman. 1962. "'Parenticipient' and Other '-Cipient' Compounds: A Suggested Terminology for a Residence Pattern." *American Anthropologist* 64:162.

Bacon, Elizabeth. 1946. "A Preliminary Attempt to Determine the Culture Areas of Asia." *Southwestern Journal of Anthropology* 2:117–32.

Baker, Elizabeth. 1958. *Case Study and Evaluation of Community Development in Cambodia.* Phnom Penh: United States Overseas Mission, Division of Education (mimeographed).

Barnes, J. A. 1954. "Class and Committees in a Norwegian Island Parish." *Human Relations* 7:39–58.

———. 1960. "Marriage and Residential Continuity." *American Anthropologist* 62:850–66.

Befu, Harumi. 1963a. "Classification of Unilineal-Bilateral Societies." *Southwestern Journal of Anthropology* 19:335–55.

———. 1963b. "Patrilineal Descent and Personal Kindred in Japan." *American Anthropologist* 65:1328–41.

Benedict, Paul. 1947. "Languages and Literatures of Indochina." *Far Eastern Quarterly* 6:379–89.

Benedict, Ruth. 1952. *Thai Culture and Behavior.* Data Paper 4 (Southeast Asia Program, Cornell University). Ithaca: Cornell University.

Bell, Hesketh. 1926. *Foreign Colonial Administration in the Far East*. London.

Bilodeau, Charles, Somlith Pathammavong, and Lê Quang Hông. 1955. *Compulsory Education in Cambodia, Laos, and Viet-Nam*. Studies on Compulsory Education 14. Paris: UNESCO.

Bitard, Pierre. 1955. "La littérature cambodgienne moderne." *France-Asie* 12(114–15):467–79.

Blanchard, Wendell, et al. 1958. *Thailand: Its People, Its Society, Its Culture*. Country Survey Series. New Haven: Human Relations Area Files Press.

Blehr, Otto. 1963. "Action Groups in a Society with Bilateral Kinship: A Case Study from the Faroe Islands." *Ethnology* 2:269–75.

Bohannan, Paul. 1957. "An Alternate Residence Classification." *American Anthropologist* 59:126–31.

———. 1963. *Social Anthropology*. New York: Holt, Rinehart and Winston.

Boskoff, Alvin. 1957. "Social Change: Major Problems in the Emergence of Theoretical and Research Foci." In *Modern Sociological Theory in Continuity and Change*, ed. H. Becker and A. Boskoff. New York: Dryden Press.

Bott, Elizabeth. 1957. *Family and Social Network: Roles, Norms, and External Relationships in Ordinary Urban Families*. London: Tavistock Publications.

Brant, Charles. 1954. *Tadagale: A Burmese Village in 1950*. Data Paper 13 (Southeast Asia Program, Cornell University). Ithaca: Cornell University.

Briggs, Lawrence P. 1951. *The Ancient Khmer Empire*. Philadelphia: American Philosophical Society.

Brohm, John. 1963. "Buddhism and Animism in a Burmese Village." *Journal of Asian Studies* 22:155–67.

Bruel, Henri. 1924. *De la condition juridique des terres du Cambodge*. Poitiers: Poitou.

Burling, Robbins. 1965a. *Hill Farms and Padi Fields: Life in Mainland Southeast Asia*. Englewood Cliffs, NJ: Prentice-Hall.

———. 1965b. "Burmese Kinship Terminology." In *Formal Semantic Analysis*, edited by E. A. Hammel, special issue, *American Anthropologist* 67(5), pt. 2.

Burtt, E. A., ed. 1955. *The Teachings of the Compassionate Buddha*. New York: New American Library.

Cady, John. 1964. *Southeast Asia: Its Historical Development*. New York: McGraw-Hill.

Cambefort, Gaston. 1950. *Introduction au Cambodgien*. Paris: Maisonneuve.

Carr, William. 1957. "Some Factors Affecting Residence Mobility." *American Anthropologist* 59:1082–85.

Casagrande, Joseph. 1959. "Some Observations on the Study of Intermediate Society." In *Intermediate Societies, Social Mobility, and Communication*, edited by Verne Ray. Seattle: American Ethnological Society.

Chassigneux, E. 1929. "Geographie de l'Indochine." In *Un empire colonial français: l'Indochine*, edited by Georges Maspero, vol. 1. Paris: G. van Oest.

Chiva, I. 1958. *Rural Communities: Problems, Methods, and Types of Research*. Reports and Papers in the Social Sciences 10. Paris: UNESCO.

Clairon, Marcel. n.d. *Droit civil khmer*. Phnom Penh: Entreprise khmère de librairie et de papeterie.

Clark, Colin, and Margaret Haswell. 1964. *The Economics of Subsistence Agriculture.* New York: St. Martin's Press.

CMCC (Commission des Moeurs et Coutumes du Cambodge): documents of reports by various informants on aspects of Khmer society and culture, filed at the Commission des Moeurs et Coutumes du Cambodge, Phnom Penh.

Coe, Michael. 1961. "Social Typology and the Tropical Forest Civilizations." *Comparative Studies in Society and History* 4:65–85.

Coedès, George. 1948. *Les états hindouisés d'Indochine et d'Indonésie.* Paris: E. de Boccard.

——. 1953. "Le substrat autochtone et la superstructure indienne au Cambodge et à Java." *Journal of World History* 1:368–77.

——. 1954. "L'osmose indienne en Indochine et en Indonésie." *Journal of World History* 1:827–38.

Condominas, Georges. 1953. "L'Indochine." In *Ethnologie de l'union française,* vol. 2, edited by A. Leroi-Gourhan and J. Poirier, Pays d'Outre-Mer, 6th series. Paris: Presses Universitaires de France.

——. 1956. "Panorama de la culture vietnamienne." *France-Asie* 13:75–94.

——. 1965. "L'ethnologie asiatique." *Revue de l'enseignement supérieur* 3:69–78.

Conze, Edward. 1959. *Buddhism: Its Essence and Development.* New York: Harper Torchbooks.

Cooke, Elena. 1961. *Rice Cultivation in Malaya.* Singapore: Donald Moore for Eastern Universities Press.

Daguin, Arthur. n.d. *Le mariage cambodgien.* Paris: Lucien Dorbon Librairie.

Davenport, William. 1959. "Nonunilinear Descent and Descent Groups. *American Anthropologist* 61:557–72.

——. 1963. "Social Organization." *Biennial Review of Anthropology* 3:178–227.

De Bary, William Theodore, et al. 1958. *Sources of Indian Tradition.* New York: Columbia University Press.

Delvert, Jean. 1958. "La vie rurale au Cambodge." *France-Asie* 15:95–104.

——. 1961. *Le paysan cambodgien.* Le Monde d'outre-mer, passé et present, Première serie, Etudes 10. Paris: Mouton.

DeYoung, John. 1955. *Village Life in Modern Thailand.* Berkeley: University of California Press.

Djamour, Judith. 1959. *Malay Kinship and Marriage in Singapore.* London School of Economics Monographs on Social Anthropology 21. London: Athalone Press.

Dobby, E. H. G. 1960. *Southeast Asia.* London: University of London Press.

Du Bois, Cora. 1949. *Social Forces in Southeast Asia.* Minneapolis: University of Minnesota Press.

Durkheim, Emile. 1947 *The Division of Labor in Society.* New York: The Free Press.

Ebihara, May. 1963. "Review of Jean Delvert's *Le Paysan cambodgien.*" *American Anthropologist* 65:1155–57.

——. 1964. "Khmer." In *Ethnic Groups of Mainland Southeast Asia,* ed. Frank LeBar, Gerald Hickey, and John Musgrave. New Haven: Human Relations Area Files Press.

———. 1966. "Interrelations between Buddhism and Social Systems in Cambodian Peasant Culture." In Manning Nash et al., *Anthropological Studies in Theravada Buddhism*, Cultural Report Series 13. New Haven: Yale University.

Eggan, Fred. 1960. "The Sagada Igorots of Northern Luzon." In *Social Structure in Southeast Asia*, edited by George P. Murdock, Viking Fund Publications in Anthropology 29. New York: Wenner-Gren Foundation for Anthropological Research.

Embree, John. 1948. "Anthropology in Indochina since 1940." *American Anthropologist* 50:714–16.

———. 1950. "Thailand—A Loosely Structured Social System." *American Anthropologist* 52:181–93.

Embree, John, and Lillian Dotson. 1950. *Bibliography of the Peoples and Cultures of Mainland Southeast Asia*. New Haven: Yale University Southeast Asia Studies.

Fallers, Lloyd. 1961. "Are African Cultivators to Be Called 'Peasants'?" *Current Anthropology* 2:108–10.

Finot, Louis. 1908. "Les etudes indochinoises." *Bulletin de l'École Française d'Extrême-Orient* 8:233–34.

Firth, Raymond. 1946. *Malay Fishermen: Their Peasant Economy*. London: Kegan Paul, Trench, Trubner.

———, ed. 1956. *Two Studies of Kinship in London*. London School of Economics Monographs on Social Anthropology 15. London: Athalone Press.

———. 1951. *Elements of Social Organization*. London: Watts.

———. 1964. "Capital, Saving, and Credit in Peasant Societies: A Viewpoint from Economic Anthropology." In *Capital, Saving and Credit in Peasant Societies: Studies from Asia, Oceania, the Caribbean and Middle America*, edited by Raymond Firth and B. S. Yamey. Chicago: Aldine.

Firth, Raymond, and B. S. Yamey. 1964. *Capital, Saving and Credit in Peasant Societies*. Chicago: Aldine.

Fischer, J. L. 1958. "The Classification of Residence in Censuses." *American Anthropologist* 60:508–17.

Fisher, Charles A. 1964. *South-East Asia: A Social, Economic, and Political Geography*. London: Methuen.

Fitchen, Janet. 1961. "Peasantry as a Social Type." In *Symposium: Patterns of Land Utilization and Other Papers*, edited by Viola Garfield, Proceedings of the American Ethnological Society. Seattle: University of Washington Press.

Foster, George. 1961a. "Interpersonal Relations in Peasant Society." *Human Organization* 19:174–78, 183–87.

———. 1961b. "The Dyadic Contract: A Model for the Social Structure of a Mexican Peasant Village." *American Anthropologist* 63:1173–92.

———. 1965. "Peasant Society and the Image of Limited Good." *American Anthropologist* 67:293–315.

Frake, Charles. 1960. "The Eastern Subanum of Mindanao." In *Social Structure in Southeast Asia*, edited by George P. Murdock, Viking Fund Publications in Anthropology 29. New York: Wenner-Gren Foundation for Anthropological Research.

*France-Asie.* 1955. "Presence du Cambodge." Special issue, *France-Asie* 12(114–15).

Fraser, Thomas. 1960. *Rusembilan: A Malay Fishing Village in Southern Thailand.* Ithaca: Cornell University Press.

Freeman, J. D. 1960. "The Iban of Western Borneo." In *Social Structure in Southeast Asia,* edited by George P. Murdock, Viking Fund Publications in Anthropology 29. New York: Wenner-Gren Foundation for Anthropological Research.

———. 1961. "On the Concept of the Kindred." *Journal of the Royal Anthropological Institute* 91:192–220.

Fried, Morton. 1967. *The Evolution of Political Society: An Essay in Political Anthropology.* New York: Random House.

Friedl, Ernestine. 1959. "The Role of Kinship in the Transmission of National Culture to Rural Villages in Mainland Greece." *American Anthropologist* 61:30–38.

———. 1963. "Studies in Peasant Life." *Biennial Review of Anthropology* 3:276–306.

Geddes, William. 1954. *The Land Dayaks of Sarawak.* Colonial Research Studies 14. London: Her Majesty's Stationery Office.

Geertz, Clifford. 1961. "Studies in Peasant Life: Community and Society." In *Biennial Review of Anthropology* 2:1–41.

———. 1963a. *Agricultural Involution: The Processes of Ecological Change in Indonesia.* Berkeley: University of California Press.

———. 1963b. *Peddlers and Princes: Social Development and Economic Change in Two Indonesian Towns.* Chicago: University of Chicago Press.

Geertz, Hildred. 1961. *The Javanese Family: A Study of Kinship and Socialization.* Glencoe, IL: Free Press.

———. 1963. "Indonesian Cultures and Communities." In *Indonesia,* ed. R. McVey. New Haven: Human Relations Area Files Press.

Ginsburg, Norton. 1955. "The Great City in Southeast Asia." *American Journal of Sociology* 60 (5): 455–62.

———. 1958. *The Pattern of Asia.* Englewood Cliffs, NJ: Prentice-Hall.

Ginsburg, Norton, and Chester F. Roberts. 1958. *Malaya.* Seattle: University of Washington Press.

Giteau, Madeleine. 1957. *Histoire du Cambodge.* Paris: Didier.

Goode, William, and Paul Hatt. 1952. *Methods in Social Research.* New York: McGraw-Hill.

Goodenough, Ward. 1955. "A Problem in Malayo-Polynesian Social Organization." *American Anthropologist* 57:71–83.

———. 1956. "Residence Rules." *Southwestern Journal of Anthropology* 12:22–37.

———. 1961. "Review of George Peter Murdock, ed., *Social Structure in Southeast Asia.*" *American Anthropologist* 63:1341–47.

———. 1962. "Kindred and Hamlet in Lalakai, New Britain." *Ethnology* 1:5–12.

Goody, Jack, ed. 1958. *The Developmental Cycle in Domestic Groups.* Cambridge Papers in Social Anthropology l. Cambridge: Cambridge University Press.

Gorer, Geoffrey. 1967. *Himalayan Village: An Account of the Lepchas of Sikkim.* New York: Basic Books.

Gourou, Pierre. 1945. *Land Utilization in French Indochina*. Washington, DC: Institute of Pacific Relations.

——. 1955. *The Peasants of the Tonkin Delta: A Study of Human Geography*. New Haven: Human Relations Area Files Press.

Groslier, Bernard-Philippe. 1957. *The Arts and Civilization of Angkor*. New York: Frederick Praeger.

——. 1958. *Angkor et le Cambodge au XVIe siècle, d'apres les sources portugaises et espagnoles*. Paris: Presses Universitaires de France.

——. 1960a. "Our Knowledge of Khmer Civilization: A Re-appraisal." *Journal of the Siam Society* 48:1–28.

——. 1960b. "Ouvrages récents sur le Cambodge." *Bulletin de l'École Française d'Extrême-Orient* 50:191–228.

Guesdon, Joseph. 1930. *Dictionnaire cambodgien–français*. Paris: Les Petit-fils de Plon et Nourrit.

Hall, D. G. E. 1964. *A History of South-East Asia*. London: Macmillan.

Halpern, Joel. 1964a. "Capital, Saving and Credit among Lao Peasants." In *Capital, Saving and Credit in Peasant Societies: Studies from Asia, Oceania, the Caribbean and Middle America*, edited by Raymond Firth and B. S. Yamey. Chicago: Aldine.

——. 1964b. *Government, Politics, and Social Structure in Laos: A Study of Tradition and Innovation*. Yale University Southeast Asia Studies Monograph Series 4. New Haven: Yale University Southeast Asia Studies.

Hanks, Jane. 1960. "The Ontology of Rice." In *Culture in History: Essays in Honor of Paul Radin*, edited by S. Diamond. New York: Columbia University Press.

Hanks, Lucien M., Jr. 1962. "Merit and Power in the Thai Social Order." *American Anthropologist* 64:1247–61.

Hart, Donn, Phya Anuman Rajadhon, and Richard Coughlin. 1965. *Southeast Asian Birth Customs: Three Studies in Human Reproduction*. New Haven: Human Relations Area Files Press.

Heine-Geldern, Robert. 1956. *Conceptions of State and Kingship in Southeast Asia*. Data Paper 18 (Southeast Asia Program, Cornell University). Ithaca: Cornell University.

Herz, Martin. 1958. *A Short History of Cambodia, from the Days of Angkor to the Present*. New York: Frederick Praeger.

Hickey, Gerald. 1964. *Village in Vietnam*. New Haven: Yale University Press.

Homans, George. 1950. *The Human Group*. New York: Harcourt Brace.

Ingersoll, Jasper. 1961. "Religious Roles and Economic Behavior in Village Thailand." Paper presented at the annual meeting of the American Anthropological Association, Philadelphia, Pennsylvania.

Johnson, Ervin. 1964. "The Stem Family and Its Extensions in Japan." *American Anthropologist* 66:839–51.

Kattenburg, Paul. 1952. *A Central Javanese Village in 1950*. Data Paper 2 (Southeast Asia Program, Cornell University). Ithaca: Cornell University.

Kaufman, Howard. 1960. *Bangkhuad, a Community Study in Thailand*. Monograph of the Association for Asian Studies 10. Locust Valley: J. J. Augustin.

———. 1961. *Village Life in Vientiane Province (1956–1957)*. Ed. Joel Halpern. Laos Project Paper 12 (mimeographed).

Kehoe, Alice. 1960. "Lactation and Pregnancy." *American Anthropologist* 62:880–81.

Kennedy, John G. 1966. "Peasant Society and the Image of Limited Good: A Critique." *American Anthropologist* 68:1212–25.

Khiang, Mi Mi. 1963. "Burma: Balance and Harmony." In *Women in the New Asia*, edited by Barbara Ward. Paris: UNESCO.

Kleinpeter, Roger. 1937. *Le problème foncier au Cambodge*. Paris: Les Editions Domat-Montchrestian.

Kluckhohn, Clyde, Henry Murray, and David Schneider. 1961. *Personality in Nature, Society, and Culture*. New York: Alfred Knopf.

Koentjaraningrat, R. 1957. *A Preliminary Description of the Javanese Kinship System*. Cultural Report Series 4. New Haven: Yale University Southeast Asia Studies.

———. 1960. "The Javanese of South Central Java." In *Social Structure in Southeast Asia*, edited by George P. Murdock, Viking Fund Publications in Anthropology 29. New York: Wenner-Gren Foundation for Anthropological Research.

Kroeber, A. L. 1909. "Classificatory Systems of Relationship." *Journal of the Royal Anthropological Institute* 39:77–84.

———. 1947. "Culture Groupings in Asia." *Southwestern Journal of Anthropology* 3:322–30.

———. 1948. *Anthropology*. New York: Harcourt Brace.

Leach, Edmund R. 1950. *Social Science Research in Sarawak: A Report on the Possibilities of a Social Economic Survey of Sarawak*. Colonial Research Studies 1. London: Her Majesty's Stationery Office.

———. 1954. *Political Systems of Highland Burma*. Cambridge, MA: Harvard University Press.

———. 1961. *Pul Eliya, a Village in Ceylon: A Study of Land Tenure and Kinship*. Cambridge: Cambridge University Press.

LeBar, Frank, Gerald Hickey, and John Musgrave, eds. 1964. *Ethnic Groups of Mainland Southeast Asia*. New Haven: Human Relations Area Files Press.

LeBar, Frank, and Adrienne Suddard. 1960. *Laos: Its People, Its Society, Its Culture*. Survey of World Cultures 8. New Haven: Human Relations Area Files Press.

Leclère, Adhémard. 1890. *Recherches sur la legislation cambodgienne (droit prive)*. Paris: Augustin Challamel, Librarie Coloniale.

———. 1894. *Recherches sur le droit public des Cambodgiens*. Paris: A Challamel.

———. 1898. *Les codes cambodgiens*. 2 vols. Paris: E. Leroux.

———. [1899]. *Le buddhisme au Cambodge*. Paris: E. Leroux.

———. 1904. "La fate des eaux au Phnom Penh." *Bulletin de l'École Française d'Extrême-Orient* 4:120–30.

———. 1914. *Histoire du Cambodge*. Paris: Librairie Paul Guethner.

———. 1916. *Cambodge: fêtes civiles et religieuses*. Paris: Imprimerie Nationale.

LeGallen, M. 1929. "Moeurs et coutumes de l'ancien Cambodge." In *Un empire colonial français: l'Indochine*, edited by Georges Maspero, vol. 1. Paris: G. van Oest.

Leichter, Hope. 1958. "Life Cycle Changes and Temporal Sequence in a Bilateral Kinship System." Paper read at the annual meeting of the American Anthropological Association, Washington, DC.

Lévi-Strauss, Claude. 1960. "The Family." In *Man, Culture, and Society*, edited by H. Shapiro. New York: Oxford University Press.

Lewis, Oscar. 1955. "Peasant Culture in India and Mexico, a Comparative Analysis." In *Village India: Studies in the Little Community*, edited by McKim Marriott, Memoirs of the American Anthropological Association 83. Chicago: University of Chicago Press.

———. 1961. "Some of My Best Friends Are Peasants." *Human Organization* 19:179–80.

Lingat, Robert. 1952–55. *Les regimes matrimoniaux de sud-est de l'Asie, essai de droit comparé indochinois*. 2 vols. Publications de l'École Française d'Extrême-Orient 34. Paris: E. de Boccard.

Linton, Ralph. 1936. *The Study of Man*. New York: D. Appleton-Century.

———. 1955. *The Tree of Culture*. New York: Alfred Knopf.

Lorimer, Frank. 1954. *Culture and human fertility*. Paris: UNESCO.

Lowie, Robert. 1948. *Social Organization*. New York: Rinehart.

Mandelbaum, David. 1966. "Transcendental and Pragmatic Aspects of Religion." *American Anthropologist* 68:1174–91.

Manners, Robert. 1957. "Methods of Community Analysis in the Caribbean." In *Caribbean Studies: A Symposium*, edited by V. Rubin. Kingston: B. W. I. Printers.

Marchal, Henri. 1956. "Les funerailles de S.M. Norodom en 1906." *France-Asie* 13:118–26.

Marriott, McKim. 1955. "Little Communities within an Indigenous Civilization." In *Village India: Studies in the Little Community*, edited by McKim Marriott, Memoirs of the American Anthropological Association 83. Chicago: University of Chicago Press.

Martini, François. 1942–45. "Aperçu phonologique du cambodgien." *Bulletin de la Société de Linguistique de Paris* 42:112–31.

———. 1955a. "Le bonze cambodgien." *France-Asie* 12(114–15):409–15.

———. 1955b. "Organisation de clergé bouddhique au Cambodge." *France-Asie* 12(114–15):416–24.

———. 1955c. "La langue cambodgienne." *France-Asie* 12(114–15):427–35.

———. 1955d. "La cuisine cambodgienne." *France-Asie* 12(114–15):399–402.

Maspero, Georges. 1915. *Grammaire de la langue khmère*. Paris: Imprimerie Nationale.

Maspero, Georges, ed. 1929–30. *Un empire colonial français: l'Indochine*. 2 vols. Paris: G. van Oest.

Mead, Margaret. 1947. *The Mountain Arapesh*. Vols. 3 and 4: *Socio-Economic Life; Diary of Events in Alitoa*. American Museum of Natural History Anthropological Papers 40.3. New York: American Museum of Natural History.

Merton, Robert. 1957. *Social Theory and Social Structure*. Glencoe, IL: Free Press.

Micaud, Charles. 1949. "French Indochina." In L. A. Mills et al., *The New World of Southeast Asia*. Minneapolis: University of Minnesota Press.

Ministère du Plan, Royaume du Cambodge. 1958. *Annuaire statistique retrospectif du Cambodge (1937–1957)*. Phnom Penh: Entreprise khmère de librairie et de papeterie.

———. 1961. *Bulletin mensuel de statistique*, nos. 1, 2, 3, January–March, 1961. Phnom Penh: E.F.I.

Mintz, Sidney. 1959. "Internal Market Systems as Mechanisms of Social Articulation." In *Intermediate Societies, Social Mobility, and Communication*, edited by Verne Ray. Seattle: American Ethnological Society.

Mitchell, William. 1963. "Theoretical Problems in the Concept of the Kindred." *American Anthropologist* 65:343–54.

———. 1965. "The Kindred and Baby Bathing in Academe." *American Anthropologist* 67:977–85.

Moerman, Michael. 1966. "Ban Ping's Temple: The Center of a 'Loosely Structured' Society." In Manning Nash et al., *Anthropological Studies in Therevada Buddhism*, Cultural Report Series 13. New Haven: Yale University Southeast Asia Studies.

Monod, G. H. 1931. *Le Cambodgien*. Paris: Larose.

Morizon, René. 1934. *L'immatriculation foncière de la propriété individuelle au Cambodge*. Paris: Editions Domat-Montchrestien.

———. 1936. *La province cambodgienne de Pursat*. Paris: Editions internationales.

Murdock, George. 1949. *Social Structure*. New York: Macmillan.

———. 1957. "World Ethnographic Sample." *American Anthropologist* 59:664–87.

———. 1960a. "Cognatic Forms of Social Organization." In *Social Structure in Southeast Asia*, edited by George P. Murdock, Viking Fund Publications in Anthropology 29. New York: Wenner-Gren Foundation for Anthropological Research.

———, ed. 1960b. *Social Structure in Southeast Asia*. Viking Fund Publications in Anthropology 29. New York: Wenner-Gren Foundation for Anthropological Research.

———. 1964. "The Kindred." *American Anthropologist* 66:129–32.

Nash, June, and Manning Nash. 1963. "Marriage, Family, and Population Growth in Upper Burma." *Southwestern Journal of Anthropology* 19:251–66.

Nash, Manning. 1963. "Burmese Buddhism in Everyday Life." *American Anthropologist* 65:285–95.

———. 1964. "Southeast Asian Society: Dual or Multiple." *Journal of Asian Studies* 23:417–23.

———. 1965. *The Golden Road to Modernity: Village Life in Contemporary Burma*. New York: John Wiley.

Nash, Manning, et al. 1966. *Anthropological Studies in Theravada Buddhism*. Cultural Report Series 13, Yale University Southeast Asia Studies. New Haven: Yale University Southeast Asia Studies.

Neuman, Stephanie, ed. 1962. *Social Research in Southeast Asia*, special issue, *American Behavioral Scientist* 5(10).

Norbeck, Edward, and Harumi Befu. 1958. "Informal Fictive Kinship in Japan." *American Anthropologist* 60:102–17.

Obeyesekere, Gananath. 1963. "The Great Tradition and the Little in the Perspective of Sinhalese Buddhism." *Journal of Asian Studies* 22:139–53.

Office National du Tourisme. n.d. *Informations touristiques Cambodge.* Phnom Penh: Imprimerie A. Portail.

Office of Strategic Services. 1944. *Civil Affairs Handbook: French Indo-China.* Section I: *Geographical and Social Background.* Washington, DC: Army Services Forces.

Olivier, Georges. 1956. *Les populations du Cambodge: anthropologie physique.* Paris: Impressions P. Andre.

Opler, Morris. 1956. "The Extensions of an Indian Village." *Journal of Asian Studies* 16:5–10.

O'Sullivan, Kevin. 1962. "Concentric Conformity in Ancient Khmer Kinship Organization." *Bulletin of the Institute of Ethnology, Academia Sinica* 13:87–96.

Padilla, Elena. 1957. "Contemporary Socio-Rural Types in the Caribbean Region." In *Caribbean Studies: A Symposium,* edited by V. Rubin. Kingston: B. W. I. Printers.

Pannetier, (Dr.), and E. Menetrier. 1922. *Éléments de grammaire cambodgienne appliquée.* Phnom Penh: Imprimerie du Protectorat.

Pehrson, Robert. 1957. *The Bilateral Network of Social Relations in Könkämä Lapp District.* Indiana University Publications, Slavic and East European Series 5. Bloomington: Indiana University Press.

Pelliot, Paul. 1951. *Mémoires sur les coutumes du Cambodge de Tcheou Ta-kouan.* Paris: Librairie d'Amérique et d'Orient.

Pfanner, David, and Jasper Ingersoll. 1962. "Theravada Buddhism and Village Economic Behavior: A Burmese and Thai Comparison." *Journal of Asian Studies* 21:341–61.

Phan, Vanput, and Richard Noss. 1958. *Spoken Cambodian.* Washington, DC: Foreign Service Institute (mimeographed).

Phillips, Herbert. 1965. *Thai Peasant Personality: The Patterning of Interpersonal Behavior in the Village of Bang Chan.* Berkeley: University of California Press.

Piker, Stephen. 1966. "'The Image of Limited Good': Comments on an Exercise in Description and Interpretation." *American Anthropologist* 68:1202–11.

Pitt-Rivers, Julian. 1961. "Interpersonal Relations in Peasant Society: A Comment." *Human Organization* 19:180–83.

Porée, Guy, and Éveline Maspero. 1938. *Moeurs et coutumes des Khmer: origines, histoire, religions, croyances, rites, evolution.* Paris: Payot.

Porée-Maspero, Éveline. [1950]. *Cérémonies des douze mois: fêtes annuelles cambodgiennes.* Phnom Penh: Commission des Moeurs et Coutumes du Cambodge, Editions de l'Institut Bouddhique.

——. 1954. "Notes sur les particularités du culte chez les Cambodgiens." *Bulletin de l'École Française d'Extrême-Orient* 44:619–41.

——. 1955a. "Les neak ta." *France-Asie* 12(114–15):375–77.

——. 1955b. "Travaux d'ethnographie au Cambodge." *France-Asie* 12(114–15):363–67.

——. 1958. *Cérémonies privées des Cambodgiens.* Phnom Penh: Commission des Moeurs et Coutumes du Cambodge, Editions de l'Institut Bouddhique, Entreprise khmère de librairie et de papeterie.

———. 1962a. *Étude sur les rites agraires des Cambodgiens*. Vol. 1. Le Monde d'outre-mer, passé et présent, Première série, Études 14. Paris: Mouton.

———. 1962b. "Le cycle des douze animaux dans la vie des Cambodgiens." *Bulletin de l'École Française d'Extrême-Orient* 50:311–66.

Potter, Jack, May Diaz, and George Foster. 1967. *Peasant Society: A Reader*. New York: Little and Brown.

Pym, Christopher. 1959. *The Road to Angkor*. London: Robert Hale.

———. 1960. *Mistapim in Cambodia*. London: Hodder and Stoughton.

Rajadhon, Phya Anuman. 1961. *Life and Ritual in Old Siam*. New Haven: Human Relations Area Files Press.

Ray, Verne, ed. 1959. *Intermediate Societies, Social Mobility, and Communication*. Seattle: American Ethnological Society.

Redfield, Robert. 1955. *The Little Community*. Chicago: University of Chicago Press.

———. 1956. *Peasant Society and Culture: An Anthropological Approach to Civilization*. Chicago: University of Chicago Press.

Redfield, Robert, and Alfonso Rojas. 1962. *Chan Kom, a Maya Village*. Chicago: University of Chicago Press.

Ricklefs, M. C. 1967. "Land the Law in the Epigraphy of Tenth-Century Cambodia." *Journal of Asian Studies* 26:411–20.

Robequain, Charles. 1944. *The Economic Development of French Indo-China*. London: Oxford University Press.

Saris-Yann, Srin. 1955. "Gateaux et friandises." *France-Asie* 12(114–15):395–98.

Schneider, David. 1965. "American Kin Terms and Terms for Kinsmen: A Critique of Goodenough's Componential Analysis of Yankee Kinship Terminology." In *Formal Semantic Analysis*, edited by E. A. Hammel, special issue, *American Anthropologist* 67(5), pt. 2.

Service, Elman. 1962. *Primitive Social Organization: An Evolutionary Perspective*. New York: Random House.

Sharp, Lauriston, et al. 1953. *Siamese Rice Village: A Preliminary Study of Bang Chan, 1948–1949*. Bangkok: Cornell Research Center.

Shway Yoe [Sir James Scott]. 1963. *The Burman: His Life and Notions*. New York: Norton.

Singer, Charles, E. J. Holmyard, and A. R. Hall, eds. 1956. *A History of Technology*. Vol. 2: *The Mediterranean Civilizations and the Middle Ages, c. 700 B.C. to c. A.D. 1500*. Oxford: Clarendon Press.

———. 1958. *A History Of Technology*. Vol. 4: *The Industrial Revolution, c. 1750–1850*. Oxford: Clarendon Press.

Skinner, G. William, ed. 1959. *Local, Ethnic, and National Loyalties in Village Indonesia: A Symposium*. Cultural Report Series, Yale University Southeast Asia Studies 8. New Haven: Yale University Southeast Asia Studies.

Smith, Roger. 1964. "Cambodia." In *Governments and Politics of Southeast Asia*, ed. G. Kahin. Ithaca: Cornell University Press.

———. 1965. *Cambodia's Foreign Policy*. Ithaca: Cornell University Press.

Souyris-Rolland, Andre. 1951. "Contribution à l'étude du culte des genies tutelaires ou 'Neak Ta' chez les Cambodgiens du sud." *Bulletin de Societe des études Indochinoises* 26:161–74.

Spiro, Melford. 1966. "Buddhism and Economic Action in Burma." *American Anthropologist* 68:1163–73.

Steinberg, David, in collaboration with Chester A. Bain. 1959. *Cambodia: Its People, Its Society, Its Culture*. Survey of World Culture Series. New Haven: Human Relations Area Files Press.

Steward, Julian. 1950. *Area Research: Theory and Practice*. New York: Social Science Research Council.

——. 1955. *Theory of Culture Change*. Urbana: University of Illinois Press.

Stewart, Charles. 1958. "The Urban-Rural Dichotomy: Concepts and Uses." *American Journal of Sociology* 64:152–58.

Swift, Michael. 1963. "Men and Women in Malay Society." In *Women in the New Asia*, edited by Barbara Ward. Paris: UNESCO.

——. 1964. "Capital, Saving, and Credit in a Malay Peasant Economy." In *Capital, Saving and Credit in Peasant Societies: Studies from Asia, Oceania, the Caribbean and Middle America*, edited by Raymond Firth and B. S. Yamey. Chicago: Aldine.

——. 1965. *Malay Peasant Society in Jelebu*. London School of Economics Monographs on Social Anthropology 24. London: Athalone Press.

Textor, Robert. 1961. *From Peasant to Pedicab Driver: A Social Study of Northeastern Thai Farmers Who Periodically Migrated to Bangkok and Became Pedicab Drivers*. Cultural Report Series 9. New Haven: Yale University Southeast Asia Studies.

Thierry, Jean. 1955. *L'evolution de la condition de la femme en droit privé cambodgien*. Phnom Penh: A. Portail.

Thiounn, Chaufea. 1956. *Danses cambodgiennes*. Phnom Penh: Institut Bouddhique, Albert Portail.

Thomas, William. 1955. "Land, Man, and Culture in Mainland Southeast Asia: A Study of the Significance of the Concept of Culture for Geographic Thought, Based upon an Analyses of the Writings on the Human Geography of Mainland Southeast Asia by American, British, German, and French Scholars." PhD diss., Yale University.

Thompson, Virginia. 1937. *French Indo-China*. New York: Macmillan.

Thompson, Virginia, and Richard Adloff. 1947. "The Cultural Institutions of Indochina Today." *Far Eastern Quarterly* 6:414–19.

——. 1955. *Minority Problems in Southeast Asia*. Stanford: Stanford University Press.

United Nations. 1951. *Demographic Yearbook 1951*. New York: Department of Economic Affairs, Statistical Office.

Vanell, Robert. 1956. "Les rites funeraires au Cambodge." *France-Asie* 13:113–17.

Vialard-Goudou, André. 1959. *Recherches sur la composition chimique, la valeur nutritive et l'emploi des plantes alimentaires du Sud-Vietnam et de l'Asie tropicale*. Toulouse: Imprimerie A. Comes.

Ward, Barbara, ed. 1963. *Women in the New Asia*. Paris: UNESCO.

Webster, Noah. 1951. *Webster's New Collegiate Dictionary*. Springfield: G. & C. Merriam.

Wittfogel, Karl. 1957. *Oriental Despotism*. New Haven: Yale University Press.

Wolf, Eric. 1955. "Types of Latin American Peasantry." *American Anthropologist* 57:452–71.

———. 1956. "Aspects of Groups Relations in a Complex Society." *American Anthropologist* 58:1065–78.

———. 1957. "Closed Corporate Peasant Communities in Mesoamerica and Central Java." *Southwestern Journal of Anthropology* 13:1–18.

———. 1966. *Peasants*. Englewood Cliffs, NJ: Prentice-Hall.

Zadrozny, Mitchell, ed. 1955. *Area Handbook on Cambodia*. Human Relations Area Files Subcontractor's Monograph 21. New Haven: Human Relations Area Files.

# MEMORIES OF THE POL POT ERA IN A CAMBODIAN VILLAGE

*May Mayko Ebihara*

# MEMORIES OF THE POL POT ERA IN A CAMBODIAN VILLAGE

My experiences and memories of Cambodia come from two disparate time periods. The first was in 1959–60, when I conducted anthropological fieldwork in a Khmer peasant village, Svay, during relatively peaceful times. The second period was some three decades later when I returned to Cambodia in 1989 and discovered that Svay, as well as some villagers whom I had known in my earlier research, had managed to survive the horrendous upheavals of civil war and Democratic Kampuchea (DK). During subsequent trips between 1990 and 1996, I gathered oral histories from villagers about their lives after 1960, especially their experiences during the Pol Pot period, and examined aspects of contemporary village life.[1]

One generally thinks of memories as existing in people's minds and, indeed, much of my research focused on collecting villagers' narratives of their recent past. Memories, in the sense of invocations of the past, are also inscribed in the landscape and on people's bodies.[2] Drawing upon both the villagers' experiences and my own recollections of Svay, this chapter explores some of these inscriptions and evocations of the Pol Pot period as they exist in multiple forms.

## BACKGROUND

Located in the countryside of Kandal province, the village as I originally knew it in 1959–60 was situated along a minor highway running from a small market town several kilometers distant.[3] I was struck from the outset by the rural beauty of the village:

This essay was first published in Judy Ledgerwood, ed., *Cambodia Emerges from the Past: Eight Essays* (DeKalb: Center for Southeast Asian Studies, Northern Illinois University, 2002).

[1] My initial fieldwork in Cambodia was funded by a Ford Foundation Foreign Area Training Fellowship; research in the 1990s was supported by grants from the Wenner-Gren Foundation for Anthropological Research, the Social Science Research Council Joint Committee on Southeast Asia, and the City University of New York Faculty Research Awards Program, to all of whom I am most grateful. I am also greatly indebted to Dr. Judy Ledgerwood, who aided my work in many ways, and to Mr. Kheang Un, Ms. Mora Chan Tho, Ms. Keriya Keo, and Ms. Siwanny Roy, who helped me with translations and transcriptions. Portions of this paper were first presented at the conference "Cambodia: Power, Myth and Memory," held at Monash University, 1996.

[2] See also Frieson 1990; French 1994; Hinton 1999. Foucault has discussed the more general issue of how power manifests itself in/on material structures and corporeal bodies, of course (see, for example, his 1995 work on prisons).

[3] Svay village as a whole had some 790 inhabitants living in three sections, or what I call hamlets, that people differentiated as West, Middle, and East. My initial fieldwork focused on West Hamlet Svay, which included approximately 159 residents in thirty-two houses. My recent research in the 1990s has concentrated on survivors from West Hamlet and their families.

the wood and thatch houses were set amid tall coconut and sugar palms, huge mango and other trees, luxuriant stands of banana and bamboo, bougainvillea and betel shrubs, kitchen gardens, and other abundant flora. South of the village there stretched what always strikes me as a quintessential Cambodian landscape: a patchwork quilt of rice paddies extending as far as the eye can see, the flat expanse punctuated by towering palms growing on the dikes. The villagers were primarily subsistence rice cultivators, smallholders averaging about one hectare of paddies per household, who made ends meet with a variety of part-time activities, such as making palm sugar. At the eastern edge of Svay was the Buddhist *wat*, a small but beautiful compound with its graceful temple, an open pavilion (*sala*) used for meetings and ceremonies, a residence for the monks, and a pond for bathing.

Villagers say that their lives proceeded without major upheavals until the early 1970s when the first conflicts began to erupt. Khmer Rouge began to make forays into the region from their strongholds to the south, and villagers were caught in the crossfire between rebel and Lon Nol government troops stationed near the village. Two respected elders were accidentally killed by gunfire; artillery shells demolished several houses; and it became dangerous, then impossible, for villagers to cultivate their fields. The civil war intensified over time, and this general region also underwent massive U.S. bombing, notably in the summer of 1973 when (according to articles in the *New York Times*) at one point it was bombed every day for an entire week. Svay's villagers gradually fled during the early 1970s to what then seemed to be the relative security of Phnom Penh and its environs, surviving with various menial jobs. But this safety became illusory as the Khmer Rouge encircled Phnom Penh ever more tightly and artillery shells destroyed homes and killed members of several families from Svay.

In April 1975, when the Khmer Rouge captured and evacuated Phnom Penh, a number of villagers made prolonged and arduous journeys back to their former homes in Svay, only to find an overgrown wilderness (*prei*) where their houses had once stood. Forbidden by DK cadre to remain there, the former inhabitants of Svay were forced to camp—along with numerous (possibly a thousand or more) other evacuees from urban centers—in a desolate, flat wasteland several kilometers away near a place called Kok Pring. In the words of one survivor:

> When we arrived at the *prei* near Kok Pring, it looked like a sea of people's heads. It was very hot [May], and there was only one source of water nearby. We built crude shelters of thatch roofing over some poles. There were many deaths there; many people from West Hamlet are buried there: Ta Neung, Yeay Man, Soi, Sokhom, Kmav, and her child, others. . . . We used to sneak over to the Svay area to try to find food or fruit, despite the mines and bombs left in the fields, because we were so hungry.[4]

Without adequate food or water, the villagers suffered an initial wave of deaths from starvation and illness. After several months they were allowed to return to Svay, which was now turned into a commune. Some former inhabitants remained there for the duration of DK, while others were dispersed to various communes to the south

---

(Note: in earlier works I gave the pseudonym "Sobay" to this community. I am now using its real name because various colleagues in Cambodia studies are familiar with the village.)

[4] This and other quotations are translations from the Khmer. Some quotes are virtually verbatim, while others are close approximations or edited translations of what villagers said. Actual names are not used in order to protect informant confidentiality.

or, later, were sent further afield to toil in Pursat province under dreadful conditions that few survived.

Although the villagers had originally come from peasant backgrounds, the fact that they had not been in DK base areas before 1975 defined them as "New People" who had not joined the revolution. Their experiences during DK thus paralleled those of countless other "April 17 People": they were segregated by age and gender into different kinds of work teams; labor was exacted from them relentlessly; draconian discipline was used; family and kin ties were ruptured; malnutrition and illness were rampant; and deaths, including executions, were commonplace. The mortality rate was appalling: of the 139 West Svay villagers I had known in my early research who were still alive in 1975, 50 percent (70 persons) died during DK.[5] Of the thirty-two families I had known, some perished completely and others were left with only one or a few survivors. Since I have discussed these points at greater length elsewhere (Ebihara 1990, 1993a, 1993b), I will give no further details here but will turn my attention to how memories of civil war and DK were and still are inscribed on the landscape, on people's bodies, and on their minds.

## LANDSCAPE

Particular aspects of the landscape can carry certain cultural meanings. In Khmer, the word *prei* can be translated as forest/jungle, wilderness, or uninhabited area, and it connotes a Lévi-Straussian sense of nature versus culture, wild versus tame (see also Smith 1989; Chandler 1996). In the early days of the revolutionary movement, the Khmer Rouge hid in mountainous or forest regions known as *prei* (and, indeed, they occupied such regions again after their ouster from power in 1979). It is intriguing that Svay villagers, having fled from the countryside to the city during the civil war, were (ironically) expelled back into the countryside in 1975 and returned to Svay to find that their abandoned village had become, in their words, *prei*. They were then forced to live for several months in another *prei* area before DK cadre permitted them to return to Svay, now reconstituted as a commune where life was to be radically different. The situation of the abandoned village deteriorating into *prei*—its houses destroyed by fighting during the civil war or subsequently torn down by the Khmer Rouge to be used for firewood or construction materials, and its flora left untended—could be said to symbolize the destruction of the old community and its way of life. Then, the months at Kok Pring, another *prei*, served as a transition, a kind of Turnerian liminal period (Turner 1967) between the old society and the DK regime that inverted or destroyed most of the villagers' former ways of life and thrust them into a new revolutionary order.

Just as aspects of the landscape can be culturally conceptualized, the physical setting can be, of course, literally constructed and materially altered by human actions. My return visits to Svay in 1989 and the early 1990s occurred some ten years after the rout of DK forces. Yet I was startled to see a number of changes in the landscape that were mute but tangible reminders of the depredations wrought by the civil war and by DK. The road into the village, which had once been a smoothly paved, two-lane road in prewar times, had deteriorated into an obstacle course full of huge potholes and jarring ruts. Within the village, I was shocked in the early 1990s to find virtually everyone

---

[5] This figure takes into account only the 139 villagers I knew during my original research. It does not include spouses and children from marriages that occurred after I left Svay in 1960, but certainly there was high mortality among those groups as well.

living in small thatch houses with dirt floors built directly on the ground, something that was unthinkable even for poor families in prerevolutionary times, but common-place for New People during DK.[6] (In a neighboring community, however, there still stands a row of neat wooden houses raised on piles that had been built for cadre.)

The village temple had been damaged during the civil war and subsequently blown up with mines during DK; the debris was used to fill in the *wat*'s pond to culti-vate plants. The *sala*, or meeting hall, had been left standing and was used as a hospital during DK; what used to be the monks' residence was also intact but pockmarked with scars and bullet holes from the civil war. In 1990, efforts to erect a new temple (*vihear*) were just beginning, and I recall the poignant sight of three statues of Buddha sitting on a mound of dirt, sheltered only by a crude tin roof as they awaited a proper temple.

Similar destruction occurred at another *wat* several kilometers down the road that had been frequently attended by both villagers and visiting city folk. The large com-pound had been famous for a forest-like growth of huge trees populated by chattering monkeys, but in 1990 I found only scattered palms and a pile of soil where the main temple once stood. As one villager recalled:

> There used to be so many trees that you couldn't see the sky, trees so big that you couldn't get your arms around them. The monkeys went away when the big trees were cut, and probably some were eaten. Several [bombs or shells] from the Khmer Rouge landed on the grounds in 1973. Later they used mines to blow up the temple, but they also used people to smash up stones [fragments of the struc-ture] to get steel rods to reinforce the gates for irrigation canals and large pieces [of stone/cement] for construction at the irrigation project.

Walking Svay's rice fields, I saw evidence of DK's massive attempts to increase and rationalize agricultural production throughout the countryside. Just as DK tried to remodel people into new revolutionary entities, so also they attempted to reconfig-ure the landscape with large dams and extensive irrigation systems that would sustain several harvests a year on huge fields laid out in neat grids. South of Svay there are still traces of the enormous rectangular paddies that consolidated and smoothed over the small plots of varied shapes and sizes typical of former times. A number of palm trees on the dikes are decapitated or bullet-marked from fighting before or after DK. Skirting the paddies and village are the remains of some of the canals that had been part of a huge regional irrigation system built during DK. Several kilometers from the village on a nearby river, remnants of the huge dam that controlled the irrigation are slowly crumbling away. DK forced people to build such dams and fields with Hercu-lean manual labor, and many villagers spoke of their efforts in terms similar to the following:

> I was put in a young women's work group [*kâng neari*] sent to distant places. There were about fifty women divided into smaller teams of ten. The small team was given ten meters of land to work—one cubic meter per girl per day—digging

---

[6] In prerevolutionary times, villagers thought of houses built directly on the ground as being a Vietnamese rather than Khmer practice. Khmer houses are customarily raised on pilings, and this had been true of all dwellings in Svay in 1959–60, even though poorer homes had supports that might be only several feet tall.

irrigation ditches. Sometimes there were two people [responsible] for two cubic meters: one dug and the other carried off the dirt. . . . [I also] pulled out rice seedlings [from nursery beds] and transplanted them. . . . Six people had to transplant one hectare per day; if we couldn't finish, the Khmer Rouge would blame us and say we were lazy.

People's worth was measured in terms of how many cubic meters of dirt they moved. We had to dig canals: measure and dig, measure and dig. I'd fall carrying heavy loads. You had to work and walk until you fell, so you'd walk and fall, walk and fall. Even when you got sick you didn't dare stop working because they'd kill you, so you kept working until you collapsed. They used people without a thought as to whether they would live or die.

In the early 1990s near Svay there were also graphic reminders of the civil war preceding DK. Next to the village the stark remains of buildings that had been part of a teacher-training center during my original research were now roofless, crumbling walls scarred by bullet holes and artillery, their gaping window frames like eye sockets in a skull. Similar destruction was evident in a nearby town that had once had thriving markets, shops, and district (*srok*) government offices but now looked like a ghost town with a few weather-beaten and war-torn buildings lining muddy streets.

Near Svay there are also certain locales that embody chilling associations. The desolate *prei* area at Kok Pring, where people were herded after the evacuation from Phnom Penh, evokes thoughts of villagers who died and were buried there. Some who succumbed while Svay was a DK commune were buried in a patch of uncultivated ground around the shrine of the local *neak ta*, the community's guardian spirit.[7] The land behind the sub-district (*khum*) office was a local killing field, and a small collection of bones and pieces of clothing are stored (but not displayed) in a small wooden shed here. As one villager explained:

The local *khum* office was also the *khum* headquarters during Pol Pot time, and lots of people were killed there [in a stand of trees behind the office buildings]. A number of former officers, soldiers, and wealthy people were killed soon after the evacuation from Phnom Penh in 1975, around the month of May. Personal histories had been taken, and many had answered honestly. They were told they were going to be taken back to Phnom Penh, but they were actually tied up and killed. Later, university students were rounded up and told the same thing about going back to school in Phnom Penh, but were killed. . . . The villagers were still in Kok Pring [the *prei*] at this point. [Later during DK, some villagers were also killed at this headquarters.]

Several kilometers south of the village near Tonle Bati are the remains of a school that had been turned into a DK regional headquarters, prison, and execution center. In one room hundreds of skulls and bones are heaped on a platform and spill over onto the floor. A wooden signpost in the midst of the skulls states that 18,318 persons had

[7] In another interesting aspect of landscape or locality, villagers say that this *neak ta* left the area during DK, although he returned ("in an oxcart like everyone else") after Pol Pot. It is also said that the Khmer Rouge had shot at and tried to blow up the shrine—now pockmarked and scarred—but failed to destroy it. A small humanlike statue of the *neak ta* disappeared during the turmoil, but villagers believe that the guardian spirit is still there, and they pay obeisance to it.

been imprisoned here, of whom 5,111 died. It was a wrenching experience to visit this site on a gray drizzly day with some villagers who had lost family, kin, and friends at this prison. One of them noted:

> People were killed in the stand of bamboo behind that building. [After DK], rains washed away dirt and exposed the remains of bodies. . . . When the mass graves were being dug up, one could see that the bodies in earlier burials, when not so many people were being killed, had well-made manacles. Later, as more and more were imprisoned and killed, the manacles became cruder. Many of our kinfolk [*bâng-b'aun*] died here: Kue, Koey, Noi, Pruk, Kun's husband, Au's husband, Rin's husband.

In various places the landscape not only held remains of the dead but also became literally deadly to the living due to unexploded shells and mines left buried from the civil war period. After people returned to this area in 1979, several were wounded or killed by accidental detonations. Even in the early 1990s there were occasional explosions in the fields around Svay, though fortunately without casualties.[8]

## BODIES

Democratic Kampuchea's power was quite literally "embodied" in its stringent control over people's physical beings and lives. What Foucault has written in his work on prisons is applicable as well to DK where New People lived in virtual prison camps in which virtually every aspect of one's existence—clothing, food, language, speech, emotions, work, sleep, movement, marriage, ideology, and more—were subject to rigid discipline and constraints. Punishments for infractions (real or alleged) included constant harassment, starvation, beatings, manacles, torture, imprisonment, and, finally, being "taken away" (*vay haol*) for execution. What Foucault has written about prisons is also applicable to the situation in DK:

> The body is . . . directly involved in a political field; power relations have an immediate hold upon it; they invest it, mark it, train it, torture it, force it to carry out tasks, to perform ceremonies, to emit signs. This political investment of the body is bound up . . . with its economic use; it is largely as a force of production that the body is invested with relations of power and domination; but on the other hand, its constitution as labor power is possible only if it is caught up in a system of subjection . . . ; the body becomes a useful force only if it is both a productive body and a subjected body. This subjection is not only obtained by the instruments of violence of ideology; it can also be direct, physical . . . bearing on material elements . . . ; it may be calculated, organized . . . ; it may be subtle, make use neither of weapons nor of terror and yet remain of a physical order. (Foucault 1995:25–26)

---

[8] Unexploded mines remain a major problem in parts of Cambodia and still maim or kill thousands of people. One Svay villager lost his leg to a mine in 1988 when he was called up for government work duty to carry supplies to People's Republic of Kampuchea (PRK) government troops in the mountains of northwestern Cambodia near the Thai border. When the Khmer Rouge captured his work unit, he managed to escape into the jungle but, unfortunately, stepped on a mine the next day. Luckily, he was rescued and survived.

While Svay's inhabitants had come from peasant backgrounds, the fact that they had fled to the city before 1975 meant that they were classified—along with other urban residents from higher socioeconomic strata—as "New People," "Lon Nol People," "April 17 People," and the "Enemy."[9] As such, they were subject to the harshest of conditions. Their narratives of "the time of Pol Pot" (*sâmay Pol Pot*), with its lack of food and literally backbreaking work, report skeletal figures suffering desperate hunger and exhaustion, endemic illnesses, and ineffectual DK medicines that villages say "looked like shit." These brief excerpts from villagers' accounts testify to the manifold ways in which DK controlled, constrained, and weakened bodies.

> We had no freedom to do anything: to eat, to sleep, to speak. We hid our crying, weeping into our pillows at night. We watched our children become beasts of burden. We had to say the opposite of what was true: that something was delicious when it wasn't.
>
> We were always looking for bits of food to pick up, but you'd get hit if they saw you. They'd hold out roasted corn, but when you grabbed it, it'd be hot and burn your hand so you'd drop it, and then they'd hit you again for wasting food. Sometimes there was no water, so you saved your own urine to drink.
>
> One man saw some potato plants and dug up two or three. [The cadre] caught him and made him wear the potatoes around his neck and beat him while he was paraded around the village. They were going to kill him, but upper echelon cadre stopped them; this was in 1975 when people were not yet being killed. But they tied him up and got in a circle around him and struck him until he fell, and then they kicked and beat him some more; even female cadres hit him. He went almost crazy from the beating.
>
> I was in a special work group for relatives of soldiers [her father was in the Lon Nol and army] and rich people. If we denied [our background] or didn't work, we'd be reported and taken away to be executed. I survived because I worked very hard and didn't say anything, so they couldn't blame me [for anything]. In the special group there was no time for rest. We slept from 9:00 p.m. to 4:00 a.m., got five minutes for the midday mean at 12:00 or 1:00 p.m., no rest and back to work until 7:00 p.m., stop fifteen minutes for supper, and sometimes we continued work until midnight or 1:00 a.m., depending on the job. Every now and then there were political meetings at night after work. If you were sitting in the front it was hard to stay awake, but you had to. The same things were said again and again, though no one was listening. There were also criticism sessions: self-criticism and criticism by others. These could last three hours or so, depending on the amount of criticism.
>
> We worked so hard planting and harvesting; there were piles of rice as big as this house, but they took it away in trucks. . . . We raised chickens and ducks and vegetables and fruit but they took it all. You'd be killed if you tried to take anything for yourself. You could *see* food, but you weren't allowed to eat it.
>
> The children had swollen faces and feet but were just bones through the rest of the body and arms and legs.

---

[9] Before 1975, some Svay families—although none from West Hamlet Svay—voluntarily went south to join Khmer Rouge camps that had been established in Takeo province. One couple from West Svay did become involuntarily associated with the Khmer Rouge because they had fled the village in the early 1970s and took refuge with relatives in an area near Oudong (northwest of Phnom Penh) that came under rebel control before 1975. They were, therefore, technically classified as Old People.

Women had no periods, their breasts shriveled up, and everyone was thin because there was no food. All the young women looked like old grandmothers.

I lost a baby when I was [several] months pregnant because I had to throw dirt up and out. I miscarried, but I didn't know what it was that came out of me and took it home. At the meeting that night I was accused of leaving work, so I showed them the fetus.

Carrying heavy loads, my uterus fell out [while I was working.] I pushed it back inside and took a lime to close up the hold. I was afraid to tell anyone . . . because if you said you were sick, you'd be punished. When I returned to the commune my sarong was all wet; my children saw that and cried. But I didn't tell anyone I was too sick to work any longer. I couldn't sit. I went to the hospital for three months.[10]

Even now, villagers say that they suffer from constant fatigue, difficulty walking, weak limbs, faulty memories, impaired vision,[11] and other physical problems that are due to beatings or overwork endured during DK. They often note such difficulties as:

My legs are still weak; sometimes they collapse and I fall down.

They beat me on the head, shoulders, and back; I never recovered, and now I can't lift heavy things.

I've forgotten how to read or write Khmer since Pol Pot.

I'm still sick in the chest from all the work.

People also explain the deaths of several villagers in the 1980s as due to illnesses caused by conditions under Pol Pot. They also say that one villager, who was relocated during DK to a distant province with especially harsh conditions and saw most of her family die, went "crazy" from stress and grief. At present, though she functions quite capably in daily life, she herself feels that the DK made her emotionally unstable, noting that "sometimes I laugh or cry for no good reason." I see, however, no other evidence of mental instability in Svay, although many villagers doubtless carry deep psychic wounds from DK that are perhaps somaticized as various ailments (see Mortland 2002).

## MEMORIES

Memories of other kinds are also indelibly etched in villagers' minds, but they are expressed—or repressed—in different ways. When I collected narratives of the Pol Pot period, some villagers spoke about their experiences stoically, while others broke

---

[10] According to a British midwife I consulted in Phnom Penh, the muscles supporting the uterus can become weakened from multiple births and heavy work (both of which this villager had experienced), resulting in a prolapsed uterus that collapses and falls out of the body.

[11] This is not the hysterical blindness that has been reported for some Khmer refugee women in the United States. One Svay man lost virtually all his eyesight, but his symptoms were similar to cases of detached retina, and the decline in vision was preceded by a fall from a cart. A Khmer medical technician at the sub-district medical clinic suggested that vision problems during DK were due to overwork, malnutrition, irritation from dust in the eyes, and long exposure to glaring sun.

down and wept. One man said he had never before disclosed his experiences during DK to anyone but, knowing that I was recording village history, he wanted to tell me. In some cases, an individual gave me one painful but perhaps cathartic account and subsequently did not wish to talk about DK any further.

I have elsewhere discussed several dominant themes in villagers' oral accounts of their lives under Pol Pot: the lack of food, unrelenting Sisyphean labor, endemic sickness, and the constant specter of death, whether from illness or being "taken away" for execution (see especially Ebihara 1993a). I shall not repeat here the substantive details of these major themes but suggest that these narratives have acquired a mythic quality. Let me emphasize immediately that the term "mythic" is not meant to imply something that is a creation of imagination. Rather, I use it in the sense that the villagers' narratives, like classic myths, tell of individuals who managed to survive—with remarkable courage, quick-wittedness, and indomitability—the extraordinary hardships and ordeals of a period when a mysterious and terrifying power called Angkar inverted or destroyed the conventional norms and patterns of Khmer society and culture.[12] Indeed, some Cambodians thought that DK was the fulfillment of terrifying prophecies in the *Put Tumneay*, ancient scriptures, that there would be an apocalyptic age of destruction and death (see also Smith 1989; Mortland 1994).

One might also suggest that DK has assumed a "mythic" quality in contemporary Cambodian national/cultural consciousness as a reign of horror against which subsequent regimes have defined themselves. Memories of DK are kept alive in the Tuol Sleng Museum of Genocidal Crimes and collections of bones at the killing fields of Choeung Ek and other local memorials, such as the one south of Svay at the former regional prison and execution center (see also Ledgerwood 1997; Chandler 1999; and Hawk 1989).[13] There is also an annual observance called the National Day of Hatred, when people are called together to revile DK. On one such day at the village level, officials and schoolchildren from the region around Svay were summoned to ceremonies at which they heard speeches and burned paper effigies of Pol Pot.

After the 1979 rout of DK, Pol Pot and his top officials remained in people's consciousness as mysterious and still-threatening figures in remote hideaways with sizeable contingents of armed troops. Throughout the 1980s and the first part of the 1990s, there were battles between government soldiers and DK holdouts in various regions, and it was common knowledge that certain roads and regions were dangerous. While there were no Khmer Rouge forces in the immediate vicinity of Svay, they were said to be present in mountains to the south from which thumps of distant

---

[12] On another point, while I do not want to attempt any discourse analysis, it is intriguing to note certain recurring themes/phrases in people's narratives of the Pol Pot period that resemble repetitive locutions in myth and folklore. I must stress again that I do not mean that villagers fabricated stories; rather, I simply point out that certain expressions appear in various accounts. These include stock descriptive phrases (e.g., "There were piles of rice as big as this house, but they were taken away in trucks"), common sayings of both the Khmer Rouge and their subjects, and stories of events that may or may not have been factually true but were nonetheless "real" in people's minds (e.g., the rumor that in some provinces, the Khmer Rouge called people to political meetings and then blew them up with mines). On common expressions, see Marston 1994.

[13] Hawk 1989 has striking pictures of Tuol Sleng, Choeung Ek, and some regional sites where bones of DK victims have been amassed. The memorial south of Svay is on a smaller scale but similar to one shown on the fourteenth page of Hawk's "photographic record" (the pictures have no pagination).

explosions were sometimes heard. In the early 1990s, villagers remained apprehensive about the Khmer Rouge and the possibility of their return to power. Some families even dug foxholes, frightened that there could be renewed fighting.

## LAYERED MEMORIES

Fears that the Khmer Rouge might regain control of the country gradually diminished in the latter part of the 1990s after the UN-sponsored general elections and especially after Pol Pot's death and the defection or capture of major leaders and their troops.[14] Also, during visits to Svay in the mid-1990s, I was heartened to see many instances of reconstruction that have, sometimes quite literally, layered over the nightmarish past as aspects of prerevolutionary Khmer life have been restored. In the landscape around Svay, the huge rectangular rice fields constructed during DK were broken up into small paddies that reflect the redistribution of land to individual owners in the 1980s.[15] Bomb craters from the 1970s civil war period are now shallow depressions where grass has grown. Trees are also a sign of hope. In the years immediately after DK, villagers did not try to replace trees that had been destroyed because they feared that conflict might force them to abandon the village again. But in the early 1980s, as people became relatively reassured that they could stay put, new trees were planted and were producing an abundance of mangoes (*svay* the village's name), coconuts, and other fruits by the 1990s. Clusters of broad-leaved banana stalks, stands of bamboo, bushes of betel leaves and other plants, house gardens with vegetables, and flashes of bright flowers have restored verdancy to Svay.

During the mid- to late 1990s there was a good deal of material (re)construction in and around Svay. The village looked increasingly attractive as more and more villagers replaced their thatch huts built directly on the ground with traditional Khmer-style houses raised on piles. Such homes are, I believe, extremely important both materially and symbolically for villagers as tangible signs of breaking away from years of deprivation and dislocation.[16] The revival of Buddhism, once again recognized as the state religion, is reflected in the considerable efforts to rebuild *wats*. At both the village *wat* and the other one down the road, it was amazing and gratifying to watch the central temples (*vihear*) being rebuilt literally from the ground up, on what were mounds of

---

[14] Fears of the Khmer Rouge often remained strong, however, among Cambodian refugees abroad. One former Svay resident became a refugee who now lives in the U.S.'s Washington state. Over the years she was frightened of returning to her homeland to visit her aged father because of her deep-seated fear that there were Khmer Rouge still in the area, despite repeated assurances (in our phone conversations and in her father's letters) that there were none. Even after she finally screwed up her courage to visit Cambodia, she was afraid to stay overnight in Svay because of her anxiety that Khmer Rouge might attack.

[15] After DK, the PRK (1979–88) initially instituted a semi-socialist economy with communal production and distribution of rice and certain other foodstuffs, with private production for other activities. The communal system, which villagers greatly disliked, deteriorated in favor of household production on de facto private fields. In 1987, the government authorized local officials to formally allocate paddies and house sites within the village to individuals, and land-ownership was reinstated in the State of Cambodia constitution of 1989 (for more details, see Ebihara 1993a).

[16] Even small houses are expensive for poor villagers to build. Some families have received financial help from relatives who are refugees living abroad, while others have taken several years to accumulate sufficient building materials and funds (which necessitates borrowing money) to erect a house.

dirt in 1990. In both instances, the temples have been constructed in classic style and are, in some ways, even more magnificently beautiful than the prewar *vihear*. Each *wat* also has a contingent of resident monks, including some young novices. As well, the war-scarred remains of former school buildings near the village were rebuilt in the mid-1990s and have been neatly refurbished as the local district (*srok*) offices.

Village subsistence and social organization are similar, though not identical, to prerevolutionary existence. Families (or what remained of them) have been reunited; rice cultivation continues; a market economy has been restored; Buddhist ceremonies and life-cycle rituals are once again faithfully observed. While some observers have stated that DK has left legacies of widespread increase in domestic violence and the breakdown of social bonds between kinsmen and neighbors (e.g., Frings 1993; Ovesen, Trankell, and Öjendal 1996; Zimmerman, Men, and Sar 1994), neither domestic abuse nor isolated households were evident in Svay. DK did indeed affect family life in terms of the high death rate (especially male mortality that left many widows), but the basic moral norm of concern for kin (and close friends) remains, as does the ethic of reciprocal labor exchange for cultivation and compassionate aid in times of need.[17]

It would be simplistic to say that contemporary village existence has simply revived prerevolutionary practices, because "traditions" have had to be reinvented (to paraphrase Hobsbawm and Ranger 1983) and necessarily transformed due to changed and still changing social, political, and economic circumstances. For instance, there is still cooperative work exchange among kin and friends for rice cultivation, but various households nowadays hire help (a rarity in prerevolutionary times) because DK left them with too few able-bodied family members to participate in widespread reciprocal labor exchange. Weddings are still as festive and elaborate as a family can afford, but some of the customary rites are now truncated or even omitted because "young people get bored with them." Nonetheless, just as Khmer-American refugees invoke customary Cambodian conceptions while in fact their lives are adapting to new circumstances and ideas (Ledgerwood 1990, 1994), so Svay villagers also evoke "tradition." Thus, people talking about contemporary village life would often say in various contexts, "It's like [it was] before (*dauch pi mun*)"—and, indeed, the broad outlines of life in Svay looked quite similar to what I had known in prerevolutionary times. But at some level, villagers know that things are not exactly *dauch pi mun* because there have been modifications in various domains of life (for more details, see Ebihara 1993a). Yet this conception is an important means of implying that Pol Pot's attempt to construct a revolutionary new society did not succeed and that Cambodian life has returned to a relative normalcy "like before."

Memories of "Pol Pot time" obviously remain vivid for those who lived through it, but one wonders what place DK will have in the minds of younger generations of Cambodians born after 1979. Children and adolescents hear references to and stories about conditions during DK that often crop up in ordinary conversations among their elders, and the infamies of Pol Pot will also be kept alive by Tuol Sleng and other institutionalized reminders of DK so long as the incumbent government maintains them. But what further social and political developments may layer over the memories of Pol Pot?

---

[17] Reports of similar social bonds in other communities can be found in, for example, Kim 2001; Uimonen 1996; McAndrew 1997; and Meas 1995. For further discussion of this issue, see also Ledgerwood 1998; Ebihara 1993a; and Ebihara and Ledgerwood 2002.

REFERENCES

Chandler, David P. 1996. "Songs at the Edge of the Forest" [1978]. In *Facing the Cambodian Past, Selected Essays, 1971–1994*, 76–99. Chiang Mai: Silkworm Books.

——. 1999. *Voices from S-21: Terror and History in Pol Pot's Secret Prison*. Berkeley: University of California Press.

Ebihara, May. 1990. "Return to a Khmer Village." *Cultural Survival Quarterly* 14(3):67–70.

——. 1993a. "'Beyond Suffering': The Recent History of a Cambodian Village." In *The Challenge of Reform in Indochina*, edited by Börje Ljunggren, 149–66. Cambridge, MA: Harvard Institute for International Development, Harvard University Press.

——. 1993b. "A Cambodian Village under the Khmer Rouge, 1975–1979." In *Genocide and Democracy in Cambodia: The Khmer Rouge, the United Nations and the International Community*, edited by Ben Kiernan, Southeast Asia Studies Monograph 41, 51–63. New Haven: Yale University Southeast Asia Studies.

Ebihara, May, and Judy Ledgerwood. 2002. "Aftermaths of Genocide: Cambodian Villagers." In *Annihilating Difference: The Anthropology of Genocide*, edited by Alexander L. Hinton, 272–91. Berkeley: University of California Press.

Foucault, Michel. 1995. *Discipline and Punish: The Birth of the Prison*. Translated by Alan Sheridan. 2nd ed. New York: Vintage Books.

French, Lindsay C. 1994. "The Political Economy of Injury and Compassion: Amputees and the Thai–Cambodia Border." In *Embodiment and Experience: The Existential Ground of Culture and Self*, edited by Thomas Csordas, 69–99. Cambridge: Cambridge University Press.

Frieson, Kate. 1990. "The Pol Pot Legacy in Village Life." *Cultural Survival Quarterly* 14 (3):71–73.

Frings, Viviane. 1993. "The Failure of Agricultural Collectivization in the People's Republic of Kampuchea, 1979–1989." Working Paper 80, Monash University Centre of Southeast Asian Studies.

Hawk, David. 1989. "The Photographic Record." In *Cambodia, 1975–1978: Rendezvous with Death*, edited by Karl D. Jackson, 209–14. Princeton, NJ: Princeton University Press.

Hinton, Alexander Laban. 1999. "Genocidal Bricolage." Paper presented to the Anthropology Section of the New York Academy of Sciences, December.

Hobsbawm, Eric, and Terence Ranger. 1983. *The Invention of Tradition*. Cambridge: Cambridge University Press.

Kim Sedara. 2001. "Reciprocity: Informal Patterns of Social Interactions in a Cambodian Village near Angkor Park." Master's thesis, Northern Illinois University.

Ledgerwood, Judy. 1990. "Changing Khmer Conceptions of Gender: Women, Stories, and the Social Order." PhD diss., Cornell University.

——. 1994. "Gender Symbolism and Culture Change: Viewing the Virtuous Woman in the Khmer Story "Mea Yoeung." In *Cambodian Culture since 1975: Homeland and*

*Exile*, edited by May Ebihara, Carol A. Mortland, and Judy Ledgerwood, 119–28. Ithaca: Cornell University Press.

———. 1997. "The Cambodian Tuol Sleng Museum of Genocidal Crimes: National Narrative." *Museum Anthropology* 21(1):82–98.

———. 1998. "Rural Development in Cambodia: The View from the Village." In *Cambodia and the International Community: The Quest for Peace, Development, and Democracy*, edited by Frederick Z. Brown and David G. Timberman, 127–48. New York: The Asia Society.

Marston, John. 1994. "Metaphors of the Khmer Rouge." In *Cambodian Culture since 1975: Homeland and Exile*, edited by May M. Ebihara, Carol A. Mortland, and Judy Ledgerwood, 105–18. Ithaca: Cornell University Press.

McAndrew, John P. 1997. *Interdependence in Household Livelihood: Strategies in Two Cambodian Villages*. Phnom Penh: Cambodia Development Resource Institute.

Meas, Nee. 1995. *Towards Restoring Life: Cambodian Villages*. Phnom Penh: NGO Forum on Cambodia.

Mortland, Carol A. 1994. "Khmer Buddhists in the United States: Ultimate Questions." In *Cambodian Culture since 1975: Homeland and Exile*, edited by May M. Ebihara, Carol A. Mortland, and Judy Ledgerwood, 72–90. Ithaca: Cornell University Press.

———. 2002. "Legacies of Genocide for Cambodians in the United States." In *Cambodia Emerges from the Past: Eight Essays*, edited by Judy Ledgerwood, 151–77. Dekalb: Northern Illinois University Center for Southeast Asian Studies Southeast Asia Publications.

Ovesen, Jan, Ing-Britt Trankell, and Joakim Öjendal. 1996. *When Every Household Is an Island: Social Organization and Power Structures in Rural Cambodia*. Uppsala: Uppsala University.

Smith, Frank. 1989. *Interpretive Accounts of the Khmer Rouge Years: Personal Experience in Cambodian Peasant World View*. Wisconsin Papers on Southeast Asia, Occasional Paper 18. Madison: University of Wisconsin, Center for Southeast Asian Studies.

Turner, Victor. 1967. *The Forest of Symbols: Aspects of Ndembu Ritual*. Cornell Paperbacks 101. Ithaca: Cornell University Press.

Uimonen, Paula. 1996. "Responses to Evolutionary Change: A Study of Social Memory in a Khmer Village." *Folk: Journal of the Danish Ethnographic Society* 38:31–51.

Zimmerman, Cathy, Men Savorn, and Sar Samen. 1994. *Plates in a Basket Will Rattle: Domestic Violence in Cambodia, Phnom Penh, December 1994*. Phnom Penh: Asia Foundation.

# Index

CPSIA information can be obtained
at www.ICGtesting.com
Printed in the USA
LVHW02s2321030418
572146LV00009B/185/P